Great Mysteries of the Past

Great
Mysteries
of the Past

Experts Unravel Fact and Fallacy
Behind the Headlines of History

Reader's Digest

The Reader's Digest Association, Inc.
Pleasantville, New York/Montreal

EDITED BY
GARDNER ASSOCIATES

Editorial Director: Joseph L. Gardner
Art Editor: Barbara Marks
Contributing Editors: Charles Flowers,
   Wendy Murphy
Research Editors: Denise Lynch (Chief),
   Mary Elizabeth Allison, Guadalupe Morgan
Copy Editor: Felice Levy
Indexer: Cynthia Crippen
Translators: M.C. Hellin, Sabine Thomson

PROJECT STAFF FOR READER'S DIGEST

Editor: Suzanne E. Weiss
Art Editor: Evelyn Bauer

READER'S DIGEST GENERAL BOOKS

Editor in Chief: John A. Pope, Jr.
Managing Editor: Jane Polley
Executive Editor: Susan J. Wernert
Art Director: David Trooper
Group Editors: Will Bradbury,
   Norman B. Mack, Kaari Ward
Group Art Editors: Evelyn Bauer,
   Robert M. Grant, Joel Musler
Chief of Research: Monica Borrowman
Copy Chief: Edward W. Atkinson
Picture Editor: Richard Pasqual
Rights and Permissions: Pat Colomban
Head Librarian: Jo Manning

Adapted from *Wie geschah es wirklich?*, published in
Germany in 1990.
Copyright © 1990 Verlag Das Beste GmbH

The credits and acknowledgments that appear on pages
440–441 are hereby made a part of this copyright page.

Library of Congress Cataloging in Publication Data

Wie geschah es wirklich? English
   Great mysteries of the past / Reader's Digest.
      p.   cm.
   Rev. translation of: Wie geschah es wirklich?
   Includes index.
   ISBN 0-89577-377-5
   1. History — Miscellanea. 2. Curiosities and wonders.
I. Reader's Digest Association. II. Title.
D24.W4713   1991   90-48005
001.9'4 — dc20

Printed in the United States of America

About This Book

*E*veryone loves a mystery. But when a famous person is involved or when questions about great historic events remain unanswered, the tale takes on an added dimension — one that no work of fiction contains. This collection of 91 stories lets you journey into a dramatic past where greed, secrecy, intrigue, treason, passion, folly, and murder all too often affected the course of history and left a baffling maze of puzzles that scholars are still seeking to solve.

Spellbinding tales and a kaleidoscope of pictures go straight to the heart of strange-but-true events and introduce you to some of the most fascinating and infamous characters of the past few centuries. The featured stories are arranged topically rather than chronologically and are accompanied by numerous boxes that investigate related events and introduce similar personalities. It all adds up to a cavalcade of suspense, revelation, and important new information.

"They Vanished Without a Trace," the first of seven sections, relates how the two ships of Sir John Franklin's Arctic exploration disappeared so completely that no evidence of his fate was found for more than a century; why Mao wanted to get rid of a challenger to his domination of Red China; and what probably happened to famed bandleader Glenn Miller on his flight to France in 1944. "Deaths Under Dubious Circumstances" reveals that U.N. Secretary-General Dag Hammarskjold, Wolfgang Amadeus Mozart, and Soviet dictator Joseph Stalin were among those who met myste-

rious ends. Among the fascinating figures introduced in "Strange and Enigmatic Characters" are Lawrence of Arabia, the sinister monk Rasputin, Lord Byron, and Benedict Arnold.

"Guilty or Not Guilty?" This is the question still being asked about the anarchists Sacco and Vanzetti, World War I spy Mata Hari, and President Nixon in the Watergate affair. Their stories and others are scrutinized in the fourth section. King Arthur at Camelot, Count Dracula, Lady Godiva, Romeo and Juliet — historians and literary sleuths help separate fact from fallacy in "Half Truth, Half Legend." Did the United States know Japan was going to attack Pearl Harbor? Who really wrote Shakespeare's plays? How could Rutherford B. Hayes become president after losing the election of 1876? Why did the Soviets shoot down a Korean passenger plane in 1983? Experts' opinions are offered in "Unanswered Questions." And in the concluding section, "Fateful Blunders," you will learn why Hitler's invasion of Russia in 1941 failed, what made Custer attack the numerically superior Sioux Indians at Little Big Horn, and how Napoleon's battle strategy at Waterloo went wrong.

The editors of Reader's Digest have gone behind the headlines of history to select the most interesting events and the most intriguing characters for this you-are-there look at the past. Puzzles, enigmas, and riddles are probed; the opinions of the experts are presented; the answers to questions and solutions to mysteries are offered — demonstrating once more that truth really is stranger than fiction.

Contents

3

Strange and Enigmatic Characters

4

Guilty or Not Guilty?

Half Truth, Half Legend

Unanswered Questions

7

Fateful Blunders

1

They Vanished
Without a Trace

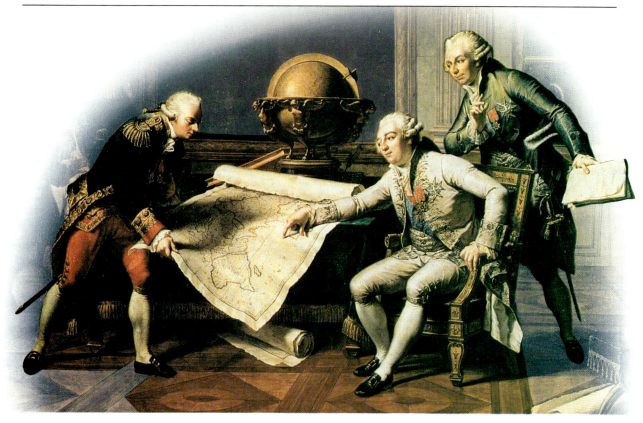

La Pérouse (left) explains his expedition's itinerary in an interview with King Louis XVI.

Destination: Great South Sea

La Pérouse's voyage of exploration was to take four years, with a return to France in the summer of 1789. His two ships were last seen headed northeast from Australia; none of the more than 400 men aboard the vessels was ever found.

"I have the honor to report that *La Boussole* and *L'Astrolabe* have departed at four o'clock this morning under northwesterly winds. Two sloops have been ordered to accompany the ships until they reach the open sea. Thus, on this day, the journey around the world of La Pérouse has begun." With this message of August 1, 1785, Admiral Jean François de Galaup, Comte de La Pérouse, informed King Louis XVI that he was leaving the French port of Brest to sail across the Atlantic Ocean and into the Great South Sea, as the Pacific Ocean was then known.

Although discovered nearly 300 years earlier by the Spanish explorer Balboa, the Pacific was only now being extensively explored and charted — thanks largely to the three voyages of Britain's Captain James Cook between 1768 and 1779. La Pérouse's expedition was meant to secure a rank for France alongside Britain, then the leading seafaring nation.

A Veteran Seafarer

Just short of his 44th birthday when he left Brest, La Pérouse was at the peak of a naval career that had started with his enlistment as a midshipman at age 15 in 1756, at the outset of the Seven Years' War between France and Britain. In 1783, a veteran of 18 campaigns in the service of his country, he had withdrawn to his family estates in the south of France — only to be called out of retirement to head the expedition that was to discover "all the lands which had escaped the vigilance of Captain Cook."

No efforts had been spared in outfitting the expedition. Provisions for a four-year voyage were stowed aboard the two 500-ton frigates — well-named *La Boussole* ("Compass") and *L'Astrolabe* ("Astrolabe," a device for measuring the distance of stars above the horizon). The latest charts and the records of previous voyages were obtained for the ships' libraries, and a portable observatory was brought aboard. Among the gifts and barter items for natives were 600 mirrors, 2,600 combs, 1,260 pounds of glass beads, and 50,000 sewing needles.

Competition was keen for the 400-odd berths on the two vessels. Among the applicants was a 16-year-old second lieutenant from the military academy at Paris: a Corsican named Napoleon Bonaparte. Although he was on the preliminary list, he failed to be chosen and remained behind in France — with enormous consequences for the history of his country.

The moment of departure arrived at last. To the cheers of well-wishers and the boom of a gun salute, *La Boussole* and *L'Astrolabe* sailed out of Brest in the predawn darkness of that August day. The voyage into the unknown had begun.

Tragedy in Alaska

On January 25, 1786, the two ships — having stopped at several islands in their journey across the Atlantic Ocean — rounded Cape Horn and

After rounding Cape Horn, La Pérouse's two ships entered the Pacific early in 1786. Their route across and around the rim of the ocean, ending in shipwreck at Vanikoro, is traced on the map below.

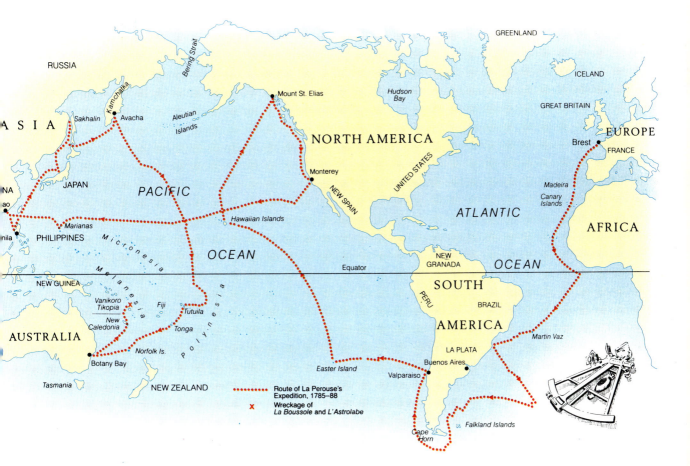

Cooperation Among Enemies

Most of La Pérouse's naval career was spent in fighting the British. Yet, as an explorer, he received the support and cooperation of his erstwhile enemies — thanks to a humane act during the American War of Independence.

Britain's fur trade in Canada was an important source of wealth; destroying it would be to the advantage of the rebellious colonists and their French allies. When Captain La Pérouse received the order to attack Britain's fur factories in Hudson Bay in 1782, he moved quickly and decisively. He seized and destroyed the forts but spared the lodgings of those British who had fled into the hostile Canadian wilderness; when he departed, he even left them food and provisions to survive the approaching winter. To have acted otherwise, La Pérouse said in explanation of such clemency, would have been inhuman.

Although his superiors in Paris may not have appreciated La Pérouse's commendable mercy, his actions were not forgotten in Britain. Thus, three years later, when he was about to launch his expedition to the Pacific, the British readily agreed to cooperate with his scientific quest.

A French go-between was allowed to look at all the charts, surveys, and reports of Captain James Cook, who had established himself as the greatest explorer of the age during his three Pacific voyages between 1768 and 1779. Among Cook's papers were 20 densely written pages about the prevention and cure of scurvy — then the most dreaded disease among seafarers. That La Pérouse learned a lesson from Cook is indicated by the fact that none of his crew is known to have suffered from scurvy during the three years of his voyage from which records survive.

When he left Brest in 1785, La Pérouse took with him two "dipping needles," or compasses, that had gone around the world with Captain Cook. He had received them as a gift of Britain's Royal Society and treated the mementoes, he wrote, "with feelings bordering almost upon religious veneration for the memory of that great and incomparable navigator."

Mighty glaciers rise above the Alaskan bay where La Boussole *and* L'Astrolabe *anchored in 1786. The drawing is by expedition artist Duche de Vancy.*

Mount St. Elias, at the north tip of Alaska's panhandle, provided the first sighting of the North American coastline. As they were charting the coast to the south, disaster struck the French expedition. Two reconnaissance boats taking soundings off the entrance to a bay were overturned by waves with the loss of 21 men, including six officers. Nevertheless, La Pérouse continued his coastal surveys through the summer, getting as far south as Monterey, California.

From California the French expedition headed due west across the Pacific and on January 3, 1787, reached the Portuguese colony of Macao at the mouth of China's Pearl River. After repairing his ships and taking on supplies in the Philippines, La Pérouse headed north in April to chart the Asian coastline, skirting Taiwan, passing between Korea and Japan into the Sea of Japan, and sailing through the strait separating Japan from Russia's Sakhalin Island.

Toward the end of their second full summer of exploration, the ships reached Russia's Kamchatka Peninsula. There La Pérouse left a Russian-speaking officer named de Lesseps with the mission to cross Siberia to Europe bearing reports of the expedition's accomplishments to date.

Second Disaster, Chance Encounter, Silence

By September 1787 the expedition was once more in southern latitudes. It stopped to take on

entered the Pacific. After putting in at Valparaiso, Chile, they reached Easter Island on April 8. The next stop was Maui in the Hawaiian Islands, discovered only eight years earlier by Captain Cook (and where the British explorer had been killed by hostile natives). Landing on May 28 in a bay that still bears his name, La Pérouse declined to take possession in the name of Louis XVI. "The customs of Europeans on such occasions are completely ridiculous," he said.

fresh water at Tutuila, today the chief island of American Samoa. Armed only with clubs and stones, natives attacked the longboats and killed 12 men, including Fleuriot de Langle, captain of *L'Astrolabe* and La Pérouse's second in command. Forty-three men, half of them seriously wounded, managed to swim to safety. The French made a hasty withdrawal and headed for Australia's east coast.

Sailing into Botany Bay at the end of January 1788, the French were surprised to find a British squadron. This was the famous First Fleet of seven vessels carrying some 750 British convicts — men, women, and children — who were the founders of Australia's first colony. With the British returning home, La Pérouse sent more reports and letters; in one of them he promised to be home by June 1789.

On March 10 the two ships left Australia, heading in a northeasterly direction. They were never seen again. "He has vanished trackless into the blue immensity," the Scottish essayist Thomas Carlyle was to write of La Pérouse; "and only some mournful, mysterious shadow of him hovers long in all heads and hearts."

An Aborted Rescue

By the summer of 1789, it had been more than a year since any word of La Pérouse's whereabouts had been received, but France had more important worries than concern over a missing explorer. On July 14 a Parisian mob stormed the infamous prison known as the Bastille — the opening event in a revolution that would keep the country in turmoil for the remaining years of the century and end with Napoleon Bonaparte crowning himself emperor.

Only two years later did the French government get around to posting a reward for any news of La Pérouse and dispatching a search expedition to the Pacific. On September 25, 1791, Rear Admiral Joseph Antoine Bruni d'Entrecasteaux left Brest with two ships — six years after La Pérouse had departed with such optimism.

Combing the Pacific for La Pérouse, d'Entrecasteaux made a number of scientific and geographic discoveries. Then, in May 1793, he called at Vanikoro, an island in the Santa Cruz group northeast of Australia.

The crew noticed smoke rising from several elevated places on the heavily wooded, mountainous island. Could it be a signal from shipwrecked

South Sea islanders were generally friendly to the French explorers. However, those of Tutuila in the Samoan group made a surprise attack on a party coming ashore for fresh water. Today, some island women of the Pacific wear flower leis around their necks (inset below) to welcome visitors.

Europeans, hoping for rescue from a passing vessel? D'Entrecasteaux was convinced he had found La Pérouse or at least survivors of his expedition. But when his ships narrowly missed running aground on Vanikoro's treacherous reefs, d'Entrecasteaux was forced to leave without sending a search party ashore. The admiral took ill and died two months later; that autumn his vessels were seized by the Dutch in Java, for by then revolutionary France was at war with Holland and most of the rest of Europe. No further rescue missions were sent by the French.

Four Decades Later: First Clues

In May 1826 an Irishman named Peter Dillon — cruising about the South Pacific in search of trade and adventure — put in at the tiny island of Tikopia in the Santa Cruz group. When he asked the natives where they had obtained their necklaces of glass beads, he was shown other articles obviously of European manufacture: a silver fork and spoon, knives, teacups, iron bolts, and a silver sword guard with the initials "J.F.G.P." The items, Dillon learned, had been obtained in trade with natives of Vanikoro, two days' sail away.

Dillon quickly guessed that the initials on the sword guard stood for Jean François Galaup de La Pérouse. But he was thwarted in his attempt to reach Vanikoro when his ship was first becalmed and then started taking on water, and so he retreated to Java. By the end of the summer he had backing for a search to find survivors of La Pérouse's expedition, but it was another year before he succeeded in actually reaching Vanikoro.

Many years ago, an old native told him, two ships had run aground on the island's reefs during a storm. One ship had sunk immediately, most of its crew drowning or being eaten by sharks. But the second ship hung on the reef, and from its timbers the survivors managed to make a small boat in which "after many moons" they sailed away. Two of the strangers — one a "chief," the other his servant — had stayed behind, surviving until only a few years earlier. All about the island Dillon's party found evidence of the French occupation, including an engraved ship's bell and a plank carved with the French fleur-de-lis.

Final Proof

In February 1829 Dillon reached Paris with the pathetic relics of La Pérouse's ill-fated expedition. On hand to authenticate them was the same de Lesseps who had been put ashore at Kamchatka in late summer 1787 with reports of the first two years of the expedition and who had spent a year crossing Siberia.

A Brawl over Venus

The discovery of the remains of La Pérouse's two ships was far from the most important find of Dumont d'Urville's career as a naval explorer.

In 1819–20, nearly a decade before his stop at Vanikoro Island, the young officer was serving in a French expedition to the Greek archipelago. Stopping at the island of Melos (or Milo), he chanced upon a statue recently unearthed by a peasant and stored in a goat pen. The well-educated Dumont d'Urville recognized the female figure as Venus, or Aphrodite, the Greek goddess of love; in her hand was the apple given by Paris in judging her the most beautiful among three rival goddesses. Although the price asked by the peasant was too high for him to pay on the spot, Dumont d'Urville recognized the statue's worth. An unknown sculptor of the second century B.C. had

Even armless, the Venus de Milo commands a place of honor in Paris's Louvre Museum. It is one of the world's most admired works of art.

created a masterpiece in which the softness of the goddess's exposed torso contrasted with the rich folds of the drapery covering her lower body. The statue had to be acquired for France.

He convinced the French ambassador in Constantinople to send with him on his return to Melos a diplomat with a commission to buy the statue. Unfortunately, the peasant had sold it in the meantime to a Turkish official, and the treasure was already packed. After a generous bribe from Dumont d'Urville, the peasant managed to remember that the statue had been presold to the French and could not be delivered to the Turks. The crated Venus was placed on a stretcher and rushed to the beach for loading on Dumont d'Urville's ship. Pursuing Turks attacked; and, in the ensuing brawl, the statue lost both arms — never to be recovered.

The Pacific is a vision of paradise (above); yet most of its islands are surrounded by treacherous coral reefs like those off Vanikoro, which proved a graveyard for La Boussole and L'Astrolabe (left). The latter's ship's bell is at right.

Rumors of Dillon's discoveries had reached Paris long before he did, and an official search mission under the command of Jules Sébastien César Dumont d'Urville had already been sent to the South Pacific. Early in 1828 Dumont d'Urville anchored off Vanikoro.

Natives showed him a channel through the reef which they still called "False," or "Wreck Passage." On that stormy day so many years ago, La Pérouse's flagship *La Boussole* had led the way to an apparent safe harbor only to be wrecked on the jagged coral just below the water's surface. Coming to her rescue, *L'Astrolabe* had been stranded. "Lying at the bottom of the sea, three or four fathoms below the surface," Dumont d'Urville wrote, "our men saw anchors, cannons, shot, and a huge quantity of lead plates." All doubts that he had found the graveyard of La Pérouse's two ships were removed when Dumont d'Urville's crew managed to salvage from the cor-

al undisputed relics from them. Before departing, he set up a monument on Vanikoro to La Pérouse and the 400 men of his ill-fated expedition.

Although further discoveries on Vanikoro were made as late as 1964, no one will ever know whether La Pérouse survived the shipwreck, remained on Vanikoro where two Frenchmen were reported living up until three years before Dillon's arrival in 1826, or sailed away on the makeshift boat a few months after the final disaster.

The Pacific Ocean keeps its secrets, but across its vast reaches La Pérouse is remembered in the name that he gave to geographic features from Easter Island to Hawaii, Japan, and Australia.

Missing Nazi War Treasures

**As Germany collapsed, its fascist masters tried to hide
$7.5 billion in gold and thousands of priceless stolen masterpieces.
Much of the hoard has never been recovered, although —
astonishingly — some was found in a small Texas town in 1990.**

"Bombs away! Doors closing! Let's get the hell out of here!" cried a young U.S. Air Force bombardier on February 3, 1945, as 950 bombers unleashed 2,265 tons of explosives on Berlin, the capital of Nazi Germany. This bombardment, the heaviest of World War II, killed about 2,000, left another 120,000 homeless, and leveled whole districts. Many important government buildings, including Adolf Hitler's headquarters, were razed or severely damaged.

On this fateful Saturday, a working day, 5,000 employees of the Nazis' principal bank, the monumental turn-of-the-century Reichsbank, cowered deep in a basement bunker as 21 separate payloads pounded the imposing edifice, finally demolishing it. When the horrific assault was over, all Reichsbank workers and their world-famous president, Dr. Walther Funk, had sur-

At war's end, Germany's parliament, the Reichstag, was a hulking ruin in the midst of Berlin's devastated landscape.

vived, but the devastation of the warrior nation's financial nerve center set in motion a bizarre series of events that would produce one of history's most intriguing unsolved mysteries. Ostensibly, Germany's wealth would be spirited away for safekeeping as the Allied forces drove across the country. In fact, greedy officials would try to skim off millions for themselves, hiding bullion and currency so well that it has never been found.

The Reichsbank vaults held the major part of Nazi Germany's gold reserves, estimated to be worth about $7.5 billion by today's standards, including about $1.5 billion of Italian gold.

A Secret Stash of Billions

One glance at the rubble and smoldering fires was sufficient for Dr. Funk. He immediately determined to transfer top bank officials to other towns to run the Reichsbank, and he ordered gold and monetary reserves shipped to a huge potassium mine 200 miles southwest of the capital. The isolated Kaiseroda Mine, 30 miles away from the nearest town of any size, offered a hiding place half a mile below ground. There were five separate entrances to its 30 miles of underground passages. The secret transfer of the bulk of Nazi resources, about 100 tons of gold and 1,000 sacks of paper marks, required 13 railway cars.

Within only seven weeks, however, the U.S. 3rd Army under General George S. Patton was advancing toward the area. Incredibly, the Easter holiday made it impossible to find enough trains to rescue the gold, but Reichsbank representatives were able to retrieve 450 sacks of paper money. On April 4 the Americans arrived. Two days later a pair of MPs driving along a country road encountered two French women, displaced persons, and, following orders to restrict civilian movement, escorted them back to the town of Merkers. As they passed the Kaiseroda, one woman said, "That's the mine where the gold bullion is kept."

On April 7, U.S. officers took an elevator 2,100 feet down into a cave hewn from salt rock and found a billion reichsmarks in the 550 bags left behind. After dynamiting the steel door to Room No. 8, they discovered more than 7,000 numbered bags in a room 150 feet long, 75 feet wide, and 12 feet high. The hoard included 8,527 gold bars, gold coins from France, Switzerland, and the United States, and still more stacks of paper money. Gold and silver plate, smashed flat for easier storage, was packed in boxes and trunks. There were suitcases filled with diamonds, pearls, and other precious stones robbed from death camp victims along with sacks stuffed

A Room Disappears

Still unknown today is the fate of the remarkable "amber room of the czars," an entire room made from ornately carved amber. Originally owned by King Frederick William I of Prussia, it was given in 1716 to his Russian ally, Czar Peter the Great, who had been struck by the "inexpressible charm" of the lustrous furnishings. Peter installed this lavish gift in a palace outside his capital of St. Petersburg, expanding it to banquet-hall size and adding 24 mirrors and a mother-of-pearl floor. Two centuries later, during their World War II invasion of Russia, the Germans reclaimed the gift and took it home for reconstruction in Königsberg's castle. Briefly on display to the public, it was crated and taken down to the cellars before the town was destroyed by British bombs in August 1944.

After the war no trace of the unique treasure was found in the bombed-out castle cellars. Rumors abounded that the Nazis had spirited away the room on a ship sunk by a Soviet submarine. Finally, testimony in 1959 seemed to indicate that the amber room had been hidden in a salt mine used to store other works of art. When investigators neared the supposed hiding place, however, a mysterious explosion occurred, flooding the mine shaft and making salvage impossible.

with gold dental bridges and fillings. Added to minor amounts of money from Britain, Norway, Turkey, Spain, and Portugal, the entire cache proved to be one of the richest deposits anywhere in the world at that time. It represented an astonishing 93.17 percent of Germany's entire financial reserves as the war reached an end.

But that was not all. In other tunnels that webbed through the soft rock, investigators found 400 tons of art, including paintings from

15 German museums, and important books from the Goethe collection from Weimar. Under heavy guard, the treasures of the mines were placed in 11,750 containers and loaded onto 32 10-ton trucks for transport to Frankfurt, where they were stored in the vaults of the Reichsbank branch there. Despite persistent rumors about the disappearance of one of the trucks in the convoy, none of the gold or art was lost in transit.

A Treasure Vanishes

To Hitler's propaganda chief Joseph Goebbels it was Funk's "criminal dereliction of duty" that had put the nation's treasures in Allied hands, but the führer approved an attempt to evacuate the reserves that were left. In fact, the plan was originated by his personal security officer, a police colonel named Friedrich Josef Rauch. Following the lead of the Gestapo — which had already started transferring its gold, jewels, art, and paper currency to mines, lakes, and other hiding places throughout the mountains of southern Bavaria and northern Austria — Colonel Rauch suggested that the 6.83 percent of official gold reserves remaining in the Reichsbank be sent to Bavaria for safekeeping. The Reichsbank gold bars and coins to be sent would probably be worth about $150 million today.

During the next few months, Allied bombing disrupted communications, and individual scheming created a complicated scenario that has never been satisfactorily explained. Currency was put aboard two trains, while a truck convoy was readied to transport gold bullion and coins. Owing to the chaos of a collapsing empire, the trains took two weeks to make the 500-mile journey south to Munich. Along the way, Dr. Funk's colleague Hans Alfred von Rosenberg-Lipinski had bags of paper currency off-loaded and transferred to the truck convoy. Eventually, the trucks carried the money, gold coins, gold bars, and foreign exchange to a tiny town in the Bavarian Alps while the trains made it to Munich. Meanwhile, Rosenberg-Lipinski retained one sack of foreign currency and five small boxes "for certain reasons." It is not known what happened to them, but it seems likely, given the impending disaster for Nazi Germany, that the bank official was preparing for a comfortable future.

Others followed his example. The treasure-laden trucks drove through the heavily forested Karwendel Mountains to an infantry training establishment. While harried officers debated where to hide the nation's dwindling treasure, it seems that the Reichsbank's Emil Januszewski took two gold bars (worth almost half a million

dollars today). Someone unable to light a fire in a stove in the school's officers' mess found them blocking the flue, and the aging, highly regarded Januszewski committed suicide. By the time of this discovery, the rest of the gold cache had been buried in watertight holes near an isolated alpine chalet known as the Forest House. The paper currency had been divided into three caches and buried on three different peaks. Subsequently, the two recovered gold bars and a great deal of currency wound up in the care of a certain Karl Jacob, a local functionary. They were never seen again. Several other lower-level Nazis involved in hiding the treasure, including distinguished military men, apparently succumbed to temptation.

Soon Dr. Funk and other high Nazi officials were in Allied custody, but none confessed to knowing where the missing gold reserves were hidden. Eventually, the U.S. military recovered about $14 million worth of Reichsbank gold and some $41 million of German gold from other government agencies, but the Forest House treasure could not be found. For four years American investigators tried diligently to solve the mystery, but they eventually had to report that approximately $3.5 million ($46.5 million today) in gold and about $2 million ($12 million today) in paper money had vanished without a trace.

The Plunder of the Victors

Germans were not alone in taking advantage of the surprising opportunities afforded by the wide dispersal of gold, cash, and irreplaceable art. To the horror of officers like General Patton, who was scrupulous in dealing with all Nazi treasure and who said, "I don't want anybody ever to say that sonuvabitch Patton had stolen any part of it," a disturbing number of American soldiers had sticky fingers. In about 300 known cases, valuable artworks were illegally taken back to the United States. The culprits were prosecuted for taking stolen property and either jailed or given dishonorable discharges from the service.

Then, in 1990, the world was shocked to learn that German art treasures, including one of the most valuable and historically significant works of medieval art still in existence, were unaccountably being offered for sale by the heirs of an obscure veteran from a small farm town in Texas.

Until his death in 1980, orchid fancier and hardware store owner Joe T. Meador had reportedly kept a priceless 9th-century manuscript of the four Gospels wrapped in a blanket, frequently showing it to friends and relatives in his hometown of Whitewright, about 65 miles north of Dallas. Bound in finely worked silver and gold,

Stolen: The Artistic Legacy of Europe

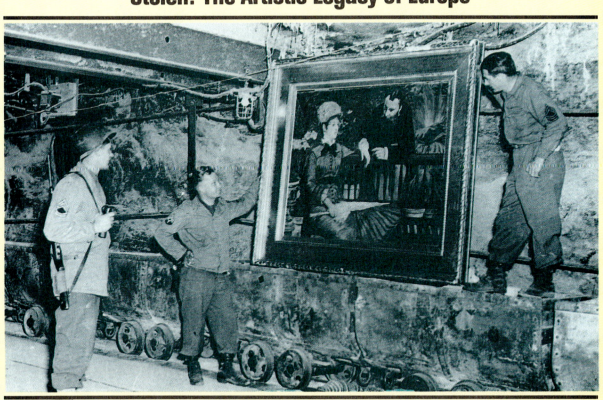

The amazing find in the Kaiseroda mine brought a visit from Allied Supreme Commander Dwight Eisenhower and four of his generals, including George Patton. When this irrepressible officer recalled his first sight of the priceless oil paintings, he wrote, "The ones I saw were worth, in my opinion, $2.50, and were the type normally seen in bars in America." Others took a different view, for the collection included masterpieces by Renoir, Titian, Raphael, Rembrandt, Dürer, Van Dyck, and Manet (above). Even these artistic landmarks were outshone by Germany's single most valuable work of art, the famed 3,000-year-old portrait bust of ancient Egypt's beautiful Queen Nefertiti. Still more treasures were found in other mines nearby.

Nazi warlords had accumulated vast holdings of art from private citizens and the museums of conquered countries. Many works apparently were destroyed during the wartime conflagration, but a number of others were restored to their rightful owners, thanks to the assiduous efforts of curatorial teams assigned to work with the U.S. departments of state and defense. Still, thousands have never been found, and one recent compilation in Munich lists some 4,000 European paintings as missing.

The theft of a defeated enemy's national art treasures is a familiar theme throughout history, recorded as early as the annals of the armies of Assyria, Egypt, Greece, and Rome and continuing down through the campaigns of Napoleon and Britain's colonial conquests. The imposing red porphyry pillars of Hagia Sophia mosque in Istanbul, for example, were stolen from the Persepolis of the Persians by conquering Romans. The famous four horses that reared atop St. Mark's Cathedral in Venice before they were removed to protect them from pollution were booty from ancient Constantinople.

In 1907 The Hague Land Warfare Convention expressly permitted "the salvaging of art treasures from all battle zones," but rapacious Nazi officials went much further, taking millions of dollars worth of art from subjugated countries. Some were exhibited in German museums, but others were stored secretly or displayed in the opulent homes of luxury-loving members of Hitler's entourage.

Special confiscation units included the extremely efficient Bildende Kunst (Fine Arts), which had 350 librarians, archivists, and art historians. It was their task to register and catalog the invaluable loot, carefully crate it for damage-free shipment, and, in many cases, find hiding places as the Third Reich began to crumble. It is quite possible, according to experts, that some missing art will never be found because much of the documentation of caches was lost or destroyed during the final days of World War II fighting.

Whitewright, Texas, was the unlikely post-World War II repository of a German church's art treasures, including a priceless illuminated manuscript of the Gospels (below).

the illuminated and illustrated 1,100-year-old manuscript came from a church in Quedlinburg, Germany. Suddenly, it was sold in Switzerland for a "finder's fee" — some would call it ransom — of $3 million.

"Absolutely a national treasure," commented the secretary-general of West Germany's Cultural Foundation of the States. Estimated to be worth up to $30 million, the manuscript is 600 years older than the Gutenberg Bible. It was written in gold for the imperial court and donated to the cloister in the medieval castle town late in the 10th century, perhaps by Emperor Otto III and his sister, Adeleid, abbess of the convent.

Meador's trove, it turned out, also included a 1513 manuscript with an ornamental gold and silver binding and a 9th- or 10th-century reliquary decorated with gold, silver, and precious stones. Others in the collection were shaped like a heart and in the form of a plate, but the most valuable was a rock crystal flask shaped like a bishop's head and thought to contain a lock of hair from Mary, the mother of Jesus. There were also gold and silver crucifixes, a 12th-century comb of Henry I, and numerous other art objects with important historical and religious significance.

The treasures had been taken from the Quedlinburg church and hidden in a mine shaft for safekeeping as Allied forces moved toward the area in the closing days of World War II. In April 1945, according to U.S. Army records, officials who inventoried the cache found "all pieces intact and present." Some days afterward, however, it was discovered that several of the art objects

had disappeared. Although an investigation was launched immediately and reports continued to be filed for the following three years, no clues were ever obtained. When Germany was divided in 1949, it became a crime for any East German to make contact with the West, so the church was unable to pursue the theft.

Apparently, Meador, then a lieutenant in the Army, took the objects and shipped them back to the United States, successfully carrying off one of the largest art thefts of the 20th century. A frustrated art teacher who was forced by personal circumstances to work in his family's hardware store, he once told a friend that he was torn between feeling guilty and deeply enjoying the beauty of the priceless masterworks.

After Meador's death, when his heirs started to offer Quedlinburg objects on the market, such United States agencies as the IRS and the FBI began investigating. After months of legal maneuvers, the heirs agreed to relinquish the entire treasure for a total payment of $2.75 million, $1 million more than the down payment already received for the Gospels. Although Germany said that the case was thus amicably resolved, many criticized the settlement.

Secrets of the Tower

*Less than a month after succeeding to the throne of England,
12-year-old Edward V entered the Tower of London and was later
joined there by his younger brother. They never emerged,
and their mysterious disappearance remains unsolved.*

*O*n April 9, 1483, King Edward IV of England died suddenly just short of his 41st birthday. His older son and heir was only 12, and in his will Edward had named his younger brother Richard, duke of Gloucester, as protector of the realm.

For nearly 30 years the British Isles had been wracked by a dreary civil war between the House of York, which had among its badges a white rose, and the House of Lancaster, symbolized by a red rose. The seesaw contest was later romanticized as the War of the Roses. As the York champion, Edward IV had had the three previous Lancaster kings declared usurpers, but his rule was by no means secure, and he must have known that there would be challenges to his youthful heir, Edward, Prince of Wales.

Richard had proved himself a loyal and resourceful soldier in the service of his brother, Edward IV, and had sworn an oath of fealty to the Prince of Wales. Now he moved quickly to take charge of a realm left with a power vacuum at its center. On April 29 Richard intercepted the entourage taking young Edward to London, arrested the boy's maternal uncle, who had been in charge, and accompanied his nephew the remaining distance to the capital. The coronation of Edward V, originally set for May 4, was postponed to June 22 as the boy-king was installed in the royal apartments at the Tower of London.

The Tower of London, scene of many sinister events — including, perhaps, the murder of two princes.

The sons of Edward IV were supposedly suffocated as they lay sleeping at the Tower of London. Was their uncle, Richard III (right), the hunchbacked villain depicted by his Tudor successors?

Suspicious of her brother-in-law's motives, Edward IV's widow, Elizabeth Woodville, sought sanctuary at Westminster Abbey with her younger son and daughters. In mid-June the protector succeeded in persuading Elizabeth to surrender the son, nine-year-old Richard, duke of York, sending word that the boy-king was lonely in the Tower and needed his brother for a playmate there.

Then, on the Sunday that was to have been his coronation day, Edward V was barred from succession. A Cambridge doctor of theology named Ralph Shaa preached a sermon outside St. Paul's Cathedral in London that challenged the legality of the succession. Dr. Shaa claimed that Edward IV was already legally betrothed at the time of his marriage to Elizabeth Woodville, that the union with her was thus invalid under current law, and that their children — including the boy-king —

were illegitimate. Two days later one of the protector's staunchest supporters repeated the claim before a group of London's leading citizens, adding the lament "Woe is the realm that has a child to their king."

After a brief show of reluctance, the duke of Gloucester accepted the crown on June 26 and was proclaimed Richard III. The boy-king's reign had lasted less than three months.

Accused: Richard III

Through July the uncrowned Edward V, now contemptuously referred to as "Edward bastard," and his brother were occasionally seen at play in the Tower yards. But then, according to one contemporary witness, the two boys were taken into the innermost rooms, seen more and more rarely behind barred windows, "until at length they ceased to appear altogether."

By the fall of 1483 it was widely rumored that the two princes had been murdered in the Tower — but by whom? In January 1484 the French chancellor warned of the dangers of a minority kingship — the French king, Charles VIII, being only 14. Edward IV's sons, he stated authoritatively, had been killed by their uncle and the crown had thus passed to the assassin.

Meanwhile, Elizabeth Woodville had forged an alliance with Richard's enemies, offering her eldest daughter in marriage to the Lancaster pretender, Henry Tudor. In August 1485 Richard III met Henry Tudor in battle at Bosworth Field. At a critical moment in the contest one of the king's supporters deserted to Henry, and Richard was killed. The deserter took the crown from the fallen king and placed it on the head of Henry VII. The War of the Roses was ended; England was about to enter a period of unprecedented growth under the House of Tudor.

As Richard III had been plagued by rumors that he had murdered the princes, now Henry VII was tormented by stories that they were still alive and potential rivals to the throne. Eventually he succeeded in establishing the story that, by order of Richard, the boys had been suffocated under feather mattresses and buried under stones at the foot of a staircase in the Tower.

The convenient scapegoat was one Sir James Tyrell, tried and executed for "unspecified treason" in May 1502. Only later was it announced that Tyrell had confessed to the murder of the princes before his beheading. The tale was accepted and entered the history books with Sir Thomas More's biography of Richard III, published in 1534 and subsequently used by Shakespeare as a source for his drama *Richard III*.

Shakespeare's Villain

Although his reign was one of the shortest in England's history, Richard III has been reinterpreted by almost every subsequent generation of scholars — being depicted alternately as heroic warrior king or deformed devil. In the present century, Richard III societies have been founded to defend his name. But theirs is a losing battle against the genius of William Shakespeare. Already accused of the murder of the two princes in his own lifetime, Richard III gained immortal notoriety a century later as the villain of one of Shakespeare's earliest plays, the historical drama *Richard III*.

Writing in the 1590's, during the reign of Queen Elizabeth I, Shakespeare not surprisingly told a story favorable to Elizabeth's grandfather, the first Tudor king, Henry VII. He portrayed Richard as a venomous usurper who does not hesitate to order a henchman to murder the "Foes to my rest and my sweet sleep's disturbers . . . those bastards in the Tower." The deed done, Richard cold-bloodedly determines to woo the little princes' older sister, already promised in marriage to his rival, Henry Tudor. A minor malformation — apparently one of Richard's shoulders was slightly higher than the other — was magnified so that Shakespeare's Richard becomes a self-pitying hunchback or, in the words of his intended bride, "a lump of foul deformity." At the play's happy conclusion on Bosworth Field, Henry Tudor declares, "the bloody dog is dead. . . peace lives again."

Belated Burial

In 1674, some 200 years after the supposed murders, a wooden box containing the skeletons of two children was found during construction work at the Tower of London. Accepted as the remains of the murdered princes, the bones were interred at Westminster Abbey.

In 1933 the bones were given to medical experts for examination. The verdict: The skeletons were those of boys the ages of Edward V and his brother at the time of their disappearance. The cause of death could not be established, but the jaw of the elder boy showed a major deterioration.

One of the princes' last visitors at the Tower of London had been a royal physician, called in to treat Edward V's toothache. The boy-king, the doctor reported, had been praying and doing penance daily in the belief that he faced death. "Alas," he said, "I would my uncle would let me have my life yet, though I lose my Kingdom."

Everyday life in Beijing. Behind the scenes in the autumn of 1971: a fierce power struggle.

A Political Crash Landing

*He was the second most powerful man in China, officially
designated as the heir to aging Mao Zedong. But was Defense
Minister Lin Biao willing to wait patiently for the succession — or
would he try to seize power in a military coup?*

Darkness had fallen over Beijing's Tiananmen Square. During the afternoon martial music had blared from loudspeakers as thousands of students and schoolchildren rehearsed for the parade that would mark the 22nd anniversary of the founding of the People's Republic of China on October 1, just two and a half weeks away. But now the square was quiet and all but deserted.

Suddenly the nocturnal calm was broken by the sound of racing engines as up to 50 black limousines swept into the square and pulled up to the Great Hall of the People, a building reserved for the most important government meetings. Out of the cars stepped the leading figures of China's government and ruling Communist Party — all, that is, except Defense Minister Lin Biao.

Later that same night, some 170 miles east of Beijing, a Trident jet airplane took off from an airport near the seaside resort of Beidaihe. Flying on a northwest course, the plane passed over the border with the Mongolian People's Republic and crashed about 2:30 A.M. Inside the wreckage were found nine half-burned corpses and weapons, documents, and equipment that identified the aircraft as belonging to the Chinese air force. At the request of the Chinese government, the bodies were buried at the site of the crash.

The anniversary celebrations for October 1, which would have placed Lin Biao next to Communist Party Chairman Mao Zedong, were canceled without explanation. Lin's name as well as those of other high-ranking military commanders were no longer mentioned in the government-controlled press.

These were the events of September 12–13, 1971 — as observed and reported at the time. But was there a link between the late-night gathering of China's leaders, the airplane crash the next morning, and the cancellation of the celebration? The story that emerged during the next dozen years is still not completely understood — at least, outside of China.

Reaching for the Top

A veteran military commander of the communist forces that had defeated Chiang Kai-shek in 1949, Lin Biao had been made minister of defense in 1959. Seven years later he was also named vice chairman of the Communist Party and in 1969 was officially designated as the successor to Chairman Mao. His rise was marked by apparently total dedication to Mao — for example, Lin was credited with compiling *Quotations from Chairman Mao Zedong*, the "little red book" carried by rampaging student Red Guards during the Great Proletarian Cultural Revolution launched by Mao in 1965.

Directed against "those people in authority *within the party* who are taking the capitalist road," the Cultural Revolution mobilized China's youth in defense of communism. Coincidentally, it led to the ouster of Liu Shaoqi as head of state while reinforcing Mao's supreme power as head of the Communist Party. When the political unrest threatened to erupt into bloody civil war, Lin stepped in with the military forces at his command to restore order to the troubled nation.

Watching from the sidelines was Premier Zhou En-lai, who disdained the futile ideological controversies of the Cultural Revolution and only desired to restore strength to China's faltering economy. But when Zhou began reappointing party functionaries expelled during the political unrest, he put himself on a collision course with Lin, who wanted the military to wield decisive power. Unlike Lin, Zhou realized the danger of being Number Two to the power-obsessed Mao and was content to bide his time as the Number Three or even Number Four in the power lineup.

No longer satisfied with his designation as Mao's eventual successor, the 62-year-old Lin made a bold move at a party gathering in August 1970. In shameless flattery, he first proposed that the constitution be amended to canonize Mao as a "genius." He next moved that the vacancy created by Liu Shaoqi's purge be filled and that Mao be named head of state as well as head of the party. If Mao declined, Lin urged that someone else — presumably himself — be named to the position. Even Mao balked at the first suggestion. "Genius does not depend on one person or a few people," he said with uncharacteristic modesty. "It depends on a party, the party which is the vanguard of the proletariat." And, in turning down the additional post of head of state, Mao declared that it should remain vacant. It was clear to all that the party chairman was displeased by Lin's transparent maneuvers.

Target: Chairman Mao

This rift between Mao and Lin, according to one theory, marked the beginning of a conspiracy that was to reach a climax on the night of September 12–13, 1971. "If there is no post of chairman of the state," Lin's wife and political confidant, Ye Qun, complained, "what can Lin Biao

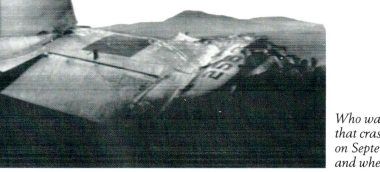

Who was in the airplane that crashed in Mongolia on September 13, 1971 — and where was it headed?

The French Revolution's Reign of Terror

The purge of Liu Shaoqi at the beginning of the Great Proletarian Cultural Revolution and the mysterious death of Lin Biao in 1971 were not unique events in the short but turbulent history of the People's Republic of China. Nor are such sudden falls from power and deaths unique to revolutionary China. Indeed, parallel events took place almost 200 years earlier in the wake of the French Revolution.

Two years after the storming of Paris's notorious prison, the Bastille, touched off the revolution, King Louis XVI was captured while attempting to flee France. The next year, on September 21, 1792, France was declared a republic; the king was executed in 1793. Soon near-dictatorial power fell to the republic's nine-member Committee of Public Safety.

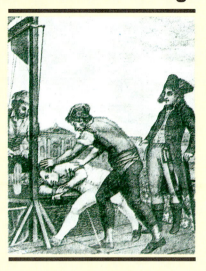

Robespierre, who had sent his chief rival, Danton, and so many others to their deaths, meets the guillotine, the revolution's efficient engine of death.

Vying for leadership of the committee were Georges Jacques Danton and Maximilien Robespierre. With his gift for oratory, Danton had called for a revolutionary tribunal that would purge enemies of the republic. In what came to be known as the Reign of Terror, the tribunal's victims were quickly decapitated by the guillotine set up in Paris's principal square. In April 1794 Robespierre succeeded in having Danton arrested, tried, condemned, and executed.

Robespierre survived his former rival by less than five months. At the end of July, he and some 100 of his followers were executed. With most of the revolutionary leaders now dead, the people demanded an end to the violence. The guillotine was dismantled and the square where executions had taken place was renamed Place de la Concorde.

---

do? Where can he be put?" Even at age 77, Mao Zedong showed no signs of tiring or even thinking of stepping down from his supreme leadership of the country. Her husband had three choices, Ye Qun said: wait patiently for the inevitable death of Mao; give up his dream of power; or eliminate Mao and seize control of the People's Republic.

In the fall of 1970 Lin Biao sent his son, Lin Liguo, whom he had raised to a high-ranking air force position, on a secret mission to China's largest cities. His task: to organize a network of loyal and trustworthy military officers to be known as the Joint Fleet. By the spring of 1971, the conspirators had a plan for a military coup that would topple Mao Zedong from the pinnacle of power to which he so tenaciously clung. It was code-named Project 571, since the Chinese words for these three numbers are also contained in the phrase "armed uprising." Mao was called "B-52" for the U.S. bomber. Lin was pro-Soviet Union and thus anything linked to the United States was an object of hatred to him.

Three attempts on Mao's life were tried: an airplane attack on the chairman's residence in Shanghai; the destruction of his private train en route from Shanghai to Beijing; the dispatch of an assassin disguised as a courier to his home in Beijing. When all three failed — the last on the eve-

ning of September 12, Lin Biao, his wife, his son, and several other conspirators scrambled to board the Trident at the airport near Beidaihe.

Escape to the Soviet Union

The seizure and confession of the courier had implicated Lin in the conspiracy. Uncertain as to the extent of the defense minister's support among the military establishment, Mao and Zhou En-lai called the late night meeting at the Great Hall of the People. As they deliberated, the Trident took off. Although Lin had planned to fly south to gather military support for his coup, he apparently changed his mind once he was airborne and decided to seek refuge in the Soviet Union. He had spent three years there recovering from World War II wounds and was reasonably certain of at least ideological support from his Russian friends for the challenge to Mao. Instead, Lin Biao and his party all died in the crash in Mongolia.

That, at least, was the version of the story first reported in the press outside of China and more or less confirmed the next year by the Chinese government. A different and far more shocking account appeared in 1983 with publication in the United States of a report smuggled out of China and attributed to an insider given the pseudonym Yao Ming-le.

Staging a Mock War

According to Yao, there were two separate conspiracies. The first, Project 571, was organized by Lin Liguo and merely called for Mao's assassination. This was cancelled by Lin Biao in favor of a more elaborate plan code-named Jade Tower Mountain for the cluster of luxurious villas outside Beijing inhabited by the power elite. There Mao was to be trapped.

Lin's dangerous scheme called for secret assistance from the Soviet Union in staging a mock attack on China. This would give him the excuse to declare martial law, take Mao and Zhou En-lai into "protective custody," eventually having them killed, and seize power for himself.

Then, in July 1971, a startled world learned that U.S. Secretary of State Henry Kissinger had secretly visited China and negotiated with Zhou En-lai for an easing of the tension that had marked relations between the two countries since the communists came to power in 1949. Early the next year President Richard Nixon was to visit China. The apparent reconciliation with the United States — and a further deterioration of the already soured relationship with the Soviet Union — made it imperative that Jade Tower Mountain be launched as soon as possible. The date chosen

China's ruling triumvirate in a harmonious pose (left to right): Lin Biao, Mao Zedong, Zhou En-lai. Behind them, the Cultural Revolution's Red Guards brandish their "little red books."

Theater as Politics

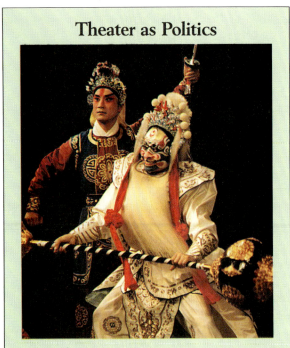

European visitors to China in the 19th century were attracted yet puzzled by a unique popular entertainment that mixed music, song, pantomime, and acrobatics. There were few props, but the performers wore magnificent costumes and ingenious masks. Since the performances blended drama and singing as in the opera with which they were familiar, the visitors called it the Peking Opera — Peking then being the name for Beijing.

Mao Zedong well understood that literature and art could be powerful propaganda tools to spread his communist message. "Literature and art are for the masses," he wrote as early as 1942, "... they are created for the workers, peasants, and soldiers and are for their use." Mao's fourth and last wife, Jiang Ching, undertook a reform of the Peking Opera during the Cultural Revolution, asking why the dramas involved the nation's handful of landlords, rich farmers, and bourgeois elements while ignoring 600 million workers, peasants, and soldiers. Revisionists led by the purged head of state Liu Shaoqi, she charged, had turned the Peking Opera into an "independent kingdom." Jiang Ching wanted to sever all ties to the theatrical past and create new art forms that would celebrate communism.

Following the death of her husband in 1976, Jiang Ching and three of her fellow leaders of the Cultural Revolution were reviled as the Gang of Four, tried, and given commuted death sentences. The radical break with the past she had dictated for the arts did not outlast her brief period of ascendancy. Today traditional Peking Opera is once more ensconced in China.

was the day Mao returned from a trip south, on or about September 11.

Meanwhile, however, Zhou En-lai had apparently tricked Lin's daughter, Lin Liheng, into revealing her brother's conspiracy if not that of her father. Zhou alerted Mao to the danger and the two set a trap for Lin.

Dinner at Chairman Mao's

On the evening of September 12, Lin Biao and his wife were guests at a festive welcome home dinner for Mao at the chairman's Jade Tower Mountain villa. Mao himself launched the celebration by uncorking a bottle of imperial wine sealed in a Ming dynasty vase 482 years earlier. At the banquet delicacies flown in from all across China were served. At one point, Mao used his chopsticks to pluck tiger tendons from a platter and place them on Lin's plate. After a dessert of fresh fruit, Ye Qun mentioned that it was growing late; she and her husband should be leaving so that the chairman could rest from his trip. But Mao seemed reluctant to break up the jolly gathering and urged them to stay on another half hour. Just before 11 P.M. Mao saw the couple to their waiting car. Minutes later, on the road descending from Mao's villa, rockets fired by an ambush party recruited from the chairman's private guard destroyed the car and its passengers.

Zhou En-lai personally verified that the charred bodies were indeed those of Lin Biao and Ye Qun, suggesting to the chairman that a proper explanation for the defense minister's disappearance be concocted so that Lin would not end up "looking like a hero." Without emotion over the death of the man who had served him and the Communist Party for more than four decades, Mao told the premier to handle the details of the cover-up as quickly as possible.

In this account of the conspiracy, it was Lin Liguo only who fled in the Trident. When pursuing Chinese fighters launched a successful missile attack, the plane crashed just over the border in Mongolia. Later, the Chinese authorities let stand the general assumption that the parents as well had perished in the crash — a much tidier story than that of a dinner party ending in death.

Whichever version one chooses to believe, Mao had eliminated his rival. The next year he welcomed President Nixon to Beijing, faithful Premier Zhou En-lai at his side. At his death in 1976, the 83-year-old Mao Zedong still controlled the China he had helped create. To the very end he had avoided sharing power or designating a successor to his rule of the world's most populous country.

Australia's Most Wanted Man

Although Australia was discovered by the Dutch in 1606, the interior was still largely unexplored two and a half centuries later when a German adventurer set out to cross the continent from east to west. He was walking into a great unknown.

Even in his native Germany, the name Ludwig Leichhardt is known today only to students of the history of exploration. But in Australia he has been granted lasting fame by his controversial exploits on that continent and by his mysterious disappearance there.

A river, a waterfall, a mountain range, a mountain peak, and a district in Sydney all bear his name. His statue was erected in that city, and just a few years ago the Ludwig Leichhardt Foundation was established. Australia's Nobel Prize-winning novelist Patrick White incorporated the explorer's story into his novel *Voss*, later the basis for an opera. Nine major expeditions and countless smaller searches have combed the continent since Leichhardt and his party of six disappeared on his last expedition in 1848. "Their fate is the great mystery in the history of the discovery of my country," says Australian writer Gordon Connell. Leichhardt's celebrity is all the more curious when one probes his background and tries to judge his accomplishments.

Leichhardt may have been the first European to see Australia's forbidding Macdonnell Ranges.

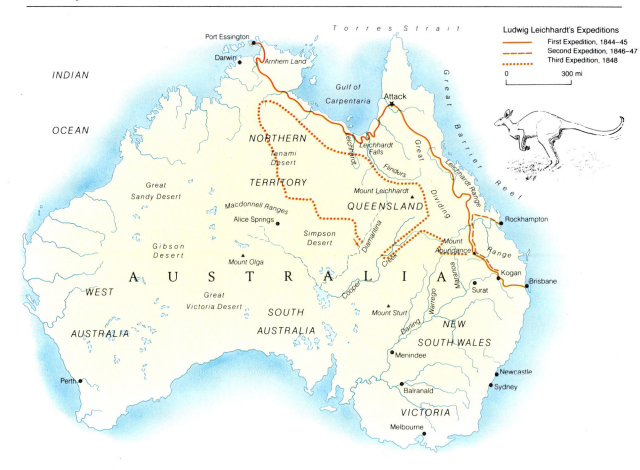

Ludwig Leichhardt's three expeditions are traced on the map of Australia above.

A Student's Wanderlust

Born in Prussia on October 23, 1813, Ludwig Leichhardt was the son of a farmer with slight prospects for an exciting future. But his scholarly nature won him admission to the University of Göttingen, where he was supposed to receive training to become a high school teacher. Two fellow students, English brothers named John and William Nicholson, must have perceived Leichhardt's potential and persuaded him to switch to the study of science and medicine at the University of Berlin — even offering to support him during his studies.

After only two years in Berlin, still not prepared for a profession and wanting to avoid compulsory military service, Leichhardt joined William Nicholson in London in May 1837. Later the two roamed about France, Switzerland, and Italy and hatched a plan to go to Australia — a largely unknown continent opened to settlement by the British only a half century earlier. When the time for departure came, Nicholson changed his mind about going but paid his friend's passage and gave him some money with which to start a new life. Thus endowed, Ludwig Leichhardt — or,

as he now liked to call himself, Doctor Leichhardt — set out on his own for the long voyage to the Southern Hemisphere in October 1841.

The Making of an Explorer

The 28-year-old German who arrived in Sydney on February 14, 1842, was described by a contemporary as "being more than six feet tall, with a high intellectual forehead, small gray, intelligent eyes, and dark brown hair. The lower part of his face was hidden by a bushy beard and moustache, the nose slightly curved. . . ."

During the next two years, Leichhardt supported himself by lecturing on botany and geology and made minor field trips to collect plants, insects, and rock samples. About this time he conceived the notion of achieving fame by exploring the interior or what he called "that kernel of the dark continent." Although he made an epic overland walk of 600 miles from Newcastle to Brisbane, Leichhardt was scarcely qualified to become an explorer. He was nearsighted, terrified of firearms, and had little sense of direction. His services, not surprisingly, were spurned by the surveyor general of New South Wales.

At Brisbane, Leichhardt heard that a government expedition across northeastern Australia to a military outpost at Port Essington had been called off for lack of funds. Yet the coastal farmers remained eager to learn of suitable agricultural land in the interior. Seizing the opportunity, Leichhardt returned to Sydney, announced his plan to lead a private expedition as replacement for the canceled government undertaking, and soon had five recruits as well as the necessary financial backing.

Setting a Leisurely Pace

Back in Brisbane, Leichhardt added four more men to his expedition; and thus it was a party of ten (two soon turned back) that set out from the last outpost of civilization on October 1, 1844, cheerfully singing "God Save the Queen." Their goal — Port Essington — was 2,000 miles to the northwest as the crow flies, but Leichhardt planned to follow rivers just inland from the coastline and avoid the interior, which his only map showed as a blank.

To transport the expedition's 1,200 pounds of provisions, Leichhardt had exchanged some of his horses for slow-moving bullocks, which could also be slaughtered for meat en route. Incredibly the expedition carried only one two-gallon water container in addition to individual canteens — and this dictated Leichhardt's "water strategy." At the first water hole, camp was set up as a search party was sent to find the next one and return to lead the others to it. Although it guaranteed a safe advance, it did not promise speed.

By February 1845 Leichhardt calculated that one-quarter of the journey had been completed although three-quarters of the food supplies were gone. Once, the leader himself — accompanied only by one of the expedition's two Aboriginals — was lost for several days, surviving on two pigeons the native shot. "I swallowed the bones

Successful Crossing — at a Terrible Price

Thirteen years after Ludwig Leichhardt disappeared trying to cross Australia from east to west, an Irish-born police officer named Robert O'Hara Burke succeeded in traversing the continent — but this time from south to north.

On August 20, 1860, Burke left Melbourne with a well-provisioned party of 14. Brave but inexperienced and unable to control his men, Burke left half the expedition at the northernmost settlement of Menindee on October 19 and pressed on with a smaller party. In mid-December he further divided his expedition, leaving William Brahe to guard a depot of supplies at their camp on Cooper Creek and taking three men with him on a 700-mile dash to the Gulf of Carpentaria.

Almost within sight of the sea but blocked from reaching it by a swamp, Burke turned back on February 21, 1861. The return journey was a nightmare. Burke had to beat one man for stealing rationed provisions and accused him of feigning illness; three weeks later the man was dead of hunger, exhaustion, and dysentery. On April 21 the three survivors reached Cooper Creek. They found a cache of provisions and a note from Brahe; after waiting a month longer than instructed, he had left only a few hours earlier! Burke never caught up with Brahe. By the end of June, Burke and one more companion were dead; the sole survivor of the crossing, John King, returned to Melbourne to tell the ghastly tale.

One of the "L trees," possibly marked by Leichhardt (right) during his third expedition into the Australian interior — a journey from which he never returned.

they passed. Early in May the party left the last river flowing eastward and struck out northwestward for the Gulf of Carpentaria and their destination on the north coast.

By the end of June the party was approaching the Gulf of Carpentaria when spear-throwing natives made a nocturnal attack on the tents. John Gilbert, the expedition's naturalist, was killed and two other men were wounded. After only two days' rest, they continued the journey, badly shaken but determined to reach their goal. On December 17, 1845, after a 14½-month trek of nearly 3,000 miles, the Leichhardt expedition marched into Port Essington.

Australia's Hero

The explorers returned to Sydney by sea and were given a hero's welcome, greeted as if back from the grave. "I thought the whole town would go mad with joy," Leichhardt wrote. He had mapped a considerable portion of northeastern Australia and revealed it to be "an excellent country, available, almost in its whole extent, for pastoral purposes." A grateful citizenry rewarded Leichhardt (the first money the 32-year-old explorer had ever earned) and raised an additional sum to be shared among the six others.

With such acclaim now his, Leichhardt had little difficulty in raising funds for a second expedition — this one to traverse the northern half of the continent and then travel south along the western coast to Perth. Accompanied by six white men and two Aboriginals, and with a caravan that included 270 goats, 108 sheep, and 40 oxen, as well as mules and sheep dogs, Leichhardt embarked on his second expedition on December 7, 1846.

Experiencing the full rigor of the rainy season, the men were soaked through night and day as their lightweight tents were torn to shreds. Soon the entire party was stricken with fever and ague, sometimes with only cold, muddy water to drink since no one was strong enough to light a fire and make tea. When they did have food to eat, they ended up swallowing "about 20 flies" with each mouthful. In temperatures of up to 107 degrees the men had to ride fully covered to avoid the stinging bites of sandflies; their horses often streamed with blood from the insect attacks.

Within six months the party returned, having traveled only 500 miles through what one member of the expedition called "the most horrible country the foot of a white man ever trod." Illness and dissension — Leichhardt was accused of taking food from the sick — had doomed the expedition from the start.

and the feet of the pigeon, to allay the cravings of my stomach," Leichhardt wrote. Soon goannas, possums, emus, kangaroos, and birds of all kind were happily consigned to the stewing pot. "It is remarkable how soon man becomes indifferent to the niceties of food," the expedition leader observed. From the rivers they caught crayfish and eels to vary their diet; nests of native bees provided "the sweetest and most aromatic honey we had ever tasted." Wild herbs gave extra strength to tea and soups, and, by cautious experiment, Leichhardt found that certain plants growing near water holes could be cooked and eaten to ward off scurvy — though severe diarrhea was an unfortunate side effect.

Through March and April the explorers continued their stately progress, attaching names of friends back on the coast to rivers and mountains

Australia's Native Peoples

The native population of Australia, the so-called Aboriginals, arrived on the southern continent some 40,000 years ago via stepping-stone islands from Southeast Asia.

In January 1788 the first British colonists — 736 male and female exiled convicts — arrived at Sydney Harbor aboard the 11 vessels of the First Fleet. They were much less fit for survival in their new homeland than were the Stone Age people they encountered. These hunter-gatherers roamed about nearly naked, boomerang, spear, stone axe, and firestick their main hunting weapons. There were perhaps 300,000 natives, divided among 600 tribes with differing languages and customs. All were deeply rooted in nature — men being patient and skilled hunters, women being discriminating plant gatherers. Each tribe had an area that supported its members; these territorial rights were strictly respected.

The fate of the Aboriginals, like that of North America's Indians, is a painful episode in the history of European discovery and settlement of new worlds. The British assumed sovereignty over land needed for the penal colonies, with little or no regard to the territorial claims of the tribes. The official goal was to establish a peaceful relationship with the Aboriginals; in reality, few of the convict-settlers shared such humanitarian goals. "Wheresoever the European put his foot down," Charles Darwin wrote after a visit to Australia in 1836, "the death of the natives seems to follow." Deprived of their hunting grounds, infected with new diseases, corrupted by al-

Few of Australia's native peoples still maintain the hunter-gatherer lifestyle.

cohol, conscripted for cheap labor, their children forced into missionary schools, hunted down and killed in the interest of "pacification," the Aboriginals suffered a devastating decline. By 1901 the population had dropped to 66,950 and by 1921 to 60,479.

World War II marked a turning point in Australia's treatment of the native peoples. With thousands of soldiers sent overseas, the country's work force was depleted. Aboriginals found new employment opportunities, in many cases receiving cash wages for the first time. In the postwar years they obtained citizenship and the right to vote, better education and health care, the right to hold land, and a choice between remaining as Aboriginals or assimilating with European Australians. A population surge brought their strength to 144,465 in 1981.

The Last March

Leichhardt was not the man to give up his dream of crossing the continent and — despite the miserable failure of his second expedition — had another party ready early in 1848. On April 4 he wrote his last letter, from a sheep station some 250 miles inland from Brisbane, before setting out in a northwesterly direction with four white comrades and two Aboriginals, 50 bullocks, 20 mules, and 7 horses.

Two and a half years passed with no news of the Leichhardt expedition — not yet cause for concern to his friends and sponsors who understood the enormity of the undertaking. But toward the end of 1850 an Aboriginal appeared at Surat, a sheep station less than 50 miles south of Leichhardt's jumping off point, with an alarming story. From another native in the interior he had heard of a massacre of several white men and two blacks just west of the Maranoa River, which would have been directly in Leichhardt's line of march. Attacking at night, the natives had killed the entire party, slaughtered the animals, and made off with pots and blankets.

Trees Marked with an "L"

A ship was sent to Port Essington, in the event that Leichhardt might emerge in that vicinity after retracing his earlier, successful expedition, but he had not been seen there. Surveying in the northwest, John McDouall Stuart reported finding mysterious footprints in an area not known to have been previously penetrated by white men. The footprints, Stuart said, "were long and narrow, with a high arch at the sole's inner side and a strongly pronounced big toe . . . more like the footprint of a white man than the one of an Aboriginal." Finally, after a settler named Gideon Lang confirmed reports of a massacre beyond the Maranoa River, the government voted funds for a search which, because of a drought, was not undertaken until 1852.

When the designated leader of the search party was washed overboard and drowned en route from Sydney to Brisbane, leadership fell to Hovenden Hely, a member of Leichhardt's second expedition. Now convinced that the explorers had been killed west of the Maranoa River, Hely concentrated his search in that area. Other natives repeated the massacre story, saying that the attack had been provoked when the two Aboriginals among Leichhardt's party had molested some local native women.

Moving on to the Warrego River in mid-June 1852, Hely found traces of an old campsite and a tree into the trunk of which had been carved the letter "L" and over it "XVA." Could the "L" stand for Leichhardt and the "XVA" be read as 15 April, a date only 11 days after the expedition was last seen? Nearby were two other trees similarly marked. Hely abandoned his search and returned with a report that the missing men undoubtedly had been killed by Aboriginals.

The Wild White Man

Two more searches were dispatched before the end of the decade and in April 1861 came the report — from the same Stuart who had found the footprints a decade earlier — of an abandoned hut near Mount Sturt in the northwestern corner of New South Wales; it seemed to have been built by a white man rather than an Aboriginal. Other "L trees" were found. Then in 1871, after repeated rumors of a wild white man living among Aboriginals in western Queensland, a police officer named J. M. Gilmour led a new search. He returned from the interior with six pairs of men's trousers, parts of a tent, remains of woolen blankets, a bag made of human hair — straight and thus from a white man, and bones that also proved to be of white men. Relics of a missing expedition undoubtedly; but which one? Leichhardt was not the only explorer to have vanished in these years.

In 1938, 90 years after Leichhardt's disappearance, yet another search — the ninth — was organized, prompted by reports of bones found at the edge of the Simpson Desert. The bones proved to be those of Aboriginals, but two British coins minted before Leichhardt left England were also recovered. Could they have been his?

Death at the Diamantina River

After painstaking research and evaluation of all previously accumulated findings, Gordon Connell published his conclusion about the fate of Ludwig Leichhardt in 1980; it has been largely accepted by the experts.

Unable to follow his intended route across the northern half of the continent, Leichhardt reached Arnhemland but then turned south — perhaps to retrace his steps back to Queensland. At a water hole near where the Diamantina River crosses the border into South Australia, he and his men were ambushed and killed. Bones of white men have been found there.

If Connell is correct, Leichhardt would have covered some 3,000 miles — more than any other explorer up to that time. Yet, apparently, tragedy overtook him only 500 miles from his departure point. Any knowledge of the continent's interior comes not from Leichhardt but from the many search parties sent to find him.

The End of a Romance

**On a summer night in 1694 a handsome young soldier
was summoned to the chambers of his beloved,
the unhappily married crown princess of Hanover.
He never returned from their tryst.**

Around 10 o'clock on a Sunday night Philipp Christoph, Count Konigsmarck, left his residence in the north German city of Hanover and, under cover of darkness, hurried to the castle on the river Leine. That morning he had received a note asking him to pay a late night call on Sophia Dorothea, the young wife of the crown prince of Hanover. Even though the letter was written in an unknown hand, Philipp eagerly accepted the invitation to a clandestine rendezvous with his beloved, for it had been many weeks since they had had the chance to be alone together. Perhaps he was also aware of the significance of the date: July 1, 1694, four years to the day since they had first exchanged love letters.

Although she had neither written nor dictated the note, Sophia Dorothea was agreeably surprised to see her lover so unexpectedly. They may have had a suspicion that the letter was a trap, but their joy at being reunited outweighed any inclination to exercise caution in holding such a dangerous meeting. At any rate, they must have reasoned, the hide-and-seek game was about to end. At the break of dawn on the following morning, a coach would come to fetch Sophia Dorothea. At last she would be able to abandon the pretense of a loveless marriage to her cousin, Georg Ludwig, and leave forever the

Secretly, Count Konigsmarck enters Hanover castle for a rendezvous with the crown princess. It was to have been the last time for such a meeting, for in the morning they were to elope.

castle in which she had never been at ease. Tomorrow she would start a new life with Philipp.

The final details of the carefully planned escape were arranged before the lovers parted; now they only had to count the hours until daybreak. But Sophia Dorothea waited in vain the next morning. Philipp never arrived, nor did he send any message to explain his failure to do so. He had vanished, never again to be seen.

In despair and fearing the worst, Sophia Dorothea turned to the court privy councilor and begged him to investigate Philipp's disappearance. "I am trembling with anguish that Count Konigsmarck could have fallen into the hands of that lady. . . ." Which lady was Sophia Dorothea afraid of and why? And what *did* happen to Philipp after he left her chamber? To solve the riddle, it is necessary to investigate the background of an unhappy marriage against which the fatally romantic affair developed.

Marriage: A Political Maneuver
Arranged marriages among rival dynasties were customary in a Germany that was then divided among a number of duchies and petty kingdoms. Love played no part in such alliances. But rarely have a bride and groom felt such deep dislike for each other as did Sophia Dorothea and Georg

There was no love in the marriage between Georg Ludwig (below, left) and his cousin, Sophia Dorothea (right), and the crown princess never felt at home in the castle on the river Leine (bottom). It is not surprising that she quickly succumbed to the charms of a childhood friend, Philipp Christoph, Count Konigsmarck (center).

Ludwig. Going back beyond their childhood acquaintance, the mutual disdain was rooted in the previous generation of their two families.

The bride's father, Duke Georg Wilhelm of Brunswick-Celle, had once been engaged to another Sophia, this one a princess of the nearby Rhineland Palatinate. Unwilling to relinquish his bachelor lifestyle, Georg Wilhelm dissolved the engagement and handed over his fiancée to his younger brother, Ernst August. To make the arrangement more attractive to the pair, he signed a contract in 1658 promising that he would never marry and that upon his death the duchy of Brunswick-Celle would be reunited with the duchy of Brunswick-Luneberg, which Ernst August had inherited.

A few years after signing the agreement with his younger brother, the confirmed bachelor Georg Wilhelm fell in love with a Frenchwoman named Eleonore d'Olbreuse. Not content to keep her as a mistress, he determined to nullify his contract and enter a lawful marriage with Eleonore. He appealed to Leopold I, who ruled in Vienna over the loose association of German states known as the Holy Roman Empire. Not until 1676, however, was his petition granted. Eleonore thus became the duchess of Brunswick-Celle and their daughter, Sophia Dorothea — already ten years old — was made legitimate with the rank of crown princess.

At Ernst August's court in Hanover these developments were regarded with suspicion. The promised reunification of the two duchies now seemed threatened. Happily, the two brothers found a solution to the problem: the marriage of Sophia Dorothea to her cousin, Ernst August's eldest son, Georg Ludwig.

Politically, the solution seemed ideal; to Sophia Dorothea it was anything but satisfying. Unused to the strict protocol and both puzzled and disturbed by court intrigue, she never felt at ease in Hanover. Even worse, her husband had a mistress — as did her father-in-law. In the peculiar etiquette of the day, Duke Ernst August's mistress, the Countess Platen, claimed a higher court rank than the crown princess. After Georg Ludwig fathered a son in 1683 and a daughter four years later, he completely ignored his wife. Little wonder, then, that Sophia Dorothea quickly succumbed to the charms of the handsome Count Konigsmarck when he appeared at court in 1688.

Love with Mars and Adonis

Philipp Christoph, Count Konigsmarck, was 23 when he arrived in Hanover, a year older than Sophia Dorothea. Of German origin, his family had achieved wealth and power in the service of the Swedish kings.

According to his rank, Philipp was to be educated as a cavalier and man of the world. To this end, he and his older brother, Karl Johann, were sent in 1680 to London to learn such arts as dancing, riding, and fencing — with plans to round out their education with more intellectual pursuits at Oxford. The glittering lifestyle of the English capital proved their downfall. Philipp incurred horrendous gambling debts, while Karl Johann was implicated in the death of a prominent man with whose wife he was having a dalliance. Karl Johann was able to escape punishment and leave England, but the scandal made Philipp's social position untenable. He returned to Germany in 1682 and the next summer entered the imperial army of Leopold I, then engaged in wresting Hungary from the Turks.

When his regiment was disbanded in 1688, Philipp had to seek other employment and thus traveled to Hanover to apply for a military post. He arrived during the pre-Lenten carnival season and at one of the many court parties encountered the woman who became his fate: the unhappily married Sophia Dorothea. The two had actually known one another since childhood, but now Sophia Dorothea was looking at a dashing soldier in his prime. According to a contemporary descrip-

A Sister's Destiny

Count Konigsmarck's disappearance changed the course of life for his younger sister, Maria Aurora, and ensured that she too would have a place in history — even if only as a footnote.

Despite the evidence to the contrary, Maria Aurora was convinced that her brother remained alive after he vanished on the night of July 1–2, 1694. Her unshakable belief was based on a horoscope predicting that in that very year Philipp would survive a disaster unharmed. To help find him, she turned to Friedrich August, elector of Saxony, whose services Philipp was supposed to be entering. In the fall of 1694 she arrived at the Dresden court.

Maria Aurora's reputation for beauty and intellect had preceded her. Among her many admirers were two dukes, one aged 60, the other a boy of 17. The French philosopher Voltaire, born in the year that proved so fateful for the Konigsmarcks, was later to praise her as "the most famous woman of two centuries."

The youthful elector of Saxony was no exception to the rule of men falling in love with Maria Aurora at first sight. After what a biographer would call "short resistance," she submitted to his passionate wooing and in October 1696 gave birth to Friedrich August's son. Not until 1711, however, did the elector recognize the boy as legitimate and allow him to call himself Hermann Maurice, count of Saxony. In 1720 Hermann Maurice entered French service and in time held that country's highest military rank.

tion, Philipp was "admirably well built, tall, handsome, with flowing hair and lively eyes, in a phrase: a well-balanced mixture of Mars and Adonis [the mythological figures for war and male beauty]."

Sophia Dorothea at first found Count Konigsmarck an attentive listener and a trusted friend in whom she could confide all her worries, large and small. With him she could give vent to her anger at the scheming Countess Platen, the object of her fear and loathing.

There was a problem, however. Shortly after his arrival at court, Philipp had begun an affair with the countess. Too late, he came to regret his mindless indiscretion and realized how difficult it would be to end the relationship without exposing both himself and Sophia Dorothea to the countess's wrath. To free himself from this embarrassing entanglement, Count Konigsmarck volunteered for active duty and left the court.

Returning to Hanover at the end of his first

campaign, Philipp mistakenly thought that Countess Platen had lost interest in him and believed that it was safe to begin seeing Sophia Dorothea again. By the spring of 1690 he must have declared his love for the crown princess. Between July 1 and the night of his disappearance exactly four years later, Philipp and Sophia Dorothea exchanged more than 300 letters — tender notes of their love, happiness, and longing for each other.

On the Edge of an Abyss

But Countess Platen had not lost her ardor for Philipp, easily saw that Sophia Dorothea was the reason for her rejection, and plotted revenge. She had the young lovers watched closely, missing letters and broken seals on envelopes alerting them to her spying. By 1693 there could be no doubt that the affair had been discovered. In a rash attempt to pacify Countess Platen, Philipp began courting her again — though his letters indicated how much he hated doing this.

More and more, Philipp and Sophia Dorothea talked about fleeing Hanover together to escape the untenable situation at the court. Yet, there was an enormous obstacle to such a plan: lack of money. Philipp was already living beyond his means, and Sophia Dorothea had surrendered all her wealth and personal property at the time of her marriage to Georg Ludwig.

In May 1694 Philipp once more left Hanover, this time to seek a generalship in the army of the elector of Saxony in Dresden. The contract he negotiated allowed him to return to Hanover the next month with more favorable financial prospects. By that time most of the court had moved to a summer palace outside Hanover, and the absence of Sophia Dorothea's husband and her mother-in-law would make it easier for the lovers to make their escape. Only the elderly Ernst August and Countess Platen remained in the castle the night Philipp called upon Sophia Dorothea, confirmed their elopement plans, bid his fond farewell — and vanished forever.

No Scandal — at Any Cost!

The news of Count Konigsmarck's disappearance spread throughout Hanover at lightning speed and soon reached the other German courts as well. Only two years earlier the duchy had been given new importance when Ernst August had been named elector of Hanover, one of the German rulers who had a vote in the selection of the Holy Roman emperor. A court scandal in Hanover would have repercussions across Europe, stretching even to England.

Rise and Fall of a Favorite

A tragedy with striking parallels to the one in Hanover was enacted three generations later in Denmark. The prologue took place in 1766, the year that 17-year-old King Christian VII of Denmark married Caroline Matilda, the 15-year-old sister of King George III of Great Britain and a great-granddaughter of George Ludwig and Sophia Dorothea.

The real plot began two years later, when Christian chose a German doctor named Johann Friedrich von Struensee as his personal physician. Apparently, the young doctor not only knew how to win the confidence of the mentally disturbed king but was also able to gain the affection of the unhappily married queen. His rise at court was inevitable; soon his political ambitions were apparent to all. In 1770 he was named a minister of

Characters in a tragedy: Struensee and the queen playing chess, as the oblivious king lounges on a sofa.

state with unprecedented power.

Struensee's affair with the queen was an open secret, but the king did not seem to mind the disgrace. At this point the king's stepmother, Maria Juliana, formed an alliance with the alienated aristocracy. A scandal involving Christian and Caroline Matilda, she speculated, would enhance the chances of her own son succeeding to the throne.

During the night of January 16–17, 1772, a group of conspirators entered the king's bedchamber and forced him to sign arrest warrants for Struensee and the queen. The ensuing trial failed to prove the various charges of official misconduct made against the doctor. But when he admitted — presumably under torture — to having committed adultery with the queen, he was condemned to death.

Like her unlucky great-grandmother, Caroline Matilda was divorced and exiled — ironically to the very castle in Germany where Sophia Dorothea had been born more than a century earlier.

The jealous Countess Platen could not forget that Philipp had left her for the younger crown princess, but she had to wait four years for her revenge. Though she did not wield the murder weapon herself, as in this lurid version of the attack on Count Konigsmarck, she most likely plotted the death of the young cavalier.

Ernst August's wife, the elder Sophia, was a granddaughter of James I of England. She had one aim in life: to secure the English throne for her descendants. A murder involving both her son's wife and her husband's mistress could destroy this prospect. The normally indiscreet Sophia grew reticent about the case, writing two weeks later to a female relative: "On the wood market where one hears all the news, there is talk that the witches of Dresden have lured away Konigsmarck."

But it was not witches who made Philipp vanish. A close study of contemporary diplomatic records concerning the events in Hanover reveals bits and pieces of a puzzle that can be put together to show what actually happened that night.

Apparently, Countess Platen's spies had informed her of the lovers' plan to flee the court on July 2. She took the story to the old elector, Ernst August, who gave her an order for Count Konigsmarck's arrest. Either upon leaving Sophia Dor-

othea's chambers that fateful night or upon returning early the next morning, Philipp was met by four cavaliers with drawn swords. In the ensuing scuffle, one of them inflicted a mortal wound. The body was hastily disposed of — flung into the river Leine, according to one story; burned or buried in the castle, according to other versions. Whether the four men had explicit orders to kill Konigsmarck is not known; at any rate, his death was most welcome.

Within six months Sophia Dorothea and Georg Ludwig were divorced, though Konigsmarck's name was never mentioned in the proceedings. The disgraced crown princess was exiled to nearby Ahlden Castle, denied any visitors except her mother, and kept in seclusion until her death 32 years later in 1726. Meanwhile, the elder Sophia had her final triumph. In 1714, the year of her death, Georg Ludwig succeeded to the throne of Great Britain as George I. His direct descendants rule the kingdom to this day.

Into the Green Hell

***Driven by an unshakable belief that
Brazil's jungles hid a city lost for millennia, a British
colonel set off in 1925 to discover the origin
of South American civilization.***

Mato Grosso in Portuguese means "dense forest" — a fitting name for the land-locked Brazilian state nearly three times the size of Texas. Until the second half of the present century, Indians were the only inhabitants of its nearly impenetrable rain forests, and few white men had attempted to chart its terrain.

Into this steaming wilderness filled with animal species still unfamiliar to zoologists and native tribes whose existence was not even suspected, three explorers dared to advance in April 1925. They would be facing poisonous snakes, flesh-eating fish, clouds of biting, stinging insects, and an uncertain welcome from the natives — all in pursuit of an elusive lost city known to them only by an enigmatic code name: "Z." Five weeks after leaving the capital, Cuiaba, the party's leader wrote home to his wife in England from the ominously named Dead Horse Camp (where his mount had died on a previous expedition): "We hope to get through this region in a few days. . . . You need have no fear of any failure." It was the last message ever received from the jungle explorer.

Penetrating the Veil

Colonel Percy Harrison Fawcett had been obsessed with solving the mysteries of the Brazilian jungle for nearly two decades. He had been commissioned by the Bolivian government to survey its boundary with Brazil in the years 1906–09 and had returned to the forbidding wilderness popularly called "the green hell" several times in the years since then.

South America's Spanish conquerors had never found fabled El Dorado or the land of the warrior women known as Amazons, but stories about them would not die. In 1911 came the electrifying news of the discovery by an American, Hiram Bingham, of the lost city of the Incas, Machu Picchu, nestled in Peru's Andes Mountains.

There were other lost cities, natives kept telling Fawcett on his subsequent surveys and explorations. In Chile he heard of a still inhabited City of the Caesars, its streets paved in silver, its buildings roofed with gold. The inhabitants supposedly led a blissful existence under the rule of an enlightened king. Some magic property made it invisible to undesirable adventurers from outside. In Rio de Janeiro, Fawcett found a report of the long forgotten discovery in 1753 of the ruins of a monumental stone city; there was no record of it ever having been visited again.

Given a 10-inch tall figure carved of black basalt, Fawcett had it evaluated by a psychometrist, one who claims he can divine an object's origin by holding it. Undoubtedly, he was told, it came from the lost continent of Atlantis, taken along when its inhabitants had fled destruction to find refuge and build a great city in the Brazilian wilderness. Since the name was unknown, Fawcett called it "Z" for convenience. A civilization older than Egypt's waited to be uncovered.

"The existence of the old cities I do not for a moment doubt," Fawcett wrote in 1924, as he prepared for another expedition. "Between the outer world and the secrets of ancient South America a veil has descended"; he who penetrated that veil would advance knowledge of the past immeasurably. At age 57, Fawcett knew this would be his last chance to be that person.

Raising funds from various scientific societies and selling the story of his exploration and expected discoveries in advance to the North American Newspaper Alliance, Fawcett was ready for the grand adventure early in 1925. He would take with him only his 21-year-old son, Jack, and a young friend named Raleigh Rimell. They would probably be gone until the end of the following year. But, if they didn't emerge from Brazil's "green hell," no rescue parties were to be sent. If Fawcett, with all his experience, couldn't survive, there was little hope for others. For that reason, he declined to give a precise route for his exploration.

Tantalizing Clues

In 1927 Fawcett's younger son, Brian, met a French traveler in Lima, Peru. En route across the continent by automobile, the Frenchman had encountered an old, sick, and apparently confused man along a road in Minas Gerais, a Brazilian state between Mato Grosso and the Atlantic. The man had said his name was Fawcett. Not having heard of the lost explorer, the Frenchman did not insist that the stranger join him.

Brian was unable to raise money for a rescue party and not until the following year did the North American Newspaper Alliance send a party under George Dyott to investigate Fawcett's disappearance. A native chieftain told Dyott that he had seen an older white man accompanied by two younger men, both lame. They were headed east, toward the Atlantic. For five days smoke from their camp fires could be seen, but thereafter there was no trace of them. Dyott returned with the belief that Fawcett and the two young men had been killed by the Indians, but the colonel's family refused to accept this.

Four years later a Swiss trapper named Stefan Rattin emerged from the Mato Grosso with a tale that Colonel Fawcett was being held as a prisoner by Indians. Brian later learned that a half-white native boy claimed to be the son of his brother Jack. All such clues, including bones produced as those of Fawcett, were dead ends. The fate of his father, Brian sadly concluded, would remain a mystery; the riddle of "Z," forever unsolved.

"Whether we get through and emerge again or leave our bones to rot in there, one thing's certain," Colonel Fawcett had told Brian. "The answer to the enigma of ancient South America — and perhaps of the prehistoric world — may be found when those old cities are located and opened up to scientific research. That the cities exist, I know. . . ."

Not greed for gold had driven Colonel Fawcett into the rain forests of the Brazilian interior but rather the search for a lost culture. Today thousands work in gold mines there under the most arduous conditions; few are lucky enough to find nuggets like the ones below.

Wanted: Raoul Wallenberg

*Memorials have been dedicated to him, streets named after him,
honorary U.S. citizenship bestowed on him, books written
about his life — but the final events of that life
in a Soviet prison or penal camp remain unknown to this day.*

A few months before the end of World War II, the Swedish diplomat Raoul Wallenberg stepped into his car in Budapest, the war-ravaged capital of Hungary. The German occupying forces had fled and the Soviet Union's victorious troops were pouring into the city. Since his arrival the previous summer, Wallenberg had tirelessly devoted himself to protecting the Jews of Budapest from the Nazis' "final solution to the Jewish problem." Now he wanted to ensure their continued safety and was going to Russian military headquarters in Debrecen, 130 miles northeast of the city, to negotiate with Marshal Rodion Malinovsky. Pointing to two Russian soldiers on motorcycles with an officer in the sidecar of one,

he told a friend that he didn't know if the escort "is to protect me or if I am under arrest."

His flippant comment proved to be a grim forecast: Neither Wallenberg nor his driver, Vilmos Langfelder, was ever again seen in the West. What happened to them from that day on is shrouded in mystery and marked by rumors, speculation, half-truths, and deliberately false statements from behind the Iron Curtain.

Who was this Raoul Wallenberg whose disappearance has been repeatedly investigated over the past four decades and whose sad destiny has captured the sympathy of people in many countries? Born on August 4, 1912, he was a member of one of Sweden's wealthiest families — often

Did Raoul Wallenberg die behind the walls of Moscow's infamous secret police headquarters, Lubyanka?

referred to as the Swedish Rockefellers; from its ranks had come bankers, industrialists, diplomats, and churchmen. Although he studied architecture at the University of Michigan, Raoul was slated to work in the family's bank and in 1936 was sent to learn the business in Haifa in what was then called Palestine. Raoul's great-great grandfather was a Jewish convert to Christianity; the young man once boasted that as a Wallenberg and "half-Jewish" he could never be defeated. In Haifa he lived in a kosher boarding-house and became acutely aware of the rising Nazi threat to Europe's Jews, for refugees had swelled the city's Jewish population to 50,000.

Back in Sweden at the outbreak of World War II in 1939, Raoul entered the food import/export business as the partner of a Hungarian-Jewish refugee, Koloman Lauer, who needed a trustworthy, multilingual gentile free to travel to the countries overrun by the Nazis. Appalled at what he saw in his travels, Wallenberg eventually became dissatisfied with his work and eager to do something worthwhile with his life. In 1942, seeing a British film about a seemingly absent-minded professor who outwits the Nazis to rescue Jews, Raoul told his sister that that was "just the kind of thing" he would like to do.

Wallenberg Against Eichmann

Throughout Nazi-occupied Europe, the Jews had been sentenced to follow a trail of sorrow into the concentration camps and gas chambers. But few even among Germany's enemies spoke out against the atrocities or extended a helping hand to those seeking to flee the terror. Not until January 1944 — and then only because of the prodding by Secretary of the Treasury Henry Morgenthau, Jr. — did the American government take action with creation of the War Refugee Board. That agency sent Iver Olsen, a Treasury Department official with connections to the Office of Strategic Services (OSS, the wartime predecessor to the CIA), to neutral Sweden with a plan to rescue Europe's last large Jewish community, the more than 700,000 Jews of Germany's ally Hungary.

Up to this point, Hungary's government had resisted Nazi pressure for the massive deportation of Jews, many of whom were converts to Christianity and who played a critical role in the country's economic life. Sensing that its ally was wavering, Germany sent troops to Hungary in March 1944 and installed a puppet regime; among the Germans dispatched to Budapest was Adolf Eichmann, architect of the "final solution" and a man described by a colleague as "complete-

ly obsessed with the idea of destroying every single Jew he could lay his hands on." Henceforth, Hungary's Jews would have to wear the yellow Star of David; soon they were being rounded up for transport to the death camps.

In Stockholm, Iver Olsen enlisted 31-year-old Raoul Wallenberg in the American plan to block Eichmann. With secret American funds but traveling as a Swedish diplomat, Wallenberg arrived in Budapest on July 9. He carried two knapsacks, a sleeping bag, and, somewhat unusual for a diplomat, a small revolver — "to give myself courage," he told a colleague. Wallenberg knew that his mission was dangerous and that he would have to act quickly. Eichmann was intent on putting all Budapest Jews on trains to the death camps; Wallenberg would try to get as many as possible off.

There wasn't much time left for Wallenberg. With the Russian army relentlessly advancing from the east, Eichmann stepped up his frantic efforts to exterminate Hungary's Jews. In October, when the Hungarian government offered to negotiate a truce with the Soviets, the pro-Nazi Arrow Cross Party seized power. As the roundup of Jews continued, Wallenberg's efforts to save them took on a new urgency.

Attempting to bargain with the Nazi official, Wallenberg invited Eichmann to dinner at his apartment in December. In a conversation punctuated by the sound and light of Russian artillery on the eastern horizon, the Swede told his guest that Nazism was doomed. Eichmann was unmoved. "Don't think we're friends," he said in parting; "we're not. I plan to do everything to keep you from saving your Jews. Your diplomatic passport won't protect you from everything. Even a neutral diplomat can meet with an accident." Soon thereafter a German truck "accidentally" crashed into Wallenberg's car; fortunately, the Swedish diplomat was not a passenger at the time, and so he escaped harm.

The day after Christmas the Russians surrounded Budapest. Eichmann had managed to slip out of the Hungarian capital, but Wallenberg remained behind with his Jewish charges.

Into the Void

On January 13, 1945, a Russian patrol found Wallenberg in a building under the protection of the International Red Cross. The young diplomat asked to be taken to Soviet military headquarters, where he hoped to present his plan for the continued protection of Hungary's Jews and for their postwar rehabilitation. Four days later he was on the road to Debrecen.

No sooner had the car left Budapest than Wallenberg and his driver, Langfelder, were handed over to the Soviet secret police, the dread NKVD. Instead of meeting Marshal Malinovsky, they were put on a train for Moscow. The Soviet Foreign Ministry notified the Swedish ambassador there that "measures have been taken to protect Mr. Raoul Wallenberg." The Russians' "protective custody" was actually imprisonment, first at NKVD headquarters, Lubyanka, later at Lefortovskaya prison. Langfelder was not seen or heard from after March. But from Wallenberg's former cellmates who somehow later found their way to the West, it is known that the Swedish diplomat was in the Moscow prison until the spring of 1947 — after which time he was presumably deported to Siberia.

Meanwhile, the Soviet ambassador in Stockholm had assured Wallenberg's mother that he was safe and would come back; perhaps it would be best, the ambassador later told the wife of the Swedish foreign minister, not to make a "fuss" about the matter.

On March 8, 1945, Wallenberg's friends in Budapest were stunned by an announcement on the Soviet-controlled radio: The Swedish diplomat had been killed en route to Debrecen on January 17, presumably by the Germans or their Hungarian allies. The story was greeted with extreme skepticism in the West.

Cold War Diplomacy

From Moscow the Swedish ambassdor, Staffan Soderblom, wrote to his superiors in Stockholm: "One of the troubles that lies on my heart is, of course, Wallenberg's tragic disappearance." Yet, he rebuffed an offer of assistance from the American ambassador, W. Averell Harriman, saying that there was no reason to doubt the Russians. "We do not require American intervention," Soderblom brusquely added.

Wallenberg (right) courageously opposed the efforts of Adolf Eichmann (below, left) to exterminate Hungary's Jews (shown in a Nazi roundup at center).

Raoul Wallenberg had become the first victim of the Cold War. Because of his dealings with Eichmann, the Swedish diplomat was at first suspected of being a Nazi agent. Learning of his sponsorship by the U.S. War Refugee Board and his links to Iver Olsen, the Russians apparently then decided that Wallenberg was an OSS operative. Anxious to preserve his country's neutrality between the United States and the Soviet Union, Soderblom did little to pursue the inquiry. It was entirely understandable, he reported home, that Wallenberg could have disappeared in the chaos of the war's last months in Hungary.

Before leaving his Moscow post in June 1946, Soderblom sought an audience with Soviet leader Josef Stalin. Although convinced that Wallenberg was dead and that Soviet officials had no information regarding his fate, he asked Stalin for an official confirmation. "This would be very much in your own interests," he told the Russian dictator, "as there are people who, in the absence of such information, will draw incorrect conclusions." Stalin wrote down Wallenberg's name and promised that the matter would be investigated and cleared up. "I shall see to it personally," he pledged.

Fourteen months later, in August 1947, the new Swedish ambassador in Moscow was informed by the Soviet Foreign Ministry that "Wallenberg is not in the Soviet Union and is unknown to us."

The "Prison Telegraph"

In the West the case remained open. A monument to Wallenberg's relief efforts was commissioned by his admirers in Budapest. Albert Einstein joined others in proposing him for the Nobel Peace Prize. Most important, however, was the arrival of former cellmates who could confirm Wallenberg's imprisonment between January 1945 and April 1947. Among these were two Germans named Gustav Richter and Horst Kitschmann. Both reported that they had been interrogated about Wallenberg at Lefortovskaya prison on July 27, 1947, and that their interrogations had been followed by solitary confinement.

During his two-year imprisonment in Moscow, they revealed, Wallenberg was allowed out of his cell only for a daily 20-minute exercise period in a courtyard measuring 10 by 15 feet and surrounded by a fence that prevented prisoners from seeing each other. But like all inmates, he soon learned to use the "prison telegraph." Pipes linking the cells provided effective conductors for the messages that prisoners tapped out with their toothbrushes. Simplest of the codes used

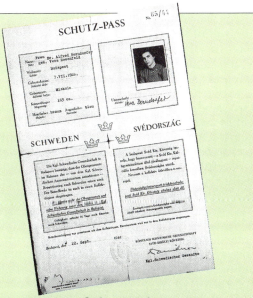

Hero of the Holocaust

By the time Raoul Wallenberg arrived in Budapest, in July 1944, Adolf Eichmann had already succeeded in transporting some half million of Hungary's Jews to the concentration camps. Yet, more than 200,000 Jews had survived his extermination net, most of them in the capital.

In order to save as many of them as possible, Wallenberg began issuing "protective passes" (see above), documenting that the bearer was cleared for repatriation to Sweden and was under the protection of the Royal Swedish Legation in Budapest. At first the passes were granted only to those with family or business connections in Sweden; later Wallenberg dropped such qualifications in handing them out. On at least two occasions he boarded trains bound for the death camps, asked for a show of "Swedish" hands, and removed several hundred people.

But Wallenberg's activities extended beyond distributing the passes. In time he had built an organization of 335 people and 40 physicians who staffed two hospitals, soup kitchens, children's nurseries, and, above all, 32 safe houses flying the Swedish flag. When the pro-Nazi Arrow Cross stormed one of the sanctuaries, the resourceful Swede put his most "Aryan-looking" charges into German uniforms and posted them in front of the safe houses. By early December, 13,000 Jews were under his custody.

With their war effort collapsing, he told the Germans and their Hungarians allies that any further persecution of the Jews would lead to trials as war criminals. He, in turn, could not be threatened: "My life is one life, but this is a matter of saving many lives." At war's end, there were 120,000 Hungarian Jews, perhaps 15,000 to 20,000 personally rescued by Wallenberg.

was the so-called "idiot system" — one tap for A; two for B; three for C; etc. More sophisticated was the "five-by-five" or "square system" in which the letters of the alphabet were imagined as if on a grid five letters across and five down — A to E on the first row, F to J on the second, etc. Two sets of taps were given, first for the row across and then for the column down. Two taps followed by five taps stood for the letter J, second row across, fifth column down.

A returned Italian prisoner named Claudio de Mohr recalled his astonishment upon hearing on the "prison telegraph" that a neutral diplomat was being kept at Lefortovskaya. Three German diplomats, following their release, told of having helped Wallenberg — again, via the "prison telegraph" — compose a letter in French to deliver to Stalin. Whether it was ever delivered, they did not know. Then, in the spring of 1947, Wallenberg tapped out his last message at the prison: "They are taking us away."

Lost in the Gulag Archipelago

Along with some 50 other prisoners — almost all Russians, most of them accused of "counterrevolutionary activities" — Wallenberg was deported to the Vorkuta labor camp, 70 miles north of the Arctic Circle. In the next dozen years, based again on the testimony of other prisoners repatriated to the West, he was shunted from camp to camp in the notorious network that came to be known as the Gulag Archipelago.

A doctor remembered certifying him for construction work in the summer of 1948; Wallenberg was then 36 years old. A Hungarian professor met him at a prison back in Moscow in 1951; he was in transit between a camp 1,500 miles southwest of the capital to another 1,000 miles east. A former Polish military attaché saw him boarding a boxcar at a camp in Siberia in 1953. A Swiss prisoner exchanged tapped messages with Wallenberg at a prison in Vladimir, a city 120 miles east of Moscow, in 1954; an Austrian told of being placed by mistake in Wallenberg's cell there the next year. If he was ever released, the man was urged, just tell any Swedish legation

Under Stalin there were thousands of penal colonies and work camps in the Soviet Union. If the statements of former prisoners can be trusted, Wallenberg's trail led through several of them.

Soviet prisons

Work camps and penal colonies where Wallenberg was reported seen

The Gulag Archipelago

According to cautious estimates, there are between 1,500 and 3,000 work camps and penal colonies in the U.S.S.R.; among the 2 million inmates are at least 20,000 political prisoners. Strung across the Soviet landmass like a chain of islands, the camps are collectively referred to as the Gulag Archipelago, the letters GULAG being the abbreviation in Russian for Central Administration of Prison and Work Camps.

Life in the camps has been vividly described by the Nobel Prize-winning writer Aleksandr Solzhenitsyn, who was a prisoner for 11 years. In two works, *One Day in the Life of Ivan Denisovich* and *The Gulag Archipelago*, he reveals the inhuman conditions under which the unfortunate inmates live and work. For up to 16 hours a day, six days a week, often without sufficient

Because of his revelations about the camps, Aleksandr Solzhenitsyn was expelled from the U.S.S.R. He now lives in the United States.

nourishment or any safety precautions, the camp inmates are forced to perform hard labor. In the 1970's, for example, prisoners were employed in uranium mines without protective clothing. Thousands died and more suffered serious damage to their health. In addition, prisoners were subjected to humiliation and even torture.

Such places of exile for criminals and political prisoners also existed in Russia under the czars. But the network was greatly expanded under Stalin's reign of terror, during which 10 million people are thought to have perished in the camps. Writing in *The Gulag Archipelago* of what he called "40 years of unprecedented Soviet state terrorism," Solzhenitsyn drew upon the memoirs of witnesses and dedicated his massive work "to all those who did not live to tell it."

---

that the "Swede from Budapest" was still alive. A political prisoner from the Soviet republic of Georgia reported sharing a cell with Wallenberg off and on between 1948 and 1953. But reliable sightings of Wallenberg dwindled toward the end of the decade; reports became blurred; the facts about his possible survival became confusing and all too often contradictory. Among the last to see him was the Polish military attaché, who reported Wallenberg as looking "young and fit" when they met again in October 1959.

Hope that Refused to Die

Despite the firm Soviet denial of knowledge about Wallenberg's whereabouts in August 1947, the diplomat's family did not give up hope. Pressed by them and other concerned citizens, the Swedish government made no fewer than 15 written and 34 oral requests for information to the Soviet Union during the period 1952–54.

In April 1956, heading the first official Swedish visit to the U.S.S.R., Prime Minister Tage Erlander handed a letter for Raoul from his mother and a file of documents to Premier Nikolai Bulganin. "This is a waste of time!" shouted Bulganin. "We don't have time for this kind of nonsense."

"If you won't even accept the material that I have brought," Erlander said, "how can you be so

sure that this whole affair is a falsification, an unimportant sideshow to embarrass you?"

"I don't want to hear any more of this!" Bulganin thundered. Party Secretary Nikita Khrushchev calmed Bulganin who, "as a gesture of our goodwill toward Sweden," agreed to examine the evidence. "You will have our reply as soon as possible," he promised.

On February 16, 1957, the Swedish government had its answer from the Soviets. A handwritten note found in the files of the Lubyanka infirmary reported the death in his cell, apparently the victim of a heart attack, of "prisoner Wallenberg." The date on the note – July 17, 1947 – was a convenient 10 days before the interrogations of Richter and Kitschmann that had revealed knowledge of his presence in the U.S.S.R. up to that point.

Even this belated admission by the Soviets that Wallenberg had indeed been a prisoner of theirs immediately after the war did not satisfy those who wanted a complete revelation and still nourished hopes for Wallenberg's survival.

Confirmation — then Denial

In 1961 there was an apparent breakthrough. The highly respected doctor and medical professor Nanna Svartz was invited to Moscow by an

On October 5, 1981, President Ronald Reagan signed the document conferring honorary American citizenship on Raoul Wallenberg. His half-sister, Nina Lagergren, is at left; his half-brother, Guy von Dardel, is at right; Tom Lantos stands behind Reagan.

old acquaintance, A. L. Myasnikov, chairman of the Soviet Academy of Medical Science. During a conversation, in German, she asked about Wallenberg. Myasnikov revealed that he knew "a great deal about the Wallenberg case." The hero of Budapest was in a mental institution, "extremely tired, nervous, and depressed." He had been called in to attend Wallenberg two years earlier when the Swedish prisoner had gone on a hunger strike and only recently reexamined him.

Dr. Svartz passed the astonishing information to the Swedish government, and Prime Minister Erlander wrote Khrushchev asking the Soviet leader to return Wallenberg to Sweden. The Soviets stuck to the report of Wallenberg's death. "For the third time we now inform you that the subject has been completely exhausted," Khrushchev told the Swedish ambassador who delivered Erlander's letter. Any attempt to pursue the matter would only worsen relations between Sweden and the Soviet Union.

On subsequent visits to Moscow, Dr. Svartz pressed Myasnikov for details. Alternately angry that a confidence had been betrayed and insistent that she had misunderstood his German, the Soviet doctor at last confirmed that Wallenberg had died in 1965. This time sworn to secrecy, Dr. Svartz broke her silence only in 1981 following an international hearing on the Wallenberg case in Stockholm, a hearing that she believed incor-

rectly endorsed the false hope that Wallenberg was still alive in the Soviet Union.

Raoul's mother, who had remarried when he was six, and his stepfather, Fredrik von Dardel, were among those who refused to abandon hope. When they died within two days of one another in February 1979 at the ages of 86 and 93, they bequeathed the quest for Wallenberg to their children, Raoul's half-brother, Guy von Dardel, and his half-sister, Nina Lagergren. Although they too were unable to solve the mystery, they had the satisfaction of posthumous recognition for their brother — from an unexpected source in the United States.

Honorary American Citizenship

In the fall of 1980 Tom Lantos, a Hungarian-Jewish refugee, was elected to the U.S. House of Representatives from California. He and his wife were among those who owed their survival to Wallenberg and so, fittingly, it was Tom Lantos who introduced the bill in Congress to make Raoul Wallenberg an honorary citizen of the United States — only the second such person, after Winston Churchill, to be so honored. Nina Lagergren and Guy von Dardel were among those present to witness President Reagan signing the bill into law in October 1981.

Raoul Wallenberg was again in the news during the summer and autumn of 1989. Soviet government officials told a U.S. press team that the case was being reopened. Next, at a Paris human-rights conference, a Russian delegate admitted that the Swedish diplomat's disappearance was "a dark page in Soviet history." The Soviet weekly *New Times*, while expressing sympathy with his friends who still hoped for a miracle, said "there is no undoing the past." Finally, in October, the Soviet government invited Mrs. Lagergren and von Dardel to Moscow, where they were given Raoul's passport and notebooks, the first tangible proof that he had ever been in Russia. However, the Soviets stuck with the story that Wallenberg had died in July 1947 and blamed his arrest and imprisonment on the excesses of the Stalin regime.

Meanwhile, in May 1987, the long-planned memorial to the hero of the Holocaust was erected in Budapest. Chiseled in granite is a Latin saying: "As long as luck smiles upon you, you have many friends; in harder times, you are alone." Raoul Wallenberg, as it turned out after four decades, had friends in adversity as well as in good fortune. Although his death may never be explained, the memory of his heroism lives on.

The Lost Colony

*An English colony of more than 100 men, women, and children,
which Sir Walter Raleigh had founded in 1587 on an island
at the entrance to North Carolina's Albemarle Sound, disappeared
within three years — leaving only a tantalizing clue to its fate.*

As the English privateer *Hopewell* approached Roanoke Island on August 17, 1590, Captain Abraham Cocke fired a cannon to announce his arrival and that of Governor John White. Three years earlier, acting on behalf of Sir Walter Raleigh, holder of a royal commission from Queen Elizabeth I, White had established what was meant to be the first permanent English colony on the eastern coast of North America. Leaving his settlers at Roanoke, the governor had sailed for England — and badly needed supplies — on August 28, 1587.

But it had taken White these three years to return, and he must have thought that his arrival would be joyously greeted by the anxious settlers. The *Hopewell*'s passengers saw smoke rising from the island and assumed that it came from a fire maintained by Roanoke's colonists. As the ship's sailors rowed White to the island, they shouted, sang, and blew trumpets to get the attention of those left behind in 1587. Going ashore at the northern tip of the island, they found the settlement deserted. The smoke came from an untended brush fire.

*Roanoke Island in a period representation: To the right is the settlement surrounded
by palisades. Below right: The* Elizabeth II, *a replica of a 16th-century
ship moored near Roanoke, is a museum ship commemorating the first voyage
to North Carolina.*

Landing at the Wrong Spot

An earlier, abortive attempt to found a colony on Roanoke Island had been made by Sir Richard Grenville, a cousin of Raleigh's, in the summer of 1585. Leaving more than 100 men on the island, Grenville had departed for England toward the end of August but promised to return by Easter 1586. The colonists — under Governor Ralph Lane and including John White as the expedition's artist and cartographer — explored the area, searching for mineral resources. But soon they clashed with the local Indians and food became scarce. Growing impatient for the overdue arrival of Grenville, the settlers seized the opportunity to return to England with Sir Francis Drake, who unexpectedly stopped at the island in June 1586 following raids against Spain's New World colonies to the south. Two weeks later — but too late — Grenville arrived with supplies and 15 additional colonists. He left these men on

Roanoke to hold the position until reinforcements could be brought from England.

The reinforcements were led by John White, named governor of a new colony to be established on Chesapeake Bay. On April 26, 1587, White left Portsmouth, England, with 117 colonists — this time including women and children — in three ships. One of the passengers was the governor's pregnant daughter, Elinor, married to a settler named Ananias Dare. On July 22 the expedition reached Roanoke, where White planned to pick up the 15 men left behind the previous year before continuing north to Chesapeake Bay to found his colony. The arrival at Roanoke was somber. Of the 15 men left behind, only the bones of one were found. The fort had been razed, but some houses, though overgrown with vines and infested with wildlife, were still standing. White was anxious to move on but was blocked by the expedition's nautical leader, a Portuguese pilot named Simon Fernandez. The two had already fallen out during the three-month-long voyage, and now Fernandez abruptly announced that he was unloading the settlers at Roanoke and would return to England in the largest of the three ships.

It was too late in the year for the sowing of grain, so the colonists would have to depend on the generosity of local Indians. But they too had left Roanoke and moved to the mainland, appalled and offended by the behavior of the English who had arrived earlier. Therefore, White would leave one of the remaining small ships with the settlers and return to England for supplies in the third. The colonists were supposed to be relayed north to Chesapeake Bay in their ship, keeping a party of 25 men on Roanoke to direct White to the new settlement upon his return.

Before leaving, White had cause to celebrate. His daughter gave birth on August 18 to a girl whom he named Virginia. This first European child born in North America outside the Spanish dominions was appropriately named for the colony and the Virgin Queen, Elizabeth I.

Belated Return

Things did not turn out as White had planned, and the six to eight months stretched into three years. Not until March 1590 did Raleigh manage to get the governor onto the privateer *Hopewell*

Settling along North America's eastern coast, the English called their first colony Virginia, after the Virgin Queen, Elizabeth I; today the region is divided between the states of Virginia and North Carolina.

Early Reports from the New World

In the second half of the 16th century, England became a maritime power. Not only music and literature flourished in Elizabethan England; shipbuilding too was thriving. No longer would the English accept the so-called division of the world between Portugal and Spain: under the Treaty of Tordesillas in 1494, Portugal claimed Africa and Brazil; Spain, the largest part of the New World and its riches. Eager to "singe the beard of the King of Spain," English privateers — most prominently, Francis Drake — were successfully attacking Spanish fleets bringing gold and silver home from the New World. But England wanted a colony, like the ones that were bringing such wealth to Spain.

In 1584 Walter Raleigh, favorite of Queen Elizabeth I, received a concession from his sovereign entitling him to discover and appropriate countries not yet ruled by "any Christian Prynce." That year Raleigh sent his first expedition to explore what is today North Carolina.

One of the leaders of that expedition, Arthur Barlowe, sent Raleigh a long report describing the new land in blazing colors: the soil was fertile and produced corn, peas, and melons; the woods were full of game; the vines were heavy with grapes. The native peoples he found to be "gentle, loving, and faithfull, void of all guile and treason . . . such as lived after the manner of the golden age."

Among the first colonists sent by Raleigh in 1585 was Thomas Hariot, only 25 and just out of Oxford but already regarded as one of England's leading naturalists. It would be his task, during the year 1585–86 spent on Roanoke, to begin the scientific exploration of North America. His book, *A Briefe and True Report on the Newly Found Land Virginia*, was published in 1588 with beautifully detailed illustrations by John White.

Most of the colonists had little if anything good to say about Virginia. Not so Hariot and White, who became ardent propagandists of colonization. Hariot's book, translated into Latin, French, and German — and with White's watercolors engraved by Theodor de Bry — was for a century one of Europe's principal sources of information about the New World. In his first chapter, Hariot listed the "Amenities for the Trading Profession": alum, civet cat, silkworms, tar, wine, cedar wood, otter skins, copper, and much more. There was also an abundance of nourishment for the prospective settlers, including fish, fowl, and turtles.

Hariot's chapter about the native inhabitants reads like a prophecy of the next 300 years. The Indians, he wrote, were a poor people; they regarded European trinkets as great treasure; they had no comparable arms nor appropriate battle techniques. In skirmishes with the Roanoke settlers, the Indians' "best defense was to show us their heels."

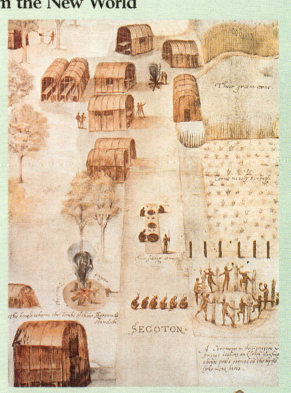

An Indian village as drawn by John White. To the right is a cornfield; at top, the cooking area, with food being served at center. Indians perform a ritual dance at right; in the large hut at bottom left are buried chieftains. At right: John White's watercolor of a tattooed North Carolina native.

Disputes arose in many of the villages the white men visited; in some, small thefts were reported. Often the white men took swift action to establish their authority and punish such transgressions. But worse punishment often occurred after the settlers had left: the death of Indians from measles and smallpox introduced by the Europeans. From this fatal encounter, the Indians came to regard the white men as powerful if cruel and vengeful gods — but gods against whom they must eventually rebel.

and load it and four smaller ships with provisions for the stranded colonists.

Thus on August 17, 1590 — almost three years to the day since he had left — White was back at Roanoke. The *Hopewell* and its sister ship *Moonlight* anchored off the barrier island separating Albemarle Sound from the Atlantic Ocean and sent two rowboats ashore. The first, from the *Moonlight*, capsized in the rough surf, and the captain and six men were drowned — just before White found the deserted settlement.

Where had the colonists of 1587 gone? There was a clue: two similar signs. On a tree at the entrance to the palisade built around the settlement the word CROATOAN had been carved; on another tree by the road leading to the mooring place were carved the three letters CRO — most likely an abbreviation of the first.

Indeed, the colonists had agreed to leave a sign in a prominent place giving their destination if they had to abandon Roanoke Island. Should they be in danger, they were to have added a cross to the sign. Since there was no cross on either sign, it would have seemed that the group had voluntarily moved on to Croatoan, an island 50 miles to the south known to be inhabited by

John White's granddaughter, Virginia Dare, is baptized on Roanoke Island in 1587; she was the first English child born on American soil but disappeared with her parents and the other Roanoke colonists.

friendly Indians. White wanted to sail there immediately. But the weather took a turn for the worse, and the *Hopewell* broke loose from its anchor and began drifting out to sea. Because of this danger, the short voyage to Croatoan was never made and the two ships set sail for England. By October 24 White was back in Plymouth.

None of the 117 men, women, and children left on Roanoke Island in 1587 was ever seen again. In history books the group appears as "The Lost Colony." What had happened to them?

Murdered by the Spaniards?

In 1586 the famous English buccaneer Sir Francis Drake sacked St. Augustine, Florida, the northernmost Spanish settlement in the Americas, and headed north along the coast en route home. Rumors reached the Spanish governor of Florida, Pedro Menendez Marques, that the English were building a fort — perhaps even establishing a colony — to the north. That would allow English fleets to remain in the New World through the winter months. Up to this point, the Spaniards could count on some seasonal relief from the feared raiders who were forced to return home at the end of each summer.

What Menendez Marques could not have known was that Drake merely stopped in Virginia that year and removed the stranded Grenville colonists from Roanoke. Nor apparently did the Spaniard learn of the second colony, left at Roanoke by White in 1587. But he was resolved to

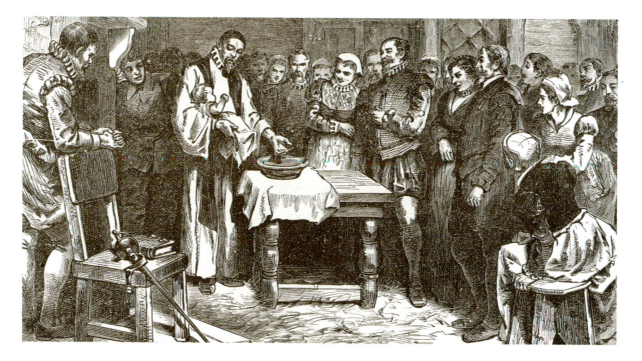

Carved on a tree at the entrance to the deserted Roanoke settlement, the word CROATOAN *is shown to Governor White upon his return in 1590.*

find out what the English were up to and in June 1588 sent a small ship commanded by Vincente Gonzalez northward.

The Spaniards searched Chesapeake Bay without finding any trace of English colonists but on the return south chanced upon Roanoke Island. There they found a landing place for boats and some barrels but neither a fort nor any settlers. With this information Gonzalez returned to Havana, where Menendez Marques had independently received news of the colony at Roanoke and had orders from the Spanish king to destroy it at the earliest possible opportunity.

The opportunity never came. The English buccaneers harassed the Spaniards so relentlessly that every vessel was needed to protect the treasure fleets taking gold and silver home from the Americas. Concentrating efforts on protecting bases to the south, Spain at times even contemplated surrendering the Florida colony. Thus, it can safely be said that, if Governor White never found his colony, the Spaniards cannot be blamed for the disappearance.

Killed by the Indians?

Did, in fact, the English settlers have to fear the Indians of the region? John White, artist and cartographer of the colony left at Roanoke in 1585, had memories of the warm welcome the white men received from the natives. Without the help and hospitality of the Indians, the English would not have survived that first winter. The Indians gave them seeds, showed them how to plant corn, and helped them make weirs to catch fish.

The settlers repaid this kindness in their own fashion. Because a silver cup had vanished from one of his boats, Sir Richard Grenville destroyed Indian cornfields and burned a village. Hearing that a local chieftain named Wingina was planning to attack, Governor Ralph Lane made a pre-emptive strike on his village and killed Wingina and his counselors. Perhaps White's lost colonists of 1587 were punished for these or similar acts.

Yet, the settlers had left no cross next to the sign CROATOAN as an indication that danger had driven them from Roanoke. Nor did White in 1590 find any bodies or burned buildings. There is simply no evidence that the settlers were the victims of Indian retribution.

What Really Happened?

Most probably, the larger number of Roanoke settlers followed the original plan and moved north to settle near the entrance to Chesapeake Bay at a place called Skicoac. Chesapeake Indians living there would have given the colonists some protection from the hostile natives led by chief Powhatan, who lived farther north and west.

But a small group of settlers may have remained at Roanoke for a while, as agreed. Perhaps threatened by increasingly hostile Indians, fearful of the Spaniards, and despairing of White's return, they may have moved south to Croatoan, where friendly Indians lived. As more years passed, they would of necessity have adapted to the Indian lifestyle and finally merged with the native peoples.

And what happened to the larger group who had moved north to Chesapeake Bay? Presumably, its members also lived and merged with the Indians, the Chesapeakes in this case. But one day, disaster struck. Advised by his priests, Powhatan decided to eliminate the danger coming from the white man as well as from the Chesapeake tribe, which had never submitted to his authority. In April 1607 he attacked the settlement at Skicoac and destroyed it completely. A month later, the first permanent English settlement was established at nearby Jamestown. Its settlers found no trace of the Roanoke colonists.

A memorial stamp issued on the 400th anniversary of the first voyage to Roanoke Island in 1584.

Major Glenn Miller Is Missing On Flight From England to Paris

Former Orchestra Leader Had Been Conducting Bands of the Army Air Forces Since Enlistment—Won Many Honors

I'VE FOUND GLENN MILLER'S PLANE

Riddle of bandleader's lost body

RAF bomb 'killed band king Miller'

By CHESTER STERN and MARTIN LEVENE

One-Way Flight to France

*In the last year of World War II, the disappearance of famed
bandleader Glenn Miller — en route from England to entertain
troops on the European continent — shocked his fans. For four
decades the mystery has remained unsolved.*

On December 15, 1944, Major Glenn Miller climbed into a single-engine Norseman aircraft at a military airstrip near Bedford, some 40 miles north of London. He was scheduled to lead his acclaimed United States Army Air Forces Band in a Christmas concert for Allied troops the next week in liberated Paris. At the last moment he had asked for a change in his orders so that he could precede the band to France. A chance encounter at an officers' club the previous evening had earned Miller space on the small plane that was defying the rain and fog to make this hop across the English Channel.

Always nervous about flying, Miller expressed doubt about the single-engine plane. His fellow passenger, Colonel Norman Baesell, reminded him that Lindbergh made it across the Atlantic Ocean on one engine; they were flying only to Paris. "Hey, where the hell are the parachutes," Miller asked. "What's the matter, Miller, do you want to live forever?" the colonel joked in reply. Shortly thereafter, the Norseman took off in the dense fog and disappeared forever.

Not until December 24 — after Miller's wife back home in New Jersey had been notified — was it announced that the famous bandleader was missing. Preoccupied with far larger problems in this decisive phase of the war in Europe, the American high command assumed that the Norseman had crashed into the Channel when its wings iced over or its engine failed. There was no search or inquiry into the tragedy.

Friends and fans of the popular swing musician were not satisfied with the official explanation. Wild rumors were soon circulating: Miller's plane had been shot down by the Germans and

In December 1944 a single-engine Norseman like the one at left, above, vanished with bandleader Glenn Miller (far left) aboard. Newspaper headlines gave different versions of the disappearance.

the horribly crippled and disfigured bandleader was hidden in a hospital somewhere; he had been killed in a brawl in a Parisian brothel; Colonel Baesell, involved in a black-market delivery, had shot both Miller and the pilot and landed the plane in France; the high command had terminated Miller as a German spy. Despite the absurdity of such stories, the disappearance has never been fully explained, and legends about the lost musician who entranced millions with his smooth rhythms continue to thrive.

Glenn Miller at the Top

Success had come to Glenn Miller in 1939 at the age of 35. A college dropout, he had joined Ben Pollack's band as a trombonist and arranger 15 years earlier on the West Coast. He later performed with such well-known bands of the 1920's and 1930's as those of Tommy and Jimmy Dorsey, Red Nichols, Smith Ballew, and Benny Goodman, the "King of Swing," who called Miller "a dedicated musician."

The slender, serious looking young man with rimless glasses brought a meticulous perfectionism to music-making as he worked on developing a distinct sound: velvety soft, smooth, supple, independent of soloists. After failing to make the big time with his first orchestra, Miller formed a second group in 1938 and early the next year got prized bookings at the Glen Island Casino in New Rochelle, New York, and the Meadowbrook in Cedar Grove, New Jersey.

In the autumn of 1939 the new Glenn Miller band went on national radio, and before long young people from New York to San Francisco were dancing cheek to cheek to such hit tunes as "In the Mood," "Pennsylvania 6-5000," "Tuxedo Junction," "String of Pearls," and the Miller theme song, "Moonlight Serenade." In 1940 his gross income was $800,000, and the next year his band made the first of two movie appearances in

Sun Valley Serenade, starring Sonja Henie. Miller's recording of the film's hit song, "Chattanooga Choo Choo," sold a million copies and earned him a gold disc from RCA Victor. Humorously modest about his success, he once joked, "It's an inspiring sight to look down from the balcony on the heads of 7,000 people swaying on a dance floor — especially when you are getting $600 for every thousand of them." Asked if he wanted to be the new "King of Swing," he said, "I'd rather have a reputation as one of the best all-round bands. Versatility, more than anything else, is what I want to accomplish."

Swing Goes to War

Eight months after America entered World War II, Glenn Miller gave up his phenomenally successful career to volunteer his services to the military; in the autumn of 1942, he was commissioned a captain in the U.S. Army. Seeking out other musicians drafted or volunteering for service, Miller formed the U.S. Army Air Forces Band, which by the next year was playing for cadets training at Yale University in New Haven, Connecticut. But when he introduced swing music into marches, a senior officer reminded him that John Philip Sousa's music had been good enough for World War I. "Are you still flying the same planes you flew in the last war, too?" he asked. The military accepted swing.

On cross-country tours, the AAF Band raised millions for the war-bond drives, but nonetheless Miller felt that he was not doing enough. Finally, in June 1944, he got approval to take his band overseas to play for the troops stationed in England. In the next five and a half months, the band played 71 concerts — the biggest morale booster for his men, one general commented, "next to a letter from home." The concerts were broadcast over the Allied Expeditionary Forces Network, beamed at troops in Britain and on the European continent. Programs on the British Broadcasting Company quickly ended, however, when a director insisted that the band play at a constant volume; listeners in remote areas weren't hearing the softer music. Nonetheless, Glenn Miller gained some "civilian" fans as well. Presented to the queen of England, Miller learned that the princesses Elizabeth and Margaret Rose listened to his broadcasts almost nightly.

In December came the orders to take the show to France. Sitting up almost all night on the 14th,

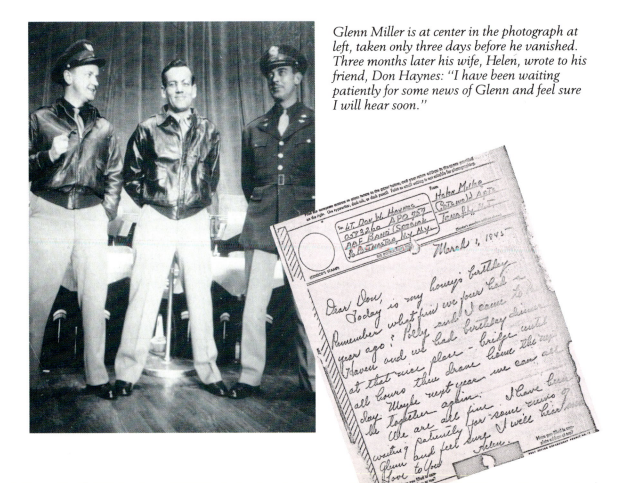

Glenn Miller is at center in the photograph at left, taken only three days before he vanished. Three months later his wife, Helen, wrote to his friend, Don Haynes: "I have been waiting patiently for some news of Glenn and feel sure I will hear soon."

A Passion for Flying

Only a few months before Glenn Miller vanished in a military airplane, another celebrity met his death in an unexplained accident. On July 31, 1944, the French writer and aviator Antoine de Saint-Exupéry disappeared on a reconnaissance flight over the Mediterranean Sea. It is still not known whether he crashed owing to a mechanical failure of his airplane or was shot down by enemy aircraft.

Born in 1900, Saint-Exupéry earned a pilot's license while serving in the French air force in the early 1920's. Later, as a commercial pilot, he helped establish airmail routes across North Africa, the South Atlantic, and South America. In 1939 he rejoined the French air force despite disabilities from earlier air crashes and, after the fall of France the next year, of-

French aviator and author Antoine de Saint-Exupéry disappeared during a World War II reconnaissance mission over the Mediterranean Sea.

fered his services to the Free French forces in North Africa.

In a series of novels, essays, and diaries Saint-Exupéry passionately recounted his adventures in flight. He wrote of almost mystical experiences that bound him to the brotherhood of pilots risking their lives in the dangerous new profession. Although he considered the 1939 collection *Wind, Sand and Stars* his most important book, he is probably best remembered for *The Little Prince*.

Charmingly illustrated by the author, this classic tale is about "a most extraordinary small person" from a distant, minuscule planet whom the narrator encounters after a crash landing in a desert. Described as a child's fable for adults, *The Little Prince* reminds the reader of such tested homilies as giving is better than receiving.

Glenn Miller discussed with a friend his plans for a postwar band and eventual retirement on a ranch he had bought in California.

A Desperately Ill Man

"Glenn Miller did not die in a plane crash over the Channel but from lung cancer in a hospital." With this startling statement the bandleader's younger brother, Herb Miller, broke a nearly 40-year silence in 1983. Miller had indeed boarded the Norseman at the airstrip outside of London on December 15, 1944. But when the airplane landed a half hour later, he was taken to a military hospital where he died the following day. It was Herb Miller who fabricated the story about the crash because his brother had wanted to die as a hero and not "in a lousy bed."

Herb Miller tried to substantiate his story with a letter that the chain-smoking musician had written in the summer of 1944: "I am totally emaciated, although I am eating enough. I have trouble breathing. I think I am very ill."

Because there was no crash, the younger Miller claimed, there was no need for a search or an inquiry. Moreover, the official weather report for December 15 listed a temperature of 5 degrees Celsius (41 degrees Fahrenheit) — not cold enough to have caused the wings to ice over. Both

the pilot of the Norseman and Glenn Miller's fellow passenger, Colonel Baesell, had died later in battle with the Germans. His brother was probably buried in a mass grave at some military cemetery in Britain.

Supporting this story is the fact that Glenn Miller seemed to be depressed, irritable, and exhausted during the last few months of his life, suffering from what he described as repeated sinus attacks. According to Don Haynes, Glenn Miller's executive officer and manager of the AAF Band, the bandleader had lost a lot of weight and his tailor-made uniforms "didn't fit him well at all. They merely hung on him." George Voutsas, the director of his military radio programs, remembered a late-night discussion of postwar plans. "I don't know why I spend time making plans like this," Miller sighed. "You know, George, I have an awful feeling you guys are going to go home without me. . . ."

Getting at the Truth

Herb Miller's version of his brother's death has not been substantiated by U.S. military authorities, but former British airmen have come up with a more plausible explanation for the famous musician's disappearance. A 30-year-old movie prompted the revelation.

Entertaining the Troops

Glenn Miller was justifiably proud of his contributions to the war effort; he felt that his band was bringing a touch of home to America's fighting men. The greatest sound coming out of his concerts, he said, was "the sound of thousands of G.I.'s reacting with an ear-splitting, almost hysterical happy yell after each number."

The American high command attached great importance to keeping up morale and enlisted stage, screen, and radio personalities to entertain the troops both during training in the United States and later overseas in the war theaters. Among the most popular stars was German-born Marlene Dietrich, who appropriately appeared in the film *Follow the*

Boys. North Africa was the starting point for an extended tour of encampments that took her through many European countries. To cheers and applause she came onstage in a close-fitting khaki uniform that discreetly revealed her famous legs and entranced the men with her husky-voiced renditions of such songs as "See What the Boys in the Back Room Will Have." She asked for no special treatment and often shared the troops' rationed fare. Nasty rumors that Dietrich had been sent to the camps to raise the troops' morale by "raising her skirts" were quickly squelched when it became known how dedicated she was to the war effort.

Germany also recognized the significance of music and entertainment in maintaining morale. As early as October 1939 — only a month after the outbreak of war — the Germans began broadcasting a program called "Request Concert for You on All the Fronts." In addition to playing the musical requests of the troops, the program broadcast messages and greetings to and from their families.

One popular World War II song made the journey from Axis to Allied lines. Lale Andersen's plaintive song about a soldier's farewell to his bride at the garrison gate, "Lili Marleen," was eventually judged to be demoralizing for German troops and was banned by the Third Reich in 1942. Thereupon, it became enormously popular among American troops in an English-language version.

Sultry Marlene Dietrich strikes a provocative pose with Allied servicemen (left). Promoted to major two months after his arrival in England, Glenn Miller (below) leads the AAF Band before an audience of G.I.'s.

5

In 1955 James Stewart and June Allyson co-starred as Glenn Miller and his wife, Helen, in the film *The Glenn Miller Story*. After seeing it, a former Royal Air Force navigator, Fred Shaw, tried to present his own theory about the fate of the Norseman to the press but was rebuffed. Not until 1984 did Shaw, then living in South Africa, see the movie again. This time he succeeded in getting his story published.

On December 15, 1944, Shaw was aboard a Lancaster bomber returning from an aborted raid on Germany. Approaching the south coast of England, the bombardier jettisoned his payload including a 4,000-pound bomb called a "cookie," which exploded several feet above the surface of the sea. As Shaw looked out to see the explosion, he spotted a Norseman flying below. A moment later, the rear gunner called over the intercom: "Did you see that kite [slang for plane] go in?" Shock waves from the explosion, Shaw explained, could have knocked the small aircraft out of the sky.

In England a member of the Glenn Miller Appreciation Society wrote the British Defense Ministry and placed an advertisement in the *R.A.F. Association Journal* for information that would confirm Shaw's story. The Lancaster's pilot, Victor Gregory, answered the ad.

Although he himself had seen nothing, Gregory confirmed that his navigator, Shaw, had seen a Norseman flying below and that the rear gunner, since deceased, had reported it falling into the sea. Since his mission had been aborted, there was no debriefing, and Gregory never mentioned the incident to his superiors. "Don't think me unsympathetic or callous, but when I heard of the plane going down, I would have said that he shouldn't have been there — forget him." His concern was getting home safely from the raid.

Shaw's story led to an investigation by the British Defense Ministry's Air Historical Branch. Up until that time, the R.A.F. had considered Miller's disappearance strictly an American matter. Yet the Norseman in which Miller had vanished took off from a British airfield and was known to be headed for France — although no flight plan was filed. The Norseman and the bombers could have crossed in flight, the report concluded, or they could have been miles apart.

The Melody Lingers On

The true story of Glenn Miller's disappearance will probably never be known — and perhaps, after all these years, it may not really matter. What is important is his music.

On January 17, 1946, only 5 months after the

James Stewart and June Allyson co-starred in The Glenn Miller Story, *a popular film of 1955;* Miller's *mother insisted that the famous movie star was not nearly as good-looking as her son had been.*

end of World II and 13 months after the Norseman vanished, the Glenn Miller Orchestra under the direction of Tex Beneke made its successful debut at New York's Capitol Theater. For the next five years it continued to delight audiences with the familiar and well-loved songs of the Swing Era. Later, the success of *The Glenn Miller Story* led to a reissue of many old recordings and a revived Glenn Miller Orchestra in 1956. What most delighted the band members playing into the 1970's were audiences too young to have heard Glenn Miller himself but who clearly wanted to continue hearing the smooth Glenn Miller sound.

Death in the Arctic Ice

*In May 1845 Sir John Franklin started a search for the elusive
Northwest Passage, long thought to link the Atlantic and Pacific oceans
north of Canada. Almost a century and a half later, scientists
unearthed the bodies of three expedition members.*

*I*n August 1984, on Beechey Island at the entrance to Wellington Channel in Canada's far north, scientists — having chipped through nearly five feet of gravel and permafrost for four days — opened the first of three graves left from a mid-19th-century arctic expedition. What they saw made them gasp: in icy ground unthawed even by the summer sun lay the almost perfectly preserved body of a young man who had died 138 years earlier. He and his two companions buried nearby were crew members of the ships *Erebus* and *Terror*, which had come there under the command of Sir John Franklin.

Amidst great fanfare, the two well-provisioned ships of the Franklin expedition had left England in the spring of 1845. His objective was to find and traverse the long-sought Northwest Passage, a sea route through Canada's arctic islands from the Atlantic Ocean to the Pacific. The three dead men on Beechey Island are the only members of that doomed voyage of exploration ever to have been found and identified.

350-Year Search
The Franklin expedition, sponsored and equipped by the British Admiralty,

was intended finally to answer a question that had puzzled the English for 350 years: Is it possible to pass through open waters north of the American landmass in order to open a new trade route from east to west? With the Panama Canal decades in the future, the only sea route from the Atlantic to the Pacific was around South America's dangerous, storm-prone Cape Horn. Would it not be more advantageous — in terms of time and distance — to find a sea passage north of Canada and Alaska and then through the Bering Strait into the Pacific Ocean?

This tantalizing notion had intrigued the English since the late 15th century. John Cabot — actually Giovanni Caboto, an Italian contemporary of Columbus's — crossed the North Atlantic in 1497 in the service of King Henry VII; upon his discovery of Newfoundland rested England's claim to North America. But Newfoundland was not Cathay, or China, as Cabot supposed,

Eyes open, teeth bared in a deathly grimace, John Torrington of the Franklin expedition stares out at the Canadian scientists who unearthed his grave in 1984.

and he had not found the Northwest Passage. Others followed, among them the Portuguese, French, and Dutch — all looking for a northern sea route to the Pacific. Henry Hudson, William Baffin, and others put their names on the map, but none of them reached the continent's western coast. On the first of three voyages between 1819 and 1825, William Edward Parry came close to victory when he reached Melville Island, just short of the Beaufort Sea north of Alaska.

Finally, in 1844, another attempt to discover the Northwest Passage was announced. But who should lead the following year's expedition, charged also with surveying and charting the unknown areas of the Canadian north? When Sir John Franklin offered his services, the lords of the Admiralty hesitated. They did not question his ability, perseverance, and knowledge of the north polar regions; his experience and character were well known. But the age of this highly decorated naval officer was disquieting: 59. "No, no, gentlemen. Not at all," Franklin corrected them calmly. "I am only 58!" He got the command.

The Royal Navy was Sir John's home. From childhood on, Franklin — born on April 16, 1786 — yearned to go to sea. At 14, he entered the navy; at 19, he fought at the Battle of Trafalgar. He first encountered arctic ice as a member of an expedition to Spitsbergen, an experience that helped shape the rest of his life. From that time on, he was obsessed by the idea of exploring the Canadian arctic.

Commissioned by the Admiralty, Franklin started to survey land along the northern coast of the North American continent east of the Coppermine River in 1819. After three and a half years of incredible privation and unimaginable suffering, he returned home — only to set out again for the land of eternal ice and snow in 1825. This time, he went down the Mackenzie River to the Beaufort Sea in order to explore the western part of the continent's north coast. Having surveyed and charted hundreds of miles of arctic coastline and published his description of Indian and Eskimo lifestyles, he was something of a national figure; in 1829 he was knighted for his services to the nation. Later, he took on quite different duties as lieutenant governor of a penal colony on the Australian island of Tasmania.

The Call of the Arctic

Even as Franklin was approaching his 60th birthday, his urge to explore had not diminished. And when the opportunity presented itself in 1844, he was quick to seize it. One more time, he determined to challenge the far north, endure the ice, cold, and storms of the arctic, and reach the goal Britain had set for him: discovery of a northern sea connection between the Atlantic and the Pacific oceans.

Everyone in Britain was convinced that the enterprise would be successful, since it had been so meticulously prepared. The sailing vessels *Erebus* and *Terror* had been reconstructed as screw steamers, the first ever sent to penetrate the arctic. Provisions for three years were stowed aboard. The crew — 129 men altogether — had passed special tests to qualify. To the cheers of an enthusiastic London crowd, the ships sailed down the river Thames and out to sea on May 19, 1845; the Franklin expedition was launched.

An early message from Sir John maintained the national euphoria: "We are assured of our success. The next position will be Hong Kong, China." Next, a whaler saw the *Erebus* and *Terror* sailing on a westerly course in Baffin Bay between Greenland and Canada. But their trace was lost after the two ships entered Lancaster Sound.

A year passed, then two, without any message from the expedition — scarcely an extraordinary silence for such a venture in those days of limited communications. But by the spring of 1848, after the third winter, the question in Britain was raised ever more anxiously: "Where on earth is Sir John Franklin?"

Reward for Franklin

The British Admiralty posted a reward of £20,000 for anyone who found the expedition and rescued its members. To that sum, Lady Franklin added £3,000 from her own funds. Thus began one of the most extensive searches in history: 40 expeditions in the next 10 years at a cost of $4 million. Several ships sailed to Baffin Bay, where the *Erebus* and *Terror* had last been sighted, and then followed routes Franklin might have taken. Others searched from the west, coming through the Bering Strait into the Beaufort Sea north of Alaska, where the expedition should have emerged on its journey to the Pacific. Each search party left food depots en route and deposited messages under stone markers. Additional messages were placed in small barrels or engraved onto neckbands that were put on foxes caught for that purpose and then released.

The journeys by land as well as by sea through this hostile territory surpassed the greatest feats of exploration made in the arctic to that time. Unknown islands were discovered, coastlines charted, straits explored. Many blank spots on maps disappeared. But nothing was found of the Franklin expedition — neither ships nor survivors nor even bodies.

The First Trace

The year was 1851. From a ship anchored at Beechey Island, the crew went ashore, searched, and came upon the remainder of a well-equipped depot — Franklin's depot! Empty bottles, canned meat, and coils of rope had been left there by the expedition. The first trace had been found. Apparently, Sir John and his men had spent the winter of 1845–46 — their first since leaving England — on Beechey Island. Nearby were found, but not opened at this time, the graves of three crew members. One gravestone bore the name John Torrington, a noncommissioned officer on the *Terror*; the two others buried there were an able seaman named John Hartnell and Royal Marine William Braine, both of the *Erebus*. (These were the three graves rediscovered and opened in 1984.) But nowhere could the search party find an indication of the route Franklin had taken from Beechey Island.

On the map below are traced the routes taken by the Franklin expedition, 1845–47; the search parties of McClure, 1850–54, and McClintock, 1857–59; and the first traverse of the Northwest Passage by Roald Amundsen, 1903–06.

In January 1854 the men of the Franklin expedition were officially declared dead. All hope had been lost of finding other traces, much less survivors of the ill-fated exploring party. But nine months later, Dr. John Rae, a physician of the Hudson's Bay Company, returned to England to shed some new light on the tragedy.

Ghastly Evidence

In Rae's luggage were parts of clocks, compasses, and silver spoons and forks, as well as a small plate engraved with the name "Sir John Franklin." He had bought these objects from some Eskimos on the west coast of Boothia Peninsula, some 300 miles south of Beechey Island. The Eskimos had told Rae that in the spring of 1850, on nearby King William Island, they had met 40 white men making their way toward the Canadian mainland with a boat and a sledge. Unable to communicate properly with the Eskimos, the men had indicated by sign language that their ships had been crushed by ice and that they were hunting for something edible — whereupon the Eskimos sold them a small seal.

That summer, as Rae had also learned, other Eskimos discovered several graves and more than 30 bodies on the mainland as well as 5 more bodies on an adjacent island. The official report that

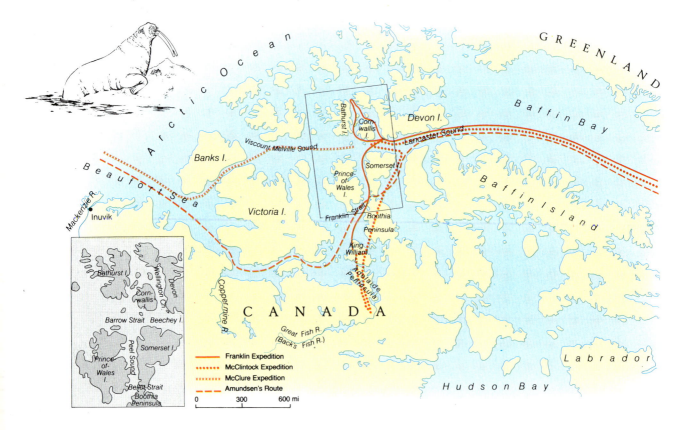

Rae submitted to the Admiralty contained some grim news: ". . . from the mutilated state of many of the corpses, and the contents of the kettles, it is evident that our wretched countrymen had been driven to the last resource — cannibalism — as a means of prolonging existence." Some of the men seem to have survived until the arrival of wild geese and ducks toward the end of May, since shots had been heard by the Eskimos and bones and feathers had been found in the vicinity where the last sad events occurred.

A journey of horrors, it seems. But had Franklin been part of the final act? This and many other questions remained unanswered. However, for the Admiralty the case was closed; all searches were suspended; and Dr. Rae was awarded £10,000 for his efforts.

The Last Search

Although it was now virtually certain that all members of the Franklin expedition had perished, Lady Franklin wanted a final, exhaustive search "for each and every one of them, for the bones of the dead, their diaries, notes, and last written words." With the remainder of her fortune, she bought the schooner-rigged, screw

Sir John Franklin eagerly undertook the commission to locate the fabled Northwest Passage, heading an expedition of 129 men on two ships that left England in the spring of 1845. None was to return to the home country, all meeting death in the white infinity typified by the view at top.

steamer yacht *Fox* and entrusted Captain Francis Leopold McClintock — veteran of the initial relief party in 1848 — with the command.

The Northwest Passage Is Discovered

The explorer's luck that eluded Franklin favored the relief expedition led by Robert Mc-Clure. Sent to find Franklin and his men, McClure entered the arctic through Bering Strait in the summer of 1850. He passed south of Banks Island into Prince of Wales Strait, which leads to Viscount Melville Sound and beyond it to Barrow Strait — a known route from the Atlantic. Realizing that he had discovered the Northwest Passage, McClure uttered a fervent "Thank God!"

Yet it was not McClure's fortune to traverse the passage he had discovered, for his ship became trapped in the ice and — after the third winter — had to be abandoned when another Franklin search party offered passage home. Court-martialed for leaving his ship, McClure was later forgiven

With the help of an icebreaker, the Standard *Oil Company's supertanker* Manhattan *reached Alaska's oilfields from the Atlantic in 1969.*

and knighted for his discovery.

More than 50 years had to pass before the Norwegian explorer Roald Amundsen successfully completed the passage. Coming from Baffin Bay in his tiny ship *Gjoa*, with a crew of only seven, Amundsen sailed into Lancaster Sound in the summer of 1903. After two winters comfortably spent on the very same King William Island that had been Franklin's death trap, Amundsen resumed his voyage, hugging the Canadian mainland. A third winter was spent just short of Alaska and the voyage completed as *Gjoa* passed through Bering Strait on August 30, 1906.

In 1969 the supertanker *Manhattan* became the first commercial ship to complete the transit. However, Canada rejected the route on the basis of the negative environmental impact.

On July 1, 1857, nine years after his departure on the first search, McClintock left on yet another dangerous journey. Could the tiny ship with a crew of 25 succeed where much larger, far better equipped vessels had failed? Consisting only of volunteers, half of them with arctic experience, McClintock's party was highly motivated. Their unbreakable resolve helped them not only to win the battle with the all-powerful ice but also to penetrate the long-hidden mystery of the Franklin expedition's disappearance.

The *Fox*'s search was to be concentrated in the area south of Bellot Strait, the passage between Boothia Peninsula and Somerset Island to the north. According to Rae's reports, the answer to the riddle would have to be found there or on adjacent King William Island. No sooner had the *Fox* reached Baffin Bay, however, than she was locked in by pack ice. Trapped for eight months, the *Fox* drifted some 1,000 miles south. After the *Fox* was finally freed and had taken on fresh supplies in Greenland, McClintock sailed to Beechey Island to place a memorial tablet at the previously discovered depot and gravesite. He then rounded Somerset Island into Peel Sound. When it proved impenetrable, McClintock tried an approach from the east. He reached but was unable to enter Bellot Strait by the onset of the second winter of his quest.

Impatient for the spring to arrive, McClintock ordered the search continued by dogsled, and he and his men explored much of Boothia Peninsula and encircled King William Island. On April 20, 1859, McClintock came upon Eskimos carrying objects from the *Erebus* and *Terror* who could at last provide information about the fate of the two ships. One of Franklin's ships had been crushed by ice masses off the northwestern coastline of King William Island; the other one, heavily damaged, had been pulled ashore, abandoned, and later used as a fuel supply by the natives.

Another of McClintock's land searches, led by Lieutenant W.R. Hobson, made a significant find at Victory Point on the northwest coast of King William Island. Under a stone marker, in a message signed by Lieutenant Graham Gore and dated May 28, 1847, was the report that all was well after the second winter and that Franklin still commanded the expedition. But a year later captains Fitzjames and Crozier had added a mournful postscript: "H.M.'s ships *Terror* and *Erebus* were deserted on the 22nd April [1848], having been beset since 12th Sept. 1846 . . . . Sir John Franklin died on the 11th June 1847, and the total loss by death in the expedition has been to this date 9 officers and 15 men. . . . Start on tomorrow 26th for Back's Fish River."

£20,000 REWARD Her Majesty's Government DISCOVERY SHIPS SIR JOHN FRANKLIN £20,000. £10,000. £10,000. W. A. B. HAMILTON.

The Franklin tragedy came near to being repeated with one of the search parties. Leading the expedition of 1850–54 that actually discovered the Northwest Passage, Robert McClure had to abandon his ship Investigator *when it became trapped in ice off Banks Island. Unlike Franklin, he and his crew were rescued — by yet another search party.*
Left: The British government offered a reward of £20,000 for the discovery and relief of the Franklin expedition's ships and £10,000 for information leading to the relief or proof of its members' fate.

Hobson soon after found a small boat mounted on a sledge; in it were two skeletons. Nearby were scattered such items as watches, books, toiletry articles, and what McClintock called "a quantity of articles of one description and another truly astonishing in variety and such as [could be considered] . . . dead weight, but slightly useful and very likely to break down the strength of the sledge crews." The only food found was a little tea and 40 pounds of chocolate. From this point, apparently, the 105 survivors began what would become a death march south.

The Franklin Expedition's Last Journey

Finally, it was possible to reconstruct what had happened to Sir John Franklin's search for the Northwest Passage.

In July 1845, two months after leaving Britain, and as reported by the whaler that had last seen them, the *Erebus* and *Terror* sailed into Lancaster Sound. With Barrow Strait ahead still blocked by ice, Franklin looked for a passageway farther north and found one in Wellington Channel. But it took him too far north when his destination was west, so he turned back to spend the winter of 1845–46 on Beechey Island. In the spring the journey continued. Since Barrow Strait was still partially closed, Franklin chose a route south along the western coast of Somerset Island and the Boothia Peninsula to King William Island.

Where to now, farther south or west? Since his map showed King William not as an island but as part of the Boothia Peninsula, Franklin would have thought he had no choice but to head west. This misinformation was the beginning of the disaster. The two ships headed west and into pack ice that by September 12, 1846, had trapped them, never to let go.

On May 28, 1847, Lieutenant Gore, exploring by sled, left his message that all was well. Two weeks later Franklin was dead. During a second winter locked in ice north of King William Island, several crew members died of contaminated food supplies. On April 22, 1848, as noted in the postscript to Gore's note, the 105 survivors abandoned their ships and began their desperate, unsuccessful attempt to reach the Canadian mainland. Their destination, the Great Fish River — renamed for George Back, a member of Franklin's two earlier expeditions who had mapped it in 1834 — would have led to Hudson's Bay Company outposts.

Rumors persisted for another decade that some survivors still lived with friendly natives, having given up all hope of rescue and a return to home. Gradually, it was said, these men adopted the northern lifestyle, their origin betrayed only by wistful blue eyes. But no such "white natives" were ever found. It seems instead that, one by one to the last man, the members of the Franklin expedition succumbed to the hostile environment of the frozen North.

What Was Accomplished?

The Franklin tragedy rekindled the interest of navigators and explorers in the arctic, the unprecedented search providing an opportunity to chart vast reaches of the Canadian north. One of the early search parties, that led by Captain Robert McClure, succeeded in discovering the northern sea route for which Franklin had given his life.

The victory was a hollow one. The Northwest Passage proved to have no commercial value, frozen solid as it was for much of each year. Eventually, several alternative routes across Canada's desolate north were found. The Norwegian Roald Amundsen succeeded in following the one closest to the mainland to become the first navigator to make the sea voyage between the two oceans — though it took him nearly three years to complete the journey. His route, Amundsen reported, was so crooked and narrow that it would be of little use to any but fur traders or missionaries. There would be no quick and easy trade route to the vast markets of Asia. Yet this did not put an end to arctic adventure. But henceforth the focus would be on the dauntless and often solitary hero who braved hideous hardships of hunger, malnutrition, monotony, frostbite, and gangrene to achieve his impossible goals.

Although he failed in his goal of discovering the Northwest Passage, Sir John Franklin is commemorated today in the name of the entire district of Canada's Northwest Territories through which he journeyed and in names also given to a lake, a bay, and a strait. The faithful widow, Lady Franklin, is remembered in the name bestowed upon a promontory on Victoria Island, midway through the Northwest Passage her husband had so bravely sought.

The Causes of the Tragedy

Contaminated food supplies, it has now been demonstrated, sealed the fate of the Franklin expedition. Near the first skeletons of the crew found in the 1850's were loaded guns and provisions — food that was still well preserved and presumably edible. Why then, if they had food and ammunition to bring down game, did all the men perish? For more than a century the mystery remained unsolved.

Anthropologist Owen Beattie found the answer in the bodies exhumed on Beechey Island in 1984. The corpses contained unusually high amounts of lead, apparently ingested with food coming from imperfectly soldered tinned goods among the ships' provisions. Lead poisoning results in loss of appetite, exhaustion, weakness, and disorders of the central nervous system that produce erratic behavior and paralysis. It also makes the victim more susceptible to such common illnesses as pneumonia.

He boarded a ship in Naples harbor and vanished: Ettore Majorana.

Escape into Another World

*He was standing on the threshold of a promising career as a
physicist. Ettore Majorana, however, mysteriously disappeared.
Is he still living behind monastery walls? Did he emigrate
to Argentina? Or did he possibly throw himself into the sea?*

On the evening of March 25, 1938, a 31-year-old Italian physicist named Ettore Majorana boarded the overnight mail ship at Naples bound for Palermo, Sicily. Before his departure, he had written two letters.

The first letter, left behind in his room at the Hotel Bologna, was addressed to his family. In it he made a peculiar request: "I only have one wish, that you will not wear black on my behalf. Should you want to observe the social customs, wear any other sign of mourning — if you must — but for no longer than three days. After that, you may remember me in your hearts and, if you are capable of doing so, forgive me." The message had the ominous tone of a suicide note.

The second letter, sent by mail, seemed to confirm that Majorana had decided to do away with himself. It was addressed to Antonio Carrelli, director of the physics institute at the University of Naples, where the young scientist had been lecturing since January. "I have made a decision that was unavoidable," he wrote Carrelli. "There is not a grain of egoism in it; yet I am well aware that my unexpected disappearance will be an inconvenience to you and the students. Therefore, I ask you to forgive me — above all, for having cast aside the trust, sincere friendship, and kindness you have shown me."

Before Carrelli received the letter, a telegram from Majorana was delivered. Sent from Palermo, it said to disregard the letter posted from Naples. The telegram was followed by a second letter, dated March 26 and also sent from Palermo. "Dear Carrelli," Majorana wrote, "The sea rejected me. I will return tomorrow to the Hotel Bologna. However, I intend to give up teaching. I will be at your disposal for further details."

The second letter to Carrelli would seem to indicate a bungled or abandoned suicide attempt. Yet it did not herald a renewed life for Majorana. Neither Carrelli nor members of the physicist's family ever saw or heard from him again.

A Brilliant Perfectionist

According to the unanimous verdict of his contemporaries, Ettore Majorana possessed an extraordinary intelligence. His mentor, the Nobel Prize winner Enrico Fermi, went so far as to mention his name alongside those of Galileo Galilei and Isaac Newton. Born in Catania, Sicily, on August 5, 1906, Ettore was already solving complicated mathematical problems in his head with incredible speed at the age of four. It was a gift that would puzzle and astonish those around him time and time again as he pursued his education.

First tutored at home, he was later sent to a Jesuit school in Rome but completed his secondary schooling at the Liceo Torquato Tasso before he was 17. In the autumn of 1923 he entered the University of Rome's school of engineering, where his fellow students included his elder brother, Luciano, and Emilio Segrè. It was the latter who persuaded Majorana to switch to the study of physics, and in 1928 he transferred to the Institute of Theoretical Physics, then under the direction of Enrico Fermi. A year later, he received his doctorate with distinction but continued to work with Fermi on solving problems in nuclear physics for the next five years.

Although Majorana's total scholarly output consists of nine papers published between 1928 and 1937, his work still excites wonder and admi-

A professor at Rome's Institute for Theoretical Studies (above) from 1927, Enrico Fermi (left) sought political refuge in the United States after accepting the Nobel Prize in 1938. He taught at Columbia University and later worked on the Manhattan Project, which created the first atomic bomb.

ration in the scientific community. The papers reveal a thorough knowledge of experimental data, a facility to simplify problems, a lively mind, and an uncompromising perfectionism. His criticism of the works of others earned him the nickname "The Grand Inquisitor." But he was equally harsh on himself, which may account for the slow pace and comparative paucity of his scholarly production in his postdoctoral years.

At Fermi's urging, Majorana left Italy early in 1933 on a grant from the National Research Council. In Leipzig, Germany, he met Werner Heisenberg, another Nobel Prize winner. In the letters he subsequently wrote Heisenberg, Majorana revealed that he had found not only a scientific colleague but a warm personal friend. Heisenberg urged the young Italian to publish more quickly, but he seemed reluctant to do so.

A Crisis Develops

In the fall of 1933, Majorana returned to Rome in poor health, having developed acute gastritis in Germany and apparently suffering from nervous exhaustion. Put on a strict diet, he grew reclusive and became harsh in his dealings with his family. To his mother, with whom he had previously shared a warm relationship, he had written from Germany that he would not accompany her on their customary summer vacation by the sea.

Appearing at the institute less frequently, he soon was scarcely leaving his home; the promising young physicist had become a hermit. For nearly four years he shut himself off from friends and stopped publishing. Only in 1937 did Majorana return to what could be termed a "normal" life. In that year — after the long silence — he published what was to be his last scientific paper and applied for a professorship of physics. In November he was named professor of theoretical physics at the University of Naples.

Unfortunately for Majorana's self-esteem, his lectures in Naples were poorly attended. Most of the students simply could not follow what he was trying to explain. On January 22, 1938, he asked his brother to transfer all his money from a bank in Rome to one in Naples. In March he asked for a lump sum of his professorial salary, untouched in the months since his appointment. With this money and his passport, Majorana boarded the ship on March 25 — and vanished forever.

Looking for Clues

The investigation conducted in the weeks immediately following the physicist's disappearance turned up several promising leads. But all proved to be dead ends.

Only a Literary Solution?

The mysterious disappearance in March 1938 of physicist Ettore Majorana had long been forgotten by the public when the Italian writer Leonardo Sciascia published *The Majorana Case* in 1975 — a work that he described as a "philosophical mystery novel." Sciascia's previous novels and short stories deal almost exclusively with the socioeconomic, political, and moral conditions in his native Sicily.

Sciascia only became aware of the mystery surrounding Majorana in 1972. That year the National Research Council — which had financed the young physicist's trip to Germany in 1933 — commissioned Erasmo Recami, professor of theoretical physics at the University of Catania, to put Majorana's scientific estate in order. In so doing, he came upon previously overlooked clues and turned these over to Sciascia. In following up these leads, the novelist began pondering the motives that might have led Majorana to flee Italy and came up with an intriguing theory. Because of his superior intelligence, Majorana had recognized earlier than most of his colleagues the enormous destructive power of atomic energy and did not want to have any part in developing an atomic weapon for Mussolini's fascist regime.

Sciascia's thesis stirred up considerable controversy in Italy. The leading voice of the opponents was Eduardo Amaldi, who completed his doctoral studies under Fermi a year after Majorana. In his opinion, no scientist in the 1930's was able to foresee the end result of nuclear research in the prewar decades. Erasmo Recami, knowing Majorana's work as no one else does, declines to rule out the theory. It is, he feels, but one of many possibilities.

On March 26, the day he sent the telegram and a second letter to Carrelli, Majorana presumably boarded the mail ship returning from Palermo to Naples. According to the shipping company authorities, a ticket in his name had been surrendered at dockside. Later, when asked to produce the evidence, they claimed that the canceled ticket had been lost. A witness first claimed to have shared a cabin with Majorana, then said that he could not be certain that his traveling companion was the missing physicist. On the other hand, a nurse who knew Majorana well insisted that she had seen him in Naples subsequent to the return of the ship on March 26.

Into a Monastery?

Majorana's family published a missing person announcement with Ettore's photograph. In July they had a response. The abbot of the monastery Gesu Nuovo in Naples came forward to say that a young man closely resembling the one in the photograph had come to see him in late March or early April, asking to be taken into the monastery as a guest. When the abbot hesitated in granting the request, the young man had left and never returned. Unfortunately, the abbot could not pinpoint the date, so it was impossible to determine whether his visit had been before or after the trip to Palermo.

Next, it was established that on April 12 a young man matching the photograph of Majorana had applied for admission to the monastery San Pasquale de Portici. There, too, he had been turned down and left.

Based on these tantalizing if inconclusive reports, a theory was proposed by the writer Leonardo Sciascia some 40 years after the event. Weary of the world and the obligations his scientific work imposed upon him, perhaps disillusioned by his apparently unsuccessful teaching career, Majorana sought escape in the religious life. Somewhere he had found a refuge where he could live incognito and devote the remaining years of his life to prayer and contemplation.

Escape to Argentina?

The final, and perhaps most intriguing, trace of Ettore Majorana leads to South America. In 1950 the Chilean physicist Carlos Rivera was living in the Argentine capital Buenos Aires, temporarily housed in the home of an elderly lady. By chance one day, she discovered the name Majorana among Rivera's papers and told her tenant that her son knew a man by that name. He was no longer working in the field of physics but had turned to engineering. Rivera had to leave

Buenos Aires before he could follow the lead.

Curiously, the Chilean scientist once more stumbled upon Majorana's tracks in Buenos Aires. In 1960, while dining in a hotel restaurant, he absentmindedly scribbled mathematical formulas on a paper napkin. A waiter approached him and said, "I know somebody else who shares your habit of scribbling mathematics on napkins. He comes here from time to time. His name is Ettore Majorana, and he was an important physicist in Italy before the war when he fled his country to come here." Again, a clue led nowhere. The waiter could not supply an address for Majorana, and Rivera once more had to leave without solving the mystery.

Three Old Ladies Keep Their Secret

Through the scientific grapevine, news of Rivera's tantalizing discoveries in Argentina at last reached Italy in the late 1970's. Physics professor Erasmo Recami and Maria Majorana, a sister of Ettore's, set out to pursue the leads. During the course of their search, they came upon yet another track leading to Argentina.

Visiting Italy, the widow of Guatemalan writer Miguel Angel Asturias heard about the renewed efforts to clarify the decades-old matter of Ettore Majorana's disappearance. She offered the information that she had met the Italian physicist during the 1960's at the home of the sisters Eleonora and Lilo Manzoni. Majorana, Mrs. Asturias said, had been a close friend of Eleonora, who was a mathematician.

But the solution to the puzzle, almost in hand at last, vanished like a puff of smoke. Asked to supply additional details, Mrs. Asturias backed down. She had not really met Majorana in person but had only heard from others of his contact with Eleonora Manzoni. But Mrs. Asturias said that her sister and Lilo Manzoni could supply evidence, Eleonora having died in the meantime. The two elderly ladies were unable or unwilling to answer questions. Had they and Mrs. Asturias formed a pact to keep the secret of Ettore Majorana among themselves?

Because two totally unrelated clues led investigators to Argentina, it is highly likely that the Italian physicist fled there in 1938 — rather than retreating to a monastery or committing suicide. The reason for his abrupt flight remains unclear and will perhaps never be known.

Perhaps Enrico Fermi was right with his dry comment on the unsuccessful investigations into the disappearance. Had Ettore Majorana decided to vanish without a trace, he could easily have done so, given an intelligence such as his.

2

Deaths Under
Dubious
Circumstances

The Mad Monarch

At age 18 the tall, handsome prince ascended the throne of Bavaria as Ludwig II to the wild acclaim of his subjects. By 40 he had become a fat recluse, obsessed with his fairy-tale castles. A few days after being judged incompetent and insane, he met death by drowning.

When the psychiatrist, Dr. Bernhard von Gudden, and his royal patient had not returned from their evening walk by eight o'clock, Gudden's assistant, Dr. Müller, grew alarmed. He had suggested that the two be accompanied by orderlies, as they had been on their morning stroll; but Gudden had refused. The king was behaving in a rational, almost normal manner. Apart from his ceaseless questions, he was presenting no problems to the doctor. "He is just a child," Gudden remarked.

Rain began falling from lowering clouds, bringing a premature twilight to the long summer evening. Dr. Müller sent a single policeman, then in quick succession two more, to look for the missing pair along the shore of Starnberg Lake where they had last been seen heading. As concern turned to panic with the coming of darkness, he enlisted the entire staff of Castle Berg for a torchlight search of the grounds. To the court in Munich he sent a telegram announcing the disappearance of the monarch and his doctor.

Sometime after 10 o'clock shouts announced the first discoveries: two umbrellas lying by a bench and the king's hat nearby. Dark objects were seen floating at water's edge; they proved to

be the king's jacket and overcoat. Rowing out into the lake, searchers soon found the lifeless bodies of Dr. Gudden and King Ludwig II, drifting in shallow water no more than 20 yards from the shore. The king's watch had stopped at 6:54 P.M. on that Sunday, June 13, 1886.

When the two bodies were examined, it was noted that Dr. Gudden's face had been scratched and that above one eye was a bruise, most likely the result of a blow from a fist. Marks on his throat suggested a strangulation attempt. The king's body showed no injuries. Had Ludwig tried an escape and killed Dr. Gudden when the psychiatrist attempted to restrain him? Or had the king drowned the doctor and then flung himself in the water to commit suicide? Had the king murdered Gudden and suffered a heart attack? Whatever the facts, it was a tragic and shocking end to a life that had begun so auspiciously 41 years earlier.

Prince Charming Becomes King

Bell-ringing and cannon shots in Munich marked the birth of a son, on August 25, 1845, to Crown Prince Maximilian of Bavaria and his wife, Marie. The infant was first named Otto, then Ludwig — after his grandfather, King Ludwig I. Three years later the king was forced to abdicate over the scandal caused by his liaison with the dancer Lola Montez; Maximilian took the throne; and young Ludwig became heir apparent. A younger brother, Otto, was born the next month.

The two princes, as was the custom of the day, were strictly disciplined and subject to a rigorous private education. But the classroom bored Ludwig, aside from the stories his French governess told him about King Louis XIV and his magnificent palace Versailles. His happiest days were spent at Hohenschwangau, a castle overlooking a lake in the Bavarian Alps 55 miles southeast of Munich. Reading the German sagas, roaming the dense forests, withdrawing into daydreams, Ludwig conceived for himself a role in life: builder of palaces to rival Versailles. A sketch he made at age 14 shows an extraordinary crenellated castle rising over a lake on which floats a swan very nearly as large as the building itself.

On March 10, 1864, just short of his 19th birthday, Ludwig became king upon the prema-

The news of Ludwig II's death, at left as announced in a newspaper "extra," shocked and dismayed his subjects — even though he was a remote and indifferent ruler. A simple cross marks the place in Starnberg Lake where his body was found.

ture death of his father. "Max died too soon," Queen Marie wrote in her diary; she knew that her son was not ready for the throne. To the people staring at Ludwig as he marched in his father's funeral procession, however, Prince Charming was now king. Tall, slender, with thick, wavy dark hair and piercing blue eyes, he carried himself erect and moved with an almost feminine grace. No matter that he seemed proud, even arrogant. His subjects fell in love with their new monarch. Women sighed as he passed, throwing flowers into his open carriage. Sonnets were written and sent off to the royal residence.

Who would be Ludwig's consort? It was his royal duty to marry and provide an heir; and, when his choice fell on his pretty cousin, Sophie, early in 1867, the country seemed pleased. Stiffly posed for the photographers, Ludwig and Sophie made a handsome couple. But the August wedding was postponed to October, and the engagement abruptly broken off by the king a few days before the scheduled ceremony. To a courtier, Ludwig confessed that he would rather drown himself in an Alpine lake than marry.

Turning Night into Day

Ludwig had never made a secret of his disdain for court life in Munich and, as the years passed by, spent more and more of his time at one or another of his mountain lodges. For dinner he preferred the company of sculpted busts of Louis XVI and of Marie Antoinette, beheaded in the French Revolution; unlike human guests, the king explained, the statues came only when invited and could be removed at his will. Turning night into day, Ludwig slept from midafternoon until midnight and then went for long, solitary rides in an ornate gilded sleigh pulled through Alpine snows by four white horses. Elaborate theatrical productions were staged at the court theater with the king as the only member of the audience.

After the brief romance with Sophie, Ludwig came to prefer the company of handsome young officers and actors. Published only after his death, the king's diaries — written in a jumble of German, French, and Latin — reveal the agony of apparently unsuccessful attempts to repress his homosexuality. Most of his attachments to male companions were transitory; but one, with his head groom, Richard Hornig, lasted nearly 20 years. Hornig's marriage, the king is supposed to have said, was harder for Ludwig to bear than the Franco-Prussian War.

In July 1870 France declared war on Prussia only to be quickly defeated by a combination of German states, including Bavaria. Prussian

Chancellor Bismarck prevailed upon Ludwig to call for the formation of a German empire to be headed by King William I of Prussia. Although allowed to maintain a separate army and diplomatic service, as well as to issue its own stamps and coinage, Ludwig's kingdom of Bavaria was absorbed into the German empire that was proclaimed early the next year in the Hall of Mirrors at Versailles.

A Building Mania

With the independence of Bavaria sharply limited, Ludwig had less to do as a monarch — which bothered him not at all. In the summer of 1867 he had traveled incognito to France and, seeing Versailles at last, resolved to build palaces just as magnificent in his homeland. He began Neuschwanstein in 1869, Linderhof in 1870, and Herrenchiemsee in 1878. Only Linderhof would be completed within the king's relatively short lifetime. These fairy-tale castles have been described as vulgar, artificial, exotic, and a riot of borrowed architectural styles. To the king they were places where he could forget that he was king.

Perhaps most representative of Ludwig's penchant for excessive display is Neuschwanstein, built on a lofty crag not unintentionally overlooking and dominating his father's palace Hohenschwangau. It was to be, he wrote Richard Wagner, a replica of the medieval castles that were the settings for the operas of the composer he so admired. There was a two-story audience hall in the style of a Byzantine basilica — except that a throne stood where one might have expected to see an altar; a minstrels' gallery; and, off Ludwig's fourth-floor study, an artificial cave complete with waterfall and indoor moon. Neuschwanstein was a place, he confided to Wagner, where "the outraged gods will take their revenge and sojourn with us on the steep summit, fanned by celestial breezes."

The king's second fairy-tale castle, Linderhof, began as a one-bedroom extension to a simple hunting lodge in a valley some 15 miles west of Neuschwanstein. But Ludwig soon became obsessed with the goal of recreating in Bavaria a replica of the Grand Trianon, the elegant royal pavilion that stands amid gardens as a satellite of Versailles. "Oh! It is essential to create such paradises," he wrote a friend, "such poetical sanctuaries where one can forget for a while the dreadful age in which we live." A compact white stone building, Linderhof was adorned with statues set into niches in the facade and along the roof line. As ornate as the exterior appears, a critic has written, "by comparison with the interior it may

be considered a model of restraint." Linderhof's rooms are studded with gilt, mirrors, porcelain, and semiprecious stones. In the gardens Ludwig had an artificial grotto erected; entered through a doorway concealed in the rocks, it contains a miniature lake on which the king could be rowed by a servant.

Ludwig's ultimate building project — or folly, as skeptics would have it — was Herrenchiemsee, built on an island in Bavaria's largest lake, the Chiemsee, 45 miles west of Munich. Here at last Ludwig could indulge his fantasy of duplicating Louis XIV's magnificent Versailles, including its famous Hall of Mirrors. Left incomplete at Ludwig's death, Herrenchiemsee cost 16 million marks, more than Neuschwanstein and Linderhof together. Ludwig spent exactly 10 nights there, in the autumn of 1885.

Desperate for Funds

The king appeared in public in Munich for the last time in August 1875. Pressed to visit the capital for the 700th anniversary of his family's rule of Bavaria in 1880, he exclaimed, "No! No! I can't come out of my shell — not ever again!" To his once devoted subjects he was now a man of mystery. To his ministers he was a cause for growing concern. Built without taste, the palaces were apparently also being built without financial limitations. Although the king received an annual allowance of 4.5 million marks, he was 7.5 million marks in debt to the royal treasury by the spring of 1884; a year later the debt had risen to 14 million marks. When the finance minister cautioned the king to exercise fiscal restraint, Ludwig brushed aside the suggestion and instead asked for a loan of 20 million marks. Neuschwanstein and Herrenchiemsee were unfinished, and he had in mind to build one or two more castles.

Turned down by his own government, Ludwig appealed to his fellow European monarchs and sought loans from the Rothschilds and the House of Orleans, no longer reigning in France but still quite wealthy. As security, he offered his family's property in Bavaria. He once suggested that robbers be hired to break into the banks of Frankfurt, Berlin, and Paris and even threatened to dig up his father's body so that he could box his ears — apparently for failing to provide him with an adequate fortune.

A Monarch Gone Mad

Apart from his building mania, Ludwig began displaying other, even more alarming signs of instability. Moments of cheerful tranquility were followed by uncontrollable rages. He ordered of-

The Ludwig myth: a handsome Prince Charming crowned king (left, an 1865 portrait), who built fairy-tale castles (at top, Neuschwanstein) and went for midnight sleigh rides through the Alpine snow, accompanied only by liveried servants (above).

An Odd Couple: The King and the Composer

At first Richard Wagner thought that the visitor was employing a ruse to see him, that it was an attempt by one of his many creditors to serve him with legal papers. What business could the secretary to the king of Bavaria have with him and how had he tracked him down to a friend's house in Stuttgart? He refused to see the man. The messenger was persistent, however, and on a second attempt presented the composer with the monarch's photograph, a ruby ring, and an invitation to come immediately to Munich.

Less than two months into his reign, Ludwig II met his musical idol for the first time on May 4, 1864. Wagner was 51 and — though the composer of such notable operas as *The Flying Dutchman* and *Tannhaüser* — in despair owing to poverty, a failed marriage, and political disgrace because of his alleged republican activities. The young monarch, not yet 19, had been addicted to the composer's

music since attending a performance of *Lohengrin* three years earlier; the experience had left him in tears. Reading the libretto for Wagner's incomplete and as-yet unperformed four-opera cycle *The Ring of the Nibelung*, Ludwig had vowed to be the royal patron with enough money and authority to bring the giant work to the stage.

In ecstasy at the meeting, Wagner wrote to a friend that the king loved him "with the fire and tenderness of a first love; he knows and understands everything about me -- understands me like my own soul." Ludwig promised to make up for all that Wagner had suffered in the past, to banish from his life all petty cares "so that you will be free to spread the mighty wings of your genius in the pure air of your rapturous art."

Ludwig put a country villa at Wagner's disposal and moved to Castle Berg to be nearby. When they were not together planning the operas to be composed and produced over the coming years, the pair were exchanging what can only be called love letters — though there was never any suspicion that Wagner shared Ludwig's suppressed homosexuality. "Unseverable is the band tying us together, steadfast, eternal, holy and deeply enchanting is the love burning for you in my soul," wrote the monarch. "I am nothing any more without you," replied the composer. "Oh, my King, you are divine!" Wagner could not have been unaware that his royal patron had no ear for music; it was the fantasy world of the stories that appealed to the king.

Wagner conducted a performance of *The Flying Dutchman* in Munich on December 4, 1864; the king was in the royal box to share the composer's triumph. The premier of *Tristan and Isolde* the next year was an equal success. But even lovers have tiffs and when news reached Ludwig that his idol had referred to him as "my lad," he temporarily barred Wagner from the royal presence. More serious were rumblings of discontent from court circles. At first there was resentment that the king was lavishing public money on Wagner to support the composer's extravagant lifestyle. Then, in November 1865, Wagner indiscreetly criticized the government — an unforgivable offense for the sensitive Bavarians, who considered the Saxon-born composer a foreigner. Members of the king's family joined in an ultimatum on December 1: Ludwig had to choose between Wagner and "the love and respect of your faithful people." The king chose the people, and 10 days later Wagner was on a train for Switzerland — the disgraced musician having announced that he was going there for his health. The idyll of king and composer had lasted 18 months.

Wagner settled into a productive life in Switzerland, while the king continued his encouragement and financial support from afar. Ludwig contributed to the building of a magnificent theater for performances of Wagner's operas at Bayreuth and was on hand for the first full presentation of the *Ring* cycle there on four successive days in August 1876; it was the first time in eight years that the two had met. At the conclusion of the fourth opera, the reticent monarch was persuaded to rise and step forward in the royal box so as to share in the ovation bestowed on Wagner.

When he learned of the composer's death in Venice on February 13, 1883, Ludwig said, "Wagner's body belongs to me," and had it transported to Bayreuth for burial. "It was *I* who was the first to recognize the artist whom the whole world now mourns," he announced; "and it was *I* who saved him for the world."

fending courtiers to be flogged, tortured, imprisoned, exiled to America, or even beheaded but showed no surprise or displeasure when the sentences were not carried out. After losing his temper and striking a servant, the king would try to atone with expensive gifts or cash. Grown fat and becoming neglectful of his clothing, he would attempt to recapture his lost good looks by hiring hairdressers to wave his hair. No one could approach within 18 inches of him or look at the food he was served. A dumbwaiter was installed in his bedroom so that meals could be served without the king having to see anyone. Finally, he began shouting orders from behind closed doors and communicating with his ministers — whom he referred to as rabble, vagabonds, and vermin — only in writing. Official papers were left unsigned or lost. In one lucid moment of self-appraisal the king confessed, "I wouldn't be my own cabinet minister for all the world."

Moonlight rides with servants often ended in

Did Dr. Gudden try to prevent the king from drowning himself during the course of their lakeside stroll at Castle Berg?

picnics, even if there was snow on the ground, and children's games that lasted till dawn. And if the weather interrupted one of his nocturnal excursions, he would impose himself and his entourage on astonished peasants. Upon leaving or returning to Linderhof, Ludwig passionately embraced a certain pillar; during his circuits, he bowed to a one particular tree and politely greeted a hedge. There were voices that only he could hear and hilarious conversations that he carried on with himself.

The Conspiracy to Replace Ludwig

By early 1886 it was apparent that something had to be done about the increasingly mad monarch. There was, however, a serious problem with the succession. At the time of the Franco-Prussian War, Prince Otto had begun showing signs of insanity. "He behaves like a madman," Ludwig wrote of his younger brother, "makes terrible faces, barks like a dog, and sometimes says the most indecent things; and then again he is perfectly normal for a while." In 1875 Otto had been locked up as incurably insane.

Undeterred, the ministers decided to make Otto king in name only; real power would go to the king's 65-year-old uncle, Prince Luitpold, as regent. First, however, they had to remove Ludwig. They turned to the eminent psychiatrist Dr. Gudden, who was persuaded to take on what he called "the painful task" of finding the king of Bavaria insane.

After gathering evidence from former and present members of the royal household, Dr. Gudden issued a 19-page report on June 8, 1886. "His Majesty is in a very advanced state of mental

disturbance," Dr. Gudden concluded; his sickness "must be pronounced incurable and a further decay of his mental faculties is certain." Since the condition would last for the remainder of Ludwig's life, "His Majesty must be considered as incapable of exercising government."

Dr. Gudden never examined the king in person, apparently satisfied with collecting second-hand information. Positive testimony was ignored, for there were servants who attested to his kindnesses. Among the peasantry he remained a beloved if somewhat odd figure. There were two souls in Ludwig's breast, a courtier wrote in sadness, "the soul of a tyrant and the soul of a child." Shown a copy of Gudden's harsh report, Chancellor Bismarck dismissed it as "rakings from the king's wastepaper basket and cupboards."

A Farcical Arrest

Toward midnight on June 9 a commission headed by Foreign Minister Baron von Crailsheim arrived at Castle Hohenschwangau to inform Ludwig that he was to be deposed. Learning that the king was at his fantasy palace Neuschwanstein nearby, the commissioners decided to defer their unpleasant task until the following morning. And so they sat down to a seven-course dinner washed down with 40 quarts of beer and 10 bottles of champagne and afterward went to bed.

At three o'clock in the morning, Baron Crailsheim awakened his fellow commissioners. A coachman named Osterholzer had slipped out of the castle and was thought to be headed for Neuschwanstein to warn Ludwig of his impending arrest. Through the darkness and a heavy rain the commissioners drove off up the winding road to the king's lair — only to be met at the gate by a police guard barring entrance. When a group of peasants loyal to Ludwig showed up and began threatening the commissioners, the party retreated to Hohenschwangau.

No sooner had the commissioners reached what they thought was the safety of the castle than they were arrested and forced to walk back to Neuschwanstein, where they were locked into individual rooms. The infuriated king had ordered their death, they were told.

By midday, his mood changed from anger to resignation, Ludwig released the commissioners, who scurried back to Munich. What should he do, he asked a loyal courtier. He was advised to appeal to the people by appearing in the capital or to flee across the border into Austria. Instead, the king asked for poison and, when it was denied, for the key to the tower. He preferred death from drowning, Ludwig remarked, since it was

less disfiguring than would be a plunge from the tower. The fearful servant told him the key to the tower was lost. Ludwig ordered brandy and champagne and proceeded to get drunk.

A second commission, this one headed by Dr. Gudden, arrived at Ludwig's mountain retreat in the early hours of June 12. With the aid of a servant, the king was lured to the tower staircase, where he was apprehended by orderlies from the Munich insane asylum. "Your Majesty," said the doctor, "the mission I have come to carry out at this time is the saddest of my life." Because of his mental condition, Ludwig was being replaced by Prince Luitpold and would be taken under custody to Castle Berg. "How can you pronounce me insane without even examining me first?" the king asked. An examination was totally unnecessary, Dr. Gudden replied, in view of the vast amount of evidence he had collected.

End of the Reign

Around four o'clock in the morning, the deathly pale king said goodbye to his faithful servants at Neuschwanstein and stepped into a carriage from which the inner door handles had been removed. Asylum orderlies sat outside, front and back; a carriage preceded and another followed the royal vehicle on the eight-hour drive to Castle Berg.

The lakeside palace had been converted into a royal prison, with iron grates attached to the windows of Ludwig's suite and peepholes drilled in the doors. Ludwig took it all quite calmly and retired after lunch, asking to be awakened as usual at midnight. His order was ignored and the king seemed irritated when he awoke toward dawn. Although Ludwig was not allowed to attend Sunday Mass, Dr. Gudden did agree to accompany him on a stroll later in the morning; two orderlies followed at a discreet distance. So pleased with his patient was Dr. Gudden that he dispensed with the orderlies for the second walk in the late afternoon. It proved to be a fatal mistake.

Since there were no witnesses to the deaths of Ludwig and Dr. Gudden, the true story will never be known. At least one of the king's biographers reached the conclusion that Ludwig killed the psychiatrist and then committed suicide; far from insane, the king realized that the future held nothing but disgrace and confinement for him. One of his contemporaries would have agreed. Hearing of her cousin's death, Empress Elizabeth of Austria sadly remarked, "The king was not mad; he was just an eccentric living in a world of dreams. They might have treated him more gently, and thus perhaps spared him so terrible an end."

Death at Ndola

Fighting had broken out between U.N. forces and mercenaries in the Congo's secessionist province, Katanga — requiring the personal intervention of Secretary-General Dag Hammarskjold. His flight for peace ended in a fatal crash.

*I*n the summer of 1960 the United Nations faced the gravest challenge in its 15-year history: preventing civil war in the newly independent Republic of the Congo.

There had been virtually no preparation for the independence of the former Belgian colony on June 30. Following anticolonial protests the previous year, Belgium had made hasty arrangements to relinquish power. As a result of elections in May, the new government was to be a fragile partnership between President Joseph Kasavubu and his rival Prime Minister Patrice Lumumba. In a country more than three times the size of Texas, with a population of some 30 million, there was not a single African doctor, engineer, or trained administrator; its army's officers were all Belgians. In a defiant independence day speech Lumumba reminded Belgium that his people had known "ironies, insults, and blows which we had to endure morning, noon, and night because we were blacks." Yet there was no national consciousness among the republic's populace; loyalties were primarily tribal.

It was not surprising, in such a tense and hostile environment, that violence soon erupted. On July 5 Congolese troops in the capital of Leopoldville mutinied against their Belgian officers. When the uprising spread to major cities in other provinces, Belgian troops intervened to protect the remaining white population. On July 11 the leader of mineral-rich Katanga, Moise Tshombe, announced the secession of his province and declared it to be an independent state. Kasavubu and Lumumba called on the United Nations, to which the Congo had just been admitted, for help in restoring order.

In April 1953, when the 47-year-old Swedish diplomat Dag Hammarskjold had been elected the second secretary-general of the United Nations, only four African states were members of the international body. By late 1960 — as Europe relinquished its colonial control of the continent — there were 26. Other than the perennially turbulent Middle East, there was no more pressing problem facing Hammarskjold than Africa. The crisis in the Congo would require a major re-evaluation of the U.N.'s role in world affairs, bring Hammarskjold into direct conflict with the Soviet Union, and ultimately cost him his life.

The last photo: Dag Hammarskjold (center) about to board the aircraft at Leopoldville on September 17, 1961, for the flight to Ndola.

Calling the U.N. Security Council into session on the evening of July 13, Hammarskjold pressed for a quick response to the Congo's appeal. The Soviet Union wanted a condemnation of Belgium's so-called aggression; France, Britain, and the United States objected to criticism of their NATO ally. Yet by 3:25 A.M. on the morning of July 14, the Security Council had adopted a compromise resolution that authorized the secretary-general to call for the withdrawal of Belgian troops and to dispatch a U.N. force to the Congo. By dawn he had his plan in operation.

Hammarskjold had previously decided to call first on other African states for military support, and within five days he could report that 3,500 troops from Tunisia, Ghana, Morocco, and Ethiopia had arrived in Leopoldville and were being deployed around the country.

Under Double Attack

The arrival of the U.N. troops in the Congo did not resolve the crisis there nor end Hammarskjold's problems at U.N. headquarters in New York. On September 5 Kasavubu dismissed Lumumba, who promptly announced that he was deposing the president. Army Chief of Staff Joseph Mobutu intervened in the dispute by seizing power for himself. One of his first acts was to expel the Soviet-bloc embassies, suspecting that they were poised to meddle in the Congo's affairs. Although Kasavubu remained nominal head of the government, Lumumba was arrested, delivered to his enemies in Katanga, and, early in 1961, brutally murdered. Meanwhile, Tshombe persisted in his defiant secession and began enlisting European mercenaries to bolster Katanga's independence.

The U.N. General Assembly that convened in New York on September 20 attracted 57 foreign ministers and 23 heads of state — including President Dwight D. Eisenhower, Britain's Prime Minister Harold Macmillan, India's Jawaharlal Nehru, Cuba's Fidel Castro, and the Soviet

At right, Secretary-General Hammarskjold inspects Swedish soldiers of the U.N. force in the Congo; above, battle scenes in the troubled African nation.

Union's Nikita Khrushchev. The Soviet leader accused the former colonial powers of "doing their dirty work in the Congo through the secretary-general" and proposed that Hammarskjold's position be abolished and replaced with a three-person executive, or *troika*, representing communist East, capitalist West, and neutral states. In reply, Hammarskjold pledged to remain in his post — and received a standing ovation from the General Assembly. But by year's end, the overwhelmed secretary-general was describing his job as "a bit like fighting an avalanche; you know the rules: get rid of the skis, don't try to resist but swim on the surface, and hope for a rescuer."

On February 17, 1961, the Security Council strengthened Hammarskjold's mandate to prevent civil war in the Congo, and that summer a coalition government in Leopoldville brought all factions together — with the notable exception of Moise Tshombe. Katanga's independence was to some extent supported by Belgium, France, Britain, the United States, and the neighboring British protectorate of Northern Rhodesia.

By late August, with some 16,000 U.N. troops in the Congo, Hammarskjold decided to take action, authorizing the roundup of European mercenaries in Katanga and the seizure of key points in the provincial capital of Elisabethville. And now it was the West's turn to attack the secretary-general, accusing him of being pro-communist and anti-Western. On September 12, confiding to a U.N. colleague that he would resign if he was unable to solve the Katanga problem, Hammarsjkold left New York for Leopoldville.

Rendezvous with Tshombe

By the time the secretary-general arrived in the Congo the next day, fighting had broken out between U.N. troops and Katanga's mercenaries, and Tshombe had disappeared across the border into Northern Rhodesia. Convinced that only his personal intervention could win over the secessionist leader, Hammarskjold offered to meet Tshombe at Ndola, just across the frontier.

Sending the British diplomat Lord Landsdowne ahead in the DC-4 that had been reserved for his use, Hammarskjold decided to make the trip in another U.N. plane, a faster DC-6B named the *Albertina*, that had just arrived from Elisabethville. Most likely the secretary-general did not know that the *Albertina* had been hit by rifle fire upon takeoff from Katanga and, though repaired, had been standing without guard on the field for four hours before he and his party of nine took off just before 5 P.M. on Sunday afternoon, September 17. To avoid Katanga, the *Albertina*

Lumumba: African Nationalist

The arrest of Patrice Lumumba by his political opponents in December 1960 and his death early the next year made him a martyr to African nationalism. Unlike his political rivals Joseph Kasavubu and Moise Tshombe, who represented large tribes and drew their support from their home regions, Lumumba was a member of one of the Congo's smaller tribes, which accounts for his advocacy of a strong, unified state.

Born in 1925 and educated at a Protestant mission school, Lumumba worked as a postal clerk, accountant, and part-time journalist. But at the age of 30 he joined the trade union movement and began showing an interest in politics. In 1958 he helped found the Congolese National Movement and attended an all-African conference in Ghana, where he met leaders pressing for the independence of other European colonies. The next year he was arrested by Belgian authorities for inciting a riot but was released to attend a meeting in Brussels early in 1960 that paved the way for the Congo's independence on June 30. With his party a victor in the May elections, Lumumba was named prime minister but was forced to share power with Kasavubu.

When the U.N. force failed to act quickly enough to end Katanga's secession, Lumumba appealed to the Soviet Union — a move that led to his dismissal by Kasavubu. Fleeing "protective custody" in Leopoldville, he sought to reach his supporters in the interior but was caught and handed over to the Katanga secessionists (above). Lumumba's death, in which Tshombe was implicated, was confirmed in February 1961. In tribute to the slain African leader, the Soviet Union established in Moscow the Patrice Lumumba People's Friendship University.

flew due east, then south over Lake Tanganyika toward Northern Rhodesia.

Shocking News from Africa

After erroneously reporting on Monday that the secretary-general had met with Tshombe at Ndola, *The New York Times* ran a banner headline on Tuesday, September 19: "Hammarskjold Dies in African Air Crash; Kennedy Going to U.N. in Succession Crisis." The President pledged American support to build the U.N. into "the effective instrument for peace which was Dag Hammarskjold's great ambition."

Details about the crash were slow to emerge. Having maintained air silence for four hours, the *Albertina* radioed its expected arrival time at Ndola as 12:35 A.M. on September 18. Ten minutes after midnight it reported that the airfield lights were in sight and that it had begun the descent for the landing. After passing over the airfield at an elevation of about 2,000 feet, lights flashing and wheels and flaps lowered, the *Albertina* flew on to complete a required circling maneuver. It never reappeared.

Not until the following afternoon was the wreckage of the *Albertina* discovered about nine miles west of the airport. Apparently coming in too low, the aircraft had brushed the treetops, dipped to the ground, and cartwheeled into flames. All six crewmen and eight members of the U.N. party were dead, most of them charred in their seats. Two of the passengers had been thrown clear: a U.N. security officer, Sergeant Harry Julien, still alive but so seriously injured that he would die five days later; and Dag Hammarskjold, dead of multiple injuries but not burned at all. The secretary-general had lived for a short time after the crash, his hand clutching a bunch of grass plucked in agony.

Unanswered Questions

As is always so in the sudden deaths of public figures, rumors began to circulate about the crash of Hammarskjold's plane. There were many people who opposed the secretary-general's efforts to end Katanga's secession, including the British in Northern Rhodesia, who saw Tshombe and his European mercenaries as a bulwark against black nationalism. The Soviet Union had openly called for his replacement at the U.N.; several Western powers charged him with being pro-communist.

Hammarskjold's last flight: From Leopoldville the U.N. aircraft headed east toward Lake Tanganyika, then south to Ndola in Northern Rhodesia.

— Hammarskjold's Flight

The wreckage of the Albertina *litters the forest near Ndola, where it crashed just after midnight on September 18, 1961.*

The Murder of Olof Palme

Late on the evening of February 28, 1986, Olof Palme, Sweden's popular prime minister and a leader of the international disarmament movement, was shot dead while leaving a Stockholm movie theater with his wife, Lisbet; a second bullet grazed Mrs. Palme's back. Three years later Carl Gustav Christer Pettersson, a 42-year-old drifter with a history of drug and alcohol abuse, violent crime, and compulsory psychiatric treatment, was formally charged with Palme's murder.

No one saw the shots fired, though several witnesses — including Mrs. Palme — put Pettersson at the scene of the crime. But after initial questioning, he was released; no motive for the slaying could be attributed to Pettersson. For more than a year Swedish authorities acted on the assumption

Mourners gather at the site on a Stockholm street, strewn with flowers and set off with a barrier, where Olof Palme was fatally shot in 1986.

that Palme's death had been a politically motivated assassination. When nothing turned up, the police again sought out Pettersson and, in December 1988, arrested him. Mrs. Palme, viewing a videotape, positively identified him as the man she believed responsible for the shooting. "His face, eyes, and that terrible look are the same," she said.

Principally on the strength of Mrs. Palme's testimony, a judicial panel found him guilty on July 28, 1989. Six lay jurors voted to convict; the two professional judges voted for acquittal. In October an appeals court overturned the conviction and freed Pettersson. Since Mrs. Palme had said that she was certain Pettersson was the killer, legal experts pointed out that she could never testify against any other suspect in the case.

A U.N. commission of inquiry reached the noncommittal conclusion that there was no evidence of sabotage, attack, or mechanical failure — though none of the three could be excluded as a cause of the crash. Curiously, the reports of natives on the ground were dismissed as being unreliable. Yet these witnesses recalled seeing two airplanes, a small one in pursuit of a larger one that crashed after being hit by fire.

A Possible Suicide?

A few years after Hammarskjold's death a bizarre story was advanced: despondent over the failure of his peace efforts and frustrated by the growing opposition to his power at the United Nations, the secretary-general had committed suicide. With a gun pointed at the captain's head, Hammarskjold had forced a diversionary maneuver over the Ndola airport that caused the crash.

The evidence for this farfetched version was said to include a manuscript left in his New York apartment with instructions for publication only after his death; a will made out shortly before his departure for the Congo; and — as final reading — on the bedside table in his Leopoldville hotel room the 15th-century German religious classic by Thomas à Kempis, *Imitation of Christ*, the place marked by a copy of Ham-

marskjold's oath of office as secretary-general.

Working against this hypothesis is the fact that Hammarskjold's will was made years before his death and not changed before he left New York. The manuscript, a sort of spiritual diary on which he had been working at least since 1956, was published under the title *Markings* in 1964 and revealed the inner man as one committed to religion, poetry, and public service — not someone likely to take 15 other lives in committing suicide. He took with him for work on the flight a book he was translating from German into Swedish and a clean shirt and toothbrush that he would scarcely have needed if contemplating putting an end to his life.

Honor in Death

On Tuesday, September 19, the day after Hammarskjold's death was confirmed, the United Nations General Assembly convened in New York. To the right of the assembly president was the secretary-general's empty chair. After the world's delegates were asked to rise for a moment of silent prayer, a U.N. staff member said, "Never was a minute so long, a silence so silent, or a chair so empty." The following month Dag Hammarskjold was posthumously awarded the Nobel Peace Prize.

Killed in a Barroom Brawl

A fight over the bill for a day of carousing in an English inn led to the death of Christopher Marlowe, England's most promising playwright of the late 16th century. The real story may be much more interesting and complex — as documents uncovered more than three centuries later have revealed.

*I*n London the plague is raging, as four men gather on a Wednesday morning for a day of eating, drinking, and talking at an inn operated by the widow Eleanor Bull in Deptford, a village about three miles southeast of the city on the opposite bank of the river Thames. The unlikely quartet consists of Ingram Frizer, a confidence man whose devious schemes kept him in perpetual litigation; Nicholas Skeres, Frizer's frequent decoy in those plots; Robert Poley, a government secret agent of dubious and unsavory character; and Christopher Marlowe, only 29 years old but already considered England's leading dramatist. The date is May 30, 1593.

Following a short walk in the afternoon, the four men resume their drinking and talking. Late that night, after dinner, a fight breaks out between Frizer and Marlowe over the bill — presumably a large one for such a long day of carousing. Both witnesses — Skeres and Poley — agree that it was Marlowe who started the fight, grabbing Frizer's dagger and lunging at him without provocation. After receiving two cuts on the head, Frizer manages to wrest the weapon from Marlowe and stabs his frenzied adversary above the right eye. The young playwright falls dead on the floor.

Guards are called and by morning the coroner of the queen's household arrives. Although Frizer is arrested for the slaying, an inquest quickly exonerates him of wrongdoing; it was clearly a matter of self-defense. By the end of June, the prisoner is freed. Meanwhile, Marlowe has been buried within 48 hours of his violent death.

This, then, is the official version of the abrupt end of a promising career and was so accepted for more than three centuries. Then, in 1925, the report of the coroner's inquest was found in an archive where it had been lying unnoticed for 332 years. A close reading of the document raises a number of questions.

Why had Marlowe been buried so quickly? Why did the inquiry take so little time and why were the statements of the two witnesses accepted so readily? Was a barroom brawl the only explanation for the slaying? Could it not have been a conspiracy of the three men to kill Marlowe? Frizer's head wounds, it appeared, were so slight that they could have been self-inflicted to make him seem the victim of a drunken attack. Were the three shady characters acting in their own behalf or were they stand-ins for someone in power? Was there a plot to get rid of a man who knew too much?

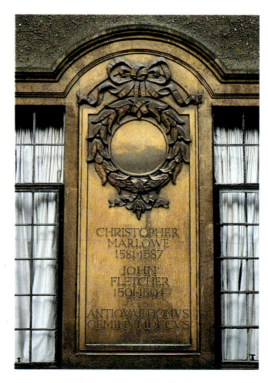

A memorial plaque in Cambridge's Corpus Christi College commemorates a famous graduate, the dramatist who died too soon.

This last possibility must be given serious consideration, since it is now known that the fledgling dramatist was leading a double life as an agent of the queen's secret service.

Christopher Marlowe (right) entered Cambridge under a scholarship meant for the training of Anglican clergymen.

Young Man in a Hurry

Christopher Marlowe was born in February 1564, two months before the man whose longer, more successful career would so quickly eclipse his own: William Shakespeare. But while Shakespeare was still living in quiet obscurity at Stratford, Marlowe was awarded a scholarship to Corpus Christi College at Cambridge and earned a bachelor's degree at the age of 20. He continued his studies there, perhaps with the goal of becoming an Anglican clergyman. But the Cambridge authorities refused at first to grant him an advanced degree, having grown suspicious of his frequent absences from the university.

England's golden age during the reign of Queen Elizabeth I (1558–1603) was also a time of tumultuous change. Succeeding her Catholic half-sister, Mary, Elizabeth had reestablished the Protestant Church of England instituted by their father, Henry VIII. Elizabeth's move brought down upon her head the wrath of King Philip II of Spain, Mary's widower and an implacable defender of the Catholic faith. By the time young

Marlowe was at Cambridge, England was under threat of Spanish invasion and Catholic students were fleeing to France. Could his absences be a prelude to such a flight? Was the university harboring a secret Catholic? In 1587 Elizabeth's privy council intervened. The scholar "in all his actions . . . had behaved himself orderly and discreetly whereby he had done Her Majesty good service"; his qualifications should not be questioned "by those who are ignorant of the affairs he went about." Cambridge awarded him the master's degree.

Within a year of leaving Cambridge, Marlowe's first play was performed, the two-part drama *Tamburlaine the Great*. The would-be clergyman had become a man of letters. In a career of only six years, he produced a half dozen plays, a long narrative poem, and translations from the Latin. But he was also gaining a reputation as an impulsive and headstrong young man, inclined to settle arguments by a resort to force.

In 1589 he was briefly imprisoned for his part in a street brawl during which a man was killed. Three years later he was summoned to appear in court for assaulting officers of the law. In the spring of 1593 Marlowe was charged with a far more serious offense.

Denying Jesus

To protect her kingdom from Spanish invasion and her throne from her Catholic rival, Mary, Queen of Scots, Elizabeth relied on the elaborate secret service organization of her resourceful secretary of state, Sir Francis Walsingham. Often spending his own money, Walsingham employed a network of spies at foreign courts to keep informed of any threats to his sovereign. It was Walsingham who uncovered Anthony Babington's plot against the queen's life in 1586 and secured the conviction and execution of the Queen of Scots in 1587. It was also he who forewarned Elizabeth of preparations for the Spanish Armada that same year and urged her in vain to take defensive measures.

Although Philip's great invasion fleet was defeated by the English in the summer of 1588, there was a renewed threat from Spain in the spring of 1593. When seditious posters began appearing overnight on London walls, the privy council appointed an investigative commission with power to enter private homes in search of treasonous activities. During this sweep, on May 12, the commissioners found the papers of Thomas Kyd, another young playwright with whom Marlowe had shared lodgings.

There was no evidence of treason among Kyd's papers, but the seized documents contained statements denying the divinity of Jesus Christ. This was blasphemy, punishable by death. Indeed, only a few years earlier, a fellow at Corpus Christi College had been burned to death for expressing such opinions. Kyd denied authorship of the documents but — under torture — blurted out that the papers belonged to Marlowe.

Kyd's "confession" put the secret service in an awkward position. For years Marlowe had been employed as a clandestine courier to the Continent; and, at the time of Kyd's arrest, he was a guest of Thomas Walsingham, Sir Francis's younger cousin, at Scadbury in Kent, 12 miles outside of London. On May 18 a summons to the city was served on Marlowe at Scadbury. Without explanation of the charge, he was released on bail but

As chief of Queen Elizabeth's secret service, Sir Francis Walsingham (left) employed Christopher Marlowe as a courier to the Continent. Other secret operatives may have murdered the dramatist, though the official report (below) dismissed his death as the accidental result of a barroom brawl.

A Fatal Postscript

The most famous victim of Sir Francis Walsingham's secret service network was Mary, Queen of Scots. In 1567 she had been forced to abdicate in favor of her infant son, James VI. The following year, with the collapse of an uprising meant to restore her to the throne, she rashly fled to England to seek the protection of her cousin Elizabeth I. But the unmarried, childless queen of England regarded Mary as a rival and promptly put her under arrest. Still languishing in captivity 18 years later, Mary was fatally implicated in a plot to assassinate Elizabeth and place a Catholic monarch, herself, on the throne of England.

The leader of the conspiracy was a 25-year-old country squire named Anthony Babington. Secretly raised as a Catholic, Babington had once served as a page to

Mary, Queen of Scots, was beheaded for knowledge of the Babington plot.

Mary's jailer, the earl of Shrewsbury — and possibly then fell under the spell of the captivating queen.

In the summer of 1586 he began writing Mary of his plans to rescue her and eliminate Elizabeth. Walsingham's agents intercepted the correspondence but, after reading the incriminating documents, resealed and forwarded them. To Mary's letter of July 17 Sir Francis forged a postscript, asking Babington to name his fellow conspirators. One of them, a priest named John Ballard, was arrested on August 4. Under torture, he identified the others; 10 days later Babington was seized. In mid-September the conspirators were tried, convicted, and put to death.

Elizabeth now had the pretext for eliminating her troublesome royal prisoner. Mary, too, was tried and found guilty of approving a plot to kill the queen. On February 8, 1587, she was executed in the great hall of Fotheringhay Castle.

---

told to be available at a day's notice to give evidence. Twelve days later, he lay dead on the floor of the inn at Deptford.

The Man Who Knew Too Much

If Marlowe was guilty of blasphemy, why was he set free? Why wasn't he, like Kyd, put to the torture and made to confess to the terrible crime? Why, instead, was he allowed to rendezvous with three such questionable characters on May 30?

Walsingham's secret service, it is believed, had been penetrated by double agents — men who claimed to serve the queen but in reality wanted to see her replaced with a Catholic monarch. Among these double agents was Robert Poley, who had been imprisoned in the wake of the Babington plot but released and readmitted to the secret service. Perhaps Marlowe knew of Poley's continuing treasonous activities; under torture, he also might break and reveal Poley's name and those of others disloyal to Elizabeth. For their safety, it may have been necessary to have Marlowe out of the way. Was this the reason for the gathering at Deptford? Was the barroom brawl a carefully rehearsed murder? Or was Marlowe not really the victim that night?

In 1955 a writer named Calvin Hoffman put forth the theory that the conspirators, including

Marlowe, lured a nameless sailor to the Deptford inn, murdered him, and cooked up the story of Marlowe's death in a brawl — whereupon, Marlowe assumed a new identity as William Shakespeare and for the next quarter century continued to write the plays that earned him immortality. Although the end of Marlowe's career coincides with the beginning of Shakespeare's, scholars have generally dismissed Hoffman's thesis as implausible.

No one will ever know the full truth about Marlowe's death. Among his contemporaries, there were those who hailed his death as God's punishment of an atheist, blasphemer, and "filthy playmaker." But posterity has come to lament his premature death. English literature lost a great dramatist on the night of May 30, 1593 — perhaps one as great as Shakespeare. Only the previous year, Shakespeare had left Stratford for London, where his plays began to attract a dedicated following. In one of them, *As You Like It*, he alluded to his predecessor's tragic death as "a great reckoning in a little room."

But Marlowe, unknowingly, provided his own epitaph in the epilogue to his most famous work, *Doctor Faustus*: "Cut is the branch that might have grown full straight . . . ." Dying at age 29, he perhaps left many masterpieces unwritten.

The Fate of a Family

*The Romanovs had ruled Russia for more than three centuries
when the revolution of 1917 swept them from the throne. A year
later the deposed czar — Nicholas II — and his entire family
were brutally murdered. Or did some escape?*

*I*mperial Russia proudly, almost gaily, marched
off to war in the summer of 1914 as an ally of
Britain and France against the German and
Austro-Hungarian empires. But World War I
proved to be a disaster for the country and for the
Romanov dynasty. By March 1917, with millions
dead, the country was reeling. In the capital, Pet-
rograd, people rioted for food, student demon-
strators joined workers on strike, and troops
called out to restore order mutinied instead.

Hastily summoned from the front where he
had taken personal command of the imperial armies, Czar Nicholas II was presented with an ultimatum: abdication. For himself and his frail 12-
year-old son, he renounced the throne his family
had held since 1613 — "just as simply as one
turns over a cavalry squadron to its new commanding officer," one of his officers remarked in
shocked surprise. To his diary, however, the czar
revealed his true feelings: "All around me I see
treason, cowardice, and deceit!"

The Provisional Government under Alexander
Kerensky immediately put the ex-imperial family under house arrest at Tsarskoye Selo, the elegant cluster of palaces and villas outside of Petro-
grad that had sheltered them from the realities of
war. In addition to Nicholas, his czarina, Alexandra, and the czarevitch, or crown prince, Alexei,
there were four older daughters, the Grand
Duchesses Olga, Tatiana, Maria, and Anastasia,
ranging in age from 22 to 16.

To Siberia — for Safety

Apart from the indignity of being under almost
constant surveillance, Nicholas and his family
suffered few deprivations during the months of
captivity at Tsarskoye Selo. Relieved of the bur-
dens of power, the ex-czar busied himself with
chopping wood, planting a vegetable garden, taking his children out in rowboats or walking in the

parks with them, and reading to his family in the
evenings. An inept and overwhelmed ruler,
Nicholas Romanov — as he was now called — had
always been a devoted family man. And this, in
part, had been the cause of his downfall.

It had long been an open secret in Russia that
Nicholas was ruled by his wife, Alexandra, the
German princess he had married in 1894. After
four daughters, they had rejoiced at the birth of
Alexei. But their joy turned to bitter sorrow
when the child proved to be a hemophiliac; the
slightest injury could cause uncontrolled bleeding, and the boy had to be watched constantly.

After 1907 Alexandra and her husband had
come under the influence of the sinister, lecher-
ous monk, Rasputin, to whom they attributed
miraculous cures of Alexei's many illnesses. But
on December 31, 1916, disgusted Russian noblemen had murdered Rasputin — a blow to the royal family almost as severe as the forced abdication
a little more than two months later.

By the summer of 1917 Kerensky was worried
about plots on the one hand from his leftist rivals,
the Bolsheviks, to eliminate the ex-czar and on
the other from still loyal monarchists to rescue
Nicholas and restore him to the throne. He decided to send his imperial prisoners to safety in
Tobolsk, an isolated Siberian town more than
1,000 miles away to the east beyond the Ural
Mountains. On August 14, accompanied by
some 40 servants, Nicholas, his wife, and five
children left Tsarskoye Selo on a heavily guarded
train for the six-day journey. Two days earlier the
captive family had celebrated Alexei's 13th
birthday.

"The House of Special Designation"

The revolutionary tide sweeping across Russia
soon eliminated Kerensky as a protector of the
ex-imperial family. In November the Bolsheviks

seized power and negotiated a separate peace with Germany and Austria-Hungary, the Treaty of Brest-Litovsk signed in March 1918. Among the many problems facing Russia's new leader, Nikolai Lenin, was what to do with the former czar, who was now his prisoner.

In April 1918, with a White army — pro-czarists in opposition to the Bolshevik Reds — advancing along the Trans-Siberian railway toward Tobolsk, Lenin ordered the family moved to Ekaterinburg, a city at the western terminus of the railroad. Local Bolsheviks requisitioned the solid two-story residence of a merchant named Ipatiev for Nicholas and his family, giving it the ominous name "The House of Special Designation."

The lower floor was partly underground and contained the kitchen and storage rooms; the five rooms upstairs were allotted to the ex-czar's family, their personal physician, Dr. Eugene Botkin, and the few servants still left to them. Cut off from public view by a wooden palisade and with the windows whitewashed so that no one could look in or out, the house was heavily guarded at all times by a detachment of local Bolsheviks. Mostly former factory workers, the guards were under the command of Alexander Avdeyev, a loutish and often drunken workman who delighted in referring to the ex-czar as "Nicholas the Blood-drinker."

Family and servants ate their two meals a day out of a common pot, from which the guards often helped themselves over the shoulders of the

The power of the Romanovs was already undermined by Alexandra's domination of Nicholas when the family photograph at left was taken in 1910. Standing to the czar's left is the czarina, while their four daughters — (from left) the grand duchesses Olga, Maria, Anastasia, and Tatiana — and the sickly czarevitch, Alexei, encircle the imperial couple. Below, the Bolsheviks storm a government stronghold in the second revolution of 1917.

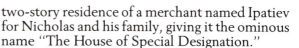

After the czar's abdication in March 1917, the former imperial family was kept under guard at Tsarskoye Selo, outside of St. Petersburg. Here, Nicholas (second from right) and two of his daughters work at planting a garden.

diners. The former grand duchesses were even escorted to the toilet, the walls of which had been defaced with obscene pictures of their mother and Rasputin. Feebly protesting such mortifying treatment, Nicholas was threatened with hard labor by Avdeyev.

By now, Alexei was so weak that he had to be carried outdoors by his father for a daily ride in a wheelchair through the dusty garden. Nicholas, at 50, was beginning to show white hairs in his beard, but he always dressed neatly in a simple soldier's khaki uniform. Alexandra, one of the guards remarked, "had the appearance and manner of a grave, haughty woman."

A Post-midnight Summons

Early in July, Avdeyev was relieved by Yakov Yurovsky, leader of the local Bolshevik secret police. "This specimen pleases me least of all," Nicholas wrote in his diary for July 10. Two days later an emissary arrived from the Bolshevik leadership in Moscow with orders to ensure that the ex-czar did not fall into the hands of the Whites. The pro-monarchists had now been joined by a Czech force of 40,000 and were steadily moving westward toward Ekaterinburg against faltering Bolshevik opposition.

Sometime after midnight of July 16–17, 1918, Yurovsky awakened the family, ordered them to dress, and had them brought to one of the ground floor rooms. The Whites were already fighting in the streets of Ekaterinburg, he told them; outside a truck with its engine running was waiting to

take them away. Chairs were brought for Nicholas, Alexandra, and the invalid Alexei, but the four daughters, Dr. Botkin, and three servants were left standing. After reading a death warrant issued by the local Bolsheviks, Yurovsky shot Nicholas in the head — a signal to other members of his execution squad to fire at their preassigned targets. Those who did not die instantly were quickly dispatched with bayonets.

The bodies were thrown in the truck and taken to a deserted mine outside the city, where they were hacked into pieces, burned, soaked with acid, and thrown down a mine shaft. On July 17 the Moscow leadership received a coded message from Ekaterinburg: "Inform Sverdlov [a close associate of Lenin's] that all the family have met the same fate as the head. Officially family died during evacuation."

Branding the Bolsheviks

The events of that fatal night as described above is the story that has entered the history books and is largely based on an exhaustive investigation undertaken by the Whites when they seized Ekaterinburg a week later. But is it the truth?

The first investigator concluded that Nicholas had indeed been executed on the night of July 16–17 but that the ex-czarina, her son, and four

Grand Duchess or Impostor?

On the evening of February 17, 1920, a policeman pulled a young woman of about 20 out of a canal in Berlin. Since she refused to reveal her identity or answer any questions about what had apparently led to a suicide attempt, she was committed to a mental institution as *Fraülein Unbekannt* ("Miss Unknown"). Found to be suffering from "mental illness of a depressive character," the young woman at last confided to a nurse that she was the Grand Duchess Anastasia, youngest of the four daughters of Czar Nicholas II of Russia and his wife, Czarina Alexandra. Alone of her family, the young woman stated, she had escaped the massacre at Ekaterinburg on the night of July 16–17, 1918. Hers was not the only claim to be a survivor of the slaughter; there would be other Anastasias and even an Alexei who surfaced in Poland in the 1960's to say that the entire family had been able to flee Russia. But the story of the woman saved from drowning in Berlin came closest to being believed.

A number of mostly impoverished members of Russia's former imperial family were living in post-World War I Europe, somehow having escaped the Bolshevik purge. What better way to establish the true identify of the young woman from Berlin — who now called herself Anna Anderson — than to have her meet some of her would-be relatives. Only two agreed to such a confrontation: Nicho-

Did the Grand Duchess Anastasia (near right, a photograph from 1914) succeed in escaping from Russia? And who was Anna Anderson (far right), the young woman who appeared so mysteriously in Berlin in 1920?

las's sister, the Grand Duchess Olga; and Alexandra's sister, Princess Irene of Prussia. When these two aunts failed to uphold Anna Anderson's claims, the others fell into line. By 1928, 12 Romanovs and three of Alexandra's German siblings had rejected her as an impostor.

Yet Anna Anderson continued to have her champions. Tatiana Botkin, the daughter of the imperial family's physician who was executed with them, had seen Anastasia as late as her imprisonment in Tobolsk and believed Anna's story. One of Princess

Irene's sons compiled a list of questions that only Anastasia would be able to answer; Anna Anderson's replies convinced him. His mother later conceded that there was a striking resemblance between the Anastasia she remembered and Anna Anderson. Grand Duchess Olga, it was revealed years later, had wavered at the time of meeting with Anna before issuing the rejection.

The meeting between Olga and the young woman who claimed to be her niece Anastasia took place in October 1925 in a Berlin hospital, where Anna Anderson was recuperating from a severe attack of tuberculosis. At their parting, Anna burst into tears; the grand duchess kissed her cheeks and promised to write. "My reason cannot grasp it," Olga told a companion, "but my heart tells me that the little one is Anastasia." Affectionate letters from Olga followed the visit, up until Christmas. Then silence and, in January 1926, the denial. For the rest of her life Anna Anderson would ponder the about-face.

Despite publication of her book, *I Am Anastasia*, Anna Anderson never convincingly explained her escape. Her story about surviving not only bullets but bayonets and being rescued by a Bolshevik guard who later became her lover seemed more romantic fiction than plausible fact. The film for which Ingrid Bergman won an Academy Award in 1956 also apparently failed to convince West German courts, which ultimately decided after a series of rulings between 1958 and 1970 that her claim could neither be proved nor refuted.

daughters had been spared. This was not good enough to brand the Bolsheviks as brutal murderers and rouse sympathy abroad for the Romanov martyrs — and so another inquiry was undertaken early in 1919.

Nikolas Sokolov was the new official investigator for "cases of exceptional importance," and the disappearance of the entire Romanov family was certainly an exceptionally important event in revolutionary Russia. Sokolov worked quickly but methodically, uncovering at the mine site such pathetic and grim evidence as a tiny lock and bent hairpin used as a fishhook by the czarevitch, gems that had been sewn into the undergarments of the grand duchesses, the carcass of Tatiana's lap dog, and the severed finger of a middle-aged woman that was identified as that of Alexandra.

By late summer 1919, with the White cause fading, Sokolov fled eastward and eventually reached Europe via China. Not until 1924 did Sokolov publish his findings, which revealed the Bolshevik savagery of that July night six years earlier; it was a picture that much of the world was then all too willing to accept. Meanwhile, in 1921, the chairman of the Ekaterinburg Soviet, Paul Bykov, had published his version of the last days of the ex-czar, confirming the deaths.

Conflicting Stories

For nearly three-quarters of a century Sokolov's conclusion — that the entire Romanov family had been murdered on the night of July 16–17, 1918 — has been disputed by careful students of the case, who point to contradictory evidence. For example, when the Bolsheviks announced the execution of the ex-czar on July 19, they said that Alexandra and the children "had been taken to a safe place," and this was the version published four days later in Ekaterinburg. Moreover, through the fall of 1918, the Bolsheviks were negotiating with the former enemy Germany to exchange Alexandra — a German princess by birth — and her children for Russian political prisoners.

One of the first foreign visitors to Ekaterinburg after the alleged slaughter was Sir Charles Eliot, the British consul for Siberia. After talking to the Whites' first investigator, Eliot informed his superiors that he believed the ex-czarina and her children had left Ekaterinburg by train on July 17. The lurid stories of a massacre, he believed, were fabrications. About this time Alexandra's brother, Grand Duke Ernst Ludwig of Hesse, sent news via neutral Sweden to another sister in England, the Marchioness of Milford Haven, that Alexandra was safe. His source, presumably, was a German secret agent in Russia.

But when the ex-czarina and her children failed to appear, and after Sokolov's report was published, the conclusion that the entire family had been murdered gradually came to be accepted. The various people who claimed to be survi-

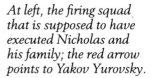

At left, the firing squad that is supposed to have executed Nicholas and his family; the red arrow points to Yakov Yurovsky.

vors of that ghastly massacre were dismissed as impostors; the legend that the Romanovs had not all perished that night was labeled sheer fantasy.

Suppressed Evidence

After the passage of several decades, it seemed highly improbable that any new leads would turn up. Yet, in the early 1970's, the British journalists Antony Summers and Tom Marigold discovered the official records of Sokolov's investigation. As they studied the documents, Summers and Marigold became convinced that Sokolov not only had omitted some critical evidence but perhaps had also falsified other information.

Sokolov had based his conclusion on five points. The first and most significant evidence was the coded telegram sent to Moscow on July 17, reporting the death of the entire family. Yet the telegram was placed in the file only in January 1919, after the first investigator had been relieved of his assignment and before Sokolov took over. Was it a convenient forgery, slyly slipped in to support the desired outcome of the pro-monarchists' investigation?

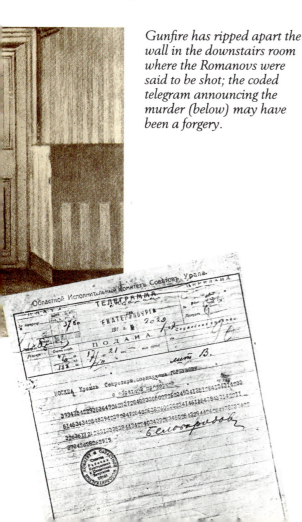

Gunfire has ripped apart the wall in the downstairs room where the Romanovs were said to be shot; the coded telegram announcing the murder (below) may have been a forgery.

Second was the statement of an eyewitness who claimed to have seen the victims immediately after the execution and may have been a participant in the murder of the ex-czar and his family. Why did this man talk so freely to the Whites, thus risking punishment for his crime? Sokolov himself never interviewed the man, who indeed died under dubious circumstances shortly after giving his deposition.

The third alleged proof was the evidence found at the abandoned mine. The first investigators found nothing; only months later did Sokolov find the grisly remains. Was he more thorough than his predecessors or only lucky?

The dog's body, identified only in June 1919, would have had to survive the rigors of a Siberian winter — unlikely in the opinion of forensic experts. The fourth proof for Sokolov's argument could have been any small animal thrown into the mine at a later date.

The fifth and seemingly irrefutable proof was the fact that no member of the ex-czar's family had been seen alive after the night of July 16–17, 1918. Yet, here again, the original documents contradict Sokolov's findings.

The Trail to Perm

Toward the end of December 1918 the Whites marched into Perm, a city approximately 175 miles northwest of Ekaterinburg. One of the White officers learned that a train had brought survivors of the massacre to Perm sometime after July 17. Among his informants were a nurse named Natalia Mutnich and a doctor named Pavel Utkin.

Interrogated three times in the spring of 1919, the nurse claimed to have heard from her brother — the assistant to one of the region's leading Bolsheviks — that only Nicholas and his son, Alexei, had been executed; Alexandra and the four daughters had been brought for safety to Perm. Moreover, the nurse said that she had seen the imperial prisoners and knew of escape attempts by Tatiana and Anastasia. Dr. Utkin confirmed Anastasia's escape attempt and said that around September 20 he had visited a severely beaten young woman who identified herself as the youngest grand duchess. Other witnesses recalled extensive searches, presumably for the escapees, in the woods around Perm that autumn.

Approximately three weeks before the Whites took Perm, according to this version, the Bolsheviks placed the five women on another train, this one headed for Moscow. And there the trail is lost. Until the Soviet Union decides to reopen the case, the mystery is likely to remain unsolved.

Royal Triangle

The new queen of England was only 25 and a desirable bride for any of several European princes. But she made it no secret to her court that she had one clear favorite: Lord Robert Dudley. Could she overcome a serious impediment to marry him?

Both his father and his grandfather had been executed for treason, but the fortunes of Lord Robert Dudley began to rise with the accession of Elizabeth I to the throne of England on November 17, 1558.

Born on the same day 25 years earlier, the two had been friends since childhood and during the reign of Elizabeth's half-sister, Queen Mary, Dudley had sold property to help support the outcast princess. Now, one of Elizabeth's first acts as queen was to name Dudley her Master of the Horse, a high-ranking court position. When she rode through London 11 days later to take possession of the Tower of London, Elizabeth was accompanied by the tall, darkly handsome Dudley — dubbed "the Gypsy" by his detractors.

The queen bestowed further favors on Dudley, awarding him property, a license to export woolen goods duty-free, and the lieutenancy of the castle and forest of Windsor. She never let him far out of her sight, boasting of his good looks and intelligence to all who would listen and defending him against any critics. Given a list of ambassadors proposed for foreign service, Elizabeth quickly crossed off Dudley's name; it was clear that she wanted him to remain at court. By spring the Spanish ambassador was writing home to say that Dudley was in such favor with the queen that he did more or less what he wished; "it is even said that Her Majesty visits him in his chamber day and night," he added.

Among the young queen's most urgent concerns was marriage and producing an heir to the throne. Henry VIII, her father, had scandalized his country and most of Europe with his six marriages and left the kingdom a disputed succession. In the 11 years since Henry's death, England had been ruled by his only son, the frail Edward VI, who died at age 16; his unpopular elder daughter, Mary, who reigned only five years and left no heir; and now, Elizabeth, daughter of Henry's unlucky second queen, Anne Boleyn.

European suitors quickly came forward, a Swedish prince, the duke of Saxony, a nephew of the king of Spain. But perhaps Elizabeth would ignore such foreign alliances and instead choose an English bridegroom. Who better than her favorite, Lord Robert Dudley?

The Inconvenient Amy Robsart

There was an impediment to a match between Elizabeth and Dudley: the handsome young cavalier was already married. Nine years earlier, just short of his 17th birthday, Dudley had married Amy Robsart, the only child of a country squire and the heiress to considerable property. Among those attending the wedding was Elizabeth, still a princess and a long way from the throne. Although the couple seemed happy at first, Dudley was more and more drawn to court life at Windsor and left his wife alone in the country for increasingly long periods of time. There were no children born of the union.

By the time Dudley was being whispered about as the young queen's lover and perhaps even future husband, his wife was living on an estate near Oxford, some 50 miles northwest of London. She and her servants occupied a suite in Cumnor Hall, a former monastery inhabited by two other families.

The rural quiet of Cumnor Hall was broken on Sunday, September 8, 1560, by preparations for departure to attend a country fair at the nearby village of Abingdon. Lady Dudley had given her servants the day off to attend the festivities but had decided to stay home in what would be a mostly deserted house. When the servants returned that evening, they were greeted with an appalling sight: their mistress lying dead with a broken neck at the foot of the staircase leading from her rooms to the main hall.

The Long Twilight of the Affair

Immediately, there were ugly rumors implicating Dudley in his wife's death, and the queen was forced to banish him from court until an investigation had been completed. "I have no way to purge myself of the malicious talk that I know the wicked world will use, but one, which is the very plain truth to be known," Dudley wrote. But what was the truth? Elizabeth's rival, Mary, Queen of Scots, was heard to say, "The queen of England is going to marry her horse-keeper who has killed his wife to make room for her!"

Elizabeth ordered the court into mourning for Lady Dudley, and two weeks after her death she was buried following services held in the royal chapel. Eventually, Lord Robert Dudley was cleared of all charges in his wife's death and allowed to return to court — still a favorite of the queen's and, no longer burdened with an unwanted wife, still considered by some as her potential consort.

As for the hapless Amy Robsart, was hers an accidental death or was she the victim of foul play? History, like the contemporary inquest, tends to vindicate Lord Robert Dudley. She was known to be suffering from cancer of the breast and had often been heard praying to God for deliverance from her agony. During the advanced stages of the disease, the cancer often moves to

Elizabeth I openly displays her affection for Lord Robert Dudley by joining him in a spirited court dance.

the spine, so weakening it that even the slightest shock can break the neck. A slip on the staircase could have resulted in the untimely death.

With Amy Robsart conveniently out of the way, the queen was free to choose between marriage to Dudley and dalliance — and she chose the latter. A few years later she made Dudley the earl of Leicester; yet when he attempted to exert power at court, she sharply rebuked him: "I will have here but one mistress and no master." Dudley remained in loyal service to the queen through the next three decades, somewhat boldly risking her displeasure by two subsequent marriages.

As for Elizabeth, she kept her kingdom and indeed all of Europe guessing about her marital intentions for most of the 45 years of her reign — even after she had passed childbearing age. And, toward the end of the century, she acquired a new favorite, the much younger Robert Devereux, the earl of Essex. But she would not marry Devereux either and, when he attempted to seize power, she had him arrested and executed. The Virgin Queen, as she was called, died in 1603, unmarried and childless, to be succeeded on the throne by the son of Mary, Queen of Scots.

Buried in an Unmarked Grave

A musical child prodigy, Wolfgang Amadeus Mozart began playing
for Europe's nobility and composed his first works at age six.
At the peak of his career 30 years later in Vienna, he died after
a short illness. Had he been poisoned?

Decades later Sophie Haibel, the younger sister of Mozart's wife, Constanze, still vividly remembered the eerie omen. On the first Sunday of December 1791, she was in the kitchen, preparing a cup of coffee for her mother. The previous day she had gone into the city of Vienna to visit her brother-in-law, who had fallen ill, but had returned with the news that he seemed better.

It was discovered only in 1964 that Mozart's unfinished Requiem was commissioned by Count von Walsegg on the death of his wife early in 1791.

Now, as she waited for the coffee to brew, Sophie stared pensively into the bright flame of an oil lamp and thought of Constanze's ailing husband. Suddenly, the flame went out "as completely as if the lamp had never been burning," she later wrote. "Not a spark remained on the main wick and yet there wasn't the slightest draught — that I can swear to." Seized with a horrible premonition, she ran to her mother, who advised her to return to Mozart's house without delay.

Constanze greeted her sister's arrival with relief, saying that Mozart had spent a restless night, and begged her to stay. "Ah, dear Sophie, how glad I am that you have come," the musician said. "You must stay here tonight and see me die." With him was a young assistant named Sussmayr, to whom Mozart was giving instructions for the completion of his last composition, a Requiem Mass. A priest was summoned, then a doctor, who ordered cold compresses to be placed on the patient's fevered brow. About an hour before midnight Mozart lost consciousness; at 12:55 A.M. on December 5, 1791, he died. The former child prodigy and prolific composer was two months short of his 36th birthday.

Always pressed for money, Mozart had been working at a feverish pace to complete important commissions through much of the year, and to his friends and family he seemed tense and exhausted from overwork. But when he took to his bed on November 20, no one suspected that it was a terminal illness. The symptoms were listed by Georg Nikolaus Nissen, Constanze's second husband, in his 1828 biography of the composer: "It began with swelling in his hands and feet and an almost total inability to move; this was followed by sudden vomiting, and this is called acute military fever." This diagnosis was confirmed in the official register of death for the city of Vienna.

Mozart himself suspected foul play. Some weeks before his death, he told Constanze that he was being poisoned: "Someone has given me aqua toffana and has calculated the precise time of my death." An odorless, slow-acting poison with an arsenic base, aqua toffana was named for Teofania de Adamo, a 17th-century Italian woman who had invented the potion and dispensed it to would-be murderers. The Requiem Mass a mysterious stranger had commissioned him to write, Mozart came to believe, was for his own funeral service.

On December 31, 1791, a Berlin newspaper reported the composer's death and speculated on the cause. "Because his body swelled up after death, people even thought he had been poisoned." In an undated memorandum, Mozart's older son, Carl Thomas, recollected that his father's body was so swollen and the stench of putrefaction so great that an autopsy was not performed. Unlike most corpses that become stiff and cold, Mozart's body remained soft and elastic, as do those who die of poisoning.

But who would have wanted Mozart dead? The widow gave little credence to the rumor of poisoning and named no suspect. And thus the tale was soon forgotten — only to be dramatically revived three decades later by none other than the rival who well may have wished Mozart dead.

The Envy of Salieri

Only five years older than Mozart, Antonio Salieri had been named court composer to Emperor Joseph II in 1774, at the age of 24. When Mozart arrived in Vienna seven years later, the Italian was the Austrian capital's reigning musician, held in high esteem by the aristocracy and a favorite with the city's demanding music lovers. Salieri was a facile and prolific composer, who was later to count among his pupils Beethoven, Schubert, and Franz Liszt. But Mozart he quickly perceived as a rival, a genius whose talent he could never match. Few in Viennese music circles doubted Salieri's envy of Mozart, and Mozart made no secret of his contempt for the court composer.

Salieri lived to see all Vienna celebrate the 50th anniversary of his appointment as court composer in 1824. But a year earlier he made a startling statement. In October 1823 a pupil of Beethoven's named Ignaz Moscheles paid a call on the elderly Salieri, by then a patient in a suburban hospital.

Able to speak only in broken sentences and preoccupied with his imminent death, Salieri gave his word of honor that "there is no truth in that absurd rumor; you know that I am supposed to have poisoned Mozart." It was pure malice, he told the shocked Moscheles; "tell the world . . . old Salieri, who will soon die, has told you." A month later, Salieri tried to commit suicide. Visitors to his sickbed reported that he was having fantasies about his responsibility for Mozart's death and wanted to confess his sin. The much honored court composer died the next year.

The Italian biographer of Haydn, Giuseppe

The unfinished portrait of Mozart below dates to 1789 or 1790 and was the work of Joseph Lange, husband of Constanze's older sister, Aloysia. Constanze thought it was the best likeness of the composer.

Only a dog follows Mozart's funeral wagon in the drawing at left, found among the papers of Ludwig van Beethoven. The unattended burial is one of the puzzles surrounding Mozart's death at an early age.

Carpani, tried to salvage his countryman's honor. He sought out a doctor consulted at the time of Mozart's final illness and got from him a diagnosis of rheumatic fever. If Mozart had been poisoned, Carpani demanded, where was the evidence? "Useless to ask. There is no evidence, and it is also impossible ever to find any."

After her husband's death, Constanze sent her younger son to take lessons from Salieri. Asked about the rumor that the court composer had poisoned his father, the boy said that Salieri had not killed Mozart but had "truly poisoned his life with intrigues." Salieri himself was heard to say that it was a pity that Mozart had died so young but perhaps just as well for other composers; if he had lived longer, "not a soul would have given us a crust of bread for our work."

A Husband's Jealousy

A second suspect in the rumored murder was Franz Hofdemel, a Masonic lodge brother of the composer, whose attractive young wife, Magdalena, was one of Mozart's last piano students. A few days after Mozart's death, Hofdemel savagely attacked his pregnant wife with a razor, maiming and disfiguring her with slashes to the face,

For the decade before his death in 1791, Mozart was a rival of Antonio Salieri (above), the highly successful Italian court composer to Emperor Joseph II. Today his once popular music is seldom played.

throat, and arms, and then killed himself. Magdalena survived and five months later bore a child who, gossips insisted, was Mozart's.

Mozart's older sister, Maria Anna, once remarked that her brother only gave lessons to young women when he was in love with them. And the prudish Ludwig van Beethoven, years after Mozart's death, refused to play in the presence of Magdalena because "too great an intimacy had existed between her and Mozart." Yet, from the observations of contemporaries and from his surviving letters, Mozart appears to have been deeply devoted to Constanze, and there is no evidence of any extramarital affairs. Finally, Empress Maria Luisa took a personal interest in Magdalena's tragedy, which she would scarcely have done if there was any truth to the stories about her baby's paternity.

Revenge of the Freemasons?

Yet another rumor was spread in the months following Mozart's death: The composer was marked for punishment because he had revealed secrets of the Freemasons in *The Magic Flute*. The allegorical opera was given its premiere in Vienna on September 30, 1791, with Mozart himself conducting, and was a great critical and popular success. Among the admirers was Salieri, who accompanied Mozart to a subsequent performance and — as Mozart proudly wrote to Constanze — said that he had never seen "a more beautiful or pleasant production."

Although some of Mozart's fellow Masons may have been startled by *The Magic Flute*, the composer and his librettist, Emmanuel Schikaneder, used the opera to introduce the secret society's ideals of courage, love, and fraternity to a wider audience. The subject was treated with sympathy, respect, and a dash of good humor.

Far from being offended by the opera, Vienna's Freemasons commissioned Mozart to compose a cantata, which he dashed off in a few days between the premiere of *The Magic Flute* and the onset of his final illness. A few days after Mozart's death, the grand master of his lodge paid tribute to him as "the most beloved and meritorious" of its members and called his passing "an irreplaceable loss." In 1792 Vienna's Freemasons staged a performance of the cantata for the benefit of Mozart's widow and sons.

Rushed to Burial

Because Constanze was so hard-pressed for money at the time of her husband's death, she chose the cheapest funeral; its cost has been estimated as $30. At 2:30 P.M. on December 7, the body was

Freemasons: A Besieged Secret Society

In December 1784 Mozart was admitted to a small Viennese Masonic lodge known as Beneficence, which later merged with the capital's principal lodge, New Crowned Hope. Tracing its origins to the medieval guild of stonecutters and cathedral builders, Freemasonry was opened to other professions early in the 18th century and rapidly spread from England across Europe.

By Mozart's time, membership in the exclusive intellectual organization was a recognition of success and a cherished honor. The young composer was an enthusiastic participant in Masonic rituals and composed music for the secret ceremonies. In a 1787 letter to his father, he confessed that membership had helped him overcome a fear of death.

But the secret society came un-

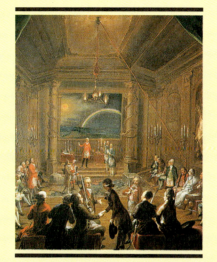

In this painting of a Masonic meeting in Vienna, about 1790, Prince Nicolaus Esterhazy (in red jacket) presides as the master of ceremonies.

der fire first from the Roman Catholic Church and later from such autocratic rulers as Emperor Joseph II, who viewed its growing power with alarm and asked the Austrian police to keep a careful watch over its activities. Mozart's last opera, *The Magic Flute*, was meant as a tribute to and defense of the besieged organization.

In the United States, Freemasonry was equally popular and counted George Washington and Benjamin Franklin as early members. The mysterious disappearance in 1826 of an upstate New Yorker named William Morgan, who had divulged secrets of his lodge, led to an investigation that revealed that many state officeholders were Masons. In a backlash, an anti-Masonic political party elected a governor or two and nominated presidential candidates in 1832 and 1836.

---

removed to St. Stephen's cathedral, where a few mourners — including, it is believed, Salieri — attended the priest's blessing in a side chapel. Rain mixed with snow was said to have deterred the witnesses from accompanying the funeral wagon to St. Mark's cemetery, about an hour's walk away; and so there was no one to note the spot where the body was placed in a mass grave. In actuality, as a diarist wrote at the time, December 7 was a mild though hazy day.

Later explaining that she had thought the church would arrange for a cross or marker at her husband's grave, Constanze erected no memorial to Mozart. Not until 1859 was a marble monument erected at St. Mark's cemetery, its precise placement there being a matter of guesswork.

Medical Detective Work

Mozart's mysterious death and hasty burial have been the subject of intense debate and speculation for two centuries. In 1966 a Swiss physician named Carl Bar dismissed the contemporary diagnosis of "acute military fever" as amateurish and unprofessional. Based on evidence handed down from Mozart's physician, Dr. Nicolaus Closset, Bar suggested rheumatic fever, an acute noninfectious disease marked by painful inflammation of the joints. In 1984 another physician,

Peter J. Davies, published an even more extensive anaylsis of Mozart's medical history and final illness.

In 1762, the year that the six-year-old musical prodigy made his concert debut and began composing, Mozart contracted a streptococcal infection of the upper respiratory system. The effects of such an infection can be delayed for months, even years. Subsequently, the boy suffered bouts of tonsillitis, typhoid fever, smallpox, bronchitis, and yellow jaundice, or type A virus hepatitis. In 1784, three years after his arrival in Vienna, the composer endured a major illness with symptoms that included violent vomiting and a rheumatic inflammatory fever.

Dr. Davies concluded his analysis of Mozart's health problems by blaming his death on a combination of a streptococcal infection contracted during an epidemic, kidney failure arising from an allergic hypersensitivity known as Schönlein-Henoch syndrome, a cerebral hemorrhage, and terminal bronchopneumonia. Among the side effects of kidney failure, Dr. Davies noted, are depression, personality change, and mental delusions — which may account for Mozart's morbid belief that he was being poisoned and that the unfinished Requiem Mass had been commissioned for his own funeral.

Lone Assassin—or Conspiracy?

On a day few who were alive at the time will ever forget,
President John F. Kennedy was shot in Dallas, Texas.
His assassin was quickly apprehended but killed in full
view of television audiences two days later. A quarter
century later, conspiracy theories still abound.

The president had been warned about going to Dallas, since it was known that he had many influential adversaries in the ultraconservative city. But John F. Kennedy brushed aside the objections. It was important that he mend his political fences in Texas and seek support from such powerful figures as Governor John Connally for his unannounced bid for reelection the next year. Upon their arrival at Dallas's Love Field, the president and his wife, Jacqueline, joined Governor and Mrs. Connally in the rear of an open car, the second vehicle in a motorcade into the city, where he was to deliver a luncheon address.

As people lining the streets cheered, Nellie Connally turned to the president and exclaimed, "You sure can't say Dallas doesn't love you." At 12:30 P.M. the motorcade slowed to make a right and then a left turn before it would pass through a triple underpass to the freeway that led to the destination. An agent in the first car said to the driver, "Five more minutes and we'll have him there." In a rear car the president's secretary, Evelyn Lincoln, remarked, "Just think — we've come through all of Dallas and there hasn't been a single demonstration." A local woman laughed; "We're not so bad," she said. A reporter in the press car, misreading the sign on the rust-colored

John F. Kennedy: Was the Mafia behind his assassination? Or was Oswald's real target Texas governor Connally?

brick building that loomed ahead, asked "What the hell is a Book Repository?" Standing between the book depository and the underpass along the motorcade route, a man named Abraham Zapruder aimed his movie camera at the presidential car. Another bystander, Charles Brend, held his five-year-old son aloft to wave at the president. Seeing him, Kennedy smiled and waved back.

Suddenly shots rang out. A bullet passed through the president's neck and on through Governor Connally's back, chest, right wrist, and left thigh. Kennedy clutched his throat; Connally, his lap full of blood, slumped onto his wife in their seats to the front. Hearing the governor scream, Mrs. Kennedy turned anxiously toward the president, as a second bullet tore off the top of his head.

Four Days

The assassination of the 35th president of the United States on November 22, 1963, stunned the nation and the world. For much of that Friday and the next three days, millions around the globe sat transfixed before their television sets as the remaining scenes of the unimaginable tragedy were enacted.

Within minutes Lee Harvey Oswald leaves the

Texas School Book Depository, where he had fired the two shots from a corner window on the sixth floor. At 1:15 P.M. Oswald shoots Dallas policeman J. D. Tippit, who had stopped him for questioning. Eyewitnesses call the police and direct them to the movie theater where Oswald had sought to hide. Arrested for killing Tippit and then accused of assassinating Kennedy, Oswald proclaims his innocence of the second charge; he is being made to take the blame for the real culprits, Oswald says.

At 12:38 P.M. Case Number 24740, a white male suffering from a gunshot wound, is admitted to Parkland Memorial Hospital, to which the presidential car had sped. A priest is called to the emergency room, but at two o'clock doctors pronounce John F. Kennedy dead. Over the objections of local authorities, Secret Service agents place the body in a coffin and transport it to Love Field. Within an hour, Lyndon B. Johnson is sworn in as president by Judge Sarah T. Hughes. Standing at his side aboard Air Force One, the presidential airplane, is Jacqueline Kennedy in her blood-spattered pink suit. That evening the presidential party arrives back in Washington, D.C., where an autopsy is performed at Bethesda Naval Hospital.

On Saturday, November 23, Mrs. Kennedy picks out a grave site for her husband at Arlington National Cemetery; the state funeral is scheduled for Monday. In Dallas, Oswald is questioned about the slaying for three hours.

At the request of FBI Director J. Edgar Hoover, Oswald is to be transferred from Dallas police headquarters to the sheriff's office on Sunday. As the transfer is taking place, shortly before noon, a Dallas nightclub operator named Jack Ruby steps from a crowd of reporters covering the event and shoots Oswald — in full view of a national television audience. He acted spontaneously, Ruby confessed, out of anger over the president's death and the wish to spare Jacqueline Kennedy the agony of an Oswald trial in Dallas.

By 9 A.M. Monday morning, November 25, a quarter million mourners have passed by the catafalque holding Kennedy's body in the U.S. Capitol. Mrs. Kennedy had asked for the building to be kept open all night to accommodate the crowds. Following a funeral service at St. Matthew's Cathedral presided over by Cardinal Cushing of Boston and attended by many of the world's leaders, Kennedy is buried at Arlington. Mrs. Kennedy lights an eternal flame at his grave.

Doubt About the Official Explanation

On the very morning of his death President Kennedy made an uncanny prediction to his adviser Kenneth O'Donnell. "If anyone wants to shoot a president," he said, "it's not a very difficult job. All one has to do is get on a high building with a telescopic rifle, and there is nothing anybody can do." And this is exactly how the assassination came to be described in the report of the Warren Commission, named for its chairman, Chief Jus-

In this frame from an amateur's movie of the shooting, a Secret Service agent vaults to the trunk of the car as Mrs. Kennedy climbs up on the rear seat to stretch out a helping hand. The presidential car was rapidly accelerating to get the victims to a hospital.

tice Earl Warren. Presented to President Johnson on September 24, 1964, the report had 26 volumes of documentation. The conclusion: John F. Kennedy was killed by the fanatic loner, Lee Harvey Oswald.

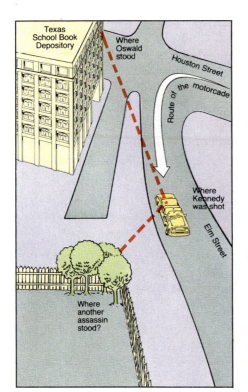

But even as the Warren Commission was conducting its exhaustive investigation, doubts were being raised. Oswald had not acted alone, some were saying, but was merely the "hit man" of an international assassination team. Behind the killer was Cuban dictator Fidel Castro, or possibly the Soviet Union's secret police. Others claimed that it was a matter of an internal power play; agents of the FBI or CIA were responsible. And, perhaps most persistent of all, there was the tale that Kennedy had been targeted by the Mafia.

The two-assassin theory is presented in the drawing at left. Standing in a sixth-floor corner window of the Texas School Book Depository, Oswald fires the shot that passed through the president's head to wound Connally. The fatal bullet comes from amid a clump of trees on a grassy knoll to the front and right of the president's car.

Standing in these trees behind a fence, a second assassin would have had a chance to make up for Oswald's failure to kill the president with his shot from above and to the rear (simulated view at left).

A Shot in the Theater

Four American presidents have been assassinated: Abraham Lincoln in 1865; James A. Garfield in 1881; William McKinley in 1901; and John F. Kennedy in 1963. Before the death of Kennedy, Lincoln's assassination was the most notorious; his passing, the most deeply mourned.

When Lincoln took office as the nation's 16th president, the long-smoldering dispute over slavery erupted into violent, protracted civil war. Between his election in November 1860 and inauguration in March 1861, seven Southern states seceded from the Union and elected Jefferson Davis as president of the Confederate States of America; four other states joined them later. The Confederate attack on Fort Sumter in Charleston Harbor on April 12 was the beginning of a four-year conflict that left

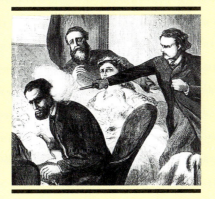

The assassination of Lincoln: Actor John Wilkes Booth fires point-blank at the president, seated in a box at Ford's Theatre in Washington.

more than 600,000 dead and nearly 400,000 wounded on both sides. Peace came to an exhausted nation with the surrender of Robert E.

Lee to Ulysses S. Grant at Appomattox Courthouse, Virginia, on April 9, 1865. Five days later the president sought relaxation from the long tension with an evening at the theater with his wife.

Waiting for him at Ford's Theatre in Washington was John Wilkes Booth, member of a famous acting family and a Southern sympathizer. Booth coolly stepped into the unguarded presidential box and fired a single, fatal shot into the back of Lincoln's head. Although he broke a leg in jumping to the stage, Booth made his getaway on a waiting horse. Two weeks later, he was found hiding in a barn in Virginia and was shot, or shot himself, as the barn was set on fire by his captors. Nine others were soon implicated in Booth's conspiracy; four were hanged, four imprisoned, and one exonerated of the crime.

Missing Evidence

Reexamining the evidence between 1976 and 1978, a House of Representatives committee charged that the autopsy performed at Bethesda Naval Hospital the day following Kennedy's assassination had not been conducted in accordance with professional standards. One of the participating doctors complained at the time that they were not allowed to lay open the track of the two bullets through the president's body because of the objections of "a high-ranking personality," presumably a military figure. Not being able to establish the trajectory of the bullets, the autopsy could not determine the angle of the shots — that is, if they both came from the window in the Texas School Book Depository or if, possibly, one had come from another direction.

The preserved brain and other autopsy materials were given to Kennedy's secretary. When these were deposited with the National Archives in 1966, the brain was found to be missing. Had evidence been suppressed?

How Many Shots?

The Warren Commission had concluded that Kennedy had been hit by two bullets, both coming from above and behind him, which was consistent with the official story of Oswald as lone assassin. The conclusion was based on an analysis of the film taken by Zapruder and on drawings made by criminal pathologists.

Late in the 1970's another piece of evidence was reexamined: the tape recorder of a Dallas policeman providing a motorcycle escort for the presidential motorcade on November 22. Due to a technical defect, the recorder had been left on during the ride from Love Field. For years it had been gathering dust with the other evidence because, apart from some faint rustling, it seemed to contain no identifiable noises.

The House committee asked acoustic experts to study the tape with state-of-the-art computer techniques. Finding noises that sounded like gunshots, the experts went to Dallas and fired guns at the assassination spot on an autumn morning in 1978. Matching new recordings to the 15-year-old tape, they were able — with a probability bordering on certainty — to isolate four distinct shots. Moreover, they claimed to be able to determine from which directions the shots had come. Three had indeed been fired from the Texas School Book Depository window where Oswald stood. (Three spent cartridges were found at the window; presumably one of Oswald's shots went astray.) The fourth shot, however, had been fired at close range from in front and to the right of the presidential car. Someone else, standing on a grassy knoll overlooking the parade route, had also been aiming for the president.

The Warren Commission had ignored or chosen to discount the testimony of witnesses who reported hearing a fourth shot. Other witnesses claimed to have seen a puff of gunsmoke coming from the knoll and men with FBI identification on their cars leaving a nearby parking lot, though the FBI said that no men had been stationed there that day. Three people had tried to catch a man running from the parking lot, but he got away.

The Zapruder film shows the president's head sinking forward, presumably after the first bullet from the rear passed through his neck. But then his entire head snaps back in a reaction that would have been consistent with a fatal bullet striking from the front and blowing away half his head as it exited to the rear. Weighing all the evidence, the House committee concluded in 1979 that Kennedy "was probably assassinated as a result of a conspiracy." Who were the conspirators? The report did not say.

Man Between Two Worlds

Despite all that has been written about him since the assassination, Lee Harvey Oswald remains an enigma, a shadowy figure whose motives for the terrible crime have never been fully explained. "It is possible to believe almost anything about him," one scholar has said, "and damned near impossible to know what's true."

A school dropout at age 16, Oswald joined the U.S. Marine Corps on October 24, 1956, six days after his 17th birthday. Following training as a radar technician, he was assigned to Atsugi Air Base outside Tokyo, Japan, the base from which were launched the U-2 photoreconnaissance flights over the U.S.S.R. Oswald had few friends and spent much of his spare time reading — in particular books about Marxism — and studying Russian. Soon, a fellow Marine later testified, he was saying that "communism was the best system in the world." Before being transferred back to the United States late in 1958, Oswald had been court-martialed twice, once for possessing an unauthorized private weapon and later for addressing "provoking words" to a sergeant. According to one of his officers, Oswald was "a little bit nuts on foreign affairs" and became an enthusiastic supporter of Fidel Castro, who seized power in Cuba in January 1959.

On September 11, 1959, Oswald received an early release from the Marine Corps in order to support his dependent mother. However, after giving her $100, he booked passage on a ship

Death of a Movie Goddess

Screen personality Marilyn Monroe died in August 1962; rumors linked her to both John and Robert Kennedy.

Like John F. Kennedy, Marilyn Monroe was a symbol of the times. Although critics scorned her acting ability, none could dispute the magic of a screen personality that made her a worldwide box office attraction. Her death during the night of August 4, 1962 — from an overdose of sedatives — was officially listed as a "probable suicide."

Exploited by gossip columnists in her lifetime, Monroe became the focus of innumerable rumors after her death. Among these rumors are stories that link her romantically to both John F. Kennedy and his brother Robert. Her alleged affair with John began in the early 1950's and lasted through the first year of his presidency. When such an involvement became too dangerous for the president, he is supposed to have asked Robert to console the emotionally dependent star.

At a Madison Square Garden birthday celebration for the president on May 19, 1962, Robert was said to have hovered around the actress "like a moth around the flame." To a friend Monroe confided that the younger Kennedy wanted to marry her. That summer she repeatedly telephoned him at the Justice Department in Washington; the attorney general refused to accept or return her calls.

On August 4 Robert Kennedy arrived in Los Angeles. According to Monroe's maid, he visited her that afternoon. Had he come to break off the affair, if indeed there was an affair? Sometime after 11 P.M. that night the actress was found unconscious in her home and rushed to a hospital where she was pronounced dead.

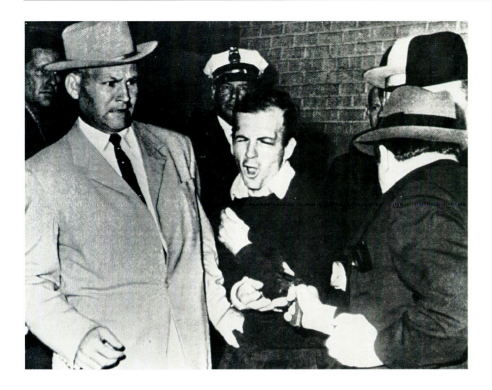

Lee Harvey Oswald at the moment he was shot by Jack Ruby. Was the nightclub operator acting alone and solely because of his outrage at Oswald's crime? Or were both Oswald and Ruby part of a larger conspiracy to eliminate Kennedy?

bound from New Orleans to Le Havre, France, and subsequently made his way across Europe to Moscow. On October 31 he appeared at the U.S. embassy there to renounce his American citizenship, saying that he was a Marxist, had applied for Soviet citizenship, and was offering the Soviets information he had acquired as a radar technician. Seven months later the Soviets shot down a U-2 aircraft. When pilot Francis Gary Powers admitted that his was a CIA photoreconnaissance mission, Soviet leader Nikita Khrushchev angrily broke off his summit meeting with President Eisenhower in Paris.

Oswald remained in the Soviet Union for two and a half years, acquiring a Russian wife but gradually becoming disillusioned with life in a Marxist state. On June 1, 1962, Oswald, his wife, Marina, and their infant daughter, June, were allowed to leave the Soviet Union. He had never received Soviet citizenship and denied having given secret information to the Russians. The U.S. Department of State overruled the Immigration and Naturalization Service to readmit Oswald, noting that "it was in the best interests of the United States to have Mr. Oswald depart from the Soviet Union as soon as possible." Was the ex-Marine's initial defection planned by the CIA; had the Soviets failed to rise to the bait of a double agent? Some questions were never asked in the official investigation of the assassination; others remained unanswered.

Fair Play for Cuba

After working at odd jobs in Fort Worth and Dallas, Oswald moved his family to New Orleans in the spring of 1963. But before leaving Texas, he purchased by mail a rifle with a telescopic sight. With it, according to the Warren Commission, he attempted to assassinate retired Major General Edwin A. Walker, an ultraconservative spokesman who was urging President Kennedy to send troops to oust Castro.

In New Orleans, Oswald set himself up as what the Warren Commission called "the imaginary president of the nonexistent chapter" of the Fair Play for Cuba Committee, a pro-Castro organization. The address he listed for the chapter, curiously enough, was a building that housed the offices of a retired FBI agent, Guy Bannister, who was said to be the coordinator of several militant anti-Castro groups. Despite the fact that Oswald was twice arrested in August 1963 for run-ins with anti-Castro Cuban exiles, he and Bannister appeared to be on friendly terms.

Apparently as disillusioned with his return to the United States as he had been by his attempted defection to the Soviet Union, Oswald went to Mexico City in September. There he unsuccessfully tried to get a transit visa to Cuba en route to the U.S.S.R. Returning to Dallas, Oswald went to work at the Texas School Book Depository in mid-October. On Tuesday, November 19, he could have read a newspaper report of a speech in Miami in which President Kennedy "all but invited the Cuban people . . . to overthrow Fidel Castro's communist regime and promised prompt U.S. aid if they do." The itinerary for the president's visit to Dallas that Friday was also published; the motorcade would pass directly in front of the building where Oswald worked.

Kennedy Versus the Mafia

If Oswald was acting for either the Soviet secret police or for Fidel Castro, why was an escape route after the assassination denied him? Or was the visitor to Mexico a look-alike, sent by the real conspirators to link Oswald falsely to Cuba and the Soviet Union? This is a theory of the most recent advocates of a conspiracy to kill the president. The conspirators? The Mafia.

Both John F. Kennedy and his brother Robert F. Kennedy were highly visible opponents of organized crime in the United States. In 1957 Senator Kennedy had sat on the Senate Rackets Committee that exposed the mob. As chief counsel to the committee, Robert Kennedy led interrogations that left witnesses squirming in their chairs. When his brother appointed him attorney general in 1961, Robert Kennedy launched a Justice Department war against crime. One of his targets was Carlos Marcello, Mafia boss of New Orleans, who was deported to Guatemala.

Secretly returning to the United States, Marcello plotted revenge. "You know what they say in Sicily," he said to a friend in August 1962; "if you want to kill a dog, you don't cut off the tail, you cut off the head." The way to immobilize Robert Kennedy was to eliminate his brother, the president. "Kennedy's not going to make it to the [1964] election," a Florida mobster told an FBI informer that same month; "he's going to be hit." By the spring of 1963 an associate of Marcello's was saying that there was a price on the president's head.

The Mafia had another reason for opposition to Kennedy: he was not acting quickly enough to rid Cuba of Fidel Castro. Upon seizing power, Castro had thrown out the Mafia, which was making profits estimated at more than $110 million annually from drugs, gambling, and prostitution in Havana. The mobsters desperately wanted that lucrative business back and were dismayed when Kennedy failed to give adequate support to the aborted Bay of Pigs invasion in April 1961. The Cuban missile crisis of October 1962 had ended when the Soviets backed down; yet the American triumph had not weakened Castro. Despite his tough talk in Miami, the pres-

ident showed little support for anti-Castro exiles in the United States and had discouraged independent raids on Cuba.

Proponents of a Mafia conspiracy have attempted to establish links between the mob and both Oswald and Jack Ruby. They fail to explain why professional gangsters would have turned to such an unlikely assassin as Oswald or such an improbable hit man as Ruby. Oswald had help, the American writer Steve Rivele claimed late in 1988, as the 25th anniversary of the assassination was bringing renewed interest in the tragedy. Rivele named three Corsicans hired by the New Orleans Mafia for the job. Unfortunately for Rivele's credibility, all three had apparently iron-clad alibis for November 22, 1963: one was recovering from an eye operation, the second was serving in the French navy, the third was in a Marseilles prison.

Was Kennedy the Target?

Yet another theory was advanced at the time of the 25th anniversary: Oswald had been aiming at Governor John Connally.

As a result of his defection to Russia, Oswald's honorable discharge from the Marine Corps was downgraded to "undesirable," only a notch above dishonorable. Realizing that this could block employment when he returned to the United States, Oswald wrote to Connally — then secretary of the Navy — from the Soviet Union asking for a reversal of the action. He was politely brushed off. In her third and final appearance before the Warren Commission, Marina Oswald expressed an opinion that the president was not her husband's target, saying that "he perhaps was shooting at Governor Connally . . . on account of his discharge from the Marines."

By the time that Mrs. Oswald volunteered this information the Warren Commission had apparently already reached its own conclusions and did not include her testimony in its report.

In a *New York Times*/CBS poll taken shortly before the 25th anniversary of the assassination, 66 percent of Americans queried believed in a conspiracy; 61 percent said that there had been "an official cover-up to keep the public from learning the truth about the assassination." Yet, 46 percent of those polled felt that it was then too late to establish the truth; 59 percent opposed further investigations.

"It does not seem likely that these mysteries will ever be solved," remarked Representative Louis Stokes, who had headed the House committee a decade earlier. "I think it's more likely than not that we'll never know."

Son Against Father

*A rebellious son, in love with his father's lovely young wife;
the autocratic ruler of half the world, responsible for the death of his
heir — this is the popular view of Prince Don Carlos and
King Philip II of Spain. The facts are quite different.*

Toward midnight on January 18, 1568, Philip II, king of Spain — sword in hand, helmet on his head — led a stealthy procession through the darkened corridors of his palace in Madrid to the apartments of his son and heir, Prince Don Carlos. Bolts on the doors had been removed in advance, the weapons the prince kept at bedside taken away. With members of the royal council as witnesses, Philip awakened his son and spoke to him no longer as father but as king. Don Carlos was under arrest. Windows were boarded up, doors locked, guards posted. Commanding that no one be allowed to speak to the prince or bring him letters, the king departed. Never again would the unhappy monarch and his only son meet.

*In drama and opera Don Carlos is portrayed as an idealistic youth defying his father
for a belief in religious freedom — and hopelessly in love with his stepmother. At left below, a
modern production of* Don Carlos; *at right, a contemporary portrait.*

The nocturnal arrest and confinement of the 22-year-old heir apparent and his death in captivity six months later not only caused a sensation at the Spanish court, it quickly became a leading topic of rumor and gossip across Europe. To his contemporaries, Philip II seemed to "bestride the narrow world like a Colossus." In addition to Spain, he ruled the Low Countries, parts of France, most of Italy, Sardinia, Sicily, and — with the exception of Portuguese Brazil — the New World south of the Rio Grande. With miscellaneous possessions in North Africa and the Philippine Islands (named after him) in Asia, Philip presided over an empire on which it could almost be said the sun never set.

Philip II inherited most of this vast realm from his father, Charles V, who had abdicated the Spanish throne to his son and the imperial crown of the Holy Roman Empire to his brother, Ferdinand, in 1555–56. After a tour of his new territories, Philip returned to Spain in the fall of 1559, never to leave the Iberian Peninsula during the remaining four decades of his life.

No detail of government seemed too small for the hard-working bureaucrat; his correspondence was voluminous. But two major concerns preoccupied his reign: preserving the Catholic faith of which he was a rigid defender; and providing an heir to the throne. These two preoccupations of Philip's intersected — with tragic consequences — in the person of Don Carlos.

Secret Lover and Rebel?

Philip's first wife, Maria of Portugal, died in 1545, shortly after giving birth to Don Carlos. Nine years later, at the wish of Charles V, he entered a loveless marriage with Mary Tudor, queen of England. He was 27; she, 38. When Mary died four years later, in 1558, without providing England with an heir to her throne, Philip married again. His choice: 14-year-old Elizabeth of Valois, daughter of the king of France.

At their first meeting in January 1560, the bright and attractive young woman was said to have stared intently at the royal bridegroom, 19 years her senior. "What are you looking at?" Philip is supposed to have asked. "To see if I have any gray hairs?" Elizabeth had previously been promised to Don Carlos, who was the same age — and this became the basis for the story of an illicit love between the two.

Philip's unwavering defense of the Catholic faith was to be most seriously challenged in the Low Countries. To suppress a rebellion of his Protestant subjects there, Philip sent a force of 20,000 under the command of the duke of Alva in the summer of 1567. Don Carlos, a secret adherent to Protestantism, determined to join the

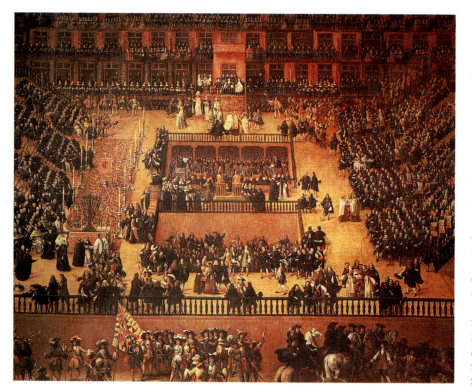

The public burnings of heretics were atrocious spectacles to which huge crowds were attracted, as at this one in Madrid's Plaza Mayor. In Philip II's Spain the auto-da-fé was considered a means of stifling Protestantism before it took root in Catholic Spain. Philip's restless provinces in the Netherlands launched a rebellion for independence and religious freedom.

A Mismatched Father and Son

Generation gaps have always existed; there is nothing extraordinary about them. However, when the family is a powerful one, such differences achieve a lasting notoriety. One of the most famous father-son conflicts was that between the so-called "Soldier King," Frederick William I of Prussia, and his son, Frederick, born in 1712.

"Instill in my son a love for the military." Such was the principal charge of the king to his son's tutors. Unfortunately, young Frederick loathed the discipline of barracks life and inclined toward a study of music, literature, and philosophy — pursuits considered effeminate by his father. With insults and humiliation he tried to mold the crown prince into his own image. The king's treatment became so intolerable that in 1730 Freder-

Crown Prince Frederick leans from a window to appeal for the life of his friend, von Katte. The king forced him to witness the execution.

ick hatched a plan to escape to England with two friends, lieutenants von Keith and von Katte.

Learning of the plan, Frederick William had his son and von Katte arrested (von Keith made good his escape) and court-martialed. The court refused to judge the crown prince but sentenced von Katte to life imprisonment. The king arbitrarily changed the sentence to death by decapitation and forced his son to witness the execution.

The crown prince had to endure 10 more years of his father's cruelty. But when he succeeded to the throne, Frederick promptly launched a war against Austria that established Prussia as a dominant power in Europe. In addition, he was a great patron of the arts. His 46-year reign easily overshadowed that of his father, and he is known to history as Frederick the Great.

rebels, a plan he unwisely divulged to his uncle, Don Juan of Austria, on December 23, 1567. When Philip learned of his son's treachery, he had the prince arrested, confined, and later — presumably — murdered. Such, at least, was the accusation made by Philip's enemies.

Two centuries later, in 1787, the great German playwright Friedrich Schiller presented this version of the story in the verse drama *Don Carlos*. In 1867 Giuseppe Verdi based his monumental opera of the same name on Schiller's play; and it is their accounts that are most widely known today. A son in rebellion against his autocratic father; an incestuous affair between the son and his beautiful young stepmother; a father's cruel revenge — but is it true?

A Disturbed Heir Apparent

In appearance, Don Carlos was scarcely an imposing heir to the world's most powerful throne. Small (at 18 he weighed but 76 pounds), with a raised shoulder that gave him the appearance of a hunchback and a speech impediment that had to be remedied by cutting his tongue ligament, the prince was unlikely to have appealed to the vivacious Elizabeth of Valois. Indeed, there is ample evidence that she was devoted to her husband, Philip. Certainly the king found his greatest

pleasure in this marriage, expressed tender love for their two daughters, Isabella and Catalina, and greatly mourned Elizabeth's death following delivery of a third daughter in September 1568.

Physical attributes aside, Don Carlos was a questionable successor to Philip. In fact, there is strong evidence that he was mentally unstable, perhaps feebleminded. As a child, he was known to take pleasure in having hares roasted alive and once in an orgy of cruelty blinded horses in the royal stable. At age 11, he had a young girl flogged for his sadistic amusement — an excess for which he was compelled to pay damages to her father. At the University of Alcalá in 1562, the 16-year-old prince fell headlong down a flight of stairs while pursuing a servant girl. In a daring and probably ill-advised operation to heal his head wound, doctors removed a piece of his skull to drain life-threatening fluids.

Following the operation, Don Carlos's actions became even more erratic and bizarre. He took to roaming the streets of Madrid, kissing attractive girls at random and shouting obscenities at respectable women. When a bootmaker delivered the wrong size boots, Don Carlos had them cut into pieces, stewed, and force-fed to the unfortunate man. Named to the council of state by his father, the prince insulted and even physically attacked the other councillors and freely told state secrets to anyone who cared to listen.

The judgment of his contemporaries at court is devastating. The imperial envoy from Vienna said that the heir to the throne had the mentality of a seven year old. A councillor to Philip, in private, referred to Don Carlos as an "imbecile."

The Would-be Commander

As for the prince's Protestant sympathies, there is no evidence that Don Carlos supported the rebellion in the Low Countries. Indeed, it is more likely that he wanted to have command of the force Philip sent north to quell the uprising. However, his wish may have had more to do with a long-standing grudge against the duke of Alva than it did with either a commitment to the Catholic cause or the hope of military glory.

As royal grand marshal, Alva had presided over the ceremony in 1560 at which Don Carlos was officially proclaimed heir to the throne. Pledging allegiance to the prince, the duke failed to kneel and kiss Don Carlos's hand — an apparent affront that sent the prince into a rage. Even though Alva asked pardon for his oversight, Don Carlos was unrelenting in his antagonism toward the veteran commander.

"Am I not a slave, the most miserable man who ever lived," Don Carlos lamented, "with no part in the affairs of state, no respect, and no occupation that would prepare me to rule?" Hearing that Alva was to head the army being sent to the Netherlands, Don Carlos impetuously sought the command for himself. When Spain's parliament, the Cortes, initiated a petition to keep him at home, the prince threatened death to any deputy who voted in its favor. Finally, he attacked Alva with a dagger when the duke came to take his leave. It was his confession to Don Juan of Austria that he was proceeding to the Netherlands against the wishes of his father that precipitated the prince's arrest and confinement a month later, on January 18, 1568.

Philip: Saddened but Resigned

Philip was aware that the action taken against his son would provoke the criticism even of his supporters and the outrage of his enemies. To his sister Maria, wife of the emperor in Vienna, he wrote the next month: "I would like to talk in all frankness about the life and conduct of the prince, the degree to which he carried on with licentiousness and confusion, and the means I used to induce him to change his behavior." Yet, he sadly concluded, all efforts to reform or cure Don Carlos had failed; what he had had to do was for the good of the realm. To Alva he confided his grief and regret, only thanking God that the people had taken the arrest so well.

The prince's reaction to his imprisonment fluctuated between silent despair and uncontrolled fits of rage, between hunger strikes and gluttony. For years the infirm Don Carlos had suffered from recurrent bouts of fever, and his confinement to the princely apartments in the palace at Madrid aggravated his condition. A crisis was reached in the summer of 1568. After fasting for three days, Don Carlos gulped down a huge meal that included a spicy partridge pie. To quench his ensuing thirst, he drank large quantities of ice water. This brought on violent diarrhea, vomiting, and an inability to retain food.

In the story of Philip as the monstrous murderer of his son, Don Carlos's dying wish for reconciliation with his father is callously denied. In actuality, when the doctors told Philip that his son's condition was hopeless, the king asked to see him. Yet it was feared that the sight of his father would send Don Carlos into a rage that would hasten death, and so Philip was dissuaded from a final meeting. Apparently the king did visit the prince's bedside after he lapsed into unconsciousness, gave his blessing, and retired to his own rooms to await the end.

The death of Philip's son was shortly followed by that of Elizabeth of Valois — and Philip was left without a male heir. To remedy the situation, the king married his 21-year-old niece, Anna of Austria, two years later. Although four of their children died at an early age, a fifth survived. As Philip III, he succeeded to the throne in 1598, when the century's most powerful monarch — so vilified by posterity — died in his 71st year.

During 21 years of his 42-year reign, Philip II occupied himself with the building of a magnificent monument: the monastery-palace El Escorial, high in the foothills of the Guadarrama Mountains, some 30 miles northwest of Madrid. In his later years the king spent much of his time in a modest apartment there, with a door that opened to the central church's high altar; even from bed, the devout monarch could follow services. Today, the rooms are open to the public, furnished just as they were during the king's residence. But what most strikes the visitor are the lifelike groupings of gilt bronze statues flanking the altar. On one side: Charles V, his wife, daughter, and two sisters. On the other: Philip II and three of his four queens (Mary Tudor is missing). And next to his mother, Maria of Portugal, is Don Carlos — the supposedly discredited son, united in death with his long-suffering father.

Intrigue in the Kremlin

When the state radio reported that the murderer of tens of millions had died of natural causes, the world was suspicious. Why had his last days been shrouded in secrecy? And who in the Soviet Union did not gain from his death?

*I*f we can believe the four wily men who inherited his vast power, Stalin, supreme dictator of the Soviet Union and puppet-master of all of Eastern Europe, suffered a fatal stroke while brooding alone in a sparely furnished room. He lay stricken and unconscious for untold hours because his bodyguard, family, and government associates were too terrified — after 27 years of his iron-fisted rule — to knock on the door.

If true, this sordid, pitiable demise contrasted dramatically with the career of a man who delighted in ordering the torture and execution of his most loyal followers. At least 30 million, and possibly double that amount, were shot, hanged, starved, beaten, or drugged to death because of his insane fear of opposition. Millions were enslaved in cruel concentration camps and forced to work for the state. Uncounted tens of millions in the Ukraine died when he forced farmers to join his collectives and send their produce elsewhere.

On the more personal level, he was amused by inviting an old colleague to dinner, flying into a carefully rehearsed rage, and ordering the hapless, bewildered victim of his sadistic cruelty to the execution chamber. It is said that he once left a Bolshoi Ballet performance of *Swan Lake* at intermission, drove over to Red Square's Lubyanka Prison to shoot some former loyalists in the head, and returned to the theater for the second act.

By early 1953, when Stalin was 73 years old, these paranoid tendencies and

Did Stalin, an old, careworn man — as the photograph silhouetted above, taken secretly in 1950, reveals — die a natural death? Only the four men at the deathwatch could answer that question: at left, Beria and Malenkov; at right, Bulganin and Khrushchev.

unpredictable explosions were increasing in virulence. "Fear and hatred of the old tyrant," according to U.S. Ambassador George Kennan, was "so thick in the air that you could almost smell it." In January a woman working as a secret agent for Lavrenti Beria, head of the State Security Service, accused Stalin's personal physician of involvement in a so-called "doctors' plot" to kill important military leaders by means of "faulty treatment." Eight other top physicians were imprisoned, most of them Jewish. Perhaps in anticipation of a pogrom, Stalin began to fan the flames of anti-Semitism.

The preceding fall, the 19th Congress of the Communist Party had, for the first time, defied the tyrant's will — if only in minor ways. Scheming surreptitiously behind the scenes, Stalin was apparently planning to purge the old-guard communists and install new men loyal only to him. The dictator's plans were intently watched by the quartet nearest him: Beria, Defense Minister Nikolai Bulganin, Deputy Prime Minister (and designated successor) Georgi Malenkov, and Nikita Khrushchev, head of the powerful Moscow city and regional party committees. Communist leaders no less entrenched than they had previously

vanished without warning under the capricious reign of "Uncle Joe."

A Drinking Party, Then Silence

Not long before his death, Stalin suddenly banished his private secretary, for decades his alter ego in all matters large and small. On February 15, his chief bodyguard succumbed to what an official announcement called a "premature death" — no doubt a euphemism for execution. Stalin's physician still languished behind bars. Meanwhile, rumors that the great man was ill had been circulating among the Moscow elite since December; but his daughter, Svetlana, was unable to get through to him, despite numerous frantic attempts. Months earlier she had seen him dwindling from the effects of arteriosclerosis.

On March 2, Stalin may have suffered a cerebral hemorrhage, but the news was suppressed by the fearful band of would-be successors. The day before, according to Khrushchev, Stalin had invited his four cohorts to his *dacha*, or summer house, in Kunzevo for a night of drinking and crude storytelling. The party broke up in the wee hours, and Stalin went to bed alone. After three in the morning of March 3, the frightened body-

At first, Stalin's death caused consternation and dismay among the Soviet Union's population. Below, masses throng Moscow's Red Square to place flowers in his honor against the Kremlin's wall; in the background, Lenin's tomb.

guards reported to the revelers that the Soviet chieftain had not appeared for about 24 hours. When they dared to enter his heavily armored inner sanctum, they found him lying prostrate on a rug, fully dressed.

Apparently surprised and alarmed, Malenkov, Khrushchev, Bulganin, and the coldly efficient Beria raced over from their separate *dachas* to find Stalin placed upon a simple couch, abnormally still. Eventually doctors were alerted, and the four colleagues, plus other members of the ruling Presidium, took turns overseeing the dictator's treatment in pairs while, presumably, making plans for the uncertain future.

A Tense Vigil

Khrushchev and the others were seen red-eyed with weeping during the ensuing days, but Beria's behavior was startling. Occasionally, his stricken leader's eyes would flicker open, and the dreaded security chief would profess his concern and affection. But when Stalin seemed to sink into his coma again, Beria horrified the others by insulting and ridiculing his old mentor. What did this bode for the others? Since 1938, Beria had headed the secret police, the true source of Stalin's omnipotence.

On March 4, Stalin suddenly woke up. As a nurse fed him with a spoon, he weakly pointed to a picture on the wall of a lamb, like him, being fed milk by a young woman. Soon, he fell into the death throes of suffocation, stared angrily at his huddled followers, then died. Beria sped back to the center of power in Moscow.

Earlier that day, 800 million people throughout the Soviet empire had learned for the first time, along with the rest of the astonished world, that Stalin was seriously ill. As if to forestall suspicion, the physicians released an unusually complete explanation of the attack and its accompanying complications. Finally, on March 6, the government radio announced that Stalin's heart had stopped beating at 10:10 the night before. A full autopsy report was read to suggest that everything possible had been done in the face of the "irreversible character of the illness."

By four in the afternoon, the body reposed in state on a huge bank of fresh flowers in the Hall of Columns of the House of the Trade Unions. Seemingly all of Moscow filed by to pay respects, perhaps 5 million in the next three days. Tragically, many were killed or seriously wounded when nervous generals trying to control the crowds gave orders that crushed the mourners against iron bars on ground-floor windows.

On March 9 all other activities in the Soviet

Against All Odds

Ironically, almost no one ever thought that plodding Joseph Stalin would rise to the supreme heights of power. A poor peasant from Soviet Georgia, the only one of four children to survive into adulthood, he had been a solitary dreamer. Born Josif Dzhugashvili, he changed his name to Stalin, or "man of steel," during his youthful days as a communist revolutionary.

When Lenin became the first head of communist Russia, Stalin moved quietly in his shadow, until the revered leader fell ill in 1921. While brilliant men like Leon Trotsky held the limelight, the clever Georgian consolidated his power and laid traps for his rivals. Eventually, Lenin became alarmed and tried to prevent Stalin from becoming a threat. From his sickbed, he dictated a secret warning against his right-hand man's "boundless power."

But the younger man would be prepared to wrest power from others and have opponents, including Trotsky, killed when Lenin died in 1924. Stalin's concentration on political intrigue was total, seemingly to the exclusion of normal human affection.

When his first wife died after three years of marriage, he said, "With her died my last warm feelings for people," and sent his toddler son to live with relatives. His second wife, an idealistic teenager, bore him two children, then became so disillusioned with his repressive policies and cruel abuse that she shot herself. After his elder son attempted suicide, Stalin ridiculed him for failing. Taken captive by the Germans in World War II, the miserable young man — hearing that his father refused to accept him in a prisoner exchange — ran headlong into a prison camp electrified fence and was burned to death.

Stalin's other two children, Svetlana and Vasily, were perhaps only marginally happier. She became world-famous when she defected to the West in 1967 but has been torn between the United States, Britain, and her homeland ever since. Vasily was a boor and a swindler, who drank himself to death at age 41.

Union were suspended for the greatest funeral service of the 20th century. Delegations filled Red Square, heads of state attended, and Stalin's successors acted as pallbearers. Communism's "Little Father" was placed alongside the founder of the Soviet state in Lenin's tomb.

Disturbing Discrepancies

The first official announcement of Stalin's fatal illness claimed that he had been stricken in his Moscow apartment. If true, how did he get back

Throughout the Soviet bloc, Stalin's death was recognized as the end of an era. When Khrushchev announced his plan of de-Stalinization, statues of the dictator were toppled (above); governments he had put in power in East Europe were challenged by spontaneous uprisings of the people.

to Kunzevo, 48 miles away? Why did the official version say the attack occurred early on Monday morning, when Khrushchev and others would report the approximate time as Sunday evening, or even sometime Sunday morning? And why would the deposed Khrushchev offer a different twist in his *Reminiscences* years later, revealing that he and his three companions did not see Stalin or call a doctor when they first rushed to the dictator's *dacha*? Instead, they went home and waited until Malenkov called hours later with the news that Stalin definitely was seriously ill.

Days before his death, as he chatted with an Indian diplomat, Stalin idly drew sketches of snarling wolves. "Peasants know how to handle wolves," he said grimly. "They exterminate them."

Was Stalin preparing a counterattack? According to his pattern, the "doctors' plot" could have been a pretext for revenge. The scenario would have the tortured prisoners "confess" to being tools of higher-ups. Stalin's recent flare-ups of

anger at Beria might have indicated that the secret police chief was in danger.

Whatever actually happened, Beria's ecstatic relief at the dictator's death and naked grab for power survived only briefly. In June he was arrested and publicly denounced as a traitor. Malenkov, who succeeded Stalin as head of both the government and the Communist Party, joined with the rest of the Presidium in denouncing and purging Beria, the genius of terrorism.

Beria was probably executed after a secret trial in December, shot to death on the spot as soon as the verdict was rendered. The Moscow grapevine soon hummed with the previously unspeakable: tales of the dead henchman's rapes of children, orgies with kidnapped young women, drunken debauches at his sylvan estate in the country.

End of an Era

Other changes were in the wind. By September, Khrushchev had taken the party chair from Malenkov; and in 1955 Bulganin assumed the office of prime minister, forcing Stalin's first deputy into virtual exile as head of a power station in the provinces. For the first time in a generation, leadership shifts did not necessarily cause an ousted chieftain his life.

Much more earthshaking, however, was the rapid turn away from Stalin's famous "cult of

The Full Flowering of de-Stalinization

The process of "de-Staliniza-tion," as it was dubbed by Western observers, was dramatically symbolized by the removal of Stalin's corpse from Lenin's tomb in Moscow's Red Square. The man who had dominated the words and imagery of the nation for more than a quarter of a century was reburied in a small cemetery beside the Kremlin walls.

But Khrushchev's fall from power in 1964 seemed to signal a retrenchment. The ruling elite, typified perhaps by Communist Party General Secretary Leonid Brezhnev, intended to keep a firm hand on the reigns of government. It was not in their interest to reject the Stalinist heritage too flagrantly.

Not until March 11, 1985, when the comparatively youthful Mikhail Gorbachev, 55, was selected general secretary, did de-Stalinization begin to flower in full force. The dictator's innocent victims were publicly exonerated, and his worst excesses were examined in the press. Aging party hacks, their political arteries hardened under Stalin's intellectual domination, were eased out so that Gorbachev's generation could tackle the realities of Soviet life with fresh views and frank appraisals. Opposition

candidates were allowed, and the world watched in wonder as the people sent powerful party bosses to defeat. Censorship of the news media, popular journals, and film was relaxed. The leadership even admitted that the Brezhnev regime's invasion of Afghanistan and suppression of a nationalistic movement in Czechoslovakia had been mistaken.

Soon, most people outside the Soviet Union learned at least two Russian words: *glasnost* and *perestroika*. *Glasnost*, translated as "openness," refers to the many different indications of loosened controls and enhanced political freedoms. Gorbachev stresses his commitment to the Communist Party but wants more citizens to participate in the making and implementing of political decisions.

The somewhat more complex concept, *perestroika*, refers to a "restructuring" of the economy and the workings of society. While the party elite leads a very comfortable life in material terms, the ordinary Russian faces continual shortages of basic goods and services and few or no prospects of individual financial advancement or the accumulation of luxuries. Increasingly, the country's vaunted science and technology are falling behind the progress of the West and the Pacific rim. *Perestroika*, in an effort to solve these problems, has already led to greater self-determination in factories and some private ownership of property.

When Mikhail Gorbachev (at right, with his wife, Raisa) assumed leadership of the Soviet government, a new generation had replaced the old. For the first time, the country was ruled by a man who did not participate as a soldier in World War II.

personality." Within two weeks of his funeral, the official press was no longer quoting and praising him ad nauseam. The "Stalinist Constitution" became the "Soviet Constitution." Even the word "Stalinist" was dropped from the official Russian dictionary. *Pravda*, the official Soviet newspaper, announced that the "doctors' plot" had never existed. Khrushchev publicly revealed that Stalin's mismanagement had left the legacy of a serious agricultural crisis.

Finally, in February 1956, the new leader of the Soviet Union delivered his famous "secret speech" to the 20th Party Congress, explicitly detailing the barbarous horrors of his predecessor's reign and formally announcing an end to state terrorism as a domestic political tool. As for the enemies in the West, Khrushchev began a reversal of Stalin's implacably hostile foreign policy. His new doctrine was heralded throughout the world as "peaceful coexistence."

A Philosopher Murdered?

*According to official statements of the Swedish court in 1650,
René Descartes died of pneumonia. For more than three
centuries, none of his biographers questioned this. Then in 1980
a startling new theory about his death was proposed.*

When a visitor to the old church of St.-Germain-des-Prés in Paris's Latin Quarter adjusts his eyesight to the candle-lit gloom, he may notice a black marble plaque set in the floor of a small side chapel. It bears the inscription Renatius Cartesius, the Latin form of the name René Descartes. There rest the mortal remains of the famous philosopher, mathematician, and scientist — born on March 31, 1596, at La Haye, a village in the Touraine region of central France; died on February 11, 1650, at the royal court of Sweden in Stockholm. Cause of death, as officially announced and largely believed at the time: pneumonia.

René Descartes made his reputation as a scientist by first doubting and then meticulously investigating what was "largely believed." In the death of another, he would have been the first to question pat explanations and then to follow up on clues to alternative possibilities. For in the palace corridors and back alleys of Stockholm, a rumor was circulating in the days following Des-

A bust of René Descartes adorns the library of the University of La Flèche.

cartes' death: the renowned man of letters, guest of Sweden's Queen Christina, had been poisoned. Like most European courts of the period, the palace of the House of Vasa thrived on rumors. The one concerning the death of the French visitor only gradually died out and then only when the brilliant and restless young queen gave her country — and indeed all Europe — something far more startling to talk about. Moreover, no one was able to identify a suspect or a motive for the murder of Descartes. And thus the official cause of death entered the history books, with biographers sadly noting the premature end of a brilliant career and the irony of an ending in so remote a spot.

Studying "the Book of the World"

Descartes was born into a French provincial family of what today would be called the upper middle class. His father was a lawyer and judge; and René as an adult would be able to live off the income of property he inherited. As a child, René was forever asking questions, so that his father began referring to him as his "little philosopher." In 1604, at the age of eight, the boy was sent off to a new college endowed by King Henry IV at La Flèche, a town some 65 miles northwest of La Haye. There, at what would eventually become one of Europe's most celebrated schools, he was tutored by Jesuit priests and placed under the care of Father Charlet, a distant relative who was to become his "second father."

During the 10 years he spent at La Flèche, René labored over the classic Greek and Latin authors, acquired skill as a writer in both French and Latin, studied music and the dramatic arts, and even mastered the gentlemanly pursuits of riding and fencing. As he grew older, he turned to science, which was then taught as little more than the 2,000-year-old theories of Aristotle as reinterpreted by medieval scholars. However, the more recent advances in mathematics and astronomy were included in the curriculum of the Jesuit school. The youth's thirst for knowledge was unquenchable, but more and more he found himself at the limits of the knowledge of his times. Discovering errors and contradictions in what his teachers said, he refused to accept blank spots in the world map of knowledge as God-given and thus beyond challenge. After two more years at the University of Poitiers, he received a degree in law in 1616.

Young Descartes' formal studies were ended, but he declined to enter the law profession as he was expected to do — and for this failure he would later be scorned by his father as "only fit to be bound in calfskin." Nor would he be satisfied with the solely contemplative life of a scholar. Instead, he announced his plans to continue seeking knowledge by travel and observation, to learn from what he called "the book of the world."

A Soldier's Dreams

In 1618 what would become known as the Thirty Years' War broke out, throwing Europe into one of the deepest crises of its history. It started as a religious controversy between Catholics and Protestants in Bohemia and ended with wars of conquest by Sweden and France fought on German soil. Curiously, the devastating conflict offered Descartes just the chance he needed to pursue his ambitious goal of seeking truth and wisdom beyond classroom walls.

Between 1618 and 1628 Descartes moved about Europe, frequently in the service of one combatant or another. Although present at the decisive Battle of the White Mountain near Prague in November 1620, Descartes saw little action and disdained camp life as one of "idleness and dissipation." For him the most profound experience of the decade occurred during the night of November 10, 1619, at Ulm, Germany.

Deep in meditation, Descartes conceived the notion that all knowledge could be brought together in a single universal science, "capable of solving in a general manner all problems." That night he had three visionary dreams. In the first dream the philosopher found himself lame and seeking shelter in a church; in the second he experienced a violent storm; in the third he opened a Latin text and read the words, *Quid vitae sectabor iter?* ("Which way of life shall I follow?"). The dreams, he was convinced, were telling him that it would be his quest in life to discover the universal science and master it.

When he was not wandering, Descartes made Paris his home, and there he began establishing a reputation for himself as a deep and imaginative thinker. At one scholarly gathering he was able to refute the proponent of a new philosophy by applying arguments so precise that they appeared to be mathematical proof for his position. A high churchman told Descartes that he had a duty to use his intellect to complete the search for knowledge that he had undertaken. But the French capital proved distracting, and in the autumn of 1628 he went first to northern France and then to Holland, where he was to live for the next two decades. There he formed a rare personal attachment, with a Dutch servant girl named Helen, who bore him a daughter. The child's death in 1640, at age five, was a bitter blow.

Descartes had few friends at the Swedish court (left); to other scholars there, he must have been a feared rival. Did his early morning lessons help convert the Protestant queen to Roman Catholicism? Shortly after his arrival, he mentioned in a letter that his stay in Stockholm would be a short one; it was a grim prophecy.

But for the most part, his life in Holland was the lonely one of a scholar. His years there were spent in studying, meditating, corresponding with other great thinkers of the day, and eventually writing and publishing the works that earned him a lasting place among history's most influential philosophers.

"I Think, Therefore I Am"

By 1633 Descartes had completed the first draft of a comprehensive work to be called *Le Monde* (*The World*). But then news came that the astronomer Galileo had been condemned by the Catholic Church in Rome for endorsing the theory that the earth revolves around the sun, a position Descartes too had adopted. He put aside his manuscript and spent the next three years writing the book that defined his scientific method in a way that he hoped would be acceptable to the church's theologians. At a time when most scholarly books were written in Latin, Descartes published this volume in French as *Discours de la méthode* (*Discourse on Method*). Yet, the saying for which he is most remembered comes down to us in Latin. It is the philosopher's ringing proof of the power of the mind: *Cogito, ergo sum* ("I think, therefore I am").

Descartes' *Discourse* of 1637 gave four rules for scientific inquiry: 1) never accept as true anything that cannot clearly be seen as such; 2) divide difficulties into as many parts as possible; 3) seek solutions of the simplest problems first and proceed step by step to the most difficult; 4) review all conclusions to make sure there are no omissions. He then applied these methods to three subjects: optics, in which he formulated the law of refraction; the weather, for which he sought a scientific explanation; and mathematics, to which he contributed the foundations of analytical geometry.

Descartes' method was revolutionary doctrine in an age when a scientist or philosopher was merely expected to back up his theories with biblical quotations and citations from the works of church fathers, and he soon had many critics. Eventually the man who had so diligently sought to remain faithful to his Catholicism found his *Discourse* and the other works that followed through the 1640's placed on the Catholic Church's list of forbidden books.

But he also had many influential supporters, and among these was Sweden's Queen Christina, who obtained Descartes' works through the French ambassador to her court and started writing to him in 1647. Christina had inherited the throne upon the death of her father, King Gustavus II Adolphus, when she was only six. While a regent governed the country in her name, Christina was raised in a rural setting away from the court — but given the education generally reserved for boys.

Foreign visitors had been barred from her father's funeral, "less they witness our poverty," the ruling council explained. Crowned at the age of 18 in 1644, Christina was determined to correct Europe's unfavorable image of her country. And so the young queen set out to make her court the center of art and learning in northern Europe, importing musicians and artists from Germany and Italy. But the star in this intellectual firmament was to be Descartes. She was determined to woo the famous French scholar away from his self-imposed exile in Holland and establish him as the resident philosopher at her court in Stockholm. Reluctantly, the 53-year-old Descartes gave in to Christina's pressure and in the fall of 1649 boarded a ship bound for what he called "the land of bears, between rock and ice."

Predawn Seminars and Frozen Thoughts

Ceremoniously received in Stockholm, Descartes was initially given the assignment to write French verses for a ballet. But his major obligation was to tutor the young queen at, for him, the uncivilized hour of 5 A.M. This was cruel punishment for a man who was used to sleeping 10 hours a night and often spent mornings in bed reading and thinking. He found his royal student to be bright and sincere in her wish to acquire knowledge. But Christina was scarcely a profound thinker and life at her court offered the French philosopher little in the way of intellectual stimulation. Moreover, the winter proved unbearable, a time — he complained — when even "men's thoughts freeze." On February 1, 1650, only four months after his arrival in Sweden, Descartes caught a chill that turned into pneumonia — or so it was said at the time; 10 days later he was dead.

As a Catholic in Protestant Sweden, Descartes was buried in a cemetery normally reserved for unbaptized children. On the tombstone the French ambassador had carved an enigmatic inscription: "He atoned for the attacks of his rivals with the innocence of his life."

Who were the rivals? Certainly other courtiers had reason to envy the prominence bestowed on the French visitor; he was clearly the first among the scholars and artists Christina had attracted to Stockholm. But was there also a religious motive for wanting Descartes out of the way? Secretly, the Protestant queen had been leaning toward Catholicism and is supposed to have written to the pope and subsequently have received two secret emissaries from Rome. Could Descartes have influenced the queen in her spiritual quest? If so, there would have been many in Stockholm who feared his power over the impressionable young ruler and who would have had strong reasons to wish him removed.

Death from Arsenic Poisoning?

As announced at the time, Descartes died of pneumonia early in 1650. The disease starts with a chill and shivering fits, high fever, and piercing chest pains; typical subsequent symptoms include coughing, breathlessness, and a rust-colored expectoration. In contrast, the contemporary letter of court physician Johann van Wullen to a Dutch colleague gives a totally different picture of the philosopher's condition: "During the first two days, he was in a deep sleep. He took nothing, no food or drink nor any medication. The third and fourth day, he was sleepless and very agitated, also without nourishment or medication. On the fifth day, I was called to his bedside but Descartes did not want to be treated by me. Since the unmistakable signs of approaching death were obvious, I gladly kept my hands from the dying patient. When the fifth and the sixth day had passed, he complained of dizziness and of having an internal fever. On the eighth day, hiccups and black vomit. Further on, unsteady breathing, the eyes wandering, all of it harbingers of death. On the ninth day, everything was amiss. On the tenth, early in the morning, he returned his soul to God."

This description of the progress of Descartes' final illness, in fact, matches the symptoms of acute arsenic poisoning much better than those of pneumonia. If van Wullen's letter is to be trusted, Descartes may have been murdered.

Symptoms of Descartes' Illness	Acute Arsenic Poisoning
First/Second Day: 48 hours deep sleep without food or drink	Fainting spells Lack of appetite
Third/Fourth Day: Insomnia and strong agitation; no nourishment	Restlessness Considerable nausea
After the Fifth/Sixth Day: Dizziness Internal fever	Circulatory collapse Shivering fit
Eighth Day: Hiccup Black vomiting Unsteady breathing Eyes wandering	Hiccup Vomiting black blood Irregular breathing Strong vertigo
Ninth Day: Agony	
Tenth Day: Death	

A Queen Departs

The rumors of foul play in the death of Descartes were short-lived; there was more important news in Sweden that year. Christina was squabbling with her parliament and resisting pressure from her advisers to marry and produce an heir. Instead she had her cousin Charles declared the heir apparent. To her innermost circle of advisers, she revealed her restlessness on the throne and began hinting of a renunciation of her crown. Four years later — at the age of 28 — she scandalized Europe by abdicating, converting to Catholicism, and leaving Sweden for Italy.

Scholars have never adequately explained Christina's bizarre decision. Some say that Protestant orthodoxy was too harsh and rigid for the intellectually curious young queen. Perhaps she was drawn to the rarefied view of religion held by Descartes — though there is no evidence that he personally had anything to do with her conversion. Other writers point out that a person as interested in the arts as Christina would more likely find happiness in the congenial setting of Italy. Although she twice returned to Sweden to visit properties granted for her support, she was ever after viewed with suspicion by her countrymen. In Italy, there was talk of making her queen of Naples or putting her on the throne of Poland, but nothing came of such schemes. Instead, she established her own court in exile at Rome, where she died 35 years later — taking the secret of her strange life to the grave.

The Wandering Remains

Belatedly, France reclaimed its illustrious son. In 1666 Descartes' bones were exhumed, placed in a copper coffin, and transported to Paris for reburial in the church of Ste. Geneviève-du-Mont. Disinterred again during the French Revolution at the end of the next century, the remains were to be placed in the Panthéon, the imposing basilica dedicated to the nation's notable thinkers and writers. Instead, in 1819, Descartes' coffin was taken to St.-Germain-des-Prés. Before being placed in its final resting place, the coffin was opened and a macabre discovery made: Descartes' skull was missing.

Sometime later the skull turned up at an estate auction in Sweden; apparently, the head had been severed at the time the remains were first disturbed, for on the skull was found an inscription: "Skull of Descartes, taken into possession and carefully kept by Israel Hanstrom in the year 1666, at the occasion of the corpse's transportation to France, and henceforth hidden in Sweden." Whoever Hanstrom was, he clearly believed that the philosopher belonged at least in part to the country of his death. But the skull too was returned to France and since 1878 has been registered in the inventory of anatomical specimens at the Musée de l'Homme in Paris. Unfortunately, head and body remain separated to this day by the river Seine.

A Medical Report — 330 Years Later

In 1980 the German publicist and scientist Eike Pies was sifting through the correspondence of his 17th-century ancestor Willem Piso in the archives of the University of Leiden in Holland. Suddenly, he came upon an eyewitness account of Descartes' death, 330 years earlier. It was in a letter written by Queen Christina's physician, Johann van Wullen, to Piso, a renowned doctor of the day.

Through sheer coincidence, the German scientist Eike Pies came across evidence of poisoning in the death of Descartes; the philosopher's skull may contain proof.

Victim of a Macabre Science

Shortly after Joseph Haydn was buried, his corpse was violated by followers of an obscure and dubious science. Skull and bones would be separated for 145 years.

What have Descartes and Austrian composer Joseph Haydn in common? A missing head.

The beloved musician — the first great master of the symphony and quartet, referred to by Mozart as "Papa Haydn" — died on May 31, 1809, at the age of 77. Eleven years later, Haydn's coffin was to be removed from its first resting place in Vienna to Eisenstadt, a town some 25 miles to the southeast that had been his home for 30 years. But before this was done, the coffin was opened to reveal to horrified onlookers that under the composer's white wig was — nothing.

A criminal investigation led to the dubious Viennese phrenology circle, disciples of one Franz Joseph Gall. They subscribed to his theory that spiritual and mental faculties could be inferred from a study of the size and shape of the brain and skull. In 1802 the so-called "Gall system" had been forbidden by imperial decree. The ban, however, failed to discourage the adherents to the bizarre pseudoscience, and rumors abounded of graves plundered for heads.

Although two of the phrenologists admitted to having had Haydn's head temporarily in their possession, Austrian police were unable to locate the composer's missing skull. It had vanished.

In 1895, Haydn's skull — having passed through several way stations — appeared among the possessions of a professor of anatomy. Upon his death, his sons gave the relic to the Society of the Friends of Music. Another 59 years passed before the strange wanderings came to an end, and the skull and bones of Haydn were reunited.

"As you know, several months ago Descartes came to Sweden to pay his respects to Her Serene Highness the Queen," van Wullen wrote to Piso. "Just now, at the fourth hour before dawn, this man has breathed his last. . . . The Queen wanted to see this letter before I send it. She wanted to know what I had written to my friends about Descartes' death. She strictly ordered me not to let it fall into the hands of strangers." His curiosity aroused, the 20th-century descendant read on. What followed was a detailed description of Descartes' final illness. But why, Eike Pies asked himself, did the Swedish court physician find it necessary to write his colleague in Holland about the course of such a common illness as pneumonia? And why did the queen herself impose censorship on the news of her renowned guest's death?

Wishing another opinion, Pies translated the letter, leaving out names, places, and dates, and gave it to a criminal pathologist. The verdict: the symptoms described in van Wullen's letter are those of acute arsenic poisoning. Through injury to the intestinal tract, arsenic poisoning causes considerable nausea and stomach pains. The mucous membranes swell, blood vessels burst, and blood mixing with gastric acid forms a black mass that is excreted through the intestines or vomit. These symptoms are not those generally associated with pneumonia.

How does one go about solving a three-century-old crime? There is little chance of finding the culprit and no question of a trial. Yet, evidence could be gathered, for arsenic is deposited in the bones, nails, and hair of a victim and can be traced long after death. Should Descartes' remains once more be exhumed? Many would protest yet another disturbance in the remote chance of discovering that a murder took place so long ago. As for finding a culprit — if indeed there were foul play in the philosopher's death — the chances would seem to be nil.

Yet Descartes was the first champion of scientific investigation. Applying the four rules he set forth in *Discourse on Method*, one could say the following: 1) his death from pneumonia is not clearly known to be fact; 2) the problem could be divided into at least four parts — was he poisoned, how, by whom, for what motives? 3) the simplest problem to solve is the cause of death, and this could be tackled before the more difficult, if not insolvable, problems; 4) a review of conclusions to make sure no errors were committed might add a fascinating footnote to history and a more interesting conclusion to the biography of one of its most profound thinkers.

Emperor in Exile

*Once Europe's most powerful leader, Napoleon ended his days
in exile on a South Atlantic island. He died in 1821, convinced
that his British captors were killing him. In 1978 came a sensational
new charge: murder by one of his French companions.*

"*I* die prematurely, murdered by the English oligarchy and its hired assassin." Three weeks before his death on May 5, 1821, Napoleon Bonaparte added these words to his last will and testament. Sitting up in bed with a piece of cardboard for a desk, the desperately ill former French emperor painstakingly copied in his own hand the words previously dictated to an aide, making sure that his normally illegible handwriting could be read. The words were meant as a reproach to the nation that had sent him into exile to the island of Saint Helena in the South Atlantic and an accusation against the island's governor, Hudson Lowe.

On the afternoon following the ex-emperor's death, seven British doctors gathered at the exile's residence as his personal physician, Francesco Antommarchi, performed a two-hour autopsy. Six of the British doctors were from the military establishment and thus subject to Governor Lowe. Although Napoleon's will was unknown to them, they were well aware that his death might have international ramifications. Unable to agree on the findings of the autopsy, the doctors submitted four separate reports. Dr. Antommarchi's conclusion that death was due to a cancerous ulcer of the stomach is the one generally accepted. When news of the death reached Europe, there was a collective sigh of relief that the man who had dominated the continent for a quarter century was gone. Napoleon's accusation, later divulged, was disregarded as the vengeful paranoia of a dying man.

A Sensational Accusation

In the years following Napoleon's death, innumerable books about him were published, including the memoirs of several persons who had joined him in exile on Saint Helena. The last book to document the emperor's final years was the autobiography of his devoted valet, Louis Marchand, written for his daughter "to show you — and later your children — what the Emperor was for me" and published by a grandson in 1955. The book was eagerly read by Sven Forshufvud, a Swedish dentist, toxicologist (specialist in the study of poisons), and admiring student of Napoleon's career.

Many historians had questioned the official version of the emperor's death, but none could provide sufficient evidence to mount a challenge. Marchand's memoirs, Dr. Forshufvud came to believe, contained information that proved Napoleon had been poisoned. His investigations took him across Europe, to North America, and to Saint Helena and led to a sensational charge published in 1978, 157 years after the exile's death. Napoleon, he claimed, was the victim of arsenic poisoning. The murderer? Not Hudson Lowe, the English governor so despised by Napoleon, but rather someone from within his own entourage, a French companion in exile.

Deadly Boredom

After conquering most of Europe, Napoleon unwisely invaded Russia in June 1812 and was forced to retreat ignominiously with a loss of half a million men. An alliance of his enemies turned on France and forced the emperor's abdication in April 1814. A year later Napoleon left his exile on the Mediterranean island of Elba, but his attempt to regain power ended with a final, crushing defeat at Waterloo on June 18, 1815, and a second abdication.

Hoping to find asylum in England, Napoleon surrendered to his most persistent foes, the British. Instead, he was put aboard a warship for the long voyage to Saint Helena — a "death sentence," the furious ex-emperor called it.

The remains of an extinct volcano, Saint Helena is a 47-square-mile island 15 degrees south of the equator and 1,200 miles from the west coast

Napoleon, the heroic conqueror of Egypt surrounded by adoring soldiers, is depicted above in battle at the Pyramids in July 1798. In exile on Saint Helena (right), the lonely and despondent ex-emperor was constantly guarded by British soldiers.

of Africa. It had been discovered by the Portuguese but granted to the British East India Company as a water-supply stop for vessels en route to and from India. The population of 4,000 included a garrison of 1,000; the force sent to guard Napoleon would triple the number of troops on the island. Seeing the island for the first time on October 15, a British doctor aboard Napoleon's ship described it as "the ugliest and most dismal rock conceivable . . . rising like an enormous black wart from the face of the deep."

Napoleon had been allowed to take a small group of friends and servants into exile with him, including Henri-Gratien Bertrand, the former grand marshal of his palace, and Count Charles-Tristan de Montholon, a member of the prerevolutionary aristocracy. Bertrand had served at Napoleon's side since 1798, but Montholon was a more recent adherent — a man who had rushed to offer his services to the restored monarchy after Napoleon's first abdication but who had switched sides again when the emperor returned from Elba. He brought with him his attractive young wife, whose attentions to Napoleon and postmidnight visits to his room soon became the subject of island gossip.

The entourage lived in the garden house of a local merchant until a 23-room yellow stucco villa called Longwood House could be made ready.

In the savage cartoon at left, the exiled French emperor — in exaggerated imperial garb — rules a kingdom of rats on Saint Helena; one of his "subjects" drills troops under the French flag.

The brooding Napoleon (right) met his nemesis at his final place of exile: Saint Helena's governor and his jailor, Hudson Lowe (left). The ex-emperor died convinced that Lowe was poisoning him.

Napoleon's Nemesis

Major General Sir Hudson Lowe arrived at Saint Helena on April 14, 1816. As the new governor, he was, in effect, Napoleon's jailor. Known for his indecision and frequent changes of mind, Lowe was characterized by his former commander as "wanting in education and judgment . . . stupid . . . suspicious and jealous." Napoleon took an instant disliking to him, saying that Lowe had "a most villainous face."

For his part, Lowe seemed terrified that his famous prisoner would escape. He imposed severe limitations on Napoleon's freedom of movement, screened all visitors, censored mail and newspapers, and began cutting down on the expenses allocated for maintaining Longwood House. At a stormy interview on August 18, Napoleon told Lowe that his job was that of an executioner. "I have to obey my orders," the governor said. "So, if you were ordered to assassinate me, you would obey?" Napoleon asked. "No, the English are not assassins," Lowe replied and angrily rode away. The two never met again, all further communications between captive and keeper being made through intermediaries.

The faithful Bertrand took up Napoleon's case against the governor. "Do you or do you not wish to kill the Emperor?" he wrote. "If you persist in

Situated on an upland plateau some miles away from Saint Helena's port, Longwood was an inhospitable, dreary place, its walls covered with green mold and infested with rats. The daily routine offered little variety, with Napoleon spending most of his days dictating his memoirs or retracing his military exploits on maps and globes placed in the former billiard room. After dinner the exiles played cards and chess or listened to the ex-emperor read aloud until he would abruptly announce that it was time to go to bed. One of the attendants characterized the week as boredom from Monday through Saturday and "great boredom" on Sunday.

your conduct, you will have answered in the affirmative; and, unhappily, the object will probably be obtained after some months' agony.'' Bertrand was referring to the restrictions placed on Napoleon's movement about the island, but the exile had a more serious charge to make.

Napoleon became convinced that he was to die a slow death from skillfully administered poison. He registered his complaints with Dr. Barry O'Meara, the Irish physician who had attended him since leaving Britain. Gout prevented him from getting exercise; he was constantly cold, but sunlight gave him headaches; his gums were sore and bled at the slightest touch.

Lowe apparently succeeded in deceiving emissaries from the European powers about the deteriorating state of the ex-emperor's health. Learning that the doctor was sending secret messages to Britain, the governor had him dismissed in July 1818. Back home, Dr. O'Meara reported that Governor Lowe had spoken to him of ''the benefit which would result to Europe from the death of Napoleon.''

The Final Illness

On August 15, 1819, Napoleon turned 50, but there was no celebration at Longwood House. His entourage was shrinking and among the defectors was Count Montholon's wife, who left for Europe with her three children — the youngest of whom, a daughter named Napoléone, had been born on the island and was rumored to be the ex-emperor's child. The exile had grown fat and flabby and was depressed. He expected to die soon, he told his valet Marchand.

A year after Dr. O'Meara's departure, Napoleon had a new private physician. Francesco Antommarchi, a young Corsican doctor, arrived on September 19 with two priests and a cook sent from Rome by the ex-emperor's uncle, Cardinal Fesch. Napoleon told Dr. Antommarchi that his father had died of cancer and asked if it was hereditary. Trying to allay his patient's fears, the doctor prescribed gardening as exercise and for a time the exile appeared to be in improved health.

On July 19, 1820, Dr. Antommarchi noted in his diary that Napoleon was experiencing ''shivering, fever, pain in the head, nausea, dry and frequent coughing, and vomiting of a bilious quality.'' These symptoms marked the onset of the illness that ended in death 10 months later. His deteriorating condition was recorded in the memoirs of Marchand, so avidly studied by Sven Forshufvud after publication in 1955.

Adding Marchand's eyewitness account to earlier testimony, the Swedish dentist was able to

New Royalty for Europe

Napoleon was born into a Corsican family of Italian origin. As he rose from military cadet to emperor of France, he began making his large family into a new dynasty to rule the countries he conquered. His older brother, Joseph, was named king of Naples, then king of Spain. Two of his younger brothers, Louis and Jerome, were placed on the thrones of Holland and the German kingdom of Westphalia. His sisters were married to princes. None of their reigns outlasted Napoleon's fall from power, but one of Napoleon's generals had better luck.

Jean Baptiste Bernadotte was born of landed gentry in southwestern France. His father, like Napoleon's, was a lawyer; but, like Napoleon, Bernadotte sought a military career and rose from the ranks to become a marshal of France in 1804. The next year Na-

King Charles XVI Gustavus, his wife, a German commoner he met at the 1972 Olympic Games in Munich, and their three children in 1987.

poleon named Bernadotte prince of Ponte Corvo.

The two were far from close, and Bernadotte is said to have opposed Napoleon's seizure of power. But in 1798 he had married Napoleon's former fiancée, Désirée Clary, the sister of Joseph Bonaparte's wife, and this connection may actually have spared him punishment.

In 1810 the Swedish parliament, perhaps hoping to curry favor with Napoleon, chose Bernadotte as heir apparent to the childless King Charles XIII. Although Bernadotte did not immediately succeed to the throne, he directed Sweden's affairs from the start. He united Norway with Sweden and initiated the withdrawal of his new country from the affairs of Europe, a policy of neutrality that persists to this day. Three years after Napoleon went into exile on Saint Helena, Bernadotte was crowned King Charles XIV John of Sweden. His direct descendant, Charles XVI Gustavus, currently occupies the throne of Sweden.

In a gesture of reconciliation King Louis Philippe allowed Napoleon's body to be brought back from Saint Helena in 1840; en route to the burial site at the Hotel des Invalides, the cortege passes through the monument to his battles, the impressive Arc de Triomphe, in Paris.

track the course of Napoleon's final illness in minute detail. In so doing, he came upon some startling new evidence that supported his charge of arsenic poisoning. Between March and May 1820 Napoleon was given a tartar emetic that would have weakened his stomach; orgeat, a drink flavored with bitter almonds; and a strong dosage of calomel, a drug that reacts fatally with bitter almonds. This was a prelude to administering arsenic, Dr. Forshufvud claimed, "the classic method of poisoning . . . the killing of the weakened victim that leaves no trace of arsenic."

The Enemy Within

Among his final wishes, Napoleon had asked that his heart be removed from his body before burial on Saint Helena and sent to his wife, Marie-Louise, and that locks of his hair be bestowed on various favorites. Governor Lowe denied the first request, but snippets of the ex-emperor's hair were handed down as souvenirs in several families, including that of Louis Marchand. From Marchand's relic Dr. Forshufvud obtained hair that, subjected to testing in 1960, revealed the presence of "relatively large amounts of arsenic" in Napoleon's body prior to death.

It took Dr. Forshufvud another 14 years to identify the assassin. The murderer, he claimed, was Count Montholon, acting on behalf of the Bourbon monarchy. At Longwood House, Napoleon was invariably served a South African wine imported in casks and bottled at Saint Helena; only he drank this wine. As wine steward, Montholon kept the ex-emperor's private supply under lock and offered a half bottle at each meal. On the two occasions that the wine was given to another by mistake, both parties became ill.

In 1840, with the Bourbons gone, France sent a delegation to Saint Helena to exhume Napoleon's body for return to Europe and ceremonious reburial in Paris. Most of the surviving members of his entourage in exile were at graveside when the coffin was opened. Count Montholon was not among them

The count had squandered his legacy from Napoleon and had been received in secret by King Charles X of France. By 1840, however, he had enlisted in the service of Louis Napoleon, a nephew of the former emperor's who was later to rule France as Napoleon III. If Montholon had been on Saint Helena to see Napoleon's coffin opened, he would have been startled. Although the clothing was in tatters, the body was well preserved. Would the count have known that arsenic prevents decay, especially of a body exposed to chronic doses of the poison?

The Unwanted Consort

Theirs had been a love match, the vivacious young queen and her tall, handsome stepcousin. Within months of the marriage, Mary, Queen of Scots, was thoroughly disillusioned. Was she guilty of her husband's murder two years later?

Merriment marked the last Sunday before the beginning of Lent at the court of Scotland in Edinburgh. In the morning the queen's favorite valet was married, and she joined the wedding dinner at noon. Later, after a second dinner for the ambassador of Savoy, the queen and her entourage spent a pleasant evening at Kirk o'Field, the house where her husband, King Henry, was recuperating from smallpox. As the queen chatted quietly with her consort, courtiers still in carnival costume played dice; a guitarist provided background music. Around 11 o'clock the queen, reminded that she was due back at Holyrood Castle for the valet's wedding entertainment, mounted a horse for the ride of less than a mile. Startled at the sight of a page in soiled garb, she said, "Jesu, how begrimed are you!"

At two in the morning an explosion with the force of 30 to 40 cannon shots awakened most of the city, including the queen. Kirk o'Field was reduced to a pile of rubble. In a nearby garden bodies of the king, clad only in a nightgown, and a servant were found; both had been strangled. The obvious murder on February 10, 1567, in which the queen was to be implicated even if only indirectly, was the beginning of the rapid, tragic downfall of the legendarily beautiful and romantic Mary, Queen of Scots.

Six days after her birth on December 8, 1542, Mary had inherited the throne of Scotland upon the death of her father,

King James V. Sent by her mother to be raised at the court of France, Mary was married at age 15 to the crown prince and became queen of France the next year when her husband succeeded to the throne as Francis II. It is unlikely that the marriage to the sickly adolescent, two years her junior, was ever consummated; and, after Francis died in 1560, the 18-year-old widow returned to Scotland. There she had to reconcile her strong Catholic beliefs with the Protestant faith of her subjects; curry favor with Queen Elizabeth I of England; and find a suitable consort so that an heir to the Scottish throne could be provided. The first task forced her to walk a political tightrope. The second proved to be a lifelong challenge, for Elizabeth knew that Mary, as a granddaughter of her father's sister, also had a claim to the English throne. As for the third, it was solved with the appearance at court in the spring of 1565 of her handsome young stepcousin, Henry Stewart, Lord Darnley.

Not yet 19, Darnley was four years younger than Mary and of a slender, delicate physique. But, important to the unusually tall queen, he was some three or four inches taller than she. As Mary confided to a courtier, Darnley was "the properest and best proportioned man" that she had ever seen. The two made a handsome couple. When Darnley contracted measles, Mary scandalized the court by spending so much time in his sickroom,

Mary, Queen of Scots, did not know that Darnley's handsome appearance concealed a weak character.

often lingering until past midnight. Ignoring her advisers, the queen married Darnley in July. As a widow, she wore black.

The new King Henry soon revealed his true colors. Vain, greedy, untrustworthy, Darnley made a spectacle of himself by excessive drinking and humiliated the queen — soon pregnant — by clandestine liaisons with court ladies and open womanizing with lower types. By autumn, Mary had fallen out of love just as quickly as she had fallen in.

First Victim: David Riccio

Behind her back, Darnley was conspiring with Protestant nobles to be named co-regent. The conspirators were not yet bold enough to strike directly at the queen. Instead, they chose as their first victim Mary's private secretary and court musician, an ill-favored, middle-aged Italian named David Riccio. Rumored to be both a secret envoy of the pope and, improbably, Mary's lover, Riccio proved to be an easy target.

By late winter of 1566 advancing pregnancy and ill health confined Mary to her apartments at Holyrood Castle. On a Saturday evening, March 9, Mary was entertaining several courtiers, including Riccio, at an intimate dinner party when Darnley suddenly burst in, accompanied by an armed nobleman, Lord Ruthven. When the queen protested this invasion, Ruthven pulled a dagger — apparently a signal for other conspirators to rush in. To the horror of Mary and her attendants, Riccio was dragged from the chambers and stabbed to death.

Mary was convinced that she was the target of the assassins and knew that she needed Darnley's help to escape her protective custody at Holyrood. Somehow, during the course of the next two days, she won over her weak-willed consort, and on Monday night the two left the castle through back passages and servants' quarters for a five-hour horseback ride to Dunbar Castle. A week later she returned to Edinburgh at the head of an 8,000-man army; at her side, more sulky retainer than royal consort, rode Darnley.

Desired Heir; Unnecessary Spouse

On June 19, 1566, after protracted labor, Mary gave birth to a son, the future James VI of Scotland and, as successor to the childless Queen Elizabeth, James I of England. One of her first public acts was to present the infant to Darnley at a ceremony in which she proclaimed that "this is your son and no other man's son." Thereafter, she had little or nothing to do with her husband.

By early 1567 it was known that Darnley was seriously ill, officially suffering from smallpox

The Casket Letters

The so-called Casket Letters played an important role in the controversy over whether Mary, Queen of Scots, had an affair with the earl of Bothwell before Darnley's death — and whether she was an accomplice in her husband's murder or the innocent victim of vicious rumors. The evidence is contained in eight letters and twelve sonnets allegedly written between January and April 1567, a month before and two months after the assassination of the king. The documents were found in a silver box, or casket, being carried by one of Bothwell's servants from Edinburgh to his master at Dunbar Castle. They served not only to discredit Mary in the eyes of her Scottish subjects but also to arouse the suspicions of Queen Elizabeth I of England.

The silver casket contained only copies in another hand; the original documents were never found. Thus the most obvious means of establishing their authenticity — by a comparison of handwriting — is impossible. Moreover, the content and style of the letters raise serious doubts as to Mary's authorship. None of the letters bears a date or a signature, and the letters lack either a reasonable beginning or a meaningful conclusion. Yet the queen was known to take great care with her correspondence, always putting her characteristic signature, "Marie," at the end. The sonnets bear no resemblance to surviving examples of Mary's poems. History's verdict: The Casket Letters are forgeries. The identity of the forger, however, remains a mystery.

but widely believed to be dying of syphilis. At the end of January the queen brought him back to the capital and installed him in a comfortable if modest house, Kirk o' Field, a short distance from Holyrood. It was there that he met his death early in the morning of February 10.

Gunpowder Plot and New Consort

The servant Mary saw when leaving Kirk o' Field on the fatal Sunday evening, it later transpired, had been engaged in the dirty task of moving gunpowder into the rooms immediately below those of Darnley. His employer was the earl of Bothwell, one of the lords who had rallied to the queen after the murder of David Riccio.

Bothwell was charged with plotting to blow up Kirk o' Field; when the king escaped the explosion, it was said, his confederates had strangled both Darnley and his servant. But in a seven-hour trial on April 12, Bothwell was acquitted. A week later a group of churchmen and nobles signed a manifesto asking that Mary take Bothwell as her new husband. When the queen refused his impetuous proposal, Bothwell seized Mary and took her as a virtual prisoner to Dunbar Castle.

After Bothwell's wife was conveniently granted a divorce by a Protestant court and the marriage annulled by a Catholic archbishop, Mary was wed to her abductor on May 15. The sordid marriage to the suspected assassin of her husband was too much for Scotland. Within a month Mary was the prisoner of rebels, and Bothwell had fled. The queen, accustomed to receiving the adulation of her subjects, now heard soldiers shouting, "Burn her, burn the whore."

Although Mary avoided death at this time, her fate was sealed. She was forced to abdicate in favor of her year-old son and was imprisoned at a castle on an island in Lochleven. Her half-brother, the natural son of James V, was named regent. The next year Mary escaped but an uprising in her favor quickly collapsed. Rashly she sought refuge in England, putting herself at the mercy of Queen Elizabeth. But Mary, instead of being a guest, became Elizabeth's prisoner.

Mary lived another 19 years in captivity. On February 8, 1587, at the order of Queen Elizabeth, Mary was executed at Fotheringhay Castle in England. It took two blows of the executioner's axe to sever her head, and witnesses swore that her lips continued moving in prayer for 15 minutes after her death. She was 44 years old.

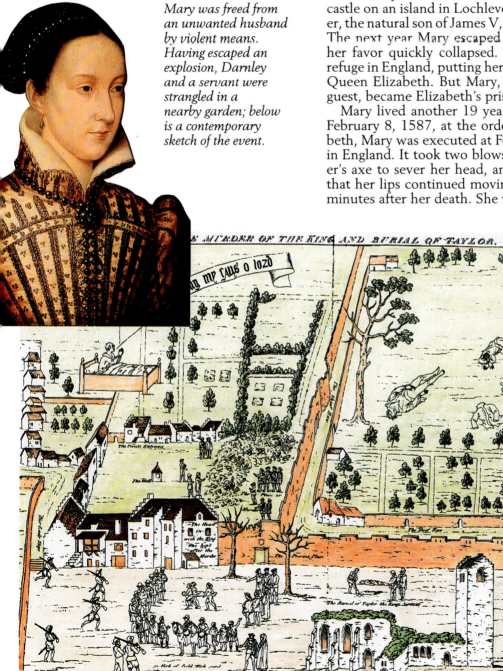

Mary was freed from an unwanted husband by violent means. Having escaped an explosion, Darnley and a servant were strangled in a nearby garden; below is a contemporary sketch of the event.

A torchlit funeral procession takes the body of Archduke Rudolf from Mayerling, the hunting lodge near Vienna where he met death in January 1889.

Tragedy at Mayerling

The heir to the throne of the Austro-Hungarian empire left Vienna for the privacy of the imperial hunting lodge, Mayerling. An unannounced guest was the 17-year-old Baroness Marie Vetsera. Were their deaths that night the result of a suicide pact?

"You must not admit anyone to my room, not even the emperor himself," Archduke Rudolf told his valet, Johann Loschek, before retiring to his bedroom shortly before 2 A.M. on Wednesday morning, January 30, 1889. The servant assumed that the heir apparent to the throne of the Austro-Hungarian empire merely wanted an undisturbed night with his voluptuous new mistress, the 17-year-old Baroness Marie Vetsera. The two had arrived at Mayerling, the imperial hunting lodge 18 miles south of Vienna, on Monday afternoon. The crown prince, traveling without guards and presumably alone, had ostensibly come for some recreational shooting with his friend Count Hoyos and his brother-in-law, the prince of Coburg. Marie, secretly spirited out of the capital and her presence at the lodge kept from the other guests, had been brought there for a romantic interlude.

At 6:30 A.M. Loschek was startled awake by his

master, who asked to be called for breakfast within an hour before withdrawing again to his private bedroom. After repeated knocks on the door between 7:30 and 8 failed to get a response, the valet grew alarmed and summoned Count Hoyos and the prince of Coburg. When they ordered him to break down the door, Loschek blurted out the secret: Archduke Rudolf was not alone in the room; Marie Vetsera was with him.

Taking an axe to the door, the valet hacked open a hole through which they could peer at the horrifying sight. Lying fully dressed on the bed, both the archduke and Marie were dead. The young woman held a single rose; her lover sat half upright but slumped toward a night table on which a mirror stood. After putting a bullet through Marie's head, Rudolf had used the mirror to take aim at himself. Their mingled blood on the sheets was only partly dried.

Count Hoyos raced by carriage to the nearest train station, flagged an express, and arrived at the palace in Vienna about 10:15 A.M. Lacking the nerve to approach Emperor Francis Joseph with the true story, the count told Empress Elizabeth that Marie had poisoned herself and the heir apparent. Relayed to the emperor, this was the first false story in an unsuccessful attempt to keep the awful truth from the public and spare the monarchy a dreadful scandal.

On Thursday, January 31, a banner newspaper headline on a black-bordered front page soberly announced that the 30-year-old crown prince was dead. The cause of death was first said to be a stroke, then a heart attack, finally an accidental gunshot wound. Not until the following day was it revealed that Rudolf had committed suicide; nothing was said about Marie Vetsera.

A Revolutionary Crown Prince

As the only son of Francis Joseph, Rudolf had been educated from boyhood to inherit the vast, polyglot empire that sprawled across central Europe. In addition to being emperor of Austria and king of Hungary, his father, Francis Joseph, ruled much of what is now Czechoslovakia and Yugoslavia; the crafty old emperor well knew that only a strong army could sustain what was known as the Dual Monarchy. And thus Rudolf — a sensitive, intelligent, and quick-witted young man — was subjected to the rigors of military life at an early age; he had to be trained for the day that he would command the imperial army.

A free-spirited woman who escaped court routine by traveling incognito throughout Europe with but a single lady-in-waiting, Empress Elizabeth intervened. She hired a tutor named Joseph

Latour von Thurnburg for her son. This man of liberal, humanitarian views made certain that Rudolf learned more of life than barracks routine and military maneuvers and introduced his young pupil to other visionary scholars. Rudolf came to see that he was living in changing times and caught an unpleasant whiff of the musty, decaying odor of his father's improbable domain.

"The empire is but a powerful ruin, at present still standing but eventually condemned to collapse," the crown prince wrote in an academic paper at age 15. "Although the monarchy has lasted for hundreds of years, as long as the people blindly accepted its authority, its function has now ended. All mankind is destined to be free, and during the next storm this ship is fated to sink." This was revolutionary doctrine coming from one so close to the throne — and when he heard of his son's views, Francis Joseph took steps to exclude Rudolf from the affairs of state.

A New Vision for Europe

Undeterred by his father's disapproval, Rudolf bombarded the emperor with memos in which he contrasted the authoritarian Hapsburg family rule with the yearnings for democracy surging across Europe. Francis Joseph simply refused to read the memos, but he found it more difficult to ignore the anonymous articles his son was contributing to *Neues Wiener Tagblatt* [*New Vienna Daily*], a radical newspaper founded by the crown prince's friend Moritz Szeps. The identity of the writer was soon known not only in Vienna but in Berlin, where German Chancellor Bismarck ordered secret agents to keep a watch on the potentially troublesome heir to the Austro-Hungarian throne.

Along with many Austrians and Hungarians, Rudolf viewed with alarm his country's close links to a Germany newly united under the Prussian house of Hohenzollern. Instead, he suggested, the Dual Monarchy should placate its Slavic subjects by reaching out to Russia, Germany's enemy. For a time, he consoled himself with a vision of a Europe united in tolerance and cooperation. This would come to pass when he and two other liberal-minded heirs apparent ascended their thrones: Prince Frederick in Germany and Edward, Prince of Wales, in Britain. It was not to be. Frederick succumbed to cancer within a year of being crowned, and his bombastic son, William II, scarcely shared Rudolf's hope for a peaceful and united Europe. Edward would have to wait until 1901 for the death of his mother, Queen Victoria.

After years of being the people's favorite, Rudolf by 1888 found himself more and more isolated as a popular clamor arose for Austria-Hungary's unification with the German reich. An ugly anti-Semitism surfaced as opponents were labeled not only traitors but captives of the Jewish money interests. "We believe, after all, in a great, beautiful future," Rudolf had once said to Moritz Szeps. No longer able to cherish the notion, the crown prince acknowledged his defeat in politics and—in what proved to be the last year of his life—surrendered to debauchery.

A Morbid Desire

The handsome crown prince had never lacked for female companionship—before and after his marriage in 1881 at age 23 to Princess Stephanie, a daughter of the king of Belgium. The sober, rather unattractive 16-year-old that his father had picked for him was far from Rudolf's taste in women. Their only child, a daughter barred from succession, was born two years later. Stephanie, apparently having contracted syphilis from her husband, was unable to bear other children, and the two were soon living in separate quarters at the palace—only maintaining the semblance of a marriage as court etiquette required. Losing himself in drink, drugs, and women of the demi-

monde, the crown prince soon conceived a morbid death wish.

Among the young women who captured Rudolf's fancy was Mitzi Caspar, who was registered in the heir apparent's retinue as "household assistant"; she was, according to Rudolf's sister-in-law, "a sweet girl," seemingly devoted to the crown prince. But when Rudolf suggested that she enter a suicide pact with him, Mitzi had first laughed at what she thought was a joke, then refused when she saw that he was serious. The disturbed heir apparent found a more gullible accomplice in October 1888.

Baroness Marie Vetsera—or Mary, as she preferred to be called—was a dark-haired beauty of Greek and Czech-Austrian descent, with soulful eyes beneath heavy eyelids and a small but sensuous mouth. "A lithe, well-developed figure," said Countess Wallersee-Larisch, her friend and sponsor at court, made her seem older than 17; she had a "graceful, irresistibly seductive" walk. It was rather widely known that she had already had several lovers.

The baroness was introduced to Rudolf at the races on October 7 by England's Prince of Wales, whose acquaintances with pretty young women were legion. A week later, as directed by Countess

The handsome crown prince appears at left in uniform; he became infatuated with the seductive Baroness Marie Vetsera (right). Above, the two riding in an open coach.

Queen Victoria, Europe's Grandmother

In sharp contrast to Francis Joseph's long reign was that of his contemporary, Queen Victoria of Great Britain. Her monarchy is considered a model of political success and domestic bliss. Only 18 at her accession to the throne, Victoria ruled for nearly 64 years — from June 20, 1837, until her death on January 22, 1901. Although her power was largely symbolic, she presided over Britain's unprecedented rise to world leadership in the 19th century. In 1876 she was also crowned empress of India, a title signifying Britain's vast colonial holdings; in Victoria's time, it was said, the sun never set on the British empire.

Three years after becoming queen, Victoria married her first cousin, Albert of Saxe-Coburg-Gotha. Theirs was a true love match, Victoria writing that she

The devotion of Queen Victoria to her husband, Prince Albert, is clear in this photograph of 1861, the year of his death from typhoid fever at age 42.

felt "paralyzed" when her husband was away. She bore him nine children and was devastated when he died in 1861 in the 22nd year of their marriage. Before his death, Prince Albert saw their eldest daughter, Victoria, married to Prussian Crown Prince Frederick, thus instituting the marital politics that would make his widow "Europe's grandmother."

The younger Victoria reigned but briefly as empress of Germany, but her son, William II, was the German kaiser of World War I. Through the marriages of her other children, Queen Victoria became grandmother to Russia's last czarina, Alexandra, and to the wives of the kings of Norway, Romania, Sweden, and Spain. Her eldest son and successor, Edward VII, is the great-grandfather of Britain's Queen Elizabeth II.

Wallersee-Larisch, she placed herself in a theater box near Rudolf's at a gala opening night. By the end of the month, the two had their first tryst. As Rudolf's driver skillfully opened doors to both the imperial carriage and that of the countess, which had pulled up alongside, Marie slipped from one vehicle to the other without being seen by passersby. As Rudolf's discreet driver closed his ears and looked the other way, the blissful couple had their first moments together.

Before long the countess was accompanying Marie to the crown prince's private apartment, both ladies swathing their faces in feather boas so as not to be recognized. Kept waiting in Rudolf's study one day, Marie found herself staring at a revolver placed next to a skull on his desk. She had picked up the skull for closer inspection when the crown prince entered the room. Seeing the concern in his eyes, she told him that she wasn't afraid of death. In mid-November, he gave her an iron ring engraved with the letters ILVBIDT; they stood, he told her, for the phrase "*In Liebe Vereint Bis In Den Tod*" ("By love united unto death"). She wore the ring on a chain around her neck but concealed beneath the bodice of her dresses.

To her former governess Marie wrote, "If I could give my life to make him happy, I would gladly do it, because I do not value my own life."

In fact, she added, they had made a pact. "After a few happy hours at a place nobody knows, we will enter death together."

Treason in the Imperial Family?

The affair between the crown prince and the alluring baroness was not consummated, if one can believe what Marie wrote to her governess, until January 13, 1889. The enraptured young lady promptly ordered a gold cigarette case for Rudolf, inscribed with the momentous date and the phrase, "in gratitude to destiny."

A round of court activities kept Rudolf busy for much of the final two weeks of the month. But no matter how late the party, on most mornings he was up early to go hunting in the country. He also found time to edit the second volume of an illustrated history of the Dual Monarchy and to correspond with Hungarian friends who were challenging Austria's dominance of the empire. There had once been talk of Rudolf's becoming king of a separate Hungary, and the emperor kept a close watch on his son's possibly treasonous political activities. On January 26 the two had a stormy meeting.

The argument may have started with Francis Joseph's reproach to his son for his increasingly notorious lifestyle. Or perhaps the emperor was only inquiring about the shattered marriage with Stephanie; he had learned of his son's overtures to the Vatican concerning an annulment. Could he really be thinking of remarriage to such an adventuress as Marie Vetsera? Inevitably, the talk would have turned to politics and Rudolf's dangerous flirting with Hungarian separatists. Seeing Rudolf later in the day, one of Stephanie's ladies-in-waiting described the crown prince as looking "terribly distraught, totally wasted"; the hand in which he held a general's hat was visibly trembling. A servant told her of the audience with Francis Joseph, a meeting that had ended when the infuriated emperor shouted, "You are not worthy of becoming my successor."

The Fateful Tryst at Mayerling

Somehow, Rudolf got through the weekend, with a Saturday dinner at the palace in honor of the German emperor's birthday and a Sunday reception marking the anniversary at the German embassy. In a tense, awkward moment at the latter affair, Marie Vetsera was presented to Crown Princess Stephanie — and paused just long enough before curtsying to silence the chatter of apprehensive onlookers. After the reception, Rudolf called upon Mitzi Caspar and stayed with her until 3 A.M. Monday morning. That very day, he told her, he was going on another hunt, the final one. As they parted, he made the sign of the cross on her forehead.

Late on Monday morning, January 28, two carriages left Vienna by the same route but at an interval of half an hour. In the first was Marie Vetsera; in the second, Rudolf, discreetly followed by a secret police detachment. As the crown prince's carriage slowed upon entering a thicket of woods, Rudolf deftly jumped down and disappeared into the trees. When his coach turned and headed back for Vienna, the police followed. Rudolf made his way through the woods to an inn that was closed for the winter, where Marie Vetsera's carriage was waiting for him. Laughing at the easy deception, the couple drove on to Mayerling, which they reached just before the early twilight.

On Tuesday morning the crown prince's hunting guests arrived but were not told of the baroness's presence. Rudolf, feigning a cold, excused himself from hunting that day and in the afternoon sent a wire to Stephanie. Explaining that his indisposition would prevent him from attending a palace dinner that evening, he asked her to beg the emperor's pardon "most obediently." He would stay at Mayerling another day.

The crown prince appeared to enjoy dinner with his hunting friends, who retired to another part of the compound about 9 P.M. Shortly thereafter, Marie Vetsera appeared, looking a bit disheveled in the same dress she had worn for the ride out from Vienna the previous day and impatiently asking for her own dinner. A servant was summoned to sing and whistle popular tunes for them, and they lingered in apparent happiness until the wee hours of Wednesday morning — at which time Rudolf gave his instructions not to be disturbed and retired to his private chambers with the young baroness.

The Reason Why

The crown prince left several farewell letters — to his mother, to his wife, to Mitzi Caspar, to his valet Loschek. In none of them did he give a reason for the suicide pact. "Now you are free from my presence and torture," he wrote Stephanie. "I face death calmly, as it is the only way I can save my good name." He thanked Loschek for his many years of service and asked that a priest be summoned. "I have no right to go on living," he wrote to Empress Elizabeth, apparently after shooting Marie Vetsera but before turning the gun on himself; "I have killed . . . ." He asked that he be buried with his mistress in the nearby Heiligenkreuz monastery.

To Francis Joseph, Rudolf wrote nothing. Perhaps the old emperor needed no explanation. All the reasons for the tragedy had been revealed just four days earlier in the last, bitter meeting between father and son.

A Bizarre Exit

Not until Thursday morning, January 31, did the emperor learn the real cause of his son's death. Only displaying momentary shock, he made two quick, irreversible decisions. Despite any clerical objections, Rudolf was to be given a full church burial. Marie Vetsera's body was to be disposed of as quickly as possible; her name was to vanish as completely as her person.

To avoid any appearance of a death other than Rudolf's at Mayerling, no hearse was sent to the hunting lodge. Instead, two of Marie's uncles went in a carriage late that afternoon to claim the body. All caked blood washed from the face and fully dressed in hat and coat, the corpse — by now stiffened with rigor mortis — was "walked" from the lodge to the carriage and seated there between the two uncles. A broomstick up the back of her dress kept Marie Vetsera's body from toppling forward during the short ride to Heiligenkreuz monastery where she, unaccompanied by Rudolf, was to be buried.

Bewhiskered Francis Joseph and his lovely empress, Elizabeth, are seated at left in this family portrait. A shadow in the imperial household, Crown Prince Rudolf has been blanked out of the photo. Determined that his heir's death would not cause scandal, Francis Joseph ordered a secret burial for Marie; at right, the telegram announcing, "All done."

A waiting policeman later wrote of his shock: "Just as the tower clock was striking midnight, a carriage appeared — not the hearse I was expecting. As I stepped forward in the darkness to see who it might be, a mocking illusion from hell greeted me. Seated between two gentlemen in the back seat was Marie Vetsera, fully dressed and upright. But also quite dead!"

When the secret burial was complete, the officer in charge sent a cryptic telegram to Vienna: "All done." No death certificate was issued; only weeks later would an entry be made in the parish death registry. Somehow escaping the imperial censor's watchful eye, a provincial newspaper reported that Baroness Vetsera had died suddenly in Venice and been buried in a family plot in Bohemia. As long as Francis Joseph remained emperor of Austria-Hungary, however, her name would never again appear in print there.

Honored in Death

As for Rudolf, court physicians ruled that an autopsy on his body had revealed abnormal mental disturbance at time of death. Not having been lucid, he could not be held responsible for committing suicide. There could be no church objection to burial in the Hapsburg family crypt at the church of the Capuchin fathers.

Dressed in a white general's uniform, the head swathed to conceal the terrible wound, the crown prince's body was put on public display. Thousands poured through the court chapel to view the remains. Elizabeth and Stephanie took to their beds in grief, but Francis Joseph remained at his desk, personally revising all acknowledgments of condolences drafted by his secretaries and attending to every last detail of the funeral to be held on February 5.

Foreign delegates were barred from the funeral. "At this profoundly moving ceremony of mourning," they were told, the emperor wanted "none but the closest members of his family." It

Unhappy Austria

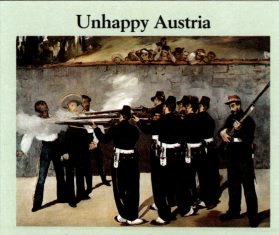

Prior to the long reign of Francis Joseph, it was said that "happy Austria" had only to marry off the sons and daughters of the ruling Hapsburg dynasty to maintain its power in Europe, while other countries had to go to war. This notion was utterly destroyed in the 19th century.

Proclaimed emperor in December 1848, the handsome 18-year-old Francis Joseph brought renewed strength to the centuries-old monarchy. His marriage six years later to his radiant young cousin, Elizabeth of Bavaria, carried the promise of a contented family life. But the hard-working autocrat was unable to contend with two overwhelming adversities: the rise of Prussia and personal tragedy.

After a humiliating defeat by the upstart north German kingdom in 1866, Austria was powerless to resist the tide of German unification under the Prussian Hohenzollerns. When the German empire was proclaimed in 1871, Austria was eclipsed.

The suicide of his only son in January 1889 was not the first nor the last painful family tragedy for Francis Joseph. During the United States' preoccupation with the Civil War, France had installed the Austrian emperor's brother, Maximilian, as a puppet ruler of Mexico. But when the French withdrew their support, Maximilian was executed by the Mexicans (above). In 1898, while on a visit to Geneva, his beloved empress, Elizabeth, was assassinated by an Italian anarchist. Rudolf's successor as heir apparent, the emperor's nephew, Francis Ferdinand, was fatally shot on June 28, 1914 — an event that precipitated World War I. Neither Francis Joseph nor his empire survived the war. On November 21, 1916, the 86-year-old emperor died, a few weeks short of the 68th anniversary of his accession to the throne. Defeated by the Allied Powers, Austria-Hungary was broken up into several independent states; Francis Joseph's successor, a grandnephew who reigned briefly as Charles I, was sent into exile.

took special tact and firmness to discourage the attendance of the German emperor, William II. "Accept our warmest thanks for your loyal friendship and also for your intention to come here," he wrote Kaiser William. "If I ask you not to do so, you may judge how deeply crushed my family is if we have to address this request even to you." The only foreign royalty invited to Vienna for the services were Stephanie's parents, the king and queen of Belgium.

The banning of foreign visitors, however, did not prevent masses of private subjects of the realm from lining the streets of Vienna on Tuesday, February 5, as the hearse carried Rudolf's body from the palace to the Capuchin church. The silence of the city was broken by the mournful toll of church bells, the clatter of hoofbeats from the military honor guards, and the creaking of wheels on Hapsburg family carriages.

According to an ancient ritual, the court chamberlain sought admission to the church by rapping on the door with a golden staff. "Who is there?" asked a friar from within. "The crown prince Rudolf," the chamberlain replied. The door remained closed, as it did when question and answer were repeated. Then, in answer to a second repetition of the question, the chamberlain responded, "Your brother Rudolf. A poor sinner." The door swung open to admit the casket and the accompanying mourners.

At the conclusion of the simple ceremony, the emperor broke tradition to kneel at his son's coffin and whisper a prayer. Rising, Francis Joseph dried his eyes with a handkerchief and made a brisk exit. There would be three months of official mourning at court — categorized in the rigid court etiquette of the day as "deepest," "deep," and "limited mourning." For Francis Joseph there was another quarter century of authoritarian rule ahead.

Anything but the Truth

As the official explanations for Rudolf's death changed — from death by stroke to heart attack to accidental gunshot wound to self-destruction under "acute mental derangement" — Francis Joseph remained adamant that the full story never be published in his empire. "Anything is better than the truth," he said.

Mayerling has long ceased to be a retreat of royalty. The imperial hunting lodge is now a Carmelite convent, and the room where Rudolf and Marie Vetsera met their deaths a century ago is the cloister's chapel. The real sequence of events that led to the tragedy there on January 30, 1889, is unlikely ever to be known.

The Kremlin, built about 1500, was once the magnificent residence of Russia's czars.

Impostor on Russia's Throne?

**In 1591 Dimitri, the 10-year-old son of Czar Ivan
the Terrible, died under mysterious circumstances.
Twelve years later a servant in Poland insisted that he was
the crown prince, a claim that threw Russia into turmoil.**

The new century got off to an inauspicious start for Russia and its insecure new ruler, Czar Boris Godunov. In 1601 exceptionally heavy rainstorms during the late spring and early summer and a devastating August frost completely destroyed the harvest. The ensuing hunger and poverty reduced the population to a state of deep misery. After two more bad harvests, there was not even seed grain left; and uprisings were suppressed with violent force.

In the midst of these catastrophic events, the czar received profoundly upsetting news. A young man in Poland was claiming to be the rightful heir to the Rus-

*The man who claimed to be Dimitri ruled
Russia for 10 months.*

sian throne; Boris Godunov was no more than a power-hungry usurper. The rumor created chaos at the Moscow court — and resurrected long forgotten suspicions.

In 1584 the feebleminded Feodor I had succeeded his father, Ivan IV — known to history as Ivan the Terrible — as czar of Russia. But real power fell to two boyars, or noblemen: his uncle, Nikita Romanov, and his brother-in-law, Boris Godunov. In 1591 Feodor's half-brother and potential heir, Dimitri, died at the age of 10, an apparent victim of foul play. When Feodor died without issue seven

In the contemporary version of the tragedy at Uglich below, the czar's widow grieves over her dead son while his assassins flee the scene. At rear, a crowd enters the palace courtyard.

To Boris Godunov (left) the czarevitch's death was most convenient, since a legitimate heir to the throne would have endangered his position as regent to Feodor I, Dimitri's dim-witted half-brother. Although an investigating commission ruled the death an accident, rumors that Dimitri had been killed on Godunov's orders would not die.

years later, in 1598, Boris Godunov was elected to fill the vacant Russian throne. But had Dimitri really been killed?

A Slap Reveals a Secret

Sometime after 1600 — the dates and details of the story are vague and even contradictory — a youth in his late teens entered the service of a Polish nobleman named Adam Wisniowiecki as a valet and groom for his horses. The young man, according to this version of the tale, soon made himself an indispensable member of the household staff. In the fall of 1603, however, a dispute between the nobleman and his servant led to an extraordinary revelation. During their argument, Wisniowiecki slapped the young man in the face,

whereupon he cried out in great excitement: "If you knew, Prince Adam, who serves you, you would not treat me like this. I am the czarevitch [crown prince] Dimitri, son of Czar Ivan."

When asked about the reported death of Dimitri in 1591, the servant declared that Boris Godunov had plotted to kill the czarevitch and thus rid himself of the only legitimate candidate for the throne he coveted. However, the boy and his mother, Czar Ivan's widow, were forewarned and able to evade the assassination attempt. After substituting another boy for her son, the mother placed Dimitri in the care of a physician who took him from one hiding place to another in monasteries across Russia during the course of the next few years. When his protector died, Dimitri fled to Poland. There he had worked as a private tutor for a Polish nobleman before entering the service of Wisniowiecki. A baptismal cross studded with precious stones, which the young man produced from among his possessions, seemed to confirm the astonishing story.

The news that the czarevitch was alive and, after a silence of 12 years, laying claim to the Russian throne, spread rapidly. Numerous witnesses came forward to testify that the youthful servant was, in fact, the czarevitch long thought dead.

Whatever belief could be given to these statements, the valet's age and looks supported his claim. According to contemporary descriptions, the young man who claimed to be Dimitri was of small stature, had reddish blond hair, pale blue eyes, and a broad face with high cheekbones. Some of the people who could still remember Ivan the Terrible thought that they saw in the youth a resemblance to the late czar. Others said that the youth's prominent facial moles, birthmark on his right hand, and arms of uneven length were all known to be physical attributes of the czarevitch Dimitri.

The sudden appearance of a claimant to the Russian throne suited Wisniowiecki and other members of the Polish nobility admirably, since they were embittered by Boris Godunov's policies and longed for an opportunity to avenge themselves on the hated ruler in Moscow. Wisniowiecki assured his servant that he would support his claim to be Dimitri—whether out of conviction that the youth was telling the truth or out of political calculation remains unknown.

An Assassination?

Was this Dimitri a cunning impostor, or did he speak the truth? The answer to the riddle had to be sought in Uglich, a town on the Volga River some 120 miles north of Moscow, once the center of its own principality and still boasting its own castle. It was to Uglich that, after the death of Ivan the Terrible in 1584, the all-powerful Boris Godunov had banished the czar's widow, Maria Nagaia, and her young son, Dimitri.

Seven years later, toward noon on a Sunday, May 15, 1591, bells usually rung as a storm warning started tolling in Uglich. Alarmed, the people ran to the castle and found in the courtyard a horrifying scene: the little czarevitch lying on the ground, presumably dead of a knife wound. Nearby, his despairing mother and her brothers were loudly accusing the son of Michael Bitiagovski, one of Godunov's financial civil servants, of having committed the gruesome crime. The crowd was so incensed that its members threw themselves on young Bitiagovski and beat him to death on the spot.

Four days after the dreadful events, an investigating commission, appointed by Godunov and headed by the boyar Basil Shuiski, arrived. After interrogating numerous witnesses, the commission issued a report two weeks later. The investigators concluded that the czarevitch had somehow inflicted the fatal wound upon himself during an epileptic seizure. Dimitri's death had been God's will; the vengeful mob had shed innocent blood, and its members had to be punished. Meanwhile, Maria Nagaia had revoked her accusations and was begging for mercy. The czar's widow was placed in a distant nunnery, but her brothers were either killed or banished along

with thousands of their supporters from among the townspeople. Anyone caught libeling the czar by implicating him in Dimitri's death had his tongue cut out. Uglich became a ghost town.

The evidence that the czarevitch was dead seemed to be overwhelming. Indeed, there were no doubts on this point at the time. Yet, certain details of the tragedy did not make sense. For instance, neither the czar's widow nor her brothers were ever questioned about the accident—either before or after the accusations of foul play were withdrawn. More strangely, the boy's body was left untended for four days after the presumed death—or until the time the investigating commission arrived. When the body was hastily buried by order of the commissioners, no one was asked to confirm that it was that of Dimitri.

A Runaway Monk

The news from Poland of a living Dimitri was more dangerous to Boris Godunov than renewed rumors that he had given orders to have the little czarevitch murdered in 1591. In order to counter the rapidly spreading belief in the servant's tale, the czar made it known throughout his empire that the alleged heir to the throne was actually one Grigori Otrepiev, a monk who had run away from the Tchudov monastery.

Godunov's story was greeted with skepticism. The claimant Dimitri played the part of a legitimate successor to the throne far better than could be expected of a simple monk. He spoke Polish and Russian with equal fluency, understood some Italian, and wrote well—signs of a good education. Furthermore, he was particularly well versed in the history of Russia and its important families. A monk could have been taught all of these things, of course, but this Dimitri also excelled at diversions of the nobility, being a remarkable horseman and a skilled hunter. Where could a monk have acquired those abilities?

At the Turning Point

Despite his attempt to fight rumor with rumor, Boris Godunov could not halt the erosion of his support. Moscow's old, powerful aristocratic families eagerly embraced the renewed doubts about Godunov's legitimacy. In their eyes he was still only a minor nobleman of Mongolian descent. A czar who had had himself elected to the throne, as he had done, was no rightful czar according to their standards.

Still in Poland, the would-be Dimitri was advancing his cause. In March 1604 he was presented to King Sigismund III at his court in Krakow. After some hesitation, the cautious ruler recognized the former servant as the czarevitch and granted him an annual pension — without, however, promising any direct assistance toward gaining the throne of Russia.

Sending appeals in every direction, Dimitri soon had gathered a small army with which he planned a march on Moscow to claim his crown. And, before leaving Poland, he forged an important alliance by promising to marry Marina, the beautiful daughter of an influential Polish nobleman named George Mniszech.

The Pretender's Triumph

Marching into Russia late in the summer of 1604, the pretender threw the country into a turmoil that would later be known as the Time of Troubles. En route to Moscow, Dimitri's band was joined by deserters from Godunov's waning cause. In their initial clash Dimitri's troops defeated Godunov's army, despite being outnumbered three to one. Many of the czar's soldiers fought only half-heartedly, secretly fearing to challenge the man who might be the next occupant of the throne. Although the czarist army was able to win the second battle, fate came to Dimitri's aid. On April 13, 1605, Boris Godunov died suddenly from the consequences of a hemorrhage brought on, it was said, by poison — per-

Members of the Russian court nobility were known as boyars. When Feodor I died without an heir in 1598, the boyar Boris Godunov succeeded in having himself elected czar of Russia.

haps self-administered. Some among his enemies would later say that the burden of guilt for the murder of Dimitri so many years earlier brought on his death.

Godunov's son, with his mother as regent, was placed on the throne as Feodor II, but his reign was to be short-lived. In May the remaining czarist troops deserted to Dimitri, and on June 1 the citizens of Moscow stormed the Kremlin, seized Feodor II and his mother, and later executed the last of the Godunovs. Basil Shuiski, who had directed the investigation at Uglich in 1591 that certified the czarevitch's death, now said that Dimitri was alive. His earlier testimony had been a lie, he confessed, made out of fear of Godunov.

On June 20, 1605, Dimitri marched into Moscow to the cheers of an exultant crowd and immediately visited the grave of his father, Ivan IV. Weeping, he said: "Oh, beloved father! You left me in this world an orphan, but your saintly prayers helped me through all persecution and has led me to the throne." The people were deeply moved by his words. If there were any doubts about his identity, they were now to be put aside.

Legitimized by a Kiss

Dimitri appears to have set out immediately to demonstrate that he did not pretend to be a figurehead of the aristocracy. And this may have been the reason for Shuiski once more to change his story — this time reaffirming the validity of his 1591 report. Arrested and condemned to death for plotting a palace revolution, Shuiski was already bound and with his head on the axeman's block when Dimitri changed the sentence to exile. Perhaps the would-be czar wanted to prove his self-confidence by this noble deed.

And now he resolved to remove the last suspicions about his identity. Who would be more qualified to end the doubts than Ivan's widow, Maria Nagaia, confined in a convent since 1591? The meeting was carefully prepared. The czar's widow was summoned to Moscow, but before she could reach the capital an impatient Dimitri set out to meet her — accompanied by a large crowd of well-wishers and the merely curious. In one version of the story, their meeting took place in a festive roadside tent that had been erected for the reunion of mother and long lost son. Dimitri and Maria Nagaia were alone in the tent for some time, and what passed between them will never be known. But when they emerged, they embraced affectionately and kissed before everyone's eyes. The crowd burst into cheers.

On July 30, 1605, Dimitri was crowned in the Kremlin's Cathedral of the Assumption. One of

The Heavy Burden of Conscience

During his short reign (1598–1605), Czar Boris Godunov was unable to stifle the suspicion that he had ordered the murder of Dimitri, the legitimate heir to the Russian throne. And it is this rumor that haunts him through the pages of history and literature. Not long after Godunov's death, the Spanish poet Lope de Vega wrote the first dramatic treatment of the story, *El Gran Duque de Moscovia*. More than a hundred versions were to follow.

Whether Godunov was responsible for the czarevitch's death is at the center of any literary interpretation. The most famous telling of the tale undoubtedly is Aleksandr Pushkin's play *Boris Godunov*, completed in 1825. The author, considered by many to be Russia's greatest poet, presents Godunov as a noble, intelligent man who ac-

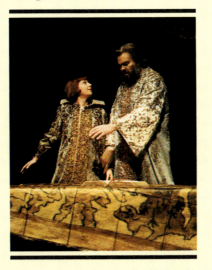

Musorgski's opera Boris Godunov, *which depicts a czar tormented by guilt, is still performed by many of the world's opera companies.*

cepts the burden of guilt for the murder of Dimitri. Yet, the crown gained by such unlawful means proves to be a heavy weight.

If Boris Godunov is today remembered in the West at all, it is through the opera composed by another Russian, Modest Musorgski, based on Pushkin's drama and first presented in 1874. Musorgski stresses the guilt theme more than does Pushkin and depicts Godunov as dying from overwhelming remorse. In the opera the vision of the murdered boy covered in blood terrifies the czar, finally driving him to madness. The czar's famous "fear monologue" in the second act is considered to be one of the most impressive arias in the opera repertoire, giving to Godunov's horror and confusion a gripping immediacy that brings the tormented ruler to life.

the new czar's first official acts was to abolish certain elaborate and highly disliked court ceremonies. In order to reinforce his popularity with his subjects, he held audiences twice a week for anyone who wanted to come and patiently listened to all complaints of injustice and petitions for redress of grievances.

Marriage and Downfall

To consolidate his rule, Dimitri had to establish the succession to the throne. In so doing, he committed a grave error. Dimitri insisted on marrying the Polish princess Marina Mniszech despite the fact that Russia's Orthodox Christians took exception to her Catholicism and were offended at the thought of a foreigner as czarina.

It cannot be said when and why Dimitri's initial popularity ended. The populace registered strong disapproval of the dissolute life of the czar and the numerous foreigners, mainly Poles, at the Moscow court. And now it became apparent that the aristocracy had needed Dimitri only to get rid of Boris Godunov.

The czar failed to heed warnings from his confidants and never seemed to realize that his clemency toward Shuiski left the conspiracy of the boyars with a potential leader. In the early hours of May 17, 1606, the czar was awakened by tolling

church bells, but it was already too late for him. Conspirators had entered the palace and easily overcome its guards. Trying to save his life, Dimitri jumped from a window but succeeded only in breaking his leg. He was trying to negotiate with the conspirators when one of them dispatched him with a bullet.

The body was publicly exhibited, then cut into pieces and burned. There was a belief that a sorcerer such as Dimitri seemed to be could rise from the dead. Therefore, his ashes were mixed with cannon shot and fired westward — toward Poland. Dimitri had ruled Russia for less than 10 months. Whether he was impostor, runaway monk, or legitimate successor to the throne will never be known.

His death, however, did not bring an end to the Time of Troubles. During the course of the next seven years, three more Dimitris appeared to claim the throne, but all met fates similar to his. Shuiski had himself proclaimed czar but was deposed and sent off to exile in Poland. Both Poland and Sweden sent armies to interfere in Russia's affairs. Finally, in 1613, Michael Romanov was elected to the czar's throne by a national assembly — thus founding a dynasty that was to rule Russia for 300 years, or until the revolution of 1917 that brought the Soviets to power.

Suicide or Murder?

Shots are fired at night in a lonely cabin in the Tennessee wilderness. The next morning Meriwether Lewis is found dying. Did the famed explorer and territorial governor, who was known to be depressed, kill himself? Or was it murder?

When Meriwether Lewis died at the age of 35 on October 11, 1809, America lost a national hero. Only three years earlier he and William Clark had returned from their epochal overland journey to the Pacific Ocean — the first expedition to cross North America and one that helped set a continental destiny for the United States. In 1807 Lewis's patron President Thomas Jefferson had named the young officer governor of the Louisiana Territory, those lands recently purchased from France lying north and west of the present state of that name.

Accusations, Then Confusion

In the summer of 1809 a new administration in Washington began questioning some of the governor's expenditures; and on September 4 Lewis left St. Louis for the capital to defend himself against the charges of impropriety. Accompanied by his servant, John Pernier, the governor boarded a boat for the voyage down the Mississippi River to New Orleans, where he planned to take an oceangoing vessel bound for the east coast. But at Chickasaw Bluffs he changed his mind and decided to strike out overland.

Captain Gilbert Russell, commander of Fort Pickering at Chickasaw Bluffs, later testified that the riverboat crew told him that Lewis had twice tried to kill himself and had been put ashore in a state of mental confusion, perhaps brought on by excessive alcohol consumption. Russell persuaded the governor to remain at the fort for a few days to recover. On September 16, the day after his arrival, Lewis wrote a letter to President James Madison. Although containing a number of erasures, the letter was certainly not the incoherent babbling of a deranged person. Rather, Lewis explained that he was exhausted from the heat and fearful that papers he was carrying might fall into the hands of the British if he continued his journey by sea. Satisfied that his official conduct would receive the president's "approbation and sanction," Lewis promised to lose no time in reaching Washington. Not until September 29 did Lewis and his servant, joined by Major James Neelly and Neelly's slave, set out on the overland journey. Neelly, an agent for the Chickasaw Indians through whose territory they would be passing, also later claimed that the governor at times appeared deranged. Crossing the Tennessee River, the party joined the Natchez Trace, the principal road north to Nashville.

Death on the Natchez Trace

During the night of October 9 two horses ran away. Neelly stayed behind to search for them the next day as Lewis, Pernier, and the slave proceeded along the wilderness trail to find lodgings. Toward sunset Lewis came upon a clearing in which stood two log cabins placed at right angles to one another and joined by a 15-foot breezeway. The lone woman there, Mrs. Robert Grinder, explained that her husband was away harvesting at their farm some 20 miles distant, but that she could accommodate the party. The governor would sleep in the main house, she would move to the kitchen cottage, Pernier and the slave would bed down in the stable. Before dinner Lewis paced up and down, muttering about the injustice of his treatment from Washington. But

The air rifle (opposite), which belonged to Meriwether Lewis (below), was considered a magic weapon by Indians because it could be fired in rapid succession without gunpowder.

Today restored steamships like the one above carry sightseers along the Mississippi River that was Meriwether Lewis's highway to New Orleans and the sea. But at Chickasaw Bluffs (today's Memphis) he made a fateful decision to travel overland.

the meal seemed to calm him, and afterwards he sat quietly smoking his pipe before retiring. Mrs. Grinder later gave three different versions of what happened that night.

When Neelly reached the scene, Mrs. Grinder told him that she had been awakened about three o'clock on the morning of October 11 by pistol shots coming from the main house. Although she heard Lewis crying for help, the terrified woman did nothing until daybreak. Then, fetching Pernier, she entered the main house to find Lewis lying terribly wounded on the bed. "I have done the business," he gasped to Pernier. "My good servant, give me some water." Shortly after sunrise he died.

Barely six months later she described the events somewhat differently, now saying that Lewis had asked his servant to put him out of his misery. And 30 years later Mrs. Grinder revealed that three unknown men had appeared at her clearing on the night of the governor's death, that their arrival greatly upset her guest, and that three, not two, shots had been fired. The next morning Pernier was wearing his master's traveling suit (an added detail had Lewis buried in his servant's shabby garments), as if he knew the governor was dead. The body was found outside, not in the bed of the main house.

The Curse of a Wicked Deed

Although it was widely accepted that Lewis had committed suicide, the ensuing fate of the persons involved in the tragedy encouraged speculation that it had been murder. Six months later John Pernier was dead in Washington, an apparent suicide from an overdose of opium. In 1812 Major Neelly was removed from his post; what happened to him thereafter is unknown. Robert Grinder, a few years later, was able to pay $250 — not an inconsiderable amount in that day — for a new farm. Lewis, known to have been carrying more than $120 in cash, had been found with but 25 cents in his pockets.

Nearly 40 years were to pass before the grave of Meriwether Lewis was marked by a simple column, broken at the top to symbolize his early death. At the base was an inscription paraphrasing Jefferson's praise of the explorer: "His courage was undaunted; his firmness and perseverance yielded to nothing but impossibilities; a rigid disciplinarian yet tender as a father of those committed to his charge; honest, disinterested, liberal, with a sound understanding and a scrupulous fidelity to truth."

A Death Foretold

*By 1943 the leader of the Polish government in exile had become
a liability to the allies against Hitler's Germany. When General
Sikorski died in an airplane crash, he was officially mourned
though not really missed. Was his death really an accident?*

On May 24, 1943, General Wladyslaw Sikorski — prime minister of the Polish government in exile and commander in chief of the Free Polish Forces allied with Britain, the United States, and the Soviet Union against Hitler's Germany — left England on a flight bound for the Middle East. Two days later his office in London received several anonymous telephone calls. "General Sikorski's airplane has crashed at Gibraltar," a voice in Polish informed several staff members. "All passengers have perished." The calls were dismissed as the work of a crank; the office had already learned of Sikorski's safe arrival at Gibraltar, an intermediate stop en route to his destination, Cairo.

Six weeks later, during the return flight to London, Sikorski's aircraft again stopped at the British military bastion guarding the entry to the Mediterranean Sea. Departing on July 4, the airplane crashed into the sea shortly after takeoff. Sikorski and 15 other passengers died; only the pilot, wearing a life jacket, managed to swim clear of the sinking wreckage, though both his legs were broken.

In London the telephone calls were recollected with fear and puzzlement. How had the mysterious caller known in advance of the crash? Was the general's death a carefully planned and successfully executed assassination? And if so, who wanted him removed from the World War II political and military scene?

Polish Patriot, Troublesome Ally

Sikorski, the uncompromising defender of Polish independence, had managed to make a number of enemies even among his allies. According to Winston Churchill's British government, the Polish leader's hostility toward the Soviet Union was a threat to the alliance against Hitler. Germany, on the other hand, probably regarded him as a useful propaganda weapon, a figure likely to stir

up dissension among its opponents pressing in from both east and west. The apparent contradiction in these views of General Sikorski can be traced back to World War I.

During that protracted conflict Poland was but a pawn between czarist Russia and the Central Powers, Germany and Austria-Hungary. Both sides declared support for an independent Poland — as long as it was one that they could control. By early 1918 the Bolsheviks had seized power in Russia and made peace with the Central Powers. On November 3, a week before the collapse of the Central Powers, a Polish republic was proclaimed with General Joseph Pilsudski as provisional president. At the Versailles peace conference the next year, Lord Curzon, the British secretary of state for foreign affairs, won Allied acceptance of an eastern border for Poland — the so-called Curzon line — that left a sizable Polish population in the Soviet Union. This was not satisfactory to Pilsudski, who demanded territory in the east seized by Russia at the end of the 18th century. In 1920 Poland went to war with the Soviet Union to win back what was considered part of the Polish patrimony.

One of the heroes of that war was Wladyslaw Sikorski. Not yet 40, Sikorski commanded a Polish army corps that repulsed a Russian cavalry attack on the capital, Warsaw, and helped secure the desired lands in the east for the new republic. In 1921 he was appointed chief of staff and served as prime minister for five months in 1922–23, during which time he gained big-power acceptance for Poland's eastern border. But after holding other military posts, Sikorski had a falling out with Pilsudski in 1928 and retired to France to write and court French support for his country's fragile independence. On April 1, 1939, back in Poland, he published an article warning that Hitler was out to conquer the world. Few paid heed to his cannily accurate prediction.

Polish general Wladyslaw Sikorski perished in an airplane crash at Gibraltar (above), the British military outpost at the entrance to the Mediterranean Sea. Examination of the wreckage (right) failed to explain the cause of the disaster.

A Government in Exile

When Hitler attacked Poland on September 1 — the event that precipitated World War II — Sikorski volunteered for military service but failed to get an assignment before his country was overrun at month's end and once more partitioned between Germany and Russia. Fleeing to France via Romania, Sikorski assumed leadership of a Polish government in exile and by November was commander of the Free Polish Forces as well. Largely recruited from expatriate Polish miners in France, Sikorski's army soon added 100,000 men to the Allied forces.

After the fall of France in June 1940, Sikorski moved his headquarters to London. With British assistance he managed to take with him the Polish air corps and 34,000 Polish infantrymen. The next year he visited the still officially neutral United States to confer with President Franklin D. Roosevelt and seek both public and private support for Polish independence. In Chicago he was enthusiastically greeted by a crowd of 75,000 people of Polish descent. As a goodwill gesture, the Canadian government promised to set up units of Polish-born citizens within its army.

Alliance with an Old Enemy

On June 22, 1941, Hitler made perhaps his biggest blunder of World War II: invading the Soviet Union without warning and thus repudiating the nonaggression pact signed between the two powers two years earlier. The U.S.S.R. became an ally of Britain; Germany was now facing enemies on two fronts.

For Sikorski it was a chance to restore Polish integrity. He succeeded in getting the Soviets to renounce the partition of Poland — or so he thought. By the end of the year he learned that Russia planned to reinstate the Curzon line as Poland's eastern border and, after the defeat of Hitler, compensate a liberated Poland with territory seized from Germany to the west.

The Polish leader protested, pointing to the Atlantic Charter signed on August 14, 1941, by President Roosevelt and Prime Minister Churchill. The agreement pledged no postwar territorial changes without the approval of the people affected. Sikorski firmly believed that Britain and the United States (which was to enter the war by year's end) would surely support Polish territorial claims in the east. As an ally in the fight against Hitler, he suggested, the Soviet Union should also subscribe to the Atlantic Charter.

Churchill did not quite see it the way Sikorski did. By early 1942 Britain was barely managing to keep Germany from invading; the United States was reeling from Japan's attack; and the Soviet Union was engaging more German forces than all the other Allies combined. The important issue was the defeat of Hitler; Polish borders were incidental to the worldwide contest of arms that was far from decided.

A Forest Massacre

A crisis in relations between the Soviet Union and the Polish government in exile was reached in the spring of 1943. In April the German propaganda ministry announced the discovery of mass graves in the Katyn forest, west of Smolensk, a Russian city then occupied by Hitler's forces. The 4,000 bodies discovered in the graves proved to be the cream of Poland's prewar officer corps; the burials dated to the time before the German invasion. The perpetrators of the crime, as subsequently confirmed: the Red army.

Sikorski demanded full disclosure from the U.S.S.R. and — without first informing his allies of the action he was about to take — called upon the International Red Cross to send a commission to the Katyn forest. The Soviet Union broke off diplomatic relations with Sikorski's government. Suddenly the outspoken Polish leader was a liability to the grand alliance against Hitler.

Mourned but Not Missed

A few weeks after his blunt accusation against the Soviet Union, Sikorski left London on the trip to

Poland: Prey of the Great Powers

The partition of Poland between Germany and the Soviet Union at the outset of World War II was nothing new in that country's unhappy history.

In 1772 Frederick the Great of Prussia endorsed a Russian seizure of Polish territory in the northeast to be compensated for by allocations of lands in the south to Austria and in the northwest to his own country. Poland was thus stripped of about one-third its territory and one-half its inhabitants. Two decades later, in 1793, Russia and Prussia seized further sizable chunks of Polish land for themselves. It was too much for the Poles, who rose in revolt against their foreign oppressors in March 1794. Proclaimed leader of the uprising was Thaddeus Kosciuszko, already a hero of the American Revolution.

In 1776, at the age of 30, Kos-

In a caricature of the first partition of Poland, Joseph II of Austria, Catherine II of Russia, and Frederick the Great trace the division on a map.

ciuszko had gone to America to offer his services to George Washington and was appointed a colonel of engineers. By war's end, in 1783, he was a brigadier general. Following his return to Poland the next year, he went into rural retirement but answered the call to arms after Poland's second partition. It was an unequal struggle that Kosciuszko led against both Prussia and Russia. After several initial successes he was defeated and captured by the Russians in October 1794. In the third partition among Russia, Prussia, and Austria a year later, Poland disappeared altogether.

As for the hero of two rebellions, Kosciuszko was released by Russia in 1796 and made his way to the United States, where a grateful Congress repaid him for his wartime services with cash and a land grant in Ohio. In 1798, however, Kosciuszko returned to Europe to continue his determined but futile efforts to secure Polish independence. He died in exile in Switzerland in 1817.

Legend:
- :::::: Poland in 1939
- —— Curzon Line
- —— Poland after 1945

0   100   200km

the Middle East from which he failed to return. In Washington, President Roosevelt said that Sikorski's death in the air crash was "a severe loss to all freedom-loving people" and revealed that the Polish leader had sent him a Fourth of July greeting before his departure from Gibraltar. Rising in the House of Commons, Churchill eulogized Sikorski as "a man of remarkable preeminence, both as a statesman and as a soldier." Sikorski, according to Churchill, had lived in the conviction that all else must be subordinated to the common struggle against Hitler yet had faith that a better Europe would arise from the conflict, one in which "a great and independent Poland would play an honorable part."

The man who succeeded Sikorski, Stanislaw Mikolajczyk, was promptly informed by his allies that individual initiatives such as the call to the Red Cross would no longer be tolerated. Anthony Eden, the British secretary of state for foreign affairs, ordered the Polish government in exile to accept Soviet territorial claims and resume diplomatic relations with the U.S.S.R.

Mikolajczyk was not invited to the Teheran conference of late 1943 at which Soviet leader Joseph Stalin agreed with Churchill and Roosevelt to set up a postwar advisory commission to study European territorial questions. But in April 1945, only weeks before victory over Hitler's Germany, the Soviet Union installed a puppet Polish government in Moscow. Over the ineffectual protests of Britain and the United States, it was this government — not Mikolajczyk's — that

At the outset of World War II, Germany and the Soviet Union divided Poland between them. At war's end the U.S.S.R. claimed territory in the east, compensating Poland with land seized from Germany in the west.

In a November 1941 ceremony, King George VI and Queen Elizabeth joined General Sikorski (center) in consecrating the Polish flag that he had brought to British soil.

The Doubts Persist

Despite the report of the official investigation, doubts remain about the cause of the crash at Gibraltar on July 4, 1943, in which General Wladyslaw Sikorski perished. Not only historians have questioned the finding that no sabotage was involved.

In the mid-1960's the German dramatist Rolf Hochhuth published a play entitled *Soldiers* that touches upon the accident. (Above, a photograph of the first performance.) In examining the possibility that Sikorski's death was the result of foul play, Hochhuth makes a shocking charge: The Polish leader was killed at the command of Winston Churchill.

Hochhuth claimed that he had received proof for his thesis from a high-ranking member of the British secret service. Together with British historian David Irving, Hochhuth had searched archives and interviewed survivors of the period familiar with the events. Irving independently published his findings in a book called *Accident: The Death of General Sikorski*.

Another book dealing with the theme refutes Hochhuth and Irving, concluding that their evidence was insufficient and incorrectly researched. In *The Defamation of Winston Churchill*, Carlos Thompson upholds the pilot's explanation that a failure of the aircraft's controls caused the crash. Thompson argues that Hochhuth's thesis that the British secret service had been instructed to eliminate the Polish leader dishonors Britain's wartime leader.

assumed power in Poland at the conclusion of hostilities with Germany.

Conflicting Evidence

The British investigation of the crash at Gibraltar disclosed some peculiar facts — none, however, that could either establish or disprove the theory that General Sikorski was the victim of an assassination plot.

The pilot of the fatal aircraft was one of the British Royal Air Force's most experienced ferry pilots, a Czech named Edward Prchal. He had flown more than 4,000 hours on this particular route and had 400 hours of flying time in "Liberators," American-made bombers, one of which had been converted to a passenger plane for Sikorski's mission. As was his custom with heavily loaded aircraft, Prchal had lowered the plane immediately after takeoff that day in order to gain speed for the actual ascent. This time, Prchal told investigators who visited him in the Gibraltar hospital a few days after the crash, he initiated the descending maneuver only some 135 feet above the ground. When he tried to regain the ascent, the control stick had jammed. He was unable to prevent the plunge into the sea.

Had excess baggage come loose, blocking or jamming the aircraft's controls? Prchal had accepted an additional passenger at Gibraltar on the condition that he not bring any luggage. But crew members on flights to and from the Middle East were known to load their aircraft with smuggled goods. In the wreckage washed ashore after the crash — in addition to the usual personal luggage of travelers and bags of diplomatic mail — were new cameras, furs, a box of jewelry, cigarettes, and cases of sherry and whiskey. Such severely rationed consumer goods were in great demand on the black market in wartime Britain and most likely were contraband.

Another question raised by the inquiry: Why was Prchal wearing a life jacket that day when he normally disdained such a precaution? And who was the second person in a life jacket, observed from shore climbing onto a wing of the downed airplane before being washed away? Was it the copilot and had he and Prchal planned to jettison the aircraft? Acknowledging that the crash was due to a failure of the plane's controls, the official report categorically stated that no sabotage was involved. And there the matter rested.

Yet, had it not been for the untimely death of General Sikorski, Poland might have had a more resolute advocate at war's end. The Soviet domination of their country, which it took the Poles 44 years to overthrow, might have been avoided.

3

Strange
and Enigmatic
Characters

Lawrence of Arabia

*The selfless champion of a primitive people's drive for independence,
a stubborn opponent of big-power politics that robbed his
followers of victory — this is the public image of T. E. Lawrence, celebrated
in books and an acclaimed film. Is it the truth?*

Thousands of cheering people lined the streets of Damascus on the morning of October 1, 1918, as the rebel army marched into the liberated city. When the Ottoman troops had withdrawn the previous day, the ancient Syrian city had passed from Turkish to Arab control. The cheers were directed not only at the victorious tribesmen but also at a young Englishman who — dressed in flowing desert robes rode among them. The rebellion and its British mentor had become inseparable.

Seeking British Support

In June 1916 Hussein ibn-Ali, the sharif of Mecca, had raised the flag of revolt against the four-century-old Ottoman domination of the Arabian Peninsula. As governor of the Hejaz, the desert province bordering the Red Sea, he controlled Islam's holiest place, Mecca, which gave him spiritual leadership of the Arab peoples. Yet Hussein's rebellion soon stalled in front of Medina, where Turkish troops were assured of supplies via the railway to the north.

Before proclaiming the rebellion, Hussein had sought support from the British. He later claimed that they had promised guns, ammunition, and technical assistance in cutting the rail link. From the outset, the British intended to control the revolt and deliberately withheld supplies to make Hussein "more modest and accommodating." But when it began to appear that Hussein might be driven back to Mecca and forced to capitulate, the British realized that it was time for a firsthand report. The man they sent from Cairo was a 28-year-old intelligence officer who spoke Arabic and already had some years of experience in the Middle East: Thomas Edward Lawrence.

Education of a Warrior

The home into which T.E. Lawrence was born, on August 16, 1888, was scarcely a stereotype of Victorian England. Four years earlier, Thomas Chapman had left his wife and four young daughters in Dublin to set up house with the girls' governess, Sarah Maden. Moving about from Ireland to England, Wales, Scotland, and France, Thomas and Sarah had four sons over the next nine years (a fifth was born in 1900). Settling down in Oxford under the assumed name Lawrence, the couple at last achieved an outward respectability; their sensitive second son, Thomas Edward, however, suffered a lifelong embarrassment over his illegitimacy.

At the age of 12 or 13, young Lawrence broke a leg. Whether due to the slow-healing fracture or to an adolescent bout of mumps, the boy stopped growing when he reached a height of 5' 5½". With a disproportionately large head, he looked much shorter than that when he entered Oxford University's Jesus College in the fall of 1907. Perhaps to compensate for his small stature, Lawrence developed several affectations — among them a shrill, nervous giggle that many found annoying. In a man's world, he seemed asexual if not effeminate.

At Oxford, Lawrence was most influenced by David George Hogarth, a Middle Eastern scholar and archaeologist. Hogarth encouraged him to write his degree thesis on the Crusaders' military architecture and gave the student detailed instructions when he sailed for the Middle East in June 1909 to conduct his field research. Traveling through Syria alone and on foot, "living as an Arab with the Arabs," Lawrence fell in love with the region and its people. Back at Oxford, he took first-class honors in history and left the university in the summer of 1910.

Through Hogarth's recommendation, Lawrence received a postgraduate award to join an archaeological dig at Carchemish, an ancient ruins on the west bank of the Euphrates River. Except for summer months when heat forced a suspen-

The exploits of British Colonel T. E. Lawrence (right) during the Arab uprising of 1916–18 were the basis for David Lean's award-winning film of 1962, Lawrence of Arabia. *Above, a still photo from the motion picture faithfully recreates the Bedouin tribesmen riding to battle in the Hejaz, the Arab province bordering the Red Sea.*

sion of work, Lawrence spent most of the next four years in Syria — the happiest years of his life, he would later say. Stripped to his shorts, he quickly tanned in the blazing sun and learned how to handle the 200 workmen in his charge by chatting and joking with them in Arabic. But archaeology did not completely account for Lawrence's deep interest in the area; sometime before January 1914, he had become a spy.

Espionage in the Desert

Since the mid-19th century, the Ottoman Empire had been known as "the sick man of Europe." With Germany, France, and Russia all eager to replace the crumbling empire as the power broker of the Middle East, Britain moved to secure its own interests. Having seized Egypt in 1882, the British controlled the Suez Canal, the lifeline to their Indian empire. But they had to monitor closely any political activity east of the Gulf of Suez and across the Red Sea.

Under the respectable sponsorship of the Palestine Exploration Fund, Lawrence joined archaeologist Leonard Woolley and British army captain Stewart Newcombe in a survey of the Sinai Peninsula early in 1914. Ostensibly, they were seeking to trace the 40-year wanderings of the Israelites following the exodus from Egypt. In reality, they were looking for evidence of Turkish military activity in the border region.

World War I erupted in August 1914, and for a time it looked as if the Ottoman Empire would remain neutral. But when the Turks attacked Russia, Britain's ally, Lawrence volunteered for service in Egypt. By December he was in Cairo, helping to set up an intelligence network in the area he had come to know so well.

Arabia in Revolt

Lawrence would never be a conventional soldier. Of his first meeting with the boyish junior officer, Lawrence's commander in Cairo could later recollect only his intense desire to tell the young man to get his hair cut. Yet his military colleagues were impressed with his keen mind, infectious enthusiasm for the work, and "extraordinary capacity to get his own way quietly." But he soon grew bored with the routine of mapmaking, issuing geographical reports, and interviewing potential espionage agents.

In 1915 two of his brothers were killed fighting in France. In contrast, Lawrence wrote in February 1916, "We do nothing here except sit and think out harassing schemes of Arabian policy." The next month, however, he was sent on an extraordinary secret mission to Mesopotamia [present-day Iraq], where a British-Indian army was besieged by the Turks. He was to offer a bribe of £1 million to the Turkish commander to raise the siege and, on the sly, sound out local Arab tribes about joining a revolt against the Ottoman Empire. Both efforts failed, and Lawrence returned to Egypt, as he complained, once more to be "nailed within that office at Cairo."

When news of Hussein's revolt of June 1916 reached Cairo, Lawrence wrote home to say how good it was "to have helped a bit in making a new nation." In October he was sent to the Hejaz to meet the Arab rebels. Although capable of providing moral leadership, the dignified Hussein was clearly too old to be a military commander. His first, second, and fourth sons, Lawrence judged to be "too clean," "too clever," or "too cool." But in Hussein's third son, Faisal, Lawrence found "the man I had come to Arabia to

At the beginning of World War I, the Ottoman Empire controlled much of the Arabian Peninsula, with the central desert remaining largely uninhabited.

seek — the leader who would bring the Arab Revolt to full glory." Comrades in arms, the short, fair Englishman and the tall, dark Arab would ride to glory together during the next two years.

"Aurens": Going the Whole Way

To win the confidence of the Arabs, Lawrence took to wearing native attire and learned to endure long hours on camelback. "If you wear Arab things at all," he wrote, "go the whole way. Leave your English friends and customs on the coast, and fall back on Arab habits entirely." His adoption of an Arab lifestyle won over the normally suspicious tribesmen, who would greet his arrival in camp with repeated shouts of "Aurens! Aurens!" — the closest they could come to pronouncing a name so alien to their language.

Accompanied by Lawrence and his retinue of 25 servants and bodyguards, Faisal launched the offensive that would end in Damascus. Under Lawrence's tutelage, he developed a strategy suitable to the terrain and his men's fighting ability. Moving up the Arabian Peninsula, the rebels waged guerrilla warfare that terrified their enemy and won recruits from other tribes en route. They bypassed Turkish strongholds to strike repeatedly at the Hejaz Railway — dynamiting bridges and track, derailing trains, disabling locomotives. "This show is splendid," Lawrence wrote; "you cannot imagine greater fun for us, greater vexation and fury for the Turks."

In January 1917 the Red Sea port of Wejh was captured and, with the surrender of Aqaba in July, the campaign in the Hejaz ended in victory for the Arabs. The British commander in Cairo suddenly became aware that the Arab rebels were holding down more Turkish troops than were the British and, as Lawrence observed somewhat maliciously, "began to remember how he had always favoured the Arab revolt." Faisal's men, henceforth, would be the right flank to General Allenby's Allied armies thrusting north through Palestine.

Twice during 1917 Lawrence made dangerous secret forays behind enemy lines to rouse Arabs in Syria. At the village of Deraa, in November, he was briefly detained by the Turks, who probably did not realize his identity. What happened there is still the subject of controversy.

According to the account in his postwar memoirs *Seven Pillars of Wisdom*, Lawrence was horribly tortured and sexually abused by his captors. The lurid tale was dismissed by a prominent American historian as "most implausible"; but one of his fellow officers remembered him returning from Deraa greatly distressed and was convinced that he had experienced some "horrible nightmare." Nonetheless, within three weeks of his return from Deraa, Lawrence was recovered enough to ride with Allenby into Jerusalem on December 9, 1917.

Through 1918 the Allies continued to advance north, with Lawrence and the Arabs on their right flank. As Allenby prepared for the assault on Damascus in September, he had 250,000 men under his command. Although the Turks nominally had an equal force, Lawrence's 3,000 Arabs were pinning down 50,000 of the enemy east of the Jordan, while an additional 150,000 Turks were spread out across Mesopotamia in a vain at-

Wilhelm Wassmuss: A German Lawrence

The biographies of T. E. Lawrence and Wilhelm Wassmuss, a German liaison officer in Persia during World War I, contain surprising parallels. Although nominally neutral in the war, Persia [today's Iran] was actually divided into Russian and British spheres of influence — Russian forces occupying towns in the north; British, established on the gulf coast to the south — with a buffer zone between.

Into this potential hot spot in January 1915 stepped Wilhelm Wassmuss, former German consul at the port of Bushire. Familiar with the language and customs of the Persian tribes, Wassmuss had as his task the kindling of hatred against the British in order to provoke a rebellion. This would force the British to divert troops from other campaigns and possibly allow for a German-Turkish thrust

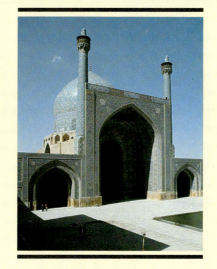

By the time of World War I, Persia had become "the apple of discord" among European powers. Only such structures as the mosque at Isfahan attested to its former glory.

toward India. Through the efforts of Wassmuss and other agents in the interior, German influence was soon predominant. But two Turkish invasions of Persia early in 1916 were stopped by the Russians, and in March the British sent Sir Percy Sykes to organize a native force to restore order in the south. Running out of funds, Wassmuss ended his mission in the fall of 1917. By that time the Turks had withdrawn from Persia, the Bolshevik revolution brought an end to Russian intervention, and Persia was in chaos. By war's end in November 1918, Britain was in control of the country. The following year it signed a treaty with Persia that assured British ascendancy.

As for Wassmuss, an impoverished, defeated man back home in Berlin, he sadly concluded that his efforts had done nothing to help the cause of Persian independence.

After their victory in the Hejaz, the Arabs assumed a more conventional military role as the right flank of the Allied armies moving north through Palestine; above, on guard in a desert trench.

tempt to check other Arab uprisings. With his five-to-one superiority, Allenby moved confidently toward victory on October 1.

Big-Power Politics

In May 1916 Britain and France had signed a secret accord — known as the Sykes-Picot Agreement, after the two negotiators — that called for a postwar division of Turkey's Middle East territories into British and French spheres of influence. Any Arab state in the region would be subject to British and French administrative control.

Two days after the triumphant entry into Damascus, Faisal learned the bitter truth about the limitations to Arab independence. Insisting that he had known nothing of the secret accord, Lawrence demanded that Allenby relieve him of his military duties and that he be permitted to return to England. "Not being a perfect fool," he was to write bitterly in *Seven Pillars of Wisdom*, "I could see that the promises to the Arabs were dead paper." He regretted having let his men risk their lives for such a meaningless reward; "instead of being proud of what we did together, I was continually and bitterly ashamed." Henceforth, Lawrence realized with a shock, his battles were to be fought in the corridors of power rather than on the sands of the desert.

Back in England and uncomfortably dressed in uniform, Lawrence appeared before a committee of Britain's war cabinet on October 29. His proposal: scrap Sykes-Picot to keep the French out of the Middle East and divide Mesopotamia and Syria into three kingdoms ruled by three of Hussein's sons, with Faisal presiding in Damascus. While he awaited a government decision, Lawrence wired Hussein, suggesting that he send Faisal as his representative to the peace conference to be held early in 1919 in Paris. But once more, Lawrence had unpleasant news for Faisal. Meeting his ship at Marseilles on November 26, he informed his wartime comrade that the French had vetoed his participation in the peace conference.

During December and January, Faisal was in Britain, where Lawrence introduced him to Chaim Weizmann, the Zionist leader to whom the British had promised a postwar Jewish homeland in Palestine. Looking upon Semitic Jews and Arabs as "an indivisible whole," Lawrence hoped for their cooperation in developing the Middle East. In return for uncontested entry to Palestine, the Jews were to lend Faisal money to establish his kingdom in Syria.

The war in the Middle East had always been secondary to the struggle with Germany on the Western Front; and Lawrence's campaign with the Arabs had been called "a sideshow to the sideshow." Nonetheless, the boyish Colonel Lawrence was, an American delegate remarked, "the most winning figure" at the peace conference that convened on January 18, 1919. With Faisal denied a seat at the conference, it became Lawrence's task to ensure that his Arab comrade remained loyal to Britain.

Escape from Fame

Lawrence's postwar career is as strange and puzzling as his legendary feats during the Arab revolt. In August 1922 the ex-colonel joined Britain's Royal Air Force under the assumed name John Ross. He humbly submitted to the tyranny of his training officers. But when the press published the story of Lawrence's self-humiliation in the ranks, he was discharged.

Unable to find employment because, as he almost cheerfully confessed, "no one will offer me a job poor enough for my acceptance," Lawrence took pleasure only in riding his motorbike about the countryside. Through the intervention of friends, he was readmitted to the armed services in March 1923, this time as a private in the tank corps and under another assumed name, T. E. Shaw. Two years later, he succeeded in transferring to the R.A.F., where he served as an airman for the remaining 10 years of his life.

On May 13, 1935, Lawrence apparently lost control of his motorbike while speeding along a narrow, curving road in the south of England and was catapulted over the handlebars. Six days later he died of head injuries. Just before the accident a black car traveling in the opposite direction passed Lawrence. At that moment two boys on bicycles appeared on a rise in front of him, and Lawrence swerved to avoid them.

To Lawrence, it was the French who were now the enemy; his own hope was "that the Arabs should be our first brown dominion, and not our last brown colony." Few shared his vision, either British or Arabs. Britain had a new interest in establishing a mandate over the Middle East: oil. And the government was not about to turn on its wartime ally, France. Reluctantly, Faisal agreed to the terms of the Sykes-Picot Agreement that postponed true Arab independence.

The Fight Ends, the Legend Grows

Defeated at the peace conference, Lawrence tried to win public support with a blizzard of newspaper articles and letters and later became Winston Churchill's adviser on Arab affairs at the Colonial Office. It was all to no avail.

Proclaimed king of Syria in March 1920, Faisal was deposed by the French in July — as the British stood by doing nothing. In 1921 the British placed Faisal on the throne of Iraq, which remained under British domination for the next decade. Meanwhile, his brother Abdullah was installed as emir of Transjordan, another British protectorate. In 1924 Hussein was forced to abdicate as ruler of the Hejaz, to be replaced by the leader of another tribe, ibn Saud.

Disgusted with politics, Lawrence meanwhile had retired to Oxford to write his revealing memoirs. Why had he done it all? The epilogue to *Seven Pillars of Wisdom* gave four motives. First and strongest was a personal one, "omitted from the body of the book, but not absent, I think, from my mind, waking or sleeping, for an hour in all those years." It was, scholarly detective work has revealed, Lawrence's love for an Arab boy named Dahoum, whom he had befriended at Carchemish in 1913; freedom for the boy's people, he wrote elsewhere, would be "an acceptable present." A few weeks before Damascus was taken, he learned that the boy had died of typhus — "so my gift was wasted," he noted in sorrow. Lawrence's second motivation was patriotism, to help Britain win the war. Third was intellectual curiosity, "the desire to feel myself the inspiration of a national movement." And fourth was personal ambition, "to sum up in my own life that new Asia which inexorable time was slowly bringing upon us."

Was Lawrence a hero? Or was he a shameless self-promoter? Was he truly dedicated to Arab nationalism? Or was he merely using gullible Arab tribesmen to help perpetuate British imperialism? Or was this a story not about dedication to a people and their cause, but rather one of obsession with an unobtainable love?

The Unholy Monk

Appearing seemingly out of nowhere, a self-proclaimed holy man achieved a strange hold on Russia's imperial couple in the years before World War I. Was his ability to heal that of a saint — or was he a fraud and an impostor?

*F*ear and anguish permeate the palace at Tsarskoye Selo, the imperial residence outside Russia's capital of St. Petersburg. Czarevitch Alexei, not quite three years old, has fallen at play and now lies in painful agony, terrible blue swellings under his pale skin marking the course of internal hemorrhages that threaten his life. The boy is a hemophiliac, suffering from a disorder inherited from his mother, Czarina Alexandra, that hinders blood clotting; even the slightest injury can bring uncontrollable bleeding.

With court doctors at a loss for a medical treatment, Alexandra and her husband, Czar Nicholas II, pray at the bedside on this July night in 1907 — and wait for a secret visitor.

Two years earlier, they had been introduced to a holy man named Grigori Efimovich by the grand duchesses Militsa and Anastasia. According to these two women, each married to a cousin of Nicholas's, Grigori possessed mysterious healing powers. At their urging, the imperial couple has summoned him to the palace, taking care that

Rasputin's path led from a Siberian village to the palace at Tsarskoye Selo.

his arrival will go unnoticed by palace guards. Toward midnight, the wild-looking man with dark gray hair and a tangled beard makes his appearance in the crown prince's nursery.

Falling to his knees, Grigori prays before a sacred icon. When he rises, he makes the sign of the cross over the czarevitch, runs his coarse hand over the boy's feverish brow, and says in a deep, melodious voice: "Now don't be afraid, Alexei, everything is all right. Tomorrow you will be well again." Then, after calming the enraptured boy with Siberian fairy tales, he leaves. "Believe in the power of my prayer," Grigori tells the anxious parents, "and your son will live." Alexei recovers, as Nicholas and Alexandra give thanks to God for sending them the holy man with such remarkable healing powers.

The Dissolute One

Virtually nothing is known about the life of Grigori Efimovich before he appeared in St. Petersburg late in 1903. He was then between the ages of 33 and 40, the son of a Siberian peasant and known in his village as Rasputin, the Russian word for dissolute. His drinking, fighting, and carousing with loose women were legendary. But at some point, he spent several months in a local monastery and, after his experience there, assumed the identity of a starets, an itinerant holy man who was supposed to live in poverty and solitude, dedicating his life to helping relieve others of pain and spiritual uncertainty.

But Rasputin's enemies would later say that he had been a member of the Khlysty, an underground sect that expressed their religious fervor at nocturnal orgies. It would certainly appear to be in keeping with the unholy monk's unique philosophy, for Grigori preached that the way to redemption was through abandonment to sin followed by repentance.

Rasputin — he did not disown the name — acquired a wife, who bore him four children. One of his sons died in infancy; the other was feebleminded and remained at home with his mother in their Siberian village. But after he gained influence at court, the self-proclaimed starets brought his two daughters to St. Petersburg to live with him and be educated there.

A Pilgrim at the Czar's Court

The unlikely starets first arrived in St. Petersburg in 1903 and presented himself as a repentant sinner to Father John of Kronstadt, the city's most revered churchman. Father John and other clergyman were impressed with Rasputin's humility, sincerity, and ability as a spellbinding preacher; they seized upon him as the instrument to reach out to Russia's illiterate peasantry. Before long, Rasputin was being accepted in court circles and, in 1905, was introduced to the czar and czarina by the two grand duchesses.

Everyone who met Rasputin remembered his eyes. Prince Yusupov, with whom Rasputin was to have a fatal rendezvous, recalled them as "glittering, phosphorescent beams of light." A young woman whom he tried to seduce recalled her horror at discovering the "mysterious, crafty, and corrupting"

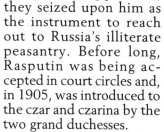

The starets' ability to heal the czarevitch (above, with his mother) has been attributed to hypnotism; at left, the unholy monk raises his hand in blessing.

man who looked out from eyes that at first had appeared to radiate only goodness and gentleness. The French ambassador to the czar's court wrote that the monk's entire personality was concentrated in his eyes: "They were pale blue, of exceptional brilliance, depth and attraction. His gaze was at once piercing and caressing, naïve and cunning, far-off and intent."

Rasputin's strange combination of raw sensuality and infectious piety won for him an adoring coterie of court ladies. After his nocturnal visit to the czarevitch's bedside, his greatest champion was Alexandra. In her eyes he could do no wrong; she would not hear of his heavy drinking and disgraceful carousing.

What pleased Alexandra also pleased her devoted, weak-willed husband. At first relying only on Rasputin's mysterious ability to heal their son, Nicholas and Alexandra were soon taking his advice on affairs of state. When it was no longer possible to contain the scandal of the starets' hold on the imperial couple, Nicholas's close relatives forced the czar to banish Rasputin from the capital. It proved to be only a temporary exile, for once more the unholy monk proved his healing powers — this time by a telegram from Siberia, reassuring the frantic parents that Alexei would recover from another attack of internal bleeding.

The Enemy of War
By the spring of 1914, the nine-year-old Alexei appeared to be in good health. In contrast, the Russian empire — so long neglected by the preoccupied czar — was tottering on the brink of war. On June 28 the assassination of the heir apparent to the Austro-Hungarian throne set off the long chain of events that led to the outbreak of World War I in August. By a curious coincidence Rasputin narrowly escaped death only a day earlier, when a crazed woman stabbed him in the stomach, crying out, "I have killed the Antichrist!" Recovering from his injury, the starets wrote in a shaky scrawl to Nicholas that war must be avoided; it would bring only "disaster, grief. . . a whole ocean of tears and so much blood." Rasputin's grim prophecy was ignored as Russia, along with most European countries, marched off to destruction.

Two years later, the war at a stalemate, there were renewed rumors about the starets and the imperial couple. The so-called man of God, it was said, had convinced Alexandra — and through her, of course, Nicholas — to make peace with Germany. A group of nobles determined to rid Russia of the unholy monk.

The Fatal Invitation
The leader of the conspiracy was 29-year-old Prince Felix Yusupov, heir to Russia's largest fortune and married to a niece of the czar's. Sharing the starets' love of carousing, he and Rasputin

Despite his indecision, blundering, inattention to official business, and preoccupation with family affairs, Russia's last czar was revered by the masses; below, soldiers kneel to Nicholas II, at center on horseback.

The Dutch Court's Own Rasputin

The joy of the Netherlands' Crown Princess Juliana and her consort, Prince Bernhard, at the birth of their fourth daughter early in 1947 quickly turned to sorrow. The infant — christened Maria Christina, but called Marijke — had been born semiblind, perhaps as a result of the German measles her mother had contracted during pregnancy. Although doctors managed to save the vision in one eye, the girl was threatened with sightlessness. As Alexandra had done four decades earlier, Juliana turned to a faith healer.

In 1948, the year Juliana succeeded to the throne, Prince Bernhard brought a 53-year-old former factory worker named Greet Hofmans to the palace to work one of the wonder cures for which she was becoming famous. When there was no improvement in Marijke's

In 1946, Greet Hofmans claimed, God offered her healing power. "Of course, I accepted," she said.

sight, the prince grew disillusioned and ordered her out of the palace. The queen ruled the country, Bernhard is supposed to have said; he ruled the home.

But Juliana had become dependent on Hofmans — even, it was said, taking her advice on affairs of state. The queen's rift with her husband and her ministers was kept secret until 1956, when a German magazine broke the story. Reluctantly, Juliana accepted the recommendation of a panel of elder statesmen and agreed to a reconciliation with Bernhard and an end to her dependency on the ineffective faith healer.

Juliana thus avoided a royal crisis and continued to be regarded with loyalty and affection by her subjects through a 31-year reign that ended with her abdication in favor of her eldest daughter, Beatrix.

had frequently met in notorious St. Petersburg night spots; on one occasion, the prince had gone to him for a cure of some illness. Late in December 1916, Yusupov invited Rasputin to a postmidnight supper at his palace.

The usually slovenly starets had washed with cheap soap and dressed himself in an embroidered silk blouse and velvet pants for the occasion. But when he arrived at the Yusupov palace, the prince took him to a basement room. Upstairs, four conspirators played a phonograph to simulate the noise of a party at which, Rasputin was told, his hostess was temporarily detained. While the two waited, Prince Felix plied the starets with cyanide-laced cakes and urged him to wash them down with wine, also poisoned. To the prince's horror and amazement, Rasputin showed no ill effects from dosages that should have been enough to kill several men.

After two and a half hours, the prince excused himself to check up on the "party" upstairs. Following a conference with the other conspirators, Yusupov returned with a concealed pistol. Directing Rasputin's gaze to a crucifix on the wall, the prince told him to say a prayer and then fired point blank into his back. As Rasputin toppled over onto a white bearskin rug, the other conspirators burst into the room. One of them, a doctor,

solemnly pronounced that their victim was dead.

As the assassins were congratulating themselves, the starets opened his eyes, jumped to his feet, and scrambled up the stairs and out into a courtyard. But before he could reach the gate, another of the plotters shot him, hitting him once more in the back and also in the head. Yusupov beat the collapsed figure with a club until there was no further sign of life. Wrapped in canvas and bound with ropes, Rasputin's body was dumped through a hole in the frozen river Neva. When the corpse was recovered from the water three days later, Rasputin's lungs were found to contain water; he had still been alive when thrown into the river.

There was rejoicing in the streets of St. Petersburg at the news of Rasputin's death. Prince Yusupov and the other conspirators were either banished, sent for military service, or acquitted. But Rasputin had the last word. In the final month of his life he had written to Alexandra, predicting that none of her family would survive his death by more than two years. In March 1917, with the war going badly for Russia, Nicholas II was forced to abdicate. Sixteen months later, Nicholas, Alexandra, Alexei, and his four sisters were reported to have been assassinated by the Bolsheviks who had seized control of Russia.

Idol of an Era

*Desperately insecure or grossly manipulative, the poet Lord
Byron shocked a nation by his scandalous affairs. But the free spirit
of his poetry and the heroics of his life inspired an entire
generation throughout Europe.*

The bright sun of July 12, 1824, washed over an eerie procession. As hushed crowds gathered to watch in sorrow, ebony-black horses dressed with somber black plumes slowly pulled a great hearse through London's major streets. Immediately behind were three carriages filled with loyal friends of the deceased. Then, one by one, clattered by the 47 coaches of England's noblest families; appropriately bizarre symbols for the funeral of a poet honored by the world but scorned in his own country, the coaches were empty. From houses along the way, respectable women dared view the odd ritual only from behind their window curtains. Even though he now lay dead in a coffin draped with black velvet, George Gordon, Lord Byron, was nonetheless still shunned by high society.

For four days the hearse, now accompanied only by undertakers, made stately progress northward to Nottingham. Respectful commoners gathered in each little town en route, undoubtedly surprised that this most popular poet of the day had been denied the honor of burial in Westminster Abbey's Poets' Corner. Instead, his body would be interred in the family vault in a humble church near his ancestral home.

*At his ancestral seat, the somber, half-ruined Newstead Abbey, the melancholy poet could
indulge his thoughts of world-weariness and fatigue with life.*

Dead at 36, Byron had been adored and despised, feared and emulated, for more than 15 years. His influence defined an age, and his ideas and personal behavior anticipated our 20th-century conceptions of national independence and individual identity.

A Mad and Mixed Ancestry

Debauchery was something of a family trait, often practiced enthusiastically at Newstead Abbey, a 3,000-acre estate and former monastery that had been seized by King Henry VIII when he overthrew the Roman Catholic Church in the 16th century. Byron's grandfather, an explorer and naval officer known as "Foul-weather Jack," was so appalled by his son John's vices — perhaps including incest — that he disinherited him. But "Mad Jack," as the son was known, eloped with a rich woman. She and two of her children died in France, but a daughter, Augusta, survived to play a flamboyant role in the poet's life leading to his exile from polite society decades later.

Ever the survivor, "Mad Jack" returned to England, where he wooed and won a wealthy but remarkably unattractive Scottish woman named Catherine Gordon. Remarriage did not end his carousing, however, and his unhappy wife suffered from wild shifts in mood. Into this strange household George Gordon, the future Lord Byron, was born on January 22, 1788.

The infant was born encased in a caul, or membranous sac, and afflicted with dysplasia, a condition in which a withered calf muscle had distorted and deformed his right foot. The caul was harmless and easily removed, but Byron later seemed to delight in regarding it as the omen of a cursed destiny. The twisted foot, however, caused him a lifelong trauma, a cruelly ironic contrast to the beautiful countenance that became his legend.

His childhood was wracked with excruciating pain, since his credulous mother paid quacks to stretch and pull his muscles. As if to compensate for his handicap, the youth would push himself to excel as a boxer, horseman, and swimmer. For everyday life, he created a kind of gliding walk to cover his limp. Either seriously, or because he characteristically engaged in self-dramatization, he spoke of having the offending foot amputated.

"Mad Jack" left home when the boy was two, so he was subject to his mother's unpredictable temper and unreasonable demands. Meanwhile, a great-uncle had inherited the peerage and Newstead Abbey. Abandoned by his wife because of his sexual escapades, the great-uncle disinherited his son for foolishly marrying for love rather than money. His own finances were so strained that he entertained himself at the crumbling abbey by holding cockroach races. Nonetheless, when he died, the property was still intact for his great-nephew to inherit; at age 10, George Gordon became the 6th Baron Byron.

Wine from a Skull

Self-important now, the youth became an arrogant, headstrong pupil at Harrow, his preparatory school, and a colorfully rebellious student at Cambridge University. He once brought a bear on campus to twit the administration for barring his pet dog. But he was already writing poetry with extraordinary facility and published his first volume of verse, *Hours of Idleness*, in 1807 while still at Cambridge. At the university, it also became obvious that he had an unusual capacity for attracting devoted friends and passionate lovers.

Like many another country gentleman of the time, Byron would spend entire days doing nothing but riding, fencing, rowing, and shooting, and long nights in revelry with college friends and his estate's band of winsome and willing servant girls. Eagerly dramatic, he passed round wine after dinner in a skull set in gold. When everyone else passed out for the night, he liked to write into the wee hours of the morning.

After being seated in the House of Lords when he turned 21, the bored young wastrel embarked on an unusually adventuresome trip to southern Europe, including stops in Portugal, Spain, Malta, Greece, and Albania. Picturing himself ro-

The eccentric Lord Byron sought adventure in travel to southern Europe and Asia Minor. During the course of his wanderings he also perfected his gifts as a poet and in Albania began writing the verse novel Childe Harold's Pilgrimage *that would make him famous overnight. Below, lines from the epic in Byron's own handwriting.*

Created on a Dare

One of history's most boring evenings gave birth to a fictional character that has inspired terror and fascination the world over. On a stormy night in 1816, a notorious band gathered at Lord Byron's Villa Diodati on Lake Geneva was reading ghost stories aloud beside the fireplace as winds howled over the waters and rain spattered against the windowpanes. Byron was host to the poet Percy Bysshe Shelley and his wife-to-be Mary Godwin, Mary's half-sister Claire Clairmont, and his personal physician and traveling companion, Dr. John Polidori.

Vexed by the bad weather and bored by this makeshift entertainment, Byron suggested that they compete to see who could write the best horror story. Sometime later the group, pondering the possibility of understanding the secret of life itself, discussed whether or not electricity could "bestow the spark of life and make one living entity from the sum of dead parts."

Long after midnight, as was their custom, the residents of the villa retired. Mary, in a state of unnatural excitement, dozed but fitfully. Halfway between sleep and waking, she had a terrifying vision: "I saw the pale adept of wretched arts kneel beside the creature he had assembled. I saw the abominable phantom of a man lying stretched out and suddenly, with the help of an enormous machine, show signs of life and move in an awkward fashion." Startled fully awake, she had found her horror story. Published two years later, Mary Shelley's *Frankenstein* has endured well into a second century and has spawned sequels and imitations in both fiction and film.

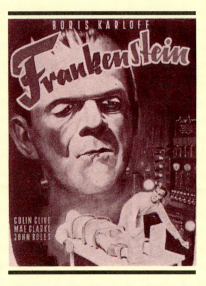

Boris Karloff starred in the first, and greatest, film Frankenstein, *creating a frightening yet pitiful monster.*

---

mantically as a "doomed youth condemned to exile," he felt immediately at home when he touched Greek soil and was soon at work on a verse tale, *Childe Harold's Pilgrimage.*

At the time, the area was ruled by a vicious tyrant, the Turk Ali Pasha, who was much taken by Byron's good looks and gave him gifts, seeking an amorous rendezvous. The young nobleman artfully declined, though he was apparently bisexual and did not necessarily scorn homoerotic experiences. Not long afterward, Byron was shipwrecked on the Albanian coast near Parga and fell in with an exotically attired band of brigands, the Suliotes, whose proud theme song was "Robbers all at Parga!" They escorted him back to Missolonghi, where fate would unite him with the band at the end of his life.

The Girl in the Sack

Gradually, Byron was becoming a convert to Philhellenism, the idea that Greece should be allowed independence from Turkish rule. The native Greeks were poverty-stricken and harshly oppressed. One Greek patriot had been tortured for three months and then cut in quarters; Byron had seen his separated arm hanging from a tree.

His deepening political concerns ran parallel to his increasing personal indulgences. Back in Athens, he became sexually involved with an untold number of women, girls, and even boys. One memorable day he encountered a group of Turks taking a squirming sack toward the Aegean Sea. Inside was a girl convicted of adultery with a Christian man. The Woiwode, or governor, of Athens had condemned her to be drowned, according to Turkish custom. The wealthy young Englishman bribed the guards, released the girl, and had her smuggled to freedom. According to a rumor that would never die, when the bag was opened, the startled Byron recognized the girl from one of his own amorous adventures.

Despite such diversions, he had finished two cantos, or sections, of his poetic novel, the *Pilgrimage.* In fleet verse using everyday language in complicated patterns of rhyme, the supposedly frivolous ne'er-do-well had created an unforgettable literary character. Harold, the model for romantic heroes to come, is passionate yet reflective, egocentrically proud yet deeply lonely, eager for adventure yet weary of the world. He is, in fact, the clone of his creator.

Famed and Fondled in London

In February 1812, back in England, the 24-year-old peer gave his maiden speech in the House of Lords, an overwrought defense of Nottingham weavers. Few noticed. Soon, however, the fledgling politician was a famous poet, quite literally overnight. The first edition of *Childe Harold's Pilgrimage* sold out within three days, and the poet was besieged with invitations to the principal houses of London.

Byron was ready to play his part to the hilt. He always dressed in black and pretended to exist on nothing but soda water and biscuits. (In fact, he would sneak off to obscure pubs to wolf down heartier fare of meat and potatoes.) He was ever ready to shock his hostesses and their guests with an improper or suggestive remark.

Soon his affairs with beautiful married women and backstairs servants were the talk of the town. But such dalliances were conveniently ignored in an upper-class world that considered adultery its favorite indoor sport. In 1813 Byron would flout even those loose standards of propriety.

Augusta, the half-sister from "Mad Jack's" first marriage, was so much like him in outward appearance and temperament that he grew to consider her as his alter ego, his mirror-image. She was restless in an unhappy marriage and drifted into an affair with Byron. When they became lovers, the poet thought that he had reached the "grand goal" of his life, a perfect union with another. Augusta gave birth to a daughter who may have been his.

Byron's openness about the affair was too explosive for even an indulgent society, and he tried escaping into a conventional marriage with the young, rich, and inexperienced Annabella Milbanke. They had a daughter, but Annabella left him after only a year of marriage, apparently angered by his mistreatment and repulsed by his sexual demands. For reasons that have never been explained, Byron and Augusta went together to a reception given by the aristocratic Lady Jersey. As one, the women disappeared from the room and the gentlemen refused to shake hands. The country's most famous poet had become a social outcast.

Escape to Europe

Once again Byron sought relief and excitement abroad, leaving on April 24, 1816, from the English Channel port of Dover, where society ladies disguised themselves as chambermaids at his hotel in order to catch a glimpse of the notorious celebrity. Scorned at home, he was lionized abroad.

He settled for a time in Venice, throwing himself with undiminished fervor into sexual liaisons of all types and indulging in other forms of debauchery. Vain, he worried increasingly about thinning hair and thickening waistline. He would binge and then diet severely, no doubt harming his health. And for the last time he fell deeply, passionately in love. Young, beautiful, and married, Countess Teresa Guiccioli was his match in melodrama, and their trysts took place from the Grand Canal to seashore retreats, in castles and rented houses in hillside towns.

During these years Byron wrote a third canto of the *Pilgrimage*, *Manfred* and other well-known poems, and the beginning of *Don Juan*, another

An intimate friendship existed between Byron and the younger poet Percy Bysshe Shelley. In the summer of 1822 Shelley encountered bad weather while sailing in Italy's Gulf of Spezia and was drowned. Although Byron was not present — as this painting would have it — when the 30-year-old poet's body was found, he did attend the cremation of Shelley's body on the beach at Viareggio a month later.

Illness of an Epoch

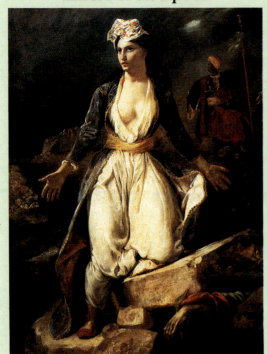

Lord Byron rose to prominence as poet and hero in an era of widespread disillusionment. At the end of the 18th century, the first stirrings of the French Revolution had aroused hope that men and women everywhere would respond to the clarion call of "liberty, equality, fraternity." Instead, the revolution turned into a manic bloodbath. Napoleon, coming to supreme power in France in a time of chaos, brought yet another promise of freedom for the oppressed. But he had himself crowned emperor and embarked on a plan of conquest that killed millions.

But if most people had lost hope in finding true liberty and full scope for self-expression, Byron's voice seemed to prove that one man, at least, was determined to live life to the fullest, even while feeling the same melancholy and world-weariness that prevailed throughout society. His hero Harold might feel despair, but he could also shout: "On with the dance! let joy be unconfined; No sleep till morn, when Youth and Pleasure meet to chase the glowing hours with flying feet." To find meaning in life by pursuing pleasure, to live only for the moment might disgust or horrify their elders; but a generation thrilled to such sensuously indulgent lines as, "Let us have wine and women, mirth and laughter, sermons and soda water the day after."

Not wholly unlike the assassination of President John F. Kennedy, few ever forgot where they were the day they heard of Byron's death.

epic that would draw heavily on his own personal feelings and experiences. Always fascinated by death, he found more cause for feeling morbid. In 1822 Allegra, his illegitimate daughter by Claire Clairmont, died of swamp fever at age five. Not long afterward he learned that his good friend and frequent companion, the poet Percy Bysshe Shelley, had drowned while sailing during a storm on the Gulf of Spezia.

The loss of his friend may have deepened Byron's disenchantment with life itself. He plunged into literary activity, fueled always with wine or watered gin. But poetry could no longer give solace to his overwhelming sense of emptiness.

Bard of Greece

In part because of Byron's stirring appeals over the years, public opinion in England and across western Europe had come round to the side of the beleaguered Greek people. Money had been raised, and when the London Greek Committee asked the literary lion to become actively involved, he responded with vigor.

On July 16, 1823, Byron set out to sea on the *Hercules*, a chartered ship outfitted with two cannons and loaded with medical supplies, weapons, and ammunition. Byron's melancholy vanished on the long voyage from Italy to Greece. Early the following year he was at Missolonghi, the marshy, mosquito-infested town where he had last seen the hardy Suliotes more than a decade earlier. He immediately hired 600 of them, but the "robbers of Parga" saw his treasure ship as prey. They schemed endlessly to get money and weapons and had to be bribed to fight their enemies, the Turks. The ship's crew mutinied, reinforcements from England were delayed, and the politics on the Greek mainland proved to be impossibly complex and unpredictable.

More than once, Byron was the commanding presence who risked his life to prevent a riot and brought peace between rivals in the rebel camp. But nature achieved what men and guns could not. Soaked one day while riding horseback in a freezing rain, Byron contracted a lingering fever. Urging the physicians not to draw pints of blood, the standard treatment of the day, he joked, "The lancet has killed more people than the lance." He was overruled, however, and his condition, not surprisingly, worsened as the so-called cure progressed. His ordeal lasted for weeks. Toward the end he whispered to his doctor, "So you actually believe that I fear for my life? Why should I deplore it? Have I not enjoyed it beyond measure?"

Lord Byron died on April 19, 1824, the anniversary of Allegra's death.

Faith in the Stars

Many would have been dismayed by the character reading Albrecht von Wallenstein received from a famous astronomer and mathematician. But the unknown young officer saw in it a prediction of military triumph and great power in the future.

The opposition of Mercury to the conjunction of the planets Saturn and Jupiter in Wallenstein's horoscope was said to be the reason for his hesitation at a critical battle.

*I*n 1608, at the age of 25, an officer in the service of the king of Bohemia had his horoscope cast by Johannes Kepler. Like most of his contemporaries, the young man believed that the position of the planets and stars at the time of birth determines a person's character and that the signs of the zodiac hold the clues to one's fate in life. Since the officer had used an intermediary to approach the famous astronomer and mathematician, Kepler did not know the identity of the person whose character he was being asked to analyze. And even if he had known, the name would have meant nothing to him. For Albrecht von Wallenstein, fame and fortune were still far in the future.

Born at 4:36 P.M. on September 24, 1583, Wallenstein was a Libra. According to Kepler's interpretation, the subject of the horoscope was "alert, lively, eager and restless, curious of every kind of novelty, unsuited to the common manner and behavior of mankind, but striving after new, untried or extraordinary ways." Saying less than he thought or perceived, the taciturn individual had a melancholy streak, or what the astrologer described as "a bent toward alchemy, magic, and enchantment, community with spirits, scorn and indifference toward human ordinances and con-

ventions and to all religions, making everything proposed by God or man to be suspected and despised." Furthermore, Kepler predicted, the subject would be "unmerciful, without brotherly or matrimonial love, caring for no one, devoted only to himself and his desires, severe upon those placed under him, parsimonious, covetous, deceitful, inequitable in his dealings, usually silent, often impetuous, also belligerent and fearless."

It was not an attractive profile. Yet Kepler offered hope to the unknown subject of his forecast: "Most of these flaws will disappear with maturity; so unusual a nature will be capable of important deeds." Because of his great ambition and thirst for power, the individual thus described would make many enemies; but in most instances he would be able to defeat them.

Young Wallenstein was deeply impressed with Kepler's horoscope and kept it with him constantly, comparing major occurrences in his life with the predictions. Born and raised a Protestant but a cynical convert to Catholicism at the age of 23, Wallenstein lacked serious religious conviction; his faith was in the stars. Throughout life he would often seek the advice of astrologers, making important decisions only after the stars had been read for him.

Making a Name for Himself

Three years after his conversion to Catholicism, Wallenstein's Jesuit confessor arranged his marriage to an elderly Czech widow with huge estates in Moravia. Her convenient death a few years later allowed the young officer not only to live comfortably but also to make himself valuable to King Ferdinand II of Bohemia. When Ferdinand appealed for help in his war against Venice in 1617, Wallenstein raised and trained a force of 260 cuirassiers and musketeers with money out of his own pocket. Leading the cuirassiers on horseback, Wallenstein pierced an enemy line encircling a fortress loyal to Ferdinand whose defenders were on the point of starvation or surrender. As the foot soldiers kept open the breach his cavalry had made, Wallenstein had the wounded and starving put in wagons for transport back to camp. The fortress was saved, and Wallenstein's military reputation was made.

The outbreak of what came to be known as the Thirty Years' War offered Wallenstein his next opportunity to achieve military glory. It started as a rebellion of Ferdinand's Protestant subjects against their Catholic ruler, dramatically demonstrated when the insurgents threw two royal governors out of the palace window at Prague on May 22, 1618. Falling 50 feet into a ditch below, the two escaped with their lives; but the challenge to Ferdinand had to be met.

This time Wallenstein financed an entire cavalry regiment in the service of the king. When the Moravian subjects of Ferdinand's cousin Holy Roman Emperor Matthias joined the rebellion, Wallenstein was named a colonel in the Austrian army and sent against the very people from whose lands he drew his fortune. He boldly seized the Moravian war treasury and turned it over to the emperor in Vienna — an act considered treasonous by the Moravians, who confiscated his property and exiled him for life from their country. It did not bother Wallenstein at all.

The 36-year-old commander was quickly learning that not only glory but wealth could be

At the Battle of Lützen in Saxony, the Swedes lost both their cavalry commander and King Gustavus II Adolphus. Failing to press his advantage, Wallenstein suffered defeat in his last major contest of arms. It was the beginning of the end for him.

The Persistent Belief in Astrology

The tradition of being guided by astrology neither began nor ended with Albrecht von Wallenstein. Despite the universal scoffing of scientists, the belief that character is determined by date of birth and that favorable and unfavorable signs can be read in a horoscope persists.

Joseph Goebbels, Hitler's propaganda minister, maintained an astrology department to aid his skillful if insidious manipulation of the media. Indian prime minister Indira Gandhi was said to have made no important decisions without consulting a personal guru. And three weeks before his fall, the shah of Iran sought advice from a Jerusalem astrologer. Having read in the stars of the imminent, unpreventable end of the shah's regime, the man declined to make the journey to Teheran. Cambo-

Upon first reading Ronald Reagan's chart, Joan Quigley said, "Wow!" To her it meant that he would accomplish great things. Above, the Reagans.

dia's president Lon Nol relied less on the advice of his generals than he did on his astrologers.

The best known recent adherent to astrology is Nancy Reagan, wife of the ex-president — thanks to the far from flattering revelations of former White House chief of staff Donald T. Regan in his 1988 memoir, *For the Record*. According to Regan, Mrs. Reagan's reliance on horoscopes, and the influence that her belief in them had on the president's schedule, "was probably the most closely guarded domestic secret of the Reagan White House." In 1981 San Francisco astrologer Joan Quigley convinced Mrs. Reagan that the assassination attempt on the president of March 30 could have been predicted. Thereafter, presidential appointments were determined by favorable horoscopes from Mrs. Quigley.

---

gained from being on the winning side of a war. Wallenstein was about to become one of the greatest wartime entrepreneurs of all time. He was not naïve enough to think that Ferdinand or Matthias would ever repay him the money he spent on raising and training troops for their cause. What he expected and got from them was more valuable: titles, land, and the prerogatives that went with them.

To the Summit

At the Battle of the White Mountain near Prague on November 8, 1620, the Protestant forces were decisively beaten. Ferdinand, who had meanwhile been elected to succeed Matthias as emperor, named Wallenstein military governor of Bohemia and partner in a syndicate authorized to issue coinage in Bohemia, Moravia, and Austria. With the new currency reduced first to 50 percent, then to a third of its former value, Wallenstein started buying up the estates of executed or banished Protestant noblemen. In rapid succession he married the daughter of the emperor's closest court adviser and was named duke of Friedland. He was the wealthiest man in the realm.

To his contemporaries Wallenstein appeared arrogant, sinister, and tyrannical — the very embodiment of Kepler's ominous horoscope. He

was notorious for the command, "Let the brute be hanged," an order given at the slightest provocation and generally carried out by fearful underlings. His hot temper was legendary. On one occasion, it was said, he ran a sword through an officer trying to deliver a message while he was engaged in conversation with his architect.

Meanwhile, the crushing of the Bohemian revolt had not ended the war, which entered a new phase in 1625 when King Christian IV of Denmark assumed leadership of the Protestant cause. Backed by the Netherlands, France, and England, Christian hoped to drive Ferdinand's Catholic league out of North Germany. The emperor knew exactly where to turn.

Wallenstein offered to raise and support an imperial army of 24,000 men; all he asked in return was power to levy taxes and collect tribute from any conquered lands. As commander in chief of the imperial forces, Wallenstein went from victory to victory in the next three years, forcing the Protestant dukes of Germany to submit to Ferdinand one by one.

Meeting a Challenge

Wallenstein's triumphs on the battlefield were not universally appreciated in the Catholic camp. Maximilian of Bavaria, for one, envied and feared the independence Ferdinand had gained by the exploits of his successful general. Soon, there would be no place left for him or other leaders of the Catholic league.

When Wallenstein learned of the dissension, he forced a showdown. If his command of the imperial forces was not renewed and he was not given a mandate to stifle opposition with an army that would be the scourge of all Europe, he would resign from Ferdinand's service. Despite the fury of Maximilian and the other Catholic leaders, he got his way and was allowed to increase the size of his army to 70,000 men. The emperor's general was also empowered to enforce an edict that returned to the Catholic Church all ecclesiastical property seized in Protestant lands and outlawed all Protestant sects except Lutheranism.

On May 22, 1629, Christian signed the Treaty of Lübeck, whereby he agreed to withdraw from German affairs in return for restoration of Danish lands conquered by Wallenstein and other Catholic generals. Among Christian's abandoned allies were the dukes of Mecklenburg, whose lands and titles were bestowed on Wallenstein. At the peak of his power, Wallenstein no longer considered himself a servant of the emperor and began pursuing an independent policy.

An Opposition Takes Shape

His campaigns in Denmark had made Wallenstein aware for the first time of the importance of sea trade and naval power, and he got himself named leader of an imperial armada operating in the North and Baltic seas. He even dreamed of establishing a postwar trading company that would rival those of England and the Netherlands. But when his siege of the Baltic port of Stralsund failed, he had to abandon that plan.

"One has to teach the German princes morals," the arrogant general had once proclaimed. "Only the emperor is to be master in this house." Wallenstein's failure at Stralsund encouraged the leaders of the Catholic league to strike out at the emperor, using Wallenstein as their ostensible target. At an electoral diet meeting in Regensburg during the summer of 1630, the princes demanded that the emperor dismiss his general. Their grievances included the size of Wallenstein's army; his practice of supporting it by confiscating provisions from the lands through which he marched, be the territories Protestant,

During the initial phases of the Thirty Years' War, Emperor Ferdinand II was triumphant — thanks to the wealth and skill of his commander in chief, Albrecht von Wallenstein (on horseback, opposite). But when the general failed in battle and entered secret negotiations with the enemy, Ferdinand had to eliminate Wallenstein. The imperial crown (right) is today only a museum display in Vienna.

Catholic, or neutral; cruel and arbitrary acts of vengeance; and the barbaric and un-Christian manner in which he enriched himself by impoverishing others.

To save his imperial seat, Ferdinand gave in to the princes on August 13. He agreed to Wallenstein's dismissal and named as his replacement 71-year-old Count von Tilly, the victor of White Mountain 10 years earlier and field commander of the Catholic league headed by the envious and restive Maximilian of Bavaria.

All that remained was the unpleasant task of bearing the news to the imperial commander in chief. Wallenstein received two messengers sent from the emperor in his splendid military tent. To their immense surprise and relief, the general did not erupt in a fit of rage. Instead, he pointed to a piece of paper on which astrological calculations had been made. The stars of Bavaria, he pointed out, were at present in ascendancy over those of Austria. Maximilian was more powerful than Ferdinand; the emperor had no alternative but to acquiesce to the demands of the Catholic league. He kept to himself any belief that, at a future point in time, Ferdinand's stars — and his own — would again be in ascent. Wallenstein

would bide his time until the inevitable recall to leadership of the imperial armies.

A Swedish March of Triumph

Even as the imperial electors were meeting at Regensburg, the Thirty Years' War was entering a third though not final phase. Landing on the Baltic coast of Pomerania, Sweden's King Gustavus II Adolphus assumed the leadership of the Protestant cause surrendered at Lübeck by Christian a year earlier. The Swedish ruler was outraged by Catholic oppression of his fellow Protestants, annoyed that his offer of mediation at Lübeck had been rejected, nervous about the emperor's maritime ambitions, and determined to restore the lands and titles of his relatives, the dukes of Mecklenburg.

Gustavus Adolphus seemed invincible as he marched south, soon forming an alliance with the elector of Saxony. At Leipzig on September 17, 1631, the Swedes and Saxons, with a combined force of 40,000, met and defeated Tilly's imperial army of about the same size. After their brilliant victory, the allies parted — the Saxons moving southeast into Bohemia; the Swedes sweeping southwestward toward the river Rhine. Panic struck Ferdinand's court in Vienna.

Once More, the Indispensable General

Embittered by his removal from command of the imperial forces, Wallenstein had plotted revenge on both Maximilian and Ferdinand. Beginning in November 1630, he entered secret negotiations with Gustavus Adolphus. As he had so often done before for the Catholic side, Wallenstein offered to recruit and train an army at his own expense — but this time to serve the Protestant cause. All he asked in return was to be named viceroy of any domains conquered from Ferdinand and to have support in his bid to become king of Bohemia. The Swedish king hesitated, understandably wary of casting his lot with a turncoat — no matter how brilliant the record of his service.

The news of Wallenstein's offer to change sides reached Ferdinand, who maintained his silence in the face of the Swedish-Saxon advance. Following the setback at Leipzig, the emperor overcame whatever reservations he may have had and recalled his former commander. Wallenstein coolly agreed to provide an army of 40,000 men within three months but only on condition that his full powers as commander in chief be restored. When Tilly was further defeated and mortally wounded in battle at the river Lech in the spring of 1632, Ferdinand had no choice but to give in to Wallenstein's exorbitant demands.

The Last Campaigns

Initially, the restored commander in chief was wildly successful, sweeping the Saxons out of Bohemia and driving the Swedes back north. By July 1632 he was confronting Gustavus Adolphus in a fortified camp at Nürnberg. For 11 weeks he declined to counterattack though easily repulsing Swedish assaults on his entrenchments. Disgusted, Gustavus Adolphus withdrew, freeing Wallenstein for a move into Saxony. His brutal occupation of Saxony had the desired result of dispiriting the Swedes' allies and driving a wedge between Ferdinand's opponents.

On November 16 Gustavus Adolphus at last had his chance to engage Wallenstein in battle, attacking a slightly smaller imperial army at Lützen. The Swedish cavalry commander and the king both fell in battle, but Wallenstein failed to press his advantage. The day ended in a rout of the Catholic army.

Had Wallenstein been defeated by the stars? As always on the eve of important battles, he had consulted an astrologer. The reading was unfavorable. And so, at this climactic moment in his military career, Wallenstein was overcome by his faith in astrology. The man whose original horoscope had bestowed upon him such decisiveness and thirst for powerful deeds had become so dependent on the reading of the stars that he had become hesitant and fearful of action.

Intrigue, Betrayal, and Downfall

With his military reputation tarnished by the defeat at Lützen, Wallenstein decided to become a peacemaker. But in order to become the arbiter between Ferdinand and Gustavus Adolphus, he had to maintain control of his sizable army and use it as a bargaining chip in any negotiations between the two sides. Setting up winter quarters in Bohemia and Moravia, Wallenstein once more relied upon the local population to support his troops' needs. This was too much for Ferdinand, who asked the general to disband his army. Wallenstein called a war council of all his generals, who supported his determination to ignore the imperial command. Ferdinand did not press the issue, though he began seeking a way to get rid of his troublesome general.

For much of the 1633 campaign season, Wallenstein remained inactive as the Swedes continued their conquests, capped by the conquest of the key fortress of Regensburg in November. Though pressed by the emperor, Wallenstein was unwilling or unable to relieve the pressure on Maximilian in Bavaria and once more went into winter quarters in Bohemia.

A Dynasty of Mercenaries

Albrecht von Wallenstein is often referred to as the last condottiere, the Italian name for a leader of professional soldiers who sold their services to various princes and city-states throughout Europe between the 14th and 16th centuries. Among the most famous of those mercenaries was Francesco Sforza.

The illegitimate son of a peasant who rose to be a soldier in the service of Pope Martin V, Sforza was already a famous warrior when he married a daughter of the duke of Milan in 1441. Nine years later he seized the duchy from his father-in-law and ruled much of northern Italy until he died peacefully in bed at the age of 65 in 1466. Sforza's talents as a statesman equaled his military skill, and he maintained the duchy's security by a clever policy of alliances with neighboring states. Under his rule Milan

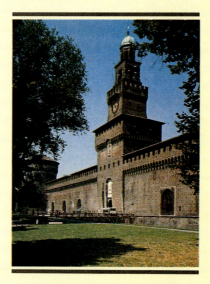

Francesco Sforza began the construction of Castello Sforza in 1450, the year he seized power in Milan. Today the fortress houses a museum.

became a prosperous center of the arts, industry, and science — a position it holds to this day.

Milan was not so lucky in Francesco's successors. His son, Galeazzo Maria, proved to be a cruel, dissolute tyrant, who was assassinated in 1476. Galeazzo Maria's unscrupulous younger brother, Lodovico, at first served as regent for his minor nephew, Giangaleazzo. But after five years he threw his nephew in prison and took over the duchy for himself. Giangaleazzo's death in prison was said to be at the order of his uncle. Lodovico ruled Milan until 1499, the year in which he was defeated and taken prisoner by the French. Apart from his military exploits and his support of a silk industry that came to employ 20,000 workers in Milan, he is best remembered for his patronage of the artist Leonardo da Vinci.

On the night of February 25, 1634, Wallenstein met his fate. Standing at a window, he cries for mercy as the assassins break into his bedroom. The astrological amulet (below) could not protect him.

Throughout the year the wily general had been secretly negotiating with the enemy, which now included France. Ruled by his faith in astrological readings more than ever, he frequently offered contradictory terms to the various parties for his support. In the end he lost credibility with both sides and came to be viewed with alarm and distrust by many of his own generals.

On January 12, 1634, Wallenstein coerced his generals into a pledge of support "so long as he remained in the emperor's service"; the document they were asked to sign, however, omitted this key phrase. When one of the generals reported the omission to Ferdinand, the emperor issued a secret decree dismissing Wallenstein and naming Matthias Gallas as his successor. Gallas was empowered to arrest and, if necessary, kill the treacherous commander in chief and any officers remaining loyal to him. In mid-February the decree was made public. Wallenstein was accused of treason, conspiracy, and barbaric behavior and was stripped of all lands and titles.

With three loyal followers, the generals Trcka, Ilow, and Kinsky, Wallenstein left his winter camp at Plzen on February 22 and made for the border — perhaps seeking to join the Swedes. Two days later they reached the fortress city Cheb, where they believed themselves to be safe.

On the evening of February 25, the town commander invited the four fugitives to a banquet in the castle. Trcka, Ilow, and Kinsky accepted, but Wallenstein remained in his quarters and thus avoided a trap. The three unarmed guests were summarily executed by command of an officer loyal to Ferdinand.

What to do about Wallenstein? It was 10 P.M. and a snowstorm had set in. After drinking up some courage, an English captain named Walter Devereux and six dragoons stormed the commander in chief's lodgings. They found Wallenstein standing by a window, perhaps peering in vain at the heavens to confirm the position of the stars. As Devereux thrust forward with his halberd, Wallenstein pleaded for mercy. It was too late. The point of the weapon passed through his chest, and he dropped dead on the spot.

"All the princes and dukes, yes, everybody, I have to turn into an enemy for the sake of the emperor," Wallenstein had remarked five years earlier. That the emperor himself would become his enemy he had not anticipated — or been able to read in the stars.

Prophet or Charlatan?

A skilled physician fascinated by the occult, Nostradamus risked the wrath of the Roman Catholic Church to predict 20 centuries of future history. Was he really a visionary, or is his legendary accuracy merely an enduring myth?

The lively little fellow with the long, thick beard cut a curious figure at the sumptuous Renaissance court of King Henry II of France. Known as the son of converted Jews, a dabbler in astrology and other questionable arts, Nostradamus had been invited to Paris in 1556 to provide exotic diversion. But his prophecies about the ruler were destined to make him internationally famous. One of them seemed straightforward but obviously preposterous, suggesting that "a one-eyed man" would soon be king. The other

was characteristically cryptic, open to interpretation: "The young lion will overcome the older one, in a field of combat in single fight. He will pierce his eyes in their golden cage; two wounds in one, then he dies a cruel death."

On July 1, 1559, as the king jousted in a knightly tournament, a freak accident sent his friendly opponent's lance through the royal gold helmet into his left eye. The horrified Comte de Montgomery was younger than his sovereign; the splintering weapon made a second gash in

"The blood of the just will be claimed from London, ravaged by fire, when three times twenty plus six is written." With these words Nostradamus is said to have predicted the fire of London in 1666.

the king's throat; and Henry would endure agonizing pain until his death 10 days later. During that period, he would become — and has remained — the only one-eyed ruler of France.

The words of Nostradamus were recalled with awe. Implacably opposed to magicians and sorcerers, leaders of the Roman Catholic Church were inclined to burn this dangerously accurate prophet at the stake. Peasants, thinking the prediction had actually been a curse, set him ablaze in effigy. Only the protection of the widowed Queen Catherine saved him from execution.

Hero of the Plague

Born Michel de Notredame on December 14, 1503, at Saint-Rémy in Provence, history's most controversial seer set out to become a physician. However, his studies were abruptly curtailed when bubonic plague swept through the south of France in 1525. As many of the area's doctors fled in panic, Michel bravely traveled about to treat the victims of the highly contagious disease. Nonetheless, he was almost denied a license upon his graduation four years later, perhaps because of charges brought by jealous colleagues. But the gratitude of the peasantry and respect of his fellow students led to his reinstatement.

Setting up practice in Agen, a town on the Garonne River, in 1533, he married a young woman said to be "of high estate, very beautiful and admirable." They were raising a son and daughter when the Inquisition, the church office bent on suppressing heresy, intervened in their lives. Nostradamus (as he now called himself) had been ordered to appear before a church court, purportedly for making a disrespectful remark about a statue of the Virgin Mary. When he returned, a resurgence of the plague claimed the lives of his wife and both their children. For the next decade the compassionate physician once again became an itinerant caregiver, acquiring the reputation of a miracle-worker. After being awarded a lifetime pension, he settled in Salon, halfway between Marseilles and Avignon, set up a business producing cosmetics, and married a wealthy widow who bore him six children.

Revelations in the Attic

As his newfound financial security made continued medical practice unnecessary, Nostradamus turned to the mystical arts. The small-town "barbarians," as he called his neighbors, viewed his interest in magic and astrology with suspicion. He converted his attic into a celestial observatory where, perched on a tripod, he contemplated the starry vaults of the heavens and claimed to re-

A Bloody Century Predicted

To many interpreters, the *Centuries* of Nostradamus are rife with prophecies of the violent and savage events of our own day — from the rise of Hitler to the assassinations of both President John F. Kennedy and his younger brother, Robert. The supposed references to the Third Reich were so widely believed in Germany, in fact, that both England and the Nazis created counterfeit quatrains favorable to their side and dropped them from planes as tools of propaganda. On the other hand, one of the authentic quatrains struck many as prefiguring the war itself: "Living fire and death hidden in globes will be loosed, horrible, terrible; by night enemy forces will reduce the city to powder."

Most recently, there has been a flurry of renewed interest in the Renaissance seer because of the climactic events in Iran when the ruling shah was forced off his Peacock Throne by a populace devoted to the Ayatollah Khomeini, who had been exiled to France. According to one translation, Nostradamus had written: "Rain, famine, and war will not cease in Persia; too great a faith will betray the monarch. Those [actions] started in France will end there, a secret sign for one to be sparing." An accurate prediction, or tortured interpretation? Does it add credence to the prophecy slated to come true in the near future, one of the few with a specific date? "In the year 1999 and seven months, from the sky will come a great and terrible king. . . . Before and after his coming, war will rule at full blast." Time will tell, in due course, but the timorous can take some comfort from the many discredited interpretations of the past.

For the early 19th century, it seemed that Nostradamus had predicted that Napoleon would successfully invade England and rule Britannia long and serenely. In fact, of course, he died a prisoner of the victorious British.

Chateau Chaumont on the Loire River exudes medieval charm; Nostradamus, however, looked not into the past but to the future when he was received there by Queen Catherine of France. He foretold the sad fate of a mother who would survive all her sons — a prophecy that came true in her case.

ceive the secrets of the future from "the internal light, the voice."

At first, he confined his predictions to the pages of a series of almanacs he began publishing in 1550, as was common practice at the time. Gradually, however, he completely lost interest in the mundane pursuit of forecasting the weather and changes of the moon.

Shrouded in Obscurity

Teetering on the brink of religious civil war, France offered fertile soil for the grim and cryptic prophecies Nostradamus published in 1555 — the first 100 of nearly 2,000 he would have in print by 1557. These *Centuries* were an instant success and led to his court appointment.

Admitting that he had purposely chosen "a secretive way of expression," Nostradamus wrote in an obscure argot, grounded in contemporary French but larded with words and phrases from Italian, Greek, Spanish, Hebrew, and Latin. Each of the predictions was a four-line verse, or qua-

train, though none reveals a flair for poetry. The seer himself claimed that this nearly unfathomable style protected him from the punishment of the mighty, who were not always likely to be pleased with what he saw in their futures. More skeptical observers have suggested that the vagueness was a deliberate evasion, leaving the writing open to various interpretations after the fact. In consequence, perhaps, almost 400 different interpretations of the *Centuries* have been produced, each trying to unlock the specific secrets of prophecies that continue up to the year 3797. "My writings will be better understood by those who come after my death," wrote the sage.

Adviser to Royalty

In troubled France there were many, like Queen Catherine, who did not feel the need to wait for history's vindication of the prescient physician. His prediction about her late husband was enough. Undoubtedly, she was responsible for his appointment as physician-in-ordinary to her son, King Charles IX.

According to one popular story, Nostradamus once summoned an angel named Anael and asked him to reveal the fates of the queen's children in a magic mirror. Her three sons were shown reigning briefly, while her despised son-in-law Henry of Navarre appeared as a future leader for 23 years. The depressed queen called a halt to the unpleasant spectacle. In fact, Nostradamus probably visited her court only to cast horoscopes for her and her children. It seems likely that he would have been careful to couch any disconcerting readings in ambiguous terms, since absolute monarchs — no matter how well disposed initially toward soothsayers — have been known to punish the messenger for delivering his message.

A Controversial Celebrity

One of France's greatest poets, Pierre de Ronsard, wrote of his contemporary: "Like an ancient oracle, he has for many years predicted the greatest part of our destiny." Clearly, the prophet delighted in the respect paid by royalty and the fame that continued to grow until his death in 1556. Inevitably, many remained highly skeptical of his work or, worse, considered him nothing but a clever charlatan, preying on the credulous.

In the interpretation of some scholars, Nostradamus also predicted the manner of his own death: "Close to bench and bed will I be found dead." After announcing one evening that he would not survive the night, he succumbed to gout and was discovered dead the next morning alone in his bedroom, near his writing desk.

Father of the Atomic Bomb

A brilliant physicist and gifted leader of other scientists, J. Robert Oppenheimer helped contribute to U.S. victory in World War II. But his hidden personal life led to charges of treason and a premature end to his government service.

After an early morning flurry of air-raid sirens, the all-clear sounded. Bright golden sunshine beamed over the rush-hour bustle of teeming Hiroshima, highlighting the slender green leaves of the city's famous legions of willow trees. On this August day in 1945, the businessmen racing to work, children skipping off to school, housewives beginning the day's traditional chores well knew, after many bombing runs,

that the two or three U.S. B-29 bombers off in the distance posed no threat. A serious attack would fill the sky with planes.

Suddenly, as a survivor would recall, "A blinding flash cut sharply across the sky . . . the skin over my body felt a burning heat . . . dead silence . . . then a huge 'boom,' like the rumbling of distant thunder." At 8:14 A.M. local time, the bomber *Enola Gay* had released its single payload,

J. Robert Oppenheimer energetically led the wartime effort to build the first atomic bomb. After Hiroshima, he came to regard the weapons with extreme skepticism.

"Little Boy," and banked sharply away. Minutes later, the atomic bomb detonated, creating a white-hot glare that lit the heavens and giving rise to fierce winds. From a fireball that raged a quarter of a mile in diameter rose a mushroom cloud soaring to 30,000 feet. The incredibly intense heat, perhaps 3,000 degrees Celsius, instantly turned thousands of human beings into smoldering bits of black carbon. Thousands more lived a few seconds longer, until knocked dead by flying debris or buried beneath toppling buildings. Panicked, many dived into river waters that had become scalding hot. In the fiery maelstrom perhaps as many as 200,000 died, up to half the city's daytime population. Something like 60,000 structures vanished. Scattered fires grew to conflagrations sweeping across the ruined city, and radiation poisoning began its silent work of bringing horrible, lingering death.

On that day, August 6, 1945, a stunned world learned that man had harnessed the power locked within the atom in order to create an unimaginably destructive weapon. Until that epochal explosion, only a few top military and political leaders had known the true story: For years, desperately straining to meet a deadline, a team of research scientists and technicians had been secretly trying to build this "doomsday weapon." They had just barely succeeded, in large part because of the intelligence and inspiration of the distinguished theoretical physicist, J. Robert Oppenheimer, then only 41 years old.

The Prodigy

Born in New York City to well-to-do parents of German-Jewish origin, Oppenheimer thrived in a family that respected art, music, and intellectual curiosity. He entered Harvard College in 1922 and earned his undergraduate degree summa cum laude in only three years, majoring in chemistry. For the next few years, the precocious young man traveled in Europe, where he worked with several physicists who were in the exciting forefront of investigating atomic phenomena in the light of new theories. Only a year out of col-

In the early 1940's the nuclear research center at Los Alamos was a top secret; not even nearby New Mexico residents had an inkling of what scientists there were working on — until news of the bomb dropped on Japan in August 1945.

First Step into the Atomic Age

Quietly working in a lab in Berlin in 1938 as the world poised to erupt in war, chemist Otto Hahn and his pupil Fritz Strassman had unwittingly made an epochal discovery that would lead to that conflict's final act of destruction. After bombarding samples of uranium with neutrons, one of the atom's constituent particles, they found atoms of a different element, barium, within the uranium metal. According to what was then known, Hahn assumed that the "barium" was actually a form of radium, but finally had to go with the evidence before him: The bombardment of uranium somehow produced barium.

Meanwhile, Hahn's colleague at the Kaiser Wilhelm Institute, Lise Meitner, who had never hidden her Jewish origins, was forced to escape from Germany as the Nazis

At this simple work table Hahn and Strassman succeeded in splitting a uranium atom – though at first they were unaware of what they had done.

began to enforce their racial laws. Settled at the new Nobel Institute in Stockholm, Sweden, she recalled Hahn's strange findings and

wrote him for confirmation. Discussing his data with her nephew, O. R. Frisch, Meitner began to suspect that Hahn had actually halved the uranium atom, which was more than twice the mass of a barium atom, into two atoms of barium. She and Frisch surmised that the bombarding neutron "split" the uranium atom in an action that would release a large amount of energy. Thus was "nuclear fission," the chain reaction that makes possible atomic weaponry and peacetime uses, discovered. Within a fraction of a second, as the reaction snowballs, all of the atomic nuclei in any given amount of uranium would be split apart. From a kilo of uranium the energy could become the unprecedented force of an atomic bomb or the fuel of a plant able to provide virtually limitless nuclear power.

---

lege, Oppenheimer published a scientific paper that showed his complete understanding of the new methods. He soon developed, along with the famed Max Born, an essential part of the quantum theory known as the Born-Oppenheimer method. His remarkable Ph.D. dissertation won him international fame in 1927.

Physics, Romance, and the Left

In 1929 the rising scientific star accepted positions at two of the several universities that vied for him. He would teach the spring term at the lively young California Institute of Technology in Pasadena, fall and winter at the Berkeley campus of the University of California, where he would be the first professor to lecture on quantum mechanics. In fact, the erudite scientist would have to undergo a period of adjustment, gradually learning to pitch the level of his discussion to the capabilities of his bewildered students.

In 1936 he fell in love with Jean Tatlock, a troubled and moody young woman whose passionate idealism had found an outlet in the Communist Party. Their stormy romance coincided with an unsettling time in the affairs of the world, from the grinding Depression in the United States to the unnerving actions of dictators like Hitler, Mussolini, and Franco in Western Europe.

Like many thoughtful people of the time, Oppenheimer investigated left-wing ideas as a possible solution, although he did not join the Communist Party, as did his younger brother, his sister-in-law, and many of his friends.

His interest in politics, like his ability to read Sanskrit, was the natural result of his continual probing for concepts and information in many areas. By his own account, he was also deeply worried about the anti-Semitism in fascist Germany and Spain and contributed as much as $1,000 a year of his annual $15,000 income to causes associated with communist groups. When he broke off his relationship with Tatlock after meeting Kitty Harrison, the woman who would become his wife in 1940, he also moved away from her circle of leftward-leaning friends.

The Nazi Threat

The United States learned in 1939 that Hitler's Germany, gearing up for cataclysmic war, had discovered nuclear fission. Oppenheimer and other experts immediately guessed that German experimenters would try to produce a controlled chain reaction that would make possible a bomb infinitely more destructive than any conventional explosive. Concerned scientists alerted President Franklin D. Roosevelt to the danger in a famous letter, after enlisting the support of the renowned scientific genius Albert Einstein, himself a refugee from the Nazi regime.

Under strictest secrecy, the president acted, authorizing the funding of projects aimed at the construction of the unproved weapon. Ironically, many leading scientists forced to flee from their home countries of Germany, Italy, and Hungary joined with American researchers to work in labs across the country. Some university teams explored the feasibility of building a nuclear reactor, while others tackled the problem of separating the uranium isotopes necessary for the release of energy in a chain reaction. It was not until early 1942 that Oppenheimer, who had become fascinated by the theoretical problems, was asked to organize the widely dispersed efforts.

"Expensive Loonies"

Code-named the Manhattan Project, the United States Army's top-priority program to invent an atomic weapon was headed by 46-year-old Colonel Leslie R. Groves, a heavy-set, tough-talking military professional. Groves — who would characterize the scientists at work in atomic energy as an "expensive collection of loonies" — recognized that Oppenheimer had the potential, heretofore untapped, for leading his disputatious colleagues in a high-pressure situation. The physicist suggested that all researchers be brought together at one lab at the obscure little town of Los Alamos, New Mexico, an area he knew well because he owned a ranch nearby. By March 1943 a boys' boarding school had been converted into a tightly guarded secret installation with Oppenheimer as scientific director.

Insisting that all information be freely exchanged among the isolated scientists, whose travel outside was severely restricted, Oppenheimer fostered an atmosphere of trust and mutual respect that yielded amazing progress. Driving himself unsparingly, he stayed on top of all developments in the complex effort, though his private life suffered terribly. His wife, hating the constrictions, began drinking heavily and became abusive to their two young children. But to the mixed assemblage of scientists — among them about a dozen current or future Nobel Prize winners, few of whom lacked strong ego — Oppenheimer was considered a leader of rare devotion and diplomacy. Most would give him the lion's share of credit for the project's eventual success.

By December 30, 1944, Groves, now a general, could predict that the $2 billion spent on his assignment would yield a fully operative bomb by August 1 of the following year. But when Ger-

When Oppenheimer and General Groves visited the site where the test bomb had been exploded, they found virtually nothing left of the steel scaffolding weighing tons that had supported the device.

many accepted defeat in May 1945, many of the Los Alamos researchers began to have second thoughts about actual use of the weapon. Would Japan not capitulate soon, regardless? Should the United States be the first country in the world to employ such a terrible device? Harry S Truman, who had succeeded to the presidency when Roosevelt died in office, appointed a committee including Oppenheimer to examine the likely consequences of setting off a nuclear bomb. The experts decided to recommend, with Oppenheimer's concurrence, that the first atomic bomb be dropped, without warning, on a major Japanese military target.

"The Destroyer of Worlds"

All of these concerns would be moot, of course, if the bomb did not work. The long-anticipated test of the world's first atomic weapon took place on July 16, 1945, some 50 miles from the U.S. Air Force base at Alamogordo, New Mexico.

A Time of Fear

Although Oppenheimer was never called to appear before the notorious Senator Joseph McCarthy, his treatment by the FBI, the White House, and the AEC was undoubtedly the result, at least in part, of fear that the Wisconsin politician would eventually find the physicist a tempting target. The so-called "McCarthy era," which would scar or destroy the lives and careers of innocent Americans, began in 1950. Only days after President Eisenhower announced that the Soviet Union had an atomic capability, the senator announced, "I have here in my hand a list of 205 that were known to the secretary of state as being members of the Communist Party and who nevertheless are still working and shaping the policy of the State Department."

In 1953 McCarthy became chairman of the Senate's Investigations Subcommittee, where staff members soon became aroused by a *Fortune* magazine article, unsigned, claiming that Oppenheimer had tried to discredit the Strategic Air Command and had once written a "veiled suggestion that Air Force doctrine was based on the slaughter of civilians." Before McCarthy made a move, however, he checked with FBI director J. Edgar Hoover, who warned that "this was not a case which should be prematurely gone into solely for the purpose of headlines." For the moment the senator pledged cooperation and backed off, but Hoover and the next AEC chairman, Lewis Strauss, knew that the publicity-seeking politician would not be stilled forever. Strauss had classified documents removed from Oppenheimer's files in Princeton, an act considered by some to be the first step in a surreptitious campaign leading to the AEC loyalty hearings on Oppenheimer in 1954.

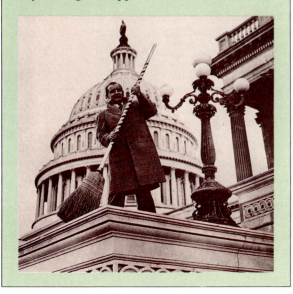

The test device, called "Fat Man" for its bulbous shape, was attached to a steel tower erected on the desert plain. Precisely at 5:30 A.M., a remote control detonator set off the bomb. With a resounding roar, a huge violet-green and orange fireball flamed over a mile-wide area. The earth shook from the chain reaction, and the tower dissolved into thin air. As a white pillar of smoke rose swiftly toward the heavens, it grew ever wider, forming an awesome mushroom shape about seven miles above the ground.

This first man-made nuclear explosion amazed, then exhilarated, scientific and military observers near the site. Some crowded around the director, shouting congratulations. But Oppenheimer was reminded of the Bhagavad-Gita, an Indian epic poem: "I am become Death, the destroyer of worlds." For the rest of his life, his satisfaction with the scientific coup was tempered by a profound sense of responsibility for the consequences.

Scorpions in the Bottle

Three days after "Little Boy" hit Hiroshima, a twin of the original "Fat Man" was dropped on the town of Nagasaki. Japan surrendered unconditionally on August 15, its resolve shattered by this devastating new weapon. The invention of the atomic bomb was seen as the climax of the victory of the United States over its enemies in World War II, perhaps sparing the lives of a million soldiers who might otherwise have been killed in an invasion of the island nation. Already, however, the voices of skeptics could be heard, and Oppenheimer himself, two months after Hiroshima, predicted that "mankind will curse the names of Los Alamos and Hiroshima." Nonetheless, he accepted appointment as president of the science council of the Atomic Energy Commission (AEC) the following year, thereby becoming the most influential adviser on nuclear matters to the government and the military.

As the West and Stalin's Russia dug in for the postwar political stalemate called the Cold War, each side focused on a new arms race. Earlier than predicted, on August 29, 1949, the Soviet Union exploded its first nuclear device. Although many scientists involved in the Manhattan Project did not support the creation of new weapons, Oppenheimer's former collaborators Edward Teller and Ernest Lawrence came to believe that the national security of the United States required the speedy development of a hydrogen bomb.

Oppenheimer was aghast. In his view, the two nuclear powers were already facing off like "two scorpions in a bottle, each capable of killing the

To
J. Robert Oppenheimer
with every good wish
Lyndon B. Johnson

Only four years before his death from lung cancer, Oppenheimer received vindication for his disgrace: On November 22, 1963, the very day he was assassinated, President John F. Kennedy announced he would award the Fermi Prize to Oppenheimer; the award was made by Kennedy's successor, Lyndon Johnson.

other, but only at the risk of its own life." With a proliferation of the projected new bombs, wars would no longer have winners and losers — only victims. The so-called father of the atomic bomb announced publicly that he opposed the proposal to develop the superbomb.

Always uneasy with Oppenheimer and apparently envious of his achievements, Teller campaigned to lead the new project, while suggesting that Oppenheimer no longer need be in the picture. He told FBI investigators that his rival's influence had kept researchers from work on the hydrogen bomb and revealed that the young Oppenheimer had suffered fits of severe depression. When President Truman agreed in 1950 to fund development of the superbomb, Teller could rest satisfied in his personal victory. But others, as it soon became clear, had been waiting for an opportunity to strike at Oppenheimer.

Hysteria and Disgrace

Could the Soviet Union have discovered how to build an atomic bomb without spying upon the U.S. efforts? Could there have been treason at Los Alamos? In 1954 FBI director J. Edgar Hoover produced a report for the White House back-

ing accusations that Oppenheimer was an "espionage agent." President Eisenhower agreed to restrict the scientist's access to secret information while the AEC deliberated the charges.

Intended as a secret proceeding in order to forestall a political outcry, the AEC hearings lasted three weeks, called 40 witnesses, and produced 3,000 pages of testimony and investigative material. Oppenheimer cooperated fully, being subjected to grueling, hostile cross-examination for three days, but his lawyers were denied access to relevant documents and even to portions of their client's testimony for security reasons.

On the witness stand the day's most respected nuclear physicists and other pillars of the establishment, including the retired General Groves, testified to Oppenheimer's absolute integrity and loyalty. The notable exception was Teller, who claimed that it "would be wiser not to grant [security] clearance." On June 29, the AEC's special security committee voted 4 to 1 against restoring Oppenheimer's security clearance, though not finding him guilty of actually giving away secrets to foreign nations. His friendships in the 1930's, his love affair with Tatlock, and his opposition to the superbomb all weighed against him.

Seeker of Troy

Born poor, he amassed four great fortunes. Uneducated, he taught himself 17 languages. But his greatest triumph came late in life, when he proved to skeptics around the world that Homer's tales of the Trojan War had actually happened.

Heinrich Schliemann's childhood memories were grim. Born in 1822 to parents who despised each other, he grew up among superstitious peasants in an obscure German village near the Polish frontier. His mother died in childbirth when he was nine. His stern, self-centered, impecunious father, the town pastor, was hounded out of the pulpit for his frenzied womanizing. Heinrich was separated from Minna, his adored childhood sweetheart, and apprenticed at 14 to a degrading job as a grocer's assistant.

But one interlude in his early life stood out with a golden glow. On bitter winter evenings, the pastor amused his children by telling them stories from *The Iliad*, the famous epic poem about the Trojan War by the blind Greek poet Homer. The children thrilled to the accounts of the heroic deeds of Hector and Achilles, the ruses of the meddling gods, and the beauty of Helen, the prize for which the Greeks had laid siege to the great city of Troy. When Heinrich was seven, his father gave him an illustrated history of the world, and the boy immediately looked up ancient Greece. He never forgot what he saw. In an engraving of the burning of Troy, Aeneas — looking exactly like the flamboyant pastor — carried his father to safety from the conflagration. The boy became hungry for more

knowledge about the glories of ancient Greece.

Convinced that fate directed his path, the mature Schliemann believed that a heavy cask filled with chicory saved him from a lifetime of drudgery at the grocer's. When he coughed up blood from the strain of lifting, he quit and walked to Hamburg, where he spent a few days completing a year's worth of accounting courses. Certain that the Americas of the 1840's offered the promise of great riches, he sold his watch and boarded a ship bound for Venezuela. When a fierce December storm sank the ship and he was thrown naked into the freezing sea, a cask once more floated into Schliemann's life. He clung to it for hours, until he was spotted and pulled aboard the stern boat with 13 other survivors. The miserable party reached the Dutch coast, where they discovered that only Schliemann's luggage had floated intact to the beach, with his belongings and papers safely inside.

Taking opportunity as it arose, he found an accounting job in Amsterdam and began the work habits that would bring him enormous wealth and

In The Iliad *Homer tells the tale of the wooden horse the Greeks used to outwit the Trojans. A copy of the horse stands amidst the ruins of Troy, discovered by Heinrich Schliemann, who listened to the poet and not to alleged experts.*

profound loneliness for decades to come. Deciding to spend nothing on entertainment or women, he lived frugally, concentrating his free time on educating himself and sharpening his considerable powers of memory. In little more than a year, he became fluent in Dutch, English, French, Spanish, Italian, and Portuguese. The new skills led to a job with a huge import-export firm. After he taught himself Russian to handle correspondence in a language no one else there could read, he was rewarded at the age of 25 with the post of chief representative of the company in St. Petersburg. Earning more money than he had dared dream possible, he could at last write for Minna's hand in marriage.

Her father replied that she had just recently been married to a farmer. The capable young businessman with an extraordinarily bright future was devastated by the news.

Cold Comforts of Success

For the next few years, mourning the loss of Minna, he traveled constantly, worked like a man possessed, and dreamed of escape. When a younger ne'er-do-well brother ran off to California, made a small fortune in the Gold Rush, and then died, Schliemann decided to retrieve the legacy and make it grow. He sailed to New York and then to Panama, which in those days had to be crossed by muleback — a journey that offered alligators, yellow fever, and murderous brigands. After sailing up to California, he discovered in Sacramento that his brother's partner had vanished with the inheritance. Undaunted, Schliemann opened a business in gold dust trading. Within nine months he had been caught in the catastrophic San Francisco fire, suffered two life-threatening bouts of yellow fever, and managed to put aside a profit of $400,000. Perhaps because he found Americans discourteous and the women unappealing, he headed back to Russia. This time the crossing of the Isthmus of Panama almost proved fatal. As he and his party trudged through a continual downpour, their guides fled. They had to capture iguana lizards and eat them raw, and many died of dysentery or of fever. Lost, starving, at each other's

Heinrich Schliemann came from a humble background; above, the house in which he grew up as the son of a village pastor. His eventual wealth is typified by the palatial residence he built for himself and his beloved second wife, Sophia, in Athens. He designed it as a modern reconstruction of the ancient palaces he unearthed.

A Passion for Riches

"When I grow up," said John D. Rockefeller as a schoolboy, "I want to be worth $100,000." Not unlike Heinrich Schliemann, this sober, determined child of modest circumstances concentrated his sharp intelligence and formidable energies on the goal of making money. At his death in 1937, he left a fortune of $26.5 million.

It says a lot about Rockefeller's sense of priorities that September 26 became an annual family holiday. On that date in 1855, after the impoverished young man had applied to every possible employer in Cleveland, Ohio, he finally got a job. Even though he had to work three months on trial before beginning to earn a salary of $4 a week, he always recalled the occasion as "a great day for our family." Writing down every meager expense in

John D. Rockefeller not only amassed one of history's great fortunes, he also gave generously to charity — beginning a family tradition of philanthropy.

a little ledger, including the gift of a tenth of his income to the Baptist Church and to charities, Rockefeller lived frugally and planned cannily for the future. With a partner he began a small wholesale business at the age of 28, but it was the fortuitous discovery of oil at Pithole, Pennsylvania, in 1865 that gave him his opportunity to amass unprecedented riches. Eventually John D. Rockefeller controlled about 95 percent of the U.S. oil industry. He had become, in the eyes of many, the image of capitalism at its worst.

Addicted to hard work, yet benevolent with his millions, Rockefeller, like Schliemann, would be linked to riches that lay hidden underground. But it was nature's ancient resource rather than the works of man that brought him lasting fame.

---

throats, his companions became a threat to Schliemann, who stayed up every night with his dagger and revolver, guarding his gold bars and bank drafts even as a leg wound throbbed with the pain of gangrene. But he survived.

Hopeless Passion

Back in St. Petersburg, he took a step that brought 17 years of another kind of misery, a loveless marriage to Ekaterina Lishin. Although he wrote on the eve of their wedding in October 1852 that she was "very good, simple, clever, and sensible," in fact Ekaterina was so unresponsive and dismissive of him that this passionate man went literally to the brink of madness. Within weeks of the wedding night, he had thrown himself into work, making yet another fortune in the indigo trade. Although the unhappy pair produced three children, Schliemann henceforth lived only for business, speculating and gambling where others moved cautiously.

Toiling six days a week, as always, he set aside Sunday for serious study of Greek. "I am intoxicated by this language!" he would exult. Having superbly weathered the international financial crisis of 1857, he sought the passion missing in his marriage by traveling to the lands of his dreams — Greece, Egypt, Palestine, India, China, Japan.

Confused, lonely, continually dissatisfied and unfulfilled, Schliemann had the money and leisure to consider one life change after another, from becoming a full-time writer to settling on a small farm to becoming a student at the Sorbonne in Paris. Instead, on another trip back to the United States, he learned that Indiana was about to pass a new divorce law — offering a way out of his marital dilemma. He started a profitable starch business in Indianapolis and within a year became an American citizen.

The Plains of Mythical Troy

Meanwhile, Schliemann was oppressed by the emptiness of his life. In the summer of 1868, seized by a new scheme to become an archaeologist, he journeyed to Ithaca and mounted a small and amateurish expedition to unearth the castle of his hero, Ulysses. He garnered just enough ancient bric-a-brac to convince himself that he had happened upon the bedchamber of Ulysses and his faithful wife, Penelope. As would happen often, his enthusiasm caused him to leap to conclusions that others could not accept.

Next, he traveled to the plains near Constantinople, where tradition had set the mythical city of Troy. The few who believed that the city might actually have existed as described by

Homer had settled upon a place called Bunarbashi as the likely site, though it was 10 miles from the Aegean Sea. Based upon events in *The Iliad*, Schliemann preferred a hill called Hissarlik, rising much nearer the shore. With his characteristic energy and obsessiveness, he began bombarding the Turkish government with requests for permission to begin digging.

At Last, a Worthy Soulmate

Schliemann was not too busy, however, to turn his attention to the lifelong problem of finding his own Penelope. Back in Indianapolis to set his divorce from Ekaterina in motion, he decided that he must have a Greek wife. Writing to an old friend in Athens, he asked for the photograph of any young woman who was beautiful, appreciative of Homer's poetry, in need of money, and able to give love to the man chosen as her husband. The friend proposed Sophia Engastromenos, the 17-year-old daughter of an Athens draper.

At the first meeting, the would-be husband asked the lovely teenager if she would like to go on a long journey, if she knew the date of the emperor Hadrian's visit to ancient Athens, and if she could recite by heart any passages from Homer. The answer was "yes" on all counts, but the frank girl's honest answer to another question almost scuttled the engagement. When Schliemann asked her privately why she would want to marry him, she replied, "Because my parents told me you were a rich man." The captain of finance sulked like a wounded adolescent for days, but Sophia brought him round, revealing the unusual sensitivity and native wisdom that would make their marriage strong, warm, and lasting.

Schliemann's first dig at Hissarlik was a disappointment. After some exploratory trenches were laid, the local owners of the property chased him off, and the Turkish government continued to turn a deaf ear to his frantic appeals for official permission to continue his excavation.

A Golden Hoard from the Bronze Age

Over the next few years, he endlessly assaulted the bureaucracy, then dug at the site with or without permission, withdrawing periodically to Athens to contemplate his puzzling and unsatisfying finds. For the most part, as his workmen

Schliemann claimed to have found King Priam's treasure within the palace walls of ancient Troy (excavation at right). Unfortunately, that treasure has since been lost so his claim cannot be proved. The so-called Mask of Agamemnon (above) survives, though it dates back to 300 years before the Trojan War.

The Treasure of Priam

"Come at once. It is vital. Be silent." That was the unspoken message the loving Sophia detected when the tensely controlled Heinrich Schliemann softly whispered her name one hot, dusty morning amidst the digs at Troy. The exact date in 1873 is not known, because neither of the Schliemanns ever revealed the truth about what happened next. Striking metal as he dug by himself, Schliemann instantly guessed that he had achieved the goal of a lifetime. "You must go at once and shout *paidos!*," he hissed, suggesting that Sophia tell the workmen that an unexpected rest period was being granted in honor of his birthday. As the diggers drifted away, Heinrich and Sophia dug quickly and furtively, uncovering a large copper box. Inside he glimpsed the glittering gold that would become the greatest archaeological find of the 19th century.

Deftly, Sophia scooped up thousands of tiny pieces in her skirt and carried them off to their little house near the site for inspection behind drawn curtains. Placing one of two dazzling gold diadems on Sophia's head, Schliemann exclaimed, "Adornment worn by Helen of Troy now graces my own wife."

Skeptics charged that the treasure was assembled from different levels of the excavation (hence, from different ages in the history of the site); the most carping of critics accused Schliemann of secretly amassing the collection by going through antique markets. Unfortunately, it is impossible to use today's technologically sophisticated techniques of determining the age of archaeological discoveries to verify the find. The so-called Treasure of Priam was given by the Schliemanns to a museum in Berlin. During the chaos of World War II, it was moved to a bunker for safekeeping but by 1945 had disappeared without a trace. The treasure that may have lain underground for 3,000 years saw the light of day only briefly before, no doubt, vanishing forever.

sank their pickaxes into the dusty soil and Sophia watched eagerly with him, only minor relics from antiquity were discovered.

Schliemann's fourth expedition proved fateful. Probably on May 30, 1873, Schliemann found the stash of 10,000 gold objects that he believed was the treasure of Priam, the last king of Troy. Barely eluding Turkish officials and guards, he smuggled the remarkable hoard to Greece, where Sophia's numerous relatives hid the precious goblets, diadems, earrings, and so forth in their farm buildings. In a book Schliemann revealed the story to an astonished world, proving to skeptical academic experts that Homer's city had actually existed. The Turkish government, of course, was outraged.

As could be expected, Schliemann stood firm, claiming that he had saved the legacy of Troy from larcenous guards and bureaucrats. As the Turks brought a lawsuit in a Greek court, the Schliemanns blithely began another excavation, for Heinrich had long thought that academic opinion was mistaken about the location of the royal tombs of Mycenae.

This important hilltop city had been ruled by Agamemnon, who was Helen's brother-in-law. Scholars believed that any important graves would lie beyond the outer walls of the city, but Schliemann's intuition suggested a site near the inner walls, not far from the famous Lion Gate. He was proved spectacularly correct. Under the watchful gaze of the Greek officials, he and Sophia found tombs that contained beautiful gold funerary objects, including haunting masks.

Laurels in the Twilight Years

For the last 10 years of his life, Schliemann lived contentedly with Sophia and their children in an Athens house designed to resemble the palaces he had uncovered. Scholars debated his findings, but he was lionized all over Europe.

Despite all of the success, he was to die alone and almost without medical attention. In Naples he collapsed in a public square, but, because he carried neither money nor identification, the hospital turned him away as an indigent. By the time his physician found him, Schliemann was paralyzed and unable to speak.

He died on December 26, 1890, just short of his 69th birthday. His grieving widow wrote, "I had the divine opportunity to delve deeply into the meaning of life. All this I owe to my dearest husband, Henry." After monumental travail against great odds, Schliemann had accomplished his dreams — great wealth, enduring fame, and the love of a remarkable woman.

The Repentant Despot

*Because of his wars, political terrorism, and personal vices —
including the murder of a son — Russia's first czar is known as Ivan
the Terrible. He began his reign determined to make Moscow the
"third Rome" and died offering prayers for his victims.*

Ivan IV was only three years old when he succeeded his father, Basil III, as grand prince of Moscow in 1533, and for five years his mother served as regent while the boy was educated in statecraft. But when she died — possibly a poison victim — he became the center of a power struggle among several factions of boyars, or noblemen. At the age of 13 he made a decisive move, ordering one of the rivals arrested in his presence and later executed. It was a cruel age.

The Good Times . . .

Fortunately, there was a restraining influence in the person of the metropolitan Makary of the Russian Orthodox Church. At 16, Ivan took the churchman's advice on two critical matters: his coronation as czar (a shortened form of "caesar") of all Russia on January 16, 1547, and his marriage a month later to Anastasia Romanova. It was Makary's goal to make Moscow the new center of Christianity, a "third Rome" (after Rome and Constantinople). "Two Romes have fallen," he proclaimed, "but the third stands and a fourth there will not be." Ivan was thus said to be not only the direct descendant of the Roman emperor Augustus but also the principal temporal ruler of Christendom. To bolster his grandiose plan, Makary scoured church documents for legends of Russian holy men and convened two church synods to proclaim Russian saints.

In addition to this religious resurgence, political reform was in the air. Guided by a group of advisers known as the Chosen Council, Ivan instituted a new legal code, tried to improve the terms of military service, and gave local governments more power.

As for the marriage, it was apparently a happy one. Before her death in 1560, Anastasia bore six children, although only two survived infancy. She had a calming influence on her husband, helping to curb his appetites for crude entertain-

ment, heavy drinking, cruel sports, and wanton displays of power.

. . . and the Reign of Terror

Leaving Moscow in charge of Makary, Ivan took to the field against the Tatars in a series of campaigns between 1547 and 1552 that destroyed the power of these Turkish invaders from the southeast and annexed their lands along the Volga River. Returning to his capital in triumph, he told the boyars, "Now I no longer fear you!" Henceforth, he would rule as an autocrat.

There was, however, one last challenge from the squabbling noblemen. When Ivan developed a raging fever early in 1553, the boyars demanded that he name a successor in case of premature death. Not wishing to endure another regency for a minor, they protested Ivan's designation of his infant son, Dimitri, and proposed a cousin, Vladimir. The czar was adamant, summoned the boyars to his bedchamber, and demanded that they kiss a cross in allegiance to Dimitri. Upon his recovery, Ivan made a pilgrimage of thanksgiving to a remote shrine.

Ivan's next campaign — a drive to give landlocked Russia an outlet to the Baltic Sea — ended in stalemate, and he was forced to call upon Pope Gregory XIII to mediate with his adversaries, Poland and Sweden. At home, following the death of Makary in 1563, the czar sought even more absolute power with the institution of what was called the *oprichnina*.

In this bizarre government reform, Ivan divided his kingdom in two. One half was to be ruled in the traditional manner, with support of the boyars. But the other — called the *oprich*, or widow's part — was to be treated as his personal possession, defended by a force of 1,000 to 6,000 men. For the Russian people it became a reign of terror. The czar himself was said to participate in the torture and murder of opponents.

A Ruler Gone Mad

Paralleling the czar's state terrorism was the chaos and tragedy of his family life. Although he had been genuinely devoted to Anastasia, he announced within two weeks of her death that he would wed again — this time seeking a political alliance through marriage to a sister of the king of Poland, Sigismund II Augustus. When Sigismund turned him down, Ivan married an Asiatic beauty named Maria, the daughter of the Circassian ruler Temgruk. Their only child, a boy, survived but five weeks, and thereafter Ivan showed no interest in her. Following Maria's death, Ivan took a third wife, Marfa, who died after 16 days, their union probably an unconsummated one. There were rumors of poison in both deaths.

Although it was against church regulations, Ivan took a fourth wife, a commoner named Anna, within two months of Marfa's death. After three years, the barren Anna was sent to a nunnery. Two more wives — mistresses in the eyes of disapproving churchmen — followed in quick succession before Ivan took Maria Nagaia, the daughter of a boyar, as his consort in 1580. The next year she gave birth to a son, Dimitri (Anastasia's son, Dimitri, having died).

In 1581 Ivan's oldest son and namesake, the czarevitch Ivan, was 27 and married for a third time. His first two wives had been banished by the czar and the third, Elena, was equally displeasing to him. When Ivan reprimanded his pregnant daughter-in-law for immodesty of attire, the czarevitch intervened. As their voices rose in anger, Ivan lunged out with an iron-pointed staff and mortally wounded his son with a blow to the head.

Overcome with remorse, Ivan began compiling a list of the victims of his terror — a list that grew to more than 3,000 names before his death in 1584. Copies of the list, along with donations, were sent to Russia's principal monasteries with instructions that prayers be offered for the repose of their souls.

Ivan IV is depicted below with the iron-pointed staff that became a tragic weapon; at left is Moscow's St. Basil's cathedral, built to commemorate his conquest of Kazan.

The Hero Turned Traitor

*A bold and fearless leader in battle, Benedict Arnold turned
bitter over his failure to win promotion and charges that he had
misspent government funds. In need of money to support an
extravagant lifestyle, he offered to surrender West Point to the enemy.*

In the rolling hills of Saratoga National Historical Park, north of Albany, New York, stands a
curious, nameless monument consisting of a
soldier's boot on a short column with an enigmatic
inscription: "In memory of the most brilliant soldier of the Continental Army, who was desperately wounded on this spot . . . 7th October 1777,
winning for his countrymen the decisive battle of
the American Revolution and for himself the
rank of Major General." The unnamed hero is
none other than Benedict Arnold, a name that is
synonymous with treason in the United States.

The surrender of British
general "Gentleman John-
ny" Burgoyne at Saratoga
seven days after the battle
was the first capitulation of
an entire army to the American rebels and a turning
point in the struggle for independence. News of the
victory helped Benjamin
Franklin, an American
commissioner in Paris, succeed in his efforts to get the
French to sign treaties of
alliance and commerce
with the fledgling nation.

Benedict Arnold's im-
petuous attacks at Sara-
toga were credited with
providing the margin of
victory, and the wounded
hero was welcomed home
in Connecticut as Ameri-
ca's "fighting general."
None of his admirers could
have predicted that Arnold
had fought his last battle or
that his military career
would end so infamously.

*A soldier's boot on a short column
marks the memorial for Benedict Arnold
on the Saratoga battlefield; his name
is missing from the monument.*

A Rapid Rise to Military Glory

Born in Norwich, Connecticut, on January 14,
1741, Benedict Arnold was an energetic youth,
endowed with unusual strength, agility, and
stamina. At age 14, he ran away from home to
join colonial troops fighting in the French and Indian War of 1754–63. But the lure of a soldier's
life soon faded, and the boy deserted to return
home — only his youth sparing him the punishment of a court-martial.

By the age of 21, Arnold was established as a
druggist and bookseller in New Haven, and before long he was investing
in trade with the sugar
plantations of the West Indies. In 1767 he married
Margaret Mansfield, by
whom he had three sons in
the next five years.

Arnold was a captain in
the Connecticut militia
when news reached New
Haven of the first battle of
the American Revolution,
fought at Lexington, Mas-
sachusetts, on April 19,
1775. Wasting no time to
volunteer his services to
the patriot cause, he
reached the Boston area
with a volunteer force 10
days later. Commissioned
a colonel, he proposed an
assault on Britain's Fort Ticonderoga on Lake Cham-
plain. In conjunction with
Ethan Allen and his Green
Mountain Boys from Ver-
mont, Arnold took the
fort — and its desperately
needed cannons — on May

10. When a dispute with Allen arose over the command and after Massachusetts failed to reimburse him for money out of his own pocket spent on the campaign, Arnold returned home in July. In his absence his wife had died.

Despite his personal sorrow and his disenchantment with the authorities, Arnold returned to Massachusetts in August and presented himself to the new commander in chief, George Washington. His bold proposal for a strike against loyalist Canada was enthusiastically embraced by Washington.

As one small army pushed up Lake Champlain, captured Montreal, and moved down the St. Lawrence River, Arnold took his men through the swamps and forests of Maine toward Quebec. Under the command of Richard Montgomery, the two forces assaulted Quebec on December 31 but were thrown back with a loss of nearly half the men. Montgomery was killed, and Arnold was wounded in the leg. With the soldiers left to him, Arnold maintained the siege until May 1776, when British reinforcements made it prudent for him to withdraw.

By now a brigadier general, Arnold built a fleet of small ships that blocked a British invasion via Lake Champlain in October. Britain's strategy, to be repeated the following year and end with defeat at Saratoga, was to cut New England off from the mid-Atlantic and southern states and thus crush the revolt piecemeal. Arnold would twice be instrumental in preserving colonial unity.

General Arnold is shown astride a white horse in this period painting of the battle at Saratoga in 1777, the high point of his military career in the Revolution.

Injured Pride

Not everyone in the military establishment shared Washington's esteem for Arnold, and in February 1777 he was passed over for promotion to major general, a rank bestowed on five officers junior to him. Only the personal plea of the commander in chief prevented him from submitting his resignation. That spring Arnold repulsed a British invasion of Connecticut, for which he was belatedly made a major general, though not given seniority over the five promoted earlier. To the proud Arnold, it was a tainted reward.

The blow to his pride was nothing compared to what came next. The Continental Congress began investigating Arnold's handling of finances during the Canadian campaign of 1775–76. He had failed to account for some $55,000 of the $66,671 allocated for the expedition, his excuse being that he had lacked a paymaster to handle the "multiplicity of accounts." Indeed, Arnold said in self-defense, he had often drawn on personal credit to pay his troops. On July 11, 1777, he submitted his resignation from the army. That very same day Congress received a letter from Washington in which the commander in chief stated his need for "an active, spirited officer" to

After George Washington named him commander at West Point, Arnold offered to surrender the American fortress to the British. On the night of September 21–22, 1780, he met with Major John André, the adjutant to the British commander in chief, Sir Henry Clinton, to hand over plans of the Hudson River stronghold. In the contemporary representation of the fateful meeting at right, Arnold tells André to hide the documents in his stockings.

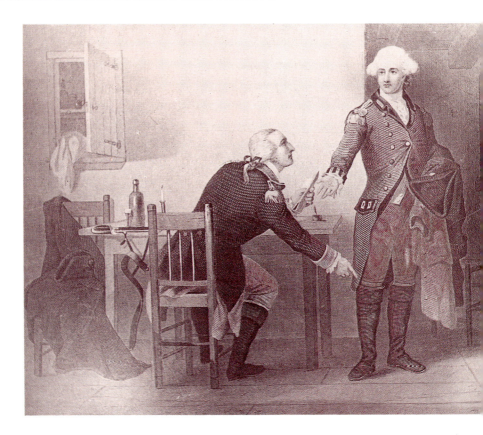

help check the renewed British attempt, under Burgoyne, to split the colonies. The man he asked for: Benedict Arnold.

Arnold withdrew his resignation and joined Horatio Gates's army in time to share in the triumph at Saratoga in October. As a reward for his role in the victory, Congress at last restored his seniority. Shot in the same leg that had been wounded at Quebec two years earlier, Arnold went home for the winter to recuperate.

A Bride for the General

By May 1778 Arnold had recovered enough to rejoin Washington's army at Valley Forge and the next month, when the British evacuated Philadelphia, was made military commander of what then became the American capital. His injuries making a return to combat doubtful, Arnold developed social ambitions. He bought a luxurious home in the capital, kept several servants, and drove about in an elegant carriage — luxuries that his military pay did not support.

Sometime during the summer he met vivacious 18-year-old Peggy Shippen. She had reveled in the British occupation and was furious at not being permitted to attend a farewell ball for General Howe. She particularly missed a hand-

some young officer, Captain John André, a would-be poet and artist who had escorted her to a number of parties. By November, however, she was paying attention to Arnold's suit, which caused a society matron to remark, "Cupid has given our little general a more mortal wound than all the host of Britons could." Despite the 20-year difference in their ages, Arnold and Peggy Shippen were married on April 8, 1779.

At the time of the wedding, however, a cloud was hanging over Arnold's head. In February the Pennsylvania Council had brought serious charges of official misconduct against Arnold — among them that he had issued an illegal permit to unload a captured privateer, the *Charming Nancy*, and had requisitioned 12 army wagons to transport its cargo to Philadelphia for sale. Arnold had received half of the proceeds from the questionable transaction.

On May 5 Arnold heatedly wrote to Washington: "If your Excellency thinks me criminal, for heaven's sake let me be immediately tried and, if found guilty, executed. I want no favour; I ask only justice." He demanded the judgment of a military tribunal.

Not until January 26, 1780, however, did the court-martial issue its verdict: guilty on two of the eight charges, punishable by a reprimand from the commander in chief. Washington's censure was guarded. The issuing of the permit he found "peculiarly reprehensible"; the use of the army wagons, "imprudent and improper."

The Road to Treason

Within days of writing his impassioned letter to Washington — and long before the court-martial verdict — Arnold entered into a secret correspondence with the British. The man with whom he was negotiating his defection from the patriot cause was John André, now a major and serving as adjutant to the British commander in chief, Sir Henry Clinton, in New York.

Later in life, Arnold would try to argue that he had valid motives for changing sides in the rebellion. Among these were doubt of the ability of the Americans to achieve independence, objection to what he considered the tyranny of Congress, and outrage at the French alliance. Historians have added more personal and less selfless motives: pique at the slowness of Congress to promote him, smoldering resentment at the repeated charges of misconduct that culminated in his court-martial, and the need for funds to support his new lifestyle.

In one of his first letters to André — written in a code and sent through intermediaries — Arnold made it clear that he expected to be paid, asking for "a revenue equivalent to the risk and service done." The sum mentioned: £10,000. The information about American troop movements and French naval dispositions that Arnold sent that summer was not what the British needed. "Permit me to prescribe a little exertion," André wrote Arnold at the end of July. "It is the procuring of an accurate plan of West Point."

The Fatal Rendezvous

The American stronghold on the west bank of the Hudson River some 50 miles north of New York was the principal block to a British thrust upriver to Lake Champlain and Canada; the British had still not abandoned hope of cutting off New England from the other rebellious colonies.

By fall the negotiations had broken off, and Arnold spent a few uneasy months waiting for the court-martial verdict. The reprimand from Washington was delivered on April 6, 1780. The next month Arnold reopened his traitorous correspondence with the British.

In August, after considerable lobbying, Arnold succeeded in persuading Washington to give him command of West Point. By the end of the month he had a letter from André offering £20,000 if he would surrender the post with its 3,000 men, artillery, and stores to the British. Sometime between midnight and 1 A.M. on Friday morning, September 22, Arnold and André met at a point along the Hudson River roughly halfway between West Point and New York. As dawn approached, the two prepared to part — their business concluded. But when the waiting British ship *Vulture* came under American fire, André was forced to return overland to New York. Arnold gave him a pass, as "Mr. John Anderson" to go through American lines.

Exchanging his uniform for a civilian disguise, André set out on a circuitous route to New York after dark that evening. In his stockings were tucked documents in Arnold's handwriting. Saturday morning, between 9 and 10 A.M., André was stopped by three self-styled militiamen who were aiding the patriot cause by robbing British sympathizers. Disappointed that André was car-

En route back to New York from his rendezvous with Arnold, Major André — disguised in civilian clothes — was seized by American militiamen. Arnold's treason was thus exposed, and the young British officer was executed as a spy.

The Fame of West Point

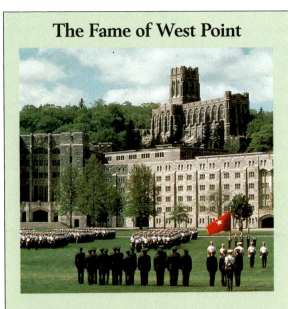

Established in 1778, the Hudson River military post at West Point was of enormous strategic significance. Had the British succeeded in winning it through Arnold's treachery, the river and lake route north to Canada would have been open to them. Twice before, the British had attempted but failed to secure this passage in a divide-and-conquer strategy.

After the war, West Point took on another role when, by act of Congress in 1802, the United States Military Academy was established there with 10 cadets in its first class. Initially a school for gunners and engineers only, the academy had a precarious existence in its first few years. Not until Major Sylvanus Thayer took over as superintendent in 1817 did anything like the West Point of today begin to take shape.

The academy grounds cover more than 16,000 acres, where some 4,400 cadets receive both a military and an academic education in four years. In small classes of 12 to 15, students receive instruction in the humanities and the social, physical, engineering, and military sciences. Candidates, most of whom are appointed by members of the United States Senate and House of Representatives, must be between 17 and 22 years of age, unmarried, and physically fit; they also must meet the academic requirements for university admission. Since 1976 women have been admitted as cadets.

Since the War of 1812, West Point graduates have served with distinction in all of America's wars. Among its most renowned generals have been Robert E. Lee, Ulysses S. Grant, John J. Pershing, Douglas MacArthur, and Dwight D. Eisenhower. Two cadets who won fame in nonmilitary careers were the poet Edgar Allan Poe and the painter James McNeill Whistler.

rying so little money, they forced him to strip and thus found the incriminating documents.

At breakfast on Monday morning, Arnold received a letter telling him that "John Anderson," bearing a pass with his signature and carrying certain documents about West Point defenses, had been captured. The papers had been forwarded to Washington, who was en route to West Point from Connecticut. Arnold bolted from the table, ordered his horse saddled, and galloped away. At the Hudson he leaped aboard a barge and ordered it rowed downstream to the *Vulture*. Arriving at Arnold's house within a half hour of the traitor's flight, Washington was given the documents. "Whom can we trust now?" the commander in chief sadly asked of his aides.

Swift Punishment and Bitter Reward

Tried as a spy and convicted, John André was hanged on October 2, 1780. His plea that, as an officer, he be executed by a firing squad was denied — though Washington would characterize the 29-year-old André as "more unfortunate than criminal."

As for Arnold, his short-term gain was followed by years of frustration. Upon his arrival in New York, the turncoat was given £6,315, well below what he had expected to receive for turning over West Point but nonetheless a handsome sum — estimated by one modern historian to be worth about $55,000. Clinton promptly made him a brigadier general of provincial troops and sent him off on a marauding expedition to Virginia, where Governor Thomas Jefferson offered a reward of £5,000 for his capture. In September 1781 he further tarnished his reputation by leading a raid against his former neighbors and putting a torch to the town of New London. Two months later, and following Cornwallis's surrender at Yorktown that effectively ended the war for independence, Arnold sailed with his wife and family for England.

The remaining 20 years of his life were spent in trying to vindicate his role in the American Revolution, but he learned that many British scorned his treason no less than did the Americans. Three times Arnold offered his services to Britain in the Napoleonic wars, and each time he was turned down, complaining to his wife that he was not to be allowed the dignity of a soldier's death. Although he received a substantial land grant in Canada, he left a debt of £5,000 when he died in London on June 14, 1801. Only 60, the vigorous officer had become a flabby, stooped old man, hobbling about on a cane; his death was ascribed to dropsy and a lung ailment.

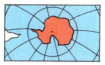

Drama on the Ice

*Britain's Robert Falcon Scott failed to achieve his goal of being
the first man to reach the South Pole; the heroic attempt cost him his life.
Yet, instead of returning home a second best, he was celebrated
as the embodiment of courage and determination.*

Among the mail waiting for Captain Scott when he arrived in Melbourne, Australia, on October 12, 1910, was a terse telegram: "Beg leave inform you proceeding Antarctic. Amundsen." Thus the British officer learned that his long-planned assault on the South Pole was to be a race with Roald Amundsen, the Norwegian Arctic explorer who had been the first to traverse the Northwest Passage five years earlier.

Two months after Scott's departure from England, Amundsen had left Norway on what was announced as a scientific expedition to the Arctic Ocean. Instead he headed south. Stopping at the Portuguese island of Madeira, he informed his crew of the change of plans and left the message for Scott. Aboard his diesel-powered ship, the *Fram* ("Forward"), were 97 Greenland dogs, a prefabricated hut, and provisions for two years. Without stopping at any other ports, Amundsen made for Antarctica's Ross Sea.

The route to the South Pole leads up
the glaciers of the Transantarctic
Mountains to the polar plateau (above).
The British on skis insisted on pulling
their own supply sleds (left).

In shirtsleeves and a Panama hat, the expedition commander, Robert F. Scott, leads one of the ponies from the Terra Nova *at McMurdo Sound's Cape Evans. The ponies initially were employed to pull sleds laden with equipment to the base camp some one and a half miles inland and were later used on the trek to the South Pole.*

"What do you think about Amundsen's expedition?" one of Scott's officers wrote his mother. "If he gets to the Pole we shall come home with our tails between our legs and no mistake." Asked about his rival, Scott told reporters that he had wanted to give Amundsen a good-luck message but didn't know where to send it.

Destined for the Antarctic

Although he was unaware of it at the time, Robert Falcon Scott had been picked to carry the British flag to the South Pole when he was only 18. In March 1887, as a midshipman, he had sailed his cutter to victory in a race off St. Kitts in the West Indies. Clements Markham, the squadron commander's cousin and guest, was watching and, after being introduced to the victor, wrote in his notes that Scott "was the destined man to command the Antarctic expedition."

At this point, such an expedition was no more than a dream of Markham's — but one that he would pursue singlemindedly for the next quarter century. Elected president of the Royal Geographical Society in 1893, Markham announced his goal of equipping and dispatching an expedition to Antarctica. Ahead of him were years of planning and fund-raising.

On June 7, 1900 — a day after his 32nd birthday — Scott was appointed to lead a British Antarctic expedition. In accepting, he insisted on complete command of both ship and shore parties and consultation on all appointments.

Scott's ship, the *Discovery*, was christened in March 1901 and the next four months were spent in outfitting and provisioning the vessel for 47 men who were expected to be gone for three years. King Edward VII and Queen Alexandra came aboard to wish Scott well before he put out to sea on August 6.

The First Attempt

After exploring the Antarctic coastline south of New Zealand early in 1902, Scott decided to spend the winter at McMurdo Sound. On April 23 the sun dipped below the horizon, the beginning of four months of winter darkness. At the arrival of the Antarctic spring, in September 1902, Scott began sending out short dogsled parties — trial runs for a major land expedition in the summer. Scott himself did not set the goal of reaching the South Pole, but surgeon and zoologist Edward Wilson wrote in his diary that "Our object is to get as far south in a straight line on the Barrier [Ross Sea ice shelf] as we can, reach the Pole if possible . . . ."

On November 2, Scott, Wilson, and 2nd Lieutenant Ernest Shackleton set out by dogsled for the journey into the great unknown. By the end of the month, they had crossed the 80th parallel, the farthest south ever reached. But the men were suffering from hunger and snow blindness, and their dogs were starving. "We cannot stop, we cannot go back, and there is no alternative but to harden our hearts and drive," Scott wrote in his diary. His determination was not to be rewarded with success. Only 480 miles short of the

South Pole, the three turned back and reached McMurdo Sound on February 3, 1903.

Before the onset of a second winter, Scott sent a number of men home aboard a relief ship, among them Shackleton, who was suffering from scurvy. In February 1904 the *Discovery* was pried out of the ice into which it had been locked for two years and was set on a course for England.

An Unexpected Rival

Welcomed home as a hero, Scott was invited to shoot grouse with the king in Scotland. But he did not get the knighthood many thought he deserved. Put on naval half-pay, the explorer gave lectures to supplement his income.

Early in 1907 Scott wrote the Royal Geographical Society, proposing a second expedition to Antarctica at a cost of £30,000. Before he got his answer, Ernest Shackleton notified the press that he had pledges of £30,000 for his own expedition to the South Pole and was asking for the society's support. It may have been a coincidence, Scott confided to a friend, "but it looks as though he had an inkling of my intentions and has rushed to be first in the field."

Scott met with Shackleton in May and got his former subordinate to agree not to use the base at McMurdo Sound but to launch his attack on the pole from Edward VII Land at the opposite end of the Ross Sea ice shelf — which would actually have put him 60 miles closer to his goal. Two months later Shackleton left for Antarctica. Failing to find an adequate harbor in the designated area, Shackleton broke his promise to Scott and set up his base at McMurdo Sound. The following year he and three of his men succeeded in getting within 113 miles of the South Pole before turning back. When Scott heard the news he said, "I think we'd better have a shot next."

"I am prepared"

Showing no rancor that Shackleton received more acclaim — including a knighthood — than he had received upon his return five years earlier, Scott was first in the receiving line at Charing Cross Station the day of his rival's return. Presiding at a dinner in Shackleton's honor a few days later, Scott said that the prize of reaching the South Pole must go to an Englishman. "Personally, I am prepared, and have been for the last two years, to go forth in search of that object." In September he announced his plans to raise £40,000 to outfit a private expedition.

Still short of the necessary funds, Scott left En-

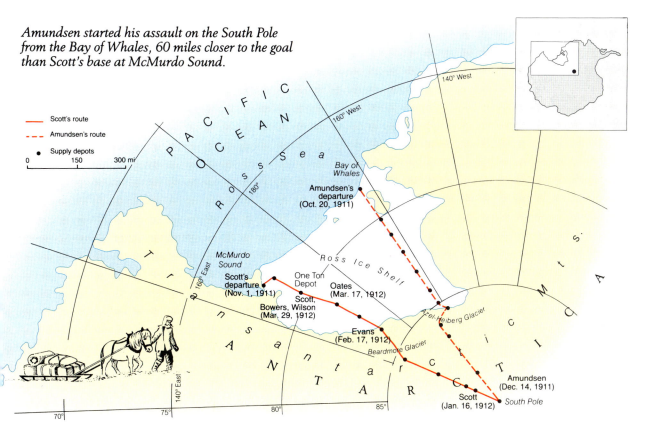

Amundsen started his assault on the South Pole from the Bay of Whales, 60 miles closer to the goal than Scott's base at McMurdo Sound.

Towering over the British base is 12,450-foot-high Mt. Erebus, an active volcano. A festive dinner marked the 43rd birthday of Captain Scott (center) on June 6, 1911 — his last.

gland in June 1910. But his new ship, the *Terra Nova*, was well provisioned, and the expedition would have a few veterans of the earlier voyage, including Edward Wilson.

The telegram received from Amundsen on October 12 was Scott's first warning of a challenge. A second came in February 1911, after he had set up his base at McMurdo Sound. Exploring eastward along the ice shelf, the *Terra Nova* came upon Amundsen's ship anchored at the Bay of Whales, the very place Scott had designated for Shackleton. "There is no doubt that Amundsen's plan is a very serious menace to ours," the commander wrote in his diary.

Dogs, Ponies, Motor Sledges

For his assault on the South Pole, Scott had equipped his expedition with Siberian ponies as well as dogs and had added a novelty: motorized

sledges. The sledges would be used to carry heavy equipment across the ice shelf, as the men set up supply depots along the route the polar party would follow. Ponies and dogs would be taken as far as the lower reaches of the glacier the explorers planned to follow for the dangerous ascent of the Transantarctic Mountains. As the animals gave out, they would be slaughtered and their meat cached along the way for sustenance on the return. The men would be on their own for the dash across the high plateau to the final goal.

Scott's faith in ponies as supplementary to dog transport proved misplaced. The poor animals bogged down easily in the wet snow and too often had to be rescued. Finally, in comparison with Amundsen's men, the British never really mastered the dog teams. In the end it came down to brute human strength and stoic endurance.

A Dismal Walk

After spending the winter of 1911 at McMurdo Sound, Scott made final preparations for the overland journey to the South Pole and set November 1 as the date of departure. Amundsen, he suspected, would have left earlier and have a better chance of traveling faster with his well-trained dog teams.

The round trip to the South Pole was nearly 1,800 miles. On schedule, Scott and nine others set out on November 1, each man leading a pony that pulled a sledge of provisions; two men with the motorized sledges had preceded them; two men with the dogs followed. The motor vehicles gave out almost immediately, ending the dream of a mechanized advance.

"It is always rather dismal walking over the great snow plain when sky and surface merge in one pall of whiteness," Scott wrote. Temperatures hovered below zero Fahrenheit and, with a haze masking the sun, navigation proved difficult in a featureless landscape. Spring snowfalls were wet and sticky, piling up drifts that trapped the ponies. Two weeks out, the party reached a major camp, named One Ton Depot for its huge cache of stores, and Scott called a day's rest.

On November 24 the first pony was killed and butchered. Noting the amount of fat-larded meat the beast provided, Scott said, "May we all do our work as well as he did." But now his worries switched to the weather. A gale from the south turned into a blizzard on December 5, and the men were confined to their tents for four days.

When they resumed their march, it proved almost impossible to get the ponies to move and on December 9 the remaining ones were shot. Two days later, at the foot of the glacier, the two men with the dogs were sent back. With each man pulling 200 pounds of supplies, they started up the 100-mile glacier that would take them 10,000 feet above the ice shelf. One day they made no more than four miles in nine hours of agonizing toil. Trying to ignore the Norwegian challenge, Scott set for his party the goal of beating Shackleton's progress toward the South Pole three years earlier.

A Fatal Choice?

Scott had not chosen the names of the three men he would take with him on the final dash to the South Pole, wisely waiting to see who would prove to be most fit when the time came to make a decision. On December 20 he sent four of his remaining 11 men back to McMurdo Sound and on January 3, 1912, made a startling announcement: there would be five, not four, in the polar party. Joining Scott on the final lap would be his companion of the earlier expedition, Edward Wilson, Captain Lawrence Oates, Lieutenant Henry Bowers, and seaman Edgar Evans.

When the five men said goodbye to the three sent back, they were only 169 miles from the South Pole. Another 10 or 11 days of easy trekking across the high plateau would get them to

Commuter Between the Poles

An American triumph in the Arctic cost Robert Scott his victory in the Antarctic. On April 6, 1909, after years of striving, Robert Edwin Peary reached the North Pole by dogsled with his black servant, Matthew Henson, and four Eskimos.

In Norway, Roald Amundsen was preparing to launch an assault on the North Pole. News of Peary's achievement was a blow. "If I was to maintain my prestige as an explorer," he wrote, "I must quickly achieve a success of some sort. I resolved upon a coup." The coup: Head for Antarctica to beat Scott to the South Pole.

Few explorers were as qualified as the 38-year-old Amundsen when he left Norway in August 1910. Thirteen years earlier, he had joined a Belgian expedition to the Antarctic. Next, with a crew of only seven, he had sailed his tiny

In his polar expeditions, Roald Amundsen shunned heavy woolens and dressed as did the natives in lightweight but warm furs.

ship the *Gjoa* through the Northwest Passage in 1903–06.

Amundsen's joy at his success in Antarctica was subdued: "Since my youth, I had been fascinated with the area surrounding the North Pole; and now I was standing at the South Pole."

In the following years he returned to the Arctic. Between 1918 and 1920 he took his ship *Maud* across the northern coast of Siberia, thus being the first to complete the voyage around the Arctic Circle. Attempting to be the first to fly over the North Pole, he was forced down within 170 miles of the goal in May 1925. But the next year he joined the Italian aeronautical engineer Umberto Nobile in a dirigible crossing from Spitsbergen to Alaska. In 1928 Amundsen disappeared while flying to the rescue of Nobile, whose dirigible had crashed in Spitsbergen.

their goal. "I think it's going to be all right," Scott wrote in a note sent back to his wife. What buoyed him most was the absence of any trace of the Norwegians; it had been assumed that Amundsen would also be following the route blazed in 1908–09 by Shackleton.

"This is an awful place . . ."

On January 6, Scott's party passed the line where Shackleton had been forced to turn back. But it was colder than expected for midsummer; clouds blew in from nowhere; the snow was too soft for easy movement. "I never had such pulling," the usually stoic Scott bitterly wrote in his diary.

"Feeling that tomorrow would see us at our destination," Scott moved his party out on an afternoon march after lunch on January 16. Two hours later Bowers saw an alien shape in the landscape ahead; it was a flag tied to a man-made cairn. The Norwegians had beaten them. "All the daydreams must go," Scott wrote; "it will be a wearisome return." In shaky, inch-high letters, Scott headed his diary entry for the next day, "*The Pole*" and complained that none had slept well after the shock of the discovery. "Great God! This is an awful place," he added, "and terrible enough for us to have laboured to it without the reward of priority."

Amundsen and four companions had reached the South Pole by skis and dogsleds on December 14, 1911, a month before Scott arrived. Following a different route, they had made the journey in 21 days less than the British. On the day Scott stood at the South Pole, Amundsen was within a week of his base at the Bay of Whales. Unlike the British, the Norwegians had been favored with uninterrupted good weather and averaged 19 miles a day. The victory was largely attributed to superb handling of the dogs.

A Dream Turns into a Nightmare

Temperatures dropped to -28° F on the second day of the return journey. The good weather at the South Pole appeared to be breaking up; "If so God help us," Scott wrote. Oates complained that his feet were perpetually cold; Evans began to appear confused and incapable of such simple tasks as putting on ski boots. Despite the fact that they were making up to 22 miles a day, the men were constantly tired and subject to mishaps. Both Scott and Evans fell into a crevasse; Wilson pulled a leg tendon; the commander stumbled and bruised a shoulder.

On February 7 they were at the head of the glacier leading off the plateau. The descent was a nightmare. For hours the men plunged through a terrible maze of crevasses and fissures, not knowing which way to turn. On the 14th, Scott confided to his diary that "There is no getting away

Scott and his men arrived too late! When the British reached the South Pole, a Norwegian flag was fluttering over a tent left by Amundsen a month earlier.

Space: The Ultimate Challenge

Along with most explorers, Captain Robert F. Scott was motivated in part by a desire to achieve fame and honor for his country, Britain. Today the quest is much more ambitious: the conquest of space; and it requires enormous expenditures that only such superpowers as the United States and the U.S.S.R. can make.

The Space Age can be said to have begun on October 4, 1957, when a stunned world learned that the Soviet Union had succeeded in launching the first man-made satellite, Sputnik I. For the United States, accustomed to being first in the post-World War II era, the notion of a Russian satellite circling Earth was humiliating. But before Americans were able to put their first satellite in orbit three months later — Explorer I, derided by the Russians as "a grapefruit" — the

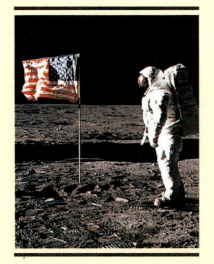

As photographed by Neil Armstrong, "Buzz" Aldrin draws to attention at the American flag planted on the moon's surface in July 1969.

Soviets sent Sputnik II into space with the dog Laika aboard.

Even more startling evidence of Soviet superiority in space technology was the flight of Yuri Gagarin on April 12, 1961. Not until February 1962 did the United States succeed in sending its first astronaut into Earth orbit: John Glenn. Meanwhile, only a few weeks after Gagarin's flight, President John F. Kennedy stood before a joint session of Congress and pledged that America would put a man on the moon before the end of the decade.

Although he did not live to see the moment, Kennedy's dream was fulfilled on July 20, 1969, when Neil Armstrong and Edwin "Buzz" Aldrin stepped from Apollo 11 onto the surface of the moon. In the next three years, the United States sent five more Apollo crews to the moon.

---

from the fact that we are not going strong." Two days later, after a light breakfast and an eight-mile morning trek, Evans collasped with vomiting and giddiness.

Evans insisted on resuming the march on February 17 but fell out in little more than half an hour to adjust his ski boots. When he failed to catch up, the others turned back to find him crouched in the snow, babbling incoherently. Camp was hastily made and the comatose seaman placed in a tent; he died that night without recovering consciousness.

At the end of the first week in March, they began anxiously peering ahead for the dogsleds that were to have come out to meet them. Indeed, two men had reached One Ton Depot by dogsled on March 2 but had headed back to McMurdo Sound on March 10. Scott and his three companions were 72 miles away at Mt. Hooper.

Eleven Miles Short

Oates had been silently suffering the agony of gangrenous feet and knew that he could only slow his teammates' progress. On the morning of March 16 or 17 — even Scott had lost track of the date — Oates asked to be left behind in his sleeping bag. The others refused and urged him a few miles farther that day. In a blizzard the next

morning, he rose and announced, "I am just going outside and may be some time." The others realized that he was walking to his death.

The three remaining explorers made their last camp on March 19, only 11 miles short of One Ton Depot. Scott's right foot was so badly frostbitten that he knew amputation was the best he could hope for. Bowers and Wilson offered to push on to the goal and return with food and fuel, but a blizzard trapped them in their tent. "The end cannot be far," Scott wrote on March 29. "It seems a pity, but I do not think I can write more."

On March 7, 1912, news of Amundsen's triumph had reached London. The following month a cable from New Zealand said that Scott had been within 150 miles of that goal on January 4. It was widely assumed that, though beaten by the Norwegians, the British expedition would return after another Antarctic winter. Early in 1913, Mrs. Scott set out to meet her husband, crossing the United States and taking ship for the South Pacific. On February 19 she was summoned into the captain's cabin and handed a telegram: a search party sent out from McMurdo Sound had found the frozen bodies of Captain Scott and his two companions in their tent the previous November 12; they had been dead for nearly eight months.

The Would-be Peace Pilot

*Peacemaker, madman, or scapegoat? Rudolf Hess claimed that
his famous flight was an act of statesmanship, but he angered
Hitler, Churchill, and Stalin, bringing his own life to ruin.*

*I*t was bizarre. Every month, for more than 20 years, a military detachment of 54 officers and men from four countries — the United States, the Soviet Union, France, and Britain — took its turn at guarding one prisoner. Weak with age, afflicted with painful ailments, and quite possibly insane, he lived in a cell 8 feet 10½ inches long by 7 feet 5 inches wide. A single barred window more than 5 feet above the floor could be opened for light and air. The stone walls were almost 2 feet thick. This was one of the cells in Berlin's Spandau Prison, built in 1876, a grim red-brick pile that could hold up to 600 prisoners. Five guard towers were built into the impregnable high walls, which were encircled by a death-dealing electrified fence and a 10-foot-high barrier of barbed wire.

Adolf Hitler, the Nazi führer, had kept the ugly fortress alive with activity. Political foes were processed there on their way to death camps or executed on the premises, which featured facilities for hanging up to eight victims at the same time. In a curious twist of fate, it would be used to house seven of the dead dictator's closest surviving advisers after the war. Yet by 1966, all except Rudolf Hess had been freed.

He alone continued to be kept entirely secluded from the outside world, although it is true that he did not express the wish to see anyone from his past. He remained subject to strict prison regulations, receiving a "new" secondhand overcoat after 16 years or being forced to sleep with a light on so that guards could open a peephole in his steel door and check up on him during the night.

Rudolf Hess was an enthusiastic aviator who, despite Hitler's orders, liked to fly solo in the Messerschmitt 110, the aircraft that he later used on his dramatic flight to Britain in May 1941.

Occasionally, a news photographer with a tele-photo lens managed to snap a candid photo of the stooped, broken old man, puttering in his garden in a courtyard of the vast, empty prison. On August 17, 1987, the 93-year-old Hess finally tricked his watchful captors and hanged himself with an electrical cord.

What had he done to earn such cruelly protracted punishment and the tight security provided by the four nations that had been allies during World War II?

Fanatic Devotion

Rudolf Hess riveted the attention of millions in 1941 with one mysterious and astonishing act. Although he was officially second in succession to Adolf Hitler, he secretly boarded a small plane and soloed across the North Sea to Britain, convinced that he could persuade the leaders of Germany's enemy to agree to stop fighting on peace terms he would outline. Was he actually following a plan cleared by Hitler? Had he become disillusioned with his leader and decided to act on his own? Had he lost his mind and become dizzied by paranoid fantasies, as his former colleagues immediately claimed?

The mystery of Rudolf Hess is rooted firmly in his character, which puzzled and disturbed many people long before his startling flight. Born in 1894 into a comfortably well-off German family living in Alexandria, Egypt, Hess enjoyed a traditional middle-class upbringing. At age 12, he was sent to a rigorous boarding school in Germany, but he summered every year with his family at a Bavarian estate built by his prosperous father. A gifted student, he volunteered for the infantry when World War I broke out and sustained three wounds, including a lung injury that rendered him short of breath for the rest of his life. He completed training as an officer pilot in the Imperial Flying Corps, but the armistice ending the war was signed before he saw aerial combat. Photos capture a darkly handsome young man of serious mien, a square-jawed, forceful visage that hints at a tendency to brood.

Refusing always to drink, smoke, or dance, the war-hardened Hess threw himself into politics. Domestic chaos after the humiliating defeat in history's first global war was threatening the very existence of Germany as a nation. Fearful of communist subversion encouraged by Soviet Russia, Hess joined the Free Corps, a group of right-wing youths devoted to suppressing leftist movements with brute force. In a 1919 street brawl with communists in Munich, he received a leg wound, an incident that apparently fueled even more

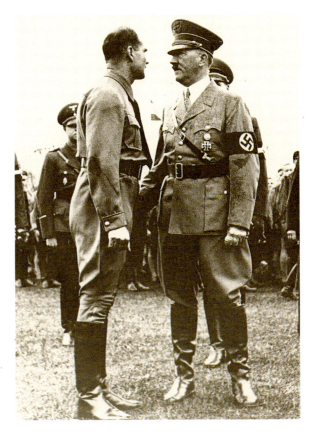

The führer and his deputy: Always eager to anticipate Adolf Hitler's wishes and to see that they were fulfilled, Hess may have believed that he was actually carrying out the führer's plans with the peace mission to Britain.

hotly his hatred for communists in his own country and in Russia as well.

In 1920 and 1921, Hess met the two most important personages in his life. As a student at the University of Munich, where he was already making his anti-Semitic feelings clear, he wrote a prize-winning essay arguing that national unity could be reestablished only under the authority of a man of the people. He added, "When necessity commands, he does not shrink before bloodshed. Great questions are always decided by blood and iron." This chilling description, of course, fitted the violent, up-and-coming young Adolf Hitler, guiding light of the infant National Socialist German Workers' Party. Earlier, Hess had enlisted as the 16th member of the group, known to history as the Nazi Party.

Hess also came under the influence of Professor Karl Haushofer, whose course in geopolitics was based on his theories of how geography affects the political history of countries. The impressionable Hess, obviously eager to hear an optimistic projection of the German future, thrilled to the idea that Germany and England, populated by the Anglo-Saxon "master race," should join together to rule the world. Germany, according to the professor, was held back by the need for more living-space (*Lebensraum*).

Apparently, the ideas of Hitler and Professor Haushofer intermingled in the dour young man's mind, and he became passionately involved in the hope of resurrecting his country's economic, political, and military power. In 1923 Hitler failed to gain control of the government in his famous "beer-hall putsch" in Munich and was jailed. Hess, who had been in charge of rounding up Jews and other likely opponents during the abortive coup d'etat and had won Hitler's praise for his effective brawling, escaped to Austria. He voluntarily gave himself up to serve time with his leader when it turned out that Hitler's chauffeur, though slavishly devoted, was an inexpert secretary. The cell blocks of Landberg Prison soon reverberated with the clacking of Hess's Remington typewriter as he took down dictation for *Mein Kampf*, the infamous blueprint for the regeneration of Germany under the Nazis.

Hess's parachute landing in Scotland created headlines throughout Britain. He asked to present his peace plan to the duke of Hamilton (right), a prewar acquaintance. Below, a Scottish officer examines the wreckage of Hess's aircraft.

It was Hess who dubbed Hitler "der Führer," or leader, and created the cult that enshrined him, popularizing the Nazi stiff-armed salute. Daily, he avidly typed such insights as "All effective propaganda must be limited to a very few points, and they should be used like slogans until the very last man in the audience is capable of understanding what is meant by this slogan." In the long-winded, repetitious book that would result, Hitler also revealed his plan to unite the Germans against both the communists and Jews by making them appear to be "a single enemy." For the taciturn Hess the experience must have been

heady, indeed. Hitler's speeches at his trial had already gained international attention, strengthening the ambitious leader's confidence, and he quickly became the center of prison life, receiving lavish presents and visitors at all hours, dominating dinner table conversation, and even being saluted with "Heil, Hitler!" by his guards. Hess was always at his side.

Shoved Aside

Years later, when Hitler had won supreme power in Germany, the loyal Hess of the lean, difficult years of struggle against great odds would be a fixture of the inner circle. Some felt that the führer trusted him with private thoughts that no one else would ever hear. Official Nazi propaganda praised him as the "Conscience of the Party."

As the German forces spread out over Europe, however, and the focus of all national effort and will was military victory, Hess began to feel shunted to the sidelines. Hitler named him deputy führer but second in the line of succession after the forceful, swaggering Field Marshal Hermann Goering. Slowly, Hess's subordinate, the sinister Martin Bormann, also began to undercut his influence. Never a wily conspirator in such bureaucratic infighting, Hess apparently thought that a dramatic gesture might reinstate him as Hitler's closest adviser and also, by shortening the war, return the attention of the party to the nonmilitary issues that concerned him most.

As deputy and cosigner of important state decrees, including many designed to exclude Jews from participating in economic or political life, Hess was deeply involved in domestic matters, charged particularly with suppressing opponents of National Socialism. But, influenced by Professor Haushofer's brilliant son, Albrecht, he came to the conclusion that Germany should make peace with England so that all of the Nazi military might could be directed at once upon the enemy he hated most, communist Russia under Stalin. Both Haushofers had contacts in Britain and in neutral Portugal and Spain, but Albrecht warned Hess that the British regarded Hitler as "Satan's representative on earth." The führer's deputy could not understand why.

Young Haushofer, however, was playing a dangerous game. Unknown to his friend and admirer, he had begun plotting with those who were organizing resistance to the Nazi regime. To placate Hess, he offered to contact a good friend, the duke of Hamilton, but stressed repeatedly that the British would not be likely to entertain any proposals that would lead to signing a peace treaty with the despised Hitler.

As far back as 1939, not long after Britain declared war against Hitler's Germany, Goering had offered to fly over to the island nation and "explain the situation." Hitler is supposed to have replied, "It will be of no use, but if you can, try it." Throughout 1940 and 1941, as a member of the wartime Cabinet Council, Hess was fully aware of the secret plans to renounce the nonaggression pact with the Soviet Union and invade Russia under the code name "Operation Barbarossa." Perhaps the seed planted by Goering was nurtured by Hess's awareness of the mammoth task of subduing the Russians and by his truly fanatical desire to serve his führer.

Apparently, late in 1940, he slipped off regularly to make training flights, perhaps as many as 30 all told, at the Messerschmitt Works airfield in Augsburg. He had worked as a test pilot and demonstration flier for the prestigious aircraft firm during the 1930's and had won aviation races, including an annual contest encircling Germany's highest peak, the Zugspitze. In fact, he had longed to join the reborn German air force, the extraordinary Luftwaffe, but in 1939 Hitler forbade him to fly for at least 12 months. When he began practicing in a Messerschmitt 110, a high-speed twin-engine fighter bomber with a maximum range of 1,200 miles, it is likely that Hitler knew. But did the führer know that, three times in 1941, his deputy tried to fly off toward Britain but had to turn back because of dangerous flying conditions? The extent of Hitler's prior knowledge of the Hess flight remains one of the unresolved mysteries of the whole affair.

Doomed Flight for Peace

"My Führer, when you receive this letter I shall be in England. You can imagine that the decision to take this step has not been easy for me, since a man of 40 has other ties in life than one of 20." Upon reading these first words of a note delivered by Hess's secretary, Adolf Hitler shrieked in pain and burst into tears. To those in attendance, he seemed both shocked and terrified to learn that his deputy had taken it upon himself to fly to Britain the night before, on May 10, 1941. "The Führer is quite shattered," reads an entry in the diary of Joseph Goebbels, minister for propaganda and popular enlightenment. Still, some historians suspect that the Nazi leader may have been playacting, waiting for the first results of the quixotic mission.

It was an unqualified disaster. Having donned a Luftwaffe uniform, Hess had taken off in the evening for Scotland. Twice, he had to dodge through the sheltering mists over the North Sea to elude interceptor Spitfires from the Royal Air Force, but he was blessed with the advantage of a swifter aircraft. He zigzagged back and forth until near sunset, possibly fearing that antiaircraft batteries would spot him by daylight, and then raced low over the British countryside, "hedge-hopping" only a few yards above ground level and waving to astonished rustics. Aiming for the Scottish countryside where his supposed friend the duke of Hamilton lived, he shot up about a mile into the air and bailed out, leaving the brand-new Messerschmitt to spiral down and crash in the rocky hills.

It was the 48-year-old deputy's first parachute jump, and it occurred in the dark after 10 P.M., factors that may explain why he cracked an ankle bone and chipped a vertebra upon landing. Hobbling to a nearby farmhouse, he introduced himself to the owner as "Hauptmann Alfred Horn" and explained that he had to go at once to the duke of Hamilton's estate, Dungavel House,

From 1947 until his death in 1987, Rudolf Hess was incarcerated in Berlin's Spandau Prison — for many of those years the solitary inmate of the citadel, guarded by the troops of four nations.

to deliver an urgent message. The suspicious Scot alerted the police, and Hess was taken into custody and handed over to the army.

Dismissed by All

By odd coincidence the duke had been on duty that night as a wing commander at Turnhouse Airport near Edinburgh and had dispatched at least one of the planes that had tried to down the German intruder. Hess probably expected a warm welcome from the titled aviator, the first to fly over Mount Everest and a luncheon guest at Hess's house during the Olympic Games in 1936. When the duke interviewed the prisoner the next day, however, he was cool and correct, noting in his official report that Hess explained Hitler's peace terms as follows: "First, he would insist on an arrangement whereby our two countries would never go to war again [and] Britain would give up her traditional policy of always opposing the strongest power in Europe."

Hess tried to bluff his way into talks with Churchill and other high-level authorities, but his fate was to be held in the Tower of London for four days and then imprisoned in a rural safe house for the next four years. After much initial bewilderment and annoyance, and not a little suspicion that this prisoner might be an impostor, the British government simply ignored Hess.

Meanwhile, the führer had recovered and put out the story that the deputy had been mentally unbalanced for years and his flight was the result of hallucinations. It was also alleged that Hess had begun to rely upon hypnotists and astrologers to interpret reality for him. Privately, the Nazi leadership worried that Hess would reveal "Operation Barbarossa" to the British. They naturally assumed that their adversaries would resort to torture of the hapless Hess.

In both countries and around the globe, mystification was the strongest reaction to the inexplicable flight. How could the all-powerful führer's most trusted aide take off without being discovered? Why would the German government tolerate a madman at the highest levels? What did Hess have to gain from the episode?

But one man thought he knew exactly what was going on. Joseph Stalin believed that Churchill wanted to make a deal with Hitler. His suspicions were confirmed, in his own paranoid mind, when Hitler proclaimed the assault upon Soviet Russia on June 22. Thus began a horrendous devastation that took the lives of millions of Russians, as the Nazis mounted a blitzkrieg reflecting their leader's conviction that "You have only to kick in the door, and the whole rotten

The Justice of the Victors

At the Potsdam Conference in 1945, the Allied leaders agreed to hold war crimes trials in Nürnberg, Germany, so that the defeated power's most important participants in the war — politicians, military officers, industrialists — could be tried before an international tribunal.

Opening on November 20 of that year, the trial brought to the dock 22 Germans, including Hess, and became a sensational exposé of the Nazi regime's worst excesses. Questions about the legitimacy of the exercise, however, are still hotly debated. Moreover, the list of charges has provoked controversy. Two were already familiar from existing international law: "actual war crimes" and "crimes against humanity." But the third, "crimes against peace," was not a charge that had been clearly defined and

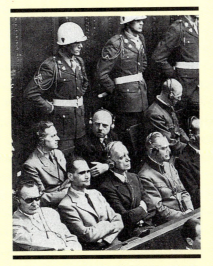

Arms across his chest, Rudolf Hess sits in the prisoners' dock at Nürnberg. He alone does not wear earphones for simultaneous translation.

recognized as punishable. It was the only charge for which Hess would be convicted.

In his final statement before his judges, Hess boasted, "I was permitted to work for many years under the greatest son whom my country has brought forth in its 1,000-year history. Even if I could, I would not want to erase this period of time from my existence." He would never be allowed to speak in public again.

Three of the Nürnberg defendants were set free, and seven, including Hess, were removed to Spandau. Twelve others were sentenced to death by hanging, but Hermann Goering committed suicide by swallowing a poison capsule, perhaps smuggled into his cell by a sympathetic guard, and Martin Bormann, who had eluded capture, was sentenced in absentia.

---

structure will come crashing down." After five months of heroic Russian resistance, the Germans were stopped. Probably, as events at Spandau later suggest, Stalin made certain that Hess's attempt to persuade Britain to betray its Russian ally was never forgotten.

Decades of Silence

The deputy führer's physical maladies, real or imagined, added to the misery of his unexpected incarceration. The British refusal to take him seriously, much less honor him with a hero's welcome, may have exacerbated his mental problems, although observers would disagree over his actual state of mind — some diagnosing acute delusionary paranoia, others suspecting an act.

Some suggested that Hess, who had waved a flag of truce when he knocked on the farmer's door, could not be held prisoner in Britain. Returning him to Germany, however, would have been tantamount to a sentence of death.

After Germany's defeat and Hitler's suicide, the discredited deputy stood trial at Nürnberg, where he confessed that he had pretended for some time to suffer from amnesia. His former colleagues seemed alternately amused and exasperated by his unpredictable behavior. Later, he prepared a paper outlining a preposterous

plan for ruling Germany when he was released from prison.

In the four decades of imprisonment at Spandau, Hess kept to himself, occasionally giving in to hypochondria and finally developing serious gastrointestinal problems. A lifelong vegetarian and practitioner of such nontraditional medicine as homeopathy, he distrusted physicians. From the beginning of his prison stay, he suspected that his warders were trying to poison him or drug him with mind-altering substances.

Possibly, his Russian guards did not resist feeding these fears, for it was obvious that they tended to be implacable and unyielding with this particular prisoner. When Hess finally agreed to see his wife and son after 28 years of imprisonment, the half-hour visit was almost canceled when the Russian representative insisted upon a minor point. Soviet soldiers bedeviled the old man by denuding his raspberry bushes, and the Russian commandant always fought the attempts of his counterparts from other nations to ease Hess's harsh life. Until the end the Russians alone resisted all attempts to parole the prisoner. To them he was a prime force in destroying untold Russian lives, not a misunderstood idealistic partisan of peace. Hitler's right-hand man was never forgiven by the heirs of Stalin.

Lonely Woman of the Forest

*For nearly two decades, she waged a passionate campaign
to save the mountain gorillas of East Africa's Virunga Mountains
from extinction. Her single-minded dedication brought conflict
with both forest poachers and the government of Rwanda.*

Dawn is enveloping Karisoke Research Station in the mist-shrouded volcanic mountains along Rwanda's border with Uganda and Zaire. Suddenly, loud clamoring breaks the silence, and a group of wildly gesticulating black men storm into the cabin where the American graduate student Wayne McGuire is sleeping. With his limited knowledge of Swahili, he does not at first understand what they are saying — until a repeated phrase registers. *"Dian kufa! Dian kufa!"* Dian is dead!

Running over to Dian Fossey's cabin, he finds her lifeless body sprawled next to the bed; her skull had been laid open by a diagonal cut from the forehead across the nose to the corner of her mouth. The weapon — a broad-bladed knife used by forest workers to hack their way through underbrush — was one she had confiscated some years earlier from poachers. The cabin was in disarray, having been ransacked by the attacker or, perhaps, upset by Fossey in an attempt to ward off her assailant. Near the door stood a Christmas tree, with presents for the staff as yet undistributed. It was December 27, 1985.

Four days later, the dead woman was buried in the station's small animal cemetery, next to the graves of some of the gorillas to whom she had given her life. Nine months later, McGuire and one of the station employees, Emmanuel Rwelekana, were charged with the murder of the 54-year-old Fossey. The native hanged himself, and McGuire, on the advice of the United States embassy in Rwanda, fled the country before he was arrested. Although he was tried and convicted in absentia, few if any accept his guilt. There were other, more obvious suspects.

Dian Fossey was a far from uncontroversial person. Yet, her most intimate friends praised her as a warmhearted, thoroughly dedicated woman and called her "Queen of the Apes." Largely through her efforts, the East African mountain gorillas are no longer an endangered species. In Rwanda's Parc National des Volcans, at least 20 gorilla families live today; in the mid-1970's, there were only half as many.

With her research into the lifestyle and behavior of the giant beasts, Fossey refuted the Hollywood-inspired myth of a fearsome, vicious King Kong. At first observing the gentle giants with the leathery faces from a safe distance, she eventually mingled among them by imitating their barking, grunting sounds and acquiring their unique body language. Thus, for example, she learned to brace her arms to signal friendliness and crouched so as never to appear larger than the family leader. In time, she was accepted by the animals almost as one of themselves and would sit for hours with them, nibbling on the wild celery they favored and being allowed to scratch and de-lice her research subjects.

The Road to East Africa

"Neither destiny nor fate took me to Africa," Fossey wrote. "Nor was it romance. I had a deep wish to see and live with wild animals in a world that hadn't yet been completely changed by humans." Her parents were divorced when she was six, and her stepfather kept her at arm's length. The lonely child sought friendship in animals but was denied all pets, except a goldfish; she cried for a week when it died.

Fossey's plan to become a veterinarian ended when she failed to master chemistry and physics at the University of California at Davis. Instead, she became an occupational therapist and worked with physically and emotionally disabled children in a Louisville, Kentucky, hospital. Her interest in Africa was sparked by a young Rhodesian suitor, but she felt that marriage was too high a price to pay for a ticket to the Dark Continent. She started saving pennies for a trip and in 1963 left for East Africa.

"She had dropped out of the human world, and it was her misfortune that she could not become a gorilla herself" — that is how a colleague characterized Dian Fossey. At left, she sits among the animals she loved perhaps too much. Below, the forest cabin in which she lived and where she was murdered.

In Tanzania she met the celebrated anthropologist Louis Leakey, who asked her what she still wanted to see. Told that her greatest hope was to see the mountain gorillas of the Virunga volcano country, Leakey asked if her interest in them was as a spectator or as a journalist. "Much more than that, Dr. Leakey," she replied. "Someday I plan to come here to live and work." A few days later, she saw her first gorillas. "They were big and imposing," she wrote, "but not monstrous at all. Somehow they looked more like members of a picnic party surprised by interlopers." When she left Africa, Fossey had no doubt that she would return to spend her life with the animals. Four years later, with a grant from the National Geographic Society, she established the Karisoke Research Station.

Scientific Research or Blind Infatuation

Nyiramachabelli, "lonely woman of the forest," is what the natives called her. She achieved much in her studies of the animals and can be credited with helping to save them from extinction. Yet, her motives and methods remained the subject of heated debate. Her highly personal relationship with the mountain gorillas surpassed both scholarly interest and the normal affection most people feel for animals. In sharp contrast to her love for the gorillas was her implacable hatred for the poachers who were destroying their habitat and wantonly slaying the beasts. She pursued them relentlessly, confiscating their tools and weapons and even flogging them personally.

Soon she was at war not only with the poachers but also with Rwandan authorities, who were hoping to open the scenic volcanic park to tourism. Fossey was firmly opposed. Her gorillas were not zoo exhibits, and she threatened to shoot any tourist approaching her station. Such stubborn dedication in time earned her many enemies — among them, no doubt, the unknown murderer who brutally killed her in December 1985.

Smithsonian Institution museums line the Mall, from the Capitol to the Washington Monument.

A Fortune for Science

The United States, and the world, are richer for the peculiar bequest of an Englishman named James Smithson, who left his entire fortune to a country he had not even visited. His reasons for doing so have never been satisfactorily explained.

A vast expanse of green, the Mall, stretches westward toward the Potomac River from the U.S. Capitol in Washington. Flanking it is an imposing array of museum buildings collectively known as the Smithsonian Institution. Its major constituents are the national museums of Air and Space, Natural History, American History, and African Art; the Freer Gallery of Art (noted for Oriental and Islamic art); the Sackler Gallery (a collection of Near Eastern and Asian art); and the Hirschhorn Museum and Sculpture Garden. Affiliated with the Smithsonian Institution are the National Gallery of Art (also on the

Mall), the John F. Kennedy Center for the Performing Arts, and the Woodrow Wilson Center for Scholars. In all there are 14 museums — 13 in Washington and one (Cooper-Hewett) in New York — plus the National Zoological Park, also in Washington.

At the midpoint of the Mall, on the south side, is a multiturreted building of red stone, a fairytale castle completed in 1855. In a chapel off the main entrance lie the mortal remains of James Smithson, an Englishman who never visited the United States during his lifetime but whose extraordinary legacy led to the foundation of what has become one of the world's preeminent scientific establishments and the repository of enormous collections of art and artifacts.

The Stigma of His Birth

James Smithson was born in 1765 in France, to which his mother had fled from the scandal of her pregnancy. For the father of Elizabeth Macie's child was Sir Hugh Smithson, married to a cousin of the wealthy widow and soon to be made the first duke of Northumberland. Elizabeth, who traced her lineage back to King Henry VII, was determined that her son overcome the stigma of his illegitimacy. When he was 10, she brought him to England and managed to have him naturalized a British subject — although he was barred from civil or military office and forbidden to accept any land grant from the crown. Denied the usual career opportunities of wealthy young men, he turned to science.

At 17 he entered Oxford University's Pembroke College under the name James Louis Macie and quickly earned a reputation as the brightest chemist and mineralogist in his class. Within four years he had a master's degree and a year later was sponsored for membership in the Royal Society by Henry Cavendish, one of the nation's most distinguished scientists. In 1791 he read his first paper before the society, a study of the chemical properties of tabasheer, a substance found in bamboo; he was 26 years old.

During his career Smithson — the name he took following his mother's death in 1800 — published 27 papers on chemical subjects. His careful analysis of European deposits of zinc ores led to the identification of zinc carbonate, a mineral named smithsonite in his honor. Yet fame eluded him as he wandered about Europe, a wealthy bachelor acquainted with all the leading scientists of the day, men whose work he could never hope to equal.

On October 23, 1826, at the age of 61, he penned a last will and testament that was to purchase immortality for him. After proudly listing his parents as the duke of Northumberland and "Elizabeth, Heiress of the Hungerfords of Studley," Smithson left his fortune to a nephew, Henry James Hungerford. But should Hungerford leave no heirs, the aging scientist bequeathed his entire estate "to the United States of America, to found at Washington, under the name of the Smithsonian Institution, an Establishment for the increase & diffusion of knowledge among men."

Helping to Build a New Athens

"The best blood of England flows in my veins," Smithson once wrote, ". . . but this avails me not.

The illegitimate son of a British nobleman, James Smithson (right) achieved the fame denied him as a scientist by his remarkable legacy to the United States.

Among the many proposals for using Smithson's bequest was a library; the collection (at left as it appeared in the 19th century) is but part of the institution's vast holdings — "the nation's attic," as it has been called.

A Troublesome Legacy

Accepting James Smithson's gift of a half million dollars did not end congressional debate on the matter. What precisely had the British benefactor in mind when he left his money to the United States for an establishment to increase and diffuse knowledge?

An experimental agriculture station, one senator said. No, exclaimed another; what the country needed was a library, "a vast storehouse, a vast treasury, of all the facts which make up the history of man and of nature." A congressman replied that libraries were but "petty antiquarian triumphs"; better a natural history collection and a school for training teachers. Rather than spending the money on a school, said ex-president John Quincy Adams, then serving as a congressman from Massachusetts, he would prefer to see it thrown in the Potomac; he opted for an observatory.

Finally, in August 1846, Congress acted to incorporate the Smithsonian Institution and authorized construction of a building "of plain and durable materials and structure, without unnecessary ornament." It would house a museum, a study collection of scientific materials, a chemical laboratory, a gallery of art, and lecture rooms. The Smithsonian's first building could scarcely be said to be without unnecessary ornament, but for the advancement of knowledge the charter was broad enough to encompass all that has been developed in a century and a half by the remarkable, wide-ranging institution.

My name shall live in the memory of man when the titles of the Northumberlands and Percys are extinct and forgotten." It is the statement of a man tormented and frustrated by the conditions under which he was born and determined to defy the society that had scorned him. But why did he choose the United States, a country he had never visited and to which he had no ties of friendship or kin? The answer perhaps lies in a visit Smithson made to Paris when he was 27.

The year was 1792, three years after a Paris mob had stormed the Bastille, the infamous prison that symbolized the decadence and tyranny of the Bourbon kings. The newly elected National Convention was about to abolish the monarchy and declare France a republic. "Stupidity and guilt have had a long reign," Smithson wrote to a friend at Oxford, "and it begins indeed to be the time for justice and common sense to have their term." Monarchy — and by extension the nobility from which he had been excluded — was a

"contemptible incumbrance"; as for himself, he was "of the democratic party."

The French Revolution, unfortunately, devolved into a reign of terror; the republic gave way to the monomaniacal Napoleon's empire. But across the Atlantic Ocean an experiment in self-government was working: the fledgling United States of America. Its capital city, the poet Joel Barlow wrote, would be a new Athens rising on the banks of the Potomac River. The great new discoveries in science, Smithson's fellow chemist Joseph Priestly declared, would be made in a republic, not under a monarchy. Turning his back on the turbulence and confusion of the Old World, James Smithson determined to have a hand in building that new Athens.

From Humble Beginnings

In 1829, three years after writing his peculiar will, James Smithson died and was buried in Genoa, Italy. Six years later his nephew died without an heir. After a lengthy debate about accepting the bequest — John C. Calhoun said that it was "beneath the dignity of the country to accept such gifts from foreigners" — Congress authorized the president to send an agent to England to collect the money. In August 1838 a boat arrived in New York City with 105 bags of gold sovereigns, at the time worth precisely $508,318.46.

Not until 1847 was the cornerstone laid for the Gothic revival building that was to be the Smithsonian Institution's first home, the red stone castle to which Smithson's remains were brought in 1904. Already the board of regents — composed then, as now, of the chief justice of the United States, the vice president, three congressmen, three senators, and six private citizens — had taken a decisive step: selecting a Princeton science professor named Joseph Henry to head the fledgling institution.

It was Henry who convinced the board that original research would be an essential function of the Smithsonian Institution; in 1848 the first volume in a series of scientific works, *Smithsonian Contributions to Knowledge*, was published. Henry enlisted volunteer observers across the country to report on the weather; his network would evolve into the United States Weather Bureau. Today Smithsonian scientists help preserve endangered species at the Washington zoo, keep a watch on celestial bodies at an Arizona observatory, conduct tropical research in Panama, and study environmental interactions in Maryland. James Smithson's goal to increase and spread knowledge has been triumphantly achieved.

4

Guilty or
Not Guilty?

The Watergate commercial and residential complex in Washington gave the political scandal its name.

Unsolved Riddles of Watergate

*A "third-rate burglary," never explained, paralyzes the U.S.
government and unlocks a Pandora's box of White House secrets.
For the first time in American history, a president is forced
to resign and his closest advisers are sent to prison.*

I t has become perhaps the most famous question ever asked in American public life: "What did the president know . . . and when did he know it?" Tennessee's Senator Howard Baker, the ranking Republican member of the Senate Select Committee on Presidential Campaign Activities, echoed the frustration of the nation in 1973 as a parade of witnesses before TV cameras told a complex, shadowy tale of intrigue, intimidation, electronic surveillance, and payoffs at the highest levels of government. The flood of sordid revelations became popularly known as

the Watergate scandal, and the resulting congressional investigations, court actions, newspaper accounts, and books would fill a small research library. But has the senator's question ever been satisfactorily answered?

The wrenching experience that President Gerald Ford would call "our long national nightmare" began as low farce. At 2 A.M. on June 17, 1972, five men were caught rummaging through the Democratic National Committee's headquarters in the Watergate complex in Washington. Carrying cameras and electronic surveillance burglars were linked to E. Howard Hunt, the CIA operative in charge of the embarrassing attempt to invade Cuba in 1961. Hunt had recently been advising Nixon's special counsel and longtime political strategist, Charles W. Colson. Even as the FBI, Department of Justice, Congress, and reporters began to focus on this inexplicable story, the president succeeded in attaining a stunning reelection victory in November.

Yet, as Nixon and his staff celebrated, the growing Watergate puzzle was becoming a national obsession. The president was soon preoccupied with explaining each bizarre new twist of the plot. Had he and his people somehow sown the seeds of their own political destruction?

"Plumbers" for National Security

On May 9, 1969, only a few months after Richard Nixon had taken the oath of office for his first term, he became infuriated when *The New York Times* reported that the United States was secretly bombing North Vietnamese bases in Laos and Cambodia. Wiretaps were ordered for the telephones of suspected informants.

Two years later, on June 13, 1971, the same newspaper began publishing excerpts from a confidential Pentagon report about the country's involvement in Vietnam. Clearly, a government insider had passed along the 7,000-page study, for only 15 copies existed. Eventually, it was learned that the report had been leaked by Daniel Ellsberg, formerly an analyst for the Department of Defense.

Determined not to have the private deliberations of his own administration noised abroad in this way, Nixon conferred with his two closest and most trusted advisers, White House Chief of Staff H. R. Haldeman and Domestic Affairs Adviser John D. Ehrlichman. Their solution was to order Egil Krogh, Ehrlichman's chief assistant, to establish a secret group charged with "plugging leaks." Inevitably, they called themselves "the plumbers." Hunt and a former small-town prosecutor and gun fancier named G. Gordon Liddy joined this enterprise but bungled their first assignment. Hoping somehow to discredit Ellsberg, they hired anti-Castro Cubans to break into the office of his psychotherapist, but the misguided burglars failed to find his treatment files.

Preparing for the Worst

In 1960 Nixon had narrowly lost the presidential election to John F. Kennedy. In his 1968 comeback he had narrowly beaten Hubert Humphrey. Pollsters said at the time that the trend of voter opinion was moving against him so swiftly to-

Carl Bernstein (left) and Bob Woodward reported the Watergate burglary for The Washington Post. *Their brilliant investigation of the unraveling scandal helped earn the newspaper a Pulitzer Prize for meritorious service in 1973.*

equipment, they had already removed ceiling panels and riffled through party files. All the men turned out to have connections with the Central Intelligence Agency. They had been caught only because an alert security guard noted that they had taped over a door lock. When he removed the tape, one of the burglars retaped it, apparently suspecting nothing.

At the time President Richard Nixon, the Republican standard-bearer, seemed headed toward an easy reelection victory over the Democratic nominee, Senator George McGovern. Even when one of the burglars turned out to be James McCord, a security agent for the Committee for the Reelection of the President (CRP), Nixon asserted that "the White House has had no involvement whatever." But Lawrence F. O'Brien, the Democratic national chairman, denounced the raid as "a blatant act of political espionage" and filed a $1 million lawsuit against CRP. Meanwhile, more and more lines of investigation led toward the White House. Two of the

Richard Nixon won a landslide victory over his Democratic opponent in the 1972 presidential election, with nearly 61 percent of the popular vote and an electoral college margin of 520 to 18. Few if any voters realized that the Watergate scandal could be traced directly to the White House.

ward the end of the campaign that he could have lost if the election had been held only a few days later. To consolidate what he feared to be a tenuous political position, Nixon established CRP, an organization dedicated to raising the millions of dollars that would fund an impressive reelection campaign in 1972. John Mitchell resigned as attorney general to become director; Liddy was hired as financial adviser; McCord was named head of security.

CRP was dramatically successful, amassing a huge war chest from corporation executives who undoubtedly wanted to be remembered at the White House after the election. But, even as it became clear that the Democrats would nominate a candidate who had almost no chance of defeating the incumbent, some operatives apper-

ently felt that unusual measures were necessary.

To this day, it is not known exactly what the burglars hoped to find at the Democratic headquarters on June 17, 1972. Did they have reason to suspect that their opponents had information that could scuttle the juggernaut of the Nixon campaign? Did they hope that "bugging" the offices would help them anticipate Democratic strategies? Ironically, the burglary attempt itself would prove to be the most damaging event of the campaign, a time bomb that would not detonate for months to come.

The Net Begins to Close

For a time, the Watergate story moved to the back pages of newspapers, but Ehrlichman, Haldeman, Mitchell, and a young lawyer named John Dean, special counsel to the president, fully recognized its explosive potential. They were working frantically to buy the silence of Hunt, Liddy, and the five original burglars. All had been promised presidential pardons, but McCord — pressured by a tough district court judge, John Sirica — confessed in March 1973 that Dean and Jeb Magruder, formerly a deputy director of CRP, had prior knowledge of the break-in.

Only a month earlier, the U.S. Senate had set in motion an investigation that would lead to nationally televised hearings into the affair. There followed a veritable avalanche of charges, countercharges, rumors, and threats. Eventually, Dean cooperated with the Senate panel, portraying a White House that was deeply involved in covering up the Watergate story. He stated that Mitchell had been urged to "take the heat" by confessing responsibility for the burglary; that Nixon knew that Hunt was asking for more than $120,000 to keep quiet about his activities; and that Ehrlichman tried to have evidence destroyed. Dean also revealed that Haldeman had ordered an aide to "remove and destroy damaging materials" from White House files.

At the heart of Dean's testimony, as if aimed in the direction of Senator Baker's fundamental question, was Dean's contention that the president had lied to the American public about his own involvement in the case. Testifying with calm precision, the self-possessed young lawyer charged that Nixon knew about the cover-up at least as early as September 15, 1972. The president had claimed that he learned about it more than six months later, on March 21, 1973, and had immediately ordered a search for the whole truth. Actually, said Dean, his boss already knew the entire story by then and was directing his energies toward saving himself.

Not surprisingly, Nixon fired Dean and regretfully asked for the resignations of his two senior advisers, Haldeman and Ehrlichman.

The Skirmish of the Tapes

Quite by accident, Senate investigators discovered that Nixon had installed a tape recorder in the Oval Office. Stored in basement archives, the tapes covered conversations dating back to the spring of 1971. Immediately, the special prosecutor appointed by the Justice Department, a Harvard law professor named Archibald Cox, cooperated with Judge Sirica and the Senate committee in efforts to obtain the taped evidence. Again citing executive privilege, Nixon refused to surrender the material and tried to force Cox, whom he called a "partisan viper," to desist. Cox, having been promised independence from the government, refused. Nixon's response was to order his dismissal on October 20, 1973.

Attorney General Eliot Richardson resigned rather than carry out the president's order. Then his deputy resigned as well. Although purposely timed to occur on the weekend, when public reaction might be muted, the action provoked, to use the term of Nixon's new chief of staff, General Alexander Haig, "a firestorm."

The Incriminating Tapes

Stunned, Nixon backed down. Of the nine tapes sought by investigators, however, he produced only seven, one of which fell suddenly silent for a gap of 18 minutes. The president's loyal secretary, Rose Mary Woods, claimed that she had inadvertently erased that section by resting her foot on a control button. When she tried to demonstrate the maneuver to reporters, however, she was un-

As the facts emerged, Nixon's removal was demanded by countless petitions (left) and White House pickets asking motorists to "Honk for impeachment."

Presidential Punishment

Perhaps because the procedure has been so infrequently used, the term "impeachment" is often misunderstood. It does not mean "conviction." Rather, the U.S. Constitution provides that the House of Representatives impeaches, or brings an indictment on charges of wrongdoing. Only the Senate, presided over by the chief justice of the Supreme Court, can convict, which requires a two-thirds vote. The only punishment is removal from office and disbarment from holding future offices.

The range of impeachable acts is described in the Constitution with a vagueness that many legal scholars find disturbing: "Treason, Bribery, or other High Crimes and Misdemeanors." In a preposterous example, Andrew Johnson, the only president ever to be impeached and tried, was charged — along with other "High Crimes and Misdemeanors" — with speaking disrespectfully of Congress "in a loud voice." Johnson's trial ended with his acquittal by one vote short of the two-thirds needed for conviction.

The Senate trial is likely to take as long as six weeks, a powerful argument for avoiding impeachment proceedings if possible. In addition, the very nature of the process pits one major branch of government against another and is susceptible to misuse as an instrument of political warfare. In fact, one of President Johnson's accusers frankly stated that "this proceeding is political in character . . . with a political object."

cause of vulgar language and national security matters, the transcripts would be edited versions rather than verbatim accounts. When the extent of the editing became known, and the transcripts were compared with the actual tapes, his credibility was further eroded.

The House committee, after public hearings, voted on July 30, 1974, to report three articles of impeachment to the full House of Representatives: obstruction of justice, abuse of the powers of the presidency, and attempts to impede the impeachment process itself. Two other articles were rejected.

In the National Interest

As late as August 5, Nixon was publicly assuring the nation that the record of the Watergate affair and his actions did not justify the extreme step of resignation. Grim reality intervened, however. Some of Nixon's oldest political friends and supporters, including the conservative senator Barry Goldwater, warned him that he was likely to be impeached by the House. Only resignation, they advised, could prevent the shameful spectacle of a subsequent trial before the entire Senate.

Thus, on the night of August 9, Nixon went on national television to announce that he would resign at noon the following day. Far from admitting any guilt or sense of remorse, he explained that his decision had become necessary only because he lacked a political base in Congress.

In an indictment that would lead to the conviction and imprisonment of many of his followers, including Mitchell, Haldeman, and Ehrlichman, the president himself was designated an "unindicted co-conspirator." The threat of prosecution lay over him until his successor, President Ford, proclaimed an amnesty "for all offenses" against the United States that Nixon may have committed during his presidency.

Ford's genial rectitude had brought him immediate popularity in the White House, but this act — which may have been motivated entirely by compassion for a disgraced and depressed human being — was viewed with suspicion by many. Some analysts think that it greatly contributed to Ford's defeat by Jimmy Carter in 1976. Although Ford hoped "to firmly shut and seal this book" by granting the pardon, in fact he added yet another fillip to the mystery. Did Nixon agree to resign only on the condition that he be promised a pardon? There is no evidence that Ford was party to any such deal, but the legacy of Watergate was a heightened distrust of high public officials. In the absence of proof, some voters seemed willing to believe the worst.

able to do so. Other gaps throughout the tapes were, in many cases, electronically enhanced by technical experts.

Therefore enough incriminating material was clearly audible, causing one of Nixon's own lawyers to whisper, upon hearing the tapes for the first time: "It's all over now." Nixon was taped in a discussion of the cover-up on June 23, 1972, only six days after the burglary and a date much earlier than that reported by John Dean.

In July 1974 the U.S. Supreme Court unanimously affirmed the right of courts to hear other tapes. The House Judiciary Committee, which had begun an impeachment inquiry, was given 19 tapes, but it wanted 42 more, covering conversations held between June 1972 and June 1973. The committee issued the first subpoena ever handed a president during impeachment proceedings.

Eventually, the White House released the tapes and approximately 1,200 pages of transcripts from them. Nixon explained that, be-

Eye of the Dawn

The name Mata Hari has come to symbolize a woman who successfully uses her feminine charms to wheedle secrets from the enemy in wartime. But was the real Mata Hari a spy? And if so, for which side was she an espionage agent?

The self-styled Indian dancer, Mata Hari. Was she German agent H-21, as the French believed? Her accusers claimed to have deciphered a code based on musical notes that she used to convey secrets to the enemy.

"*I* am not French," the woman told her accusers. "I have the right to have friends in other countries, even among those at war with France. I have remained neutral. I count upon the goodness of heart of you French officers." Thus Mata Hari summed up her defense before the court-martial in Paris on July 24, 1917. The three members of the panel retired to another room to consider a verdict. Within 10 minutes they were back. The international courtesan and self-styled Hindu dancer was to be shot as a spy.

The tortuous road to the court room had begun 41 years earlier in the northern Dutch town of Leeuwarden, where a daughter was born to a tradesman named Adam Zelle and his wife on August 7, 1876. The girl was christened Margaretha Geertruida. At the age of 14, she was sent to a convent school to be trained in the domestic arts in preparation for marriage — the proper upbringing for young women of her class. But such a conventional life was not for Margaretha Geertruida. One month short of her 19th birthday, she married Campbell MacLeod, a Dutch army officer of Scottish origin who was 21 years her senior. It was a disastrous mistake.

In quick succession, the young Mrs. MacLeod gave birth to a son and a daughter and in 1897 accompanied her husband to the Dutch East Indies, where he had been given command of a battalion on the island of Java. MacLeod drank heavily, took up with other women, and beat his wife frequently — once threatening her with a loaded revolver. Their son died under mysterious circumstances; according to one story, he was poisoned by a servant who had been mistreated by MacLeod. Shortly after the MacLeods returned to the Netherlands in 1902, Margaretha Geertruida separated from her husband (they were divorced four years later). Leaving her daughter with relatives, the young woman left for Paris and a startling new career.

Inventing Mata Hari

As a Dutch officer's wife and mother of two, Margaretha Geertruida would scarcely have taken the sophisticated French capital by storm. But as an exotic dancer from the East, she could attract the attention she craved. And so, by 1905, she had assumed a new identity, successfully passing herself off as the daughter of an East Indian temple dancer who had died in childbirth. To replace her mother, Margaretha Geertruida now claimed, she had been dedicated to the Hindu god Shiva and instructed in the erotic rituals of his worship. Tall and shapely, with blue-black hair, dark eyes, and a slightly brownish complexion, she was easily taken for an Indian. The exotic name she gave herself, Mata Hari, meant "eye of the dawn."

After a debut amidst the Oriental collections at the Musée Guimet, Mata Hari went on to score triumphs in Paris's elegant salons. She moved on to theaters in Monte Carlo, Berlin, Vienna, Sofia, Milan, and Madrid. All Europe, it seemed, was at her feet. Although members of her largely male audiences could claim that their reason for attending her performances was to learn more about Eastern religions, they came principally to see a sensuous young woman who dared appear in public virtually nude.

Not surprisingly, the voluptuous dancer had scores of admirers who willingly paid for her generously bestowed favors. By the outbreak of World War I in August 1914, Mata Hari was said to be the highest paid courtesan in Europe. Among her conquests in Berlin: Germany's crown prince, the foreign minister, and the duke of Brunswick. On the day that war was declared, she was seen riding through the streets of the German capital with the chief of police.

Fateful Journeys

By the end of 1915 Mata Hari was back in Paris — to rescue her personal belongings from her villa in suburban Neuilly, according to one story; to tend a wounded Russian lover, according to another. A third motive for the visit, espionage, was given in a cryptic message sent by the Italian secret service to their counterparts in France. The "theatrical celebrity named Mata Hari . . . who purports to reveal secret Hindu dances which demand nudity," the Italians warned, had renounced her claim of Indian birth and was now speaking German with a slight Eastern accent.

Detained by French authorities, Mata Hari ve-

A Mata Hari of the 1960's

The scandal that rocked Britain in 1963 — known as the Profumo affair — had at least one thing in common with the celebrated case of Mata Hari. The woman involved freely shared her sexual favors with several men and was accused of being a spy. Fortunately for that woman, execution by a firing squad was not the punishment for either her alleged espionage or for her indiscretions.

Not yet 16, Christine Keeler came to London in 1957 seeking escape from small-town boredom. Working in a Soho dress shop and later in a Baker Street restaurant, she aspired to be a model. Moving on as a topless dancer in a cabaret club whose clients typically included Americans and Arabs, she met Stephen Ward, an osteopath and artist. Ward ingratiated himself with the rich and famous by painting their

Christine Keeler as a photographer's model. By sharing her favors with a cabinet minister and a Soviet officer, she created a national scandal.

portraits and by introducing pretty young women to restless middle-aged men. By June 1961 Keeler was living with the osteopath. Among the men to whom Ward introduced his protégé were John Profumo, secretary of state for war in Harold Macmillan's cabinet, and Captain Eugene Ivanov, the Soviet Union's naval attaché in London.

When Keeler's jealous Jamaican lover followed her to Ward's flat and began shooting at the house in an effort to drive her out, the police investigated and discovered her relationships with the defense minister and the Soviet officer. Headlines charged that she had wrested military secrets from Profumo for sale to Ivanov. The scandal forced Profumo out of the government. On trial as a procurer, Ward committed suicide. Keeler, however, sold her story to the press for a tidy sum.

*With World War I at a stalemate in 1917
and its troops on the verge of mutiny, the French
high command needed a scapegoat. Posters like
the one at right warned that vigilance was required
since the enemy lurked everywhere. The arrest
of Mata Hari proved the point; above, a photograph
said to be of her execution on October 15, 1917.*

MÉFIEZ-VOUS
*Le boche est
sur la ligne!*

hemently denied being a German spy and impetuously offered her services as a secret agent
to France. Curiously enough, the French accepted her offer and dispatched her to German-
occupied Belgium with a list of six undercover
agents there. Shortly afterward, one of them
was captured and shot by the Germans — betrayed by a woman, it was said. Nonetheless, the
French gave Mata Hari a new assignment: neutral
Spain. She was to travel there via ship from the
Netherlands.

The British forced the ship ashore at Falmouth
on England's southern coast and arrested Mata
Hari in the belief that she was a German spy
named Clara Bendix. She gained her release by
convincing the British that she was in the employment of France. Although advised by her
captors to give up the dangerous role, she continued her journey to Madrid.

In the Spanish capital Mata Hari quickly
formed liaisons with Germany's naval and military attachés, being paid generously for her services. What exactly was the nature of her services
to the German officers remains the core of the
mystery surrounding Mata Hari.

Invisible Ink for H-21

Toward the end of 1916 Berlin advised the two
German attachés in Madrid that they were paying too much for the routine information being
supplied by "Agent H-21"; send her back to Paris
with a check payable by a French bank in the
amount of 5,000 francs, they were ordered. The
incriminating message was intercepted by the
French secret service.

On February 12, 1917, Mata Hari arrived back
in Paris and registered at the elegant Hotel Plaza-
Athénée on the Avenue Montaigne. The next
day she was arrested and charged with being a
German double agent. The evidence used to sustain the charge was an uncashed check in the
amount of 5,000 francs drawn on the bank specified in the German message and a tube containing what was identified as invisible ink — both
seized from her hotel room.

The "invisible ink," Mata Hari explained during her interrogation, was a common disinfectant that she used as a contraceptive. As for the check, she readily admitted that it was a payment from the German attachés in Madrid — but for her sexual favors and certainly not for espionage activities. Unaware of her precarious situation, she made a number of ambiguous and unconvincing statements about her travels since the outbreak of war two and half years earlier. The former toast of Europe and mistress to men in high places was taken to the Saint-Lazare prison and assigned to cell 12. Among the room's previous inhabitants had been the female assassins of a former French president and a leading newspaper editor and Margueritte Francillard, who had been executed as a spy.

An Inconclusive Trial

After months of fruitless interrogations during which Mata Hari steadfastly maintained her innocence, the trial by court-martial was held on July 24, 1917. The president and two other members of the court were already convinced of her guilt — though crowds in the street waiting for the verdict maintained that she was innocent and hoped for an acquittal.

Yes, she testified, she had viewed army maneuvers in Germany, Italy, and France — but as a guest of one or another of her many admirers. The 30,000 marks she had received from the German foreign minister? "That was the price of my favors. My lovers never offered me less." As for the 50,000 lives lost when French transports were torpedoed in the Mediterranean with information about sailings she had supplied, where was the evidence of such sinkings? The allegation was not backed up with any proof. Her use of the Dutch diplomatic pouch for messages from Paris? She was only writing to her daughter in the Netherlands. Despite the weakness of the prosecution's case, the guilty verdict was entirely predictable — given the temper of the times. The French high command desperately needed a scapegoat for the Allies' failure to break the three-year-long stalemate with Germany.

Waiting for the Summons

The death sentence was not immediately carried out; and, during the ensuing months of waiting, Mata Hari grew increasingly nervous and despondent. The only night on which she slept soundly was Saturday, since executions were never held on Sundays. On every other night she went to bed knowing that a knock on the door at daybreak could summon her before the firing squad.

An offer of her counsel to seek a stay of execution on the ground that she was pregnant by him was indignantly refused by Mata Hari. She preferred to place her hopes on a last-minute appeal for clemency to the French president. Her petition was denied. And thus, before dawn on Monday, October 15, she was awakened from a leaden sleep induced by the medication she had requested of the prison doctor. In a toneless voice her attorney told the convicted spy that she was to die that morning.

A Mock Execution?

Mindful of her reputation, the 41-year-old woman took pains with her attire. She wore a pearl gray dress, a large straw hat, her best pair of shoes. About her shoulders she loosely arranged a coat. Only after she put on a pair of gloves was she ready to leave the prison cell for the trip by car to the Château Vincennes on the outskirts of the city.

The firing squad was waiting on the rifle range at Vincennes, 12 men drawn up on three sides of a hollow square facing a tree stripped of its branches and leaves. With a firm step Mata Hari walked up to the tree. She accepted the shot of rum allowed a condemned person but refused to be tied firmly to the tree or accept a blindfold — preferring to look her executioners in the eyes. As the rising sun pierced the night's fog, the priest and nuns attending her withdrew, the men of the firing squad drew to attention at the command of their leader, the signal was given. Twelve shots broke the silence, and the lifeless body of "Eye of the Dawn" slumped to the ground.

The reason for the condemned woman's exceptional composure at the moment of execution was later explained by a bizarre story. An ardent young admirer named Pierre de Morrisac arranged to bribe the firing squad into loading their rifles with blank cartridges. The execution was to be faked, as in Puccini's popular opera of the day *Tosca*. But like the operatic execution, the one in Morrisac's plot went astray; the rifles were loaded with real bullets — and the unsuspecting victim met a quick death.

The truth of this story — or of the one that Mata Hari flung open her coat at the moment of firing to reveal her nudity beneath to the soldiers? It is impossible to say and ultimately unimportant. Both tales are but part of the glamorous legend of the Dutch beauty who achieved fame in her lifetime as an exotic dancer and a high-priced courtesan — but who achieved immortality in death as the spy she probably never was.

Conspiracy of the Cardinals

During the Renaissance the papal court in Rome was a hotbed of intrigue for luxury-loving churchmen. One of them, Cardinal Alfonso Petrucci, made too bold a grab for power.

On a July day in the year 1517, a priest made his way to Rome's Castel Sant'Angelo, the tomb built by the emperor Hadrian in the 2nd century A.D. and converted in the Middle Ages to a papal fortress connected to the Vatican by an elevated passageway. In times of warfare or domestic strife, popes could withdraw to the safety of the castle, which also served as a prison.

The priest had been summoned to give the last rites to a condemned man. It was not an ordinary prisoner who awaited him but rather one of Pope Leo X's former confidants, Cardinal Alfonso Petrucci. The cardinal refused the priest's ministrations and sent him away in haughty anger. Petrucci did not see his next visitor leave, for the pope had sent a Moor to carry out the death sentence — it being considered inappropriate for a Christian to kill a prince of the church. Drawing a noose of crimson silk around the cardinal's neck, the Moor slowly strangled Petrucci. Thus was justice administered in a time of crass materialism, fear, passion, and intrigue.

Relationships between Pope Leo X and the College of Cardinals were tense — before he put in his own men.

A Renaissance Prince on Peter's Throne

Four years earlier, in March 1513, Giovanni de' Medici had been elected pope at the age of 37. The second son of Lorenzo the Magnificent, the ruler of Florence, he had been dedicated to the church at an early age, educated by court tutors, and sent to the University of Pisa to study theology and church law. Although named to the College of Cardinals at age 17, he had to be hastily ordained a priest and consecrated a bishop following his surprising election to the papacy. Since the death of his older brother 10 years earlier, he had been preoccupied with restoring his family's control of Florence after the followers of the religious reformer Savonarola had expelled the Medicis for betraying the city's republican ideals. He had little time for church affairs, which did not necessarily count against him. In papal politics, family wealth and position were more important than theological attainment.

"Let us enjoy the papacy that God has given us," Leo X wrote his brother upon becoming pope — and immediately demonstrated his capacity for such enjoyment. The pageant staged for his coronation was more the victory parade of a Roman emperor than a sober religious ceremony. With more than 2,000 church offices for sale, money flowed into Leo's coffers to support a lavish lifestyle. Determined to make Rome a center of the arts, he dedicated himself to completing the work of his predecessor, Julius II, who had torn down the old St. Peter's basilica and begun building the magnificent edifice that today stands as the centerpiece of the Eternal City. Among the artists employed on his projects were Raphael and Michelangelo. "He would have been a perfect pope," a contemporary historian wrote, "if to his artistic accomplishments he had added even the slightest knowledge of religion."

Matching the extravagance of his courtiers, Leo hosted banquets that offered such delicacies as peacock tongues and pies from which live nightingales flew. A midget jester was employed to amuse him by eating as many as 20 chickens at a single sitting. Perhaps the most beloved member of the court was a white elephant named Hanno, a gift of the king of Portugal, that was trained to kneel in obeisance to the pontiff.

An enthusiastic supporter of Leo's spendthrift ways was the 27-year-old cardinal of Siena, Alfonso Petrucci. But Petrucci and other members of the College of Cardinals grew disillusioned as they saw the papal treasury diverted to a war against the duke of Urbino. Leo's goal was to make his nephew, Lorenzo, ruler of Urbino. But when the pope replaced Petrucci's brother in the

Charged with leading the conspiracy against the pope, Cardinal Petrucci was sent to a dungeon in the lower depths of Castel Sant'Angelo, an enormous circular edifice that dates to the 2nd century A.D. At top, the angel that gives the fortress its name.

top office in Siena with a Medici favorite and seized the family fortune, the cardinal decided that he must act.

An Ingenious Plot Uncovered

Petrucci was indiscreet in enlisting the support of other cardinals and in writing to the deposed duke of Urbino. But when he blurted out in public that he wanted to stab Leo to death, papal agents began screening his correspondence. From it Leo learned of his rival's sinister plan in mid-May 1517.

For some time the pope had been suffering from gastrointestinal problems. Petrucci bribed a Florentine doctor, Battista de Vercelli, to administer poison to the pope while operating on him and then recommended Battista's services to Leo. Forewarned, the pope instead had the doctor seized, tortured to reveal the plot, and put to a horrible death.

Next Leo summoned a consistory of the cardinals. At the conclusion of a long speech, Leo ordered the Swiss Guards to arrest the first of the conspirators, one Cardinal Riario. Without being told what was transpiring, the other cardinals were dismissed. Two weeks later, at a second

Salvation for Sale

The enormous expense of rebuilding St. Peter's basilica in Rome, begun by Leo's predecessor, Pope Julius II, led to a peculiar papal ruling. In return for gifts of money to the church, penitents were granted letters of indulgence relieving them of temporal punishment for their sins — those of the past as well as those to be committed in the future. Among the preachers who fanned out across Europe to sell the papal indulgences was a Dominican friar named Johann Tetzel, who used a catchy verse to get across his message.

"As soon as the coin in the coffer rings,
A soul from Purgatory's punishment springs."
Funds collected were to be sent back to Rome in heavy chests like the one below.

In the confessional one day, a priest and university professor in the north German town of Wittenberg was handed one of Tetzel's letters of indulgence. Outraged, Martin Luther composed 95 theses questioning the value of indulgences and condemning the practice of selling them. The pope had no power to remit punishment for sins, Luther wrote; Tetzel and those of his ilk were sowing weeds while the bishops slept. In defiance of ecclesiastical authority, he nailed his inflammatory theses to a church door on October 31, 1517.

To Leo, who had recently survived the Petrucci conspiracy, the matter at first seemed of little consequence. But when Luther refused to back down, the pope condemned him for heresy and ordered him to submit to the authority of Rome. Again, Luther refused to retract his challenge to the pope. On January 3, 1521, Leo excommunicated Martin Luther; to the pope he was but the latest heretic whose false teachings could never supplant the true religion of Rome. Eleven months later, the pope died — unaware that his brief reign had encompassed the beginning of the Protestant Reformation.

consistory, the pope announced that there were two more enemies of his in the assembly. Removing his miter and raising the papal headdress above the cardinals, he said, "In the name of this symbol of Christ, I promise to pardon them if they confess their crime." When no one stepped forward, Leo confronted each cardinal in turn: "Guilty or not guilty?" Unable to meet the pope's piercing gaze, cardinals Soderini and Adrian fell to their knees in submission.

At a tumultuous third consistory, on June 22, Leo pronounced sentences on the first three cardinals caught in the conspiracy and revealed Petrucci as the ringleader. For his crime Petrucci was sentenced to death and sent to the grim stronghold, Castel Sant'Angelo.

On July 1, deciding that he needed firm control of the College of Cardinals, Leo appointed 31 new princes of the church — most of whom had made considerable contributions to his depleted treasury. Among the new cardinals were two first cousins and three nephews. Then, pleased with a good day's work done, the pope withdrew from Rome for an extended period of stag and boar hunting at his sumptuous country villa.

The Papacy on the Brink

With Petrucci's conspiracy behind him, Leo could turn his attention to securing his family's dominance of Italy. Allied with Spain, the pope had succeeded in getting King Louis XII of France to renounce his claims to Milan and Naples. But Louis' successor, Francis I, marched back into Italy, won a stunning victory at Marignano, and forced the pope to surrender much of his power over the French church.

Next, Leo became embroiled in the squabbles over the successor to Holy Roman Emperor Maximilian I, who died in 1519. The pope opposed the claims of both Francis I and Charles I of Spain, fearing that Italy would be squeezed between either a France or a Spain united with Germany. When his candidate, Frederick of Saxony, lost out to Charles, Leo had no recourse but to back the Spanish monarch — which brought yet another invasion of Italy by France.

The real crisis of Leo's papacy, however, took place far from Rome and was scarcely recognized by him at the time. Protesting the sale of indulgences, Martin Luther had posted his 95 theses on the church door at Wittenberg castle on October 31, 1517. When news of this first salvo in what would become the Protestant Reformation reached Rome, Pope Leo is supposed to have said, "Brother Martin has a very fine talent. But all this is mere monkish squabbling."

Too Costly for a Queen

**Though notoriously extravagant, the flippant young queen
refused to buy the world's most expensive necklace.
The unexpected result was preposterous intrigue, breathtaking
larceny, and one of history's most famous scandals.**

The royal jewelers, Boehmer and Bassenge, had a frightening business problem. With painstaking care their workshop had assembled a truly astonishing necklace. Precisely 647 glittering diamonds, many as large as cherries, had been mounted in gold to suit the ostentatious tastes of Madame du Barry, the mistress of King Louis XV of France. The asking price was the equivalent of about $8 million in today's currency. Unfortunately, smallpox carried off the monarch before the deal could be concluded. His successor, Louis XVI, had married the Austrian princess Marie Antoinette. Famously frivolous and enamored of luxurious excesses, she seemed the ideal customer for the inimitable bauble but startled the jewelers and her numerous critics by rejecting it twice.

Although scornfully referred to as "Madame Deficit" by the people because of the riches squandered upon her parties and her opulent rooms at Versailles, Marie Antoinette was perhaps sensitive to the nation's budgetary problems after all. Her husband's country had spent heavily in support of the Americans and their revolution against the British.

When Boehmer wept and said that he would be ruined, even threatening suicide, the queen sensibly told him to pull himself together and break up the necklace and sell the stones sepa-

An ostentatious piece of jewelry (here reconstructed from contemporary descriptions) gave its name to the affair of the necklace in 1785–86.

rately. The stubborn jeweler tried the court of Spain but was stymied. Only royalty could afford such extravagance, and royalty was becoming scarce as the concept of democracy swept through 18th-century Europe. Meanwhile, the inexorable interest payments on the gems continued to mount. The necklace seemed destined to become the century's most expensive white elephant.

An Unholy Cardinal

Venal, debauched, arrogant, and fatuous, Louis de Rohan was a descendant of one of the most important families of the country. Despite his scandalous private life, which included many a romantic liaison, he was a cardinal in the Roman Catholic Church, the official state religion of France. From 1772 to 1774, he had been the French ambassador to Vienna, the capital of the Austro-Hungarian empire ruled by Marie Antoinette's mother, the stolid and puritanical Maria Theresa. Although his fun-loving, free-spending ways made him popular with many of her subjects, the elderly empress was outraged that a clergyman spent his days at the hunt and his nights in vulgar amusements. She besieged her daughter with complaints until Marie Antoinette succeeded in having Rohan recalled from his diplomatic post in Vienna.

The well-connected, smooth-talking cardinal rebounded by winning the post of grand almoner, thus becoming the highest ranking cleric at the court of Versailles. It was his duty to officiate at mass on important occasions and participate in other elaborate ceremonies, but Marie Antoinette so studiously ignored him that she could later claim that she had not spoken a word to him for eight years. Rohan, who was racking up huge debts as he refurbished his many inherited properties and supported his hangers-on, was mortified. A man of his birth, charm, and position deserved to be on familiar terms with the royal family, or so he believed, and he became desperate to gain acceptance at court.

The Last of the Valois

The most important, and most improbable, character in what came to be known as the affair of the necklace was the ingeniously deceitful, seductive Jeanne de Valois, the daughter of a drunken poacher and a wayward maidservant. As an unkempt young beggar girl, she had somehow convinced a noble patroness that she was the last descendant of the former royal house, the Valois. Indeed she was, but the genteel convent school to which she was then sent did not long hold her attention. At the age of 22, she ran away with a rakish gendarme, Nicolas de Lamotte. A month after they married, she gave birth to twins.

Sensing that the infamously licentious Rohan would be easy prey, Jeanne wangled an invitation to one of his castles and soon had him under her spell. The cardinal paid off her profligate husband's debts and had him promoted to captain in the dragoons. Untiring in her schemes, and almost unbelievably daring, this unscrupulous adventuress, now calling herself the comtesse de Lamotte-Valois, went to Versailles and staged a fainting fit in a reception room. When her husband explained to the astounded courtiers that she was of royal blood but was suffering from years of malnutrition, the self-styled comtesse was awarded a sizable annual pension.

Such successes merely whetted the comtesse's appetite for more mischief, and, fortuitously, yet another larcenous cohort appeared on the scene. The alchemist known as Cagliostro, who was regularly bleeding the gullible Rohan, told her that the cardinal desperately wanted to rise to a high political position but knew that the queen's dislike of him stood in his way.

Seizing upon this slender straw, the comtesse began dropping hints to the cardinal in 1784 about her "dear friend" Marie Antoinette. She promised Rohan that the queen would nod meaningfully toward him at the next court affair. The grand almoner, seeing what he hoped to see, was grateful for the imagined royal nod and rewarded his go-between with money. Next, the indefatigable comtesse enlisted the talents of another lover, her husband's friend Retaux de Villette, to act as her "first secretary" and forge notes on gilded paper decorated with the royal fleur-de-lis. This sham correspondence urged the credulous Rohan to be discreet while assuring him that the queen had at last forgiven him.

Proof of Fidelity

The cardinal was not completely hooked and landed, however, until the comtesse hit upon the daring scheme of pretending to arrange a rendez-

All threads of the scheme to confiscate the fabulous diamond necklace led to comtesse de Lamotte-Valois. Here, she and her husband examine their prize with Retaux de Villette before taking it apart to sell the gems individually on the black market.

vous with the queen near the Grove of Venus in her private gardens, which even the king could not enter without her permission. First, comte de Lamotte went to a favorite Paris hangout of prostitutes and found a dim-witted young woman named Nicole who resembled Marie Antoinette.

The clever pair dressed Nicole in a white gown that looked exactly like one in a well-known portrait of the queen and gave her a few lines to memorize. On a moonless night the grand almoner crept among the pines, cedars, and fig trees and bowed deeply when he glimpsed the supposed queen. Tentatively following the script, Nicole softly breathed, "You may hope that the past will be forgotten." But before she had to strain her thespian talents, a manservant in palace livery rushed up, warning, "Come away quickly, quickly." As Rohan ran off, he saw the man's face, as he was meant to.

Now certain that his ambitions would soon be realized, the poor cardinal was even more receptive to the machinations of the pretty Valois. When she reported that the queen wanted to help an impoverished noble family but was a little short of funds herself, he readily handed over 50,000 livres in cash. Deep in debt himself, however, he had to borrow the sum from a moneylender. When the queen supposedly asked for more money a few months later, he pawned his household goods. Of course, both of these sums were pocketed by his young mistress.

The monstrously greedy comte and comtesse began spending princely sums of money so openly that suspicions should have been aroused, but they seemed to be living a charmed life. In fact, their next victims sought them out. Believing the rumors about the close friendship between the Valois and the queen, Boehmer and Bassenge asked the consummate schemer to act as intermediary in convincing Marie Antoinette to buy the famous necklace. On December 29, 1784, the comtesse was shown the stunning creation.

Whatever a Queen Desires

Subsequent events defy belief. For that reason, much of the French populace would later suspect that the tale was a cover-up to protect Marie Antoinette. The evidence available, however, tends to support the following scenario.

The comtesse told Rohan that the queen wanted to buy the costly diamonds without letting Louis know. Moreover, thanks to Marie Antoi-

Although Queen Marie Antoinette (right) was only indirectly involved in the affair of the necklace, the scandal disastrously tarnished her name. A look-alike from the Paris demimonde was hired for the nocturnal rendezvous with the easily duped Cardinal Rohan in the gardens of Versailles (below).

nette's newfound confidence in the cardinal, she felt that only he could be trusted to carry off the deal in secret. The naïve Rohan agreed to buy the necklace by paying four installments of 1.6 million livres over a two-year period. His wily mistress allayed any doubts by taking away the purchase contract and reappearing with the word "Approved" beside each paragraph and the queen's own signature at the end, "Marie Antoinette de France." After the necklace was delivered to Rohan's house, a young man soon appeared and intoned the phrase, "By order of the queen." The jewels were handed over forthwith, for this was the manservant Rohan had been allowed to glimpse in the queen's gardens.

The First Nagging Doubts

Though briefly ecstatic, Cardinal Rohan soon became disturbed that the queen was not wearing the remarkable jewelry on public occasions. The resourceful comtesse replied that her intimate royal friend was fearful of showing off such a monumentally expensive trinket. Could the price not be lowered? The jewelers readily agreed to cut the price by 200,000 livres, and on July 12, while delivering some other gems to the palace,

At first, all of Paris laughed at the gullibility of Cardinal Rohan. But their derision soon turned to sympathy for the deceived man, whose only mistake was his pathetic attempt to win the favor of the queen at all costs. The cardinal's acquittal was greeted with loud cheers from the crowd, giving vent to their long-suppressed scorn for the "Austrian woman," Marie Antoinette.

Boehmer sent the queen a note affirming the price reduction. Characteristically, Marie Antoinette did not read the entire note and tossed it into the fireplace.

Meanwhile, a reputable diamond merchant reported to the police that valuable stones were being offered around Paris for suspiciously low prices by one Retaux de Villette. When questioned by the minister of police, the redoubtable "first secretary" honestly answered that he was acting as agent for the comtesse de Lamotte-Valois. The impressive title sufficed, but the comtesse, sensing danger, sent her husband off to London to sell the remaining jewels from the destroyed necklace.

But even this masterly tactician could not finally avert the inevitable, the due date of the first payment. Gamely, she tried a bold assault, telling the jewelers that the queen's signature was a forgery and that they must pry their money out of the rich cardinal. But Boehmer and Bassenge knew that Rohan was indebted to the limit. Desperate for the money and certain that the queen had the necklace in her possession, Boehmer went to see Marie Antoinette at Versailles.

The King Goes Too Far

The queen's name day and the important feast of the Assumption both occurred on August 15, an occasion for the ritual gathering of the entire court. When Rohan used his position as grand almoner to gain admittance to the king's chamber before the ceremonies, he was greeted by cold stares from ministers, the averted gaze of the queen, and an abrupt question from Louis: "I want to know all about the diamond necklace which you bought in the queen's name."

The king was merciful enough to consider having him taken away quietly, but the angry, tearful queen demanded that he be arrested immediately, in front of everyone. As the puzzled crowd grew fearful about the delay of the ceremony, the cardinal, resplendent in his robes of office, strode out into the glittering Hall of Mirrors. Behind him an old enemy, the Baron Breteuil, roared out, "Arrest Monsieur le Cardinal!" The horrified astonishment of the assemblage soon gave way to anger. Even as Rohan deftly smuggled a note to a servant ordering the fake correspondence destroyed, the disaffected nobility and clergy were plotting revenge upon Marie Antoinette.

The cardinal, who was connected to the noblest lines of France, was taken to a narrow stone cell in the infamous Bastille. But the queen soon became walled up within her own apartments, a prisoner of hostile public opinion. When she went to the theater, the audience hissed her.

Miracles for the Gullible

Few men in history can have held deeper contempt for others than the mountebank known as Cagliostro, for he ceaselessly invented confidence schemes to relieve the foolish of their money — and continually succeeded. Described as "small in stature, of darkish complexion, with a fat body, round head, and stiff neck," this persistent scoundrel was able to pass himself off as Alessandro, count of Cagliostro, though he was in fact the son of a Sicilian merchant.

Born Giuseppe Balsamo in 1743, he was to create various personalities and professions for himself, carefully gauging his victims in light of the superstitions of the day. Starting his career in Sicily, he soon had to flee the law and ply his imaginary trades in Greece, Egypt, Arabia, Persia, and the island of Rhodes. After taking lessons in alchemy, the pseudoscience of changing one substance into another, he won introductions to some of the most important families of Naples and Rome, where he met and married Lorenza Feliciani. This kindred spirit traveled with him throughout Europe. Under various names, the pair sold love potions to the lovelorn, elixirs guaranteed to restore youth, and secret mixtures to make unattractive women into great beauties. Perhaps because they kept on the move, they amassed large profits.

His successful duping of Cardinal Rohan led for a time to his greatest triumphs. Ironically, however, one of his sharper tricks in Paris made him seem a likely conspirator in the affair of the necklace. Often, he had offered to "enlarge" a client's diamond. After dipping the gem in an opaque liquid, he would pull out a crystal that was twice the size of the original.

A Tactical Error

Once again, Louis unwisely listened to his outraged wife on a political point and ordered that Rohan be tried before the parliament. The resulting brouhaha weakened the monarchy. Pamphleteers published slanders, and antiroyalists were heartened. As one said, "A cardinal disclosed as a thief, and the queen implicated in a most unsavory scandal . . . . The crozier and the scepter are being bespattered with mire! What a triumph for the ideas of liberty!" In the public proceedings, of course, the comtesse made wild accusations to save herself, but the unwitting prostitute, Nicole, and the "first secretary" told the truth. The comte was never seen again.

On May 31, 1786, throngs began gathering at five in the morning outside the Palace of Justice to hear the verdict, even though the deliberations were likely to take hours. Finally, by a vote of 26 to 22, Rohan was acquitted "without a stain upon his character," as was Nicole and the alchemist Cagliostro, who had been drawn into court by the comtesse's scattershot charges. Retaux de Villette was banished, and his friend, the comte, was sentenced in absentia to the galleys.

Only the comtesse would be severely punished. She was to be flogged, branded with a "V" for *voleuse*, or thief, and then confined to prison for life on a diet of bread and lentils. But this harsh punishment backfired, still further damaging the reputation of the queen. Although 13 men tried to hold down the struggling comtesse to be branded, she fought so savagely that her clothes were ripped and the branding iron scorched her breast. She fainted dead away. Reports of this horrible spectacle aroused sympathy for the prisoner, and the most fashionable people of Paris lined up their carriages to visit her in jail. When the comtesse escaped to England within weeks, disguised as a boy, Marie Antoinette's enemies suspected that she was being rewarded for keeping silent about the queen's actual role in the affair of the necklace.

But the future dealt harshly with more than one participant in the scandal. Cagliostro was banished by Louis and eventually died in prison in Italy. Rohan was barred from court and forced to live out a quiet life in the countryside. In 1791 the self-styled comtesse, apparently delirious, jumped to her death from a window of a house of ill repute. King Louis XVI and his consort, Marie Antoinette, were beheaded by the guillotine when the fires of revolution — stoked in part by the lies surrounding the affair of the necklace — swept through France and destroyed forever the old order for which they stood.

A Miscarriage of Justice

A memorandum found in the wastebasket of Germany's military attaché in Paris revealed that a French officer was selling secrets to a potential enemy. The arrest, conviction, and deportation of Captain Alfred Dreyfus divided France into bitter camps for years.

Soldiers drawn to attention line the courtyard of Paris's École Militaire as the prisoner is marched out to stand before a general on horseback. Outside a crowd estimated at 20,000 howls, "Death to the traitor! Death to the Jew!" Precisely at nine o'clock on that Saturday morning, January 5, 1895, the sentence is read, and the general shouts, "Alfred Dreyfus, you are unworthy to bear arms. In the name of the French people we degrade you."

"Soldiers, they are degrading an innocent man. Soldiers, they are dishonoring an innocent man," the prisoner cries out. "*Vive la France, vive l'armée!*" A towering sergeant of the Republican Guard steps forward, bends over the condemned officer, and strips from his cap and sleeves the insignia of rank. Next the sergeant rips off the prisoner's buttons and the stripes from his trousers. Finally, he draws the sword from the officer's scabbard and breaks it over his knee. After being paraded before the assembled troops, the disgraced man is placed in a police van and taken as a

"I accuse . . . !" is the headline given Émile Zola's open letter to the president of France in January 1898; it challenged the injustice of the Dreyfus conviction.

Following his conviction for treason, Captain Dreyfus was publicly humiliated in a ceremony at the French military academy in Paris. As General Darras (inset) watched on horseback, a sergeant stripped insignia of rank from the convict's uniform and broke the disgraced officer's sword over his knee.

common criminal to a city prison. En route, he passes the home where he had known so many happy years with his wife and children.

To his beloved Lucie, the 35-year-old ex-captain writes later that day: "Oh, my darling, do everything in the world to find the guilty one; do not relax your efforts for one instant. . . . There is a traitor, but it is not I." Two weeks later Dreyfus, in chains, is put on a train for the port of La Rochelle. There a ship awaits to take him to Devil's Island off French Guiana on the northeast coast of South America. For most prisoners the notorious penal colony is a death sentence.

"That Scoundrel D"

The conviction, sentencing, degradation, and exile to Devil's Island of Alfred Dreyfus was the climax of an espionage case that gripped France for months late in 1894. It was, however, only the beginning of what would become known as the Dreyfus affair, a shocking miscarriage of justice that preoccupied, bitterly divided, and nearly immobilized the army and government of France for the next 12 years.

Still smarting from the humiliating defeat in the Franco-Prussian War of 1870–71, the French army's counterintelligence service kept a close watch on the German embassy in Paris and, in particular, on its military attaché, Lieutenant Colonel Maximilien von Schwartzkoppen. From papers retrieved by the embassy's cleaning woman, the French learned that Schwartzkoppen had

been receiving plans of their fortifications from an agent using the code name Jacques Dubois, or "that scoundrel D," as the German officer called him. The identity of the traitor eluded the chief of counterintelligence, Colonel Jean-Conrad Sandherr, and his deputy, Major Hubert Joseph Henry, until an apparent breakthrough in the case on September 17, 1894.

On that date Major Henry received a *bordereau*, or covering memorandum, handwritten on onionskin paper, itemizing military information for sale. Included in the list were details about the new 120 mm cannon that, Henry speculated, could only have been supplied by an artillery officer on the general staff. Scanning the roster, Henry found the name Alfred Dreyfus. Handwriting on a report Dreyfus had filed the previous year, it was next discovered, bore a superficial resemblance to that of the *bordereau*. Henry quickly convinced his colleagues that Dreyfus must be "that scoundrel D." What no one mentioned openly was that, as a Jew, Dreyfus was a convenient scapegoat. To the elitist French officer corps, Jews were a foreign element. Born in Alsace, Dreyfus was thought to be pro-German — although his family had left the disputed province when it had been seized by Germany two decades earlier.

Accusation, Trial, Conviction

On Saturday morning, October 13, Captain Dreyfus received a curious summons. The following Monday morning he was to report to the chief of staff — in civilian attire. When he did so, he found himself facing two officers and two policemen; he did not know that Major Henry was hiding behind a drapery. The perplexed captain was asked to write a request for a return of "documents that I had passed on to you before my departure for maneuvers." He started to write, then paused, trembling. What could it mean?

The charade at an end, one of the officers blurted out, "Dreyfus, in the name of the law I arrest you! You are accused of the crime of high treason." On what evidence, he demanded to know. The evidence, he was told, "is overwhelming." Protesting his innocence and declaring that "an appalling plan" had been hatched against him, Dreyfus was taken away to prison.

Not until November 1 was the arrest confirmed in the Parisian press. "High Treason. Arrest of the Jewish Officer Alfred Dreyfus," shrieked an anti-Semitic tabloid. A public trial was demanded since, as another newspaper claimed, one in private would "only serve to prolong the scandal." But when Dreyfus appeared before the seven military judges of a court-martial on December 19, the public was excluded at the first defense mention of "the sole piece of evidence," the *bordereau*.

Two of the five handwriting experts asked to inspect the document said that Dreyfus could not have written it. Three said he had, one of them —

Alphonse Bertillon — refuting his own testimony that the sentences Dreyfus took in dictation at the chief of staff's office on October 15 differed from the *bordereau*. Dreyfus, Bertillon grandly proposed, had been disguising his handwriting during the dictation; the sentences four witnesses had seen him write were forgeries!

Major Henry testified that he had known for some time that there was a German spy on the general staff. "And that traitor is sitting there!" he said, pointing to Dreyfus. Asked to substantiate his charge, Henry icily answered, "There are secrets that an officer does not even share with his hat." The judges appeared to be impressed.

After four days of inconclusive testimony from prosecution witnesses and a bland, dispassionate appearance by the defendant, the judges withdrew to deliberate. At that point, a messenger arrived with a packet from the minister of war. Expecting to find new evidence, the judges instead read a virtual order from the minister to find Dreyfus guilty. Later that evening the panel of officers vot-

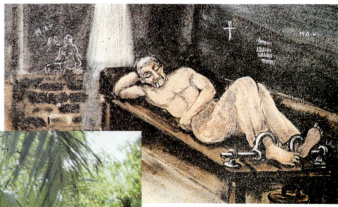

During his years of imprisonment on Devil's Island, Alfred Dreyfus was treated little better than a caged animal. As the sketch by a fellow prisoner above reveals, he was chained to his bed. Gloomy days, he wrote, were "hardly distinguishable one from another." The penal colonies were abolished in 1938; the cells today are choked with jungle growth.

ed unanimously to convict the defendant of the charge of treason.

On the Trail of the Real Culprit

In the summer of 1895, several months after Dreyfus had been shipped off to Devil's Island, Lieutenant Colonel Marie-Georges Picquart succeeded Sandherr as chief of counterintelligence. Since the military realized how weak the case against Dreyfus had been, Picquart was instructed to intercept and read all mail to and from the prisoner and, incidentally, continue to monitor the wastepaper smuggled out of the German embassy by the cleaning woman. In March 1896 he received from her torn fragments of a *petit bleu*, a special delivery letter on thin blue paper for local use in Paris. The letter, apparently torn up and tossed in a wastebasket without being sent, was addressed to Major Marie-Charles-Ferdinand Walsin-Esterhazy and asked for "a more detailed explanation than you gave me the other day on the question in suspense."

Esterhazy was the son of a French general of an illegitimate branch of the immensely wealthy Hungarian Esterhazys. Although married to a woman of independent means, Esterhazy never seemed to have enough money to support his life

of debauchery in Paris. Sensing that he was on the trail of another spy, Picquart had Esterhazy shadowed; twice he was seen visiting the German embassy. In August the chief of counterintelligence obtained two of Esterhazy's letters. The handwriting was identical to that of the *bordereau*, the sole piece of evidence in the conviction of Captain Dreyfus.

When Picquart sought to prove that Esterhazy rather than Dreyfus was the traitor, a superior officer advised him not to reopen the case. "What difference does it make to you if that Jew remains on Devil's Island?" he was asked. "I will not carry this secret to my grave," replied Picquart. Learning that his chief could prove Dreyfus innocent, Major Henry set about forging new evidence to incriminate the prisoner.

"I Accuse!"

Inevitably, there were leaks to the press about new evidence in the Dreyfus case. Moreover, there was a growing suspicion in army and government circles that another culprit was involved. Fearing that his efforts to implicate Esterhazy would be blocked by the army high command, Picquart revealed his findings to his attorney and authorized him to pass the information on to the government. The attorney told a sympathetic senator that the *bordereau* could be shown to be in the hand of Esterhazy and not Dreyfus; the senator informed Alfred's brother, Mathieu. On November 15, 1897, Mathieu Dreyfus formally accused Esterhazy of the treason for which his brother had been convicted — taking care that a copy of his letter to the minister of war also be sent to a leading Paris newspaper.

Deciding to bluff his way through, Esterhazy demanded a court-martial. The military closed ranks behind the unsavory defendant, and a judicial panel hastily acquitted Esterhazy. The verdict, according to the novelist Émile Zola, was "a final blow at all truth, at all justice."

On January 13, 1898, Zola addressed an open letter to the president of the republic, Félix Faure. Under the title *"J'Accuse . . . !"* (I accuse), it was printed on the front page of *L'Aurore*, a liberal newspaper published by the future prime minister Georges Clemenceau. In his letter Zola accused by name seven high-ranking officers and three handwriting experts of having fabricated

Newly decorated as a chevalier of the Legion of Honor, Major Dreyfus chats with fellow officers at the École Militaire in Paris following his official rehabilitation in July 1906.

A Dream Becomes Reality

As were many Jews, Theodor Herzl — Paris correspondent for a Viennese newspaper — was deeply shocked by the blatant anti-Semitism displayed by the accusers of Captain Alfred Dreyfus. The miscarriage of justice set him to thinking about the future of the Jewish people, dispersed around the globe. In 1896 Herzl published *The Jewish State*, a seminal tract in which he proposed that a Jewish nation be established in Palestine, the historic homeland from which Jews had been separated for centuries. As founder of what came to be known as the Zionist movement, Herzl devoted the remaining years of his life to this advocacy. At his death in 1904, Jews were already settling in a territory that was part of the Ottoman empire.

At the end of World War I, Britain was given a mandate over Pales-

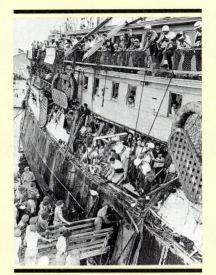

In defiance of Britain, Jewish refugees boarded overcrowded, barely seaworthy vessels to reach Palestine.

tine, which it had wrested from the Ottomans, and attempted to make good on its wartime promise to establish a Jewish state there. This brought violent protests from the Arab inhabitants, who objected to the influx of Jews. When Britain attempted to limit Jewish immigration, the Jews in turn protested — especially after the rise of Hitler in 1933 made escape to Palestine the only salvation for many of Europe's Jews.

It was not until the defeat of Germany in World War II that the drive for a Jewish state gained momentum. The United Nations voted to partition Palestine between Arabs and Jews, and on the day the British mandate ended — May 14, 1948 — the state of Israel was proclaimed. It took a bitter war with the Arabs for the Israelis to win their independence.

the evidence against Dreyfus and having conspired to cover up their guilt as the facts in the case became known.

As Zola had intended, the sensational accusation brought the novelist to trial for libel. After tumultuous proceedings in which the duplicity of the army was fully revealed, Zola was found guilty, fined 3,000 francs, and sentenced to prison for a year. While awaiting a second trial on his appeal of the verdict, Zola fled France for refuge in England and remained there until June 1899.

The Case Reopened

The trial and conviction of Zola seemed to divide the nation into two camps, defenders of the army and believers in the innocence of Dreyfus. For his role in exposing the conspiracy, Picquart was dismissed from the army — though he was later reinstated. On August 30, 1898, Henry broke down under interrogation to confess his forgeries and was placed under arrest. The next day he was found dead in his cell, having slit his throat with a razor. Esterhazy fled to London, where he admitted his guilt; he remained in exile until his death a quarter century later.

In June 1899 the verdict in the Dreyfus court-martial was set aside and a new trial ordered. Greatly aged by nearly five years of captivity, the

ex-captain was brought back to France once more to confront his accusers. His hopes for vindication, however, were cruelly dashed by a split decision of the new court-martial on September 9. Found guilty of treason but under extenuating circumstances, Dreyfus was sentenced to 10 years of detention. To Zola the verdict was one of "ignorance, folly, cruelty, falsehood, crime." Future generations would shudder, he predicted, adding that "Jesus was condemned but once."

Taking into consideration the prisoner's deteriorating health, the minister of war pardoned Dreyfus 10 days later. The act of mercy, he explained, was "to efface all traces of a painful conflict." Reluctantly accepting the pardon, Dreyfus vowed to continue seeking vindication. "My heart will not be at rest until there is no longer a Frenchman who imputes to me the abominable crime which another has committed."

After seven years of dogged efforts, Dreyfus's supporters succeeded in having the verdict in the second court-martial set aside on July 12, 1906. Dreyfus was reinstated in the army and promoted to major. In a ceremony at the École Militaire on July 20 he was officially rehabilitated and made a chevalier of the Legion of Honor. "Long live Dreyfus," rang out the cries. "No," he replied, "Long live truth."

The Imperious Wife

*In a new language and an unfamiliar ritual, a German
princess is wed to the heir apparent to the throne of Russia in 1745.
For 17 years theirs is a loveless marriage. When Peter III dies
only six months after becoming czar, his wife is a suspect.*

It had been a long and exhausting day for the 16-year-old bride. Awakened at 6 A.M., she was taken to the apartments of the empress, who personally supervised the hairstyling, jewelry selection, and dressing of the young woman about to marry the heir apparent to the throne of Russia. At noon, the groom — only a year older than his bride — arrived in the next room, and at 3 P.M. the couple set off across St. Petersburg in the imperial carriage. The ceremony at the cathedral of the Virgin of Kazan lasted several hours, followed by a 50-course banquet and a ball at which the young woman was forced to dance with one elderly nobleman after another.

But at nine o'clock the empress cut short the festivities and escorted the newlyweds to their nuptial chambers. The groom was told to await in an adjoining room, as court ladies removed the bride's heavy gown of silk brocade, dressed her in a pink nightgown from Paris, and settled her into

*On the first day of her reign, Catherine II of Russia reviewed troops outside St. Petersburg dressed in
a uniform and riding astride a white horse, as in this later portrait.*

an enormous canopied bed. At last, all withdrew, leaving the apprehensive young woman in an empty room lit by flickering candles. Now she lay in the near darkness, eyes trained on the door through which she expected her husband to enter momentarily.

An hour passed, then two. Toward midnight a lady-in-waiting popped in to announce that the groom was dining with his servants. Only after another long delay did the young husband appear, climb into bed next to her, joke that it would amuse the servants to see them together, and promptly fall into a drunken sleep. "It was the gayest marriage that has perhaps ever been celebrated in Europe," the bride's mother wrote home to her husband in Germany. For the dismayed young bride, it was anything but gay.

In Name Only

In February 1744, just short of her 15th birthday, Sophia Augusta Frederica, princess of the petty German duchy of Anhalt-Zerbst, had been brought to Russia by her mother. The unmarried and childless Empress Elizabeth had adopted her nephew Peter as heir to the throne and was anxious to see him wed so that the Romanov succession might be secured. She hoped that the petite, pretty Sophia — the marriage candidate proposed by the

influential Frederick II of Prussia — might win Peter away from his childish preoccupations with toys and pets. After suitable tutoring in the Russian language, the Orthodox religion, and court etiquette, Sophia was rechristened Catherine and betrothed to Peter. Their marriage was celebrated on August 21, 1745.

"I would have been ready to like my new husband had he been capable of affection or willing to show any," Catherine later wrote in her famous memoirs. But the thin, gangly, pale, and pockmarked Peter preferred to idle away his days playing with tin soldiers and cardboard castles. To his young wife's intense annoyance, he turned their bedroom into a kennel for his hunting spaniels. For at least nine years their marriage remained unconsummated. Meanwhile, in 1752, Catherine took a lover.

"He was as beautiful as the dawn," Catherine wrote of the 26-year-old chamberlain Serge Saltykov. "No one at court could equal him." After two miscarriages, Catherine gave birth to a son on September 20, 1754. Named Paul, the infant was acknowledged by Peter as his son and raised by Elizabeth as the second in line to the throne. Court gossips, of course, suspected that Saltykov was the father — especially after Elizabeth packed him off on diplomatic missions abroad.

Political Intrigues

With her duty as a wife and mother accomplished, Catherine was expected to lead a quiet life on the fringes of the court. Yet with Elizabeth

Empress Elizabeth chose the son of her sister Anna, Prince Peter of Holstein-Gottorp (left), as her heir. Despite her efforts to train him for his future imperial duties, the immature youth preferred to play with toy soldiers — often arranging them in mock battle across the bed he was forced to share with his unloved wife, Catherine.

aging and Peter so obviously unfit to rule, there were those in St. Petersburg — as the British envoy, Sir Charles Hanbury-Williams, reported to London — who expected Catherine to be the one to reign "in case of certain unexpected events."

Those "unexpected events" took place in 1756, when Russia joined Austria and France in war against Frederick II's Prussia. The initial Russian victories were greeted with joy in St. Petersburg by all except the infantile Peter, whose father was German and who regarded the king of Prussia as an invincible military genius. The visible decline of the empress raised fears that Peter would soon inherit the throne and conclude an ignominious peace with Prussia. As an alternative to his rule, Russian nationalists began thinking of Catherine — as regent for her young son, Paul, or as empress in her own right. "Be assured," Catherine confided to the conspiratorial Hanbury-Williams, "I have already laid my plans and shall either perish or reign."

After the troops of the regimental guards proclaimed their loyalty, Catherine took the imperial oath at the cathedral of the Virgin of Kazan (right), where she had been married 17 years earlier.

Hanbury-Williams supported Catherine's ambitions and her taste for luxury with secret "loans" and even supplied a new lover, a handsome young Polish count in his retinue, Stanislas Poniatowski. Peter, who had installed a mistress in his own apartments and was studiously avoiding his wife, took it in stride when Catherine gave birth to a daughter on December 9, 1757. "I have no idea how my wife becomes pregnant," he is said to have remarked, "but I suppose I shall have to accept the child as my own."

Confrontation and Reconciliation

No sooner had Catherine recovered from childbirth than she had to confront the consequences of her political intrigues and indiscreet behavior. On Sunday morning, February 15, 1758, she received an alarming note from her lover. Elizabeth had ordered the arrest of the Russian chancellor, Count Bestuzhev, on a charge of treason. Also arrested were an Italian jeweler named Bernardi and Catherine's Russian teacher, Adadurov — both of whom had served as go-betweens in her secret correspondence with the chancellor and the British envoy.

Shortly thereafter, Elizabeth asked that Poniatowski be recalled to Poland. The court buzzed with rumors that Catherine's turn was next. The terrified young woman wrote Elizabeth, asking for an audience. She had to endure a nearly monthlong wait before being summoned to the imperial apartments, where she also found her despised husband waiting for her.

Dramatically, Catherine fell to her knees be-

Potemkin Villages—Not Made of Cardboard

As Catherine II prepared to review troops on the day she was proclaimed empress, a young subaltern noticed that her sword was without a ceremonial knot. Stepping forward, he removed his own sword knot and gallantly handed it to the new monarch. She did not forget the young officer, and 12 years later Gregory Potemkin became her lover. Although the promiscuous empress soon turned to other men, Potemkin remained her friend and confidant until his death in 1791, five years before that of Catherine.

Among the favors Catherine bestowed on Potemkin was appointment as governor-general of the southern provinces of her sprawling empire. In an effort to stimulate colonization, he created the cities Kherson, Sevastapol, and Ekaterinoslav ("Catherine's glory").

In this satirical drawing, a log hut is made to hold the columned portico of a Greek temple for the imperial progress of "K" (for Katherine, an alternate spelling of the empress's name). The term "Potemkin village" has come to stand for a false pretense.

But Potemkin is perhaps best — if somewhat mistakenly — remembered for the ceremonial journey to the south that he arranged for his empress in 1787. To impress Catherine with the region's prosperity, the governor-general is said to have erected fake villages along her route and dressed happy peasants in new garments.

In reality, Potemkin did only what is customary to this day on the occasion of state visits — that is, show a royal visitor only the best. To this end he painted the facades of houses and garlanded them with flowers. Accompanying Catherine on the last part of her journey, Emperor Joseph II of Austria was impressed by and somewhat envious of the new cities. "The master orders, the slave obeys," he cynically remarked. "Catherine can spend whatever she pleases."

fore Elizabeth and asked to be returned to her parents in Germany. "How can you speak of being sent away?" the empress asked. "Remember that you have children." Peter interrupted to charge his wife with cruelty and stubbornness. Appalled at the squabbling between the two, Elizabeth ended the interview but indicated with a silent gesture to Catherine that the conversation would be continued in private later.

On April 21 the empress publicly toasted Catherine on her 30th birthday and the next month granted her a second interview. After swearing Catherine to tell nothing but the truth, Elizabeth asked for details about the life of the heir apparent. What the young woman said is not known for at this point in her narrative, Catherine abruptly ended her memoirs. Although Catherine missed her banished lover and soon thereafter saw her daughter die, there was no more talk of exile for the wife of the heir to the throne.

A Most Unpopular Czar

After a 21-year reign, Elizabeth died on Christmas Day, 1761, and was succeeded by her nephew, Peter III. Although six months pregnant with the child of yet another lover, Catherine knelt for hours at the late empress's bier. When Peter appeared, he joked with court ladies and made rude remarks about the priests. Cavorting behind the hearse at the state funeral, he scandalized onlookers. To cronies he confided that he planned to divorce Catherine and marry his mistress.

Fearing that the new child would give her husband just the excuse he needed to push her aside, she successfully concealed the pregnancy from him and devised an elaborate ruse to distract him at the time of her delivery. Because her simple-minded husband liked nothing better than a fire, Catherine conspired with a devoted retainer to set his house afire at the time she went into labor. Predictably, Peter rushed from the palace to watch the conflagration, and the newborn child, a boy, was smuggled to a foster home.

What finally guaranteed a short reign for Peter was the truce he decreed in the war with Prussia in March 1762, followed by a peace treaty surrendering all Russian gains and an alliance with the former enemy, Frederick II. The last straw for Catherine was a banquet held in June to celebrate the peace with Prussia. When she failed to rise for a toast to Peter's German relatives, the new czar called Catherine an idiot in front of their 400 guests. "Peter III's barbarous, senseless ferocity made it seem quite possible that he intended to eliminate his wife," a French diplomat wrote in a report sent home.

The Peasant Czar

Although the Romanovs ruled Russia for three centuries, there were numerous challenges to their dynasty. Rival claimants to the throne generally stepped forward when a czar died after a short reign or under mysterious circumstances, as was the case with Peter III.

In the eight years following his death, four false Peters appeared in the southwestern provinces of the Russian empire, but they were quickly exposed as frauds. In 1773, however, Catherine faced a serious threat from a Cossack deserter named Emelyan Pugachev. No matter that he bore no resemblance whatsoever to the long dead czar, Pugachev was accepted by the gullible peasant masses as the reincarnation of Peter III. In their naïve view, "that German woman" had murdered a sovereign who had only the interests of his great Russian people at heart. Gathering an army of fellow deserters, escaped serfs, disgruntled workers, and common thieves, Pugachev marched on the capital.

Although she feigned indifference, Catherine was soon forced to give full attention to Pugachev's rebellion, offering a reward of 100,000 rubles for his capture by the spring of 1774. Concluding a war with Turkey that summer, she turned her attention to the self-styled peasant czar and defeated his rabble force in battle at the end of August. Pugachev's own lieutenants handed him over to Catherine's army, and the former conquering hero was taken to Moscow in a cage. A huge crowd cheered his decapitation on January 10, 1775.

The Reach for Power

Catherine's allies at court were now urging her to take drastic action against her deranged and dangerous husband. Among them were her current lover and the father of her latest child, a dashing young officer named Gregory Orlov, and his younger brother, Alexis. The date they chose for their coup d'etat was the eve of the celebration of Peter's name day on June 29.

At dawn on June 28, Alexis Orlov awakened Catherine at her villa outside St. Petersburg. "Everything is ready to proclaim you empress," he said, escorting her to a waiting carriage. En route to the capital, they were joined by Gregory Orlov. By 8 A.M. the threesome had reached the barracks of the regimental guards. Stepping from the carriage, Catherine asked the carefully rehearsed troops for protection. "Long live our little mother Catherine!" they cried.

Accompanied by the soldiers, Catherine proceeded to the cathedral of the Virgin of Kazan to receive the church's blessing and take the imperial oath as Catherine II of Russia. At her side was her seven-year-old son, Paul. Early the next morning, on what was supposed to have been the celebration of his name day, Peter III obediently copied and signed a letter of abdication — "like a child who is sent to bed," the disgusted Frederick II said when he heard of it. Granted his wish to take along a servant, his violin, and a favorite dog, but denied the company of his mistress, Peter was taken to a country estate and put under the surveillance of Alexis Orlov.

A week later, on July 6, Catherine received a virtually incoherent message from Orlov. "How can I explain — how can I describe what has happened?" he wrote. Her husband was dead, apparently killed in a drunken brawl.

According to eyewitnesses, Catherine was genuinely shocked at the news, weeping and crying out that her reputation was ruined and that posterity would never forgive her for an involuntary crime. However, she quickly regained her composure, hid Orlov's note, and ordered an autopsy that conveniently found Peter to have died of a violent colic attack.

Catherine ruled Russia for 34 years and at her death in 1796 was acclaimed as Catherine the Great. To her son and heir, Paul, she was anything but a heroine, responsible — in his eyes — for the death of the man he still believed to be his father. Ordering a double funeral, he had the late czar's bones disinterred and brought for burial beside those of Catherine. At Paul's order, the man carrying the crown of Peter III in the funeral procession was Alexis Orlov.

Traitor or Patriot?

*As Britain was fighting Germany to a stalemate in World War I,
a distinguished public servant, Sir Roger Casement, was charged
with treason. To Irish nationalists, however, he was a hero
of their accelerated effort to gain independence.*

Before dawn on Good Friday, April 21, 1916, a German submarine surfaced in Tralee Bay on the southwestern coast of Ireland. From it three men started for shore in a dinghy. After a wave capsized their small boat, the men reached the shore soaked and exhausted. Pausing only to bury a crate of arms and ammunition in the sand, two of the men set off for town to find help. The third, a man of 51 who had shaved off his beard to conceal his identity, was too weak to proceed and took refuge in the ruins of an ancient fort. There, early in the morning, he was found by a local policeman who had seen the overturned boat bobbing in the surf and was taken into custody. "This is a nice way to treat an English traveler," the man protested, trying to pass himself off as a writer out for a morning stroll.

The prisoner, in fact, was Sir Roger Casement, an Irish-born British public servant who had been knighted five years earlier for his humanitarian efforts in behalf of enslaved natives in Africa and South America. More recently, however, he was a convert to the cause of Irish nationalism who hoped that Britain's preoccupation with the

*The Bay of Tralee in southwestern Ireland: Sir Roger Casement landed here on Good Friday in 1916,
hoping to prevent an uprising he thought doomed to failure.*

struggle against Germany in World War I would provide an opportunity to declare Irish independence. "When I landed in Ireland that morning, swamped and swimming ashore on an unknown strand," Casement later wrote his sister, "I was happy for the first time in over a year."

Two days later Casement was in London and was being interrogated at Scotland Yard on Monday, April 24, when news reached the capital of an aborted uprising in Dublin. A member of Parliament rose to demand that "this traitor [Casement] be shot forthwith." After a four-day trial Casement was convicted of treason and sentenced to death on June 29.

In Search of Adventure

Born near Dublin into a pro-English family of Ireland's Protestant minority on September 1, 1864, Roger Casement was secretly baptized a Catholic at his mother's wish. But both his parents died before he was 10, and he was taken to Ulster to be raised as a Protestant by a member of his father's family. Only as his political beliefs changed in mid-life did he return to Catholicism.

Casement had hoped to join the British civil service but instead was put to work as a clerk in the Liverpool office of a shipping line. "I must

have an open-air life," the tall, handsome young man told his sister, "or I shall die." Persuading the firm to make him a purser on a ship bound for West Africa, he got the chance for adventure that he so desperately craved.

Africa at the time was being carved up by the European powers. One unlikely victor in the contest for spoils was King Leopold II of Belgium, who had himself proclaimed sovereign of the Congo Free State in 1885 and ruled the territory thereafter as his personal possession. Casement got a job helping to build a transportation system in the backward region. Although he was praised for his hard work, his superiors felt that his treatment of the natives was perhaps too lenient.

By 1892 Casement was working for a British trading company in the Niger Coast protectorate. He wrote critical reports concerning his fellow countrymen's treatment of the natives that eventually reached high government circles in London. In 1895 he was named British consul in Portuguese East Africa, now Mozambique. Casement's assignment was to protect British subjects and look out for British interests, informing the home office of any moves in the area by rival Germany. But much of his work was routine, and after three years he managed to arrange

Casement won international acclaim and honors in Britain for his public service in the years before 1913.

The name Casement is inseparably linked to revelations of Belgian mistreatment of natives in the Congo.

an extended home leave to recuperate from malaria and other disabilities resulting from his service in Africa. His next posting was to Portuguese West Africa, now Angola, but in 1900 he got the assignment that was to make his reputation: establishing a new British consulate at Kinshasa in the Congo Free State and reporting home on the alleged atrocities against the natives there by the colony's Belgian rulers.

Exposing European Atrocities

Before taking his post, Casement journeyed to Brussels to interview King Leopold. Why were the natives employed as forced laborers, he asked? It was work in lieu of taxes, the king replied. And what about such atrocities as cutting off hands as punishment for disobedience? Rumors, said the king.

It did not take Casement long, following his arrival in the Congo Free State, to learn that the king had been lying. Down the Congo River came load after load of rubber produced by slave labor in the interior; upriver went only guns and ammunition to keep the natives in check. Photographs documented the ghastly mutilations of rebels. In London, Casement's reports were added to an "atrocity file" in the British Foreign Office and in 1908 were used against King Leopold to force reforms in his African possession.

Meanwhile, Casement had been posted to South America and in 1910 was sent to investigate alleged atrocities against the natives on British-owned rubber plantations along Peru's Putumayo River. His proof that the allegations were true won him his knighthood the following year.

Finding a New Cause

The years of service in tropical climates had so damaged Casement's health that he was forced to retire from the British civil service in 1913. Returning to his native Ireland, he was soon caught up in the movement for Irish independence.

Since 1801 Ireland had been ruled from London as an unwilling and restless partner in the United Kingdom. Home rule for Ireland had twice been defeated late in the 19th century, but in 1913 it was accepted by the House of Commons only to be blocked in the House of Lords. In reaction to this setback, Casement assumed a leading position in the Irish Volunteers, a resistance movement dedicated to defending the rights and liberties of the Irish people.

To raise money and collect weapons for the movement, Casement went to the United States in July 1914. When World War I erupted the following month, he sided with Germany. After his

The Irish Question

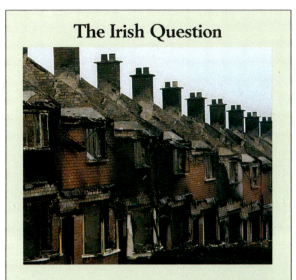

Ever since 1154, when Pope Adrian IV awarded the country to King Henry II — hoping that the English monarch would be able to reform the Irish church — Ireland has had to endure the harsh rule of its powerful neighbor. Henry himself landed there in 1171, received the homage of local barons, and later named his son lord of Ireland. But English colonists soon followed, and the Irish, little by little, were excluded from positions of political and economic power.

At first set off from the English colonists by their language (Gaelic), the Irish were separated by their religion after the reign of Henry VIII, remaining Catholic as England became a Protestant nation. Henry's daughter, Elizabeth I, liberally granted Irish estates to such favorites as Sir Walter Raleigh, giving rise to a system of absentee landownership that condemned the native inhabitants to poverty.

United with Britain in 1801, Ireland was nonetheless denied full representation in the British Parliament. By midcentury a home rule movement had been launched, but it foundered after its leader, Charles Stewart Parnell, became involved in a divorce scandal. The outbreak of World War I in 1914 at last seemed to offer Ireland the opportunity to break free of Britain.

Although the Easter uprising of 1916 failed, the nationalist movement could not be suppressed for long. The Sinn Fein party took up the political struggle, with the Irish Republican Army as its military counterpart. Although an Irish republic was proclaimed the next year, and Eamon de Valera elected the first president, it was not until 1921 that Britain signed a treaty with Ireland granting dominion status to an Irish free state consisting of 26 counties in the south and west. For the six counties of largely Protestant Ulster that chose to remain in the United Kingdom, the union has remained a troubled one.

Irish nationalists had hoped that British military forces, locked in battle with Germany, could not be spared to oppose their rebellion on Easter Monday, April 24, 1916. After only a few days, however, the British succeeded in suppressing the uprising — leaving large sections of Dublin in ruins.

experiences in the Congo, he could not accept Britain's defense of Belgium as the reason for going to war against Germany. He used the powerful Irish-American organization *Clan-na-Gael* to contact the German ambassador in Washington. It was his hope that Germany would support Irish independence as a means of striking at the British enemy from the rear.

Trusted by None

News of his activities in the United States made it impossible for Casement to return to Britain, so instead he sailed for Germany via Norway in October. He was accompanied by a young Norwegian sailor named Adler Christensen, who served as his servant and German interpreter. In Christiania, today's Oslo, Christensen apparently tried to sell out Casement to the British minister but was rebuffed. The sailor told Casement another story, alleging that the British had offered him $5,000 to lure his master to some place where he could be abducted or perhaps killed. "I am glad I brought him, indeed," Casement wrote of his servant; ". . . he is a treasure." He remained totally unaware that the disloyal Christensen continued to supply the British mission in Norway with reports on Casement's activities.

In Berlin, which he reached on October 31, Casement set himself three goals: Form a brigade of Irish prisoners of war to fight Britain; secure arms for Ireland's forthcoming struggle for independence; and win from the German government a public declaration of support for his cause. "It is not every day," Casement confided to his diary, "that even an Irishman commits high treason — especially one who has been in the service of the sovereign he discards, and not without honour and some fame in that service."

Although the German government issued a declaration of sympathy for Irish independence on November 20, Casement was not quite trusted by his new friends in Berlin. Nothing ever came of his plan for an Irish brigade, and the negotiations for the supply of arms were conducted not by Casement in Berlin, but rather by the *Clan-na-Gael* working through the German embassy in Washington. Meanwhile, thanks to Christensen's information, plans were being made to trap the defector.

The Easter Rebellion

Without Casement's participation, an Irish uprising was planned for Easter Sunday, April 23, 1916. To arm the rebels, Germany promised to smuggle 20,000 rifles with ammunition to Ireland aboard a fishing cutter to arrive at the Bay of Tralee a few days earlier. When Casement heard of the plan, he protested that the arms were insufficient and predicted that the rebellion would fail. Somehow he persuaded Germany to send him to Ireland on a submarine — ostensibly to join the uprising but in reality to prevent a premature and ill-prepared rebellion.

Casement's journey was not the only one to end disastrously. Having left Germany on April 9 with no radio aboard, the fishing cutter failed to learn of a postponement of the uprising by one day. When it arrived off Tralee on April 20, there were no Irish rebels to receive the smuggled arms. While waiting in vain for a signal from land, the cutter was detected by a British warship. Rather than be seized, the German captain ordered the crew to abandon ship and blew up the vessel. Without the arms from Germany, the Easter rebellion was indeed doomed to failure.

Following his apprehension at Tralee, Casement was brought to London for trial on a charge of treason. He was photographed leaving the court after his appeal of the conviction was dismissed.

The British were able to suppress the uprising within a few days and turn their attention to the man they thought partly guilty for it.

The Black Diaries

The guilty verdict in Casement's trial was not unexpected, and the defendant was ready with an impassioned statement objecting to the authority of the British court. His only offense had been that he had put Ireland first, Casement argued. His country was treated no better than a convicted criminal, its people subjected to inhumanities that no savage tribe would endure without resistance. "If it be treason to fight against such an unnatural fate as this, then I am proud to be a rebel and shall cling to my 'rebellion' with the last drop of my blood," he concluded.

Apparently fearful that the death sentence against Casement would never be carried out, the British authorities took steps to discredit their prisoner and thus block any efforts to win a reprieve for him. At hand were Casement's private diaries for the years 1903 and 1910, seized by the police from his London lodgings.

According to the excerpts leaked to the press, Casement's diaries contained details of his secret life as a homosexual. Once this sensational revelation had been made, prominent government and church figures in Britain and the United States withdrew their support of his appeal for clemency. On August 3 Casement was executed by hanging.

Were the so-called black diaries genuine? The argument has raged for decades — those who regard Casement as a British traitor generally accepting them as authentic; those who think of him as an Irish patriot and martyr to the cause of independence denouncing them as forgeries. According to the latter viewpoint, Casement was executed not for treason but for his lifestyle.

Not until 1948 did Ireland receive its full independence from Britain, though six of the nine counties of Ulster stayed within the United Kingdom as Northern Ireland.

After years of Irish pleading, the British released the remains of Sir Roger Casement for reburial in his native land. On February 23, 1965, the coffin was brought to Dublin, where thousands filed by to pay their respects. Warned by his doctors not to attend the graveyard ceremony, 88-year-old President Eamon de Valera insisted on going. Then, he was told, at least wear a hat in the inclement weather. "Casement deserves better than that," de Valera replied and went on to deliver a eulogy that echoed Casement's final plea in the dock for a united Ireland.

Stranger Than Fiction

The mysterious death of a New York shop girl was headline news in the summer of 1841. The following year a struggling young writer named Edgar Allan Poe published a story with striking parallels. What did he know about the true case?

On a hot summer day in 1841 the body of a young woman was found floating in the Hudson River near Weehawken, New Jersey. It proved to be that of 21-year-old Mary Cecilia Rogers, a pretty young woman well known to the writers, actors, and other celebrities who had stopped by to flirt with her at John Anderson's tobacco shop on Liberty Street, just across the river in lower Manhattan. The New York press eagerly exploited the case, publishing daily reports of police efforts to solve the mystery of her death and wildly speculating on the identity of her murderer — for there was little doubt that Mary had been the victim of foul play.

The first suspect was Anderson, Mary's employer, who had often accompanied her home evenings. Even though he could offer no convincing alibi for the day of her disappearance and presumed death, Anderson was quickly released as attention focused on Mary's fiancé, David Payne, a resident of her mother's boardinghouse in Hoboken, New Jersey. Payne admitted to having seen Mary on the morning that she disappeared, three days before the body was found.

The first evidence in the case turned up in a wooded area near the river: a slip, a shawl, a parasol, and a handkerchief with the initials "M.R." Grass at the site appeared to be trampled down, as if a struggle had taken place there. Shortly afterward, David Payne committed suicide at the site by taking an overdose of laudanum, or tincture of opium. "This is the place," Payne wrote in his suicide note. "May God forgive me for my misspent life!" Did this prove that he had murdered Mary? No, said the police, he had an alibi for the time in question. The case remained unsolved; the investigation continued.

Making Fiction Out of Fact

Among readers of the press reports was 32-year-old Edgar Allan Poe, whose six volumes of short stories and poems had brought him some recognition but little money. He was supporting his tubercular young wife on the $800 annual salary he earned as literary editor of a magazine in Philadelphia and casting about for the subject of a sequel to his first detective story, "The Murders in the Rue Morgue." He found a crime for his fictional Inspector Dupin to solve in the story of Mary Rogers. But in Poe's tale, Mary was renamed Marie Rogêt; New York became Paris; the Hudson River, the Seine.

"Under pretence of showing how Dupin unravelled the mystery of Marie's assassination, I, in fact, enter into a very rigorous analysis of the *real* tragedy in New York," Poe wrote a friend on June 4, 1842. "No *point* is omitted. I examine, each by each, the opinions and arguments of our press on the subject, and show (I think satisfactorily) that this subject has never yet been *approached*. The press has been entirely on a wrong scent. In fact, I really believe, not only that I have demonstrated the falsity of the idea that the girl was the victim of a gang, but have *indicated the assassin*."

Poe's story, "The Mystery of Marie Rogêt," was published in three issues of a women's magazine between November 1842 and February 1843. With seamless logic, Inspector Dupin (that is, Poe) proves that there can be but one murderer, the "man of dark complexion," a naval officer with whom Marie (Mary) had last been seen and with whom she had disappeared for a few weeks three years earlier. At this point, Poe ended his tale, declining to give the name of the culprit as he had done in his earlier crime stories. An editor's note explained: "For reasons which we shall not specify, but which to many readers will appear obvious, we have taken the liberty of here omitting, from the manuscript placed in our hands, such portion as details the *following up* of the apparently slight clew obtained by Dupin.

The stories of Edgar Allan Poe (right) have fascinated generations of readers and inspired countless artists to depict his characters in haunting fashion.

We feel it advisable only to state, in brief, that the result desired was brought to pass. . . .''

Was this actually the comment of the magazine's editors? Or was Poe using this device to withhold evidence in the real case? At the time his story was published, the police had not solved the murder of Mary Rogers.

Suspect: Edgar Allan Poe

It did not take long after the publication of "The Mystery of Marie Rogêt" for people to begin speculating that perhaps Poe knew more than he was willing to disclose. Could it be possible that the writer himself was involved in the death of the New York shop girl?

A frequent visitor to New York, Poe may well have met Mary at the tobacco shop and turned to her for the sexual gratification his sickly young wife could not provide. But was he capable of murder? At this period in his life, the struggling writer was oppressed by his poverty and lack of literary recognition. He was fighting an apparently losing battle with his lifelong alcoholism and reputed drug addiction. To his friends and family, he appeared physically if not mentally ill.

Poe's state of being is mirrored by the egocentric heroes of his crime and horror stories. He gave his literary creations license to indulge in every passion, allowing them to torture for pleasure and even commit murder. Death, as revealed in his stories, had a peculiar fascination for the master of the macabre. Could Poe, in a moment of frenzy, have surrendered to the darker instincts that he bottled up within himself but allowed to erupt in the bizarre and unprincipled characters that peopled his works of fiction?

Behavioral psychologists have demonstrated that criminals often give tips that could lead to their apprehension — without being aware of their subconscious desires to be punished. Was Poe doing just this when he gave his decisive hint about the identity of Marie Rogêt's murderer? The writer was dark-skinned, with a full head of black hair falling over his large forehead. Although literary sleuths have continued to speculate about Poe's involvement in the true case he transformed into fiction, there is no hard evidence to link him to Mary Rogers's murder.

What scholars have been able to prove is that Poe adjusted his story to fit the facts of the case — as revealed by the police after the first installment appeared but before publication was completed. The "man of dark complexion" was an abortionist, very likely the same one to whom the naval officer had taken Mary in 1838. In the summer of 1841, the young woman probably died as a consequence of her second abortion. When Poe revised the story for publication in book form two years later, he made 15 minor changes to accommodate the possibility of Marie's death following a bungled abortion. The writer then added footnotes to make it appear that he had been right about the case from the start.

"Nothing was omitted in 'Marie Rogêt' but what I omitted myself," Poe later wrote a friend. "The 'naval officer,' who committed the murder (or rather, the accidental death arising from an attempt at abortion) *confessed* it; and the whole matter is now well understood — but, for the sake of relatives, this is a topic on which I must not speak further.''

King James I (left) came to the throne of England in 1603 distrusting Sir Walter Raleigh (right). Within months the famed courtier was summoned to Windsor Castle (above) and charged with treason.

The Downfall of a Favorite

The handsome soldier quickly caught the fancy of England's Queen Elizabeth I when he appeared at court in 1581. But later Sir Walter Raleigh had a falling-out with the queen and, under her successor, was convicted of treason. The sentence was death.

Because of an outbreak of plague claiming 2,000 victims a week in London, the trial for treason had been moved to Wolversey Castle in Winchester, a town some 60 miles southwest of the capital. En route to the proceedings that day, November 17, 1603, Sir Walter Raleigh — a wealthy and accomplished court favorite under the late Queen Elizabeth I — had to endure the hostility of a mob that cursed him and pelted his carriage with mud and stones. Ignoring the degrading insults, the defendant calmly puffed at his pipe.

There were four charges against Raleigh: that he had sought to overthrow the new monarch, James I, and replace him with his cousin, Arabella Stuart; that he had fomented rebellion in the kingdom; that he had plotted to restore Catholicism to the realm; and that he had conspired to procure a Spanish invasion of Britain.

Despite the defendant's plea of not guilty, his reminder that the testimony of two witnesses was required for conviction, and the failure of the prosecution to produce Raleigh's single accuser, a guilty verdict was returned by the jury after only 15 minutes of deliberation. Chief Justice Sir John Popham did not hesitate to deliver the terrible sentence. Raleigh was to be hanged but cut down alive and dismembered, "then your head [is] to be stricken off from your body, and your body shall be divided into four quarters, to be disposed of at the king's pleasure: And may God have mercy on your soul!"

The Rise of a Court Favorite

It was a long, twisting road that had taken Raleigh to the courtroom at Winchester. The son of a Devonshire country gentleman, he had left Oxford without a degree in 1569 at the age of 17 to fight with the Protestant armies in France. A decade later he accompanied his half brother, Sir Humphrey Gilbert, on a so-called voyage of discovery that in reality was to be an attack on Spanish possessions in the West Indies. He only got as far as the Cape Verde Islands. Next, he helped put down an uprising in Ireland and, in December 1581, was sent to the court in Greenwich with dispatches from the front.

The story that Raleigh spread his cloak over a muddy road so that Queen Elizabeth might keep her feet dry is probably only legend. It is certain, however, that the tall, handsome soldier — not yet 30 — captured the fancy of the unmarried, 48-year-old queen with his reputation for valor, courtly manners, and ready wit. With her long-time favorite, the earl of Leicester, recently remarried, Elizabeth eagerly sought Raleigh's companionship and showered him with gifts of property, offices, and lucrative trading licenses. In 1584 she bestowed knighthood on him.

Upon the death of Gilbert, Raleigh was granted his half brother's patent to discover unknown lands in the New World and take possession of them in the queen's name. The first expedition he sent claimed the Atlantic seaboard north of Florida for England. To this territory the queen gave the name Virginia — for herself, the Virgin Queen. Later, when Elizabeth forbade Raleigh to leave the court, he sent a cousin, Sir Richard Grenville, to found a colony at Roanoke, the first of two unsuccessful efforts to establish a toehold on the North American continent.

The arrival at court of Robert Devereux, the earl of Essex, in May 1587 brought Raleigh a rival for the affections of Elizabeth, and he temporarily withdrew to his Irish estates. When he returned to court, he formed a liaison with one of the queen's maids of honor, Elizabeth Throckmorton — an affront to the jealous monarch for which both were imprisoned in the Tower of London. Eventually, the lovers were released and allowed to marry, though they were forced to retire from the court and live quietly in the country.

In 1595 Raleigh was at last permitted to leave England, leading an expedition against Spain's New World possessions and looking for gold up the Orinoco River in South America. The following year he joined in a successful attack on the Spanish port of Cadiz, and by 1597 he was not only once more in favor with the queen but was also serving as a member of Parliament.

Dawn of a New Era

By the turn of the century, it was apparent to all that the long, glorious reign of Elizabeth I was drawing to a close. With her death on March 24, 1603, the Tudor dynasty came to an end. The decades of speculation and intrigue over a successor to the childless queen were over. Within hours King James VI of Scotland — son of the hapless Mary, Queen of Scots — was proclaimed King James I of England, uniting the two kingdoms under his personal rule. For Raleigh it meant an end to his favored position at court.

Two men, both of whom he had regarded as friends, were to betray Raleigh. The first was Sir Robert Cecil, a small, sickly hunchback — "my pygmy," Elizabeth called him — who had served as the queen's secretary of state since 1596 and had been in secret communication with James VI of Scotland about the succession. Cecil encouraged James's plans to strengthen the monarchy, weaken Parliament, and end hostilities with Spain — policies, Cecil let James know, that were opposed by Raleigh. The second false friend was Lord Cobham, who would provide the sole evidence on which Raleigh was eventually convicted of treason.

When Raleigh hastened to swear allegiance to the new king, James greeted Elizabeth's favorite with marked discourtesy. Within two weeks James stripped Raleigh of his posts and his trading licenses and ordered him to move out of the London townhouse given him some years earlier by the queen. On July 14 Cecil — who had retained his position as secretary of state under James — summoned Raleigh before the king's council at Windsor Castle to be examined about his knowledge of a plot against the new monarch.

A History of the World

Sir Walter Raleigh, the impetuous adventurer and polished courtier, was also a man of considerable literary accomplishments. Much of the poetry he wrote has been lost, but several impressive prose works survive. The most ambitious and distinguished of these is *The History of the World*, written between 1607 and 1614, during his years of confinement in the Tower of London under a death sentence. Although Raleigh's name did not appear on the elaborately engraved frontispiece to the first edition (above), there was no secret about the authorship. The book was immediately banned by King James I.

Raleigh set out to write a universal chronicle that would parallel the Old Testament chronology in its initial chapters but bring the story up to his own times, in which the history of England would be related to that of the rest of the world. He got only as far as the fall of Macedonia in 130 B.C.

James's displeasure was caused by Raleigh's portrayals of Assyrian Queen Semiramis, which was seen as a tribute to Elizabeth I, and of her effeminate successor, Ninus, which the king interpreted as an unflattering caricature of himself.

Accused of Treason

Lord Cobham, Raleigh's erstwhile friend, had made no secret of his dislike for King James and his contempt for Cecil. From the ambassador of the Spanish Netherlands, Count Aremberg, Cobham obtained a loan of 500,000 crowns to finance a coup d'etat that would replace James on the throne with his pliant cousin, Arabella Stuart. Having got wind of the plot, Cecil now asked Raleigh how much he knew about his friend's treasonous activities. At first Raleigh denied any complicity in Cobham's scheme, but he later wrote to Cecil, admitting that Cobham had offered him 10,000 crowns to bring about peace between Spain and England — an offer that he had not taken seriously.

Shown Raleigh's letter, the terrified Cobham confessed to his dealings with Aremberg but named Raleigh as the instigator of the plot. It was this accusation that brought Raleigh to trial at Winchester on November 17.

Convicted on Slender Evidence

Denied legal counsel, Raleigh had to defend himself — and here his wit and eloquence served him well. According to one eyewitness, he bantered with the prosecution as if "it was the happiest day of his life." Asking if he could answer the charges one by one as they were brought against him, Raleigh was told that the presentation of evidence could not be interrupted lest it lose "its grace and vigor." Confronted with Cobham's confession, the defendant calmly produced a recantation in his friend's handwriting. The prosecutor, Sir Edward Coke, countered with Cobham's revocation of his recantation. Stymied, Raleigh demanded that his accuser be brought to court to confront him. Coke denied the request. A guilty verdict from the obviously intimidated jury was a foregone conclusion.

Some of the jurors knelt before Raleigh to beg his forgiveness. The scorned courtier of the morning had suddenly become a martyr, the victim of a judicial murder plot. A wave of revulsion at the hasty, patently unfair proceedings swept the country and led, in time, to a reform of court procedures that now distinguish the legal systems of both Britain and America. On his deathbed, one of the judges in the case said, "Never before had the justice of England been so depraved and injured as in this trial."

The Years of Waiting

Raleigh's execution was scheduled for December 10. A day before the sentence was to be carried out, the king granted a reprieve to Raleigh but

Released from a long imprisonment in 1616, Raleigh returned to South America's Orinoco River, where he had sought gold and fame two decades earlier. His new exploits brought his rearrest and execution.

Shortly before midnight on October 28, 1618, the condemned man took leave of his faithful wife, Elizabeth. That morning he had lost the appeal of his 15-year-old death sentence; the next day he was to die on the scaffold.

sent him to the Tower of London. Although allowed the company of his wife and son, Raleigh had to spend the next 13 years in prison.

After years of petitioning the king for his release and endorsement of his plan for another expedition to the New World, Raleigh was granted his freedom early in 1616. By June of the following year, he had raised enough funds for his voyage, though he was warned by the crown to avoid hostilities with the Spaniards.

The expedition was a disaster, reaching a climax with an attack on a Spanish settlement that claimed the life of Raleigh's son. Upon his return to England in June 1618, Raleigh was arrested and sent back to the Tower of London. Since he was already under sentence of death, Raleigh could not be tried for disobeying the king's order to avoid conflict with Spain. And thus, on October 29, he was taken to the scaffold for the carrying out of his 15-year-old death sentence.

Asking to see the ax that would sever his head, Raleigh ran his fingers over the edge and joked, "It is sharp and fair medicine to cure me of all my diseases." When a bystander demanded that the condemned man place his head on the block pointing toward the east, Raleigh answered, "What matter how the head lie so the heart be right" — a fitting epitaph for the court favorite who fell from grace.

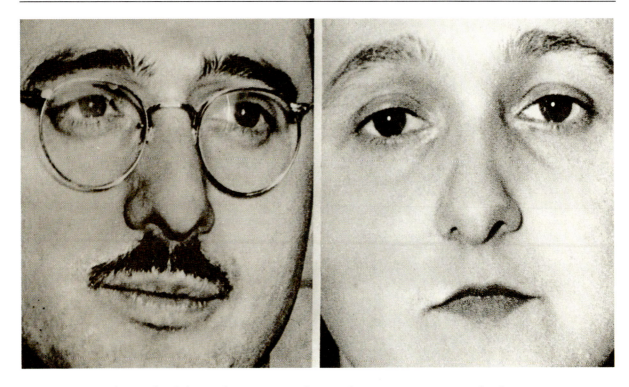

Julius and Ethel Rosenberg: Convicted spies, they spent two years on death row.

Death for the Atom Spies

**An obscure American couple with few friends was executed for
having given secrets about the atomic bomb to the Soviet Union.
But was their trial a frame-up? Were they made
scapegoats for high-level incompetence?**

Scores of police officers were on special assignment to guard New York's grim Sing Sing penitentiary just before sundown on Friday, June 19, 1953. Inside, a six-man FBI team equipped with two special phone lines to Washington waited in a secret command post, hopeful that either Julius Rosenberg or his wife, Ethel, would confess their espionage activities rather than face death in the electric chair.

Some 30 miles to the south, a crowd of perhaps 7,000 gathered in New York City's Union Square to mount a vigil. Outside the White House, some urged clemency for the couple — the only Ameri-

cans ever sentenced to death for peacetime espionage — while others held placards that read, "Death to the Communist Rats!"

After a total of 112 judges had participated in 23 appeals, including seven at the Supreme Court level, the executions ordered two years before were to be carried out. Because the appointed execution time of 11 P.M. would conflict with the Jewish Sabbath beginning at sundown, the schedule had been moved forward.

When Julius was escorted into the brightly lit death chamber shortly before 8 P.M., he looked pale and drawn. His knees buckled when he spotted the electric chair, but he said nothing. He had remained silent since issuing a last statement earlier that day that concluded, "Never let them change the truth of our innocence." After the standard charge of electricity — one short, two long — he was pronounced dead at 8:06. Soon afterward, Ethel Rosenberg was executed. The couple left two sons, aged nine and six.

Masters of Deceit?

To J. Edgar Hoover, director of the Federal Bureau of Investigation, the Rosenberg case was "the crime of the century." Allegedly, Julius Rosenberg was the mastermind of an espionage ring — perhaps two — that helped the Soviet Union develop its own atomic bomb years before the Russians could have done so unaided, thus changing the balance of power in the world.

Nothing in their backgrounds indicated that Julius Rosenberg and Ethel Greenglass were destined for international notoriety. Both were the eldest children in impoverished families struggling for a living during the darkest years of the Depression on New York City's Lower East Side. Intellectually gifted, Rosenberg entered City College of New York at age 16, majoring in engineering even though his father had wanted him to become a rabbi. Soon, outraged by the rise of Nazism in Germany and concerned about social and racial inequality in the United States, he was attracted to the professed ideals of the Communist Party and began to neglect his studies for active work with the Young Communist League.

Meanwhile, Ethel Greenglass had to forgo higher education and begin clerical work for a shipping company at age 15. She earned $7 a week. Four years later she was fired for leading 150 women in a strike, but her complaint to the National Labor Relations Board was upheld. Backstage one night at a benefit for the International Seamen's Union, Ethel met and fell in love with Julius Rosenberg, who was nearly three years her junior. Theirs was a passionate devotion that was never to waver.

With her encouragement, Julius earned his engineering degree in 1939, shortly before they married. In 1940 he was hired as a civilian engineer with the U.S. Army Signal Corps in Brooklyn. He was promoted a year later to engineer inspector, a job that required travel throughout New York and New Jersey but also brought a pay increase. During these years the couple became full members of the Communist Party, as did Ethel's younger brother, David Greenglass. In 1943, after the birth of their first son, the Rosenbergs apparently dropped out of the party, but

two years later the Signal Corps fired Julius for denying that he had been a communist.

Theft of U.S. Atom Secrets

On August 28, 1948, Stalin's Russia successfully exploded its first atomic bomb. Early the following year, an FBI counterintelligence officer discovered that the Russian secret police agency, the KGB, had a copy of a report on the Manhattan Project, America's secret plan to develop the atomic bomb. It had been written by German-born Klaus Fuchs, a brilliant physicist who had worked on the project at Los Alamos, New Mexico, and had then set up a laboratory at the Harwell Atomic Research Establishment in England. He confessed that he had joined the Communist Party in Germany in 1933 to oppose the Nazis and that he had begun spying for the Russians after escaping to England and finding employment in Britain's atomic research program.

Julius Rosenberg and Ethel Greenglass grew up on New York City's Lower East Side. The poverty of their upbringing apparently made them receptive to communist pleas for social reform.

After Fuchs was transferred to the United States, he established contact with a courier known only as Raymond. By 1945, when it became apparent that Germany was not developing an atom bomb, Fuchs — like many other scientists — questioned U.S. goals and the consequences of an escalating nuclear weapons race. Eventually, he gave Raymond written documents that described the first atomic bomb tested in the New Mexico desert.

Based upon information from Fuchs, the FBI closed in on Raymond, who turned out to be a chemist named Harry Gold, and the bare outlines of a conspiracy began to appear. According to Gold, his "control," or spy master, was Anatoli Yakovlev, Soviet vice-consul in New York City. Gold confessed that, on Yakovlev's orders, he had traveled to New Mexico in 1944 to meet with David Greenglass, who had been assigned as a mechanic to the Los Alamos project. Julius Rosenberg's young brother-in-law, it turned out, had taken $500 for drawings of the firing mechanism, lens mold, and internal structure of the atomic bomb. Why did David Greenglass and his wife, Ruth, trust Raymond? They later testified that the stranger arrived bearing coded identification from Julius Rosenberg.

Even as Gold was talking with FBI investigators, Rosenberg, according to his brother-in-law, was making plans to take his family out of the country and was frantically urging the Greenglasses to flee as well, offering $4,000 in cash to finance the escape. No one moved fast enough. On June 15, 1950, Greenglass was picked up by the FBI and confessed his role in the conspiracy, implicating his brother-in-law. On July 17 Julius was arrested. Ethel was unexpectedly taken into custody on August 11; she was even refused time to arrange for the care of her two children.

The Conspiracy of Shadows

Despite the assurance of investigators that Julius Rosenberg was the leader of a ring of spies, hard evidence did not come to light. But the climate of suspicion grew nevertheless. Two friends from student days, one mentioned in certain Soviet documents, suddenly disappeared. Another college acquaintance, Morton Sobell, fled with his wife to Mexico, but he was eventually handed over to the FBI and, like the Rosenbergs, charged with conspiracy to commit espionage.

But what did this "ring" actually accomplish? What "secrets" were passed to the enemy? The reason so many people still doubt the validity of the government's case against the Rosenbergs and Sobell is the lack of solid proof,

After Victory: A Cold War

At the end of World War II, the United States was the most powerful nation in the world — yet many citizens developed profound fears for the future. The Soviet Union, a staunch wartime ally, seemingly overnight had become a dangerous enemy, dedicated to the overthrow of democratic governments everywhere. Long dominated by Hitler's Germany, Eastern Europe now lay behind Stalin's symbolic iron curtain. Popular movements there were being brutally suppressed by the Red Army and puppet regimes installed by Moscow.

In Asia huge, populous China — another wartime ally of the United States — fell to the communist forces of Mao Zedong in 1949. The next year war erupted in Korea. That conflict would eventually find Chinese infantry fighting hand to hand with American soldiers.

At the height of the Cold War, the Soviet Union blockaded the western sector of Berlin. The United States organized an airlift to supply the city.

How had victory turned sour so suddenly? Should one look for political miscalculation and failure — as some critics of the 20 years of Democratic presidential leadership charged? Or had U.S. adversaries reaped the unfair advantage of espionage and internal treason? The shock of events during the late 1940's helped fuel a national furor in the early 1950's, the very time that charges of a conspiracy to commit espionage were brought against the Rosenbergs. Though later branded a demagogue, Wisconsin Senator Joseph R. McCarthy summed up the feelings of many: "The reason why we find ourselves in a position of impotency is not because our only powerful potential enemy has sent men to invade our shores but, rather, because of the traitorous actions of those who have been treated so well by this nation."

coupled with the reliance upon testimony from the Greenglasses. Some observers think that they saved themselves by testifying against the Rosenbergs.

"Worse than murder . . ."

In the minds of many, the trial that began on March 6, 1951, did not offer definitive answers. Both Rosenbergs chose to testify in their own defense and steadfastly protested their innocence. But Julius seemed arrogant and combative, opening himself up to clever counterthrusts from the prosecutor, Irving Saypol. Ethel perhaps undercut sympathy for her plight by relying too much

Named legal guardian of the Rosenbergs' sons, defense attorney Emanuel Bloch arranged for their adoption by Anne and Abel Meeropol after their parents' execution.

upon the Fifth Amendment privilege of not testifying about her communist past.

The verdict to convict both defendants was unanimous. Judge Irving R. Kaufman, sentencing both Rosenbergs to the electric chair, said, "I consider your crime worse than murder."

Sobell was given 30 years, and Greenglass was sentenced to a 15-year term, though he would be paroled in 1960. His cooperation, according to government files, was the basis of an implicit agreement not to indict his wife, Ruth. Gold had already been sentenced to 30 years.

For the following two years, the Rosenberg case received international attention as various appeals made their way through the court system and failed. Meanwhile, the Rosenbergs lived on death row, rarely able to communicate with each other, visited only infrequently by their sons.

After the Rosenbergs were executed, 8,000 mourners attended their funeral in Brooklyn, fully believing them innocent of the charges. Nobel laureate Harold Urey expressed his opinion that "a man of Greenglass's capacity is wholly incapable of transmitting the physics, chemistry, and mathematics of the bomb to anyone." The famous French existentialist philosopher Jean-Paul Sartre termed the Rosenberg executions "a legal lynching that smears with blood a whole nation." But Hoover considered the conviction one of his bureau's greatest achievements; and, in 1954, Congress made peacetime espionage a capital crime, legislation that inevitably became known as the Rosenberg law.

On the day the Rosenbergs were to die, June 19, 1953, pickets marched outside the White House. Since they refused to confess their guilt, no last-minute clemency was granted by the president.

Accused: The Queen

**As Prince of Wales, England's King George IV had surrendered
himself to a life of pleasure. When he tried to dissolve his
marriage to Queen Caroline and strip her of the royal title, many
people thought that a double standard was being applied.**

Because she had conducted herself toward one Bartolommeo Pergami with "indecent and offensive familiarity and freedom" and had carried on "a licentious, disgraceful, and adulterous" relationship with him, Caroline Amelia Elizabeth was to be deprived of "the title, prerogatives, rights, privileges, and pretensions" of the queen consort of the realm. Her marriage to George IV, king of the United Kingdom of Great Britain and Ireland, was to be dissolved.

Such was the accusation in a bill of Pains and Penalties introduced in the House of Lords on July 5, 1820. Since Pergami was a foreigner not subject to British law, and since the alleged offenses had not taken place in Britain, a trial for treason was not possible. The bill — a private measure introduced on behalf of an unnamed party, whom everyone knew to be the king — was

*The House of Lords during debate on the divorce bill in 1820: Although Queen Caroline attended the
proceedings, she was not called upon to testify in her own defense.*

seen as a way of punishing Queen Caroline without an actual trial. To the queen it was an opportunistic strategy on the part of her dissolute husband to deprive her of her rightful place beside him on the throne. For George IV it was a convenient way to end the marital strife that had plagued his private life for the past quarter century.

A Wayward Prince

That George should be the accuser in a matter of improper behavior was highly ironic. Born on August 12, 1762, the eldest son of King George III was a handsome youth, intelligent, affable, and discerning in his taste for art. But all too soon the Prince of Wales turned into a corpulent rake. His numerous love affairs and profligate spending dismayed his father's subjects, who took to calling him the dissolute prince.

Then, in 1784, at the age of 22, the heir apparent to the throne fell in love — virtually at first sight — with Maria Fitzherbert, a twice-widowed woman six years his senior. Unfortunately, there were insurmountable impediments to their marriage. As a commoner, Mrs. Fitzherbert was considered beneath the prince's station. As a Catholic, she was barred from marriage to an heir to the throne. And, since George was under 25, he could not marry without the consent of his father, which the king would not grant.

When the proper Mrs. Fitzherbert declined to become the prince's mistress, George feigned a suicide attempt to lure her to his London townhouse and win from her a promise to marry him. Learning of this deceit, she fled to the Continent. George's request to live abroad — as a means of economy, he told his father, but actually to be near Mrs. Fitzherbert — was summarily dismissed by the king, who had been kept informed of the progress of the affair.

After a year George succeeded in enticing Mrs. Fitzherbert back to England; and on December 15, 1785, they were married in the drawing room of her London home. The Church of England cleric who performed the illegal ceremony had been given money to liquidate his debts and the promise of being made a bishop when George became king. Although the prince thereafter was constantly seen in the presence of Mrs. Fitzherbert, and their marriage was something of an open secret, the couple continued to live separately for propriety's sake.

An Unloved Bride

The clandestine marriage did not end George's pursuit of other women or his spendthrift ways. As quarrels with Mrs. Fitzherbert became more frequent, and as his debts mounted, the prince came to realize that only an officially recognized union with a Protestant princess would save him from financial ruin. His younger brother, the duke of York, had been rewarded for a proper marriage by an increased allowance from the king. In August 1794 George told his father that he had broken off with Mrs. Fitzherbert and was willing to enter "a more creditable line of life." He was, in fact, ready for a royal marriage.

The bride George chose was Caroline, daughter of the duke of Brunswick-Wolfenbüttel and his first cousin. His mother, Queen Charlotte, was shocked, writing to her brother that Caroline "is a woman I do not recommend at all." The princess was said to be of such a passionate nature that her father would not let her go from one room to another without a chaperone. A governess had been instructed to shadow her at court dances, lest she make "an exhibition of herself by indecent conversations with men." Lord Malmesbury, the envoy sent to ask for her hand, described her as short and plump, with a head rather too big for her body. Yet she was cheerful and always laughing. Her father claimed that she was not stupid, only lacking in judgment and given to impromptu, tactless remarks and harsh criticisms of others.

Upon her arrival in England, Caroline was officially greeted by the countess of Jersey, who was rumored to have taken the place of Mrs. Fitzherbert in the prince's affections. Lady Jersey promptly told her to change her dress and apply rouge to her cheeks for her meeting with her future husband. When Caroline was presented to the prince, George dutifully embraced her, then turned abruptly away and called to Lord Malmesbury, "Harris, I am not well. Pray get me a glass of brandy." As soon as her intended husband left the room, Caroline — who had just started to learn English — plaintively asked in French, *"Mon Dieu!* Does the prince always act like this?" No more taken by him than he was by her, she added, "I think he's very fat and he's nothing like as handsome as his portrait." At their wedding, which took place three days later, on April 8, 1795, the prince appeared to be quite drunk.

A Shilling for the Princess

In January 1796 Caroline gave birth to a daughter. Three days later George, despondent, ill, and convinced that he was about to die, wrote a new will. In it he left all his money and property to his "beloved and adored Maria Fitzherbert," calling her "the wife of my heart and soul." To his infant daughter he bequeathed the jewels previously bestowed on Caroline. To his lawful wife, "her, who is called the Princess of Wales," he left exactly one shilling.

In a lengthy exchange of correspondence, the princess demanded that she and George henceforth be man and wife in name only. He must never attempt to produce another heir, even in the event of the death of their daughter. "Nature has not made us suitable to each other," the prince replied. Having reached an agreement to live separately, he added maliciously, "The rest of our lives will be passed in uninterrupted tranquility." All attempts by the king to save his son's marriage failed, yet he refused to grant the couple a formal separation.

By the summer of 1797, Caroline was settled in a country house, some hours' distance from London. Deserted by the few friends she had made in aristocratic circles, the princess surrounded herself with young naval officers, politicians, and writers. Informers told George that his spurned wife was leading a scandalous life, even that she had given birth to an illegitimate child by one of her many lovers. In December 1805 a committee of the king's council acquitted her of the latter charge. The only mistake she had ever made, Caroline blithely remarked, was going to bed with Mrs. Fitzherbert's husband.

Court painter Sir Thomas Lawrence captured Caroline's sensuous nature in this portrait of her as Princess of Wales. There were rumors that the artist had been her lover.

When Royalty Marries for Love

Marriage for members of Europe's royalty has always been a matter of duty and seldom of love. Partners, especially for heirs to a throne, are chosen from among those of equal rank who will provide the strongest political, military, or financial alliance. Marriage to a mere member of the nobility is frowned upon; marriage to a commoner, scorned.

Nonetheless, a prince could fall in love with a woman considered ineligible to be a royal spouse. To accommodate such unions, the morganatic marriage was created. The term is derived from a Latin phrase meaning "marriage on the morning gift"; the bride is entitled to no more than the dowry she receives on the morning of her wedding. She has no right to the title, coat of arms, or fortune of her husband; nor can their children inherit any of these. Such unions are also

Because of her rank, Sophie Chotek could not be buried in the Hapsburg family crypt. Instead, she and Francis Ferdinand were interred in the chapel of this Danube River castle.

called "marriage on the left hand," because the bride is made to stand to the left of the groom rather than to the right, as is customary.

Upon the death of Queen Marie Thérèse, Louis XV of France contracted a morganatic marriage with his mistress, Madame de Maintenon. Frederick William III of Prussia's second marriage, to the countess of Harrach, was another "marriage on the left hand."

Perhaps the most famous morganatic marriage of modern times was that of Archduke Francis Ferdinand, heir to the throne of the Austro-Hungarian empire, to Countess Sophie Chotek in 1900. The countess was constantly reminded of her lower rank, never allowed to enter rooms at her husband's side or sit next to him in royal processions. But on one notable occasion they were together, riding in a motorcade through Sarajevo on June 28, 1914. The assassin's bullets that took their lives that day turned out to be the first shots of World War I.

Before his dissolute life-style took its toll, the Prince of Wales (left) was judged to be quite handsome. His clandestine marriage to Mrs. Fitzherbert in 1785 could not long be kept a secret — and was the subject of the satirical drawing below in which England (personified as John Bull) sleeps through the ceremony. Since this first union was illegal, his marriage to Caroline was not considered bigamous.

Free at Last

The mental illness from which George III had long suffered at last became so prominent that the king was declared incompetent in 1811 and replaced by his son as regent. The prince used his new authority to ban Caroline from all court activities and to exclude her from the festivities that took place in London in the summer of 1814 in honor of the sovereigns who had united to defeat Napoleon. In August, traveling as the countess of Wolfenbüttel, Caroline boarded a frigate bound for France. Witnesses recalled that there were tears in her eyes as she left England.

George had hoped that she would live quietly in retirement somewhere in Europe. But Caroline was determined to discover the world, to enjoy life to the fullest, to do exactly as she pleased. Returning to Brunswick after all these years, she exhausted her hosts at suppers, dances, and gambling parties lasting to dawn. In Geneva the 46-year-old princess shocked guests at a masked ball by appearing dressed — or rather undressed from the waist up — as Venus. And in Milan she added a swarthy, robust former soldier named Bartolommeo Pergami to her entourage as a sort of valet. He was 14 years her junior. Before long, Pergami was promoted to be Caroline's chamberlain and given the title Baron della Francina. It was Pergami who organized her pilgrimage to the Holy Land, an extended tour via Sicily, Algiers, Greece, and Turkey that reached a climax when she rode into Jerusalem on an ass. Back in Europe, Caroline rented a villa in Italy and installed Pergami's family — save his estranged wife — there. His young daughter, Victorine, slept in Caroline's bedroom and called her "Mamma."

Toward the end of 1817, Caroline learned that her 21-year-old daughter had died in childbirth. Sadly, she realized that the last impediment to a divorce from George had been removed. With their child dead, she wrote her lawyer Henry Brougham, George would have no hesitation in making "false and foul accusations against my character." The next summer George dispatched a three-man commission to Milan to investigate the princess's bizarre behavior in Italy and gather any evidence of her infidelity.

Claiming a Crown

When George III died on January 29, 1820, the 57-year-old regent ascended the throne as King George IV. Refusing a generous financial settle-

On her return from a pilgrimage to the Holy Land, Caroline settled down in a villa overlooking Italy's Lake Como. It was there, according to her accusers, that she committed adultery with Bartolommeo Pergami — an offense for which she could be denied the title of queen and her marriage to George IV dissolved.

ment if she renounced her title and remained abroad, Caroline returned to England on June 5 to claim her crown as queen consort. In defiance of the unpopular new monarch, crowds rapturously greeted her arrival in London. "Long live the queen! No queen, no king!" echoed the shouts of supporters, who surged about her residence. Alarmed by the mobs who appeared outside his windows to call him Nero, the king withdrew from London to Windsor Castle. Before he left, he sent messages to both houses of Parliament, asking them to give "immediate and serious attention" to the contents of a certain green bag. It contained the report of the commission sent to Milan and was grounds for the introduction of the bill of Pains and Penalties in the House of Lords early the next month.

"Non mi ricordo"

The queen appeared in person at the House of Lords for the opening of the public inquiry — everybody called it a trial — on August 17. Although a loyal newspaper described her as looking "extremely well," less charitable observers noted how fat she had grown and how heavily she had applied makeup to her face.

In support of the bill to deprive Caroline of her title and dissolve her marriage to the king, the government had summoned numerous witnesses from Italy — including servants and workmen at her villa and sailors aboard the ship she had taken to the Holy Land — who could support the charge that she had committed adultery with Pergami. The first witness, one Teodoro Majoc-

chi, testified that he had twice seen the queen in Pergami's bedroom. Henry Brougham, acting as chief counsel to the queen, destroyed Majocchi's testimony in cross-examination, so confusing the unfortunate witness that he was reduced to replying *"Non mi ricordo"* ("I don't remember") to every question. Overnight, the Italian phrase became a popular refrain in England. Other witnesses, though offering evidence of the queen's indiscretions, were no more able than Majocchi to substantiate the charge of adultery.

On November 10 the lords voted on the bill, 108 supporting it and 99 opposing it. Realizing that such a slim margin in the House of Lords made it unlikely that the bill would ever get through the House of Commons, where Caroline was known to have more support, the government reluctantly informed the king that the charges would have to be withdrawn. London and other cities throughout the realm celebrated Caroline's victory with three days of fireworks, bonfires, dances, and parades.

George IV, however, had the last word. When Caroline appeared at Westminster Abbey on July 19, 1821, for the king's coronation, she was stopped at the door and denied admission because she did not have a proper ticket.

Almost immediately, the rejected queen took to her bed with an acute intestinal disorder, for which her doctors prescribed bleeding, opium, and castor oil — enough, said Henry Brougham, to "have turned the stomach of a horse." On August 7 she died, murmuring in French, "I die without sorrow; I die without regret."

Equal Justice for All?

*The trial, conviction, and execution of two Italian immigrants in
the 1920's became one of the most celebrated cases in
American judicial history. Were they victims of antiradical hysteria —
or, just possibly, could one of them actually have been guilty?*

Shortly after three o'clock on Thursday afternoon, April 15, 1920, the paymaster of the Slater & Morrill shoe company in South Braintree, Massachusetts, leaves the office in the company of an armed guard to deliver the weekly payroll of some $16,000 to the factory a few blocks away. Two dark-complexioned men stop them, pull out weapons, and begin shooting. The guard dies almost instantly, the paymaster some hours later. Bending over to take the guard's weapon, the second gunman drops his cap. A third assailant appears with a rifle as the two gunmen grab the money boxes. All three leap into the back seat of a dark blue touring car with two

men in front, their escape covered by the shotgun protruding from the rear window. Two days later the getaway car, a Buick stripped of its license plates, is found in a woods a few miles away. Nearby are the tracks of a smaller automobile to which the holdup party obviously had transferred their loot and escaped.

Meanwhile, police have asked all garage owners in the metropolitan area south of Boston to be on the alert for swarthy, foreign, possibly Italian men inquiring about automobiles. After nine o'clock on the evening of May 5, Simon Johnson, a garage owner in Bridgewater, several miles south of Braintree, has just retired for the night

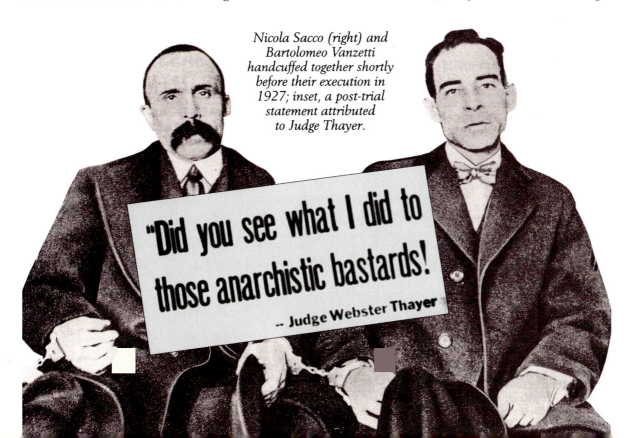

*Nicola Sacco (right) and
Bartolomeo Vanzetti
handcuffed together shortly
before their execution in
1927; inset, a post-trial
statement attributed
to Judge Thayer.*

"Did you see what I did to those anarchistic bastards!
-- Judge Webster Thayer

when a knock on the door announces the arrival of one Mike Boda, come to collect a car he had left for repairs. Peering through a window, Johnson's wife sees a second man sitting on a motorcycle and two others approaching along the street. As Johnson stalls Boda, his wife goes next door to call the police.

Apparently growing nervous at the delay, Boda offers to return the next morning to claim his vehicle. He climbs into the motorcycle's sidecar and rides away. The two other men are seen heading for a nearby streetcar stop. The Bridgewater police chief, Michael Stewart, phones his counterpart at the next town north, Brockton, and asks that the two men be detained. Just after 10 P.M., two officers board the streetcar in Brockton and arrest the suspects: Nicola Sacco, a 29-year-old shoemaker, and Bartolomeo Vanzetti, a 32-year-old fish peddler.

Both men are carrying weapons and are evasive about their activities in Bridgewater that evening. Nor, when asked, can they remember where they had been on April 15. Several witnesses to the Braintree holdup subsequently identify Sacco as one of the gunmen; others are not so sure. Only one can pick out Vanzetti. Nonetheless, five months later Sacco and Vanzetti are indicted for the Braintree slayings.

A Time of Fear

The Bolsheviks' seizure of power in Russia in 1917 and their subsequent proclamation of worldwide revolution terrified political leaders across Western Europe and in the United States. In 1919 Attorney General A. Mitchell Palmer warned that 60,000 alien radicals were poised to bring the Red rebellion to America, citing the scores of bombs mailed to public figures in April and the midnight bombings on June 3 of the homes of government officials in eight cities — including his own in Washington. The time had come, said Palmer, to put aside the "very liberal" provisions of the Bill of Rights and take action against these subversive elements.

Using Justice Department undercover agents, Palmer penetrated the Communist, Communist Labor, and Socialist parties and succeeded in coordinating meetings of these and other radical groups on the evening of January 2, 1920. In raids in 33 cities across the country that night, the attorney general's agents rounded up 3,000 persons, mostly aliens, who were accused of trying to overthrow the government of the United States. The so-called Palmer raids continued through June, with warrants issued for the arrest of 6,000 undesirable aliens and the deportation of nearly 1,000 of them. It was in the midst of this antiradi-

A Victim of Violence and Injustice

After a reign of only four years, Duke Karl Alexander of Württemberg — an unpopular Catholic ruler in a Protestant country — died of a lung ailment on March 12, 1737. That very same day his chief financial adviser, Joseph Süss Oppenheimer, was arrested and accused of several serious crimes, including treason and illicit affairs with women of the court. For Süss Oppenheimer was what was known at the time as a "court Jew," responsible for such financial transactions as lending money at exorbitant rates that church law prevented Catholics from carrying out. In his position, he was permitted to mingle in court circles and participate in affairs of state but forbidden liaisons with Christian women.

Süss Oppenheimer had encouraged the duke's absolutism, introduced state monopolies on salt,

This sketch of Süss Oppenheimer in prison was made for a broadside announcing his guilty verdict and death sentence.

leather, wine, and tobacco, founded a bank, and set up a porcelain factory in which he was said to have a private interest. He was also rumored to share in the profits of gambling casinos and coffeehouses of ill repute. He carried out the duke's orders to strip the landed gentry of their traditional privileges and to secure equal rights for Catholics — the first step, it was widely believed, toward making Catholicism the state religion. Such actions, along with his wealth and access to the duke, had earned him many envious enemies. It was these who brought about his arrest and ensured that the outcome of his trial would be a guilty verdict.

Under torture, Süss Oppenheimer confessed to all seven of the deadly sins. But asked to become a Christian, he said, "I intend to die a Jew. I am a victim of violence and injustice." The residents of Stuttgart lined the streets to jeer and rejoice as the "court Jew" was carried in a cage to his place of execution on February 4, 1738.

Thousands marched in a Boston funeral procession for the executed men, protesting what many liberals across the United States and around the world thought was a miscarriage of justice.

Some years after the executions, a bomb placed by unknown persons partly demolished Judge Thayer's house (above), injuring his wife. The judge (inset) was under continuing attack for injudicious behavior in and out of the courtroom and for resisting attempts to reopen the case.

cal and antiforeign hysteria that the holdup at South Braintree and subsequent arrest and indictment of Sacco and Vanzetti took place.

The Road to Dedham

Born in Italy, Sacco and Vanzetti had separately emigrated to the United States in 1908. Sacco, the younger by three years, married, fathered a son and daughter, and settled down as a shoemaker in Milford, Massachusetts. Vanzetti, who remained a bachelor, became a fish peddler in Plymouth. Both, in time, came under the influence of a philosophical anarchist named Luigi Galleani, who advocated the overthrow of capitalism. In 1917–18 both young men sought refuge from the World War I draft in Mexico.

At first denying their radical association to police interrogators, Sacco and Vanzetti eventually admitted that on the night of their arrest they had been seeking a car to dispose of incriminating anarchist literature in their possession. The carrying of weapons, the false and evasive statements, the leftist activities, the tentative identification by eyewitnesses were more than enough to secure an indictment in the South Braintree holdup and slayings. But before their joint trial could be held,

Vanzetti was separately indicted, tried, convicted, and given a prison sentence for his role as gunman in an unsuccessful payroll holdup in Bridgewater on December 24, 1919. The judge in the first trial, as in the second, which opened at Dedham on May 21, 1921, was Webster Thayer.

"Because the witnesses are Italians," Judge Thayer instructed the jury in the first trial, "no inference should be drawn against them. People are supposed to be honest, to be truthful, to be innocent." In the Dedham trial seven prosecution witnesses identified Sacco as one of the Braintree gunmen; four identified Vanzetti. Of the 12 defense witnesses who testified that the accused men were elsewhere on the day of the robbery and slayings, all but one were Italian. The jurors, small-town, middle-class people, were of predominantly Yankee stock. Later, one of them admitted that the conflicting testimony of witnesses more or less canceled itself out. "But the bullets," he added, "there was no way of getting around that evidence."

The prosecution was eventually able to establish that the bullets and casings found at the scene of the crime had been fired from the pistol found on Sacco at the time of his arrest. The identifica-

Though not taking a stand on guilt or innocence, Massachusetts governor Michael Dukakis signs a proclamation making August 23, 1977 — the 50th anniversary of their execution — "Sacco and Vanzetti Memorial Day." In tears at his side was Nicola Sacco's son, Spenser.

tion of Vanzetti's weapon as the one taken from the slain guard was less conclusive. The not unexpected guilty verdict of July 14, however, was far from the final act of the tragedy.

Victims of Red Hysteria?

As Sacco and Vanzetti remained in custody, the defense filed motion after motion for a retrial during the next few years. All were denied. Across the country and around the world, many protested against what they felt were convictions for unpopular political beliefs rather than for criminal culpability.

Toward the end of 1925, there appeared to be a break in the case when one Celestino Madeiros, a prisoner in the Dedham jail and under sentence of death in a bank robbery, confessed to having taken part in the Braintree holdup. The gunmen, Madeiros swore, were not Sacco and Vanzetti. Though unable to give a coherent account of the holdup and unable to identify the other participants, Madeiros did succeed in gaining nearly two years of life before his death sentence was carried out. His "confession" was of no help to

Sacco and Vanzetti in their ongoing legal efforts.

In the spring of 1927, Harvard law professor and later Supreme Court justice Felix Frankfurter published a ringing denunciation of the Dedham trial. "Outside the courtroom the Red hysteria was rampant," he wrote; "it was allowed to dominate within." Frankfurter's legal tirade brought a new wave of protests against the verdict. Bowing to pressure, Massachusetts governor Alvin T. Fuller appointed Harvard president A. Lawrence Lowell to head a three-member commission to review the case.

In what amounted to a second trial (and one lasting longer than the original six-and-a-half week Dedham trial), the Lowell commission read the stenographic record, recalled witnesses, and interviewed Judge Thayer, the prosecutor, and the jurors. The conclusion: Sacco was guilty beyond a reasonable doubt; although the evidence against him was "less strong," Vanzetti was also guilty. On August 8 the defense application for a stay of execution was denied.

The Case That Will Not Die

Shortly after midnight on August 23, 1927, first Sacco and then Vanzetti went to their deaths in the electric chair. "Long live anarchy!" Sacco cried out in Italian. "I am an innocent man," protested Vanzetti. News of the execution sparked anti-American riots around the world.

For three decades, beginning in the mid-1950's, American writer Francis Russell studied, pondered, and wrote about the Sacco-Vanzetti case. At the outset, he accepted the conventional wisdom that their trial had been a travesty and their conviction a miscarriage of justice. But by the time he published his first book on the subject, *Tragedy at Dedham*, he had taken the position that Sacco was guilty but Vanzetti had been innocent. Sacco could have spared his colleague by a confession but, to him, it would have been a betrayal of the anarchist movement. As for Vanzetti, it was apparently worth dying — not for a crime he did not commit — but for the movement.

In November 1982, Russell received what appeared to be confirmation of his thesis: a letter from the son of the last surviving member of the Sacco-Vanzetti defense committee, Giovanni Gambera. Before his death a few months earlier, the elder Gambera had confided to his son that everyone in the Boston anarchist circle knew that Sacco was guilty and Vanzetti was innocent. But no one would ever break the code of silence — even if it cost Vanzetti his life. "Between you and me," the younger Gambera wrote Russell, "this is the last word."

Suicide by Order of the Führer

**The daring and resourceful commander of Germany's Afrika Korps,
Erwin Rommel won fame as the Desert Fox. Hitler made him a field marshal
and gave him command of troops resisting the Allied invasion of France.
But was Rommel a participant in the plot to assassinate the führer?**

*U*lm, Germany, Friday, October 13, 1944. The army garrison is informed that a large wreath will arrive on the express train from Berlin the following morning. An officer should be sent to receive it. Earlier, in his villa outside the city, Field Marshal Erwin Rommel had received a telephone call from the führer's general headquarters. Hitler's chief adjutant, General Wilhelm Burgdorf, will be arriving on October 14 to discuss with Rommel "his future." Secretly, Burgdorf's personnel office is working out the plan for a state funeral.

Walking in the garden with his 16-year-old son on Saturday morning, Rommel wonders out loud about his impending visitor. "There are two probabilities today," he says. "Either nothing happens at all — or this evening I won't be here." At noon Burgdorf and his deputy, Major General Ernst Maisel, arrive at the field marshal's villa, decline an invitation to lunch from Lucie Rommel, and ask to speak privately with her husband. The three officers retire to Rommel's study and later drive off in a small car. Within 90 minutes the field marshal is dead.

Germany's renowned war hero, it is officially announced, has succumbed to the serious head injuries he sustained a few weeks earlier when his car was driven off the road by British fighter

Two generals with a grim ultimatum from Hitler appeared at Field Marshal Rommel's villa (left) near Ulm on October 14, 1944. His grave (below) is marked by a simple replica of Germany's Iron Cross, a decoration for valor.

bombers. In reality, Rommel had taken poison by command of the führer. The reason for the suicide order: his complicity in an assassination attempt on Hitler's life the preceding July 20.

An Officer's Career

Although he was the son and grandson of schoolmasters, Erwin Rommel chose a military career, joining the German army as an officer cadet in July 1910. He was four months short of his 19th birthday. As a lieutenant in World War I, he fought in France, Romania, and Italy, where he earned the respect of the men under his command and demonstrated to his superior officers a natural gift for leadership. Under the terms of the Treaty of Versailles that ended the war, only 4,000 officers were allowed to remain in the army of defeated Germany. Rommel, by then a captain, was one of them.

For Rommel the 1920's were uneventful years, except for his marriage to Lucie Mollin and the birth of their son, Manfred, in 1928. For nine years he commanded a rifle company in an infantry regiment at Stuttgart, but in 1933 he moved up to battalion command and, two years later, was named an instructor at the new infantry school in Potsdam. In September 1936 he came to the attention of Adolf Hitler, when he was asked to make security arrangements for the German leader's appearance at a Nazi Party rally in Nürnberg. The führer himself was among the readers of Rommel's manual on tactics, *Infantry Attacks*, published in 1937.

On August 25, 1939 — newly appointed a major general — Rommel assumed command of the troops guarding Hitler's military headquarters. There he learned of plans for the secret attack on Poland on September 1, an event that was to precipitate World War II.

Guarding the führer was scarcely a challenge to an officer who yearned to lead troops in battle, and Rommel succeeded in getting Hitler to overrule his chief of army personnel to win command of the Seventh Panzer Division in February 1940. Though an infantryman by training and experience, Rommel quickly saw that mechanized and armored troops would give Germany an offensive advantage. As his tanks swept through France in May and June, Rommel became known as the commander of the "Ghost Division," so swift and stealthy was its advance.

The Desert Fox

By early 1941 Italy was on the point of being overcome by the British in North Africa and desperately requested help from its German ally. The man chosen for the rescue mission was Erwin Rommel. To Lucie he wrote that a new command — wartime security made it impossible for him to give his destination — would at last enable him to do something about his rheumatism. Reading between the lines, she remembered that a doctor had told her husband, "You need sunshine, General; you ought to be in Africa."

Arriving in Libya as commander of Germany's Afrika Korps in February 1941, Rommel was on

Rommel, the Desert Fox, possessed two qualities that made him an outstanding leader of troops: He was a superb tactician, and he never demanded more of his soldiers than he did of himself. The Axis victories in North Africa are associated with his name; the final defeat there was not blamed on him.

The Shifted Briefcase

Lieutenant Colonel Klaus von Stauffenberg had little difficulty in getting past three checkpoints surrounding Hitler's "wolf's lair," the heavily guarded military headquarters set in an East Prussian forest, on the morning of July 20, 1944. He was there by order of the führer, bringing important reports from Berlin on the new divisions being rushed to the crumbling Eastern Front. Although they checked his military pass, the guards did not inspect his briefcase. Had they done so, they would have found it contained a time bomb.

On this sultry day Hitler had moved his daily briefing from a concrete underground bunker to a small wooden building whose windows were thrown open to catch any breeze. When Stauffenberg entered the room, Hitler was seated at the center of a long table, surrounded by about two dozen high-ranking officers and guards. No one seemed to see him surreptitiously place the briefcase under the table within six feet of the führer's legs. Nor did anyone take notice when he casually left the room a few moments later. But then one of the officers, trying to get a better look at the map Hitler was studying, discovered that the briefcase was in his way and moved it to the other side of the table. In so doing, he unintentionally saved Hitler's life but lost his own. Although four people were killed in the blast and several others were severely wounded, Hitler escaped with only minor injuries. (Above, officers inspect the rubble.)

Stauffenberg returned to Berlin that afternoon, convinced that the führer was dead and that the carefully laid plans to take over the government were being carried out. Instead, he was arrested and summarily executed. In the ensuing roundup of suspected conspirators, as many as 5,000 met their deaths.

the brink of his greatest military successes. For the audacity of his surprise attacks, he was nicknamed the Desert Fox by his wary but admiring foe. Driving the British out of Cyrenaica, he took their key defensive position at Tobruk and, under orders from Berlin, launched an attack across the Egyptian border in the spring of 1942.

Although Rommel was made a field marshal on June 22 — at 52, the youngest in the German army — his drive eastward was stopped by the British at El Alamein, 60 miles short of Alexandria and the Nile delta. In September an exhausted and ill Rommel withdrew to Germany for medical treatment. But, when the British counterattacked the next month, he returned to North Africa. "There is to be no retreat," Hitler ordered. "Victory or death!"

A desperate situation was made impossible in November, when an Anglo-American force commanded by General Dwight D. Eisenhower landed in Morocco and Algiers. At the risk of courtmartial, the Desert Fox ordered the retreat from Egypt and withdrew to a German bridgehead in Tunis early in 1943. When Rommel attempted to persuade Hitler that the war in Africa was lost, he was ordered home and put on sick leave. But the canny field marshal had been right. In May the Germans and Italians still fighting in North Africa were forced to capitulate to the Allies; the campaign had claimed nearly a million Axis casualties and cost Germany 8,000 airplanes and 2.4 million tons of shipping.

The Führer's Last Chance

After the Soviet Union halted the German drive east at Stalingrad in February 1943, and Italy surrendered that summer, it began to look as if a German victory was unlikely. Posted to Hitler's headquarters as a "military adviser" following a hospital stay, Rommel dared broach the subject of defeat to the führer. Hitler was furious. If the German people were not capable of winning the war, he screamed, they should perish.

With its defeats to the east and south, Germany now anxiously turned its attention to the west, where an Allied invasion across the English Channel was expected. In November, Hitler sent Rommel on a special mission to inspect coastal defenses from occupied Denmark south to the French border with neutral Spain. Taking command of all the German forces mustered to meet the invasion on January 15, 1944, Rommel ordered his troops to drive stakes into the beaches as a barrier to landing craft.

The Allies landed in Normandy on June 6. Six days later Rommel reported, "The strength of the enemy on land is increasing more quickly than our reserves can reach the front." There was little doubt in his mind as to the eventual outcome of the fighting in France.

The field marshal tried to make Hitler aware of the seriousness of the situation in two meetings. The first took place on June 17 at Soissons, France, 150 miles behind the Normandy battlefront. But when Rommel introduced the subject of making peace overtures to the Allies, the führer quickly terminated the interview. The second, on June 29 at Hitler's Alpine lair in southeastern Germany, ended on an equally bitter note when the führer told Rommel in front of his other generals that "everything would be all right if you would only fight better."

Rommel made a last attempt to avert catastrophe in a report sent to Hitler on July 15. "Everywhere our troops are fighting heroically," he wrote, "but the unequal struggle is drawing to a close. In my view the consequences of this have just got to be faced. As commander in chief of the army group, I feel obliged to make myself quite plain." To an aide he remarked, "I have given him his last chance. If he draws no conclusion, we will act." Two days later Rommel barely escaped death when a British fighter bomber drove his car off the road. He was in a hospital on July 20,

when an audacious and meticulously rehearsed attempt to assassinate Hitler failed.

A Plot Takes Shape

Ever since Hitler had come to power in 1933, there were Germans at different levels of society who were repelled by his authoritarian rule. But his various religious and political opponents were never able to forge a united movement. On the eve of World War II, members of the army's general staff hatched a plan to remove Hitler, but the führer's foreign policy successes made him too popular to overthrow. The conspiracy that reached a climax in the summer of 1944 at last brought together civilian and military groups determined to rid Germany of the Nazi dictator.

The conspirators struggled with an inner conflict. Those in the military were bound, as officers, to obey the führer's orders, but they — like Rommel — were beginning to hold Hitler personally responsible for the military debacle. Such civil servants as Karl Strölin, the mayor of Stuttgart, were responsible for the smooth functioning of the National Socialist state, but they eventually became convinced that only Hitler's removal could save Germany.

It was Strölin, a friend of Rommel's since World War I, who made the first contact with the

The White Rose: Youth in Opposition

From the time he came to power in 1933, Adolf Hitler made a bid for youthful support by outlawing independent student groups and forcing their members into the Hitler Youth. During the 1930's university students were among the most fanatical of Nazis, but they grew disillusioned when World War II did not end in the quick victory the führer had promised and began forming illegal resistance groups.

The student revolt at the University of Munich was led by a 25-year-old medical student, Hans Scholl, and his 21-year-old sister, Sophie. Encouraged by a philosophy professor named Kurt Huber, the Scholls and other students spread their anti-Nazi propaganda through so-called White Rose letters sent to other campuses. The crushing Soviet defeat of Germany at Stalingrad in February 1943

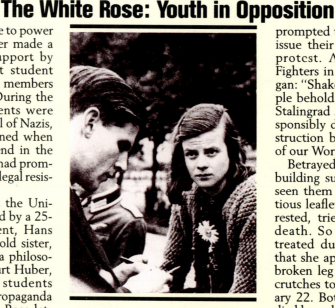

Hans and Sophie Scholl were executed for their part in an anti-Nazi student revolt at the University of Munich.

prompted the Munich students to issue their last and most famous protest. Addressed to "Fellow Fighters in the Resistance," it began: "Shaken and broken, our people behold the loss of the men of Stalingrad . . . senselessly and irresponsibly driven to death and destruction by the inspired strategy of our World War I private. . . ."

Betrayed to the Gestapo by a building superintendent who had seen them distributing their seditious leaflets, the Scholls were arrested, tried, and condemned to death. So savagely was Sophie treated during her interrogation that she appeared in court with a broken leg and had to hobble on crutches to the scaffold on February 22. Both she and her brother died bravely, Hans's last words being, "Long live freedom!" A few days later Professor Huber and several other students were executed.

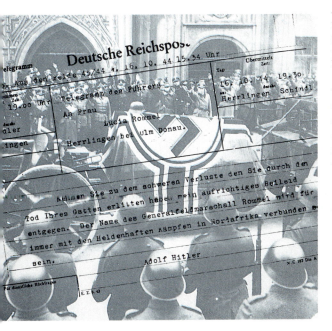

Hitler staged an impressive state funeral for the field marshal he had ordered to commit suicide, meanwhile sending a hypocritical message of condolences to the widow. The secret of Rommel's complicity in the failed assassination plot of July 20, 1944, was kept until war's end.

field marshal. In February 1944 he visited Rommel's home to tell him of the plan of certain high-ranking officers to take Hitler prisoner and force him to announce his resignation over the radio. As Germany's most popular general, Strölin told Rommel, "You are the only one who can prevent civil war. You must lend your name to the movement." Although acknowledging his duty to come to the rescue of Germany, Rommel promised only to continue applying pressure on the führer to face reality and recognize how desperate the military situation had become.

The next conspirator to approach Rommel was his chief of staff, Lieutenant General Hans Speidel. On May 15 he arranged for the field marshal to meet outside of Paris with the military governor of France, General Carl-Heinrich von Stülpnagel — at that time the only ranking officer who knew that the plot now included the elimination of Hitler by assassination. Stülpnagel's aide-de-camp, Lieutenant Colonel Caesar von Hofacker, visited Rommel on July 9 to tell him that, if Hitler refused to take the initiative for ending hostilities, he must be "coerced." Rommel brushed off the suggestion of coercion but volunteered to ask permission of Hitler to approach his old rival in

North Africa, Britain's Field Marshal Bernard Montgomery, with a peace initiative. Perhaps Britain could be persuaded to join Germany in fighting the Soviet Union, he mused.

Although Hofacker hastened to tell his chief that "Rommel has placed himself completely at our disposal," there is no evidence that he or any other of the conspirators informed the field marshal of the imminent assassination attempt. Nor is it certain that Rommel was ever told that he was slated to be either army chief of staff or president of a post-Nazi German regime.

Hitler's Revenge

Almost miraculously, Hitler survived the bomb explosion at a military conference on July 20. "Now I have those fellows," the führer said as his personal physician bandaged his wounds. "Now I can take steps!"

Nearly all the conspirators were rounded up in the wave of arrests that followed the unsuccessful coup d'etat, and few could stand up to Gestapo torture. Thus, Rommel's name soon appeared in testimony about the plot. Yet Hitler realized that there would be an unprecedented scandal if the popular field marshal were to be tried and condemned in court. He therefore ordered that Rommel be allowed to take his own life rather than face the accusation of high treason. Generals Burgdorf and Maisel were sent from Berlin on October 14 to deliver the ultimatum.

Rommel asked for only a few minutes to think over the terrible demand. "Can I take your car and drive off quietly somewhere?" he asked Burgdorf. "I'm not sure I can trust myself to handle a pistol properly." They had brought poison, Burgdorf told him; "It works in three seconds." Without any show of emotion, the field marshal took leave of his wife and son.

The driver of the car in which the three officers left the villa later recounted the final scene. Some yards away from the house, he was told to pull over and leave the car with Maisel. Five or ten minutes later they were summoned back by Burgdorf. Slumped over in the backseat and obviously dying, Rommel was sobbing. When he was dead, the driver respectfully returned Rommel's body to an upright position and replaced the field marshal's fallen cap on his head.

After the war, one of the few conspirators who escaped the führer's dragnet erected a commemorative plaque to those "who lost their lives because they participated in the plot against Hitler or had close ties to the participants." Among the names listed on the plaque is that of Field Marshal Erwin Rommel.

A Hero's Agonizing Ordeal

*When the infant son of the internationally renowned Charles Lindbergh
was kidnapped, armies of newsmen and three separate police agencies scoured
the land for clues. Was the man executed for the deed innocent,
a victim of hysteria and conspiracy?*

As cold night winds buffeted their gloomy, 10-room mansion set in wooded isolation atop Sourland Mountain, Anne and Charles Lindbergh, a romantic and adventuresome young couple who had captured the hearts of millions around the globe, were spending a quiet Tuesday evening at home. Typically, they would have already left this New Jersey weekend retreat for Englewood, where they and their infant son lived during the week at Next Day Hill, the 50-acre estate belonging to Anne's mother. Mrs. Lindbergh, a sensitive young woman on the brink of a distinguished writing career, was pregnant again. Though devoted to her husband and sympathetic to his desire to escape the hordes of fans and photographers that dogged their every footstep, she was not happy with their new house. It sat by itself 90 miles from New York City on 500 acres surrounded by swamps and thickly forested hills and could be reached only by one winding dirt road. But she knew that her husband was at peace here.

At his suggestion they had stayed over an extra two days because the weekend weather had been chilly and rainy, and their 20-month-old firstborn, Charles, Jr., had a slight cold. Usually, Anne herself would have been caring for the baby, but she had asked the weekday nursemaid to come down from Next Day Hill. As the couple read in separate rooms, their son slept in his crib in a second-story nursery that had a window shutter that could not be fastened.

It was March 1, 1932, and a crime that would shock the world was about to be discovered. At about 10 P.M., the nursemaid sought out Mrs. Lindbergh. The baby was not in his crib, so she assumed that his mother had taken him. She had not. Slightly unsettled, the two women went to Charles, who always enjoyed a romp with "Buster." To their growing horror, he was alone. When all three frantically raced up to the nursery, they found footprints near the empty crib and an envelope on the windowsill. "Anne," Lindbergh cried out, "they've stolen our baby!"

Puzzling Clues

About 75 yards from the house, the police discovered a home-built ladder with one rung snapped. It had been designed to be quickly dismantled into three parts for portability. Directly beneath the nursery window, there were holes that fit the legs of the ladder and footprints nearby. A carpenter's chisel had been dropped.

No fingerprints could be found on the ladder, chisel, or envelope. The ransom note, which demanded $50,000 in assorted small denominations, was written in curiously misspelled and nonstandard English and signed with an odd logo: Two blue circles were drawn to overlap, and the shared oval space thus formed was colored in red. This "singnature," as the note misspelled it, would appear on further correspondence. Lindbergh was warned not to tell the police and await instructions for delivering the money.

When Lindbergh nonetheless reported the crime, the New Jersey state police set up 20 phone lines in the garage and tramped through the house night and day. Some clues were ignored and others obliterated as the armies of the press moved in, competing for scoops that would satisfy the curiosity of the waiting world. Since he had flown his *Spirit of St. Louis* from New York to Paris in 1927, Lindbergh had been world famous. Now, celebrities and politicians descended upon his house, eager to share the spotlight.

Lindbergh, primarily concerned about the welfare of his son, came into conflict with law enforcement officers, who wanted his full cooperation in catching the kidnapper. The press, whom the aviator had despised since the early days of his fame, did agree to a "withdrawal," so that more ransom notes could be delivered. By March 5 two more had arrived, each bearing the telltale "singnature," but there was no word about the fate or whereabouts of the child.

An Unlikely Go-Between

Tall, stern, yet charismatic, Lindbergh ignored professional advice and went his own way, thereby unwittingly adding to the unsolved mysteries of the case. Publicly declaring that he would like to "make a personal contact" with the kidnappers, he promised to meet all demands. The notes had raised the ransom total to $70,000. Meanwhile, an eccentric retired teacher, Dr. John Condon, had taken it upon himself to advertise in the *Home News*, a local newspaper in the Bronx, a borough of New York City, that he would be willing to act as a go-between. Incredibly, he soon received a note with the "singnature" and then phone calls from a heavily accented voice. Nocturnal meetings in a cemetery followed.

Hidden in the shadows, a man claimed that he was himself "only a go-between" and handed over the baby's sleeping suit. Despite the pleas of detectives, the grieving father agreed to pay the

During the days following the kidnapping of Charles A. Lindbergh, Jr., a feverish search for the missing infant was conducted and posters seeking information (right) were widely distributed. Below, Boy Scouts comb the area surrounding the Lindbergh home.

original demand of $50,000. As Lindbergh watched and listened from an automobile one night, Dr. Condon passed the money to his contact and received a sealed envelope allegedly telling where the child could be found. "The boy is on boad Nelly It is a small boad 28 feet long. two persons on the Boad. the are innosent. You will find the boad between Horsenecks Beach and Gay Head near Elisabeth Island."

Jubilant, Lindbergh flew up and down the shores of Connecticut and Rhode Island, eagerly searching for the boat described. After a second agonizing day aloft, he realized that he had been duped. Dr. Condon placed more newspaper ads, now asking, "Have you crossed me?" But there would be no more heavily accented phone calls or notes with a "singnature."

On May 12 a trucker stopped beside a road within sight of the Sourland Mountain mansion. His interest piqued by a shallow ditch covered with leaves, he turned over the soil with the toe of his shoe and uncovered a child's hand. When a pale, gaunt Lindbergh saw the sheet-covered body in a Trenton mortuary, he asked that the cloth be lifted and stared silently, looking particularly at the dead boy's teeth. "Yes," he said finally. "I'm perfectly satisfied this is my child."

The Lindbergh baby had probably been killed instantly by a crushing blow to his skull and buried the night he was kidnapped. Purposefully murdered with the chisel? Accidentally knocked against the windowsill when the ladder broke?

The Trail to the Bronx

For months the serial numbers of the ransom money had been showing up on bills circulating in northern Manhattan and the neighboring Bronx. The FBI quickly assigned 15 men to the New York City area. Some witnesses recalled a man who resembled Dr. Condon's description of his nighttime contact: "pointed chin," "shifty blue eyes," "German accent." A tenacious expert in wood had traced the material in the bro-

A homemade, three-part portable ladder was found at the scene of the crime; above right, the police placed the ladder next to the nursery window the following morning. Arthur Koehler (above), a wood expert for the U.S. Forest Service, testified that the ladder had been made from wood removed from Hauptmann's attic. At right, the accused carpenter in custody manages a tight smile.

Fiction Born of Tragedy

Even before Bruno Hauptmann was arrested, Agatha Christie, the enormously popular English mystery novelist, had been inspired by the known facts of the Lindbergh kidnapping to craft her ingenious *Murder on the Orient Express*, published in 1934. Her fictional detective, Hercule Poirot, discovers that a murder victim on the luxury train had once headed a gang of professional kidnappers. Eventually, it becomes clear that all 12 of the likely suspects are conspirators and took turns stabbing the criminal to death.

Christie, who wrote 94 books and 17 plays, specialized in constructing slick mystery novels with unexpected conclusions based upon subtle clues deftly hidden throughout the story. In 1926 she herself became involved in a tantalizing mystery. When her hus-

Agatha Christie: A woman whose passion was writing mystery stories left her real-life mystery unsolved.

band asked for a divorce so that he could marry another woman, she suddenly vanished, leaving clues to suggest that she had either been murdered or had killed herself. Already well known for her first six books of intrigue and mayhem, she immediately became the object of a frantic nationwide hunt, including aerial searches. Suspicion of her husband intensified, but after 10 days an anonymous letter appeared, directing investigators to a resort hotel where the writer, diagnosed as suffering from amnesia, was registered under the name of the woman her husband now loved. Temporary illness? A revenge plot? A cry for help? A wily publicity scheme? The legendary author never explained and, in fact, does not even mention the incident in her autobiography.

ken ladder to a Bronx lumberyard, but the firm apparently did not keep records of its sales.

On September 15, 1934, a suspicious gas station attendant took down the license plate number of a man who paid with a $10 gold certificate, a type of currency that had become illegal the previous year. The bill was part of the ransom money. Tracing the license number, police started watching the Bronx house of Bruno Richard Hauptmann, a German carpenter who lived with his wife, Anna, and their infant son, Manfred. Finally, representatives of New Jersey, New York, and federal law enforcement agencies stopped him in his car. He was carrying a $20 gold note that was also part of the ransom currency.

Filling in the Blanks

Although Hauptmann would deny any involvement in the Lindbergh affair, the police felt that they had drawn their net tightly. Lindbergh said he recognized the suspect's voice, having heard him shout, "Hey, doctor! Over here, doctor!" Dr. Condon agreed, as did a cab driver who had delivered one of the ransom notes. Another $14,590 in ransom bills was uncovered in various hiding places in Hauptmann's garage. According to police experts, his handwriting and misuse of English matched the "singnature" notes in scores

of particulars, unlike the writing of others who were also tested. Dr. Condon's telephone number and address were found written on the wall of a bedroom closet. In his attic investigators found a piece of wood that was identical, under a microscope, with the broken rung on the ladder. A sales receipt for lumber bought at the Bronx lumberyard turned up. His professional tool kit was complete, except for a chisel.

Much of this evidence, as well as other incriminating facts and testimony that appeared at the trial, was questioned by investigative reporters. There were charges that some of it had been manufactured by newsmen or by the police, and books that seek to prove Hauptmann's innocence continue to gain respectful attention.

How could this Bronx immigrant, acting alone, know that the Lindberghs would change their weekly schedule and be in residence on March 1? Or know about the nursery window that would not close properly? Although he had become a fugitive from his native Germany after a series of burglaries and come to the United States as a stowaway, nothing in his record approached the enormity of the Lindbergh kidnapping. And he resisted all inducements to confess, apparently including a severe beating that may have led him to attempt suicide.

"Lucky Lindy"

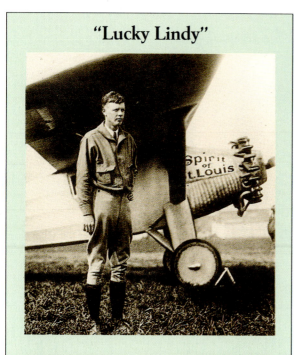

The son of a Minnesota congressman, Charles A. Lindbergh dropped out of college in 1922 at the age of 20 to take up flying — a romantic pursuit in those early days of aviation. Soon he was barnstorming about the Midwest and South, wingwalking, parachuting, and taking the adventuresome up for $5 plane rides. In April 1923 he bought his first plane, a World War I surplus trainer, for $500. The next year he entered the U.S. Army flying school at San Antonio, Texas, graduating first in his class. He was commissioned a reserve 2nd lieutenant in 1925. But flying an airmail route between Chicago and St. Louis was not exciting enough for the tall, lanky pilot. In 1927 he set his mind to winning a $25,000 prize for making the first nonstop flight from New York to Paris.

With the financial support of friends and $2,000 of his own money, Lindbergh bought a single-engine monoplane, named it *Spirit of St. Louis* (above), and took off from Roosevelt Field, Long Island, at 7:52 A.M. on May 20, 1927. He carried extra canisters of gas, sandwiches, and drinking water but omitted a radio or parachute in order to reduce weight. His 3,600-mile, 33½-hour flight was a grueling battle against fatigue and the mental confusion caused by flying alone through dense fog and icy clouds.

Tumultuous crowds greeted his arrival at Paris's Le Bourget airport the following evening. But fame also brought "Lucky Lindy" — and Anne Morrow, whom he married two years later — the unwanted attention of reporters, clamorous fans, and, perhaps, the man who kidnapped and killed his firstborn son in 1932.

An Obscene Circus

The trial that began January 2, 1935, in the quiet little town of Flemington, New Jersey, caused traffic jams for miles, as thousands of the curious came to take part in the spectacle. About a million words a day of news coverage were sent out by a team of 68 telegraph operators. Some 300 working reporters milled around the site. Hucksters sold "certified locks of Baby Lindbergh's hair" and forged Lindbergh autographs.

Bravely, Anne Lindbergh appeared twice, testifying with quiet dignity. Her husband came every day, watching intently and never revealing any emotion. He later described the defendant's eyes as "mean, shifty, small, and cruel." Hauptmann's attorney, Edward J. Reilly, known for his rude and contemptuous behavior, did not present an inspired defense. Often drunk on a gin-based cocktail known as an orange blossom, the lawyer had conferred with his client for a total of only 38 minutes.

On February 13, as crowds outside the courtroom shouted, "Kill Hauptmann," the judge accepted the jury's unanimous verdict: guilty of murder in the first degree. He handed down the death sentence forthwith.

Uncertainty to the End

The Lindberghs, though skeptical at first, eventually came to believe that Hauptmann's guilt had been proved beyond any reasonable doubt. "Everything is chance," Anne Lindbergh said in despair, believing that the unlikely events of March 1 could only be explained by the cruel play of coincidence. For her, especially, the past few years had been devastating. In 1931 her father, Dwight Morrow, who might well have been the Republican candidate for president in 1932, died unexpectedly. Her sister Elizabeth died in 1934 after an operation for appendicitis. The couple's second child, a son named Jon, was harassed by reporters on his way to nursery school. Weary of it all, the Lindberghs moved from America to Europe in December 1935.

Meanwhile, appeals had been mounted for Hauptmann, and even the governor of New Jersey became involved, thinking that the man had been railroaded. The convicted kidnapper, who had never really believed that he would face the electric chair, eventually lost hope. For three days before the end, he was "already dead," according to guards at the New Jersey state penitentiary. The first jolt of electricity coursed through his body at 8:44 P.M. on April 3, 1936. Three-and-a-half minutes later, he was officially pronounced dead.

5

Half Truth, Half Legend

In Search of King Arthur

*His reign marked a golden era for Britain, a time of
chivalry in combat and love. For centuries writers and artists embellished
his story. Modern scientists and literary scholars, however,
propose a reality far different from the legend.*

*Destined for immortality: The wounded King Arthur is borne away to the enchanted island of
Avalon in a boat rowed by silent, shrouded attendants.*

In a gloomy castle set on a rocky spit of land jutting into the sea, Igrayne awaits the return of her husband, Gorlois, duke of Cornwall. It is not he, however, who comes to her room that night but rather Uther Pendragon, king of Britain — given the appearance of Gorlois by the magician Merlin in order to satisfy the king's illicit passion for Igrayne. A son is conceived. Thus begins the story of the legendary King Arthur, a tale that has inspired numerous writers and artists and captured people's imaginations for centuries.

The infant born to Igrayne is spirited away by Merlin and given to the good Sir Ector to be raised as his own son. Although the king has no other children, Igrayne and Gorlois are blessed with three daughters — two of whom are married to other kings while the third is sent to a nunnery. This daughter, Morgana le Fay, somehow acquires magical skills and ultimately plays a fatal role in her half brother's life.

Only when the king is dead and Arthur is 16 does Merlin reveal to him his true paternity, and he does so then only after the youth has succeeded in pulling out a sword embedded in an anvil set on a slab of marble in a churchyard. All who tried had failed the test, which was to be passed only by "the true-born king of all Britain." Merlin also tells of the enchantment cast upon the infant by the fairies of Avalon, the land of mystery. Arthur is to be the best of all knights and the greatest of all kings, and he will live "longer than any man shall ever know." As the people kneel to take an oath to their new sovereign, the archbishop places the crown upon his head.

An Age of Chivalry

Under Arthur's benevolent rule, Britain enjoys 12 years of peace, a time that sees the full flowering of chivalry. To his castle of Camelot, Arthur summons the brave and faithful knights of his realm — Launcelot, Gawain, Percivale, and many others — and seats them about an enormous round table with each of their names engraved in gold at his seat, or siege. Those thus seated are instructed by Merlin to shun murder, cruelty, and wickedness, to fly from treason, lying, and dishonesty, to grant mercy to those who ask it, and, above all, to respect and protect women. From Camelot the knights sally forth to fight dragons, giants, and cunning dwarfs, their encounters with the forces of evil usually taking place in haunted castles, dark forests, and enchanted gardens. Full of pride in their accomplishments, they return to tell their tales at court.

To Camelot, Arthur also brings the fair Guinevere to be his queen. When Launcelot is unable to resist his sinful passion for Guinevere, Arthur's nephew Mordred, the son of Morgana le Fay, exposes the lovers and forces Arthur to condemn his wife to a public burning. Launcelot rescues the queen and escapes with her to France. Before taking his army in pursuit of the couple, Arthur turns his kingdom over to Mordred, who uses the king's absence to stage a coup d'etat. Upon his return to England, Arthur meets Mordred in battle and runs his spear under his nephew's shield and through his body. But before Mordred dies, he gives the king a mortal wound.

Arthur's faithful supporters place the dying king in a boat that glides off through a white mist across the sea to Avalon. "Comfort yourself," Arthur calls out to his grief-stricken knights on the shore. "Be you sure that I will come again when the land of Britain has need of me."

Britain in the Time of Arthur

King Arthur is supposed to have reigned from the late 5th century to the early 6th, with dates for his final battle with Mordred given as 537 or 542. But what actually was the political situation in the island kingdom then? And who ruled there?

A century earlier the Romans had gradually withdrawn from the British colony they had ruled since the conquest of Julius Caesar in 54 B.C. — unable to withstand the invasion of barbarian Jutes, Angles, and Saxons from the European mainland and the pressure from the north of a tribe known as the Picts. In the unsettled times that followed, various warlords came forth to confront the invaders and fight among themselves. There is no record of a unified kingdom or a ruler with anything but local power. Christianity did not gain a toehold in England until the arrival of St. Augustine and his 40 monks in 597. For Britain and for much of Europe, this was the beginning of the Dark Ages.

If the Welsh monk Nennius can be believed, a warrior named Arthur — "together with the kings of the Britons" — led the resistance to the invaders. Writing his *History of the Britons* about

Waves dash against the rocky headlands of Cornwall at the southwestern tip of England. Here, according to literary tradition and modern archaeology, the story of Arthur began — in the castle at Tintagel, where he was born of an illicit rendezvous arranged by the magician Merlin.

The Quest for the Holy Grail

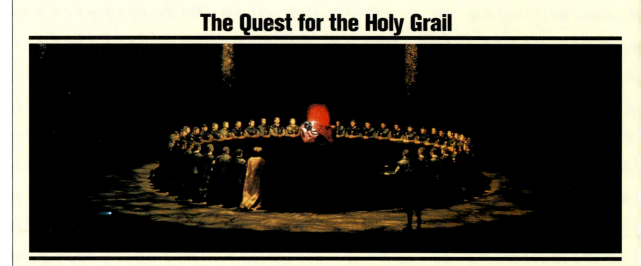

At the center of the King Arthur narrative is the story of the search for the Holy Grail, the cup from which Jesus drank at the Last Supper and which was supposed to possess miraculous powers of healing and regeneration. Along with the spear used by a Roman soldier to pierce the side of the crucified Jesus, the cup was given to Joseph of Arimathea, whose descendants brought it to Britain. According to the legend, one of these guardians of the holy relics so forgot his sacred trust that he gazed lustfully on a female pilgrim — whereupon the spear fell upon him, inflicting a wound that would not heal. The Holy Grail at this time disappeared.

Merlin sent a message to Camelot, directing King Arthur to initiate a search for the lost cup. The knight destined to find it, he hinted, would soon appear. Arthur and his knights were gathered at the round table on the vigil of Pen-

Richard Wagner used the Percivale version of the search for the Holy Grail for his monumental opera Parsifal; *above, a scene from the production at Bayreuth staged by the composer's grandson, Wieland Wagner.*

tecost when a clap of thunder and a burst of lightning announced a vision of the Holy Grail; it was covered with a rich white fabric as it floated through the hall. Shortly thereafter, an old man proposed a candidate for the last unoccupied seat at the round table. This young knight turned out to be Sir Galahad, the son of Sir Launcelot.

During their search for the Holy Grail, the knights of the round table encountered numerous adventures and were often challenged to make sacrifices that exceeded their abilities. Launcelot, however, was eventually barred from the quest because he could not give up his forbidden passion for Queen Guinevere. To Sir Galahad, as Merlin

had predicted, fell the reward of discovering the Holy Grail and dispensing the Blessed Sacrament from it. Kneeling before it, the youthful knight realized that his mission in life was accomplished. As his soul was taken up to heaven, his body lay stretched before the altar in death. Two years later to the day, the searchers returned to Camelot to tell the king of their adventuresome quest.

In another version of the story, it is Sir Percivale who completes the quest. He finds the sacred vessel at the castle of Monsalvat in the Spanish Pyrenees, under the guard of Amfortas, king of the knights of the Holy Grail. But a sorcerer has wounded Amfortas with the lance of the crucifixion, and the king lies near death, refusing to receive the sacrament of Holy Communion because of his unforgiven sins. Only when Percivale heals the wound with a touch of the lance is the Holy Grail revealed on the altar.

the year 826, Nennius listed 12 battles in which Arthur vanquished the barbarians. In his last victory he personally slew 960 of the enemy.

Some 150 years after Nennius, an anonymous Welshman compiled a chronology of British history, *Cambrian Annals*. For the year 537 he listed, "Battle of Camlann, in which Arthur and Medraut fell." It is not difficult to read Mordred for Medraut. Yet another 150 years passed before Arthur was again mentioned by a historian —

and then it was but a tantalizing reference. Writing in 1125, the monk William of Malmesbury mentions a warlike Arthur, "about whom the Britons rave in empty words, but who, in truth, is worthy to be the subject, not of deceitful tales and dreams, but of true history; for he was long the prop of his tottering fatherland, and spurred the broken spirit of his countrymen on to war." It remained for a contemporary of William's to make Arthur a sovereign.

About 1139 a Welsh deacon and later bishop named Geoffrey of Monmouth completed his monumental *History of the Kings of Britain*, a sweeping survey of Britain's rulers from Roman times. To the works of such earlier historians as Nennius, Geoffrey added colorful details drawn from local tradition, Celtic and Scandinavian myths, and even biblical history. Two of Geoffrey's 12 books are devoted to Arthur, and in them appear for the first time the enchanter Merlin and the tales of Guinevere's abduction and Mordred's treachery. By embellishing the scanty historical record with imaginative events and introducing personages about whom nothing was really known, Geoffrey established a pattern that was followed for centuries — thus turning a 5th-century warrior into a heroic king.

The Transformation of Arthur

In 1155 an Anglo-Norman cleric known as Wace translated Geoffrey's narrative into French, making it a romance in which Arthur presides over his court as a hero of chivalry. Toward the end of the century the Anglo-Saxon monk Layamon turned Geoffrey's Arthur into a fierce warrior and stern father figure. Both writers mentioned the round table. But it was probably the French poet Chrétien de Troyes, writing between 1160 and 1180, who made Arthur an arbiter of courtesy and etiquette and a model of chivalry and courtly love. Early in the following century, two German epics based on the Arthur legend appeared: *Parzival* by Wolfram von Eschenbach and *Tristan* by Gottfried von Strassburg.

The posthumously printed work of a 15th-

The Arthur story has inspired numerous artists such as Gustave Doré, who depicted the king gazing at Camelot's crenellated grandeur — a gross exaggeration of the primitive fortress proposed by archaeologists.

To avoid the jousting of knights for a seat near the head of the table, Arthur invented the round table. In the 13th century King Henry III placed this replica in Winchester Castle.

Merlin the Magician

Perhaps the strangest, most enigmatic character in the Arthur stories is Merlin, the son of a virtuous young woman and an incubus — one of those ethereal evil spirits who are said to prey upon the innocent at night. At birth Merlin was rushed to the baptismal font and thus spared his father's evil nature, though he retained certain supernatural powers. He not only knew the past but could foretell the future, and it was a simple matter to transform himself into any shape: a dwarf, a damsel, a greyhound, or a stag. But when he imparted his secret arts to the fair Viviane, his lady love used his magic against him to bind him with the veil of her headdress and thereafter imprison him in a tower where only she could visit him.

Before compiling his *History of the Kings of Britain*, Geoffrey of Monmouth wrote a brief Latin tract called *The Little Book of Merlin*, which introduced the magician to the reading public. Scholars have suggested several models for Geoffrey's Merlin, including a Welsh fortune-teller named Myrrdhin and a Scottish visionary known only as Lailoken.

by poets from Edmund Spenser in *The Faerie Queene* (1590–96) to Alfred, Lord Tennyson, in *Idylls of the King* (1859–85). A 20th-century version of the legend, T.H. White's *The Once and Future King*, served as the basis for the stage and motion picture musical *Camelot*.

Unearthing Arthur's Court

With the story of Arthur so widespread and enduring, it was inevitable that scientists would eventually seek to strip away the literary adornments and establish the truth behind the legend. In 1965 the Camelot Research Committee was formed, its founders bristling at the suggestion that they would be turning up the round table or the Holy Grail. After five years of digging in Somerset, however, the committee's archaeologists identified the ruins of Cadbury Castle near Glastonbury as Camelot.

The hilltop site was fortified in pre-Roman times, chosen no doubt for its commanding view of the plains stretching to the Bristol Channel. Rubbish embedded in a wall above the original fort revealed that Cadbury Castle had continued in use during the centuries of Roman occupation. But the most exciting discovery for the Camelot researchers was pottery suggesting that the site had been used by a British chieftain about the year 500 — after the withdrawal of the Romans and before the Saxon conquest. His headquarters were a hall, 60 feet by 30 feet, of timber construction and probably having a thatch roof. If the chieftain was not the heroic Arthur of legend and literature, he at least was a Briton who strove to preserve Roman civilization against the onslaught of the barbarian invaders. The findings of the Camelot Research Committee were not accepted by the American scholar Norma Lorre Goodrich, who proposed that King Arthur ruled not in England but to the north, in Scotland. Her exhaustive literary research pointed to Stirling, northwest of Edinburgh, rather than Cadbury Castle, as the site of Camelot.

As for Arthur's vaunted chivalry, he reigned in a time of savage warfare in defense of territorial integrity and political independence. Chivalry was far in the future, in those more settled times when historians such as Geoffrey of Monmouth and Sir Thomas Malory could appraise their own more peaceful eras and impose their standards and values on an invented past. Yet it is their Arthur, not the obscure warrior of a tumultuous era, who lives. His glorious, never to be forgotten reign, in the words of one commentator, was a "brief period of light set like a star of heaven in the midst of the Dark Ages."

century Englishman, Sir Thomas Malory, is responsible for the final transformation of Arthur into an enduring literary figure. Malory condensed, adapted, and rearranged earlier materials into a more or less coherent narrative that introduced all the major figures and pivotal events now associated with the story of Arthur. Ever since it was published in 1485, Malory's *Le Morte d'Arthur* ("The Death of Arthur") has been widely read and used as a source for other works

The Vampire Patriot

Ghostly pale, his needle-sharp teeth dripping red with blood, the ghoulish Dracula is the epitome of fictional horror. His real-life ancestor, equally bloodthirsty, is nonetheless a national hero.

"My very feelings changed to repulsion and terror when I saw the man slowly emerge from the window and begin to crawl down the castle wall over that dreadful abyss, face down with his cloak spreading out around him like great wings." Thus the young British solicitor's assistant, Jonathan Harker, glimpsed his noble host one moonlit night in Transylvania, a wild, rocky region in the Carpathian Mountains of modern-day Romania.

Previously, Count Dracula, a tall, pallid man always garbed in black, had been behaving very peculiarly indeed. When wolves were heard howling in the valley 1,000 feet below his ancient family castle, his eyes gleamed and he exclaimed, "Listen to them — the children of the night. What music they make!" When Harker cut himself shaving, the older man made a grab for his throat, his eyes blazing "with a sort of demoniac fury," but he drew back when he touched the chain of a cross around his startled guest's throat. Immediately before this episode, Harker realized

Disguised as a bat, the vampire enters the bedroom of his victim, who awaits his bite on her throat with fear and longing.

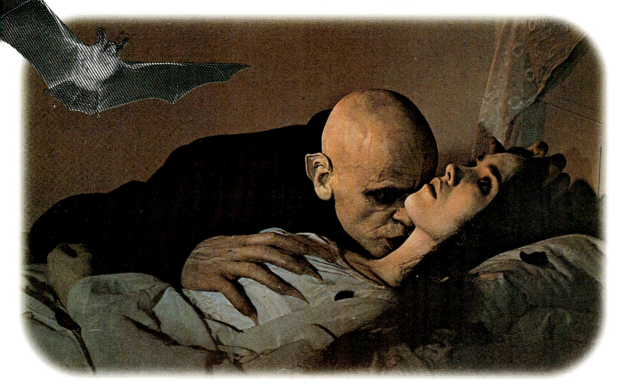

that Dracula, though standing in the room, had not been reflected in the shaving mirror.

At the Englishman's last stopover, villagers had crowded around, muttering such imprecations as *"ordog"* (Satan) and *"pokol"* (hell) and rapidly making the sign of the cross. Now, he found himself imprisoned in "a vast ruined castle, from whose tall black windows came no ray of light, and whose broken battlements showed a jagged line against the moonlit sky." His host, apparently the sole inhabitant of the gloomy fortress, appears only at night. The terrified Harker wonders if he will ever again see his homeland.

Bram Stoker's Phenomenon

Harker, of course, is the young hero in one of the most remarkably popular novels of all time, Bram Stoker's *Dracula*. It was an immediate success when first published in London in 1897 and has remained in print ever since. Several films, stage adaptations, comic books, and even a ballet have brought the story of the loathsome blood-sucking vampire count to a worldwide audience in the millions. In the novel Dracula travels to England to spread his vampire cult, but he is eventually foiled when Harker escapes from the castle and joins forces with Dr. Abraham Van Helsing, a Dutch expert on vampirism. Helsing alone seems to know that the monster cannot endure sunlight, garlic, or the symbol of the Christian cross. He also has learned that the "undead," as vampires are called, can be killed only with a stake driven through the heart.

The Enduring Legend

Stoker's vampire novel draws on the rich and widespread history of belief in the fearsome creatures, who are mentioned as far back as the literatures of ancient Egypt and Greece. Since the dying become weak from loss of blood, simple people must have assumed that drinking blood would restore strength, or even that the blood of the living could bring the dead back to life.

But the novel *Dracula* borrows most heavily from the deeply held folk beliefs of rural Romania. According to the Eastern Orthodox Church, the dominant religion there, people who die under a curse or a ban of excommunication will become walking dead, or *"moroi,"* until they are granted absolution by the church. Local superstition adds the creatures known as *"strigoi,"* demon birds that fly only at night, ravenous for human flesh and blood. Traditionally, vampires were seen as the cause of plagues in the area.

Romanian legends suggest that certain people — such as illegitimate or unbaptized children,

Bizarre Cult of the "Walking Dead"

In 1962, according to his death certificate, the Haitian peasant Clairvius Narcisse died near his home village in the Artibonite Valley. Though physically strong and rarely ill, he had begun to have difficulty breathing after a dispute with his brother over a piece of land. Weakened and nauseated, he began to spit blood and died two days later. His body was buried in a small rural cemetery.

Eighteen years later Narcisse strolled into the marketplace of his ancestral village. Along with others who were found wandering near the city of Cap Haitian, he claimed that he had been dug out of the ground by men who beat him cruelly, then forced him into slave labor as a zombie. He was one of the infamous "walking dead," long considered to be mere figments of superstition in the island nation where voudon, or voodoo, is said to

In West Indian rituals the faithful dance themselves into ecstatic trances to give their bodies over to spirits.

hold sway. After two years of this horrible servitude, Narcisse's zombie master had been killed, but the wretched young man did not dare return home until his brother died.

He knew that his sibling had arranged for the transformation.

According to experts, zombies are produced by a combination of intense psychological pressure and exotic pharmacology. Typically, the victim is condemned by his immediate family or neighbors, who treat him as if he is really dying. In addition, he is poisoned with the powerful natural anesthetic tetrodotoxin, which can indeed kill or render the subject paralyzed and apparently dead, but still conscious of what is going on.

To arouse the victim when he is disinterred, the houngan, or voodoo priest, force-feeds a paste probably made from a psychoactive plant known in Creole as "the zombie's cucumber." The new zombie enters an impotent state that resembles psychosis, toiling unemotionally until dead or deemed to have suffered enough.

witches, and the seventh son of a seventh son — are doomed to become vampires. The vampire has the power to change into animal shapes, most often that of the wolf or the bat. In some villages anyone who refuses to eat garlic falls under suspicion of vampirism. In fact, protection from night assaults by the drinkers of blood is best assured by rubbing garlic on all windows and doors.

Stoker learned about such legends from intense research in London's British Museum and in conversations with the Hungarian scholar Arminius Vambery. He was also influenced by the unsolved murders of the notorious Jack the Ripper and by his friendship with the explorer and man of letters Richard Burton, whose translations included 11 Hindu tales about vampires.

Hidden Sensuality

In the sexually repressed age of Queen Victoria, according to many literary critics, erotic feelings were often disguised. Stoker may have unconsciously sublimated strong sexual themes in his novel, blending the violent and bloody attacks of the vampires with a passionate yearning for sensual experience in mysterious nighttime settings. Harker, for example, is surely responding romantically when he is approached in his sleep by a trio of Dracula's young followers: "All three had brilliant white teeth that shone like pearls against the ruby of their voluptuous lips. There was something about them that made me uneasy, some longing and at the same time some deadly fear. I felt in my heart a wicked, burning desire that they would kiss me with those red lips. . . ."

But this erotic appeal, along with the undeniable thrill of the ancient superstitions about the bloodsucking "undead" wandering abroad in the night, is augmented in Stoker's novel by yet another fantastic element, the incredible but true story of a revered Romanian national hero. In fact, Dracula himself boasts to Harker about his warlike, patriotic ancestor, who fought valiantly against the enemy Turks: the tyrant known to history as Vlad the Impaler.

A Savage Patriot

The original Dracula was a 15th-century prince of Wallachia, a mountainous territory adjacent to Transylvania. Portrayed in surviving paintings and woodcuts as heavily moustached with a sharp beak of a nose and huge staring eyes, he was christened Vlad but nicknamed Dracula because of the family symbol, the "*dracul,*" or dragon. Coincidentally, the word also means "devil."

As a youth, Dracula was held hostage by the Turks, from whom he learned about an excruci-

Vlad Tepes (right) was the real-life ancestor of Bram Stoker's fictional Dracula. A 15th-century woodcut (above) shows the tyrant at table, surrounded by his impaled victims as a servant dismembers corpses. To prolong the suffering, Vlad often had the tips of the stakes blunted.

ating method of execution, impalement. In this barbaric punishment, a wooden stake or an iron pike is driven through the body and then set into the ground, leaving the victim to die in agony.

In 1448 Vlad, probably only 18 at the time, was set upon the Wallachian throne by the Turks, but after two months he ran away to a Christian monastery. After the great Christian capital of Constantinople fell to the Turks, Vlad returned to his hereditary throne in 1456 and began a four-year reign of uniquely inventive terror. On one occasion, for no discernible reason, he raided a friendly town and killed and tortured 10,000 of

In the novel Dracula, *the vampire count's castle is located in Transylvania's Carpathian Mountains, a nearly inaccessible forested region still inhabited by bears, wolves, lynx, and — who knows — perhaps also by those enduring creatures of legend, vampires.*

his subjects, many by impalement. He thus earned a new nickname, Tepes, or "the Impaler." In his most infamous massacre, which occurred on St. Bartholomew's Day in 1460, 30,000 were impaled in one town in Transylvania.

Was Dracula simply a sadist or did his cruel depredations have a political purpose? The answer is probably a little of both. When emissaries from the Turkish court dared to keep their turbans on in his presence, he ordered the headgear nailed to their skulls — certainly a bold gesture of independence. Barbaric or not, he achieved fame throughout Christian Europe when he recaptured fortresses along the Danube River and led his army nearly to the Black Sea.

On the other hand, once his forces were turned back, his own people forged letters that suggested he might defect to the Turks, and Dracula was summarily imprisoned for 12 years by King Mathias of Hungary. Perhaps the Wallachians had been sickened by their prince's amazing variety of punishments, which included skinning and boiling alive, burning, and mutilation.

During his incarceration Dracula, who could be insidiously charming, made friends with his guards, and they helpfully supplied him with mice and other small animals that he could impale in his cell for pleasure. Released in 1474, Dracula claimed the throne of Wallachia for the third time two years later, but he was killed only two months afterward, at the age of 45, in yet another battle against the Turks. His head was cut off, preserved in honey, and sent as a trophy to the sultan; his body lies in an unmarked grave.

The Vampire Who Will Not Die

Why did Stoker associate Dracula, or Vlad the Impaler, with vampirism? Generations of Romanian children have been threatened with the folk warning, "Be good, or Dracula will get you." Conversely, there is a traditional belief that the heroic leader of his people will return somehow whenever the nation is gravely threatened. Perhaps the persistence of the legend of the impaler was irresistible to an author who wanted to use the vibrant folklore and eerily beautiful wilderness of eastern Romania for his novel.

Certainly, Stoker's fictional Count Dracula refuses to die. Motion pictures, toys, games, and even food products bearing the Dracula image continue to do well in the marketplace. Bela Lugosi, the Hungarian actor who became the most famous portrayer of Dracula on the screen, earned a fortune in the role, but he squandered almost all of it as he fought an addiction to morphine. When he died in 1956 at the age of 73, he was buried, at his request, in the red-satin-lined black cape he used in his vampire role.

In the mid-1980's, medical accounts of an extremely rare disease, porphyria, stirred up interest in a possible basis for the legends about vampires, and press accounts made much of the "Dracula disease." In fact, only the form of porphyria known as CEP produces the "vampire-like" characteristics: pointed teeth, excessive hair, extreme sensitivity to light, and the need for blood. Only 60 cases have been reported.

Nonetheless, the excited journalistic accounts of the medical research on porphyria proved once again that public fascination with the fictional Dracula remains as deep and wondering as young Harker's question in the novel: "What manner of man is this, or what manner of creature is it in the semblance of man?"

On the Trail of a Bandit

*His name is synonymous with the common man's fight for
freedom and against the injustice of the powerful. But although his
fame has endured for more than 600 years, scholars have yet
to prove that Robin Hood ever existed.*

"Robyn was a proud outlaw," the anonymous author of the late 15th-century ballad *Littel Geste of Robyn Hode* wrote in introducing his hero. "He wente hym forth full mery syngynge, As men have told in tale."

In four related stories, the reader meets the intrepid leader of a band of merry men of the forest who prey on the rich in order to give to the poor. In the first story, Robin lends both money and his squire Little John to an impoverished knight in order to turn the tables on a greedy abbot. In the second, he tricks the despised sheriff of Nottingham into joining him in a dinner of venison poached from the lawman's preserve in Sherwood Forest; he then makes the sheriff shed his rich clothes for the outlaw band's simple livery of Lincoln green. In the third, Robin sees through the disguise of King Edward — come to investigate the lawbreakers — and, pledging his loyalty, enters the service of his sovereign. The final story of the ballad, printed about 1495, tells of Robin's return to banditry and the treachery of the prior-

An idealized Robin Hood is represented in this statue in Nottingham, England. The arrow to his bow is missing, having proved to be an irresistible souvenir for vandals.

ess of Kirklees Abbey, who bleeds him to death when he goes to her for a cure.

These are only the first documented tales of Robin Hood, tales no doubt told and retold for at least the preceding century and a half and added to during the following centuries. As late as 1819, Sir Walter Scott used Robin Hood as the model for one of the characters in his novel *Ivanhoe*, and the hero survives today in children's books, on television, and in motion pictures.

The Man Behind the Myth

It is easy to account for Robin Hood's enduring popularity. Proud and independent, he placed himself in opposition to those who used their rank and wealth — mainly officers of the law and churchmen — to cheat and oppress the common folk. But he remained loyal to the king and accepted religion, counting the earthy Friar Tuck among his followers. It was not the existing social order that he challenged, only abuses of it by the unprincipled and avaricious. So appealing is the character of Robin Hood that historians have long sought the real man behind the legend.

In the 1377 edition of his poetic masterpiece *Piers Plowman*, William Langland refers to

"rymes of Robyn Hode." His contemporary Geoffrey Chaucer mentions "hazellwood where Jolly Robin plaied" in *Troilus and Criseyde*. Moreover, "The Tale of Gamelyn," incorporated into Chaucer's *Canterbury Tales*, features a bandit hero. To literary detectives these references suggest that ballads about Robin Hood were probably already well known by the mid-1300's, some 150 years before they were first printed. They have proposed several possible candidates for the historical person on which the outlaw of Sherwood Forest could have been modeled.

The census rolls of 1228 and 1230 contain the name Robert Hood, nicknamed Hobbehod, and describe him as a fugitive from justice. A movement led by Sir Robert Thwing about that time was characterized by raids on monasteries, from which grain was seized for distribution to the poor. But the name Robert Hood was not an uncommon one, as later manor rolls reveal, and this slim evidence for so early a Robin Hood is generally dismissed. More persistent is the identification of Robin Hood as one Robert Fitzooth, a claimant to the earldom of Huntingdon, who was born about 1160 and died in 1247. Some reference works actually cite these dates for Robin Hood, but skeptics point out that contemporary records contain no mention of a rebellious nobleman named Robert Fitzooth.

Who Was Robin Hood's King?

Among the problems in dating the origin of the Robin Hood stories are the references in different versions to various English monarchs. An early historian, Walter Bower, confidently placed Robin Hood in the 1265 revolt against King Henry III led by his brother-in-law Simon de Montfort. Following de Montfort's defeat at the Battle of Evesham, many of the rebels remained in arms and lived much as did the Robin Hood of the ballads. "At this time," writes Bower, "the famous robber Robin Hood . . . rose to prominence among those who had been disinherited and banished on account of the revolt. These men . . . love to sing of their deeds in all kinds of romances, mimes, and snatches." The major difficulty with Bower's thesis is the longbow, which features so prominently in the Robin Hood ballads. It had not been invented at the time of Simon de Montfort's rebellion.

King Richard I spent less than a year of his reign (1189–99) in England, preferring adventures abroad to administrative duties at home. His link to a real Robin Hood is considered to be highly unlikely.

A Sicilian Robin Hood

Once lauded as a fighter for Sicilian independence, Salvatore Giuliano ended his life as a common criminal with a price on his head.

In September 1943, as German and Italian resistance to the Allied invasion of Sicily collapsed, a 20-year-old black marketeer named Salvatore Giuliano shot and killed a policeman while resisting arrest. It was the beginning of a life of violent crime that, by late 1949, made him Italy's most wanted fugitive — yet, one who was celebrated as a hero of Sicilian independence and a modern Robin Hood.

From his mountain hideouts, Giuliano and his band of followers swooped down upon the towns and villages to rob, kill, and seize hostages for ransom. Although more than 2,000 policemen were detailed to hunt the brigand, Giuliano's links to the Mafia protected him. Sicilian separatists named him colonel in an army seeking independence from mainland Italy. Tales of his exploits were sold in railroad stations for the amusement of travelers, and itinerant ballad singers entertained country folk with songs in his praise — until a senseless act of brutality revealed that Giuliano was not a hero. At a May Day celebration in 1947, Giuliano's brigands fired their machine guns into a holiday crowd gathered to hear a socialist speaker. Eight people died; 33 were wounded. The Mafia backed off from its support, and the central government made the apprehension of the outlaw a major goal.

Perhaps betrayed by a cousin who said that he was bringing a government offer of amnesty and a chance to flee to the United States, Giuliano was cornered by the police early on the morning of July 5, 1950, outside a friend's house. He died instantly in a hail of bullets from their automatic weapons.

A document of 1322 refers to a "stone of Robin Hood" in Yorkshire, suggesting that the ballads — if not the actual man — were well known by that date. Those who would place the original Robin Hood at this date propose Robert Hood, a tenant of Wakefield involved in the uprising that year of the earl of Lancaster, as the model for the fugitive hero. The next year, they point out, King Edward II visited Nottingham and took into service as court valet one Robert Hood, to whom payments were made during the next 12 months, or until he retired "because he can no longer work." This evidence fits in nicely with the third story in *Littel Geste of Robyn Hode*.

The reference to King Edward II would place the outlaw hero in the first quarter of the 14th century. But in other versions, Robin Hood appears as a champion of King Richard I, the Lionhearted, who reigned in the final decade of the 12th century, and as an opponent of Richard's brother and successor John Lackland — so called for the territories he lost in France.

Embellishing the Tales

What is certain about Robin Hood is the evolving nature of his legend. In the early ballads there is no mention of Maid Marian, Robin's lady love. She first appears in late 15th-century versions, at a time when folk plays and morris dances were becoming popular in May festivities. The giant Little John is with Robin's band in the initial ballads, but Friar Tuck appears only in the later tale in which he ducks Robin in a stream. The original Robin is a simple yeoman; later, he is described as a fugitive nobleman.

With so many contradictory additions to the Robin Hood legend, it is unlikely that the real hero will ever be identified. Most scholars now agree that he represents a type — the outlaw hero — that was celebrated in ballads handed down from generation to generation from at least the early 1300's. As the storytellers spun their yarns, they would freely interpolate contemporary events and the exploits of real people into the story of a man who probably never existed. Robin Hood, as one professor has written, was "the pure creation of the ballad muse," the invention of anonymous poets who wanted to celebrate a simple man who fought for justice against oppression by the high and mighty. And this accounts for his universal and lasting appeal, epitomized by the ballad maker's benediction:

Cryst have mercy on his soule,
That dyed on the rode;
For he was a good outlaw,
And dyd pore men much good.

A Pact with the Devil

Was he a powerful sorcerer who sold his soul to the devil or merely a charlatan? Amazingly, the shadowy life of the actual Faust has inspired fiction that either deplores man's sinful arrogance or celebrates his potential for achieving goodness.

The horrible uproar shook the walls of the Lion's Inn throughout the night. Shrieks, roars, and a weird rumbling frightened the neighborhood, and not until the first light of dawn did the innkeeper find the courage to knock at the room assigned to the strange man known as Faust. When there was no answer, the trembling landlord unlocked the door. There, amid broken sticks of furniture, the body of the renowned sorcerer lay sprawled and twisted on the floor, gruesomely mutilated and disfigured.

The solution to the mystery of his death reached by the townspeople can be read on a wall plaque at the inn in Württemberg, Germany: "One of the most powerful devils, Mephistopheles, whom he had called brother-in-law dur-

Faust is supposed to have kept his instruments and ingredients for experiments in this star-shaped alchemist's cabinet.

ing his lifetime, had broken his neck, as the pact had expired after 24 years, and delivered his soul to eternal damnation." The murder occurred sometime around 1540. Contemporary accounts disagree about the actual date, but all concur that Magister Georgius Sabellicus Faustus Junior, as he styled himself, had been famous for decades throughout Europe for either fraud or true wizardry.

Mountebank or Monster?

One view of Faust comes down to us from the work of a Protestant pastor, Johann Gast, who wrote that the magician's performing horse and dog were in fact evil spirits, working with their master as part of his contract with Satan. Another writer described Faust as "a disgraceful beast and sewer of many devils." On the other hand, the respected scholar and monk Trithemius, himself a dabbler in magic, dismissed his notorious contemporary as a fool and mountebank who should be horsewhipped. Others agreed, including a historian who ranked Faust with "wicked, cheating, useless, and unlearned doctors."

Despite his ability to arouse such impassioned condemnation, surprisingly little is known about the highlights of Faust's life. Probably, as Johann Faust, he graduated from Heidelberg University in 1509 and went on to study natural science in Poland. Evidently, he soon became a wandering astrologer and necromancer, for it is known that, as Georg Faust, he somehow made himself unwelcome at the University of Erfurt. In 1520 he was at the court of George III, the prince-bishop of Bamberg, casting the ruler's horoscope. Thereafter Faust advertised himself as "Prince-Episcopal Court Astrologer." Eight years later, by then known as Jörg Faustus the fortune-teller, he was thrown out of the town of Ingolstadt. For a time thereafter, he was employed as a schoolmaster at a boys' boarding school in Nürnberg, but in 1532

In German-speaking countries Faust is inseparably linked with the name of Goethe. The poet's great drama Faust *was first performed in Weimar in 1829. A noted Hamburg stage production with Will Quadflieg and Gustav Gründgens (right) was filmed in 1960.*

Itinerant theater troupes and puppet shows popularized the Faust story in the 17th and 18th centuries. Audiences were particularly fascinated by Mephistopheles.

he was dismissed and exiled from the city for corrupting the morals of his young students.

Evidently, the historical Faust had the tenacity of a natural survivor, for he continually resurfaced after disgrace and defeat. Blithely, it would seem, he passed out calling cards in which he described himself as "Fountain of the Necromancers, Astrologer, Second of the Magicians, Chiromancer, Aeromancer, Pyromancer, Second of Hydromancy." In 1536 at least two distinguished clients sought him out for a glimpse into the future: A senator in Würzburg wanted an astrological reading on the outcome of Charles V's war against the king of France, and a German adventurer, mounting an expedition to South America to find the fabled Eldorado, wanted to know his chances of success. Apparently, Faust satisfied both customers, although his prophecy to the second one probably partook more of common sense than of supernatural prescience. He told him that the mission would be unsuccessful, and indeed Eldorado was never found.

The Elusive Meaning of Science

Today it may be difficult to understand Renaissance attitudes toward the many different "sciences" practiced by Faust and other soothsayers, alchemists, astrologers, and illusionists. Astrology, even in the judgment of the most educated, was a respectable science. Some forms of magic, too, were considered acceptable, or "white," because they sought to discover and master secret forces in nature by natural means.

If legend is to be believed, Faust was one of the few who dared practice "black" magic, accepting the spiritual risks of consorting with evil spirits and demons in order to gain secret knowledge. While offensive to the pillars of secular and church society, such diabolism might well have been more impressive to the common folk, the prey upon whom Faust apparently fed with much success.

It seems likely that, like others who practiced mainstream alchemy, he was seeking the so-called Philosopher's Stone, the supposed catalyst for turning base metals into pure gold. Some historians have theorized that he may even have been one of the "true alchemists," those who strove to attain inner perfection and purify their souls in their lonely, grueling studies. According to this theory, the many gaps in his known history were periods of seclusion during which, having set aside monies earned by his fortune-telling and magical performances, he was able to study in secret. But this revisionist view has not been widely shared. Rather, by the end of the 16th century, his name had become forever linked with the black arts. Even Martin Luther, whose protests against the abuses of the Roman Catholic Church precipitated the Protestant Reformation, claimed that he required the help of God to save himself from demons set upon him by Faust.

A Legend for the Times

Whatever the truth about the historical Faust, the time was ripe for the legends about him to flourish. In an age dominated by Christianity, whether Roman Catholic or Protestant, it was assumed that the truth of divine revelations and the very different truths of human science would inevitably come into conflict. In fact, secular learning was considered so inherently evil that, as far back as the 6th century, there were legends based upon the idea that scholars must have had to sell their souls to the devil in order to gain so much knowledge. Theophilus, an archdeacon in the early Christian church, was supposed to have trafficked with Satan, and Pope Silvester II, a scholar whose erudition was far in advance of his time, was widely believed to be in league with infernal spirits. Even earlier, at the dawn of the Christian era, certain Jewish mystics had created incantations for calling on Satan, and these formulas were still to be found in books of magic available in Faust's day. It must be remembered, too, that in those days practically everyone believed in the efficacy of witchcraft. And demons were thought to be feverishly going about the devil's business at all times.

An additional factor in the enormous popularity of the Faust story was the Reformation, during which adherents of Protestantism set themselves against the Roman Catholic Church. To these reformers the established faith had become corrupt, and they were returning to the ideas and practices of the "pure word of God." To them Faust's investigations into forbidden knowledge were impious, as were all revolts of human intellect against the laws in the Holy Bible. According to orthodox Protestant belief, the necromancer deserved his eternal doom simply because he chose human over divine knowledge.

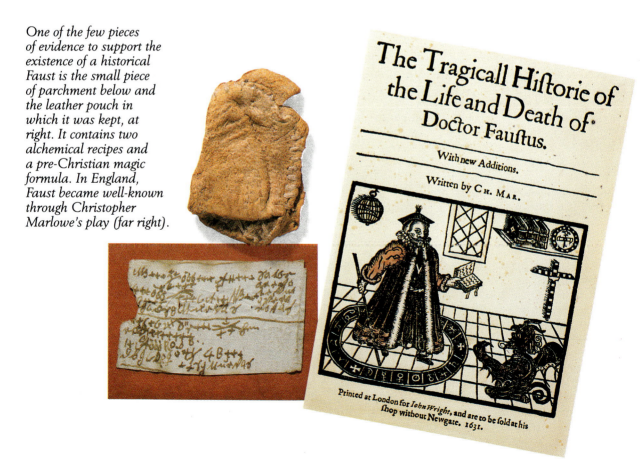

One of the few pieces of evidence to support the existence of a historical Faust is the small piece of parchment below and the leather pouch in which it was kept, at right. It contains two alchemical recipes and a pre-Christian magic formula. In England, Faust became well-known through Christopher Marlowe's play (far right).

Science in an Unscientific Age

Misunderstood as little but the foolish search to find a way of turning base metals into gold, alchemy was in fact the chemistry of the Middle Ages. It was unified by the philosophical principle that all bodies are composed of the "prima materia" combined with various mixtures of the four elements, as specified by the Greek philosopher Aristotle: earth, air, fire, and water. According to this theory, lead could be changed or transmuted to gold by subtracting qualities that are characteristic of lead, thus isolating the "prima materia," and then adding to the basic primitive matter the qualities that are characteristic of gold. Despite the Faustian associations that have come down to the present day, this process was not considered at all magical or supernatural by alchemists. On the con-

In this reconstruction of an 18th-century alchemist's workshop, many laboratory instruments still in use today can be seen.

trary, they were trying to discover the laboratory methods that would accurately mimic the changes observed in nature.

The word "alchemy" goes back at least to the 4th century, but legends credit the ancient god Hermes with creating the art. From the alchemical practice of sealing vessels with the sign of Hermes comes the phrase "hermetically sealed," used frequently today. The science as developed in classical Greece and Rome was eventually influenced by the magic and astrology known in Babylon, Persia, and Egypt. It reached western Europe in the 11th century, after the Moorish conquests brought Arabic learning to Spain. To the goal of creating precious metal was added the search for the Elixir of Life, an imagined substance that would bestow eternal youth and cure diseases.

From Satanist to Buffoon

From Germany, Faust's fame spread like wildfire because of a crudely written collection of legends, *The History of Johann Faust* (1587). This so-called Faustbook, considered by some critics to be the first important German novel, proved irresistible to popular taste and was translated into several languages. "History is composed of true and observed events," the anonymous author observes sententiously before recounting his updated versions of medieval tales about men of the occult while substituting Faust as the hero. He also adds scenes of simpleminded humor, with Faust's dupes as the butt of the jokes. Nonetheless, passages such as descriptions of eternal punishment in hell convey the intensity of sincere conviction. His portrayals of Mephistopheles as a savagely bitter fiend and Faust as a terrified sinner struck a common chord with readers. Two more versions of the book would be successfully published over the next century.

Meanwhile, the oral tradition remained strong, based upon anecdotes about the sorcerer's amazing powers. His compact with Satan was said to be abundantly evident in everyday life, as when he was able to tap a plain wooden table so that wine flowed forth or order the fiend to bring him fresh strawberries in the dead of winter. In one tale he was so hungry that he literally devoured a horse, along with its cart and load of hay. When he was bored and overheated in summer, the demonic powers brought snow so that he could take a sleigh ride.

On a night of carousing, Faust supposedly noticed four brawny men struggling to bring a heavy barrel up from the cellar. "What foolish people!" he shouted. "I can bring up the barrel all by myself!" As the innkeeper and his customers drew back in wonder, the necromancer descended the staircase, mounted the barrel, and triumphantly rode it back up the stairs into the saloon.

From Buffoon to Hero

These trivial displays may seem ridiculous, particularly when they have been earned, as the legends claim, at the price of the eternal damnation of Faust's soul. Yet the basic elements that appealed to the untutored popular mind proved to have universal meaning, inspiring great works of drama, poetry, and music.

The first widely acclaimed work premiered in England in 1594, a year after the mysterious death of its author Christopher Marlowe. Although flawed with gratuitous insults to Roman Catholicism and by oafish humor, the theme of *The Tragicall Historie of the Life and Death of Doc-*

The Saint's Orgy

One of the most famous scenes in Part One of Goethe's *Faust* is the hero's visit to the annual witches' sabbath known as Walpurgis Night. According to Germanic traditions, at midnight on May 1 the witches gather deliriously on a mountaintop to perform obscene rites.

Incredibly, the name for this bestial celebration is a corruption of the name of a saint revered in Germany: Saint Walburga, who came from England as a Christian missionary in the mid-700's. It was on the eve of May 1 that her remains were disinterred and moved to the church of the Holy Cross at Eichstatt. The apparent coincidence of the dates is one explanation for the name of the witches' sabbath, Walpurgis (or Walburga's) Night. But it is also true that her annual feast day, observed by the church on May 1, takes place the same day as an ancient spring festival that was dedicated to Waldborg, a pagan goddess of fertility.

Belief in the actual existence of witches was as prevalent in the Middle Ages and Renaissance as fear of Faustian demons, and the consequences for human beings were often grave. Forced to confess their guilt by cruel and ingenious tortures, accused witches were often executed by being burned alive.

Teufelsschloss.   Teufelsbecken.

nizes the enormity of his bargain and knows that he is unable to elude the consequences. Renaissance audiences shuddered in horror at the vision he conjured of his everlasting fate:

O, if my soul must suffer for my sin,
Impose some end to my incessant pain!
Let Faustus live in hell a thousand years,
A hundred thousand, and at last be saved.

Less impressively, many other plays and puppet shows were produced throughout the 1600's and 1700's, mostly in Germany. Generally speaking, they stressed the gruesome and silly rather than the literary aspects of the material. At the same time, manuals of magic using Faust's name were widely sold. The reader who capably followed instructions could supposedly avoid any dangerous contract with Satan or, alternatively, enter into such a pact and safely break it later.

It was almost 300 years after the death of Faust, however, that perhaps the greatest literary version of his life was completed. Johann Wolfgang von Goethe, the revered German poet, worked almost 30 years to complete his poetic drama, *Faust*. Part One appeared in 1808; Part Two, in 1832. His main character makes a clear break with the traditional interpretation. In fact, God saves him from perdition, for, "A good man through the obscurest aspiration is ever conscious of the one true way." In other words, Goethe's Faust is a hero. Unfulfilled by intellectual and scientific knowledge, he bargains his soul for one moment of experience that will give him complete satisfaction. No "low" pleasure of the senses will suffice, but he finds the meaning of life in the constant love of a simple peasant girl he has seduced and abandoned. His final salvation comes, however, because he aspires to the creation of a better society for all mankind. Goethe's message is that man can achieve nobility and goodness despite the evil in his makeup.

Perhaps no other artist has produced as profound a philosophical and psychological work from the Faust legend, but many have been inspired to create works that endure. Hector Berlioz composed *The Damnation of Faust*, a dramatic cantata that is sometimes performed on the operatic stage. Charles Gounod's *Faust* has become one of the most admired operas of all time.

Why has the violent death of a despised charlatan intrigued so many creative geniuses? Why do their works remain so popular today? Perhaps the answer lies in the wall plaque at the Lion's Inn, with its clear indication that Faust — though finally damned — did indeed for 24 years enjoy the power and pleasures of the forbidden secrets of satanic evil. Forbidden . . . but seductive.

tor Faustus would influence all serious Faustian literature for the next 200 years. The protagonist must pay with his soul for revolting against the word of God. Not simply a trickster or diabolist, Marlowe's Faust wants Satan's aid in learning about all the possibilities of human experience. The drama often soars with glorious poetry, as when the ghost of Helen of Troy appears. But the most powerful of Marlowe's lines portray Faust's doomed efforts to repent when he finally recog-

Scandal in the Eternal City: Pope John VIII is dramatically revealed as a woman.

A Woman on the Papal Throne

*The popes who ruled the Christian church from Rome in the Middle Ages
were, more often than not, far from holy men. Credulous people
were prepared to accept any tale, however scandalous, about them.*

Violent earthquakes shake southern Italy; there is rumor of blood raining down upon France; and in Rome the stench of locusts swarming over the Eternal City and falling dead into the sea so poisons the air that both people and animals succumb. Panic grips the masses. Was Charlemagne, crowned emperor only a half century earlier, the mighty ruler whose reign was to precede the end of the world? Had Mohammed been the precursor of the dreaded anti-Christ, and would the seemingly irresistible surge westward of his fanatical followers spell the end of Christianity?

The year is 857, and the people of Rome demand reassurance from Pope John VIII, whom they have grown to love during the two years of his pontificate. Throngs turn out to cheer him as he heads a procession from St. Peter's basilica to his residence in the Lateran palace on the opposite side of the Tiber River. But as the papal party enters a narrow alley between the Colosseum and the church of St. Clement, the holy father stumbles and collapses. In full view of horrified onlookers, Pope John is revealed as a woman in labor. Within moments, as she gives birth to a child, the devout crowd turns into an enraged mob. The furious onlookers seize the hapless woman and her newborn infant, drag them beyond the city gates, and stone them to death.

Such is the story told and retold throughout Europe from at least the late 1200's and widely believed for centuries thereafter.

All for the Sake of Love

Early in the 9th century, about the year 818, so we are told, a daughter named Joan was born to English missionaries in the Rhine River city of Mainz. As a child, she was noted for her beauty and remarkable intellect. Falling in love with a monk at the age of 12, Joan left her parents' home, donned male attire, and offered herself as a novice at the monastery in order to be with her lover. The days of John Anglicus, or John the Englishman, as she called herself, were spent praying or studying in the library; the nights were given over to love.

Before long, the deception was discovered, and the couple had to flee — their escape from church punishment taking the guise of a pilgrimage across Europe and south toward the Holy Land. In Athens, Joan's companion disappeared, but she went on to Rome. Still masquerading as a man, Joan took work as a notary or, in another version of the story, as a teacher. Whatever her initial employment, Joan was soon a celebrity. Students admired her eloquence, philosophers respected her wisdom, cardinals noted her theological knowledge, and papal courtiers loved her for her generosity. When Pope Leo IV died in 855, Joan was unanimously elected as his successor; she took the papal throne as John VIII.

Joan/John was able to keep the secret of her sex from all but one, and this proved her undoing. The lonely, passionate woman took her valet as a lover and was soon pregnant with his child. After the delivery in public of the infant and the swift vengeance of the mob, a new pope, Benedict III, was hastily installed. Church historians later advanced the date of his accession to 855 so as to eliminate any record of Joan's pontificate. When another John became pope 15 years later, in 872, he was given the name John VIII, not John IX.

Proof for Doubters

The story of Pope Joan most likely arose during the 10th century, when no fewer than 23 popes reigned — some for only months. The endings of their pontificates are a grim litany: imprisoned, murdered, deposed, starved to death, blinded. Behind many of these ineffectual and short-lived pontiffs stood women from Rome's noble families. If women wielded so much power, the common folk asked, why not a woman pope?

Historians find the earliest reference to Pope Joan in *The Seven Gifts of the Holy Spirit*, the work of a 13th-century French Dominican named Stephen of Bourbon. The tale told by Stephen was incorporated in *The Chronicle of the Popes and Emperors*, a widely read work by another 13th-century

The Papacy's Regiment of Women

During the Middle Ages — particularly in the 10th century, when the legend of Pope Joan probably arose — the women of Rome's patrician families wielded enormous power over the papal court. A number of popes openly kept mistresses, though any illegitimate offspring were euphemistically referred to as nieces or nephews of the errant pope. Their mothers sometimes succeeded in placing the popes' "nephews" on the papal throne, so that in time it was said that the papacy was ruled by a "regiment of women."

Among the most notorious of such women was Marozia, the daughter of a Roman senator. At the age of 15, she became the mistress of Pope Sergius III and bore him a son. At Sergius's death in 911, the boy was only six, but Marozia bided her time, married Count Alberic of Tuscany, and

Scarcely a pious figure, Alexander VI used his power to advance his children's careers.

gave birth to a second son, also named Alberic. In 931 she saw her son by Sergius, though only 25 years old, enthroned as Pope John XI. With her husband dead, Marozia married his brother, Hugo of Provence. The pope officiated at his mother's second wedding. During the revels following the ceremony, angry words were exchanged between the young Alberic and his new stepfather. In the resulting brawl, Alberic chased Hugo out of the city and imprisoned Marozia and Pope John XI. The pope died within a few years, but his mother lived to see Alberic's son, and her grandson, elevated to the papacy as Pope John XII.

A record of sorts was set some 500 years later by Pope Alexander VI, who acknowledged at least four of his illegitimate children and made one of them, a son named Cesare Borgia, a cardinal.

At the time of the legendary Pope Joan (855–57), the familiar colonnaded plaza in front of St. Peter's basilica (left) was far in the future. The odd marble chair below was said to have been used at papal enthronements for centuries after the female pope's brief reign.

Dominican, a Pole called Martin of Troppau.

Believers in the story of Pope Joan cited such evidence as the statue of a woman with a child in the alley between the Colosseum and the church of St. Clement, where the papal procession of 857 came to such a dramatic halt. The alley, because of the shame Pope Joan brought to the papacy, was avoided by subsequent processions. For more than 200 years, among the papal busts in Siena cathedral, there was a statue labeled, "Pope John VIII, a woman from England"; in the 16th century Pope Clement VIII ordered the bust renamed "Pope Zachary."

Perhaps the most bizarre evidence offered in support of the story of Pope Joan was the *Sella stercoraria*, a peculiar marble chair with a hole in the seat to be found in the basilica of St. John Lateran. From the end of the 11th century up until the 16th century, it was alleged, this chair was used at papal enthronements. Before taking office, each new pope was required to sit on the chair so that a medical examination could be performed to determine the sex of the candidate.

The Scholarly Rebuttal

So serious was the story of a female pope taken that the Council of Constance in 1415 cited it in debating the powers of the pope. The scholar pope Pius II, reigning later in that century, tried to debunk the legend — apparently with little success. Through the 16th and 17th centuries,

Protestant writers seized upon the story of Pope Joan to bolster their attacks upon the papacy. Curiously enough, however, it was a Calvinist writer, David Blondel, who made the first serious assault on the persistent tale. His 1647 treatise bears the lengthy title, *Familiar Enlightenment of the Question: Whether a Woman Had Been Seated on the Papal Throne in Rome*.

Today scholars reject the Pope Joan story. It is, they say, not a record of true events but rather a legacy of the medieval papacy — a troubled time when popes were known for anything but their holiness and nothing was too evil or too strange about them for belief. As for the marble chair, it was probably a relic of ancient Rome, a commode from one of the city's communal baths.

Vengeance for Siegfried

Bold courtship, superhuman acts of strength, and the rivalry of two queens that ends in a bloody massacre — such are the events of the medieval German epic the Nibelungenlied. Scholars still seek its literary and historical sources.

Word of Kriemhild's charming manners and incomparable beauty has spread abroad to reach the castle of Xanten in the flatlands of the lower Rhine River. When the young prince, Siegfried, tells his father that he will have no other as his bride, the king warns him about wooing the sister of Burgundy's proud monarch, Gunther. The court at Worms has many a fierce and haughty vassal who will oppose his suit. Undeterred, Siegfried sets out on his quest, accompanied by a dozen warriors — all handsomely attired and splendidly armed. The woman he seeks will be the joy of his life and also the indirect cause of his tragic death.

Thus begins the great German epic the *Nibelungenlied*, or *Song of the Nibelungs*, the work of an unknown poet completed about the year 1203. The last third of the 12th century and the first half of the 13th witnessed the first flowering of German literature, marked also by two King Arthur tales, *Parzival* by Wolfram von Eschenbach and *Tristan* by Gottfried von Strassburg.

To prevent the widowed Kriemhild from using the Nibelung treasure for her own purposes, Siegfried's murderer, Hagen, throws it in the Rhine. A statue commemorating the dramatic incident from the Nibelungenlied *was erected at Worms in 1906.*

The *Nibelungenlied* was enormously popular over the next three centuries — no fewer than 34 manuscript versions have been preserved. It is not difficult to understand its appeal: The unforgettable characters are placed in scenes of courtly love, ruthless displays of strength, and passionate acts of revenge. Lengthy descriptions of clothing, weapons, and court etiquette mirror an age of chivalry already waning by the time the poet wrote and, no doubt, were riveting to his contemporaries. For modern readers, however, the epic seems more of a fairy tale than history.

Two Princes Go Courting

The appearance of Siegfried at Worms causes a sensation. Who is the imposing stranger, King Gunther asks his cousin and vassal Hagen? He is, Hagen replies, the invincible prince who — in a previous adventure — had slain a dragon, seized the vast fortune of the Nibelungs, and snatched the cloak of invisibility from the dwarf Alberich. He should be courteously welcomed to Worms, advises Gunther's vassal, "so that we may not reap the young warrior's wrath." The Burgundians make Siegfried feel at home and channel his bellicose nature into friendly contests of strength

and knightly skills. From a latticed window, Kriemhild watches the dashing stranger and begins to form a longing for him that matches his passion for her — though the two have yet to meet. A year passes.

When news of an invasion by the kings of Saxony and Denmark reaches Worms, Siegfried offers to take arms in defense of Burgundy and returns from the campaign with the two captive monarchs in tow. At a tournament to celebrate his victory, he at last meets the fair Kriemhild. The two fall in love, and Siegfried asks her brother for her hand. Before consenting, Gunther demands that Siegfried accompany him across the sea to Isenland to help him woo and win the renowned warrior princess Brunhild. Possessed of superhuman strength, the beauteous princess has vowed to marry only the man who can throw a spear, hurl a rock, and jump farther than she can. The

At the court of King Etzel of Hungary, the Burgundians are unprepared for the slaughter ordered by the vengeful Queen Kriemhild. The concluding event of the epic poem may record a massacre carried out by Attila the Hun.

loser in any contest with her must forfeit his life.

Although Gunther suggests a host of 30,000 for his assault on Brunhild's realm and heart, Siegfried cautions a more modest approach — and thus the two, with only Hagen and a valiant warrior named Dankwart as escorts, set out by boat for the 12-day voyage to Isenland. Brunhild already knows Siegfried by reputation and is impressed that he appears as but a vassal to the unknown king who has come courting.

Brunhild demonstrates her awesome strength and skill with the sword, thrusting at Gunther's shield. But, draped in his invisible cloak, Siegfried stands beside the king, wards off Brunhild's mighty blow, and delivers a thrust she cannot meet. Impressed but angry, she congratulates Gunther before hurling a huge stone a great distance and then leaping beyond the point where it lands. The invisible Siegfried throws the stone even farther and, lifting Gunther, jumps beyond where it falls. Brunhild must accept defeat and accompany Gunther to Burgundy as his intended bride. Although Kriemhild graciously welcomes her brother's betrothed to Worms, it is clear to onlookers that a rivalry between the two beauties is all but inevitable.

Two Queens Start Quarreling

Double nuptials follow the return to Burgundy. For Siegfried, his wedding night brings rapture; for Gunther, humiliation and frustration. Brunhild refuses to allow the king in her bed, roughly seizing him, tying him with the band she wears about her waist, and hanging him from a nail on the wall. When Gunther reveals the secret of his disgrace to his new brother-in-law, Siegfried once more comes to the rescue. Under cover of darkness and speaking no word that would reveal his identity, Siegfried steals into Brunhild's chamber, subdues her with his strength, and turns her over to Gunther. But before leaving, he takes Brunhild's waistband and golden ring as souvenirs of his conquest.

At the conclusion of the wedding festivities, Siegfried takes his bride back home to the lowlands, where his father and mother abdicate in their favor. In Worms, Brunhild broods over Gunther's evasion of her questions as to why the king bestowed his sister on a mere vassal and waits in vain for tribute from Siegfried, made enormously wealthy by his seizure of the treasure of the Nibelungs. She asks Gunther to invite Siegfried and Kriemhild to Worms.

A number of springs in the Odenwald, a mountainous region in southwestern Germany, are claimed to be the site of Siegfried's murder. The one above is at Grasellenbach.

Siegfried's bath in the blood of the slain dragon was recreated in Fritz Lang's 1924 motion picture Die Nibelungen. *A leaf clinging to the hero's back marks the spot of his vulnerability.*

Medieval Singers of Love

The reverence in which women were held by the minnesingers is reflected in this charming detail from the Great Heidelberg Songscript.

The heroic epic — of which the *Nibelungenlied* is the best known example in German — was not necessarily the most popular literary form of the late Middle Ages. More elegant, and thus especially pleasing to women, were the sophisticated poems of the 12th- and 13th-century minnesingers. The term "minne" derives from the Old High German word *minna*, or "loving remembrance."

Influenced by the troubadours of France, these wandering minstrels sang of the chivalric love of knights for the married women they were sworn to defend. Because the objects of their affection were unobtainable, the love they celebrated necessarily remained platonic, and the desires such love prompted were rigorously suppressed. Their songs were called high minne, and the exemplary composer of this form was Reinmar von Hagenau, who flourished about the year 1190.

In sharp contrast were the low minne of Walther von der Vogelweide early in the 13th century. He demanded that the minnesong bring joy to the listener, and thus he dwelt upon the fulfillment of love. His most famous song is "Under the Linden Tree on the Moors" in which he playfully — if discreetly and only by innuendo — describes a night of lovemaking.

The poems of more than 160 minnesingers have survived. From them scholars have determined that these minstrels were far from spontaneous entertainers. Rather they were skilled craftsmen, who followed strict poetic conventions to create polished works that upheld the social and religious conventions of chivalry's waning age.

At the doorway to the Worms cathedral, the two queens start arguing as to which of them should enter first. She cannot give way to the wife of a vassal, Brunhild haughtily announces. If her husband is a vassal, Kriemhild retorts, then Brunhild has slept with a vassal — revealing Siegfried's wedding night victory over Gunther's reluctant bride and now showing her the ring and waistband that her husband had entrusted to her. Weeping in shame, Brunhild vows revenge.

Siegfried's Vulnerability

After slaying the dragon in his earlier adventure, Siegfried had bathed in the beast's blood so as to gain invincibility in combat. But as he bathed, a broad leaf fell on his back between his shoulder blades and left that area of his skin uncleansed. Only in that spot can he be fatally wounded.

With the aid of Hagen, Brunhild sets a trap for Siegfried. First, Gunther's trusted knight tells the visiting monarch that Burgundy is once more to be attacked by the kings of Saxony and Denmark and that his leadership is again needed to repulse the enemy. Then, he wheedles the secret of her husband's vulnerability from Kriemhild and persuades her to embroider a cross on Siegfried's garment to mark the spot. Next, he reports that the invasion threat has ended and proposes a hunt in the forest. As Siegfried bends over a spring to drink, the treacherous Hagen sinks a spear between his shoulder blades and kills him.

In the long aftermath to Siegfried's death, Kriemhild loses the treasure of the Nibelungs to Hagen, who sinks it in the Rhine, and marries Etzel, the king of Hungary. After many years she invites her brother and his court to her new kingdom on the Danube. While her guests are at table in Etzel's castle, Kriemhild orders an attack on her brother's guard outside. In retaliation Hagen kills her son by Etzel. Kriemhild offers to let her brother go in peace, if only he turns the murderer over to her, but Gunther refuses to surrender his vassal, and she orders her brother decapitated. The vengeful queen next offers to spare Hagen if only he will divulge the secret resting place of the Nibelung treasure. He refuses, and she strikes off his head, using Siegfried's sword. The horrified Etzel does nothing to prevent a retainer from putting a swift end to the rampaging queen.

In Search of Siegfried

For 300 years the *Nibelungenlied* enjoyed widespread popularity among German-speaking people, but early in the 16th century it lapsed into an obscurity that ended only in 1757, when a manuscript copy of the epic was discovered and pub-

The Scourge of God

"They are compact and strongly built, have broad necks, and are revoltingly ugly and disgusting, like two-legged beasts." Thus a 4th-century Roman historian described the Huns, who had stormed out of their homeland in the Asian steppes to seize control of a large territory north of the Danube River. The threat these invaders posed to the Roman empire was initially contained by annual payments in gold.

In 433 leadership of the Huns passed to Attila, a name meaning "little father," and his brother Bleda. After Attila had his brother murdered, he led the Asiatic horde to its greatest victories in campaigns that earned him the nickname *flagellum dei*, or "scourge of God." No longer satisfied with bribes, Attila attacked the eastern part of the empire but was turned back before he reached Constantinople. Next he directed his attention to the west, invading Gaul in 451. Although defeated by the Roman general Aëtius at the Battle of Châlons, Attila marched south into Italy, where he conquered Milan the next year. Pope Leo I — in legend supported by saints Peter and Paul — visited the Hun camp and persuaded Attila to withdraw northward. By 453 the "scourge of God" was dead, most likely the victim of assassins, though there is a romantic tale that he burst a blood vessel on the night of his wedding to a beautiful Gothic maiden named Hilda. Without his leadership the Hun kingdom quickly disintegrated.

Under his Middle High German name, Etzel, Attila appears in the *Nibelungenlied*. Scholars think that the anonymous poet may have combined Attila the Hun with Hungary's first king and patron saint, Stephen, who ruled in the first half of the 11th century.

lished. Early in the 18th century, as the tide of Romanticism swept across Europe, it was adopted as something of a German national epic. The renewed popular interest touched off a literary and historical quest.

Frustrated in their attempt to identify the author, scholars tried to discover the anonymous poet's literary sources. Three Scandinavian works — in prose, not verse — also contain the saga of the Nibelungs; two are Icelandic, and one is Norwegian. But all are later than the German poem, and at least one of the three is probably based on the *Nibelungenlied*. It is very likely that the German author and his Scandinavian counterparts drew from earlier, now lost ballads that celebrated actual historical events. With this in mind, scholars then attempted to trace the historical antecedents of the fantastic tale.

About the year 200 a Germanic tribe, the Burgundians, migrated from the East and settled along the middle Rhine River; their capital may have been at Worms. Under King Gundikar at the beginning of the 5th century, the Burgundians tried to expand their realm downriver — toward the lowlands from which Siegfried came. They were blocked by a Roman commander named Aëtius, who forced them to sue for peace. About 436 the Burgundian realm was invaded by the Huns, under the leadership of the infamous Attila. In Middle High German, Attila is known as Etzel — the king of Hungary in the *Nibelungenlied*. Contemporary sources record that Attila ordered a slaughter of 20,000 Burgundians; this, perhaps, can be linked to the bloodbath that ends the epic. A few years later Aëtius forced the remaining Burgundians to leave the Rhineland for resettlement in what is now southeastern France and northwestern Italy. So dramatic were these events that they well might have been kept alive in songs and tales handed down for centuries before they were ever incorporated into the German and Scandinavian sagas of the 13th century.

As for Siegfried, his heroic achievements are clearly legendary. He is an archetypical hero with no real-life counterpart. Yet an incident of female revenge among the Merovingians, a Frankish dynasty of the 6th century, leaves a tantalizing clue. Fredegund, the concubine of King Chilperic, murdered his wife so that she could become queen. This brought her into conflict with the queen's sister, Brunhild, wife of King Siebert of Austria. To get even with Brunhild, Fredegund arranged the murder of her enemy's husband — a deed that puts her in a class with the vengeful Kriemhild, whose savagery brings the *Nibelungenlied* to its terrible conclusion.

The Desperado as Unlikely Hero

*Leader of the most notorious band of outlaws in U.S. history,
Jesse James somehow managed to gain a reputation as a kind of American
Robin Hood — even while disrupting the social order
and killing at least 16 innocent people.*

On February 1, 1874, Missouri newspapers carried the banner headline, "The Most Daring Train Robbery on Record!" The report went on to tell of a gang of heavily armed, uncommonly tall men, riding handsome horses, who had the previous day seized the Iron Mountain Railroad flag station in tiny Gads Hill, Missouri. The writer said that the brazen bandits had thrown the signal switches, stopping the southbound express to Little Rock and taking $22,000 in cash and gold from the train's safe.

Though the gang was not identified, everyone recognized the stylish work of Jesse Woodson James and his brother Frank. In fact, the news bulletin itself was penned by Jesse, who left his handwritten press release with the train engineer just before riding off into the woods with the loot. Jesse believed in publicity, for he knew that much of his success in Missouri was dependent upon the tacit approval of its rustic citizens. Poor and struggling farmers for the most part, they idolized him and his cohorts as symbols of bold defiance against the authorities.

Learning the Trade

Jesse James learned his wild and wily ways as a teenaged guerrilla in the Civil War "army" of William Quantrill. This gang of adventurers, working nominally for the Confederate cause in Union-held Missouri, robbed Union mail, am-

*In the years following his death, the outlaw Jesse James was transformed into the
hero of such stage productions as the one advertised below.*

bushed federal patrols, and attacked shipping along the Missouri River with a speed and brutality that the Union regulars could seldom match. As Quantrill's men were never on any payroll — indeed, the Confederate army officially disavowed any connection with them — the guerrillas supported themselves by any means available, including robbery and extortion.

In 1864 the 17-year-old Jesse joined one of Quantrill's squads, a gang of cutthroats under the command of "Bloody Bill" Anderson, following his older brother Frank and his cousin, Cole Younger, both veteran bushwhackers. Anderson had much to teach them about planning raids, carrying out intelligence-gathering missions, deploying attackers for maximum advantage, and using horses and small arms to deadly effect.

Anderson soon came to regard Jesse James as "the keenest and cleanest fighter in the command," a judgment confirmed in a bloody encounter with Union troops at Centralia, Missouri, on September 27, 1864. The guerrillas halted

a passing train, stole $3,000 in Union currency, and slaughtered more than 225 armed Union troops. James, riding hard with the reins of his horse in his teeth and firing a six-shooter in each hand, reportedly killed three of the enemy.

When the war ended, Confederate guerrillas like Jesse and Frank James were not offered amnesty, as were the regulars, but were declared outlaws and ordered to give themselves up for prosecution. Frank did so and was soon paroled, but Jesse was shot by federal soldiers outside of Lexington, Missouri. Seriously wounded, he was allowed to be carried home to his mother's farm in Kearney, Missouri, presumably to die. But Jesse was soon on the road to recovery, and as his strength returned, he and Frank, cousin Cole, and three others of the Younger clan decided to take up where they had left off, plundering at will, only this time going after a different enemy: banks, railroads, and large landowners.

Pursuing a Bloody Trade

On February 13, 1866, the James brothers launched their new careers in nearby Liberty, Missouri, with the holdup of the Clay County Savings Bank. While eight gang members took up defensive positions on the main street, Frank and Jesse went into the bank, their guns drawn, and ordered the cashier to open the vault and fill the wheat sacks they carried with cash and securities. Then, with an estimated $60,000 in their posses-

In the vintage photograph below, a confident Jesse James (standing at right) poses outside a log cabin with members of his gang. Frank James — a partner from the beginning — stands at left, his hand resting on the shoulder of a recruit.

sion, the gang mounted up and rode out of town.

None of the outlaws was recognized; and, when a citizen posse attempted to follow their trail, it was stopped by a blizzard. After dividing the spoils, each of the bandits slipped back to his family homestead where he did his best to avoid attracting attention. For more than three years, the gang pursued its bloody trade deliberately but infrequently — and without serious interference. Along the way they killed the mayor of one town, several bank clerks, and a score or more bystanders, collecting enough money to live comfortably. Though many privately suspected the James and Younger brothers, there was so much local sympathy for the gang's activities that no one dared testify against its members.

Then, in December 1869, the James brothers' luck changed when they raided a bank in Gallatin, Missouri. The ordinarily cool Jesse shot the cashier, who reminded him of a despised Union officer, and the noise of gunfire drew a crowd to see what was happening. The brothers barely escaped the hail of bullets fired by the townspeople, and in the melee Jesse's mount became skittish and galloped off, throwing Jesse from his saddle and dragging him some 30 feet. When Jesse finally freed himself, he was able to climb up behind Frank on another horse and get away. But Jesse's horse was caught and its owner's identity established for certain. Jesse and Frank decided it was time to lie low, and this they did for nearly two years.

When they did resume their raiding parties, it was in the next state, at Corydon, Iowa, in June 1871. The Corydon escapade turned out to be one of the easiest holdups of their career, and the outlaws enjoyed themselves immensely. Stopping briefly at the church on their way out of town, Jesse interrupted the minister to announce that "some riders" had just robbed the town's bank. "You folks best get down there in a hurry," said the bandit to the astonished worshipers. In the next three years the James brothers grew ever bolder, as one success followed on another. On September 26, 1872, they rode into the giant fairgrounds at Kansas City and, before huge crowds, stole the cash receipts rumored to be about $10,000. Then, to be sure that their exploits were duly appreciated, they rode through the throngs, shooting over their heads like some kind of Wild West circus act.

Going for Higher Stakes

Not long after the raid on the fairgrounds, the brothers decided to try their hands at robbing trains. As the gang's first target, they chose the

Soldiers into Outlaws

When the American Civil War ended in 1865, many of the defeated Confederate states were devastated, the political, social, and economic fabric of their societies torn asunder. No less hard hit were the citizens of Missouri, which had originally entered the Union as a slave state but which had remained officially loyal to the Union during the war. As a result of split loyalties, the state's western border counties had known continual fighting between pro-slavery "bushwhackers" and anti-slavery "jayhawkers." The war simply intensified the dispute between the bitter rival factions.

To meet the menace, Union commanders instituted a series of repressive measures designed to destroy the bushwhackers and punish the civilians who were presumed to be giving them aid and comfort. The bushwhackers proved too clever for the Union regulars, but thousands of farmers were forced to flee as Union troops burned houses and slaughtered livestock.

Peace brought no end to Missouri's problems. In Cass County, where 10,000 Missourians had lived in 1860 — among them relatives of the famed Dalton gang — scarcely 600 remained in 1865. Nearby Clay and Jackson counties, where the James and Younger brothers were born, were similarly depopulated. In this atmosphere of violence and despair, survival by the gun became the order of the day. It was not surprising then that many men were drawn to outlaw gangs after the war, nor that they were uncommonly clever at their chosen trade, given the years of practice they had already had.

Chicago, Rock Island, and Pacific express, which was scheduled to run eastbound with $100,000 in gold on July 21, 1873. On a curving stretch of railbed near Council Bluffs, Iowa, the gang pulled a section of track out of line. Before the approaching train's engineer had a chance to slow down, the engine overshot the curve and ran off the tracks, the following coaches crunching one into the next. One trainman died and a dozen passengers were injured. The James brothers boarded the baggage car and ordered the clerks to open their safes, only to discover that the gold had gone through ahead of schedule and that just a few thousand in federal notes remained. In subsequent attempts they did far better. In addition to the $22,000 carried off from the Gads Hill train robbery in January 1874, they netted $135,000 in three other train robberies.

As the roster of crimes grew and local law enforcement officers did little or nothing to apprehend the outlaws, the bankers and railroad interests took matters into their own hands and hired the Pinkerton National Detective Agency. But because Allan Pinkerton himself had been closely allied with the Union cause, having set up a secret service for the Union army, his men were regarded as enemies among the large segment of Missouri society still sympathetic to the defeated Confederacy. The detectives were placed at further disadvantage by having no photographs of any of the alleged culprits to help them track their quarry without local help. The James gang, by contrast, had no trouble spotting Pinkerton men nor any compunctions about shooting them dead when the opportunity presented itself.

Three Pinkerton operatives were murdered in a single week early in 1874. Stepping up its efforts, the agency laid plans to surround the Kearney homestead where the James brothers' remarried mother, Mrs. Zerelda Samuel, lived — on the presumption that they would trap Jesse and Frank during a filial visit. Hearing rumors that the James boys were already on the premises, one of the agents lobbed a bomb into the house. But all they managed to accomplish was to blow off Mrs. Samuel's right arm and kill Jesse's eight-year-old half brother, Archie. The outlaws were safely ensconced in Tennessee at the time. The vicious bombing only improved Jesse's reputation as a social martyr.

Forced into Hiding

The gang's luck ran out during a bank robbery in Northfield, Minnesota, on September 7, 1876. Two of the James gang were killed on the spot; a third died in a fight with a posse sent after them.

The Great Coup

For most of the 1963 British train robbers, success quickly turned to humiliation and imprisonment.

Train robberies did not end in the 19th century with the downfall of men like Jesse James. In the early 1960's a British gang staged a spectacular train holdup that for bravado — and pecuniary success — would have made their American cousins take notice. The Great Train Robbery, as Britons dubbed the heist, took place in the early hours of August 8, 1963, when 14 masked men hijacked a mail train en route from Glasgow to London and grabbed 120 sacks containing £2.6 million, valued at more than $7 million. As Scotland Yard soon learned, the gang of small-time crooks had stopped the train by the simple ruse of changing a signal along the tracks, causing the engineer to bring the train to a halt near where the hijackers' truck waited.

Within a few days the authorities did manage to identify the culprits — including a house painter, a hairdresser, a flower vendor, a carpenter, a silversmith, and two bookies. All were apprehended. But except for £343,000, the loot had disappeared. The judge who sat at the trial sentenced the guilty to prison terms ranging up to 30 years, doling out maximum penalties that he hoped would prevent any of the bandits from enjoying their secreted "ill-gotten gains" for a very long time.

Most of the men did remain in jail for extended periods, their names and fates soon forgotten, but Ronald Biggs became Scotland Yard's most wanted fugitive and something of a counterculture hero for more than two decades. Escaping soon after sentencing, Biggs found his way to Brazil, took a common-law wife, sired a son, and, as father of a Brazilian citizen, became unextraditable.

The James brothers learned their trade as anti-Union guerrillas during the Civil War. In the postwar years they began as bank robbers, but they eventually turned to more profitable train holdups, in which transported cash and passengers' valuables were seized.

A vigilant eye was the trademark of the famous Pinkerton detective agency, hired to apprehend Jesse James.

The three Younger brothers were wounded and captured several days later. Frank and Jesse were the only ones to escape, and because they were now more earnestly sought by the law than ever, they decided that their only recourse was to take new names and hide out once more.

Had the James brothers remained incognito, Jesse might have died in bed of old age. But three years after disappearing, he and Frank formed a new gang and began stirring up more excitement. Missouri's new governor, Thomas T. Crittenden, put a price of $5,000 on the arrest of Jesse or Frank James, with added amounts if either were convicted for robbery or murder.

Robert and Charles Ford, two recent recruits to the James gang who felt none of the loyalty that their predecessors had known, found the offer too good to refuse. Bob Ford secretly went to Crittenden and won a promise of amnesty in return for delivering Jesse James. The two Fords then paid a social call on Jesse and his family, who were living in St. Joseph, Missouri, under the assumed name of Howard. James was delighted to see his comrades in arms and invited them to stay a while. The Fords waited several days until they found Jesse unarmed — of all improbable cir-

cumstances, the moment came one morning when the outlaw took off his gun belt, climbed up on a chair, his back to Bob Ford, and began dusting a picture on the wall. Slowly, Ford drew his weapon, aimed at Jesse's head, and pulled the trigger. The bullet killed him instantly.

Five months later, 39-year-old Frank James surrendered on his own, laying his gun belt before the governor with a ceremonial flourish. Crittenden promised him a fair trial; and, perhaps because the public had been so outraged by the treacherous nature of Jesse's assassination, Frank was acquitted of all charges. He lived out the rest of his life in peace.

The Jesse James legend lives on. To generations of Americans, the outlaw was remembered as a brazen hero who stole from the rich to give to the poor but fell victim to the unjust power of the state. It was an image perpetuated in dime novels, folk ballads, and theatrical entertainments. That he and his cohorts in fact made no distinction between rich and poor, murdered a dozen or more innocent people, and created a climate of fear and disorder in many parts of the West simply did not fit the populist image, and, consequently, was left out of the telling.

Lady of the Camellias

She was the most admired and sought-after courtesan of the day. But although Marie Duplessis shared her favors with many of Paris's wealthy and titled men, it was her liaison with an impoverished youth that brought her lasting fame.

After a day of riding in the country, the tall, broad-shouldered young man — impeccably dressed as always, though he could scarcely afford it — joined a friend for an evening of theatergoing in Paris. At the Théâtre des Variétés, Alexandre Dumas spent more time peering through his opera glasses at the attractive women prominently arrayed in the box seats than he did at the stage. In the audience that September evening were several alluring members of the demimonde, a class of women on the fringes of respectable society. Although supported by the wealthy, usually older men with whom they shared their favors, most such women craved the true love of handsome, if poor, youths. Such at least was the firmly held belief of young men like the 20-year-old Dumas.

One woman in particular caught his fancy. "She was tall, very slender, with black hair and a pink and white complexion," he later wrote. "She had a small head and elongated eyes that had the porcelain look to be found in the women of Japan. But there was in them something that indicated a proud and lively nature. . . . She might have been a Dresden figurine." The woman so rapturously described was Marie Duplessis, the most famous courtesan of the day.

The woman also noticed Dumas, for she was soon signaling a friend named Clémence Prat, with whom the young man was acquainted. At the end of the performance, Madame Prat obligingly invited Dumas and his friend back to her home — which conveniently was next door to that of Marie on the fashionable Boulevard de la Madeleine. After a short interval, Marie called

A white camellia worn by Marie Duplessis signaled her receptivity to romantic proposals; a red one advised patience.

through a window to tell her neighbor that she was bored with a visiting count and craved company. Madame Prat, the two young men in tow, scurried over. Once the count had been driven away, Marie served a late champagne supper to her three guests. Toward the end of the meal, however, she was overcome by a fit of coughing and had to leave the room. Dumas followed her, finding her collapsed on a sofa. In the water of a silver bowl nearby were traces of blood.

"Are you suffering?" the young man asked. "Very little. I have become used to this sort of thing," the lovely woman answered. "You are killing yourself," he retorted. "Why this sudden devotion? Are you in love with me?" she demanded to know. When he hesitated, she pressed him for an avowal but warned of two consequences. "Either I shall refuse you, in which case you will harbor a grievance against me; or I shall accept you, and you will find yourself with a gloomy mistress on your hands, a nerve-ridden, sick and melancholy woman, whose gaiety you will find sadder even than her grief."

The meeting of Alexandre Dumas and Marie Duplessis took place early in the autumn of 1844 and was followed by a short, bittersweet romance. But the dialogue is from a novel he published four years later, *La dame aux camélias*, or as it is known in English, *Camille*.

The Life of a Courtesan

Born in 1824, the same year as Dumas, Alphonsine Plessis was the daughter of a farmer who was rumored to have sold her to gypsies. Eventually she turned up in Paris as a dressmaker, calling herself Marie Duplessis. She did not have to work at dressmaking long, for her delicate beauty quickly attracted the attention of a restaurant owner, who set her up in an apartment. Her first lover was soon replaced by the duc de Guiche, a wealthy young man-about-town who had left the army for nominal studies at the École Polytechnique. As the duc's mistress, Marie Duplessis was the talk of Paris, besieged by would-be suitors. She was only 16 years old.

Daytime drives in her carriage, nightly visits to the opera or theater followed by brilliant parties and romantic rendezvous with men willing to contribute to her support — such was the life of a courtesan. Before long, Marie was being so well paid for her services that it was said she could spend 100,000 gold francs a year on a lavish lifestyle. Her clothes were beautiful, and she surrounded herself with flowers. But the scent of roses made Marie dizzy, and so she wore instead odorless camellias and filled her house with the

delicate flowers until, in the words of a critical observer, "She was imprisoned in a fortress of camellias." Marie had read and could discuss the many books in her library and was an accomplished pianist. Her only fault, she confessed, was lying. But this was gaily dismissed by her observation that "Lies keep the teeth white."

At the time she met Dumas, Marie was being kept by the elderly comte de Stackelberg because — as she lied to her new young suitor — she reminded him of a daughter who had died. The evenings devoted to Dumas, she disingenuously explained to Stackelberg, were spent with her friend Zélia. She apparently did not tell either of them about a third lover, the comte de Perregaux. But, her admirers agreed, Marie had a heart of gold. Yet she seemed driven to go from one man to another, "obsessed by a longing for peace, tranquility, and love," in the words of a critic of the day. Fashionably slender and pale, Marie was an ethereal beauty. She was also a sick woman,

Scarcely a woman of the streets, Marie Duplessis was a well-known theater- and operagoer — often seen in the elegant reception rooms of the Paris Opera (right). The dramatic contrast between her dark hair and pale skin was usually cited by her admirers as the principal attribute of her beauty.

haunted by the fear that her life would be short.

After only a few months of blissful romance that put him hugely in debt, Dumas began drifting away from Marie — though she offered herself to him as a friend if no longer a mistress. On August 30, 1845, he wrote to break off the affair: "I am neither rich enough to love you as I would wish, nor poor enough to be loved by you as you would. . . . You have too much heart not to understand the reasons for this letter, and too much intelligence not to forgive me."

Paying the Penalty

In the wake of her abandonment by Dumas, Marie Duplessis turned first to the composer Franz Liszt. Then, early in 1846, she accepted a surprising offer of marriage from the comte de Perregaux. They were wed in London on February 21.

Some suggested that the comte merely pitied Marie, for she was rapidly succumbing to consumption, or tuberculosis. They separated shortly after their return to Paris, and Marie was soon alone — no longer strong enough to participate in the social whirl, forced to sell off most of her possessions to ward off her creditors. She installed a small kneeling bench in her bedroom for private devotions and ultimately summoned a priest to administer the last rites of the Roman Catholic Church. The end came for the 23-year-old courtesan on February 3, 1847, as carnival revelers filled the streets outside the house on Boulevard de la Madeleine with their songs and laughter.

Meanwhile Dumas had traveled to Spain and Algeria with his father, also named Alexandre Dumas, the celebrated author of *The Three Musketeers* and *The Count of Monte-Cristo*. (The two are distinguished as Alexandre *père*, father, and Alexandre *fils*, son.) En route home, Dumas learned of Marie's death. Strolling past the house where they had first met and where they had held their romantic trysts, he saw an announcement of an auction to sell off the remaining contents of the dwelling. Not able to afford the more luxurious items, he was content with the purchase of a gold chain that Marie had once worn around her neck. The sale, incidentally, not only brought enough money to pay Marie's remaining debts, it also left funds for a small legacy to a favored niece in Normandy. The only restriction on the bequest was that the young woman never come to Paris with its temptations so fatal to her aunt.

Grief Inspires a Classic

In May, Alexandre Dumas took a hotel room, reread Marie's letters to him, and set about writing the novel that would make him famous.

Madame de Pompadour: At the King's Side

A patroness of literature and the arts, Madame de Pompadour gave her name to an upswept hairstyle.

As a courtesan, Marie Duplessis could not be received in the polite society of Paris. Only a century earlier, however, such women were accepted at the very highest levels — the most famous being Jeanne-Antoinette Poisson, for nearly 20 years the official mistress of King Louis XV of France.

When her father was forced to flee France because of a financial scandal, Jeanne-Antoinette was raised by a family friend and given an education in literature and the arts that would make her a suitable wife for a rich man. In 1741, at the age of 19, she was married to Charles-Guilliaume le Normant d'Étioles, who was wealthy enough to establish a salon in Paris where his young wife could entertain the leading intellectual and social luminaries of the day. Although the couple appeared to be happy, Jeanne-Antoinette had set her sights higher. At the age of nine, she had been told by a fortune-teller that she would one day be mistress to a king.

Not until February 1745, at a ball celebrating the marriage of the king's son, did she meet Louis XV, 11 years her senior. Almost immediately thereafter they became lovers, and before the year was over she was installed in her own apartments at the palace of Versailles. Her marriage was conveniently dissolved and the title marquise de Pompadour given her.

As official mistress of the king, Madame de Pompadour set the fashions of the day and was acknowledged even by the queen — though critics accused her of exercising too much political power. As the king turned to younger women, their romance ripened into friendship, and Louis appeared devastated by her death in 1764.

Among her lovers, Marie Duplessis counted not only the rich and titled of Paris society but also such intellectuals and artists as the composer Franz Liszt (right) and the writer Alexandre Dumas (above), who immortalized her in his novel and play La dame aux camélias.

In *La dame aux camélias*, a courtesan named Marguerite Gautier gives up the glittering life of Paris to go off to the country with a young lover, Armand Duval. Their idyll is interrupted by Armand's father, who calls upon Marguerite to express his doubts about her true feelings for his son. When bribes fail, he implores Marguerite to leave Armand for the good of the family name; he will be unable to find a suitable match for his daughter as long as the son is living with such an infamous woman. Sadly, she abandons her young lover, telling him that she prefers a rich nobleman in the city. But the return to a courtesan's frenzied life taxes the consumptive's strength, and she is soon on her deathbed. Too late, Armand learns of the deception, though he arrives in time to hold Marguerite in his arms as she sinks into unconsciousness.

Published in 1848, *La dame aux camélias* was an enormous success, and young Dumas was besieged with requests from professional dramatists to adapt it for the stage. Instead, he retired to a country house and feverishly wrote his own play. But when he suggested that his father produce it in the Paris theater of which he was principal author and director, the elder Dumas objected. The subject matter was not suitable for the stage; he would never dream of putting it on. The son pressed him to read the manuscript of the play. "Very good," the father said after reading the first act, at which point the younger Dumas was called away on business. When he returned, he found his father in tears. "My dear boy," he exclaimed, "I was entirely wrong! Your play shall be performed. . . ."

The play was first staged in 1852 and was an even greater success than the novel. But when Giuseppe Verdi transformed the story into his opera *La Traviata* the following year, Marie Duplessis gained a sort of immortality. Certainly, her notoriety stretched well into the 20th century, with no fewer than five motion pictures based on Dumas' story, the most admired of which is the 1936 *Camille* starring Greta Garbo.

The Quest for Eldorado

*An old man, most likely under torture, told the European
conquerors of Colombia's Chibcha people the story of the Golden Man.
It was enough to direct the oppressors eastward, but it also led
to centuries of searching for a mythical land.*

Hundreds of tribesmen had come from afar to gather on the shores of a deep, dark lake set in the crater of an extinct volcano some 9,000 feet above sea level. A hush fell over the assembled multitude as the solemn ceremony got under way. Attendants slowly undressed the ruler, rubbed clay over his naked body, and sprinkled him with gold dust until he became — as a Spanish chronicler wrote in 1636 — *El Dorado*, the Golden Man. They led him to a balsa-wood raft, where he was joined by four chieftains. Laden with offerings of gold and emeralds, the raft was pushed out into the lake.

Chants and instrumental music reverberated from the surrounding mountains as the ritual neared its climax. Then, silence. The chieftains threw the offerings into the water; the ruler plunged in afterward, emerging from the depths with his body cleansed of its golden sheath. The music resumed to reach a new crescendo.

The Spaniard who so vividly described the scene, Juan Rodriguez Freyle, had not actually witnessed the ceremony. Indeed, at the time he wrote, the ritual of *El Dorado* — if indeed it had

ever been held — was a thing of the past. Nearly a century earlier, Spanish conquistadores had converged on the highland area of what is now Colombia in search of its fabled treasure and had succeeded only in destroying the native culture of the Chibcha people.

Come the Conquerors

The relative ease with which Hernán Cortés had toppled the Aztec empire of Mexico in 1521 and Francisco Pizarro that of the Incas in Peru 12 years later whetted the appetites of others for conquest and plunder. In April 1536 some 900 Europeans and an unspecified number of native porters set out from the settlement at Santa Marta on the northwest coast of Colombia. Their plan was to follow the Magdalena River to its source, find a new route across the Andes Mountains to Peru, and, perhaps, discover another native empire ripe for the plucking. In command was the austere, pious deputy governor of the province, a 36-year-old attorney from Granada named Gonzalo Jiménez de Quesada.

For 11 months Jiménez de Quesada's men endured incredible difficulties, having to cut their way with machetes through the seemingly impenetrable vegetation and wade through swamps

Remote and hidden from the surrounding valleys, Colombia's Lake Guatavita (opposite) is situated at an altitude of 9,000 feet. The trench through which the Europeans hoped to drain its waters can be seen at far left. All such efforts to recover treasure from the lake proved futile. Superimposed on the photograph is a period engraving of the ritual of the Golden Man. The delicately wrought gold model above, found only in 1969, shows an outsized central figure and several attendants on a raft — perhaps an ancient depiction of the ceremony. Few such objets d'art survived Europe's plunder of the New World.

up to their waists. They were in constant peril of snakes, alligators, and jaguars. Unseen natives showered them with poisoned arrows. Many of the would-be conquistadores succumbed to hunger and fever, and the survivors subsisted on a diet of lizards and frogs. With fewer than 200 able-bodied men left under his command, Jiménez de Quesada was about to turn back when his tattered expedition stumbled onto the Cundinamarca Plateau. Before the astonished interlopers stretched carefully tended corn and potato fields, dotted with neat, obviously prosperous villages. Thin sheets of gold hung outside each doorway; twisting and tinkling in the wind, they created what the Europeans described as the "sweetest melody" they had ever heard. They had reached the homeland of the Chibchas.

Startled by the arrival of the strangers and awed by their horses, many of the natives abandoned their villages and withdrew from the dreaded encounter. Others greeted their visitors as gods descended from the heavens, offering them food, women, and the gold the Europeans seemed so intent on amassing. To the Chibchas gold was easily obtainable from other tribes by bartering the emeralds and salt they had in plentiful supply. For them it had little intrinsic value — though they prized it for the luster and malleability it offered their craftsmen who fashioned delicate ornaments for wearing and for decorating homes and shrines. But nothing seemed to satisfy the Europeans, who were soon taking by force what they were not offered in friendship. The Chibchas' clubs and javelins were no match for the Europeans' firearms. Within months Jiménez de Quesada had subdued the entire region with the loss of but a single man.

What the rapacious Europeans did not discover, however, was the source of the Chibcha gold supply. Then one day they learned from an old man, perhaps under torture, the secret of *El Dorado*, the Golden Man. Limitless treasure, he revealed, was to be found to the east, in the mountain fastness in which nestled Lake Guatavita. There, he told the credulous Europeans, a chieftain annually offered a portion of his vast wealth to the gods by throwing gold and emeralds into the lake waters. After having his naked body coated with gold dust, the chieftain dived in so that his gold could be added to the treasure. Whether a fact, a legend, or a ruse to direct the oppressors away from his country, the old man's story was eagerly accepted by the Europeans. *El Dorado* entered the annals of the conquest of the New World, being transformed in time from the story of a ruler's bizarre ritual to a goal of count-

The proud conquistador Gonzalo Jiménez de Quesada easily subdued the Chibcha population of perhaps 1 million with fewer than 200 men. Yet he never found the great riches he sought and had to settle for an honorary military title.

By coincidence, three treasure seekers met near the newly founded Santa Fé de Bogotá (today, the capital of Colombia) early in 1539. Their separate routes to the plateau are traced on the map above.

less treasure seekers: Eldorado, the land of unbelievable riches that was always just beyond the next mountain or across the next river.

Three Minds, One Thought

Before leading his men in search of the Golden Man, Jiménez de Quesada decided that he must return to Santa Marta to confirm his governorship of the highland territory he had subdued and

renamed New Granada. His departure was cut short, however, when news reached him in February 1539 that another expedition of Europeans was approaching his newly established capital, Santa Fé de Bogotá, from the northeast.

The newcomers proved to be a band of some 160 men led by a German named Nikolaus Federmann, acting on behalf of the commercial firm of Welser in Augsburg. In return for Welser's financial support of his election as Holy Roman Emperor, King Charles I of Spain had granted the German company the province of Venezuela. Also seeking another native empire to conquer, Federmann had left the coastal settlement at Coro several months after Jiménez de Quesada had departed from Santa Marta. For more than two years he had been seeking a way through the mountains to the Cundinamarca Plateau. Somewhat warily welcoming the exhausted, half-starved, and nearly naked strangers, Jiménez de Quesada offered them food and clothing and pondered how they might be used for his assault on the land of Eldorado.

He did not have long to think, for Jiménez de Quesada soon learned that a third expedition was approaching Santa Fé de Bogotá — this one from the southwest. It was led by Sebastián de Belalcázar, a deputy of Pizarro's in the conquest of Peru.

Having pursued the remnants of the Inca army north to Ecuador, where he founded Quito, Belalcázar had also learned of fabled riches to be seized in the interior. About the time Jiménez de Quesada left Santa Marta, Belalcázar set out from Quito for the long march north. He arrived at Santa Fé de Bogotá with a sturdy band of well-clad and well-armed Europeans, many mounted on fine horses. He also had a large force of native retainers, a silver dinner service, and 300 pigs — a welcome addition to their diet for the meat-starved Europeans who had reached the plateau earlier. By the most curious of coincidences, each of the three expeditions numbered exactly 166 men at the time they linked forces.

Disagreeing as to who had priority in the search for a new native empire to conquer, the three leaders simultaneously departed for Spain to present their rival claims at court. His employers having lost Venezuela to a Spanish adventurer, Federmann was out of contention and died in obscurity. Belalcázar was given command of one of the cities he had founded en route to Sante Fé de Bogotá, but he seems to have ended his career in disgrace. Denied the governorship, Jiménez de Quesada had to content himself with the honorary military title marshal of New Grenada. Although he lived to the age of 80 and never gave up on his dream of finding the land of the Golden Man, his days of glory were behind him.

Lake Guatavita Keeps Its Secrets

Even as the three rival claimants were arguing their cases before the king in Spain, the search for Eldorado was under way. Hernán Perez de Quesada, a brother of the conqueror of New Grenada, was the first to try to recover the treasure thought to lie at the bottom of Lake Guatavita. During the dry season of 1540 he set his men to bailing out the lake's waters with gourds. After three months of patient work, they actually succeeded in lowering the water level by about 10 feet. Between 3,000 and 4,000 tiny gold pieces were retrieved near the receding shoreline, but they never got to the center of the lake where, presumably, the real hoard was to be found.

Four decades later an even more sensational attempt was made to drain the lake. A wealthy merchant from Bogotá employed thousands of natives to dig a trench through one of the surrounding hills. When it was completed, the waters poured out of the lake, this time lowering the level by more than 60 feet. An emerald the size of an egg and numerous gold trinkets were found, but the rewards were scarcely worth the effort. Another treasure hunter had a tunnel dug to carry away the waters, but he had to abandon his plan when it collapsed, killing most of his workers.

The story of *El Dorado* would not die and even

Four Centuries Later, a New Mania

The Europeans' insatiable appetite for gold brought about the annihilation of New World native cultures like that of the Chibchas. Four centuries later the people of Colombia are faced with an equally serious threat: almost certain death for opposition to the powerful drug cartels of Medellín and Cali.

Fortune magazine called the illicit trade in drugs "a huge, multinational commodity business with a fast-moving top management, a widespread distribution network, and price-insensitive customers." Andean coca plants tended by Peruvian and Bolivian peasants provide the world's cocaine — to which an estimated 6 million Americans are addicted, particularly in its lower-costing, smokable version, crack.

The drug barons of Colombia finance the cultivation of coca

Because of its strength and cost, white-powdered cocaine is carefully measured out for sniffing through small hollow reeds.

plants, import a gooey base processed from the leaves, and at their secret laboratories mix it with ether and acetone to produce pure cocaine. The white powder, usually packed in one-kilogram plastic bags, is flown illegally to the United States and other destinations, where a network of distributors gets it out on the streets.

Government officials in Latin America's oldest democracy seem powerless to stop the traffic — particularly in view of the drug barons' offer of *plomo o plata* ("lead or silver"), which means a bullet in the head or a bribe. An estimated 350 to 450 metric tons of cocaine are smuggled out of Colombia annually, bringing revenues of $4 billion and making cocaine the country's biggest export. Far from being regarded as a common criminal, a founder of one cartel was elected an alternate member of the Colombian legislature in 1982 and was able to lobby there against laws that would allow extradition of suspected drug traffickers to the United States for prosecution.

caught the fancy of the German naturalist Alexander von Humboldt, who visited Colombia during the course of a scientific expedition early in the 19th century. Although his interest in the treasure was merely theoretical, he calculated that gold worth $300 million might lie beneath Lake Guatavita's waters. He reached this figure by speculating that 1,000 pilgrims, each sacrificing five gold objects, would have participated in the annual ritual during the course of a century.

A final attempt to drain the lake was made in 1912, when British treasure seekers used giant pumps to do the job. Although they removed most of the water, the soft mud beneath quickly mired those who ventured out into it. By the next day the mud had dried to a consistency as impenetrable as concrete. For their expenditure of $160,000, the British recovered $10,000 worth of gold objects. An end was put to all such futile efforts to reach the bottom of Lake Guatavita when the Colombian government declared the lake a national historic site in 1965.

The Search Redirected

In 1541, five years after Belalcázar marched out of Quito for Colombia, Gonzalo Pizarro — a brother of the conqueror of Peru — left the city in search of Eldorado, whose treasure he had heard included not only gold but the valuable spice cinnamon. He was shortly joined by a soldier of fortune named Francisco de Orellana. After their expedition crossed the Andes Mountains and descended into the tropical forests to the east, the two parted company. Pizarro eventually returned to Quito, but Orellana followed a wide, sluggish river all the way to the Atlantic Ocean. En route, he came across a tribe whose women proved to be better archers than its men. Linking them to the Greek legend of warrior women, he called his river the Amazon.

Other Spanish adventurers followed in the wake of Pizarro and Orellana, extending their quest for the Golden Man down both the Amazon and the Orinoco rivers. Among the most persistent of these seekers was Antonio de Berrío, governor of a vast tract of land between the two rivers. Like those who had gone before him, Berrío was convinced that the Golden Man could be found in a mountaintop lake. But it was not Lake Guatavita but rather one in the mountains of Guiana to which — he claimed — the defeated Incas had fled and where they had founded a fabulous new city, Manoa, whose very streets were said to be paved with gold.

Between 1584 and 1595, Berrío led three expeditions to Guiana. On the third he proceeded to the island of Trinidad, where he encountered Sir Walter Raleigh, who was attempting to restore his somewhat tarnished reputation as a colonizer. During a drinking bout the Englishman pried the secret of *El Dorado* from Berrío, temporarily imprisoned his confidant, and returned home to write rapturously of Manoa and Eldorado, as he called the Golden Man's kingdom. Believing, in Raleigh's case, did not require seeing. Eldorado's wealth, he insisted, was greater than Peru's. Indeed, he wrote, "for the greatnes, for the riches, and for the excellent seate, it [Manoa] farre exceedeth any of the world. . . ." Raleigh's book about Guiana did little to rouse interest in the area, and his own attempts to find Eldorado, not surprisingly, ended in failure.

The Tale That Would Not Die

For nearly four centuries the tale of the Golden Man — probably wrenched from a desperate native who only wanted the European conquerors to move on — has teased and tantalized treasure seekers. None of these adventurers, of course, ever found a lake whose bottom was lined with gold or a city whose streets were paved with it. The gold they did find was often in the shape of curiously wrought objects for personal adornment and interior decoration. Because these trinkets did not meet European standards of artistic merit, they were mostly melted down and sent home as gold bullion. Those relatively few objects that survived are today prized museum pieces.

In their frantic crisscrossing of South America's mountains, jungles, and savannas, European adventurers never satisfied their appetite for easily gained riches. But almost accidentally they explored and mapped an entire continent. They were driven by a greed for gold, an intoxicant that enabled them to endure the incredible hardships imposed by an unfamiliar terrain, a harsh climate, and hostile natives.

As for the natives, it was their tragedy to possess a metal that was so highly valued by Europeans. To the peoples of the pre-Columbian New World, gold was a thing of beauty to adorn person, home, and shrine. When the strangers from across the seas came, the natives simply could not understand why the metal was so desirable. It could not keep out the cold as did a blanket; it could not fill the stomach as did corn; it could not bring pleasure as did tobacco or strong drink. Yet gold is what the Europeans wanted above all else. And that is why the unwanted visitors so readily believed in *El Dorado*, the Golden Man, who — if he ever existed — had disappeared long before they went looking for him.

Father of Swiss Freedom?

Twice the renowned marksman took aim with his crossbow, and twice his arrow hit the mark. The first shot saved his life; the second launched the Swiss wars of independence — or so the story was told and widely accepted for centuries.

"Look, father!" the young boy calls. "There is a hat on top of that pole." Unimpressed, the man replies, "What has that hat to do with us? Come on!" A child's innocent question; a father's indifferent response. And yet, history was about to be made.

The scene is the marketplace of Altdorf in Canton Uri, one of the three forest cantons, or states, of the Swiss heartland. It is the early 1300's; Uri, Schwyz, and Unterwalden have only recently forged an alliance to settle disagreements among themselves by arbitration and not by warfare and to unite for mutual defense against outsiders. For centuries the cantons have been ruled by the distant Holy Roman emperors, independence being but a dream of the proud peasants who toil in nearly inaccessible mountain valleys.

William Tell is such a lover of freedom, and it is he on this day who scorns the hat placed on a pole by Hermann Gessler, the autocratic governor sent from Vienna. When he is away, Gessler has decreed, the hat represents his authority. All passersby must pause to salute it. Tell's casual disrespect is observed by a mercenary named Friesshart, who stops him with a leveled pike. "Halt there!" he cries. "I charge you in the name of the emperor." Threatened with

In a detail from the oldest-known representation of the William Tell legend, Walter courageously faces his father's arrow.

arrest, Tell is momentarily at a loss. Walter, his son, runs for help and soon returns with a number of other peasants who share his father's indignation at the outrageous demand of the governor. As the argument between Tell and Friesshart is about to erupt into violence, a figure on horseback appears. "Make way for the governor!" comes a shout.

Gessler demands to know what has happened and is displeased with Friesshart's report. He knows Tell by reputation as a master marksman with bow and arrow, a skill young Walter proudly confirms: "My father can shoot an apple from a tree at a hundred yards." A cruel smile flashes across the oppressor's face. In punishment for his disrespect to the hat, Tell is ordered to demonstrate his prowess — by shooting an apple not from a tree but from atop Walter's head. A horrified hush falls over the crowd, but Tell's pleas for mercy are ignored by Gessler. "Shoot, or die!" Gessler thunders. "You and the boy."

Slowly regaining his composure, Tell prepares for the dreadful ordeal. Walter, in supreme trust of his father, scorns a blindfold. But after he has placed the arrow in his crossbow and begun to take aim, Tell pauses, lowers the weapon, removes a second arrow from his quiver, and puts it in his belt. Only then does he perform the unpleasant task. The arrow splits the apple on Walter's head neatly in half; the boy runs to his father, who picks him up and tenderly presses him to his chest. Though complimenting the marksman, Gessler has guessed why he readied the second arrow. Tell confirms the governor's suspicion: "If my first arrow had my dear child struck, the second arrow I had aimed at you. And, be assured, I should not then have missed."

Igniting an Insurrection

For his insolence, William Tell is taken into custody by the governor. "I'll have you carried hence and safely penned where neither sun nor moon shall reach your eyes," Gessler thunders. "Thus from your arrows I'll be free."

But as the prisoner is being transported by boat across Lake Lucerne, a gale turns the waters into

Tourists are shown this sunken road near Küssnacht as the defile in which the tyrannical Gessler was ambushed by William Tell — an assassination that is alleged to have touched off the Swiss wars of independence early in the 14th century.

First Blow for Independence

It took more than an oath of confederation on the meadow at Rütli in 1291 for the Swiss to win their independence from Hapsburg domination. Indeed, this daring act of defiance against the despised Austrians had little immediate effect on relations between the proud mountain folk and their distant overlords. Apart from minor protests and desultory raids on Hapsburg castles, there was little evidence of a revolt. If the Austrians reacted at all, it was with a show of indifference. This changed, however, in January 1314 when a troop of Schwyz rebels raided the Einsiedeln abbey, a church property under the protection of the Hapsburgs. In retaliation, Frederick the Fair, duke of Austria and king of Germany, sent his brother Leopold to punish the troublemakers. Coincidentally, it gave Frederick the opportunity he needed to assert his claim to the imperial title over that of Louis IV of Bavaria, who was being supported by the people of the Swiss cantons.

Some 2,000 strong, the Austrians confidently marched up to Morgarten Pass on the morning of November 15, 1315. As the mountain slopes closed in on them, the invaders were gradually forced into a single column. Hidden above, the mountaineers of Schwyz waited until the enemy was at its most vulnerable, then loosed an avalanche of boulders that crushed men and horses alike. Unable to move in their heavy armor, the Austrians were easy prey to Schwyz pikemen.

It took three wars with the Austrians during the course of the next 73 years for the Swiss to establish their independence. But the victory at Morgarten Pass was the first convincing demonstration of Swiss arms, a display of ingenuity, discipline, and preparedness that, in time, won for Swiss soldiers the reputation of being Europe's finest fighters. No less of an authority than Napoleon said that "The best troops — those in whom you can have the most confidence — are the Swiss." Since 1515 the Swiss army has been able to defend and enforce the country's strict neutrality with but few challenges.

raging whirlpools. Recalling that Tell is also an experienced coxswain, the oarsmen beg Gessler to untie the ropes that bind him so that he can take charge of the helm. Tell skillfully steers the boat toward shore and, as it passes a rocky ledge, jumps to his freedom.

Now a fugitive, Tell plots his revenge, vowing to put an end to Gessler's capricious cruelty. Knowing the route that the governor must take to his castle, the marksman stations himself behind brushwood overlooking a depressed road through the forest. "He has no choice but through this sunken way to come to Küssnacht," mutters Tell. " 'Tis here I'll do it."

Once more, Tell's arrow finds its target. Gessler falls to the ground, finding time before he dies only to croak out the assassin's name. "You know the marksman, you need not seek another," Tell cries in glee from atop a rock. "Free are the homesteads, innocence is safe, and you will do the country no more harm." It is the opening shot in the wars for Swiss independence.

History or Drama?

The apple shot from a son's head, the escape of a prisoner during a storm on the waters, the assassination of a tyrant — such is the plot of *William Tell*, a verse drama by Friedrich von Schiller. It was first performed in 1804, some 500 years after the events it includes are supposed to have taken place. But Schiller was not merely inventing a tale to make a thrilling stage presentation. He based his play on narratives dating back to the late 1400's that, in turn, seem to have been based on earlier oral traditions.

The first reference in print to William Tell is in a ballad published in 1477, *Song of the Origin of the Confederation*. Four of its 29 stanzas celebrating the achievement of Swiss unity and independence in the previous century deal with the story of the marksman forced to shoot an apple from his son's head. There is no mention of a governor named Gessler, a hat placed on a pole, Tell's escape from captivity, or the assassination at Küssnacht. Such details are found in another work of approximately the same date.

Sometime between 1467 and 1474 an anonymous notary at Sarnen in Canton Unterwalden gathered a number of historical stories apparently handed down by word of mouth into a collection known as *The White Book* because of the color of its parchment binding. In this version Gessler is named, though identified as a bailiff. He demands respect for his hat, forces a marksman to shoot an apple from his son's head for failure to make obeisance to it, arrests him for the threat of the second arrow, and is assassinated by the escaped prisoner. However, the marksman — called Thall not Tell — is not linked to the rebellion leading to Swiss independence.

A Long Literary Tradition

A leading scholar of early Swiss history asked how Tell, or Thall, came to feature so prominently in two works published more than a century and a half after the outbreak of the Swiss insur-

According to tradition, delegates from the three forest cantons — Uri, Schwyz, and Unterwalden — met on the Rütli, a high meadow near Lake Urn to swear their oath of confederation in 1291. The dramatist Friedrich von Schiller included the scene in his play William Tell.

rection. Earlier historians of the movement made no mention of such a hero. The answer, he suggested, lay beyond the borders of Switzerland.

Until the end of the Middle Ages an ordeal was generally accepted throughout Europe as the means of establishing guilt or innocence. If guilty, the accused would perish; if innocent, he would survive the ordeal. God would so will it to happen, and men would be expected to respect his verdict. The theme of a marksman put to the test of shooting an apple from his child's head is found in the oral traditions of countries throughout Europe, including Germany, Denmark, Norway, and Iceland. The old English ballad of William of Cloudesly is remarkably similar to the 1477 *Song of the Origin of the Confederation*:

I have a sonne is seven yere olde;
He is to me full deare;
I will hym tye to a stake,
All shall see that be here;
And lay an apple upon hys head
And go syxe score paces huym fro,
And I my selfe, with a brodc arrow,
Shall cleve the apple in two.

Cloudesly's king, like Tell's governor, expresses the fear that the marksman's arrow will in time be turned on him.

The work to which the tale of the Swiss William Tell bears the strongest resemblance, however, is *Gesta Danorum*, a 12th-century Danish history by one Saxo Grammaticus. During a drinking bout the hero, Toko, or Tiki, boasts of his skill at archery — for which the cruel king Harald Bluetooth puts him to the test of shooting an apple from his son's head. As does Tell, Toko reserves a second arrow for the tyrant in case he misses. In a subsequent rebellion the marksman slays the king in a forest ambush. Whoever first wrote about William Tell may well have had Toko in mind as a model for the Swiss master marksman who defied a cruel oppressor.

Chipping Away at a Legend

As early as the 16th century the story of William Tell fell under suspicion. A chronicler of Canton Saint Gall noted that the three forest cantons "tell strange things in regard to their age and origin. . . . I suspect that much is fabled, and some again may not be likened to the truth." François Guilliman included William Tell in his 1607 history *De Rebus Helvetiorum*, even embellishing the tale with some details of his own. But in a letter to a friend, he surprisingly confessed that, after mature reflection, he had reached the conclusion that it was but a fable — invented to nourish hatred of the Austrians.

In 1760 a Swiss pastor named Uriel Freudenberg published a pamphlet linking William Tell to the Danish legendary hero; the officials of Uri ordered the blasphemous work publicly burned. A rebuttal in defense of Tell was published by a writer of Lucerne, and two noted historians of the day issued declarations in support of the tradition — though one of them privately expressed his reservations about the authenticity of the beloved tale. In composing his drama, Schiller had to confess that he was taking literary license in making William Tell the central figure in the struggle for Swiss independence.

The final blow to the legend was struck by the

A Life for the Revolution

Ernesto "Che" Guevara, who helped bring Fidel Castro's communist revolution to Cuba in 1959, had a vision of Latin America not as a collection of separate nations but rather as a single cultural and economic entity — resembling, in a way, the confederation of Swiss cantons. He gave his life for that dream.

Born in Argentina on June 14, 1928, and educated there as a surgeon, Guevara left his homeland in 1953 to escape military service. Observing political and economic conditions in the Latin American countries he visited, he became committed to Marxism and developed an anti-American bias. When the leftist regime of Jacobo Arbenz Guzmán was overthrown in Guatemala — reputedly with the assistance of the U.S. Central Intelligence Agency — Guevara took part in an abortive resistance move-

As a spokesman for Fidel Castro's communist revolution in Cuba and a critic of the United States, Che Guevara became a left-wing hero.

ment, then fled to Mexico where he met the brothers Fidel and Raul Castro. He joined their invasion of Cuba in December 1956 and was with them when they overthrew the right-wing dictatorship of Fulgencio Batista two years later. Naturalized a Cuban citizen and named by Castro to his government's top economic post, he raged against American imperialism and ignored U.S. protests against the expropriation of American property by Castro's communists. In 1962, after visiting the Soviet Union, he began speaking of exporting Cuba's revolution.

By the spring of 1965 Guevara had dropped out of sight and was later reported organizing guerrilla fighters in the Congo's civil war. In October 1967 he was captured while fighting with Bolivian revolutionaries and summarily executed by the Bolivian army.

historian Joseph Eutych Kopp in three scholarly works published between 1835 and 1853. After thoroughly searching the archives of the three forest cantons, he reached the conclusion that William Tell had never existed. The public outcry was about what could be expected if an American historian tried to prove that George Washington was only a legendary figure. Nonetheless, in time, most Swiss came to accept the fact that there had been no William Tell and that there was no one heroic father of Swiss independence. The country's best-loved story, unfortunately, had no basis in fact.

The Emergence of Switzerland

Though lacking a central heroic figure, the Swiss struggle for independence is not without drama. The pact signed in 1291 by Uri, Schwyz, and Unterwalden was not a declaration of independence — though the three forest cantons were restive under the rule of the Holy Roman emperors. They particularly resented the fact that their lands were treated as family property by the ruling Hapsburgs.

Early in 1314 Duke Leopold of Hapsburg invaded the cantons, determined to assert his family's authority over the defiant mountaineers. An inferior force of Schwyz foot soldiers, joined by some Uri confederates, trapped the Austrians in a mountain pass, hurled boulders down at them, and decisively defeated them at the Battle of Morgarten on November 15, 1315. In recognition of the role played by Canton Schwyz at Morgarten the confederation came to be known as Schweiz (in German), Suisse (in French), Svizzera (in Italian), or Switzerland (in English).

In the wake of this victory the three forest cantons were joined by other breakaway provinces until, by 1353, there were eight members of the confederation, including the cities of Lucerne, Zurich, and Bern. The Hapsburgs again intervened, hoping to check the tide of Swiss independence, but they were again defeated in two critical battles. In 1394 the Austrians signed a 20-year truce with the confederation that, in effect, acknowledged Swiss independence.

The Immortal Tell

Like all other peoples, the Swiss need their heroes, and the legendary William Tell is remembered at numerous locations throughout the country. Visitors can see the rocky ledge on Lake Lucerne to which he leaped to freedom, the sunken road near Küssnacht where he ambushed Gessler, and, of course, the marketplace at Altdorf where he shot the apple from Walter's head.

Bürglen in Canton Uri claims to be the birthplace of William Tell. It raised this monument to its famous son — appropriately set against a beautiful mountain backdrop.

As late as 1569, two and a half centuries after the alleged trial by ordeal, a lime tree stood in Altdorf's marketplace. According to tradition, Walter had faced his father from beneath its branches. In reality, it marked the place where judicial inquiries were held. Legal documents of the time carried the notation that they were signed "under the lime tree at Altdorf." When the tree withered, died, and was cut down, a fountain was erected on the spot.

As for the hat on a pole, it seems to have been unique to the Swiss version of a trial by ordeal. Since a number of Swiss families show a hat in their coat of arms, a modern historian speculates that a hat somehow symbolized authority. Putting a hat on a post — far from being the whim of a tyrant — was perhaps merely the way in which an official such as a mayor announced his presence at a public gathering.

A Ride into History

The pious wife of the earl of Mercia was celebrated for her patronage of several monasteries during the middle of the 11th century. Ironically, she is remembered today only for a notorious ride that she is highly unlikely to have made.

Along with most of the subjects of Edward the Confessor, the last Anglo-Saxon king of England, the people of Coventry were suffering from the burden of high taxes. But their pleas for relief went unheeded by their overlord Leofric, the powerful earl of Mercia, who had his own obligations to meet and who was not above passing them on to the citizenry. Instead of mercy, Coventry's inhabitants received notice of a tax increase. To meet it they would have to impoverish themselves.

Into this tense situation stepped Leofric's deeply religious wife, Godgifu, "gift of God." Filled with compassion for the desperate people of Coventry, she went before her husband — as she had on earlier occasions — to ask that he suspend the onerous levies. Perhaps angered at her persistence, and wishing to put an end to her tiresome requests, the earl made an outlandish proposal. "Mount your horse naked," he said to his wife, "and pass through the market of the town, from one end to the other, when the people are assembled." On her return from the ride, he promised, Godgifu would be granted her wish. The townspeople would be spared the burdensome new taxes.

Leofric expected his wife to withdraw in shock and embarrassment. Instead, to his astonishment, she agreed. On the next morning, completely unclothed but with her body concealed by her flowing hair, Godgifu mounted a charger and rode through the marketplace. Leofric had no alternative but to grant her wish and lift the taxes. As Lady Godiva, Godgifu rode into the pages of history — or so it came to be believed.

A Patroness Achieves Fame

About the year 1028 a wealthy widow named Godgifu or Godiva (there are 17 different spellings of her name), believing herself on her deathbed, bequeathed her considerable property to the monastery at Ely. But she recovered and a decade or so later remarried, soon interesting her new husband, the earl of Mercia, in her charitable donations. In 1043 the earl and his lady founded a Benedictine monastery at Coventry, one of the towns within his domain. On October 4 the church was dedicated to St. Peter, St. Osburg, All Saints, and the Virgin Mary, to whom Godiva was particularly devoted. Her later gifts of gold and gems made the monastery chapel one of the richest in England. After the earl's death Lady Godiva continued her patronage of the church, contributing to the support of at least half a dozen more monasteries.

Yet, it is not for such good works that the countess is remembered, but rather for the notorious ride through Coventry in the nude. The story first appears in the *Flores Historiarum* of Roger of Wendover, a historian who lived some two centuries after Lady Godiva's time. He seems to have based his account on the work of an earlier but now lost chronicle. Subsequent writers steadily embellished the piquant tale.

In one version, Lady Godiva's body is hidden not by her flowing locks but by a God-granted cloak of invisibility. In another, she orders Coventry's inhabitants to remain indoors behind shuttered windows on the morning of the ride — thus sparing herself the rude stares of the common folk. Early in the 18th century another character was added to the narrative. A tailor named Tom, it was claimed, disobeyed her command. When he peeked through a crack in the shutter of his window, Tom was miraculously struck blind. The justly punished voyeur was the original "peeping Tom."

As for Leofric's taxes, an early ballad includes a line stating that the humbled earl rewarded his wife's act of compassion by lifting all tolls on

A lissome, almost demure Lady Godiva appears in this 1898 painting by John Collier. Historians, who find no contemporary evidence for the countess's infamous ride, quibble with those depictions of the alleged event that show the heroine riding side-saddle, an equestrian style unknown in her day.

Coventry except those for keeping horses. As late as the 17th century, the town was still boasting of such a tax-exempt status.

Remembering Lady Godiva

On May 31, 1678, Coventry staged its first reenactment of Lady Godiva's ride — the countess's part being taken by a boy. The procession was repeated at periodic intervals until 1907, by which time the garb or lack of it by the person portraying Lady Godiva became a subject of civic contention. Statues of the famous equestrienne and of the archetypal "peeping Tom" still adorn the English city.

Within the past century two European dramatists have incorporated the Lady Godiva legend into their plays. In *Monna Vanna*, Maurice Maeterlinck, the Belgian winner of the Nobel Prize for literature in 1911, transformed Lady Godiva into an Italian noblewoman. To save her city of Pisa from starvation, she submits to the demands of a lustful enemy general and appears at his camp naked under her cloak. The Austrian playwright Arthur Schnitzler created another Godiva-like character in the heroine of his play *Fräulein Else*. Ordered to appear in the nude before the man who has the power to save her father,

she is incapable of resolving the conflict between modesty and self-sacrifice for a worthy cause. Else chooses death by suicide.

As recently as 1966, Lady Godiva made headline news of a wildly improbable nature. That year's edition of *Debrett's Peerage*, the definitive guide to who's who among Britain's aristocracy, took a new look at the lineage of Queen Elizabeth II. The queen, long known to count William the Conqueror among her ancestors, was now said also to be 31st in descent from Harold, the monarch William displaced.

Following her father's defeat and death at the Battle of Hastings on October 14, 1066, the princess Gytha reportedly fled to the Continent, where she met and married Volodymyr Monomakh, grand prince of Kiev. Their progeny can be traced through several European royal families. One of their descendants returned to England in the time of Edward II, the Plantagenet king brutally murdered in prison in 1327. Diligent readers of *Debrett's Peerage* were quick to note the ancestry of Gytha: Her great-great grandfather was none other than Leofric, the oppressive earl who is supposed to have sent his pious wife on a nude ride through the streets of Coventry. Queen Elizabeth can thus claim descent from Lady Godiva.

Fiction's Famous Castaway

*Robinson Crusoe has captured the imagination of millions
of readers around the world for almost three centuries. Few know that
the remarkable adventurer had counterparts in real life.*

*I*t is one of the most astonishing moments in world literature. One day about noon, as Robinson Crusoe strolls around the deserted island where he has lived alone for more than two decades, he suddenly spots a naked footprint in the sand. "I stood like one thunderstruck," writes the hero of Daniel Defoe's 1719 novel. "Nor is it possible to describe how many various shapes affrighted imagination represented things to me in, how many wild ideas were found every moment in my fancy, and what strange, unaccountable whimsies came into my thoughts."

This shock, which occurs about halfway through the story, will lead to more adventure, for the lone castaway will rescue a native from a band of cannibals and dub him "Man Friday," for the day of the week on which they met. But Crusoe has already encountered his greatest challenge at that point. Son of a successful English businessman, the young hero was seduced by the romance of the sea. Before his island adventure, he had nearly lost his life in a great storm, had been captured by Turkish pirates and sold into slavery, had escaped to Brazil where he bought a

*Scenes from an island life: Robinson Crusoe rescues supplies from his shipwrecked vessel,
discovers a cannibal encampment, and meets Friday.*

plantation, and had finally entered into the African slave trade. It was on a slave-trading trip that his ship had been wrecked upon a reef near the mouth of South America's Orinoco River. Everyone else was lost, but Crusoe was washed ashore on an apparently uninhabited island.

True to the Puritan Ethic

Until Defoe no author had ever dared to write a story about one man's solitude, but Crusoe's ordeal was intended as a celebration of British virtues. Rather than despair, Crusoe immediately sets about "civilizing" the wilderness, always ready to work hard and find a practical solution. Not only does he grow grains, construct furniture, and tame the wild goats and parrots, he also learns to make pottery. More important, he never loses his Christian faith, thanking God every morning and evening for saving him from drowning. A staunch middle-class Protestant himself, Defoe has his hero face the emptiness of his lonely life by asking, "What am I and all the other creatures, wild and tame, human and brutal? Whence are we?" Crusoe answers his own questions by recognizing that all of creation expresses God's will and that submission to Providence will lead to happiness in this life.

Self-reliant but true to the Puritan ethic, Defoe's hero foreshadowed political events in the 18th century, as the middle class grew larger, more comfortable, and more powerful. In a sense, Crusoe was a forerunner of the ideal democrat, believing both in himself and in the importance of distinguishing right from wrong.

But it is the story that readers cherish, filled as it is with naturalistic details that make it seem so convincingly real. Even though Defoe hinted that his novel was based upon his own experiences, he was thinking symbolically. His trials and tribulations had all occurred not on a faraway and uninhabited island, but rather on the large and well-populated island of England, where he spent a lifetime dodging creditors and suffering the attacks of political adversaries. As he recalled in a witty couplet:

No man has tasted differing fortunes more,
And thirteen times I have been rich and poor.

His many failures included the loss of a brick-and-tile factory, a business that may have inspired his hero's discovery of how to make ceramic ware on a deserted island. Three times, for political offenses, Defoe was sentenced to the pillory, but his spunky "Hymn to the Pillory" got the mob on his side. As they drank toasts to him, the people happily garlanded the instrument of punishment with flower blossoms. A highly productive journalist, essayist, and pamphleteer who produced 500 works, he did not turn to fiction until he was 59 years old.

Saved by a Sailor's Chest

Defoe's landmark novel was based to some extent on the actual adventures of a contemporary, Alexander Selkirk, whose dramatic story of survival had been chronicled in *A Cruising Voyage Round the World* by Woodes Rogers.

Selkirk, seventh son of a Scottish shoemaker, had run away to sea rather than defend himself against a charge of indecent behavior in church. Late in 1704 he was sailing in a fleet under the command of William Dampier. For unknown reasons Selkirk became so angry with the captain of his ship that he demanded to be put ashore on a deserted isle in the Juan Fernández group off the coast of Chile. Before the ship left, he changed his mind and begged to be taken back aboard, but his superior refused.

For the next four years the abandoned Scot survived alone, sustained only by the few necessities packed in a lowly seaman's chest. These included clothing, a little food, and a pound of tobacco, along with a musket, a kettle, an ax, and a knife. Perhaps to his frustration, he also had navigation instruments and books on the subject. According to his own account, however, it was the Bible that became the special treasure of his unrelieved solitude. Crusoe, similarly, had such basic supplies, having been able to make a raft to go out to his wrecked ship and retrieve a number of items, including three Bibles. He read the Scriptures with great care for the remainder of his stay.

As would Crusoe, Selkirk found fresh water burbling from the ground in natural springs and discovered wild goats. In addition, there were pigs and chickens to supplement his diet of fish and exotic fruits. Though oppressed by the loneliness of his exile, the resourceful adventurer contrived to sew new clothes from goat skins, using an old nail as the needle. Taking thread from worn socks and a piece of linen, he fashioned a new shirt. And, much like his fictional counterpart, Selkirk built wooden buildings for sleeping and cooking and learned how to make fire by rubbing blocks of pine wood against each other.

Early in 1709 he was rescued by Rogers, who was leading a South Seas expedition with Dampier as his navigator. Rogers made Selkirk his mate and later put him in command of a seized ship, *The Increase*. The mettlesome Scot died at sea in 1721, but before then — whenever he spent time back in his native land — his friends found him greatly changed. It was said that he had a cave dug so that he could spend long hours in solitary meditation, apparently regretting the loss of his isolated life on the tiny Pacific island.

Lost in the Rush

Coincidentally, Dampier himself had written about yet another castaway in his book *A New Voyage Round the World,* published in 1697. While he was privateering early in the previous decade around the same group of islands where Selkirk later lived, he sent some of his sailors ashore to seek out fresh water and food. Unexpectedly, a hostile Spanish frigate appeared on the horizon, heading ominously toward the English vessel. Dampier's men rushed back on board, and he speedily sailed off.

In the confusion and alarm, everyone apparently forgot about a loyal Indian, a member of the Central American Miskito tribe, who had ventured farther into the interior to hunt for goat meat. Forced to rely upon only the basic tools he had with him, the unfortunate native survived by his wits. One source of material was his rifle. After making fire with a flintstone and a small fragment of iron, he heated the barrel of his weapon so that he could more easily break it into small parts. With these he fashioned harpoons, fish hooks, spear tips, and a saw. From the skin of seals he made fishing lines and thongs.

As would both Selkirk and the fictional Crusoe, this equally energetic castaway made himself a hut and hunted goats, using the skins to cover his little home and to make simple clothes. It was three years before Dampier was able to return and rescue his crewman.

Imprisoned in Paradise

Yet another real-life source for Defoe's novel may have been the published recollections of Londoner Robert Knox, who was held against his will for 20 years in the Kandyan kingdom of Ceylon (present-day Sri Lanka). The exotic national customs and the natural beauty of the mountains and forests of 100-foot-high doon trees were fascinating to readers of Knox's 1681 account, *An Historical Relation of the Island of Ceylon.*

In 1659, when he was 19, Knox, his father, and their fellow merchant seamen were captured by the Ceylonese. But their imprisonment was strangely gentle. Never confined, they could travel freely, engage in trade, and build their own

The island of Más a Tierra is part of the Juan Fernández group 400 miles off the coast of Chile. Early in the 18th century a Scottish sailor named Alexander Selkirk was marooned there for several years — an adventure that may have inspired Daniel Defoe to write Robinson Crusoe. *In 1966 the island was renamed for the fictional hero, while another island in the group was renamed for Selkirk.*

Secret Island of the Mutineers

Pitcairn, a rugged volcanic island with rocky cliffs rising to 1,100 feet, is an isolated, forbidding spot in the south central Pacific, some 1,350 miles to the southeast of the fabled Tahiti. Amazingly, its grim facade hides a veritable paradise of fertile soil and warm, subtropical climate.

But Pitcairn is famous, or notorious, as the refuge of the British sailors who mutinied against Captain William Bligh, master of the *Bounty*, in 1789. After setting their martinet of a captain and several of his supporters adrift in an open boat, the helmsman's mate, Fletcher Christian, and eight other crew members decided to hide, since it was obvious that the British navy would search diligently to bring them to the scaffold. Accompanied by 19 Polynesian men and women, the mutineers fled to Pitcairn.

When the Bounty *left England for Tahiti in 1787, no one could have foretold the odyssey that lay ahead.*

Incredibly, Bligh survived, after sailing 3,618 miles in 41 days to the island of Timor. He was luckier than some of his adversaries. Soon alcoholism and feuding over the women led to the death of almost all of the mutineers, including Christian. One of the mutineers was captured, but King George III pardoned him. By 1800 only one rebel, John Adams, still survived on the island. He was successful in establishing a peaceful, well-structured community before his death in 1829 at the age of 68. Since 1887 the islanders have been Seventh-Day Adventists, continuing to grow subsistence crops as their forebears had done. Owing to the appeal of educational and employment opportunities elsewhere, the little community has dwindled from more than 200 to fewer than 50 people today.

homes — so long as they stayed clear of the shore, with its opportunities for escape. Knox set up a plantation, and some of his friends married local women. Always determined to return home, he bided his time in an obscure village, resisting attempts by the king to make him a court secretary. Eventually, he and a friend were able to set up a fake business trip that took them across the island to the coast, where they happened upon a British ship that was heading homeward.

Although the autocratic monarch of Ceylon could be severe when angered, and the society was based upon a strict system of caste, Knox's observations make clear that the country was civilized and peaceful. On the other hand, Defoe's most horrifying example of foreign behavior, the cannibalism that Crusoe discovers being practiced on his supposedly uninhabited island, was based upon tales told by sailors.

A Pale Precursor

Despite all of the influences, the secret of the continuing appeal of *Robinson Crusoe* lies in the particular genius of Defoe himself. He used facts that were well-known to create a work so original that he is recognized today as the father of the English novel. His achievement looms even more impressively when compared with another writer's weak attempt — 11 years before Defoe published his novel — to make a major work of fiction from the scattered reports of isolated castaways and romantic Pacific isles.

Texel, a young hero created by the Dutch author Hendrik Smeeks, finds himself alone on an island. But, unlike the resourceful and courageous Crusoe, he cannot handle the challenges and increasingly disintegrates. By contrast, Defoe's hero not only becomes master of his island, he does so with such self-confidence and natural ability that, ironically, many readers think of his island prison as a kind of idyllic paradise. If it is, that is only because Crusoe has made it so.

Later, in his *Serious Reflections*, Defoe explained that the isolation of his world-famous hero should remind readers of the spiritual isolation that we all feel, even in the midst of thronged cities and active personal lives. Whether it is indeed from a sense of that symbolic meaning, a delight in the remarkable adventures of Crusoe, or a combination of the two, critics regard Defoe's unforgettable novel as a masterpiece of physical and psychological realism. Perhaps that is why it is so tempting to believe that the story actually happened. We would like to believe, perhaps, that human beings can always be as strong and inventive as was that castaway par excellence.

For Cross and Crown

***Left in command of the rear guard as Charlemagne withdrew
from Spain, the peerless Roland gave his life resisting a Muslim attack —
or so it was written in an epic composed long after the event.***

With an ivory horn such as this, the hero Roland is supposed to have made his tardy summons for help.

For seven years Charlemagne, king of the Franks, has pressed his campaign against the Muslim invaders of Spain until just one city, Saragossa, remains in their control. Its defender, King Marsiliun, despairs of being able to resist the Christian onslaught and summons his nobles for advice. Blancandrin, the wisest among them, suggests a ruse. Tell Charlemagne that you wish to convert to his faith, he advises the king. If he will withdraw from Spain, you will follow him to France for baptism at his church in Aix. Marsiliun endorses the plan and sends Blancandrin to the French camp with the offer.

Charlemagne's nephew Roland is skeptical, reminding his uncle that once before Marsiliun had tricked the Franks. But Ganelon, Roland's stepfather, angrily intervenes to urge acceptance. "Whoever tells you that we should reject this offer, sire, does not much care what kind of death we may die." Yes, agrees another senior adviser, the war has gone on long enough; Marsiliun is defeated. "When he begs you to have mercy on him, it would be a sin if you were to go on." The king concurs and asks who should be sent on the

perhaps dangerous mission to Saragossa to accept the Muslim offer. Roland proposes Ganelon, which so angers the older man that he drops the glove Charlemagne proffers as the peace offering to be brought to Marsiliun. It is an evil omen.

En route to Saragossa, Ganelon reveals to Blancandrin his envy of Roland, saying that Charlemagne will never leave Spain as long as his belligerent nephew has his ear. By the time the two reach Marsiliun's court, the plot for treason against Charlemagne and elimination of Roland is hatched. With Marsiliun's promise of submission, Charlemagne will be convinced that it is safe to withdraw and will leave Roland in command of his rear guard — and thus vulnerable to a Muslim attack. And so it transpires.

Given the keys of Saragossa by the treacherous Ganelon, Charlemagne crosses the Pyrenees Mountains into France in the belief that Marsiliun will follow in peace. In command of the troops bringing up the rear, Roland is surprised by a vast Muslim force as the Franks enter the pass at Roncesvalles. The proud knight ignores the advice of his boon companion Oliver to

Spain's Golden Age Under the Moors

Only nine miles of Mediterranean waters separate Morocco's Jabal Musa from its twin rocky outcrop at the southern tip of Spain, the Rock of Gibraltar. In ancient times these were the Pillars of Hercules, the westernmost boundary of the known world. In 711 Tariq ibn Ziyad took his 12,000-man Muslim Arab army across the strait in four borrowed boats to launch his swift conquest of the Iberian Peninsula. Driving the Christian Visigoths before them, the Muslims reached the Pyrenees Mountains by 719. Although their invasion of France was aborted, the Moors — as the invaders came to be called — established a powerful state in Spain, al-Andalus, that was to endure for nearly 800 years.

By the 10th century the Umayyad caliphs of Córdoba were challenging the Abbasid caliphs of Baghdad for supremacy in the Islamic world. They presided over a golden age during which Muslims, Christians, and Jews lived in harmony. Trade and commerce brought prosperity; learning and the arts flourished. With a population of perhaps half a million, Córdoba was one of the great capitals of Europe, boasting libraries, schools, and hospitals. Arab scholars were pushing at the frontiers of knowledge in mathematics, astronomy, and philosophy; their works were quickly translated into Latin and Hebrew so that the accumulated knowledge of the East could be passed to the West. Arab doctors laid the foundations of homeopathic medicine, publishing the

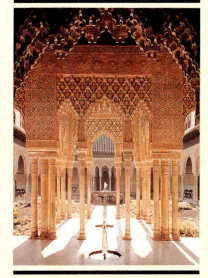

Spain's Moorish treasure, the Alhambra: Like an oasis in the desert, its Court of the Lions beckons the visitor to a cool retreat from the sun.

first treatises on medicinal plants. They also discovered the therapeutic value of music, prescribing the soothing sound of the lute to calm mental patients. Spain's arid landscape was made to bloom with vegetable gardens and citrus orchards with the introduction of revolutionary methods of irrigation.

Charlemagne's abortive excursion across the Pyrenees in 777 was only the first campaign in a centuries-long effort to reclaim Spain for Christianity. The legendary El Cid captured Valencia in 1094. Saragossa fell to Alfonso I of Aragon in 1118. Córdoba itself was taken in 1236; Seville, 12 years later. By the late 15th century the Moors remained in control of but one Spanish stronghold, Granada. Its capture by Ferdinand and Isabella in 1492 freed the Catholic monarchs from the burden of warfare and, coincidentally, allowed them to sponsor the voyage into the unknown that led to Christopher Columbus's discovery of the New World.

Although the Moors were driven out of Spain 500 years ago, the Islamic legacy is clearly visible in two architectural masterpieces. Built over the course of two centuries after the foundation stone was laid in 786, the great mosque at Córdoba overwhelms the visitor with its interior "forest of 1,000 pillars," many of them plundered from earlier Roman or Visigothic buildings. So vast is the space encompassed by the mosque that a Christian basilica, an addition following the reconquest, seems lost within it. At the core of the mosque — now preserved as a historic monument — is a gilded prayer niche pointing toward Mecca.

The palace-fortress Alhambra in Grenada is the other greatly admired wonder of Moorish Spain. Its maze of cool, darkened rooms are clustered around sunny courtyards in which splash the waters of numerous fountains. Curving arches, windows framed by pillars, dazzling mosaics on walls and ceilings everywhere meet the eye. No wonder that Ferdinand and Isabella, accepting the keys of the fortress from its defenders in 1492, knew that a great prize had been won, that a great victory was theirs.

sound the ivory horn that will bring Charlemagne to their rescue. "That would be the act of a fool!" he retorts. Soon, he promises Oliver, he will be striking the enemy so savagely with his sword Durendal that its blade will be covered to the hilt with Muslim blood.

Despite Roland's bravado and his heroic efforts to resist the superior forces of the enemy, the Franks fall one by one. Too late, Roland blows the horn, the strain of his effort bursting the blood vessels in his temple. Hearing the distant call, Charlemagne rushes back to the pass only to find his valiant if foolhardy nephew dead along with all the members of the rear guard.

A Medieval Masterpiece

Sometime late in the 11th century a poet or scribe known only as Turoldus set down the story of Roland's tragic death — or perhaps merely transcribed an already well-known legend. His

The impressive gap in the ridge of the Pyrenees Mountains at the Cirque de Gavarnie is called Roland's Breach. According to local legend, the knight commanding Charlemagne's rear guard split the solid rock with a single blow of his sword.

4,000-word-long epic poem, *The Song of Roland*, is the outstanding example of a medieval French literary form known as the chanson de geste, or song of heroic deeds. It survives in half a dozen versions, three in French and three in translations into other languages. The oldest, and considered by scholars to be the most beautiful, is a manuscript rediscovered in Oxford University's Bodleian Library in 1837.

Although in agreement with those who proclaim *The Song of Roland* a masterpiece, historians are quick to point out that the tale bears only superficial resemblance to the actual events it purports to record. Charlemagne did indeed invade Spain toward the end of the 8th century, and his rear guard was attacked at Roncesvalles as he withdrew to France. But there the similarity with the renowned chanson de geste ends.

Charlemagne in Spain

Having swept across North Africa from their base in Arabia, Muslims crossed the Strait of Gibraltar to invade Spain in 711. Within eight years they had driven the country's Christian inhabitants to the Pyrenees Mountains. But when they tried to conquer France as well, the Muslims were met and turned back at Tours by Charles Martel in 732.

Charles's son Pepin the Short was elected king of the Franks two decades later. His grandson united much of Europe under his rule and is known to history as Charlemagne, or Charles the Great. A fierce defender of the Christian faith, Charlemagne in 777 saw in the quarrel between two Muslim leaders an opportunity not only to expand his domain southward but also to restore Christianity to lands seized earlier in the century by the invaders from North Africa. That year, in response to the pleas of the governor of Saragossa for help in resisting pressure from the caliph of Córdoba, the king of the Franks invaded Spain sometime after Easter.

At first Charlemagne was successful, taking one city after another but stopping short of Saragossa. When he halted his advance to organize the Frankish administration of the lands already won, however, the governor who had invited him to Spain settled his quarrel with the caliph and even sought the assistance of Christian remnants to expel the unwanted Franks. What happened next is not clear from the scanty historical evidence. By mid-August, it seems, Charlemagne was withdrawing to France through the pass at Roncesvalles in the Pyrenees when his rear guard was ambushed. The attackers were not Muslims but rather native inhabitants, the Basques, who were mainly interested in plunder.

Among the Frankish victims at Roncesvalles was one Hruoland, identified only as "warden of the Breton March." The skirmish in the Pyrenees gets scant mention in *Vita Karoli Magni*, the life of Charlemagne composed by his court secretary some years after his death in 814, and would no doubt long be forgotten were it not for the legend that sprung from the incident.

A Time for Heroes

At the time Turoldus composed *The Song of Roland*, Christian Europe was embarking on the Crusades, the long and ultimately unsuccessful effort to wrest the Holy Land from the Muslims. Heroes were needed, chivalrous knights who were dedicated to the fight for cross and crown. Such a hero was Roland, transposed to an earlier century and given superhuman strength and courage. The church was eager to perpetuate the ideal of a knight possessing the Christian virtues expected of a soldier enlisted in the struggle against the infidels. This explains why scribes transformed an unknown soldier in Charlemagne's rear guard into a martyr for the faith.

Young Lovers of Verona

In Romeo and Juliet, *critics and public agree, Shakespeare created the most touching love story of all time. Did such a "star-cross'd" couple ever live? Or is the story of the rival Montagues and Capulets representative of something far different?*

*T*wo households, both alike in dignity,
In fair Verona, where we lay our scene,
From ancient grudge break to new mutiny,
Where civil blood makes civil hands unclean.
From forth the fatal loins of these two foes
A pair of star-cross'd lovers take their life . . .
With these words William Shakespeare begins his immortal tragedy *Romeo and Juliet*, the tale of perhaps the most famous lovers in world literature. First performed about 1595, the play was instantly and enormously popular with London audiences. The first printed version, dated 1597, carries on the title page the comment that the work "hath been often (with great applause) plaid publiquely. . . ." In four centuries the drama's popularity has never waned.

The play opens with the young Montague, Romeo, pining over the haughty Rosaline, with whom he fancies himself in love. Hearing that she is to attend a ball at the palace of the enemy Capulets, Romeo and his friend Mercutio don masks to join the party uninvited. There Romeo sees Juliet, the exquisite daughter of the Capulets, not yet 14 years old. He begs to kiss her hand, then her lips. The two fall instantly in love, though Romeo has a premonition that his passion harbors danger. When Juliet learns that the handsome stranger is a Montague, she bemoans her fate, "That I must love a loathed enemy."

After the ball Romeo steals into the orchard of the Capulets, where he spies upon Juliet at a window as she confesses her love to the night — saying that, if Romeo will not deny his father and refuse his name, "I'll no longer be a Capulet." Her suitor steps forward, and the enraptured couple vows to ignore their families' bitter and divisive hostility by entering into a secret marriage.

Thinking that the union will heal the breach between the Montagues and Capulets, the well-meaning if naïve Friar Laurence agrees to perform the ceremony the next day. But the bride and groom must part immediately afterward, promising to meet that night at the window overlooking the orchard where they had first pledged their love. Their joy is to be short-lived, however, as the first of several tragic mishaps occurs.

En route home from the wedding, Romeo encounters Mercutio being provoked by Juliet's fiery cousin Tybalt. When Tybalt turns on him, Romeo refuses to fight his new wife's kinsman. Shocked by his friend's apparent cowardice, Mercutio draws a sword only to receive a mortal wound from Tybalt. "A plague o' both your houses!" he cries as he is

Meeting at Juliet's window overlooking the Capulet orchard, Romeo and Juliet pledge their eternal love — convinced that it will overcome their families' mortal rivalry.

carried away to die. To avenge his friend's death, Romeo stabs Tybalt — a murder for which he is immediately banished from Verona.

Before leaving, Romeo keeps his rendezvous with Juliet, but they must part at dawn. As her husband climbs down from her window, Juliet shudders at a terrible vision. "Methinks I see thee . . . As one dead in the bottom of a tomb," she cries out. On the advice of Friar Laurence, Romeo withdraws to Mantua to await publication of news of the secret wedding — which the friar still believes will bring reconciliation between the warring clans.

Juliet now faces a dilemma, for her parents are urging upon her a marriage with Paris, a kinsman of Verona's ruling prince. Knowing that she cannot enter such a bigamous union, Juliet seeks the counsel of Friar Laurence. He gives her a narcotic potion that will induce a deathlike trance. After she is placed in the tomb, he says, Romeo will be summoned to take her away with him into exile. Yet another mishap foils the plan, for the friar's letter never reaches Romeo. Instead the young Montague hears that his bride has died and been buried. He secretly returns to Verona and enters the Capulet tomb only to find Paris mourning at Juliet's bier. Romeo and Paris fight a duel, ending in the latter's death. Romeo kisses the presum-

ably dead Juliet and takes a dose of poison that he has brought along for the occasion. Awakening from her trance, Juliet sees her husband dead beside her, realizes how fate has tricked them, and stabs herself with Romeo's dagger.

Gathering at the scene of the tragedy, the Montagues and Capulets are reminded by the prince that their mutual hatred has brought the scourge. The rivals make peace, Montague vowing to raise a statue in gold to Juliet; Capulet, one to Romeo. The prince has the last word:

. . . never was a story of more woe
Than this of Juliet and her Romeo.

Did They Ever Live?

So appealingly believable are the young lovers, so haunting is their tale, that readers and theatergoers were quick to assume that *Romeo and Juliet* was based on real people and events. An Italian contemporary of Shakespeare's, Giralomo della Corte, was convinced of the veracity of the story and in a history of Verona confidently if somewhat arbitrarily assigned the date of 1303 to the tragic deaths of the pair. Shakespeare himself, or at least his editor, made no claim for a historical pair of lovers. The 1597 printed version called the play "an excellent conceited [that is, ingeniously contrived] tragedie."

Renouncing a Throne for Love

Unlike Shakespeare's *Romeo and Juliet*, the most famous love story of the 20th century involves two real people: Britain's King Edward VIII and the woman for whom he gave up the throne.

As the oldest son of King George V, Edward was groomed for his future role as the British monarch from an early age. Barely 20 when World War I broke out in 1914, the Prince of Wales was given an officer's rank but kept from the front — a restriction he greatly resented. In the postwar years he assiduously carried out his duties as the king's representative in travels about the globe. The handsome, slender prince was soon being talked of as the world's most eligible bachelor. Although there were women in his life, he managed to avoid marriage with any of the European princesses who would have been considered a proper match

Photographed on the occasion of their wedding, the duke and duchess of Windsor became peripatetic socialites.

for him. Instead, early in 1931, he met and fell in love with a divorced and remarried American woman, Wallis Warfield Simpson. He was 37; she was one year his senior. When Mrs. Simpson left her husband for the prince, the scandal was initially kept from the British public by a combination of government pressure and press restraint.

At the death of his father in January 1936, Edward ascended the throne — nourishing the hope that he would at least be allowed to contract a morganatic marriage with Mrs. Simpson after her second divorce was granted. But the union was ruled out. Declaring that it was impossible for him to discharge his duties as king, Edward VIII abdicated in favor of his brother, the duke of York, on December 10. Six months later, on June 3, 1937, he and Wallis Simpson were married.

Verona traces its history to Roman times, and the 1st-century A.D. amphitheater still dominates the town (right). During summer months operatic spectacles are staged there. Visitors may prefer the more intimate setting of the palazzo balcony (below), identified as the place where Romeo and Juliet had their first rendezvous.

Literary scholars point out that such "star-cross'd lovers" are found in works as early as the 2nd-century Greek romance *Anthia and Abrocomas* by Xenophon Epehesius. Shakespeare's sources, however, seem to have been much nearer his own time.

A story similar to that of *Romeo and Juliet* appeared in the 1476 *Novellino* of Massuccio Salernitano and was retold some 50 years later by Luigi da Porto, who called his lovers Romeo and Giulietta. Da Porto's "recently discovered story of two noble lovers" contained all the major elements of Shakespeare's tragedy: a setting in Verona, two feuding families named Montecchi and

Cappelletti, a double suicide at the conclusion. Another Italian, Matteo Bandello, freely adapted the tale for his *Novelle* of 1554, which was soon translated into French by Pierre Boisteau de Launay and which appeared in the 1559 *Histoires Tragiques* of François de Belleforest.

The French version in turn was translated into English verse by Arthur Brooke as *Romeus and Juliet* (1562) and into English prose by William Paynter as *The Palace of Pleasure* (1567). Since Brooke wrote of having seen "the same argument lately set forth on the stage," scholars think that it is possible that Shakespeare was adapting a now lost play, though his masterpiece runs parallel to Brooke's poem.

Italy's Feuding Families

Although it seems fairly certain that Romeo and Juliet are but literary inventions, of whatever period or language, it has been proposed that the feuding families — the framework in which their tragedy is set — are real. The names Montecchi and Cappelletti (in Shakespeare, Montague and Capulet) were not invented by da Porto. Dante Alighieri alludes to internal strife in Italy in *The Divine Comedy* of 1320. "Come, see the Montec-

Romeo and Juliet *is not only one of Shakespeare's most popular plays, it has inspired such other works as the operas* I Capuleti ed i Montecchi *of Vincenzo Bellini and* Roméo et Juliette *of Charles Gounod and the ballet score of Sergei Prokofiev (a staging of which is shown at left).*

chi and Cappelletti. . . ." Dante wrote in the sixth canto of his epic poem's section on purgatory, "See those bowed down by grief, and those in dread; Come, cruel man, to see the oppressive rule of your own nobles; punish their misdeeds." Yet, all attempts to find valid historical references to two families named Montecchi and Cappelletti have proved futile.

An American historian named Olin H. Moore proposed a solution to the puzzle. "Contrary to popular understanding," he wrote in 1930, "the designations Montecchi and Cappelletti were the nicknames of political parties, not names of private families." These parties, he suggested, were local representatives of the rival factions that dominated Italian political life in the late Middle Ages, the Guelfs and Ghibellines.

The Guelfs, who took their name from a German family named Welf, advocated a federal state for Italy with the pope as its head. The Ghibellines, named for the ancestral home of the Hohenstaufens in Germany, supported the efforts of the Holy Roman Emperor to impose his authority over the entire Italian peninsula. The international contest of strength lasted from the middle of the 12th century to the second half of the 13th, after which it degenerated into squabbling of merely local importance.

One group of Ghibellines took the name Montecchi, after the castle Montecchio Maggiore near Vicenza where its first assembly was held, and was successful in imposing its control over the Guelf ruler of Verona, which is situated some 30 miles to the west. There is no record, however, that the Montecchi ever collided with the Cappelletti, the Guelf party at Cremona that took its name from the little hat (in Italian, *cappelletto*) that was its characteristic headgear.

How then did these two local Italian political parties become two feuding families in Verona? The fault apparently lies with early commentators on Dante's great work, who thought his references to factions were names of rival families. Luigi da Porto chose the version most convenient to his tale when he wrote the archetypal Romeo and Juliet story in 1524, the one from which later versions in French and English — most notably, that of Shakespeare — were derived.

The Immortal Lovers

Visitors to the lovely north Italian town of Verona need not concern themselves with the puzzle of whether Romeo and Juliet ever lived there. They are more likely to indulge this fantasy if they enter the courtyard of the Palazzo di Capuletti and gaze upward at the balcony where Shakespeare set his haunting love scene. In the garden of the monastery of San Francesco they can imagine themselves at the site of the furtive wedding ceremony — no matter that this was home to Carthusian monks, whereas Friar Laurence was a Franciscan. From a garden such as this, Friar Laurence could have taken the herbs to make Juliet's potion. Finally, visitors may shed a tear at the dim vault that is identified as the tomb where Romeo and Juliet died.

That it cannot be proved that the young lovers ever lived is really unimportant. What matters, of course, is the genius of William Shakespeare, who made them immortal.

6

Unanswered Questions

Was Kaspar Hauser the crown prince of Baden, born in the palace at Karlsruhe?

Cheated of His Birthright?

*In May 1828 a youth who could not say who he was
or where he came from appeared in Nürnberg, a Bavarian city in what
is now Germany. Five years later he was murdered, leaving
unsolved the mystery of his identity.*

"Went palace gardens . . . man had knife . . . gave purse . . . stabbed . . . run all I could," gasped the young man fleeing from the palace gardens as if pursued by the furies. He was found to have a deep wound in the left side of his chest. Three days later, on December 17, 1833, Kaspar Hauser, who had been living in the household of a local teacher, died from the injury.

The purse was found; and soon thereafter, the murder weapon as well: a dagger roughly 12 inches in length. But who was the murderer and what was the motive for his attack? The answer to these questions lies concealed behind the mystery concerning the true identity of Kaspar Hauser, who had appeared in the city of Nürnberg five and a half years earlier.

The Demented Stranger

About four o'clock on Monday afternoon, May 26, 1828, a "strange and funny" figure came "tottering" (in the words of two passersby) into Nürnberg's Unschlitt Square. He was wearing a gray jacket, a worn pair of trousers, an old, non-descript waistcoat, a shirt, low boots, and a cylindrical hat. His gait was unsteady, like that of a child who had just learned to walk.

When the two onlookers — cobblers by the names of Jakob Beck and Georg Leonhardt Weickmann — addressed the young man, he could only babble in meaningless words. Eventually, he presented them with a letter addressed to the commander of the 4th Troop of the 6th Light Cavalry Regiment, then stationed in Nürnberg.

The two men considered it best to take the odd stranger to the guardhouse at the city gate. Since Weickmann was going in that direction anyway, he undertook to accompany the stumbling youth there and to deposit him with the duty officer, who would be able to direct him farther.

At length, when the stranger finally reached the troop commander's house, there was only a servant on hand; he accepted the letter and advised the obviously bewildered and exhausted youth to go to the stable and rest there while awaiting the commander. Since the bizarre guest appeared to be hungry and thirsty, the servant offered him a piece of meat and a jug of beer. The young man declined both with obvious repugnance but avidly accepted bread and water. Having satisfied his hunger and thirst, he promptly fell into a deep sleep.

Around eight o'clock that evening the commander, Baron Friedrich von Wessenig, returned home. Upon hearing of the uninvited guest, the baron asked to see the letter and read it without being able to make any sense of it. He then had the stranger awakened and brought to him. But all attempts to extract from him intelligible answers to questions as to who he was, where he came from, and who had given him the letter failed; nothing more could be gotten out of him than a jumble of unconnected words.

Annoyed at the mysterious intruder, the baron decided without further ado to hand the youth over to the police. They also tried to interrogate him; but the strange figure, whom everyone at first took for a tramp, only wept and whimpered to himself, answered "I don't know" to every question, and pointed to his feet, which were obviously causing him considerable pain. His behavior was similar to that of a child — the only difference being that this child was lodged in the body of an approximately 16-year-old youth.

The interrogation failed to produce any results until one of the policemen had the notion of giving the youth pen and paper and asking him to write his name. The improbable happened, and he wrote without hesitation "Kaspar Hauser."

Kaspar Hauser's coat, with the rip (white circle) caused by the murder instrument; the assassin killed his victim with an upward thrust of the dagger, piercing Kaspar's chest to the pericardium. A skull and crossbones and an hourglass, both gruesome symbols of death, were faintly engraved on the blade of the murder weapon.

However, when instructed to write down where he came from, he could only stammer "I don't know." In the end, he was deposited in a cell in the Luginsland, the prison in Nürnberg Castle, where once again he sank into sleep.

A Remarkable Letter

Such was Kaspar Hauser's first day in Nürnberg, as far as can be ascertained from historical records. Among these records is the letter to the cavalry commander; however, instead of providing answers, it only raises new questions.

The author of the letter describes himself as a poor day laborer and father of ten children and claims that on October 7, 1812, he had taken in an abandoned child and secretly reared it; there were no details as to the child's birthplace or parentage. The letter was unsigned. Enclosed with the letter was a note, which was obviously in-

An unknown person attempted to murder Kaspar Hauser in October 1829. The man, who hid his face behind a black cloth, struck Kaspar with an axlike instrument and injured him on the forehead.

tended to create the impression that it had been written by the boy's mother and found with the infant in 1812. The note stated that she was a "poor maid" no longer able to provide for the child, who had been born six months earlier, on April 30, 1812, and christened with the name Kaspar. According to the note, the boy's father was no longer alive; he had once served with the Light Cavalry and, for this reason, the mother had requested that the boy be sent to the 6th Light Cavalry Regiment in Nürnberg when he was old enough. As in the case of the letter, the note bore no signature. Added to Kaspar's inability to answer questions about his past, the slight information contained in these two missives did nothing to clarify the situation and, indeed, created additional riddles.

How did the woman who wrote the note know that this particular regiment would be stationed at Nürnberg in 1828? In 1812 it had been stationed in an entirely different locality, and no one then could have said where the regiment was going to be 16 years later. The note was a clumsy piece of forgery; the ink and paper used for both letter and note were identical, proving that they had been written at the same time — even if not by the same hand.

This together with other inconsistencies soon aroused suspicion that a yarn was being spun deliberately to mislead people. The possibility that Kaspar Hauser himself wrote the letter and the note can be excluded by a comparison of handwritings. And, if he really were a crafty swindler who expected to gain from playing the role of a bewildered foundling, he certainly could have concocted a more convincing story.

The Foundling as Sensation

Not long after he first appeared in Nürnberg, Kaspar Hauser was moved from his cell in the prison to a small room beside the apartment of a prison warder named Andreas Hiltel. After observing his strange charge at close hand and reaching the conclusion that Kaspar Hauser was, in fact, not mentally retarded but simply totally lacking in education, Hiltel decided to take in Kaspar as one of his own family.

From the Hiltel family Kaspar Hauser learned how to sit on a chair at table, how to use a knife and fork, and the basics of personal hygiene. However, his distaste for every form of food other than bread and water could not be overcome. He played with the Hiltel children and became especially attached to 11-year-old Julius, from whom he learned new words. Indeed, Kaspar was soon able to form entire sentences.

The news about the odd stranger in the prison soon spread throughout the town, and hordes of curious onlookers streamed daily to the castle to view the "tame savage" at close range. When Kaspar's health eventually began to suffer seriously on account of all this morbid curiosity, the town council decided to put a stop to the undignified spectacle and committed him to the care of Georg Friedrich Daumer, a local schoolteacher. During the ensuing months public interest in the stranger gradually subsided; and, under Daumer's patient guidance, Kaspar slowly began to overcome the peculiar disparity between the physical and mental stages of his development.

Kaspar Hauser once again became a topic of public gossip when it was reported that a man in dark clothes had attacked him on October 17, 1829, just outside the Daumer house and had succeeded in wounding him on the forehead with an axlike instrument before fleeing.

The Solution to the Mystery?

In July 1828, a few weeks after Kaspar Hauser's appearance in Nürnberg, the lawyer and philosopher Paul Johann Anselm von Feuerbach made the acquaintance of the strange young man and began to follow the case with great interest. By 1832 he came to believe that he had the answer

The scar that remained on Kaspar Hauser's forehead after the murder attempt of 1829 is clearly visible in the portrait at right. Suspicion was voiced at an early date that the unknown youth might be the victim of a dynastic intrigue.

The parents of the unnamed crown prince of Baden, who is supposed to have died on October 16, 1812: Grand Duke Karl (above) and Stephanie (left), the adopted daughter of Napoleon.

to the question of Kaspar Hauser's identity. On January 4 Feuerbach wrote in his diary, "I have discovered that Kaspar Hauser is probably by birth a prince of the Royal House of B[aden]. . . ."

Rumors and even anonymous tip-offs to the public prosecutor had been making the rounds ever since the uncommunicative stranger had stumbled into Nürnberg. They centered on the speculation that Kaspar Hauser was the victim of a dynastic conspiracy — and that, in reality, he was the heir apparent to the throne of the Grand Duchy of Baden and had been deprived of his inheritance. But Feuerbach was the first person who tried to substantiate these rumors in a thorough and logical manner. He committed his thoughts to paper in a confidential memorandum that he sent in February 1832 to Caroline von Bayern, a princess of Baden and — if Feuerbach's theory was correct — the boy's paternal aunt.

Feuerbach's research into the history of Germany's royal families led him to the conclusion that Kaspar Hauser had been born on September 29, 1812, as the son of Karl, grand duke of Baden, and his wife, Stephanie de Beauharnais. Stephanie, the niece of French Empress Josephine's first husband, had been adopted as a daughter by Josephine's second husband, Napoleon Bonaparte. She was but one of the many relatives Napoleon installed upon European thrones before he met defeat at Waterloo.

The child resulting from the marriage of Stephanie to Grand Duke Karl, according to official sources, died within three weeks of his birth. In Feuerbach's opinion, however, the heir apparent to the throne of Baden had been secretly abducted and replaced by the infant who was reported to have died. The person behind this plot was the Countess von Hochberg, the second wife

In the dungeon a toy wooden horse (above, the one found in 1982) was the boy's only source of amusement. Above right: a portrait made of Kaspar shortly after his arrival in Nürnberg.

Kaspar Hauser may have spent his childhood in this dungeon in Pilsach Castle, totally cut off from human society. According to Kaspar, he saw his jailer for the first time only shortly before he was set loose in Nürnberg in May 1828.

of Grand Duke Karl Friedrich, who had been succeeded on the throne of Baden in 1811 by his grandson, Karl. Since the countess's rank was not high enough to ensure her children a right to the throne, she had decided to remove whatever obstacles might prevent them from acquiring royal succession. The principal obstacle would be any legitimate child of the current ruler.

Feuerbach was convinced that he had discovered the solution to the mystery surrounding Kaspar Hauser. When Feuerbach died about a year later, after a short and apparently inexplicable illness, suspicion immediately arose that he had been poisoned for having uncovered the long-suppressed intrigue.

Kaspar Hauser, Prince of Baden?

At first reading, Feuerbach's line of argument seems convincing. It is an undisputed fact that Kaspar Hauser was roughly 16 years of age when he appeared in Nürnberg in 1828. Both the letter and the note alleged that he was born in 1812, the same year in which the nameless prince of Baden had been born. Yet, could the Countess von Hochberg have been able at that point in time to reckon on installing her sons on the throne by disposing of the young prince?

In 1812 the ruling Grand Duke Karl had two uncles who were still alive and who stood in direct line of succession to the throne: Margrave Friedrich and Margrave Ludwig, both sons of Karl Friedrich's first marriage. Friedrich died in 1817, and Ludwig ruled Baden from 1818 to 1830 after the death of his nephew. Only then did the first scion of the Hochberg family mount the throne. But these developments could not possibly have been foreseen in 1812.

Apart from this objection, another question must be asked: Why was the little prince not simply murdered in 1812 instead of being abducted and replaced by another child — an action that would have added an extra risk factor to the affair? And did, in fact, such a substitution take place in the royal house of Baden?

There is no airtight evidence to prove such an event, only circumstantial evidence that one Johann Ernst Jakob Blochmann, the infant son of a working-class family, was deposited in the prince's cradle. Whether or not the Blochmann child died a natural death is a subject of controversy. However, the fact that the prince's nurse was refused admission to the nursery and that Stephanie, his mother, was also kept away from the dying child, gives reason to believe that such an exchange may have taken place. And even if there is no clear proof that the Countess von Hochberg engineered the exchange, there is no doubt that she had the chance to do so, for she had constant access to the child's room. A further cause for suspicion is the fact that the Blochmann family was employed by the countess.

But how can one know whether the Blochmann child was in fact the one involved in the exchange? Systematic research and a bit of luck have provided clues in this respect. The christening of Johann Ernst Jakob Blochmann was recorded in the parish register of the town of Karlsruhe on October 4, 1812. Under normal circumstances such an entry would be supplemented at a later date by an entry recording the person's death. In this case the death notice is missing and in its place there is an entry written between December 14 and 16, 1833, which states: "On November 27 [1833] . . . Kaspar Ernst Blochmann, soldier in the Royal Greek Corps and son of Christoph Blochmann, court servant . . . died in Munich." Investigations have since shown that there was no such soldier by the name of Blochmann in the Bavarian army.

Furthermore, the Christian names Kaspar Ernst makes one wonder — especially since an identically worded entry in the Munich register of deaths mentions only the forename Ernst. In some inexplicable way Ernst Blochmann and Kaspar Hauser seem to have merged into one and the same person. The chronology of events also gives food for thought, for the fatal attack on Kaspar Hauser in the palace gardens in Nürnberg took place on December 14, 1833.

A Life in the Dark

Kaspar Hauser's childhood and early youth remain shrouded in mystery. If indeed he was the abducted prince, he was probably raised at first by the parents of the deceased Blochmann child and taken in January 1815, by then a two-year-old child beginning to speak, to Beuggen Castle near Laufenberg in the Upper Rhine district. The castle belonged to Countess von Hochberg and could have been used as a a safe place to hide the boy since it had previously served as a fever hospital for the military and was therefore still given a wide berth by the local populace.

Reared in Isolation

Child savages is the term used for boys and girls who have grown up without any contact with human society — that is, under conditions similar to those of Kaspar Hauser's childhood.

In 1976 a boy roughly 10 years of age was found in India in the company of three wolves; he ran about on all fours, ate only raw meat, and tried to bite people. Mother Teresa, the celebrated nun and winner of the Nobel Peace Prize for her work with the poor of Calcutta, took charge of him but failed in her efforts to teach him human behavior and to make him understand such words as "God" and "love."

Another case is that of a girl, Susan W., called Genie, who was discovered in Los Angeles in 1970. Because her father could not stand the noise children make, she was tied to a chair in an almost empty room for the better part of 12

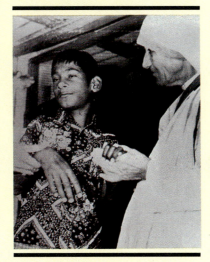

Mother Teresa with her protégé, whom she christened Pascal. The boy is said to have grown up among wolves with no human contact.

years, growing up without any human contact. She could hardly stand, far less walk, and she was incapable of speech. In the ensuing years she learned human social behavior only with great difficulty.

If one compares these children with Kaspar Hauser, who was supposed to have spent 12 years in the dungeon of Pilsach Castle, then one cannot help feeling that he adapted himself fairly quickly to human society and demonstrated remarkable progress by learning to read and write within a short period of time. Only when he was agitated did his language reflect his past. Kaspar Hauser's capacity for learning was perhaps related to the fact that he had spent at least the first two years of his life under relatively normal conditions — and those are the years that, according to scientific opinion, are crucial for an individual's later development.

A Secret Wire-Puller?

One of the most dubious characters to cross Kaspar Hauser's path was the Englishman Philip Henry, 5th earl of Stanhope. At the end of May 1831 he appeared at Nürnberg in the role of a wealthy aristocrat moved by the fate of the unknown foundling. Lavishing proof of his good will on Kaspar, Lord Stanhope succeeded through sheer tenacity in persuading the town council to appoint him as the young man's foster father. Scarcely had he achieved this goal when he deserted Kaspar Hauser, never to be seen in Nürnberg again. What was even worse, he turned against his former protégé to claim that the young man was a cheat and swindler.

Stanhope's role in the tragedy of Kaspar Hauser is indeed obscure and one of Feuerbach's sons suspected not without good cause that he "was a tool in the hands of Hauser's enemies and acted deliberately on their behalf."

It is a curious fact that Stanhope was in Nürnberg as early as 1829, only a few days after the first, unsuccessful attempt on Kaspar Hauser's life. He sought precise information about the attempted murder together with other details about what was known of Kaspar's past life.

Stanhope seems to have been on Kaspar Hauser's trail as early as 1826 and had traveled the length and breadth of south Germany, establishing contacts with the royal courts of both Baden and Bavaria. He was also in touch with the Bourbons, restored to the throne of France following the deposition of Napoleon, and with Prince Metternich, the Austrian foreign minister who had joined his country to the alliance that defeated Napoleon. The interest displayed by Stanhope, who appears to have been a secret agent, seems to confirm that Kaspar Hauser was no ordinary foundling. If he were the crown prince of Baden, then he would also have been a grandson of Napoleon's — and nothing was more dreaded in Paris and Vienna than a revival of the Napoleonic dynasty.

Kaspar Hauser dreamed repeatedly of a castle in association with a coat of arms, which — as he described and drew it — bore a close resemblance to that of Beuggen Castle. This fact alone strongly suggests that Kaspar did actually live there for a time. A further clue is a bottle that was fished out of the Rhine in 1816 containing a message in Latin: "I am held prisoner in a dungeon near Laufenberg on the Rhine. The one occupying the throne doesn't know the whereabouts of my prison." The message was signed S. HANES SPRANCIO, letters that when rearranged can spell in German "His son Caspar." Of course, a child not yet four could not have written the message; but it is presumed that one of those involved in the plot wanted for some reason or other to draw attention to the imprisoned boy.

Kaspar's next presumed place of imprisonment was Pilsach Castle, approximately 25 miles from Nürnberg. It belonged to Baron Karl von Griessenbeck, who came to Pilsach only once a year in order to check his estate manager's accounts. In Pilsach Castle there is a dungeon between the ground and second floors with an air shaft that even today is barred on the outside wall with an iron grating bearing a shape in the form of a plant. On April 24, 1829, under interrogation to glean details about his past, Kaspar drew a sort of tulip that resembled the grating emblem at Pilsach Castle. Furthermore, when Kaspar Hauser tried to describe his earlier life in a dungeon, he mentioned that he had played there with a toy wooden horse. In 1982, during renovation work on Pilsach Castle, an old wooden horse was found; still in relatively good condition, it corresponds to a remarkable degree to the description that Kaspar gave of his toy.

Should Kaspar Hauser's period of captivity in Pilsach Castle be considered as clearly proved on the basis of the above evidence, then another question arises. Why was Kaspar Hauser released from his imprisonment in 1828 and deposited in Nürnberg in such a helpless condition?

Having been deprived of his childhood and youth, Kaspar Hauser spent the remaining five and a half years of his life among caring people. He learned to speak and write, was confirmed in church, and eventually caught up on the education he had been denied up to the age of 16. But he remained haunted by his past and constantly tried to recall what had happened during those lost years. Various people continued to investigate Kaspar's numerous but fragmentary reminiscences, but the separate pieces of the puzzle did not — and still do not — fit into a clear picture of events prior to May 1828.

Surprised at Dawn

*Japan's devastating attack on Pearl Harbor early on the morning
of December 7, 1941, brought the United States into World War II against
the Axis powers. Did America ignore forewarning of the
strike to make Japan appear as the aggressor?*

Admiral Husband E. Kimmel, commander in chief of the U.S. Pacific Fleet stationed at Pearl Harbor on the Hawaiian island of Oahu, rose about 7 A.M. on that Sunday morning. He had a golf date with his military counterpart, Lieutenant General Walter C. Short. But before he had time to dress and breakfast, Admiral Kimmel received word that a destroyer on patrol at the entrance to the harbor had sighted and sunk an enemy submarine. Although there had been many false reports of submarines in the outlying areas, he promised to come down to fleet head-

quarters immediately to await further news. Meanwhile, at a mobile radar station on the north coast of the island, an Army private was startled by an echo on the oscilloscope indicating that more than 50 airplanes were rapidly approaching Oahu. At 7:30 the unidentified airplanes were within 45 miles of the coast.

Oahu was so shrouded by a morning cloud cover that the Japanese attack planes did not see the island until they were actually over it. Leading his 140 bombers and 43 escort fighters to the west and south for the approach to Pearl Harbor,

As a Honolulu newspaper proclaimed, the Japanese attack on Pearl Harbor brought war.

First wave of Japanese attack 7:55 A.M.
Second wave of Japanese attack 8:55 A.M.
American airfields attacked

The 183 aircraft in the first wave of Japan's air strike were followed by a second wave of 170 bombers from the east and south that was timed to arrive one hour later.

Commander Mitsuo Fuchida mused that it must have been "God's hand" that pulled aside the clouds directly over his target. Below was "a majestic sight, almost unbelievable": seven great ships at their moorings on Battleship Row. An eighth battleship, the *Pennsylvania*, and two destroyers were in drydock nearby. Arrayed about the harbor were 29 additional destroyers, nine cruisers, and a number of lesser craft that brought the total to 94 vessels. Fuchida only regretted the absence of aircraft carriers.

Glancing up from the deck of his flagship, the *Oglala*, Rear Admiral William Furlong saw a single plane appear in the sky above Pearl Harbor's Ford Island airfield a few minutes before 8. When it dropped a bomb on the hangars, the admiral assumed it was an error and silently cursed the "stupid, careless pilot" for not having properly secured the bomb's releasing device. But as the plane changed course to veer between his ship

and Ford Island, he saw the rising sun emblem and knew a Japanese attack was under way.

As she was preparing breakfast in the house next door to Admiral Kimmel's, Mrs. John B. Earle heard an explosion and ran to her front window just in time to see the hangars on Ford Island erupt in smoke and flame. She stepped outside for a better view and was joined by the admiral looking "completely stunned," his face "as white as the uniform he wore." As they looked on "in utter disbelief," the battleship *Arizona* rose out of the water, then sunk beneath its surface.

All Over Within Two Hours

Racing off in his staff car, Admiral Kimmel was at headquarters by 8:05, just in time to see the battleship *California* hit by a torpedo. He was powerless to do anything as, one by one, the giant ships along Battleship Row came under enemy fire. The first wave of the attack was over by 8:35, only to be followed — after a 20-minute lull — by an hour-long second wave that ended at 9:55 A.M. The toll was horrendous: 18 vessels, including all eight battleships, either sunk, capsized, or damaged; scores of Army and Navy aircraft de-

President Roosevelt signed the declaration of war against Japan on December 8, 1941, a day after the Pearl Harbor disaster.

stroyed; 2,403 lives lost and 1,178 persons wounded. By comparison, Japanese losses were minimal: 29 aircraft, six submarines, and perhaps fewer than 100 casualties.

December 7, 1941, was a day — President Franklin D. Roosevelt would tell Congress and the nation the next afternoon in asking for a declaration of war on Japan — that would "live in infamy." Following an on-the-spot investigation by Secretary of the Navy Frank Knox, Admiral Kimmel was relieved of his command on December 16, as was General Short. But were they responsible, as an investigative commission would later find, for failing to evaluate the seriousness of the situation prior to the surprise attack and omitting to take the necessary precautions to counter such an attack? It has taken five decades to begin finding answers to this question.

"Cancer of the Pacific"

Although few at the time realized it, Japan had been on a collision course with the United States for nearly a decade, or since it had seized Manchuria from China in 1931–32. In 1937 Japan invaded northern China and two years later turned south to seize the island of Hainan, casting covetous eyes on Malaya, the Philippines, and the Netherlands East Indies (today's Indonesia). Meanwhile, the United States not only supported the Chinese government of Chiang Kai-shek but also seemed to endorse British, French, and Dutch colonialism in Asia at a time the Japanese were trumpeting that "Asia is the territory of the Asiatics. . . ." Grandly speaking of a Greater East Asia Co-Prosperity Sphere, the Japanese, in fact, were desperately seeking the natural resources so sadly lacking in their island chain to feed a rapidly growing population and develop their manufacturing potential.

The fall of France in June 1940 gave Japan just the pretext it needed to send troops to French Indochina (today's Vietnam), and on September 27 it signed a pact with the Axis powers, Germany and Italy. "It seems to me increasingly clear that we are bound to have a showdown some day," Joseph C. Grew, the American ambassador in Tokyo, wrote to President Franklin D. Roosevelt, "and the principal question at issue is whether it is to our advantage to have that showdown sooner or have it later." His sympathies openly with Britain against the Axis powers, including their new ally in Asia, Roosevelt saw to it that by year's end embargoes were placed on all exports to Japan of vital war materials with the exception of petroleum. The Japanese called the ugly standoff between the two powers *Taihei-*

Admiral Isoroku Yamamoto was the mastermind behind the attack on Pearl Harbor. He used the threat of resignation to win endorsement of his audacious plan, which he believed would give Japan a free hand for its expansion in the Pacific.

yono-gan: "Cancer of the Pacific." Seeking a diplomatic solution to the dilemma, Japan called Admiral Kichisaburo Nomura out of retirement and sent him as ambassador to Washington in January 1941. Even as Nomura was traveling to the United States, another Japanese admiral was beginning to formulate a plan that would ignite war between the two nations.

Deciding the War on the First Day

On January 7, 1941, Isoroku Yamamoto, commander of Japan's combined naval fleet, wrote a highly confidential memorandum to the navy minister. Since conflict with the United States was "inevitable," Admiral Yamamoto suggested that a bold stroke was needed "to decide the fate of the war on the very first day." Specifically, he proposed a surprise air attack on the American fleet at Pearl Harbor "on a moonlit night or at dawn." By mid-April, Yamamoto's plan had been endorsed for staff study; the formation that month of the First Air Fleet gave him the force he needed to make his preemptive strike.

Enigma: Breaking Germany's Codes

When the German battleship *Scharnhorst* left Norway on a secret mission in December 1943, its fate was already sealed. Two days later the British navy sank the vessel — one of Germany's three largest — thanks to precise information it had received on the enemy's naval deployment. A large number of German submarines had met a similar fate: 287 in 1943, more than in the preceding three years combined. Germany's efforts to cut off the vital American supply line to its ally Britain had failed miserably.

The Allied victory in the North Atlantic was essentially a triumph of the British intelligence service. Even before the outbreak of war, the British knew of Enigma, a machine developed in 1923 by a German engineer named Arthur Scherbius to encode messages by

Enigma appeared about as harmless as an ordinary typewriter. In British hands it brought death to thousands of German seamen.

electromechanical means. Although they had received two such machines from their Polish allies, the British were unable to crack the codes until the spring of 1941, when they apprehended a German submarine and found aboard it an Enigma cipher machine and the necessary code books with which it could be used. The Germans remained unaware of the British windfall and were confident that they possessed the most sophisticated and safest codes in existence.

The unexpected bounty gave Britain the means of decoding German radio communications. According to some estimates, the Allies' precise knowledge of German submarine positions thereafter cost the lives of 28,000 of Germany's 39,000 submarine crew members in the crucial battle for control of the North Atlantic.

Three weeks after Yamamoto sent his memo to the navy minister, Ambassador Grew heard rumors of the plan and warned Washington. The naval intelligence office forwarded Grew's message to Admiral Kimmel in Hawaii, saying that it gave no credence to the report. Nonetheless, Secretary of the Navy Knox wrote to Secretary of War Henry L. Stimson that he believed it "easily possible" that hostilities between Japan and the United States would be initiated with a surprise attack on Pearl Harbor and asked for a joint Army-Navy buildup to thwart such a raid. Stimson agreed, as did Army Chief of Staff George C. Marshall, who said that his first concern was to protect the fleet. In Hawaii, General Short apparently thought otherwise, believing that the presence of the fleet at Pearl Harbor somehow shielded his soldiers from the potential enemy. Despite the dismissal of Ambassador Grew's warning, Admiral Kimmel took seriously the possibility of a Japanese strike against his fleet but thought that it would be launched from submarines rather than from the air.

Unaware of Yamamoto's plans, Ambassador Nomura presented his credentials to President Roosevelt, who greeted him cordially, saying that there was "plenty of room in the Pacific for everybody," and urged him to work out a settlement with Secretary of State Cordell Hull. It wasn't as easy as the president indicated, for Japan's expansionism and alliance with Germany and Italy ran counter to American foreign policy. When Japan refused to reconsider its policies, the United States took additional economic measures, freezing all Japanese assets in America on July 26 and, six days later, extending the embargo to petroleum. Without American gasoline products and crude oil, Tokyo calculated, its industries would be paralyzed within a year.

With the deterioration of relations between his country and the United States, Admiral Yamamoto argued, it was "all the more necessary" to adopt his Pearl Harbor plan. "Japan must deal the U.S. Navy a fatal blow at the outset of war." Caving in to Yamamoto's threat of resignation, the Japanese naval command approved the surprise attack on Pearl Harbor.

Purple Succumbs to Magic

To ensure success the Japanese needed accurate, up-to-date information on the fleet disposition in Hawaii. On September 24 the foreign ministry asked the Japanese consulate in Honolulu to plot the location of each ship on a grid of Pearl Harbor. Donning a Hawaiian shirt and taking along a geisha friend as a cover, a secret agent named

Takeo Yoshikawa boarded a tourist flight over Oahu to observe the fleet. From early autumn through December 6 Tokyo was kept posted on all fleet movements in and out of the harbor and was supplied with information on the exact location of all the vessels in port.

Astonishingly, Washington knew that the Japanese were keeping track of the Pacific fleet. Tokyo's diplomatic correspondence was being transmitted by a sophisticated code named Purple. Unknown to Japan, the United States had cracked the code in the summer of 1940, using a decrypting system called Magic. By July 1941 the United States had eight Magic decrypting machines. Four were in Washington, two each assigned to the Navy and the Army; and three had been sent to the British in London. An eighth machine was dispatched to the U.S. Army in the Philippines, believed to be the most vulnerable of America's Pacific outposts. Magic, however, did not break the Japanese naval codes, and thus Washington remained unaware of the messages Yamamoto sent to the First Air Fleet when it left Japan for the long voyage to Hawaii.

"This Means War"

The American economic sanctions only stiffened Japanese resolve to pursue its expansionist policies. Japan, advised Ambassador Grew on November 3, would risk "national hara kiri rather than cede to foreign pressure." Demanding that the United States lift the freeze, supply it with petroleum, and discontinue aid to China, Japan in return promised only to withdraw its troops to northern Indochina and make no further moves into Southeast Asia. Cordell Hull called the proposal "preposterous."

On November 25 President Roosevelt met with his war council. According to the notes of Secretary of War Stimson, the president said that it was likely Japan would attack by December 1. The question for the war council, Stimson wrote, "was how we should maneuver them into the position of firing the first shot without allowing too much danger to ourselves." So-called revisionist historians have seized upon Stimson's statement in their attempts to prove that the United States wanted Japan to precipitate war.

The American historian Gordon W. Prange spent 37 years investigating Pearl Harbor, interviewing survivors in both Japan and the United States. The results of his exhaustive study were presented in several books published after his death in 1980. In the first of these books, *At Dawn We Slept*, Professor Prange rejected the revisionist viewpoint. No one who examined the mass of historical evidence could doubt that the United States wanted to maintain peace with Japan as long as possible in order to remain free to assist Britain in defeating the Axis in Europe. "Make no mistake about it," Prange wrote, "Japan was going to war, and those with access to

From the early 1930's on, Japan's army and navy determined the nation's foreign policy. The Greater East Asia Co-Prosperity Sphere used the nation's need for natural resources to cloak its military expansion. In Tokyo children dressed as generals and admirals marched in the streets.

No Foreign Wars

"And while I am talking to you mothers and fathers, I give you one more assurance. I have said this before, but I shall say it again and again and again: Your boys are not going to be sent into any foreign wars." Campaign promises such as this ensured reelection to an unprecedented third term for President Franklin D. Roosevelt on November 5, 1940.

Disillusioned by the peace settlement following its participation in World War I, the United States had retreated into isolationism in the 1920's and 1930's. During his first two terms Roosevelt had been preoccupied with engineering recovery from the Depression and could do no more than stand by as he saw Europe drift toward war. Although America officially remained neutral in the European conflict that erupted in September 1939, his sympathies were clearly with America's World War I allies, Britain and France, against the Axis powers, Germany, Italy, and — after September 27, 1940 — Japan. Following his reelection, Roosevelt signed the Lend-Lease Act, which empowered him to provide goods and services to those nations whose defense he deemed vital to that of the United States — a move favoring Britain. In August 1941 the president met with British Prime Minister Winston Churchill to sign the Atlantic Charter, a joint declaration of peace aims in the war against the Axis.

Such bold moves brought Roosevelt under fire from both Congress and the public as antiwar demonstrations broke out across the nation. "Save Our Sons" became the slogan of the America First Committee, which advocated strict neutrality. As late as October 1941, an opinion poll indicated that 74 percent of Americans were opposed to a U.S. declaration of war on Germany. The Japanese attack on Pearl Harbor two months later, however, united Americans behind Roosevelt as war was declared upon the aggressor and its European allies.

Magic knew it." The problem for the United States was not to maintain peace but only to be sure that Japan be revealed as the true aggressor.

The day after Roosevelt met with his war council, Yamamoto's First Air Fleet left Japan. By 5:50 A.M. on December 7 it was within 220 miles of Oahu — launch point for the air strike — and had not been detected. The armada consisted of six aircraft carriers, two battleships, three cruisers, a squadron of destroyers, and accompanying tankers and submarines.

In Tokyo the Japanese government drafted a "final communication to the United States," to be delivered by Ambassador Nomura at 1 P.M. Washington time on Sunday, December 7. This would be 7:30 A.M. in Honolulu, half an hour before the scheduled attack. Intercepting and decrypting the message, U.S. intelligence reported the contents to President Roosevelt Saturday evening. "This means war," the president said.

The instruction to Nomura to deliver the message precisely at 1 P.M. was a tip-off to intelligence officer Colonel Rufus S. Bratton that the Japanese were planning something for that hour — but what, and where? On Sunday morning he sought out Army Chief of Staff Marshall, only to learn that the general was out horseback riding and would not be at his office until 11:30. When presented a copy of the Japanese message, Marshall agreed that a strike was imminent and prepared a warning for all outlying U.S. possessions. It was to be sent "at once by the fastest safe means," with priority given to the Philippines. Since telephone calls could be monitored, it was decided to send Marshall's message in code by telegraph; U.S. intelligence was determined that Japan not learn that Magic had broken Purple. And thus General Short did not receive his copy of the warning until after the strike.

"Tora! Tora! Tora!"

Swooping in over Pearl Harbor at 7:53 A.M. on Sunday morning, Commander Fuchida shouted into his radio, *"Tora! Tora! Tora!"* ("Tiger! Tiger! Tiger!"). It was the code word for informing the Japanese navy that the U.S. Pacific Fleet had been caught unawares.

Yamamoto had predicted that the destruction of its fleet would so demoralize the United States that it would cease its opposition to Japan's expansion. Yet, in welcoming the First Air Fleet back home on December 24, the admiral cautioned that only one operation had been completed. "You must guard scrupulously against a smug self-satisfaction with this initial success," he warned. "There are many more battles ahead."

The Unknown Genius

*Romeo and Juliet, Hamlet, King Lear, Macbeth, Othello —
their deeds and thoughts are known the world over. Curiously, little is
known about the actor-playwright who created these fictional
characters, William Shakespeare.*

His literary legacy is perhaps the richest in the world: 37 plays, 154 sonnets, 2 long narrative poems, and miscellaneous verses. Yet there are but two likenesses of him with any claims to authenticity; no letters or diaries to reveal his personal feelings; and in his own handwriting only a variety of scrawled signatures and 147 lines of a scene he contributed to a collaborative play written about the year 1595 but suppressed by the censors.

Although William Shakespeare's accomplishments as a dramatist were acknowledged by his contemporaries, he himself thought that his poems would bring whatever enduring fame he merited. The complete canon of his plays was published only seven years after his death in 1616, and some scholars still do not accept all these as coming entirely from his pen. Would-be biographers have available to them only sketchy details with which to reconstruct a life.

Who Was Shakespeare?

In the parish register of Stratford-upon-Avon, a town of some 20,000 inhabitants 21 miles southeast of Birmingham, England, is an entry in Latin for the christening on April 26, 1564, of "Gulielmus, filius Johannes Shaksper": William, the son of John Shakespeare. William was the third child

Who really wrote the immortal plays? Was it the aristocratic Sir Francis Bacon (left), the poet and playwright Ben Jonson (right), or the actor William Shakespeare (center)?

(and first son) of eight born to Mary Arden and her husband, John Shakespeare, a glove maker and sometime local officeholder. He was probably born two or three days before his christening. There are no records of William's education, but it is reasonable to suppose that he attended Stratford's grammar school — grammar meaning Latin grammar. His upbringing would have included church attendance and intensive Bible study.

In late November or early December of 1582, the 18-year-old Shakespeare married Anne Hathaway, a prosperous farmer's daughter eight years his senior. Six months later a daughter, Susanna, was born to them; and in February 1585, twins, a son named Hamnet and another daughter named Judith. From that date until he appears in London as a popular actor and burgeoning playwright in 1592, nothing is known about William Shakespeare. These are his seven lost years.

The Upstart Crow

During the years Shakespeare was growing to maturity, Stratford's town fathers occasionally financed amateur theatrical performances at Pentecost. One of them may have offered Shakespeare his first chance to act. Or perhaps he traveled to nearby Coventry to attend one of the last cycles of medieval mystery plays given by members of the craft guilds. Shakespeare would certainly have had an opportunity to see one of the itinerant bands of players who regularly visited his town. No fewer than five troupes appeared in Stratford between December 1586 and December 1587; one of them was short one player, an actor recently killed in a barroom brawl. Did the company leave Stratford with a stagestruck young recruit?

The first reference to Shakespeare as being in London is an unflattering one. In his posthumously published pamphlet of 1592, *A Groatsworth of Wit*, the prolific young dramatist Robert Greene inveighed against a theatrical Jack-of-all-trades who had the audacity to pass himself off as a playwright. Trust not this "upstart crow," Greene warned his fellow authors, ". . . that with his tiger's heart wrapped in a player's hide supposes he is as well able to bombast out blank verse as the best of you." The newcomer, Greene complained, "is in his own conceit the only Shake-scene in a country." Literary detectives point out

Since little is known about Shakespeare's early years, biographers seize on the smallest items to invent colorful incidents. A document saying that he had to appear before a justice of the peace for poaching is the source for the illustration below.

The Stratford house in which Shakespeare is thought to have been born (above) is a popular tourist attraction.

not only the punning reference to Shakespeare in this passage but also the parody of a line from one of the dramatist's earliest plays, *Henry VI, Part III*, in which the captive duke of York refers to the vengeful Queen Margaret as a "tiger's heart wrapped in a woman's hide."

The Lord Chamberlain's Men

Largely because of Greene's disparaging remark, historians list the three parts of *Henry VI* as Shakespeare's first plays. Most likely they were written before 1592, when he was a fledgling actor in one of London's theatrical companies such as the Queen's Men. But on January 28, 1593, Shakespeare's activities as an actor and playwright were temporarily halted, as were those of all his professional colleagues. Because of an outbreak of plague in London, the queen's privy council banned "all plays, baiting of bears, bulls, bowling and any other like occasions to assemble any numbers of people together (preaching and divine service at churches excepted)." The theaters were not to reopen until the autumn of 1594.

By the time the plague had abated, Shakespeare had acquired a patron, the handsome young earl of Southampton, to whom he dedicated his narrative poems *Venus and Adonis* and *The Rape of Lucrece*. Issued in 1593, *Venus and Adonis* was his first published work. And when the theaters reopened, Shakespeare was a member of the Lord Chamberlain's Men, the company with which he would be associated until his retirement from the stage some 18 years later. The account book of Queen Elizabeth's treasurer lists William Shakespeare as one of the three "servants to the Lord Chamberlain" paid for performances before the queen at her Greenwich palace on December 26 and 28, 1594.

As the comedies, tragedies, and historical dramas followed one after another, Shakespeare gained fame as well as wealth, for he was soon a shareholder in the company as well as its principal dramatist. Most likely he staged his own works, and he is known to have continued acting — in his own plays and in those of others, among them the works of his young protégé Ben Jonson. His best performance was said to be as the ghost of Hamlet's father, and Shakespeare's younger brother recalled him appearing as the aged servant Adam in *As You Like It*.

Although Shakespeare seemed relatively indifferent to publication of his works for the theater, several of his plays were published by the end of the century — with or without his consent, often without his name as author. In some cases it was necessary for the playwright to issue corrected

Theater's Golden Age

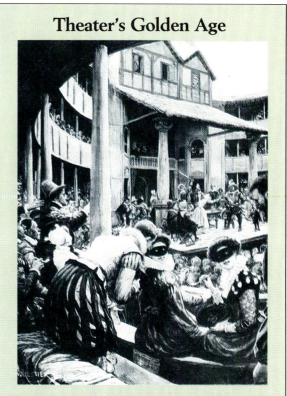

To the everlasting glory of English literature, Shakespeare and the London stage came of age at the same time. In 1574, when the future playwright was but a 10-year-old country boy in Stratford, Queen Elizabeth I licensed a troupe of actors under the patronage of the earl of Leicester to give performances in the capital city and throughout her realm. The leading player, James Burbage, promptly built the first commercial playhouse in London, an open-air amphitheater, approximately 100 feet in diameter, that could hold 3,000 spectators. Admission to his theater was one penny — a 12th of the shilling a skilled craftsman earned in a day.

Burbage's theater, modeled after the bull- and bear-baiting amphitheaters of the time, was a polygonal structure with three rings of galleries for seated spectators. Most of the audience, however, stood in the courtyard surrounding the thrust stage, which measured 40 by 27 feet.

Burbage's son, Richard, was the leading actor of the Lord Chamberlain's Men, for which Shakespeare wrote his greatest plays. The two were among the partners who built the Globe in 1599. There Richard Burbage created the title roles in *Hamlet*, *Richard III*, *Othello*, and *King Lear* — giving such compelling performances that it was widely believed the plays would not survive his death in 1619. But not even Parliament's closure of all London theaters in 1642 could suppress Shakespeare's immortal genius.

versions of plays that had appeared in incomplete or corrupted form.

In February 1599 Shakespeare joined other members of the Lord Chamberlain's Men in leasing a site on the south bank of the river Thames and erecting there a grand new theater, the Globe. That autumn the Globe opened with a performance of *Julius Caesar*.

Home to Stratford

There is no record of Anne Hathaway bringing her three children to London to live with her husband. Instead, the famous actor and playwright seems to have maintained his family in Stratford, first in a little house on Henley Street but, after 1597, in a handsome, three-story house with five gables set behind a courtyard on Chapel Street across from the church he had attended as a boy. Their son, Hamnet, died at the age of 11, but Shakespeare lived to see both of his daughters marry, and the eldest, Susanna, give birth to his only grandchild, a girl named Elizabeth Hall.

Sometime after 1612, Shakespeare retired to Stratford and, on March 25, 1616, signed his last will and testament — with its peculiar bequest of his "second best bed" to his wife of 33 years, Anne Hathaway. He died a month later, on April 23, on or about his 52nd birthday.

In Search of Shakespeare

So rich and so enduring are the works of William Shakespeare that, in time, doubts arose as to whether they could have come from the pen of a single person — especially one as relatively uneducated as the minor actor from Stratford. With their intricate plots and unforgettable characters, the celebrated plays plumb the breadth and depth of human emotions and reveal the author's knowledge of history, literature, philosophy, law, and even court etiquette. Where did this country man pursuing a profession on the fringes of society learn how aristocrats behave and lawyers talk? Was it possible that the actor allowed his name to be used by a well-educated man in high office who wished to keep his authorship of the plays a secret?

In 1781 an English churchman named J. Wilmot, after searching the records at Stratford, reached the startling conclusion that a man of Shakespeare's background lacked the education and experience to write the immortal plays. Unwilling to publish his thesis, Wilmot burned his notes although he confided his suspicions to a friend. The friend's record of their conversations did not come to light until 1932. Meanwhile, in the mid-19th century, both British and American scholars had begun advancing similar theories. In 1856 one of them, William Henry Smith, proposed Sir Francis Bacon as author of the plays. The philosopher, essayist, and statesman held high office under Queen Elizabeth's successor, James I, and was later raised to the nobility by his royal patron. Scholars on both sides of the Atlantic pounced on Smith's hypothesis to produce an avalanche of documentation for the claim.

The Baconians, as they came to be known, pointed out that Sir Francis had all the qualities the actor lacked: a classical education, a position

A visitor to Stratford inspects the Elizabethan costumes of wax figures made for a film about the playwright's times. Performances of the plays are given in Stratford by the Royal Shakespeare Company.

The Man No One Knew

It was only long after his death that the authorship of Shakespeare's plays came to be questioned. For the 20th-century novelist B. Traven, the mystery of his identity shrouded his entire career.

A stream of radical, antiauthoritarian books, obsessed with cruelty, loneliness, fear, superstition, and death, began appearing in Germany in the mid-1920's. They were later published in English as *The Death Ship, The Bridge in the Jungle, The Rebellion of the Hanged,* and *The Treasure of the Sierra Madre*. The author, B. Traven, was known to be living in Mexico, but he declined to give his publishers any photographs or biographical material. The author's reticence only whetted the appetites of journalists and literary historians, but it was only in 1990 — 21 years after his death — that his widow, Rosa

The author B. Traven remained a mystery man; above, the German cover of his first book.

Elena Luján, revealed his secret.

According to her, the novelist was the actor turned revolutionary, Ret Marut, forced to flee Germany after a failed uprising in Munich in 1919. Among the aliases he assumed in Mexico was Hal Croves, the name under which the director John Huston — filming *The Treasure of the Sierra Madre* in 1947 — hired him as a technical adviser. The Mexican passport he obtained in the 1950's gave his name as Traven Torsvan, born in Chicago on May 3, 1890, of Norwegian immigrant parents. The novelist also liked to mention the theory that he was the illegitimate son of German emperor William II. Since Ret Marut can only be traced to 1907, Mrs. Luján's revelation leaves unanswered the question, Who was B. Traven before he took on the identity of Ret Marut?

at court, a sound knowledge of the law. Unfortunately for their theory, Bacon apparently did not care for the theater and is not known to have written any blank verse.

In 1955 an American scholar named Calvin Hoffman named the Elizabethan playwright Christopher Marlowe as the author of the Shakespeare plays. Marlowe was facing imprisonment, perhaps even death, for his heretical views in 1593. According to Hoffman's theory, he staged his own murder in a pub south of London — a foreign seaman being the real victim. Fleeing to the Continent, Marlowe continued writing the type of plays that had already gained him acclaim in London and sent them back to England for production under Shakespeare's name.

Aristocratic Candidates

Not Bacon, not Marlowe, not the younger playwright Ben Jonson wrote Shakespeare's plays say other literary sleuths. The real author was a nobleman who either considered it beneath his dignity to write for the theater or feared royal displeasure for expressing controversial political opinions in public. Among the aristocratic candidates proposed — all, more or less, Shakespeare's contemporaries — are William Stanley, the sixth earl of Derby; Roger Manners, the fifth earl of Rutland;

and Edward de Vere, the 17th earl of Oxford.

Although Lord Derby displayed a great interest in the theater and even wrote a few plays, it has to be noted that he outlived Shakespeare by 26 years, and in those years no additional Shakespeare plays appeared. The problem with a claim for Lord Rutland is that he was only 16 in 1592, the year by which at least three of Shakespeare's plays had been written and produced. As for Lord Oxford, he died in 1604, whereas such Shakespearean masterpieces as *King Lear, Macbeth*, and *The Tempest* continued to appear in a steady stream up to 1612 — the year Shakespeare is thought to have retired to Stratford.

Despite such intriguing speculation about a secret author who cloaked his identity behind a rustic actor's name, most scholars now accept William Shakespeare of Stratford-upon-Avon as the true author of the great works so long attributed to him. His genius was acknowledged in his own time, and there were no contemporary challenges to his authorship. It is futile to try to explain how he acquired the experience and talent to produce such a body of work. It is far better to be thankful that the young man left his humble background behind as he set out on the road for London 400 years ago. The world is far richer for his having done so.

The Stolen Election

*When all the popular votes had been counted in the 1876
presidential election, Democrat Samuel J. Tilden appeared to have
defeated Republican Rutherford B. Hayes. But the final
outcome rested with the electoral college.*

Rutherford B. Hayes, the governor of Ohio and Republican candidate for president of the United States, is sitting in the parlor of his home across the street from the statehouse in Columbus with his wife, Lucy, and a few friends, anxiously awaiting the election returns. It is Tuesday, November 7, 1876. Throughout the evening messenger boys from the local telegraph office file in and out of the room with the latest news, which is mostly bad.

New York, which Hayes had considered a key to victory, has remained loyal to its favorite son, Governor Samuel J. Tilden, the Democratic standard-bearer. Connecticut, New Jersey, even staunchly Republican Indiana fall into the Democratic column. Since the Democrats are expected to carry the so-called Solid South, Tilden appears to have won the hotly contested race. Trying to console his wife with the observation that defeat means a more tranquil personal life, Hayes retires shortly after midnight; for him, the affair seems over. Meanwhile, in New York City, Governor Tilden is receiving congratulatory messages at his Gramercy Park mansion.

*Republicans celebrated the electoral victory of their candidates, Hayes and Wheeler (right), over
Democrats Tilden and Hendricks (left), with a torchlight procession in Washington.*

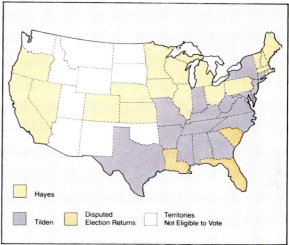

Both parties were accused of fraud in the 1876 presidential election. In the South white Democrats frequently intimidated black freedmen.

As the map below shows, Hayes carried most of the North and West. In addition to his own New York and other scattered northern states, Tilden carried the Solid South — with the dispute centering on South Carolina, Florida, and Louisiana.

Hayes	
Tilden	Disputed Election Returns
	Territories Not Eligible to Vote

Turning Defeat into Victory

However, the presidential election is not being conceded to Tilden by the managing editor of *The New York Times*, John C. Reid. An inquiry from Democratic headquarters, received in the newsroom at 3:45 A.M. on Wednesday morning, tips off Reid to the lack of accurate information on the voting in three southern states: Louisiana, with eight electoral votes; South Carolina, with seven; and Florida, with four. According to Reid's calculations, Tilden has 184 electoral votes to Hayes's 166. The Democrat is one vote short of a majority, but if those three southern states can be put in the Republican column, Hayes will be the winner. An ardent and unabashed Republican, the newspaperman forms a plan.

Rousing the Republican national leader from his sleep at the Fifth Avenue Hotel, Reid receives authorization to send messages to party leaders in the three states: "Hayes is elected if we have carried South Carolina, Florida, and Louisiana. Can you hold your state? Answer immediately." Scurrying back to the *Times*, Reid locks up the first edition of the Wednesday newspaper, in which he states that "the result of the presidential election is still in doubt." The second edition, published at 6:30 A.M., concedes 184 electoral votes to Tilden but arbitrarily consigns Louisiana and South Carolina to Hayes, giving the Republican 181 votes. The outcome, the *Times* now claims, rests with Florida's four electoral votes. It takes Reid only another day to award the election

to the Republicans. The November 9 edition of the *Times* announces without reservation that "Hayes has 185 electoral votes and is elected."

Constitutional Loopholes

The irregular and highly partisan activities of the *Times* managing editor, most historians agree, set in motion a train of events that led to the inauguration of the man who actually lost the 1876 presidential election. But Reid, and those who successfully maneuvered Hayes into the White House, were merely seizing upon two weaknesses or ambiguities in the U.S. Constitution to ensure a favorite's victory.

Under Article II, Section 1, of the Constitution, the president of the United States is actually selected by a majority vote of the electoral college, each state having the same number of electors as it has U.S. senators and members of the House of Representatives. (Thus, in 1876, populous New York had 35 electors, corresponding to its two U.S. senators and its 33 representatives; sparsely settled Oregon had but three electors, corresponding to its two U.S. senators and its single representative.) Meeting separately in their respective states after the general election, the electors certify the choices of the people and forward the state results to Washington, D.C. The candidate who carries the popular vote, by tradition at least, is awarded a state's entire electoral vote. Thus it is possible for a candidate to garner more votes nationwide than his opponent but lose out in the electoral count.

The president of the Senate, the Constitution continues, is to open the state certificates of election and count the vote in the presence of the Senate and House of Representatives. It is silent on what is to be done in the event that conflicting electoral votes are returned by any state. However, if no candidate wins a clear majority in the electoral college, the selection of a president is to be made by the House of Representatives.

Troubled Times

To understand how and why Hayes and not Tilden was inaugurated on March 4, 1877, as the 19th president of the United States, one must know something about the troubled times in which the disputed election was held. In 1876, only 11 years after the North's victory in the Civil War, the nation was but slowly emerging from the excesses of what is known as the Reconstruction period. In those southern states where the Democrats had regained control, freed slaves were often denied the vote by intimidation if not by outright physical force. In three states, however, the Republicans still held power by military force: Louisiana, South Carolina, and Florida.

In Washington, Ulysses S. Grant was completing his second term, the improprieties of his Republican administration shocking even the most devoted supporters of the popular wartime hero. But as the party in power in the White House, the Republicans were determined to repeat their decisive victories in the last two presidential elections. The Democrats hungered for an end to Reconstruction and a return to undisputed national leadership, denied them since Lincoln's surprising win in 1860. Congress reflected the nation's sharp division with a Republican Senate and a Democratic House of Representatives.

With so much at stake and passions running so strong, Tilden's supporters were not about to accept the verdict of *The New York Times*, and the Democrats promptly sent a delegation south to review the electoral process that presumably had denied the three states' votes to their candidate. The Republicans also sent emissaries south to look after Hayes's interests. President Grant, loyal Republican that he was, alerted federal troops in the southern states to the need for resisting any tampering with the returns as canvassing boards went about the business of validating the elector-

al count to be sent to Washington. Controlled by the Republicans, the canvassing boards in Louisiana, South Carolina, and Florida were thoroughly corrupt. James A. Garfield, Republican leader in the House of Representatives (and a future president of the United States), called his party's Louisiana canvassers a "graceless set of scamps." There is evidence that the Louisiana board offered to certify Tilden's election if the Democrats could come up with a $1 million bribe.

Meeting separately in the three disputed states on December 6, Hayes and Tilden electors cast votes for their candidate and each forwarded the results to Washington. If it was now up to the Republican president of the Senate to choose between conflicting electoral returns, Hayes would be declared the winner. If neither candidate could be shown to have a majority of the electoral college, the election would go to the House of Representatives, controlled by the Democrats, and Tilden would be chosen.

The suspense mounted as a further element of doubt about the electoral count was raised in Oregon. One of Hayes's three electors there was John W. Watts, a fourth-class postmaster drawing an annual salary of $268. The Democratic governor of Oregon ruled that Watts's position was one of "trust and profit under the United States" and that he was thus barred by the Constitution from serving as an elector. In his place, the governor named a Democratic elector who — if accepted by the president of the Senate — would give Tilden the final vote he needed.

Reaching a Compromise

A dignified, humorless man, Governor Tilden confined his post-election activities to compiling a learned study showing that no previous president of the Senate had ever exercised discretionary power in counting the electoral votes. He sent a copy to each member of Congress in the hope that the deadlock would be resolved by a vote in the House of Representatives, which he could be expected to win. Hayes likewise remained above the fray, though his political friends were busy behind the scenes negotiating a compromise with wavering southern Democrats who wanted federal troops removed from their states more than they wanted a Democratic president.

At last men of both parties agreed on a method of resolving the crisis. On January 29, 1877, Congress passed a law establishing a special 15-member electoral commission. It was to be composed of three Republican and two Democratic senators, three Democratic and two Republican members of the House of Representatives, and

Following his inauguration on March 4, 1877, President Hayes (third from right) was pictured in a White House meeting with his cabinet. At the extreme left is his interior secretary, the liberal Republican Carl Schurz, a champion of the civil service reform that was a major accomplishment of the Hayes administration.

two Supreme Court justices from each party. The 15th, presumably neutral, commissioner was to be an independent Supreme Court justice, David Davis of Illinois. On the very day that the bill went to President Grant for signature, Justice Davis was notified that the Illinois legislature had elected him to the U.S. Senate. The neutrality of Davis's replacement on the commission, Justice Joseph P. Bradley, was less assured.

On February 1 both houses of Congress met to begin counting the electoral returns, proceeding alphabetically through the list of states: Alabama and Arkansas, Tilden; California and Colorado, Hayes; Connecticut and Delaware, Tilden. But when Florida's conflicting returns were presented, the Senate president halted the count and referred the dispute to the electoral commission.

The night before the commission was to announce its decision on Florida, the Democratic national chairman went to visit Justice Bradley, who assured him that he would vote with the Democrats. But sometime between midnight and dawn, and after being visited by two influential Republicans, Bradley changed his mind. By a vote of eight to seven, Bradley voting with the Republicans, the commission awarded Florida's four votes to Hayes. Although the final outcome was no longer in doubt, the charade continued until — toward 4 A.M. on the morning of March 2 — the state roll call was completed. Rutherford B. Hayes was declared the victor over Tilden, 185 electoral votes to 184. Two days later Hayes was inaugurated as president of the United States.

Who Really Won the Election?

When all the election returns were in, Tilden had 4,300,590 popular votes to 4,036,298 for Hayes — a clear majority for the Democratic standard-bearer. The final vote of the electoral college, however, is still disputed among students of the period.

Most historians agree that only a technicality prevented Hayes from rightfully claiming all three of Oregon's votes. They also concede South Carolina to the Republican candidate. In awarding Louisiana's electoral vote to Hayes, the state canvassing board and later the electoral commission in Washington were ignoring the popular vote. Yet the intimidation of black voters in Louisiana helped produce a popular majority for Tilden; in a fair election, Hayes might well have triumphed. In Florida, however, it was the Republicans who perpetrated the greatest election fraud. In a fair election there, white voters — in the majority and solidly Democratic — would have given the state to Tilden. Florida's four electoral votes, if awarded to Tilden, would have put him over the top: 188 votes to Hayes's 181.

Despite the controversy of his election, Hayes proved to be a competent president, amply demonstrating in his single term that he meant what he said in his inaugural address: "He serves his party best who serves his country best." As for Tilden, he left office in 1877 after serving a single two-year term as governor of New York — convinced that he had been cheated of the presidency. He never again sought public office.

Murders Along the Thames

Swift as a cat, reveling in blood, a savage murderer
picked his victims from among the streetwalkers of a seamy London slum.
The 1888 killer was never caught, though the police declared
the case closed. Why did they do so?

With the fragment of human kidney sent in the mail to the police came a letter: "I send you half the kidne I took from one woman . . . tother piece I fried and ate. . . ." The writer's return address: "From Hell." It was the fall of 1888, and all of London instantly knew that the gruesome missive came from "Jack the Ripper," who had just slashed to death his fourth known victim, 43-year-old Catherine Eddowes.

All four women had been pathetic prostitutes, aging and worn, forced to ply their degrading trade in the slum district known as Whitechapel. A veritable cesspool of the most wretchedly impoverished people, it had narrow streets and alleys that led through a filthy maze of gin shops, brothels, and opium dens. Fewer than half the children survived to the age of five; up to seven people were packed into each tiny room of this garbage-strewn warren. To fend off starvation in such desperate circumstances, many young women had no alternative but to become streetwalkers. Such women, for unexplained reasons, were the prey of the Ripper, who was never identified nor apprehended.

Death in the Foggy Gloom

The first victim was 42-year-old Mary Ann "Polly" Nichols, whose throat was slit on the night of August 31. As she lay dying in a grimy little alley, her killer ripped open her abdomen with his 10-inch knife. Eight days later "Dark Annie" Chapman, 47, already weakened from tuberculosis, was dispatched in precisely the same manner with the same type of instrument.

Now people recalled an earlier murder of a Whitechapel prostitute. Since she had merely been stabbed to death, police saw no likely connection. But the public felt otherwise and raised a frightened outcry that put pressure on the police to send reinforcements to the slum district. Private detectives and civilian volunteers eagerly enlisted in the Whitechapel Vigilance Committee, set up by concerned London business interests.

With the mounting fear came an exposé of the dark side of Victorian life. Comfortable members of society had long ignored the cruel conditions forced upon the poor. In an age when sexual matters were not even mentioned, much less discussed, the so-called proper people had turned a blind eye on the city's numerous streetwalkers.

However, attention continued to be focused upon the killer, who had written his first letter bragging about his crimes in red ink and signed it with the name he bestowed on himself, "Jack the Ripper." His taunts that the police would not catch him seemed well-founded, though patterns in his crimes became evident.

Medical examiners determined that he was left-handed and knew a good deal about anatomy, obviously being skilled in extracting human organs with precision. And, gradually, it became clear that each murder was committed in the hours between 11 P.M. and 4 A.M. But this was not nearly enough evidence. Investigators took to hounding innocent persons, merely because they were common criminals, known sex offenders, or mentally ill surgeons and butchers. The harassment proved fruitless.

The murderer's crimes became even more daring — and more hideous. Apparently interrupted just after cutting the throat of Elizabeth "Long Liz" Stride, 45, the Ripper fleetly vanished into the night vapors shortly after midnight on September 30, leaving his victim dead but unmutilated. She was found clutching a bunch of grapes in one hand, sweets in the other. The witness who had stumbled upon the scene heard footsteps but failed to catch a glimpse of the killer.

Deprived of his familiar pleasure, the Ripper struck again within 45 minutes. His target this time was Eddowes, whom he killed and disemboweled, removing the kidney fragment sent

The phantom of the grisly murders haunted London. For three months late in 1888, Jack the Ripper terrified the British capital, as defenseless women of the night wondered who would be his next victim.

through the mail. Astonishingly, a watchman on guard only several yards away heard nothing. Somehow, on a busy Saturday night in a teeming slum, with hordes of extra-duty policemen and vigilantes primed to nab him, the presumably blood-covered killer got away once again.

A Royal Suspect . . .

For six weeks after the double murder, the Ripper did not make a move. Meanwhile, the police pursued an interesting lead.

On the night that Stride and Eddowes had been killed, an officer had detained an elegantly attired gentleman seen talking to a Whitechapel prostitute. When questioned, the well-spoken suspect — totally out of place in the dingy district — passed himself off as a physician and convinced the policeman to let him go. Suddenly, rumors were spreading unchecked. Was the murderer a member of high society who, driven by some mad compulsion, had become obsessed with the lowlife of the slums?

For nearly a century one popular suspect under this theory was the duke of Clarence, a grandson of Queen Victoria. Newspapers of the time, however, never published such speculation since the duke was the eldest son of the heir to the throne, Edward, Prince of Wales, who later reigned as King Edward VII. Yet it was known that the duke suffered from some form of mental instability. Those who support the theory that he was Jack the Ripper point out that the duke was

Persistent rumors linked the Ripper with the duke of Clarence, a grandson of Queen Victoria. Unfortunately for lovers of hidden royal scandal, recent research has proved that the duke was off shooting in Scotland at the time at least two of the murders were committed.

institutionalized after the last murder, never to be set free. He died in 1892.

... and a Convenient Suicide

The most hideous of the murders took place early in the morning of November 10. At 3:45 A.M. that day, neighbors heard screams from the room of Jane "Black Mary" Kelly, who was only 24 years old. When the landlord's servant edged inside at daylight, it was clear that the Ripper had taken advantage of the privacy afforded by his victim's quarters. Painstakingly, he had eviscerated the corpse, removed the heart and kidneys, and laid the body parts neatly about the room.

This brutal and bizarre murder was the last of-

ficially attributed to Jack the Ripper. Within weeks, the police had closed the case without an explanation to the mystified public. In private, members of the Whitechapel Vigilance Committee were told that the murderer had confessed before drowning himself in the Thames. To this day, however, the suicide note has not been shown publicly, nor have its contents been revealed. Many suspect that officials were perpetrating a cover-up to protect either the duke of Clarence or a rogue police officer.

As for the drowned man, a suicide had indeed been pulled out of the Thames after the murder of "Black Mary" Kelly. On December 3 Montague John Druitt, a struggling lawyer who had become obsessed with his mother's mental illness, killed himself by drowning. His suicide note has never been published and could well be the confession cited by the police in closing the case.

Scion of an aristocratic family in the medical profession, Druitt was well connected in England's upper-class society, having attended a prestigious boarding school. His fellow members in an elite club, The Apostles, came from the nation's first families. All who knew the lawyer agreed that he detested women.

On July 1, 1888, Mrs. Druitt was committed to a clinic for the mentally ill. Her son visited her there regularly, perhaps increasingly fearful of his own mental stability. Whether he went there from his law offices or from a boys' boarding school where he had to eke out a living as a physical education instructor, Druitt would have had to pass through the Whitechapel district to reach his mother's clinic.

Did Druitt's fears and hatred of women combine to produce the monster who called himself Jack the Ripper? By October his brother William was noticing signs of mental strain and aberrant behavior. On November 30 Druitt was summarily dismissed from his school job.

To some theorists it seems likely that The Apostles used their high social position to protect the good name of one of their own. Perhaps they encouraged Druitt's suicide or even banded together to kill him, thus putting an end to his barbaric and insatiable addiction. Then, according to this theory, they convinced the authorities to suppress the true story and close the case.

Suspected of as many as 14 murders, the unknown assailant was perhaps guilty of only five during his three-month reign of terror. Fascinated with blood, choosing his victims so that the crime sites formed a cross on the map of Whitechapel, Jack the Ripper will probably never be identified, much less understood.

Flames over Berlin

**Scarcely had Adolf Hitler been sworn in as chancellor
than the hall of Germany's lower house was set ablaze. Nazi and
communist parties each accused the other of complicity. Who, indeed, was
responsible for the dramatic act of political arson?**

O n the cold, blustery evening of February 27, 1933, the great stone edifice known as the Reichstag stood all but empty in Berlin. The deputies had gone home, leaving only a few night watchmen to turn off the lights, patrol the corridors, and guard the one portal that remained unlocked. Just after 9 P.M. a student walking in the street below heard the sound of breaking glass and, looking up, saw a figure on one of the building's first floor balconies. The figure was carrying what appeared to be a flaming torch.

The student sprang into action, running toward the nearest guard station to sound the alarm. The officer on duty, Karl Buwert, decided to confirm the report before passing it on to his superiors, so he went around to find the broken window. When he saw the opening, and the reddish glow within, Buwert realized that a fire was already burning in several places. He raced off to alert the police and government officials, and within a few minutes the fire brigades' sirens were ringing out across the city.

Now constables and watchmen were running everywhere, trying to unlock doors to let the firemen gain entry to the building. All told, 19 minutes elapsed between the time the student spotted the intruder and the time the first official was able to enter the session chamber, where the

*The Reichstag in Berlin went up in flames on the night of February 27, 1933. The Nazis exploited an
arsonist's crime to stifle opposition and consolidate their power in Germany.*

main fire was burning. They found the thick plush curtains on either side of the door aflame and some of the wooden paneling on fire. Across the room flames were also licking around the stenographer's pulpit, and dozens of smaller fires were burning on the deputies' desks. One of the constables, running back to portal five to report what he had seen, also noted several wastebasket fires, more than two dozen burning rags scattered about, and, finally, an abandoned cap and necktie. Clearly, the fires were not accidental but the work of an arsonist — perhaps several.

By 9:25 constable Helmut Poeschel and building inspector Alexander Scranowitz had arrived at the sessions chamber to see what they could do. While they were still staring in astonishment at the conflagration, a young man, shirtless, sooty, and disheveled, darted past them. The officers shouted at him to halt and put up his hands.

Through this underground passage from the ministry of the interior, the arsonist or arsonists were said to have gained access to the Reichstag — though an investigation proved such an entry to be highly unlikely. Van der Lubbe's frantic route through the building is traced in red on the floor plan at right.

The man offered no resistance and was immediately searched for weapons or other incriminating evidence. All Poeschel and Scranowitz found were a pocket knife, a wallet, and a Dutch passport identifying him as Marinus van der Lubbe, born January 13, 1909, in Leiden. It was plain to them that they had stumbled on the culprit. "Why did you do it?" Scranowitz shouted. "As a protest," the man mumbled.

As the officers led van der Lubbe away to police headquarters, 15 fire companies arrived on the scene, and soon 60 pumpers and several fire boats were pouring water onto the burning building. In an hour and a half the crews had the fire under control. The building was saved, but the session chamber was in ruins, its glass ceiling lying in exploded shards all over the floor.

A Communist Conspiracy?

Hermann Goering, the minister of the interior, was dining with Adolf Hitler, the newly elected chancellor of Germany and leader of the National Socialist Party, when news of the Reichstag burning reached him. Goering abruptly excused himself from the führer and immediately rushed across town to observe the fire. When asked by reporters who might be responsible for the crime, Goering did not hesitate. He accused the German communists, against whom the Nazis were currently waging an all-out campaign of suppression. "This is a communist crime against the new government," he charged. And when an official argued that only one perpetrator had been seized, he shot back, "One man? That wasn't just one man, but ten, twenty! This is the signal for the communist uprising!" Asked how

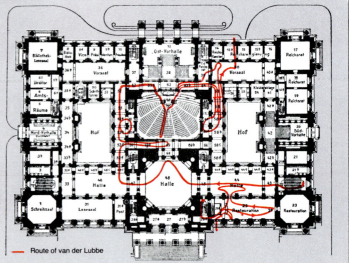

Route of van der Lubbe

The Clairvoyant Who Knew Too Much

On April 5, 1933, less than three months after the Reichstag fire, repairmen working a few miles east of Berlin came upon a bloody corpse lying in a roadside ditch. The victim was identified as the celebrated stage performer Jan Erik Hanussen.

Hanussen, born the son of a synagogue caretaker, had left the Jewish ghetto as a youngster to seek his fortune in vaudeville. He tried his hand as a knife-thrower, a strong man, and a fire-eater, succeeding after a fashion at all of them. After World War I the young trooper joined a major circus company where he discovered he had remarkable talents as a stage clairvoyant as well. He was soon enthralling audiences with mental feats that ranged from "seeing" objects in people's pockets to predicting bank robberies and fingering

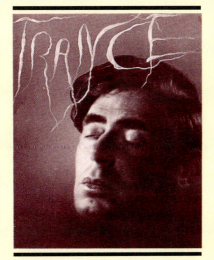

The séances of Jan Erik Hanussen were famous and his predictions eagerly awaited. He won favor with the Nazis by foretelling Hitler's rise.

the culprits. By the 1920's Hanussen's unusual abilities had made him famous, and he became a pet of the Nazi leadership.

It was not long after his spectacular rise, however, that he came to his bloody end. To this day historians differ as to what caused Hanussen's falling out with his patrons. Some say that he embarrassed party members when — on the evening of February 24, 1933, just three days before the Reichstag fire — he foretold of "a great house on fire," adding that it was a signal for some kind of popular uprising. But this explanation for the clairvoyant's murder makes sense only if the Nazis were indeed directly responsible for the arson. A more plausible theory is that Hanussen was killed by order of a Nazi official to whom he had unwisely lent a substantial sum of money.

the arsonists might have gained access to the Reichstag — and all but one of them have gotten away again — Goering suggested that they had used the underground passage that ran between his offices across the boulevard and the Reichstag. The minister, looking almost ebullient, vowed to round up and punish all 4,000 members of what he called the "Red Terror" immediately.

Legalizing Totalitarianism

Many outside Nazi circles, however, were not so sure about Goering's hasty judgment. The communists were already in a weakened state in Germany, and it was hard to imagine how the tactics of arson could possibly gain them favor with a wary populace. And the underground tunnels by which they were supposed to have gained entry to the Reichstag were under the specific control of Goering and his police; it would presumably be easy for Nazi arsonists to set the fire and retreat in good order, but very difficult for communist plotters. At the same time, there were many reasons why the Nazis might benefit from a spectacular fire, especially one in which they could implicate their archenemies on the eve of major nationwide elections. Had not Goering vowed in recent times to get the Reds by "indirect" means, but only at "the proper moment," after what he

termed a Bolshevik revolution had "flared up"?

Goering's critics also noted that the interior minister lost no time in submitting a "Decree for the Protection of People and State," which effectively gave the Nazis all the legal powers they would ever need to run a totalitarian dictatorship. The morning after the fire Goering showed up at the office of the doddering old president of the Weimar Republic, Paul von Hindenburg, to demand that he sign into law a wide-ranging decree "against communist acts of violence." Goering's decree restricted personal liberty, the free expression of opinions, including freedom of the press, and the rights of assembly and association. In their place the decree gave the government permission to control all use of the postal and telephone services, to conduct unannounced house searches, and to confiscate private property in the interests of state security.

Even while German communists were being rounded up, a few brave voices were raised among centrists who wanted the government to launch an objective investigation into the crime and to restore civil rights. In Paris a group of international communists published a document entitled *The Brown Book*. The book purported to tell the real story of how the Nazis had torched their own government building. Working from a distance, and without benefit of any direct evidence, the authors of the exposé did not scruple to invent "proof" of involvement by Goering and other high-ranking Nazis.

An Inconclusive Trial

In the end, *The Brown Book* only confused foreign opinion further, and the Nazis, thoroughly untouched by the debate, proceeded with their own plans. Goering, in particular, seemed to grow bolder as he saw public distrust of the communists becoming ever greater. "Fellow Germans," he told an assembled crowd two days before the March 5 election of deputies, "my measures will not be crippled by any judicial thinking. . . . I don't have to worry about justice. . . . This struggle will be a struggle against chaos."

On March 22, three weeks after van der Lubbe's arrest, the magistrate of the supreme court issued a statement: "The investigation has so far shown that the Dutch communist van der Lubbe . . . was in communication immediately before the fire not only with German communists but also with foreign communists." He added that the persons were under arrest and included Ernst Torgler, parliamentary leader of the German communists, and three Bulgarians.

The subsequent supreme court trial, which

was held in both Leipzig and Berlin and ran from September 21 to December 23, turned into something of an embarrassment for the Nazis, lending some credence to claims that the communists were not, in fact, behind the crime. The prosecution failed to mount a serious case against Torgler or the Bulgarians. Despite the appearance of many prominent witnesses for the state, no direct links between van der Lubbe and the four "coconspirators" were ever established. Georgi Dimitroff, one of the Bulgarians, even managed to catch Goering in a number of inconsistencies. In cross-examination, which the Bulgarian handled on his own behalf, he so unnerved Goering that the latter lost his temper, shouting death threats at his calm questioner.

As for van der Lubbe, he proved an even more difficult defendant, but for different reasons. The Dutchman was not interested in defense at all. He confessed to having set the fire at the outset, and he never wavered from that position throughout the trial. Although van der Lubbe was questioned at length about his motives and associations, all that anyone succeeded in getting from him was the proud boast that he had acted alone, that he had set every one of the several dozen fires in the Reichstag himself, and that he was impatient to be sentenced for his crime.

Carefully Contrived Scandals

Internal politics appear to have been behind Hitler's removal of two leading military officers on the eve of World War II. The first general to be swept aside was Field Marshal Werner von Blomberg, minister of war, who had repeatedly expressed doubts about the wisdom of provoking Britain or France into war. Hitler, who could not tolerate opposition, decided to arrange Blomberg's downfall.

In late December 1937 the 59-year-old widower asked Hitler for permission to marry a certain Eva Gruhn. Unbeknownst to Blomberg, Gruhn had a police record, having once been a prostitute and a pornographic model. Hermann Goering, who made it his business to know such things, saw the perfect opportunity to oust the troublesome general and so informed the führer. No sooner was the couple married than malicious ru-

Two victims of a Goering plot: Werner von Fritsch, commander in chief of the German army (right), and Werner von Blomberg, minister of war.

mors began circulating about Eva Gruhn. The general, accused of dishonoring his position, resigned.

Goering hoped to succeed Blom-

berg as minister of war. But first he had to get rid of the logical claimant to Blomberg's post, the commander in chief of the German army, Werner von Fritsch. Like Blomberg, von Fritsch had been a frequent skeptic of Hitler's plans for war in the West.

Goering enlisted the help of Heinrich Himmler, head of Hitler's personal police force. Within days of Blomberg's resignation the two intriguers stepped forward with "evidence" of von Fritsch's homosexuality. Their witness to these "crimes" was a professional blackmailer named Otto Schmidt, who testified to having had an affair with von Fritsch. Hitler demanded that the general step down for security reasons. Von Fritsch protested his innocence and was eventually exonerated of all charges. But the clamor lasted long enough for Hitler to take over as his own commander in chief.

Many who observed the lethargic figure in the defendant's dock found his statements of independent and lightning-fast action impossible to believe. Not only was van der Lubbe said to be half blind owing to a childhood accident, but he moved with difficulty. On the rare occasions that he answered his interrogators, his responses were rambling, childish, and inconsistent. On one occasion, when asked who told him to set fire to the Reichstag, he insisted that he acted at the direction of "voices in my body." As for his political convictions, it was hard to take seriously his claim to being a communist. He was unable to give evidence of any affiliation except that he had briefly joined a Dutch cell when he was 16.

Van der Lubbe's court-appointed defense counsel, whose help van der Lubbe had tried unsuccessfully to reject at the outset, painted a rather convincing portrait of a "rebellious ragamuffin," a mentally deranged vagrant who had been in trouble with the police since childhood. Van der Lubbe, the lawyer said, had tendencies toward impulsive behavior and wanted the sort of attention that capture could bring. He had no sense whatever of revolutionary ideals.

Yet, the defense counsel's picture of van der Lubbe was not totally convincing either. When questioned closely about the night of February 27, the defendant displayed a remarkable grasp of every detail; and, when the police had him retrace his steps while they timed his moves, everything tallied perfectly. Using a quick-igniting substance and shredded bits of his jacket, it was quite possible for one person to set multiple fires. Much as both sides wanted to believe in a conspiracy theory, one could argue that this eccentric, handicapped, and slightly demented young man could conceive and execute such a plan if he focused all his energies on it.

As the trial was ending, the court was forced for lack of substantiating evidence to acquit the four communists of involvement in the plot, and the men were promptly deported. Van der Lubbe, who clearly had some role in the fire, was sentenced to death. After pro forma appeals for leniency, he was executed on January 10, 1934.

A Bizarre Confession

Although the matter was officially closed with the execution of van der Lubbe, speculation as to the full story behind the Reichstag fire has never ended. Several of the defendants at the Nürnberg war crimes trials after World War II testified that Goering was definitely behind the plot. And General Franz Halder, chief of the German general staff during the early years of the war, re-

The accused arsonists in the Reichstag fire went on trial in Leipzig on September 21, 1933. Along with Marinus van der Lubbe (left), who had already confessed to the crime, the four charged as coconspirators are pictured in the newspaper above: the German communist Ernst Torgler and three Bulgarians.

called how Goering had actually boasted about his role at a party for Hitler in 1942.

When one of the guests began talking about the fateful events of 1933, Goering interrupted him. "The only one who really knows about the Reichstag is I, because I set it on fire!" But it seems probable that no one will ever know for sure whether Goering was telling the truth or engaging in yet another bit of self-aggrandizement. The only point that all can agree on is that the burning of the Reichstag proved to be a turning point in the Nazis' rise to power.

The Man in the Mask

*For 22 years — perhaps even longer — an unnamed prisoner,
his identity concealed behind the mask he was forced to wear, languished
in French prisons. What did Louis XIV, the omnipotent Sun King,
have to fear from the mysterious captive?*

*E*tienne du Junca, the king's lieutenant at the Bastille prison in Paris, made a precise yet intriguing entry in his official journal for September 18, 1698. At 3 P.M. that day the new prison governor, Bénigne D'Auvergne de Saint-Mars, had arrived from the south of France, where he had been in command of a fortress in the Bay of Cannes. With him, in a sedan chair, was an aging prisoner who wore a mask and went unnamed. Saint-Mars's mysterious charge, the lieutenant noted, had been with him from the time he had served as commandant of the fortress-prison at Pignerol in the Piedmont region of southeastern France. Since Saint-Mars's tour of duty at Pignerol stretched from 1664 to 1681, du Junca's journal entry suggested an incarceration of at least 17 years and perhaps one lasting more than three decades. During the prisoner's subsequent years in the Bastille, the mask was never removed; a name was never mentioned.

*When the Bastille fell to French revolutionaries in 1789, a chained skeleton was found in one of its
dungeons. Was it that of the man in the mask, incarcerated by command of Louis XIV?*

The unknown prisoner of the French king spent as many as 34 years under guard, in three — or perhaps four — maximum security establishments (map below). Perhaps the happiest of his years in detention were on the Isle Ste. Marguerite in the Bay of Cannes (right).

Five years after he was taken into the Paris prison, the man in the mask became ill on the way back from attendance at Mass — under guard, as always — and collapsed on the bed in his cell. Urgently summoned, the prison doctor pronounced that nothing could be done to save the man. At 10 P.M. on November 19, 1703, the unnamed prisoner died. That night every trace of his existence was eradicated. The furniture in the cell was destroyed; the man's few personal belongings were burned; the walls of the room in which he had lived were replastered. A few days later, du Junca noted in his journal that the unknown prisoner was buried in St. Paul's cemetery. The name of the deceased, according to the parish register du Junca consulted, was M. de Marchiel; his age was listed as "about 45."

Behind the Mask

Only a handful of people — among them, King Louis XIV — knew the identity of the Mask, as the anonymous prisoner was often referred to.

History tells of no more absolute a ruler than the so-called Sun King. At the death of his father in May 1643, Louis had become king four months short of his fifth birthday. As regent for her son, Anne of Austria placed the government in the hands of Cardinal Mazarin, who continued to exercise power even after Louis came of age. But in 1661, upon Mazarin's death, the young king told his astonished ministers that he intended to assume sole responsibility for ruling France. With the powers that were his, Louis could easily have arrested and imprisoned anyone he chose.

The king and his fellow conspirators took the secret of the mysterious prisoner's identity with them to their graves, leaving unsolved a mystery that has prompted speculation for generations. The prisoner was variously identified as an English nobleman forced to flee his country after the failure of a plot against King William III; the dramatist Molière, being punished for his irreverant plays; and Louis XIV's illegitimate half brother, born of a liaison between Anne of Austria and Cardinal Mazarin. The most plausible explanation, however, is that the Mask was an Italian courtier who had earned the king's wrath.

A Monarch Double-crossed

During the years Saint-Mars commanded the fortress-prison at Pignerol many prisoners were entrusted to his care. He was personally responsible to the king for one of them — referred to as simply "the prisoner" in letters from Louis' minister

The Count of Monte Cristo

In 1807, during the reign of Napoleon Bonaparte, a young shoemaker in Paris named François Picaud suffered a fate similar to that of the man in the mask. Learning that Picaud was to marry the beautiful Marguerite Vigoroux, a jealous friend named Mathieu Loupian falsely informed the police that the shoemaker was an English agent. Napoleon's police seized Picaud and threw him in prison, where he languished in anonymity until 1814.

During his seven years of captivity, Picaud befriended an Italian prelate who, on his deathbed, told him of a hidden fortune. Upon his release, the embittered prisoner found the treasure and returned to Paris a wealthy man. In Paris he learned not only of Loupian's duplicity but of Marguerite Vigor-

oux's subsequent marriage to the man who had betrayed him. Appearing in various disguises, Picaud set out to avenge himself on Loupian and his fellow conspirators — killing them one by one until he himself was slain by one of his intended victims. The story, published in 1838, caught the attention of the novelist Alexandre Dumas.

Some years earlier Dumas had been shooting on an island near Elba, the place of Napoleon's first exile. In the distance he saw a rocky islet rising from the sea. Its name was Monte Cristo. Enchanted with the vista, Dumas vowed to write a novel using the name. After reading of Picaud's tragic history, the

Dumas had his hero Dantès imprisoned in the Chateau d'If off the French port of Marseille.

novelist adapted it to create *The Count of Monte Cristo.*

Like Picaud, Dumas' hero Edmond Dantès is unjustly imprisoned owing to the treachery of friends — accused by them of being a conspirator in the plot to return the exiled emperor to power. Like Picaud, Dantès befriends a fellow inmate, an Italian prelate, and learns of a hidden treasure. But here the novelist's imagination takes over. When the priest dies, Dantès takes his place in the burial sack that is thrown in the sea, swims to safety, and is picked up by a gang of smugglers. Taken by his rescuers to the island of Monte Cristo, the hero finds a fortune in gold and jewels in an underground cavern. Posing as the Count of Monte Cristo, Dantès returns to Paris to seek revenge.

of war, the marquis de Louvois. Circumstantial evidence points to this man as the Mask.

Ercole Antonio Mattioli was a minister at the court of Charles IV, duke of Mantua, and in charge of the frontier fortress of Casale Monferrato, which Louis XIV was eager to control as a means of extending his influence to Italy. Accepting valuable gifts from the French king on a trip to Paris in December 1677, Mattioli arranged for the sale of Casale Monferrato for

100,000 crowns. Upon his return home, the courtier either had qualms about selling Italian property to France or saw a way of making more money to support his extravagant life-style. He spread word about the secret transaction to the courts of Austria, Spain, Venice, and Savoy. Suddenly, all of Europe knew of Louis XIV's designs on Italy. The mortified Sun King was forced to withdraw his bid for the fortress.

In revenge for what he considered Mattioli's

betrayal, Louis had the Italian courtier kidnapped in 1679 and delivered — wearing a mask — to Saint-Mars at Pignerol. Saint-Mars may or may not have taken his masked Italian prisoner with him to another fortress, Exiles, in 1681; but it is known that in March 1694 three prisoners, including one in a mask, were brought from Pignerol to the Isle Ste. Marguerite in the Bay of Cannes where Saint-Mars was then in command. "You know that they are of more consequence, at least one, than those who are at present on the island," the king's minister wrote Saint Mars. This sequence of events dovetails with du Junca's journal entry of 1698, which states that the Mask arrived in Paris after imprisonment in Pignerol and on the Isle Ste. Marguerite. Moreover, the St. Paul's parish register of the prisoner's burial in 1703 lists the deceased as Marchioly and not Marchiel as reported by du Junca. A French clerk unfamiliar with the spelling of Italian names could easily have made the mistake of writing Marchioly for Mattioli.

Opponents of the Mattioli theory point out that a month after the Italian's arrival at the Isle Ste. Marguerite, a prisoner with a valet was reported to have died. At Pignerol, Mattioli was known to have been allowed a personal servant; no other of Saint-Mars's charges at Cannes had one. Since he had been born in 1640, Mattioli would have been 63 in the year of the man in the mask's death, not "about 45." Finally, the skeptics say, Mattioli's arrest and confinement were no secret at the time, and Saint-Mars occasionally referred to his Italian charge in his letters, though misspelling the name as Marthioly.

The Unfortunate Twin

For those unwilling to accept Mattioli as the Mask there is a more astonishing theory: The anonymous prisoner was the identical twin brother of Louis XIV.

In his memoirs Cardinal Richelieu, chief minister to King Louis XIII, revealed that Anne of Austria gave birth to twin sons on September 5, 1638. The first infant was born around noon and was promptly declared the heir apparent. At 8:30 P.M. the queen, having gone into labor again, gave birth to a second infant. Whereas the future king's birth, according to Richelieu, "had been so splendid and glorious, that of his brother, which was kept strictly secret, was all the sadder."

Under the laws of the times, the second born of twins was considered the elder. But since the firstborn child had been named Louis XIII's heir, it was considered prudent to conceal the birth of the second infant. As the unacknowledged prince was given over to the care of a midwife, the queen was told that her second child had died. Thus the brothers grew to maturity, one at court, the other in some humble abode. In time, however, the resemblance of the second young man to King Louis XIV was so noticeable that he had to be sent abroad — to England, where he was given a royal upbringing by his paternal aunt, Henrietta Maria, queen consort of King Charles I.

According to an elaborate scenario based on Richelieu's explosive revelation, the unfortunate twin eventually learned his true identity and sought to reclaim the throne that was rightfully his. In 1669, at the age of 31, he joined forces with a French Huguenot named Roux de Marsilly, who was the secret agent of a Protestant alli-

Anne of Austria (right) is said to have given birth to twins in 1638. One became Louis XIV; the other disappeared into captivity. The mask worn by the mysterious prisoner was not of iron (below, as depicted in a film) but of black velvet.

"I am the state"

Assuming full power upon the death of Cardinal Mazarin in 1661, Louis XIV considered his reign to be a dictatorship by divine right or – as the Sun King is supposed to have said – *"L'état, c'est moi"* ("I am the state"). During his 54 remaining years on the throne, Louis brooked no opposition to his iron rule. France became the most powerful, and most feared, state in Europe.

Louis transformed his father's hunting lodge outside Paris into the magnificent palace of Versailles and forced France's leading nobility to live there with him, though accommodations other than his own were often primitive. The king's tours of the exquisite gardens – like every event in the daily routine at Versailles – became an elaborate ritual (above).

At the age of 22, the king dutifully married Marie-Thérèse, a daughter of the king of Spain, in order to cement relations between the two countries; he always treated his queen with kindness and respect. Only the first of their children survived, Louis, the Grand Dauphin. Despite the objections of the clergy, the king openly kept mistresses at Versailles, legitimizing seven offspring of one such liaison and seeing them married into great families of the realm. When the queen died in 1683, Louis secretly married the last of his mistresses, Madame de Maintenon, a pious widow who had originally been brought to court as the governess of his illegitimate children.

Louis XIV outlived his only son as well as the Grand Dauphin's son, the duke of Burgundy. At the death of the Sun King in 1715, a great-grandson ascended the throne as Louis XV.

ance against France that included England, the Netherlands, Sweden, and several Swiss cantons. In April, Marsilly was apprehended in Switzerland by Louis XIV's secret service and taken to Paris, where he died under torture. Before dying, he revealed that Eustache Dauger, the man posing as his valet in England, was in reality the king's long-lost twin.

Arriving at Dunkirk on July 19, Dauger was arrested by order of Louvois. That very day the minister of war wrote to Saint-Mars, saying that he was sending an important prisoner to Pignerol. The commandant was to keep him under the closest surveillance.

In the following years – as he was posted to Exiles, to the Isle Ste. Marguerite, and at last to Paris – Saint-Mars took Dauger with him. The prison commander always treated his charge with respect, allowing him good clothing, books, a guitar, even a personal servant. In short, Saint-Mars acted as if Dauger were a member of the nobility, if not actually of royal blood. However, he was compelled to wear a black velvet mask whenever visitors were on the prison grounds and when he traveled with Saint-Mars to a new assignment – as he did in September 1698 for the trip to Paris and his final incarceration.

A Life in Custody

Who was Eustache Dauger? After exhaustive research, a British historian published a rather prosaic answer in 1910. Dauger was the valet of Nicholas Fouquet, Louis XIV's finance minister. Fouquet was arrested for embezzling public funds in 1661, tried, convicted, and sentenced to lifetime imprisonment. He died in captivity at Pignerol in 1680. Because Fouquet had shared state secrets with his manservant during his confinement at Pignerol, the valet – Dauger, according to this theory – remained in custody after his master's death. He was the special ward of Saint-Mars until his own death in Paris 23 years later.

Servant, or disinherited royalty? There is simply not enough evidence to answer the question with any degree of certainty. Those who were in on the secret at the time – the king, Louvois, and, of course, Saint-Mars – were careful not to reveal it in writing, so there is no proof to support or refute the supposition that Dauger was the rightful heir to the throne of France.

Dauger, imprisoned and a ward of Saint-Mars from 1669; Mattioli, in custody and the special charge of the commandant from 1679: that is all the two have in common. One of them, in all likelihood, was the man in the mask. Which one will probably never be proved.

The Black Hand

*The shots fired at Sarajevo on June 28, 1914, proved to be
the first of World War I. Were the youthful conspirators the only
guilty ones? Or were others higher up involved?*

The Hapsburg heir to the Austro-Hungarian throne was joyously greeted by the inhabitants of the provincial capital that Sunday morning, June 28, 1914. But shortly after 10 A.M. a bomb was thrown at the open car in which Archduke Francis Ferdinand and his wife Sophie, the duchess of Hohenberg, were riding through the streets of Sarajevo. Raising his arm to shield Sophie from the flying object, the archduke deflected the missile so that it bounced off their vehicle to explode in the street behind them.

Although several onlookers and passengers in the following car were slightly injured by bomb fragments, it was decided that the motorcade should proceed to the welcoming ceremonies at the city hall. "Do you think there will be any more bomb throwing?" the angry Francis Ferdinand asked his host, Bosnia's military governor General Oskar Potiorek. Trying to make light of the incident, the general in turn asked his royal guest, "Does Your Highness think the streets are filled with assassins?" Nonetheless, it was decided to alter the previously published route for the remainder of the motorcade. No one informed the driver of the change in plans.

"What is this? This is the wrong way!" the general shouted, as the archduke's automobile turned off the broad Appel Quay into Francis Jo-

As the royal touring car stopped to back up, the assassin took direct aim at Francis Ferdinand and his wife.

seph Street. Confused, the driver abruptly stopped to back his vehicle out of the narrow street. The maneuver put his royal passengers directly in the assassin's line of fire. Two shots were fired. One bullet pierced Francis Ferdinand's neck; the other ripped into Sophie's abdomen. Both were pronounced dead within a few minutes.

Young Bosnia

The gunman was instantly seized, as had been the bomb thrower an hour earlier — their attempts at suicide thwarted by outraged bystanders. The two proved to be Gavrilo Princip and Nedeljko Cabrinovic, adherents of a revolutionary movement among South Slavic youth called Young Bosnia. Taking inspiration from contemporary Russian revolutionaries, these young men were dedicated to the liberation of Bosnia and the neighboring province of Herzegovina from Austro-Hungarian rule and unification with the kingdom of Serbia. Along with four other youthful conspirators, Princip and Cabrinovic had stationed themselves along the route of the motorcade with the intention of killing the archduke, the hated symbol of Hapsburg domination.

While students in the Serbian capital of Belgrade, the two had hatched their plot sometime early in the spring upon learning of the archduke's intended visit to Sarajevo. After enlisting a third youth, Trifko Grabez, the conspirators sought arms from an older Bosnia nationalist named Milan Ciganovic. He trained them to fire pistols, instructed them in the use of bombs, and provided them with cyanide capsules for committing suicide after their deed was done. Meanwhile Princip had written to Danilo Ilic, a teacher and writer in Sarajevo, who recruited three other assassins and assumed leadership of the plot.

Tracing the Deed to Serbia

Ilic, it turned out, was a member of a secret terrorist organization named Unity or Death, but unofficially known as the Black Hand. Its members were committed to using whatever means necessary to pry Bosnia and Herzegovina from Austro-Hungarian rule and unite the South Slavic population of the provinces with Serbia. At the head of the organization was Colonel Dragutin Dimitrijevic, chief of the intelligence department of the Serbian general staff, known within the Black Hand as Apis. In November 1913 Ilic had visited Serbia to discuss an assassination plot with Apis — though the target then was the military governor of Bosnia, General Potiorek. Early in 1914 Apis sent his chief deputy to a meeting of Bosnian revolutionaries in Toulouse, France, to plan the general's assassination.

How and when the Black Hand conspiracy merged with the plot of Princip and his youthful partners will probably never be known. However-er, as a frequenter of the Belgrade cafés where Serbian revolutionaries were known to gather, Princip in all likelihood met members of the Black Hand. The motives for both assassination plans were identical: to terrorize the Austro-Hungarian empire into relinquishing control of its South Slavic subjects.

The Road to War

In Vienna the Austro-Hungarian government held Serbia responsible for the assassination of the heir apparent and his consort. A month later, on July 23, the Austro-Hungarian empire sent an ultimatum to Serbia. Vienna was demanding the dissolution of patriotic organizations hostile to the empire; participation in the Serbian inquiry into its responsibility for the killings; arrest of Serbian officials known to have plotted against the Hapsburg monarchy; and explanations of and apologies for Serbian guilt.

Although meant to appear conciliatory, the Serbian reply was evasive. Led to believe that Russia would come to its rescue, the tiny kingdom began mobilizing for war. Five days after the delivery of the ultimatum, the Austro-Hungarian empire declared war on Serbia. When the Russian czar called for general mobilization, Germany — allied with the Austro-Hungarian empire — declared war on Russia. France and Britain, allies of Russia, declared war on Germany. By the end of August all Europe was at war.

The shots at Sarajevo ignited what was known as the Balkan powder keg. The fire soon spread across the map of Europe, represented in the caricature at left as a tangle of hostile and competing figures — from Britain's bulldog to Russia's voracious maw (extreme right).

Punishment and Guilt

The trial of Princip and 24 codefendants rounded up in the investigation of the assassinations opened in Sarajevo's district court on October 12, 1914. Only the local participants were in the dock. The true culprits, it was widely believed, were in Belgrade — behind enemy lines and unavailable for prosecution. Asked if he was guilty of committing a crime, Princip replied, "I am not a criminal, for I have removed an evildoer. I meant to do a good deed."

Six days after the trial ended, on October 23, the judges handed down their verdicts. Princip, Cabrinovic, and Grabez were found guilty of murder and treason. Being under 20 years of age, they could not be given death penalties but instead were handed maximum prison sentences of 20 years. All three died in prison before the end of the war they had helped spark — Princip and Cabrinovic of tuberculosis; Grabez of chronic malnutrition. Ilic and four others received death sentences, two of which were changed to imprisonment on appeal. The schoolteacher and two of his fellow conspirators were executed in February 1915. Lesser sentences were given to eight other defendants; nine were acquitted.

Gavrilo Princip (above, second from right) was seized immediately after he fired the shots that killed the archduke and his wife. The insignia of the Serbian secret organization popularly known as the Black Hand bore a skull and crossed bones.

Two years later, in a puzzling postscript to the trial, Colonel Dimitrijevic took responsibility for the conspiracy. The Black Hand leader had been accused of an attempt on the life of Alexander, Serbia's prince regent, tried, and condemned to death. In a deposition handed to the military tribunal, Apis confessed to his involvement in the plot leading to Francis Ferdinand's death. Whether he was the mastermind behind the scheme is still argued among historians. But in Yugoslavia, the South Slavic homeland that had been his goal, Gavrilo Princip is a national hero.

Blasted from the Sky

*As the Cold War eased, the United States and the Soviet Union seemed
ready to discuss their differences. Suddenly, Soviet jets shot down a Korean airliner
filled with civilians. Was it human error, provocation, or the
logical conclusion of a paranoid policy?*

"Now I will try a rocket," said a calm voice through bursts of radio static. "I am closing on the target. . . . I have executed the launch. The target is destroyed."

As the pilot of the Soviet Sukhoi-15 supersonic jet fighter searched for visual confirmation of his hit, a Boeing 747-200B began spiraling downward toward the chilly waters of the Sea of Japan at 6:26 in the morning. The hunter had bagged his quarry with two sophisticated weapons — a heat-seeking missile that took out an engine and a radar-homing missile that probably slammed into the fuselage. "Korean Air 007," the pilot of the jetliner managed to call out on his radio. Then silence. For 14 minutes the huge aircraft fell 33,000 feet, smashing into the sea somewhere west of the secret military bases on Russia's Sakhalin Island on September 1, 1983. Nearby, Japanese fishermen caught the odor of burning fuel.

On board, 269 civilian passengers and crew members perished, including 76 Koreans, 61 Americans, and citizens of 11 other countries. Most had begun the fatal flight shortly after midnight, eastern standard time, at New York's John F. Kennedy International Airport. Seven hours later the first leg ended at Anchorage, Alaska, where four passengers disembarked. The new flight crew taking over was captained by 45-year-old Chun Byung In, a veteran pilot with 10,547 flying hours, including 6,619 in jumbo jets like the 747. Delayed 39 minutes, KAL 007 lifted off at 4 A.M., local time, and headed for the Korean capital, Seoul, about 3,800 miles away.

The Torment of Uncertainty

Had KAL 007 been hijacked? Had there been an accident? For 18 hours hope mixed with dread, for there was no official explanation for the miss-

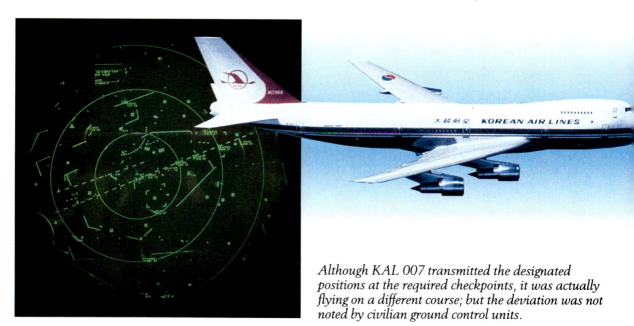

*Although KAL 007 transmitted the designated
positions at the required checkpoints, it was actually
flying on a different course; but the deviation was not
noted by civilian ground control units.*

Deviating from its prescribed route (Romeo 20), the Korean jumbo jet crossed over the Kamchatka Peninsula and the island of Sakhalin, thus violating Soviet airspace before it was shot down.

ing airliner. No one had received an SOS from the captain. Japanese air controllers had apparently not noticed that their radar showed the plane to be seriously off course. A South Korean pilot flying within 100 miles of the airliner had been unable to communicate with Captain Chun but had not seen fit to raise an alarm.

Finally, U.S. Secretary of State George Shultz stunned the world by announcing what intelligence experts had learned by examining data retrieved from computers. KAL 007 had been purposely blasted from the sky by the Soviet military. "This event shocks the sensibilities of people everywhere," said President Ronald Reagan. An American congressman spoke for many: "Attacking an unarmed civilian plane is like attacking a school bus."

For two days representatives of the Soviet Union made virtually no comment. Then, as people everywhere were expressing sympathy for the grieving and bewildered survivors of the murdered passengers, a Russian statement referred to an "unidentified plane" that had "rudely violated the state border and intruded deep into the Soviet Union's airspace." Tass, the official news agency, claimed that the interceptors had fired only warning shots and tracer shells. "Hullabaloo" was their characterization of world outrage, and there were dark hints that the flight had been on an American-directed spy mission.

Tempers flared on the international scene. South Koreans by the tens of thousands marched in protests in Seoul; communist parties in Italy and Japan demanded that Moscow explain the "crime"; and four West European nations lodged a formal protest with Soviet diplomats. "Straying off course is not recognized as a capital crime by civilized nations," stormed U.S. Ambassador Jeane Kirkpatrick at the United Nations. Delegates listened in fascinated horror as a tape of the Russian pilot's radio transmissions was played. Obtained from the Japan Defense Agency, it proved that the plane had been shot down in cold blood. Soviet Foreign Minister Andrei Gromyko reacted with belligerence: "Soviet territory, the borders of the Soviet Union are sacred. No matter who resorts to provocation of that kind, he should know that he will bear the full brunt of responsibility for it."

The Hunt for the Black Box

Deep in the waters lay one possible clue to the mystery, the so-called black box that contains recordings of a plane's flight data and cockpit conversations. Frantically, the adversarial teams of Russians and Americans rushed to the supposed site of impact, bitterly competing to find the telltale evidence. The battery-operated radio direction finder in the black box, though designed to beam up information even from 20,000 feet underwater, would lose power within about a month. At peak power, it could be heard for five miles in any direction.

In the frenzy, according to reports from the U.S. aircraft carrier *Stertett*, only pure luck saved the various ships from colliding with each other in the waters west of Sakhalin. It was all wasted effort. The black box was never found; instead, the cruel sea cast up only fragments of metal, items of personal use, and scattered human remains, none identifiable.

Despite inclement weather and the great depth of the ocean canyons, the searchers persisted until November 7, when all operations were discontinued. The truth would have to be ascertained from the recordings and computer infor-

"The Target Is Destroyed"

Some four hours after leaving Anchorage, KAL 007 established high-frequency radio contact with Tokyo and reported its progress on the flight to Seoul as if it were still on course. At 1707 (5:07 P.M. Greenwich mean time; 5:07 A.M. on Sakhalin Island) it reported that it had just passed over control point NIPPI; in fact, it was passing over Russia's Kamchatka Peninsula, headed for Sakhalin. At 1815 the Korean jumbo jet requested clearance from Tokyo for a climb to 35,000 feet. Permission was granted, and Tokyo received confirmation that the maneuver had been completed. Minutes later, Tokyo heard the last, incomplete message: "Korean Air 007. . . ." Only silence greeted Tokyo's request that the Korean plane switch channels so as better to be heard on the ground.

Meanwhile, another air-to-ground conversation was taking place — that of Russian pilot 805 to Soviet air defense command on Sakhalin Island. Voice-activated tape recorders in Japan picked up the messages. Excerpts follow:

1812:10 I see it visually and on [radar] screen.
1813:05 I'm locked on to the target.
1813:26 The target isn't responding to inquiry.
1813:40 [Weapons system] is turned on.
1819:02 I am closing on the target.
1819:08 They do not see me.
1820:49 I am firing cannon bursts.
1823:37 Now I will try the rockets.
1826:20 I have executed the launch.
1826:22 The target is destroyed.

mation that had been culled from top-secret equipment and intelligence agency observers during KAL 007's final hours.

Spies for the United States?

Eight days after the crash, Soviet Chief of Staff Nikolai Ogarkov went on state television with a new story. Admitting implicitly that his country's fighters had "stopped" the airliner with two air-to-air missiles, he offered two contradictory justifications. On the one hand, he claimed that Soviet ground controllers had confused KAL 007 with a U.S. spy plane that was flying in the area. On the other, he charged that the Korean airliner had been involved in espionage for the United States. The strictly military decision to destroy the 747 had been made by a commander in the Soviet Far East, he explained, not at the highest levels of the military or the civilian government.

Western observers scoffed at both notions. Indeed, a U.S. RC-135 reconnaissance plane had passed within 86 miles of KAL 007 a couple of hours before the shooting, headed in the opposite direction. The 747, half again as large as an RC-135, was seen by the Russian fighter pilot, according to the tapes, and he had twice reported that he could see its navigation and strobe lights.

As for the espionage charge, there are some intriguing factors. Captain Chun, like most pilots for Korean Air Lines, had a military background and had once been selected to fly the personal plane of the Korean president. Also, he had taken his airliner off course over an extremely sensitive area. Sakhalin Island was home to a naval center and six vitally important air bases. The Kamchatka Peninsula, a target area for test firings of long-range missiles, was crucial to the Russian defense perimeter. The Sea of Okhotsk, lying between the two, was a haven for nuclear submarines whose missiles were designated for U.S. targets.

Despite all of these indications, however, experts could see no need for endangering civilians on a secret spy mission. The 747, flying at night at a high altitude, could not gather information of any substance unless it was physically altered and festooned with large antennas that would have been immediately visible. Even in that event, it could not have provided the kind of detailed intelligence that was routinely being collected by RC-135 flights and U.S. orbiting satellites. Korea's president Chun Doo Hwan testily dismissed Marshal Ogarkov's contention: "Nobody on earth but the Soviet authorities would believe that a 70-year-old man or a 4-year-old child would be allowed to fly in a civilian plane that had the objective of violating Soviet airspace in order to engage in espionage."

Inexplicable Deviation

Why, then, had a skillful pilot using state-of-the-art equipment strayed deep into Soviet territory? A $100,000 set of three Inertial Navigation Systems (INS) used gyroscopes and acceleration meters to guide the craft on its preprogrammed flight path. For greater accuracy, the three computers were to be fed information separately. Were all three given incorrect coordinates? Did the crew neglect to check the INS coordinates with those on the flight charts, as is required? Did the experienced pilot fail to ensure that the plane's true location coincided with the checkpoints registered by the INS along the way?

Captain Chun confidently reported in his last radio contact with Tokyo that he was 113 miles southeast of the Japanese island of Hokkaido. In fact, he was exactly 113 miles to the north of the island. Why didn't the ground controllers inform him that he was mistaken? Could he have purposely flown over the forbidden Russian territories in order to save expensive jet fuel for his cost-conscious employers? Already, he was flying the route called Romeo 20, so close to the Soviet Union that pilots ordinarily used weather radar to ensure that they did not cross the border. Endangering his plane by altering his route would not have saved much money, and records show that the regularly scheduled flight had never before deviated from the assigned flight plan.

In addition, South Koreans had particular reason to know the perils of going off course. In 1978 the Russians had fired on another straying Korean airliner and forced it to land. Pierced by a heat-seeking missile, the 707 fell out of control for 32,000 feet before leveling off and crash landing on a frozen lake above the Arctic Circle near Murmansk. Two passengers were killed. The Soviets rescued the survivors, including 13 wounded, then billed the South Korean government $100,000 for expenses.

A Hasty Judgment?

That incident had left a residue of suspicion in the minds of the Soviets, who had been deeply embarrassed that the 707 had flown undetected into their skies. This time, they had been watch-

At a press conference on September 9, 1983, Soviet Chief of Staff Nikolai Ogarkov explained the parallel flights of KAL 007 and an American RC-135 on a reconnaissance mission — the reason, he said, for the downing of the Korean jumbo. Crowds around the world protested the Soviet action; below, outraged Koreans demonstrate in Tokyo.

ing the radar blip made by KAL 007 for about two and a half hours as it verged upon their airspace. The minute the airliner crossed the eastern border of the Kamchatka Peninsula, four MiG-23s and Su-15s raced to confront the intruder, although only two of the pilots would be recorded. Four more interceptors joined the chase later.

One fear facing the interceptor pilots was exhaustion of fuel. Maximum flight time for each of the craft was less than an hour, even with extra drop tanks. Pilot 805, who fired the fatal missiles, jettisoned his empty drop tanks seconds after catching sight of KAL 007, leaving him just another 35 minutes to complete his mission and return safely to base. After locking his automatic fix on the unsuspecting target from behind, 805 directed an Identification: Friend or Foe (IFF) signal to the airliner. Only a Soviet plane, however, would have been able to pick up this special frequency. At this point, the Korean 747 was probably cruising at about 540 miles per hour so Pilot 805 would not have to use his fighter's afterburner, which could propel the Su-15 at more than 1,400 miles per hour.

Pilot 805 said that he saw the Korean airliner's strobe light blinking. About seven miles away one of the MiG-23 pilots reported that he could see both the interceptor and its target. More than six miles up in the air, visibility that night should have been good, according to Western experts. Moreover, Soviet pilots, just like pilots in the United States and other Western countries, are required to learn to recognize the silhouettes of planes. With its characteristic and unusual humped profile, the Boeing 747 is unmistakable. The white-painted jumbo jet was flying above the clouds, illuminated by a half moon. Also, intelligence experts agree that the Russian radar operators would keep a log of all commercial flights scheduled to fly near their borders.

Later Pilot 805 claimed that he had fired 120 rounds of warning tracer shots. The tape of his transmissions does not support this story. Just as KAL 007 reached a point 90 seconds from international airspace — about 12 miles or so — the fuel guzzling Su-15 fired and, desperate to head home, tarried only briefly to see the results.

The Puzzling Aftermath

Despite the angry charges and countercharges of diplomats and politicians, no one wanted the incident to develop into a major-power confrontation. President Reagan spoke of the "crime against humanity," but reprisals from the United States — such as suggesting that other countries suspend air service with Russia for two months —

A Deadly Mistake

The U.S. Navy was on a peacekeeping mission in the Persian Gulf when one of its cruisers shot down an Iranian passenger jet.

Only five years after the KAL 007 disaster, "the most sophisticated ship in the world, bar none," a U.S. cruiser in the Persian Gulf, mistakenly shot down an Iranian commercial airliner, killing all 290 people on board. On the morning of July 3, 1988, the *Vincennes* under Captain Will Rogers III had already been harassed twice in the hostile waters of the Strait of Hormuz. Three Iranian boats fired on one of the ship's helicopters; then the cruiser and another U.S. ship skirmished with a flotilla of small Iranian launches, sinking two of them. Minutes later, the blue computer screens showed an aircraft headed toward the *Vincennes*.

The subsequent events were all scanned by the computers, but not actually witnessed by anyone aboard the cruiser. An Identification: Friend or Foe (IFF) scan seemed to show that the craft was transmitting signals used by the Iranian jet fighters stationed in the war-torn area. When the *Vincennes* broadcast three warnings on the civilian emergency frequency and four on the military distress frequency, the Iranian pilot did not respond. Nor did his craft change course, as the warnings demanded. According to U.S. rules of engagement, a naval commander can fire on his own authority whenever a plane comes within 20 miles. At 10:51 A.M. the aircraft crossed that line, and the Aegis computer system automatically readied two Standard-2 surface-to-air missiles.

Once again Captain Rogers sent warnings. It seemed to him that the plane began to dive and pick up speed, as if getting ready to attack his ship. His choices grew more restricted, because six miles was the minimum range of his missiles. At 10:54, as the plane reached the nine-mile mark, the captain fired the two missiles. At least one hit the passenger jet, which exploded and fell in fragments to the water.

For weeks after the disaster, Japanese military search parties combed Hokkaido beaches for debris from the crash 60 miles away. Passengers' belongings and human remains were discovered — but not the black box that perhaps could have explained how the tragedy came about.

were measured. Eleven Western nations agreed to shorter travel bans. The deaths of the innocent civilians were tragic, but the world seemed to agree that revenge or punishment could not be allowed to stand in the way of progress that could save the lives of millions. Even as the facts about the destruction of KAL 007 were first being brought to light, Soviet and American negotiators were actively working on the details of a proposed nuclear weapons treaty in Geneva. In Reagan's words, the U.S. approach would be to "show our outrage, but keep talking."

Rather than seek vengeance, experts wanted to solve the mystery. Could such a disastrous mistake in navigation occur again? Investigations, research, and speculation did not reach a consoling answer. One fairly convincing solution was suggested by the calculations of a mechanical flight simulator at the Boeing works in Seattle. When Captain Chun left Anchorage, he could not check his preprogrammed flight path with the INS system because the Alaska airport's high-frequency control beam system, used by the on-board computers, had been temporarily shut off for servicing. If the pilot had relied on his compass for takeoff, he would have set a compass course of 246. The deviation from the prescribed Romeo 20 would be only 9 compass degrees, or about 15 miles on the ground. If the captain had continued to use that setting and not switched over to the INS, his error combined with the wind drift in the upper atmosphere that night could have taken KAL 007 into the computer-ized sights of the alert Soviet interceptor jets.

Could an electrical problem on board have crippled the jumbo jet, making its crucial navigational systems, lights, and radios completely inoperable? That would have been extremely unlikely. Each of the three INS units was independently powered. Lights could be kept on by any one of four electrical generators, one for each of the craft's jet engines. Five separate radio transmitters were available on the 747. Until the fatal explosion the crew was never out of touch with ground stations along the route.

Human Tragedy on the World Stage

"Nothing special, just an ordinary flight. It was a very, very silent flight," recalled the purser for the first leg of KAL 007. Indeed, except for one U.S. congressman, who was the only occupant of the first-class cabin, the passengers were ordinary citizens, many traveling with their families. Business class was full, but about 80 seats were empty in the economy-class rear section. Most people were passing the time in the same way — sleeping the dreary hours away in the dimly lit cabin. It was all routine. Scores of commercial flights plied KAL 007's route every month.

The very ordinariness made the grief of relatives and friends all that much harder to bear. In Korea mourners were flown by KAL to Hokkaido to board ferries that took them to the waters where a child's body had been found. In honor of all of the dead, wreaths and bouquets of fresh flowers were tossed into the sea.

A Butcher's Son as King?

Italy's first king, Victor Emmanuel II, came from the ancient and highly respectable House of Savoy. But he didn't quite look or act like royalty. Was he, in fact, the illegitimate offspring of a tradesman, substituted for a royal infant who perished in a fire?

*L*ate in the summer of 1822, Charles Albert, prince of Savoy-Carignano, and his family were residing at the Villa del Poggio Imperiale just outside the Italian city of Florence. On the evening of September 16 a nurse went to the room of the prince's two-year-old son, Victor Emmanuel, carrying a candle with which she hoped to chase away the mosquitoes that were disturbing the young prince's sleep. As she bent over the cradle, lace from the child's bedding brushed against the candle and burst into flame. In her frenzied efforts to save the boy from the blaze, the nurse was burned so severely that she died a few weeks later.

The little prince, however, was saved. The official journal of the grand ducal court in Florence scrupulously recorded every event in the lives of Prince Charles Albert and his wife, Maria Theresa. In the entry for September 16 it was duly noted that their son, Victor Emmanuel, had suffered burns on three parts of his body but was expected to recover. There were no further reports about the prince and his family for nearly a month. Not until October 10 did Charles Albert attend a court function in Florence, though his corre-

spondence reveals that he returned to the city as early as September 20—four days after the unfortunate accident in the country villa.

Charles Albert's letters of the time contain expressions of his relief at his son's escape from serious injury and, initially at least, the observation that the nurse's burns were not considered to be life threatening. On October 3 a lady-in-waiting to Maria Theresa reported that the nurse, Teresa Zanotti Racca, was recovering nicely and would be accompanying the prince's family on their return to Florence the next day. As was his duty, the mayor of Santo Spirito, the village in which the villa was situated, informed the police department that the prince of Savoy-Carignano and his family had concluded their summer's stay at the villa on the evening of October 4. Two days later Teresa Zanotti Racca, having lapsed into a coma, died in Florence.

Why was there a discrepancy in the dates for Charles Albert's return to Florence? And why was the nurse said to be recovering from her burns only three days before she died? Was Teresa Zanotti Racca the only victim of the fire at the villa?

Stolid as the ornate chair behind which he stands, Victor Emmanuel II ruled Sardinia-Piedmont from 1849 and a united Italy from 1861.

The Substitute Child

In the weeks following the accident, rumors swept through Florence and the surrounding region that the prince's son had perished in the blaze and that another child had replaced him in the royal nursery. The substitute, people were soon whispering, was the illegitimate son of the butcher Gaetano Tiburzi — also called Maciaccia — and his paramour Regina Bettini.

Not long after the fire Tiburzi married another woman and built a three-story house near Florence's Porta Romana, through which passed the road leading to the Villa del Poggio Imperiale. On the ground floor of his spacious new abode, the butcher opened his own shop. The love of his youth, Regina Bettini, later married Tiburzi's younger brother, Pasquale. In a short time the butcher had enough money to build a second house, the beginning of real estate investments that left him with 43 rental properties at the time of his death in 1888. Meanwhile, he had comfortably supported a family of 17 children. Was there a hidden source of income? Had Tiburzi extended an extraordinary favor to Charles Albert and been rewarded for his silence about it?

As for the heroic nurse who had presumably given her life to save Charles Albert's son, there

Charles Albert, prince of Savoy-Carignano, held court at Florence (above). A dreadful accident occurred in his villa outside the city on the evening of September 16, 1822.

was no reward to her or her family and no official acknowledgment of her sacrifice. Indeed, all mention of the dreadful accident was soon suppressed. The Villa del Poggio Imperiale was judged to be no longer suitable for royal summer vacations and was transformed into a convent school for daughters of the aristocracy.

Reaching for the Throne

Supposing that the rumors about a substitute child were true, what could have been the motive of Charles Albert for suppressing news of his son's death? To answer that question it is necessary to look at Italy's tangled political situation in the 1820's.

Following the collapse of Napoleon's empire in 1814–15, many of the Italian peninsula's fragmented states had come under Austrian domination. One of these was the kingdom of Sardinia, which embraced not only the large island by that name but also the mainland territory of Piedmont. Although an 1821 uprising against Austria failed, the king of Sardinia-Piedmont, Victor Emmanuel I, was forced to abdicate in favor of his brother, Charles Felix. Since the childless Charles Felix was the last male offspring of the main branch of the House of Savoy, a congress of church and state dignitaries met in Verona to name his heir. One of the candidates was Charles Albert, the king's distant cousin from the Savoy-Carignano line of the royal family. With an infant son, Victor Emmanuel, Charles Albert offered the troubled kingdom a secured succession.

In this tense situation occurred the fire at the Villa del Poggio Imperiale. Without a male heir Charles Albert would be a less desirable candidate to succeed his cousin on the throne of Sardinia-Piedmont. There was indeed reason for the prince to conceal news of a tragedy in the nursery and replace his dead son with another child.

Troublesome Prince, Unconventional King

Charles Albert and Maria Theresa appeared to be far from satisfied with the intellectual and social development of their firstborn son. In a letter to her father, the princess complained that Victor Emmanuel seemed bent on driving everyone in the royal household to despair. Boisterous and disinterested in his studies, the heir apparent was the complete opposite of his younger brother, Ferdinand. Born after the tragedy at Villa del Poggio Imperiale, Ferdinand was quiet, sensitive, pious, and dutiful — the very image of his serious-minded father, Charles Albert. Victor Emmanuel, his mother confessed, did not bear the slightest resemblance to any member of the royal family. Whereas Ferdinand was of a delicate constitution (he died of tuberculosis at the age of 32), Victor Emmanuel developed into a strong, muscular youth with coarse features, uncouth manners, and — it was widely rumored — a predilection for amorous adventures that in time produced several illegitimate children.

In 1831 Charles Albert succeeded his cousin on the throne of Sardinia-Piedmont. An able administrator, he reformed the kingdom's financial system, bolstered its army, and issued a liberal constitution. But when he sought to assert independence from Austrian domination, he was defeated in battle and forced to accept humiliating peace terms from the victors. Believing that his usefulness to the country was at an end, Charles Albert abdicated in favor of his 29-year-old son on March 23, 1849. He died a few months later in exile at a monastery in Portugal. The troublesome prince ascended the throne as King Victor Emmanuel II.

Six Wives for an Heir

Through the ages it has generally been a king's first duty to secure his family's succession by producing an heir — preferably a male. In 16th-century England King Henry VIII's relentless efforts to ensure that the House of Tudor retain the throne led to a break with Rome and the establishment of the Church of England.

In 1509, the year he succeeded his father as king of England, Henry married Catherine of Aragon, the daughter of Spain's Ferdinand and Isabella and the widow of his deceased elder brother Arthur. After her first four children were stillborn or died in infancy, Catherine gave birth to a daughter, Mary, in 1516. This was not good enough for Henry, who picked comely Anne Boleyn as his next consort. Convincing himself that his union with Catherine violated biblical injunctions against marriage to a brother's widow, the king asked the pope for an annulment. When the pope refused, Henry turned to Thomas Cranmer, the archbishop of Canterbury, who obligingly declared the marriage of Henry and Catherine to be null and void in May 1533. Meanwhile, Henry had secretly married Anne Boleyn; their daughter, Elizabeth, was born in September. When Anne failed to produce a male heir, Henry had her tried and executed on trumped-up charges of treasonable adultery in 1536. The king immediately married Jane Seymour, who died giving birth to a son, Edward, the next year. Henry married three more times: to Anne of Cleves, whom he divorced in 1540; to Catherine Howard, who was executed for adultery in 1542; and to the twice-widowed Catherine Parr, who survived his death in 1547. None provided an heir.

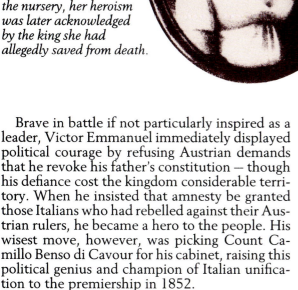

Teresa Zanotti Racca (right) was nurse to the young prince Victor Emmanuel. Although her carelessness led to a devastating fire in the nursery, her heroism was later acknowledged by the king she had allegedly saved from death.

The Villa del Poggio Imperiale (below) was abandoned as a summer residence after 1822 — the memories of the fire no doubt being too painful for the royal family.

Brave in battle if not particularly inspired as a leader, Victor Emmanuel immediately displayed political courage by refusing Austrian demands that he revoke his father's constitution — though his defiance cost the kingdom considerable territory. When he insisted that amnesty be granted those Italians who had rebelled against their Austrian rulers, he became a hero to the people. His wisest move, however, was picking Count Camillo Benso di Cavour for his cabinet, raising this political genius and champion of Italian unification to the premiership in 1852.

Yet there were those who continued to look askance at the young king's unconventional behavior. One such critic was Britain's Queen Victoria, a year older than Victor Emmanuel. "On horseback, the king appears like a savage, as well as in his life in general," she wrote with ill-concealed prejudice. "I have grown used to his strange and coarse peculiarities, as well as to his eyes, which he rolls furiously. . . . A truly eccentric type!" Clearly, she considered him an outsider among the crowned heads of Europe.

The Road to Italian Statehood

A successful farmer and businessman before entering politics, Count Cavour was cofounder in 1847 of the newspaper that became the organ for the Italian national movement, *Il Risorgimento* — which means rebirth or renewal. As prime minister of Sardinia-Piedmont, he had to fight a two-front war. In Italy he sought to reconcile the differences between two factions: those who were satisfied with a federation of existing states and those who would settle for nothing less than a new, consolidated Italy. Abroad he worked to

convince other European governments that they had nothing to fear from an Italy united under the ancient and respected House of Savoy.

Through a mixture of war and diplomacy, Cavour achieved his ambitions. On March 17, 1861, the kingdom of Italy was proclaimed with Victor Emmanuel II as its ruler. Within three months Cavour was dead. Had his great achievement been placing the son of a butcher on the throne of a united Italy?

The Doubts Persist

Victor Emmanuel was well aware of the ugly rumors about his nonaristocratic origins and apparently took extraordinary measures to dispel them. In 1860 the king visited Florence on behalf of the unification movement. Prior to the royal visit, the son of Teresa Zanotti Racca — then employed as an administrator of the king's properties in Piedmont — sent a collection of Charles Albert's letters written from the Villa del Poggio Imperiale in the summer of 1822 to the governor-general of Tuscany. On April 15, the day before Victor Emmanuel's arrival in Florence, excerpts from the letters appeared on the front page

The Dream of Unification

During the first several decades of the 19th century, Italy was obsessed with *Risorgimento*, the movement to establish a unified state. During its incorporation in the Napoleonic empire, Italy had absorbed many of the liberal doctrines of the French Enlightenment. But the Congress of Vienna — the peace conference after Napoleon's defeat — restored the conservative old order in 1815.

The leading apostle of national awareness was Giuseppe Mazzini, who was arrested in 1831 for his inflammatory advocacy of rebellion against the old order; he spent most of the remaining years of his life in exile. Meanwhile, spontaneous uprisings in various parts of the Italian peninsula had been brutally suppressed with the aid of Austrian troops. When Sardinia-Piedmont was granted a liberal constitution by King Charles Albert in 1848, Italian nationalists focused their hopes of unity on the House of Savoy — particularly after Charles Albert's son and successor, Victor Emmanuel II, chose Count Cavour as his prime minister.

Sailing from Genoa in May 1860, Giuseppe Garibaldi (above) launched an invasion of Sicily that ended with his overthrow of the Bourbon monarch in Naples. With Garibaldi's conquests in the south added to those of Victor Emmanuel in the central regions, Cavour seized the moment to have his monarch crowned king of Italy in 1861. Venetia was incorporated into the unified kingdom five years later, and in 1870 Rome fell to Victor Emmanuel's troops and was proclaimed Italy's capital.

of the newspaper *Monitore Toscano*. The dreadful accident, the nurse's heroic rescue, the royal infant's miraculous survival — all were once again news, 38 years after the tragedy occurred.

How did the nurse's son come to have the letters of Charles Albert? They must have been supplied by the king. Before Victor Emmanuel left Florence, he righted a four-decade-long wrong. In recognition of Teresa Zanotti Racca's sacrifice on that evening so long ago, the king unveiled a commemorative plaque in her honor at the villa turned convent.

Yet the rumors could not so easily be suppressed, and they even followed Victor Emmanuel to the grave. Moreover, those who regarded the stories about the king's supposed humble origins as nothing more than the gossip of the uninformed and credulous got a rude shock in 1883, five years after the king's death.

Among the early champions of Victor Emmanuel was the novelist Massimo d'Azeglio. As the young king's first prime minister in the years 1849–52, he guided the inexperienced monarch through the difficult shoals of statehood and instilled in him a passion for *Risorgimento*. Some 20 years older than the king, d'Azeglio was a highly valued confidant and adviser — until something came between them, and Victor Emmanuel installed Cavour in his place.

Six months before his death in 1866, d'Azeglio confided to his friend and publisher Gaspero Barbera that he was convinced the king was indeed the son of the Tuscan butcher. Barbera included the revelation in his memoirs, published posthumously in 1883. "Kings and royal children are similar to English race horses; they have very delicate limbs," Barbera wrote. "But Victor Emmanuel? He has the arms of a butcher."

Was the publisher's comment a paraphrase of what d'Azeglio had told him? And where was the proof of the onetime prime minister's allegation? Had the king blurted out his awful secret in a moment of self-abnegation? Or was d'Azeglio trying to justify his estrangement from the king? It was well known that, before his removal from office, the prime minister had come to consider Victor Emmanuel's uncouth manners and licentious life-style unfit for the king of a united Italy.

To most Italians, the origin of their first king is relatively unimportant. In 1946 Italy abolished its monarchy, and Victor Emmanuel's great-grandson was removed from the throne — one that may have had a butcher's son as its first occupant. Nonetheless, Victor Emmanuel II, the right man for the right time, is still fondly remembered as the father of his country.

Target Hit–Sunk!

**On May 7, 1915, a German submarine sank a British
passenger ship with the loss of 1,198 lives — including 128 Americans.
Was the captain's negligence to blame? Or was there a conspiracy
to bring the United States into World War I?**

The crossing of the North Atlantic had been unusually smooth for so early in the season — the first week of May. Passengers aboard the British luxury liner *Lusitania* had whiled away the time playing cards, competing in deck games, crowding the lounges, attending concerts, strolling about, or stretching out on deck chairs to enjoy the salubrious sea air. On the seventh morning out of New York the ship ran into intermittent patches of fog off the southern coast of Ireland. Captain William Turner slowed his vessel from 21 to 18 knots per hour — at times, even to 15 knots — and ordered the fog-horn operated at 60-second intervals between 8 and 11 A.M. But toward noon the fog burned off, and many of the passengers took to the decks after lunch to enjoy the warm sunshine and admire the emerald beauty of the Irish coast.

In many minds, however, there were nagging doubts and ill-concealed concerns, for this was a wartime voyage, and the ship was entering British waters. Only three months earlier, on February 4, 1915, Germany — locked in the mortal combat of World War I with Britain — had declared the seas surrounding the British Isles to be a war zone and ordered its submarines to destroy

Lieutenant Walther Schwieger (above) commanded the U-20 that sunk the Lusitania *(left) in May 1915. Or was it exploding contraband that proved fatal to the luxury liner?*

Queen of the Atlantic

Completed in 1907, the *Lusitania* and her sister ship the *Mauretania* were the undoubted champions of the North Atlantic — frequently winning for the Cunard Line the coveted blue ribbon for the fastest crossing of the year on their voyages between New York and Liverpool, England. Luxuriously appointed, the vessels were called floating palaces and could compete with any first-class hotel in the world.

The *Lusitania* had accommodations for 2,600 passengers, whose every whim was cared for by a crew of 700. Its luxury suites boasted a living room, a dining room, two bedrooms, and a bath paneled in fine wood. Just under 800 feet in length and with a beam of only 88 feet, the *Lusitania* presented a sleek profile. Four huge funnels vented smoke from the belowdecks engine rooms, where coal-burning boilers generated 68,000 horsepower to attain speeds up to 25 knots per hour — fast enough, many passengers in May 1915 must have thought, to evade the slow-moving, unwieldy submarines of the day. Up until that point in the war, the Germans had failed to sink any ship even approaching the size and speed of the vaunted queen of the Atlantic.

enemy merchant vessels within it. By the end of April, German submarines had sunk 66 ships.

During the voyage daily lifeboat musters had been held, with eight crew members demonstrating to passengers how to get into the boats and fasten the life belts. Were such preparations adequate for an emergency, one worried passenger asked Captain Turner. "A torpedo can't get the *Lusitania*," he replied. "She runs too fast."

Just before 2:10 P.M. two passengers on deck, first spying the telltale periscope, made out a submerged hull and conning tower. "Look, there's a submarine," one cried. "My God," the other said, "we're lost!" At that moment the lookout on the starboard bow, an 18-year-old seaman named Leslie Morton, saw an enormous bubble bursting through the water's surface about 500 yards away and a white streak making directly for the ship. Seizing a megaphone, he shouted to the bridge, "Torpedo on the starboard side!"

The missile struck just forward of midship, about 10 feet below the waterline. The sharp initial detonation of the exploding torpedo was followed almost immediately by a second, more violent explosion that sent water, steam, smoke, coal, dust, and other debris through the ship's ventilators and smokestacks. Listing heavily to starboard, the *Lusitania* slid beneath the sea within 18 minutes. Although 761 passengers and crew managed to get clear of the sinking vessel, 1,198 perished in the waters off Ireland.

A Crime Against Humanity?

There was an instantaneous and enormous outcry against the German submarine attack on the unarmed passenger liner — especially in neutral America, which mourned 128 lost citizens. "Nothing in the annals of piracy can, in wanton and cruel ferocity, equal the destruction of the *Lusitania*," declared the Louisville *Courier-Journal*. "Germany surely must have gone mad," echoed the Richmond *Times-Dispatch*.

On May 10, three days after the sinking, the German government delivered a note to Washington expressing its "deepest sympathy" for the loss of American lives. But Germany placed blame for the tragedy squarely on Britain, saying that it had been forced to take such retaliatory measures to counter the British blockade of Germany, which had cut off needed supplies of food and raw materials. Moreover, Berlin claimed, the *Lusitania* was carrying 5,450 cases of ammunition and other war matériel that negated its status as a harmless passenger vessel. "Germany has a right to prevent contraband going to the Allies," Secretary of State William Jennings Bryan wrote

On May 1, 1915, the luxury liner Lusitania —
the pride of the Cunard Line — steamed out of New
York on her 202nd Atlantic crossing. Above, the
ship arrives in port on a previous voyage.

The warning below —
though dated April 22,
1915 — did not appear
until May 1, the very
day the Lusitania was
scheduled to sail. By
coincidence the German
ad ran next to the
Cunard Line's schedule
of departures in some
newspapers. Few
passengers took the
warning seriously
enough to cancel or
change their bookings.

to President Woodrow Wilson, "and a ship carrying contraband should not rely upon passengers
to protect her from attack." The official manifest
of the Lusitania's cargo had not listed the muni-
tions; only a supplemental bill of lading, signed
four days after departure, revealed the war cargo.

No one could deny that the Lusitania's passengers had been warned of the danger they were
courting. On May 1 the German government had
placed an announcement in New York morning
newspapers reminding travelers that vessels flying the British flag were subject to destruction in
the war zone around the British Isles. The ominous notification appeared the very day the Lusitania was scheduled to sail. Only a few passengers had changed their bookings.

Steaming into a Trap

On April 30 the German submarine U-20, commanded by 30-year-old Lieutenant Walther
Schwieger, departed from the North Sea naval
base of Emden. Along with two other submarines, the U-20 was under orders to search out
and destroy enemy warships, troop transports,
and merchant vessels in the waters surrounding
the British Isles. Schwieger was to operate in the
Irish Sea off Liverpool, the port toward which
the Lusitania was heading when it left New York

the next day. Passing north of Scotland and west
of Ireland, the U-20 reached the area to which it
had been assigned on May 5. That day Schwieger
sank a schooner off the south Irish coast; on May
6 he destroyed two large steamers.

Alarmed, the British admiralty in London sent
a radio message to the Lusitania advising Captain
Turner that enemy submarines were active in the
area he was about to enter. It was the first of four
messages, one of which was repeated six times,
that Turner received that evening and during the
morning of May 7. None, however, mentioned
the sinkings by Schwieger's U-20.

Turner, like all captains of British ships in the war zone, was supposed to be operating his ship under specific orders issued in February 1915 in response to the German declaration of a war zone. Among them were directives to steer a zig-zag course in midchannel and to operate at full speed. On the fatal morning of May 7, the *Lusitania* was cruising 12 miles off the Irish coast at a point where 140 miles of water separate Ireland from southern England. It was proceeding on a more or less straight course. In response to the fog, and to delay his arrival in Liverpool until he could ride the tides into the harbor, Captain Turner had slowed his ship from 21 to 18 knots (top speed was 25 knots). Had he been zigzagging at midchannel and operating at full speed, Turner could easily have evaded the *U-20*.

The Missing Escort

Captain Turner had been expecting an escort for the final hours of his voyage to Liverpool. What

Although he sent strong protests to Germany, President Wilson resisted pressure from outraged Americans to enter the war over the Lusitania *sinking in 1915 and ran for reelection the next year on a neutrality platform. He preached the need to arm for self-defense and marched in so-called preparedness parades.*

was needed was a destroyer with a ramming speed of 35 knots to sight and remove any submarines from the passenger liner's route. But the priority for destroyers was escorting troopships to France and the Mediterranean. As the *Lusitania* approached the Irish coast, only the aging cruiser *Juno* was available. Capable of making no more than 17 or 18 knots and lacking the depth charges with which to disable a submarine, the *Juno* would have been of little or no help to the *Lusitania* and would perhaps have even further slowed the vessel's progress.

In response to the *Lusitania*'s distress signal after being torpedoed, Vice Admiral Sir Charles Coke sent all rescue ships at his disposition — including converted fishing trawlers — from the nearby port of Queenstown. Reaching the scene some two hours later, the rescuers were able to pull some survivors out of the sea and tow back to port the few lifeboats that had been successfully launched. Taking longer to get under way, the *Juno* was called back to Queenstown when it was learned that the smaller ships could do all that was necessary. If German submarines were still in the area, the *Juno* would have been another tempting target. Coke, of course, could not have known that Schwieger — with but a single torpedo remaining in his arsenal — set out for home immediately after sinking the *Lusitania*.

No Guilty Conscience

Although Schwieger's mission was regarded as a great success throughout the German fleet, the young lieutenant got a frosty reception in Berlin, where the government was reeling from the backlash of world opinion. A typescript of his diary, possibly an edited version, contains the statement that he was unaware of the identity of his prey until he saw the ship's name as the vessel slipped below the waves.

Four months later Schwieger — though under strict orders by then not to attack passenger ships — sank another British liner, the *Hesperian*, this time with a loss of 32 lives. Questioned about his violation of instructions, Schwieger said that he had mistaken the *Hesperian* for an auxiliary cruiser. When he realized his mistake, he was asked, did it trouble his conscience. His answer: "a definite no." Before losing his life on a mission in September 1917, Schwieger was responsible for sinking 190,000 tons of British shipping and received the German navy's highest award.

"Strict Accountability"

Although the American government had failed to protest the British blockade of Germany in

Attacks Without Warning

According to the rules of international law accepted in 1914, a warship was permitted to stop an unarmed merchant vessel to examine its freight for contraband — that is, illegal war matériel. If a boarding party discovered cargo being shipped to an enemy, the warship could either direct the intercepted ship to a friendly harbor or sink it. But the attacker was expected to take aboard the crew and any passengers or see them safely into lifeboats. However, the advent of the submarine — in particular as it was employed by the German navy in World War I — altered the rules.

Even before the outbreak of war, Britain had begun equipping its merchant vessels with guns capable of blasting a submarine out of the water. Many surface vessels, warships as well as passenger liners like the *Lusitania*, were capable of overtaking submarines and ramming them. Winston Churchill, first lord of the British admiralty, initiated a policy of dispatching warships disguised as merchant vessels in order to lure German submarines close enough to be destroyed.

When Germany declared the waters surrounding the British Isles to be a war zone — in retaliation for Britain's blockade of its ports — neutral ships were advised to stay out of the area. Because of Britain's misuse of neutral flags, mistakes were unavoidable, the Germans said.

Because their submarines were so vulnerable to gunfire and ramming, the Germans resorted to premeditated attacks without warning — that on the *Lusitania* being the most notorious in the first year of the war. Backing off from a confrontation with neutral America, Germany announced on September 1, 1915, that no passenger liners would be sunk without warning and without making provision for the safety of passengers and crew. The resumption of unrestricted submarine warfare early in 1917, however, finally led to a U.S. declaration of war on Germany on April 6.

Space aboard a German submarine, as in this torpedo room, was extremely limited.

November 1914, President Wilson's reaction to the German declaration of a war zone around the British Isles was prompt and hostile. Germany would be held to "strict accountability" if American vessels or lives were lost in submarine attacks. The United States was prepared to "take any steps it might be necessary to take to safeguard American lives and property."

To some people — perhaps including those American citizens who sailed on the *Lusitania* despite the German warning — the president's statement implied that the flag protected Americans on the high seas regardless of the country of origin of the ship on which they sailed. To others — perhaps including figures high up in the British government — it meant that Wilson was ready to join the Allies if a German submarine took American lives. This, according to British writer Colin Simpson, led to a conspiracy involving both British and American officials to provoke the attack on the *Lusitania*.

Why did the original ship's manifest not list the contraband war matériel? And was it the exploding ammunition and not the torpedo that sent the *Lusitania* to its watery grave? Why did the British admiralty fail to provide an escort as the Cunard liner entered the dangerous waters south of Ireland? Had Captain Turner been secretly ordered to ignore the safety measures that would have kept his vessel from harm? Why was the *Lusitania*'s captain not given specific information on the sinkings just prior to the *U-20*'s attack? And precisely what did Lord Mersey, the official British investigator of the disaster, mean when he called the sinking of the *Lusitania* "a damned dirty business"?

The tragedy did not bring the United States into the war — as some people on both sides of the Atlantic may have hoped. That happened two years later, in April 1917, after Germany resumed unrestricted submarine warfare. And American intervention ultimately led to German defeat.

The Missing Dauphin

The Bourbon monarchy was swept away in the chaos of the French Revolution. Louis XVI and his queen, Marie Antoinette, met ignominious deaths on the guillotine; their son, the dauphin Louis Charles, died in prison — or so it was reported at the time.

France had been in turmoil for five years, or since a Paris mob had stormed the Bastille on July 14, 1789. The destruction of the infamous prison, symbol of the corrupt, uncaring Bourbon monarchy, marked the beginning of the French Revolution. In October a band of hungry women marched out to the palace of Versailles and forced King Louis XVI, his wife, Marie Antoinette, and their two children to accompany them back to the city, where the king was forced to endorse the modest reforms of a national assembly. It was not enough to stem the tides of change that were about to engulf the nation.

Realizing the danger to his person, Louis fled Paris with his family in June 1791, but they were stopped at the town of Varennes on the northeast frontier and taken back to the capital as virtual prisoners. On September 21, 1792, the National Convention voted to abolish the monarchy and declared France a republic. Tried for treason, convicted, and sentenced to death by a vote of 387 to 334, Louis XVI was sent to the guillotine on January 21, 1793. Marie Antoinette followed him nine months later. This period, known to history as the Reign of Terror, was presided over by an uncompromising revolutionary, Maximilien Robespierre.

On July 27, 1794, Robespierre's time came. Arrested with 21 of his accomplices, he was sentenced to death the next day on the very guillo-

After the execution of Louis XVI early in 1793, the dauphin — proclaimed king by royalists in exile — was taken from his mother (below) and imprisoned separately in the Temple (right).

LOUIS XVII

Roi de France et de Navarre

(Charles Louis Duc de Normandie)

The German clock maker Karl Wilhelm Naundorff styled himself Louis XVII, king of France and Navarre, or Charles Louis, duke of Normandy, but he was unable to prove the claim.

tine to which he had condemned so many. On that day of retribution, Paul de Barras, a leader of the National Convention who had been instrumental in removing Robespierre, hastened from the scene of execution to the Temple, a prison in the heart of the city. He was to confirm the condition of its two royal inmates, the orphans of Louis XVI and Marie Antoinette: 16-year-old Marie Thérèse and 9-year-old Louis Charles.

From Palace to Prison

Born on Easter Sunday in 1785, Louis Charles had enjoyed a privileged and carefree childhood at Versailles — until the Revolution overtook his family. Only a month before the storming of the Bastille, upon the death from tuberculosis of his older brother, the boy had become the dauphin, or crown prince, of France and heir apparent to Louis XVI. When the king was executed, exiled royalists proclaimed him King Louis XVII and named his uncle the comte de Provence as regent during his minority.

The action of the royalists posed a threat to the National Convention, which ordered the dauphin given over to the care of a shoemaker named Antoine Simon and his wife. Treating the boy as they would one of their own class, roughly and with coarse familiarity, the couple tried to make the titular king a republican — even teaching him to sing the stirring revolutionary anthem *Le Marseillaise*. For such actions, Simon and his wife would later be branded as sadistic brutes.

In January 1794 Simon relinquished his guardianship of Louis Charles, who was next assigned to the very room in a tower of the Temple that had been his father's last prison. Cared for by four guards who were rotated daily, the boy was so isolated that Marie Thérèse — held prisoner on the floor above him — became convinced that her brother was dead or had been removed from the Temple. The neglected boy that Barras visited on July 28 was despondent and sickly. Outraged, he arranged for medical care and insisted on more humane treatment of the royal ward.

Early the following year, the National Convention voted to send Louis Charles into exile but was informed that the boy was too weak to travel. On June 28, 1795, it was reported that the dauphin — Louis XVII to some — had died of scrofula, tuberculosis of the lymph glands.

A Plethora of Pretenders

The death of Robespierre and the end of the Reign of Terror did not restore tranquillity to France. The next two decades saw the rise and fall of Napoleon, the military genius and political megalomaniac who plunged all of Europe into devastating warfare. Upon Napoleon's defeat by a coalition of France's enemies in 1814, the Bourbon monarchy was restored in the person of the comte de Provence, who was proclaimed King Louis XVIII.

The new king and his younger brother and successor, Charles X, had to contend with the claims of various pretenders to the throne — as did Charles's successor, the citizen king Louis Philippe, who reigned from 1830 to 1848, until revolution once more made France a republic. In these years more than 30 men stepped forward to say they were the lost dauphin.

In 1834 one of the pretenders was put on trial in Paris. A prosecution witness electrified the court by reading a letter from the "real" Louis XVII. He proved to be an impoverished clock maker named Karl Wilhelm Naundorff who had spent many years in Germany and spoke French only haltingly. Somehow, Naundorff convinced former members of the court at Versailles that he was indeed the rightful king of France.

The Return of the Bourbons

The comte de Provence, a year younger than his brother Louis XVI, played a dangerous game during the French Revolution and a cautious one during the subsequent reign of Napoleon. Initially he expressed support for reform and scorned those members of the nobility who fled France at the outbreak of revolution. But in June 1791 — at the very time the king and his family were prevented from fleeing the country — the comte went into exile. With scant concern for the well-being of Louis,

When Napoleon escaped from Elba, Louis XVIII once more had to flee Paris. But following the emperor's final defeat at Waterloo, he returned in triumph on July 8, 1815.

Marie Antoinette, and their children, held prisoners in Paris, the comte issued counterrevolutionary proclamations, organized fellow émigrés abroad, and asked for the support of other European monarchs in his efforts to stem the rebellion. Following the execution of

the king, he was named regent for his nephew, Louis Charles, whom royalists abroad proclaimed King Louis XVII.

During Napoleon's reign, the comte remained in exile and — though hard-pressed for funds — refused either to renounce his claim to the throne or accept a pension from the emperor. His was a waiting game, which paid off when Napoleon was defeated early in 1814. On May 3 the comte de Provence — now King Louis XVIII — was joyously received in Paris.

The Adventures of a Clock Maker

The highest social circles in Paris listened in astonishment as Naundorff revealed intimate details about the family life of Louis XVI and Marie Antoinette. Asked about specific occurrences at Versailles just prior to the Revolution or in prison later, he always had the right answer. Without hesitation he called people presented to him by name, though he could only have met them decades before as a child.

And yet the clock maker could not explain exactly when and how he had been rescued from imprisonment in the Temple. The stories he did tell about the years between 1795, when he was last known to have been alive, and the year he emerged in Berlin, 1810, were the makings of a historical romance. After his abduction from Paris, Naundorff claimed, he had remained in captivity, often ill-treated by his supposed liberators. Nothing was left out of Naundorff's mesmerizing account: an ocean voyage to America, betrayal, theft, forged documents, murder, a return to Europe. Unfortunately, he could not document any of these events.

Naundorff's life after 1810, for which he did have proof, was not of a character likely to instill confidence among those supporting his claims to be the long-lost dauphin. Two years after his documented arrival in Berlin, Naundorff had moved to Spandau, where he obtained Prussian citizenship with no apparent difficulty. By 1822 he was settled with a family in Brandenburg. Soon thereafter he was brought to court on a charge of counterfeiting and fraud, accused of having set his own house on fire. Although one of the judges in the case declared him to be insane, Naundorff was sentenced to three years' imprisonment. Following his release, he moved to the Prussian town of Crossen. Sometime after 1827 he came up with the story that he was the rightful heir to the throne of France. Through newspaper reports

The dauphin Louis Charles was a delicate child, as the painting above reveals. To ardent royalists he was the uncrowned king Louis XVII. He was reported to have died in prison in June 1795, at the age of 10, and to have been buried at the cemetery of Sainte-Marguerite in Paris; a simple gravestone marked "L XVII" (right) is said to be his.

the story reached the French capital, and Naundorff was summoned to Paris.

A Sister Declines

The simplest way to convince those who continued to express skepticism about Naundorff's claims would have been to confront him with the one person still alive who had known him best in the years before 1795: his sister, Marie Thérèse. The princess had managed to survive imprisonment and was living in exile.

Although Marie Thérèse acknowledged that it was quite likely that another boy had been substituted for her brother at the Temple, she refused to receive Naundorff in person. Brusquely, she asserted that she could see no similarity between Louis Charles and the picture of the clock maker she was shown. And when Naundorff was at last able to bring his claims to a French court, Marie Thérèse firmly declined to appear as a witness. Instead of winning legal recognition, Naundorff was arrested by order of King Louis Philippe and deported to England in 1836.

Nursing his hatred of the Bourbons who had refused to accept him, Naundorff set up a chemical laboratory in England to build what he called his Bourbon bomb. Unfortunately, it exploded prematurely, causing considerable damage to his own home. Next, he predicted his ascension to the throne of France on January 1, 1840; when his prophecy went unfulfilled, Naundorff lost the support of whatever followers he still had. He died on August 10, 1845, in the Netherlands — apparently a victim of poisoning.

A Life in Exile

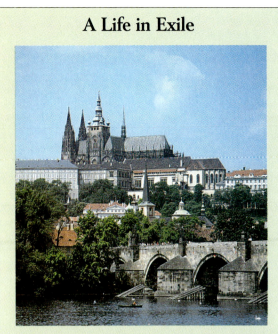

Marie Thérèse was the second child of Louis XVI and Marie Antoinette. She was two months short of her 11th birthday on the terrifying October day in 1789 when a mob forced the royal family to abandon the luxury of Versailles for a dubious future in Paris. Following the failure of the escape attempt in 1791, the princess saw first her father, then her mother taken off for execution. In June 1795 she was told that her brother, the dauphin Louis Charles, had died in the same prison where she was held captive, the Temple. Six months later, on December 19, she was unaccountably released from confinement and sent into exile. It was her 17th birthday.

The first stop on her peripatetic wanderings about Europe was Austria, the homeland of her mother. But she was not made particularly welcome at the court in Vienna by her cousin, Holy Roman Emperor Francis II, and sought escape from her loneliness with a trip to the duchy of Kurland (today's Latvia), where an uncle suggested a marriage of convenience to her cousin, and fellow exile from France, Louis Antoine, the duc d'Angoulême.

In 1814 Marie Thérèse returned to France when the Bourbon monarchy was restored and her uncle, the comte de Provence, was installed as Louis XVIII. Her father-in-law succeeded to the throne in 1824 as Charles X. Six years later, when Charles was forced to abdicate in favor of the citizen king Louis Philippe, Marie Thérèse fled to Prague and lived for a time in its castle (above). But her wanderings were still not over, and she eventually settled in Friuli, in what is now northern Italy, where she died an embittered woman of 72 in 1851.

Remarkably, Naundorff's descendants were able to carry his claims into the 20th century, stubbornly adding "de Bourbon" to their names. In July 1954 a French court of appeals definitively ruled against one of Naundorff's descendants, a circus manager who called himself René Charles de Bourbon. Louis Charles, the dauphin of France and the uncrowned King Louis XVII, was officially declared to have died in the Temple on June 8, 1795. For whatever unlikely value it possessed, the claim to France's nonexistent throne was awarded to the Bourbon-Parma branch of the former royal family.

A Changeling Captive?

Even if the claims of Naundorff remain unsubstantiated, there are historians who still question the death of Louis Charles as reported to the National Convention 200 years ago. Certain evidence, they say, strongly suggests that another boy was substituted for the dauphin.

The report of a member of the National Convention who visited the royal prisoner at the Temple early in 1795 stated that the 10-year-old boy seemed to be a deaf-mute. One of the boy's last guards described his charge as being exceptionally tall for his age; the dauphin, it is well documented, was short and slender. The physician called in to perform an autopsy tersely wrote that he had been shown a corpse that "was said to be" the son of Louis XVI; his comment leaves the impression that the doctor was unconvinced. A lock of hair taken from the body was later compared with a wisp of the dauphin's hair in a locket belonging to Marie Antoinette; they did not appear to be the same.

Had another boy been brought in secret to the Temple and Louis Charles spirited away? The wife of Antoine Simon, the dauphin's guardian in the last half of 1794, inadvertently gave a clue as to how the change might have been effected. Among the meager furnishings of their royal ward's prison quarters was a large linen basket with a false bottom; it could have been used to conceal a small boy being brought in or out.

Against all such doubts, however, is the testimony of the duchess of Tourzel, governess to Marie Antoinette's children. Despite the risk of offending the revolutionaries, she kept a miniature of Louis Charles in her sitting room. Following the reported death of the dauphin, two of his jailors visited her with the sad news. Seeing the portrait, they told the duchess that it was a likeness of their late charge. The priest who conducted the burial service also confirmed that the corpse was that of the boy in the miniature.

7

Fateful
Blunders

The Invincible Armada

*It was the greatest naval force ever assembled, and with it King
Philip II of Spain intended to oust Queen Elizabeth I from the
throne of England and restore her realm to Catholicism.
He made a fatal miscalculation.*

The duke was appalled at the commission he had received from King Philip II of Spain. Upon the death of the marquis of Santa Cruz on February 9, 1588, the king had picked him to command the expedition against England. "My health is not equal to such a voyage," the duke implored the king in a letter acknowledging receipt of the royal command, "for I know by experience of the little I have been at sea that I am always seasick and always catch cold. . . . Since I have had no experience either of the sea, or of war, I cannot feel that I ought to command so important an enterprise."

But the king's will could not be resisted. Don Alonso de Guzmán el Bueno, the duke of Medina Sidonia and captain-general of Andalusia, dutifully accepted the command. As a devout Catholic and a nobleman of ancient and impeccable lineage, he knew that he had no choice. Leaving the comforts of his home in the south of Spain, the

*The triumph of England over the Spanish armada in the summer of 1588 marked the beginning of
Britain's long naval supremacy.*

The duke of Medina Sidonia, a Spanish grandee of impeccable lineage but little naval experience, commanded the expedition against England.

Proudly setting sail from Lisbon, the armada was soon forced to land at La Coruña to take on supplies. After fighting its way up the English Channel and through the Straits of Dover, the fleet returned via the circuitous route shown on the map above.

duke made haste for Lisbon, where the naval force had been assembled. The death of the marquis had halted the frantic preparations for departure, and it was Medina Sidonia's Herculean task to bring order out of the chaos in the port. Somehow he did so, and on April 25 he went to the cathedral to accept the standard he would take into battle: a banner bearing the arms of Spain, flanked by images of Jesus and the Virgin Mary. A scroll bore the expedition's motto, "Arise, O Lord, and vindicate thy cause."

To the Spaniards this was a holy war, one they were destined to win despite the fact that the English had faster ships and better guns and were more experienced seamen. How could he be sure of prevailing, one of the duke's high-ranking officers was asked. "It's very simple," he replied. "We fight in God's cause."

Catholic versus Protestant

The conflict had been brewing for nearly 30 years or ever since Elizabeth I had succeeded her half sister Mary on the throne of England in 1558. Their father, Henry VIII, had broken with the Catholic Church over the issue of divorcing Mary's mother, Catherine of Aragon, to marry Elizabeth's mother, Anne Boleyn, and had established the Church of England. During her brief reign Mary had attempted to restore Catholicism to England and had married the heir apparent of

Spain, later King Philip II. But when Mary died childless, the crown passed to Elizabeth, no less determined than her sister to support the religion of her upbringing, Protestantism. To the ardently Catholic Philip her efforts were heresy.

According to an English patriotic myth, Sir Francis Drake and Lord Howard finished their game of bowls even after being alerted to the enemy's approach off the southwest coast.

When Elizabeth signed an alliance with the Netherlands and sent troops to support the rebellion of Philip's Protestant subjects there, the king of Spain had a political as well as a religious grievance with England. Yet he hesitated. There was one hope: that the aging, unmarried queen of England would be succeeded by her Catholic cousin Mary Stuart, the deposed Queen of Scots. But on February 18, 1587, Mary was executed by command of Elizabeth. Philip knew that he would have to take action.

The Most Fortunate Fleet

Philip's plan was to send a heavily armed fleet to the English Channel to rendezvous with an invasion force led by his commander in the Netherlands, the duke of Parma. Protected by the fleet, Parma's 30,000-man army was to cross the channel in barges for a landing at Margate and then march along the Thames River to seize London.

The naval expedition of which Medina Sidonia so reluctantly assumed command was composed of 130 ships armed with 2,400 guns, for which 124,000 rounds of ammunition had been provided. The vessels ranged in size from formidable floating fortresses called galleons to galleys that could be maneuvered by oars to swift frigates for scouting to unwieldy *urcas*, literally "hulks," that carried supplies. The ships were manned by 8,000 seamen and carried nearly 19,000 soldiers. Officially, the expedition was called *La felicissima armada* ("the most fortunate fleet"). Because of its awesome strength, the Spaniards called it *La Invencible* ("The Invincible"). On May 9, 1588, the first ships hauled anchor and began making their way down the broad Tagus River to the Atlantic Ocean.

Because of unseasonable gales, however, the entire fleet was not assembled at sea for the voyage north until month's end. By then, a serious spoilage in the food supplies had been detected — some of the meat, fish, and biscuits having been packed into casks for the original departure date of October 1587. Moreover, the water, stowed for at least a month, proved undrinkable. Reluctantly, Medina Sidonia ordered his fleet to put in at La Coruña on the northwest coast of Spain on June 19 to take on provisions and water. Not until July 21 was the voyage resumed.

Time Enough to Beat the Spaniards

Whereas the Spanish armada had been assembling since the previous autumn, the English fleet was not fully commissioned until April — and this lack of preparation curiously worked in Elizabeth's favor. The food and water aboard her ships had not turned bad; her fighting men had not grown bored with inactivity.

The queen's fleet was commanded by Lord Howard of Effingham. He had been given his post for many of the reasons as had Medina Sidonia — because he was an ardent Protestant, unquestionably loyal to Elizabeth, and from a noble family that had already provided England with three lord admirals. His second in command was the dashing privateer Sir Francis Drake.

Aware of the lengthy preparations of the Spaniards, the English had assembled a land force of nearly 30,000 men along the south coast and an additional 17,000 at Tilbury on the lower Thames. At sight of the armada, they were to follow it along the coast and attack as soon as a landing was attempted. From the tip of Cornwall to London signal fires were ready to be lit.

According to a popular legend in England, Drake was playing a game of bowls at Plymouth on Friday, July 29, when word arrived that the first Spanish ships had been sighted off the south-west coast. Calmly, he resisted the temptation to order an immediate embarkation. "We have time enough to finish the game and beat the Spaniards, too," Sir Francis is supposed to have said.

The Formidable Crescent

News of the sighting most likely reached Plymouth in midafternoon, as the tide was flooding into the sound. Not until after 10 P.M. would it be possible for Howard's fighting fleet to catch the freshening ebb tide out to sea — time enough to finish a game, if one had been under way. But in reality Howard ordered his ships to be laboriously warped out of port — that is, towed with rowboats or pulled on anchors cast ahead. By dawn of July 30 the 105 ships of the English fleet were ready to meet the armada. What the defenders saw before an evening squall and nightfall obscured their vision was the greatest assembly of hostile ships yet known to history, 125 of Medina Sidonia's 130 ships having survived the voyage from Spain. Put to the torch, the signal fires carried the news across Elizabeth's realm.

Some of the naval skirmishes between the Spanish and English fleets took place within sight of the chalk cliffs of Dover (above). The contemporary map at left shows two separate actions: the English pursuing the Spanish crescent formation and the inconclusive encounter off Portland Bill on August 2.

Fighting at Close Range

Service aboard 16th-century warships was both strenuous and hazardous. Though put to hard labor, sailors were given short, often putrid rations. Forced to work and sleep in cramped quarters, they were prey to frequent epidemics.

"Clear ship for battle" was the call beaten on drums once an enemy had been sighted; the drum above was invariably taken into battle by the English hero Sir Francis Drake. The men responding to the drumbeat knew that fighting would be at extremely close quarters, since the range of their guns was no more than about 300 yards. But at that distance the huge cannonballs could easily pierce a ship's timbers, and through openings the attackers could hurl firepots.

At even closer range, the opponents commenced firing with small arms to reduce resistance to the final phase of the fight: boarding. Grappling hooks were used to pull the enemy vessel closer so that the attackers could leap aboard for the man-to-man fight that decided the contest. The Spaniards thought that the superior size of their vessels would lead to victory in 1588; they did not reckon with their adversary's new tactics that disdained close encounters in favor of swift maneuvering that allowed the English to wreak havoc at a distance.

As Medina Sidonia moved up the English Channel, he arrayed his vast fleet in a tight crescent, its extended wings pointed toward the enemy. The Spaniards planned to lure the English ships into the thickened center where they could be boarded and subdued. With their smaller, swifter ships, the English hoped to avoid such close combat and destroy their adversary's vessels by clever maneuvering and efficient gunfire.

During a week of spirited skirmishes off the south coast of England, the Spaniards were able to maintain their tight formation. But on August 6 Howard gained numerical superiority with the arrival of vessels that had been kept at Dover to block any move across the strait by the duke of Parma. That was not the worst news that day for Medina Sidonia. Putting in at the French port of Calais, he learned that the invasion force was unprepared for the crossing.

A King Keeps His Secrets

The duke of Parma had written Philip repeatedly since the beginning of the year that he could not risk venturing to sea with his transport barges unless the armada could offer protection not only from the English fleet but from Dutch ships as well. The king never shared this information with Medina Sidonia — though the rendezvous of the two commanders was the whole point of the campaign. Perhaps, some historians have argued, Philip never seriously intended an invasion of England. Instead, he may have merely wanted to frighten Elizabeth into submission. If so, it was a costly blunder — dealing a serious blow to Spanish power and pride.

Medina Sidonia continued to ward off English attacks for a few more days, but his pursuers were driving him ever northward and beyond the point where he could lend protection to the dubious invasion. On August 12 Howard turned back, badly in need of provisions and convinced that the threat had passed. The English had not lost a single ship in the two weeks of combat.

The Spanish commander reluctantly concluded that he would have to make for home by a roundabout route: into the North Sea, between the Orkney and Shetland islands off northern Scotland, and along the west coast of Ireland before heading south. The journey turned into a disaster, as unseasonable storms sent many of his ships widely off course or to destruction on rocky shores where survivors were captured and often put to death on the spot. On September 21 Medina Sidonia's flagship limped into the port of Santander. Only 67 additional vessels — a little more than half of the invincible armada — ever reached Spanish ports.

"I sent my ships to fight against men," King Philip is supposed to have remarked upon receiving news of the catastrophic defeat, "and not against the winds and waves of God." It was perhaps the only opinion of his with which Elizabeth would ever agree, composing as she did a song for the victory celebrations:

He made the winds and waters rise
To scatter all myne enemyes.

The Blitzkrieg That Failed

When Hitler's crack troops invaded the Soviet Union in 1941,
a Nazi victory seemed inevitable. Mysteriously, the führer halted
his armies outside Moscow, a mistake that caused disaster
and showed that the Third Reich was not invincible.

Stalin, suspicious of the capitalist West, would not believe the rapidly accumulating evidence that Hitler intended to launch a surprise invasion of Russia in 1941. Shocking the world, the dictators of the Soviet Union and Nazi Germany, self-proclaimed messiahs of diametrically opposed political systems, had signed a non-aggression pact on August 23, 1939. The stated term of the agreement was 10 years, during which time both sides were to settle disagreements by peaceful means. Nine days later, on September 1, the Germans invaded Poland, having secretly agreed to split the helpless nation with Russia. The attack precipitated World War II.

As war ravaged Western Europe and the astonishing Nazi armies marched implacably toward the Atlantic, Stalin clung desperately to the illusion that his vast but struggling nation would be spared. "It is best to hold aloof from the conflict," explained an official of the international communist organization known as the Comintern, "while remaining ready to intervene when the powers engaged therein are weakened by war, in the hope of securing a social revolution." For his part, the Soviet leader supplied his untrustworthy ally with such essential raw materials as grain, oil, and iron ore.

But after conquering France and tightening his

Without warning, on June 22, 1941, German soldiers (below) leapt from their trenches for the massive assault on the Soviet Union. Despite warnings, Stalin was caught totally unprepared.

Owing to the surprise of their attack, Nazi Germany's tanks almost effortlessly swept through the vast and vital grainfields of the Soviet Union's Ukraine (above).

grip on Europe, the führer was stymied by the stalwart resistance of Britain, which had surprised him in the summer of 1940 by enduring the onslaught of his huge air force, the Luftwaffe. During the Battle of Britain, Hitler told his top military brass that he had decided that communism in Russia must be defeated once and for all. By removing Russia as a possible ally, he hoped to win Britain by smashing its last hope. Also, after brooding over the decision for a year, he had come to believe that the Soviet Union was becoming dangerously strong.

On December 18 Hitler's top-secret Directive 21 ordered preparations for a blitzkrieg ("lightning campaign") into Russia the following summer. Operation Barbarossa, named for a German emperor who had prevailed in the East during the Middle Ages, was expected to last no longer than four months, if that. It would require at least 3 million German soldiers, 3,400 tanks, and about 3,000 aircraft — making it the greatest land campaign in all of history.

Meanwhile, Stalin had decreed that his minions not provoke Germany, even by reacting to Nazi reconnaissance flights over Soviet territory. He dismissed warnings from Britain's Prime Minister Winston Churchill as capitalist trickery and ignored the grim and accurate predictions of his own spy network operating in Germany. On June 22, 1941, a freight train loaded with Russian grain for the Germans crossed the border at about 2 A.M. An hour and 15 minutes later, without bothering to declare war, Hitler hurled his armies across the border and sent them racing toward Moscow. The nonaggression pact had endured for 22 months.

Hitler's Miscalculation

Hitler and his Nazis despised the Russian people as *untermensch*, less than human beings. He believed that communism was the work of Jewish intellectuals and wanted the supposed Jewish-Bolshevik class exterminated. His desire to dominate the world and create a new order could be realized, he thought, by controlling the extraordinary natural resources and agricultural production of Russia — even if millions of people starved to death as a result. Opting for a policy of unprecedented cruelty, the Nazi dictator told his military leaders that the ordinary rules of war could be ignored since the Soviets had not signed the Geneva convention. Terror would be the princi-

It was Hitler's aim to have the Soviet Union at his mercy by year's end, and his initial advance to Moscow was swift. In haste, Stalin made his capital ready for the onslaught; below, civilian workers dig tank traps.

By October 1941 rains had turned Russian soil into seas of mud, slowing the seemingly inexorable German advance on Moscow to a crawl. Much of the invaders' equipment had to be surrendered to the invincible "General Mud."

The Miracle of Dunkirk

More than a year before the Battle of Moscow, Hitler had also hesitated on the brink of victory, again giving his adversary the opportunity to regroup. On May 20, 1940, French and British forces were trapped as the advancing Germans closed in on Flanders. Evacuation by sea was the only possible escape. Operation Dynamo, using military and civilian craft, began at Dunkirk, an ancient city that was France's third largest port. Astonishingly, Hitler ordered his tanks to halt about 12 miles outside Dunkirk on May 24, allowing the rescue effort to begin.

First, the 28,000 men assigned to communications and training were successfully ferried back across the English Channel to the chalk cliffs of Dover. Then, as some soldiers waited patiently in water up to their necks, Allied forces by the

In May 1940 British and other Allied soldiers were forced to wade from the sands at Dunkirk to the craft that would take them to safety in England.

thousands were picked up by boats both large and small. This extraordinary flotilla numbered 848 vessels, including 45 passenger ships, 230 fishing boats, and more than 200 private launches. On May 26 Hitler ordered the tanks forward again, and the fighting became fierce. When the operation was brought to a halt on June 3, a total of 338,226 British, French, Belgian, and Dutch soldiers were safe in England. Dunkirk, with about 40,000 men left behind, was surrendered at 9 A.M. that day.

Why did the fabled German intelligence not report to Hitler that the channel was virtually teeming with rescue craft as his tanks stood still? Whatever the explanation, the escape of the Dunkirk forces — miracle or not — was another critical missed opportunity for the armies of the Third Reich.

---

pal weapon against the people. The Nazi party and the SS would immediately take over the administration of captured territories. All Soviet commissars, civilian or military, were to be shot upon capture.

Viciousness aside, this policy was a serious miscalculation, for many noncommunist Soviet citizens viewed the Germans as their liberators from Stalin's institutionalized atrocities. In the Ukraine villagers toasted the invaders and gave thanks in the churches Stalin had closed. But as the brutal enemy swept across the plains, the shocked citizenry began to fight back.

The Russian people were caught between horrible alternatives. On July 3 Stalin, speaking publicly for the first time in his long rule (and surprising Russians by his thick Georgian accent), eschewed the usual party propaganda and called for sacrifice in the name of Mother Russia. Many rallied to this patriotic ideal, but their loyalty was backed up by the secret police, the NKVD. Officers who ordered strategic retreats were shot, sometimes in the back. They, in turn, sometimes shot their own men. The average soldier was at once the target of the advancing enemy and his own superiors in the rear.

Before the end of the year, Hitler boasted that 17,000 Russian airplanes had been shot down. As

early as July 19, more than 400,000 Soviet troops had been taken prisoner. Even more startling, by July 3 German forces had penetrated 320 miles into Russia, halfway to Moscow. "For all practical purposes," Hitler noted the next day, "the enemy has lost this campaign."

The Scourge of Interference

Soon, however, nature intervened, just as the Germans saw victory in their grasp. Heavy rains in July produced seas of mud that stalled the Nazi vehicles. The few roads and rail lines in the underdeveloped country groaned under the demands of supplying the invading armies. Although Russian losses were heavy, because incompetent leaders had stationed so many troops at the front, the reserves kept coming, drawn from the huge native population.

But these hints of future disaster seemed unimportant as the German war machine racked up one victory after another. By July 19 Hitler's forces had taken the natural gateway to Moscow and had pushed to within 200 miles of the exposed capital. Decisive victory seemed imminent. Then Hitler countermanded his generals.

Rather than seize the capital, the führer — who typically preferred to wage war in flanking movements — decided to go after Leningrad to the

The Germans launched a three-pronged attack on the Soviet Union: in the north, toward Leningrad; in the center, toward Moscow; and in the south, toward the industrial region of the Don, the oil fields of the Caucasus, and the Crimea.

north and the rich industrial, coal, and oil regions to the south. Capture of Leningrad would be an enormous psychological victory, he thought, and the raw materials were vital to his expanding war effort. He expected both goals to be accomplished before the onset of winter. Later, military historians assessed this period of inaction as the seed of failure for the entire campaign.

At first, despite the fears of his military advisers, the plan went well. In the south, Kiev was occupied by September 20, and 700,000 prisoners were taken off to camps. In the north, the frightened citizens of Leningrad worked day and night to prepare for the inevitable. Cut off from outside help, the lovely metropolis created by Peter the Great was considered doomed. The Germans did not even bother to mount an assault, assuming that a debilitating siege had broken the will of the people within.

Now, after a monthlong hiatus, Hitler was ready to polish off Moscow. In two months of war he had lost 409,998 combatants, including 87,489 fatalities. More than half of his critically important tanks were out of commission. To his generals' surprise, their intelligence about enemy strength had proved woefully inadequate. Expecting to face a total of 200 Russian divisions, they had already encountered 360. Yet Operation Typhoon, the attack upon the Russian capital itself, began with promise. In two preliminary battles, 663,000 Soviet soldiers were captured; thousands more deserted, demoralized by the victories to north and south. No war in history had seen such enormous numbers of prisoners and military booty, including tanks and guns.

Nature: The Final Adversary

In October the rains came again, enlisting the famed "General Mud" against the invaders, whose lightning speed slowed to a crawl. Thousands of vehicles became mired. In July the Germans had averaged 28 miles a day; now there were days when they could advance only a single mile. During the breathing space afforded by Hitler's decision not to attack earlier, Stalin had been able to bring in 30 Siberian divisions as reinforcements to the undefended capital.

In addition, the Russians could now throw in their new T-34 tanks, acknowledged today as the best tanks employed anywhere in World War II. Katyusha rockets, known as Stalin's pipe organs, rained on the enemy. In Moscow perhaps 100,000 citizens, mostly women, dug defensive trenches, built pillboxes, and put up barbed wire fences. Approximately 2 million Muscovites had fled eastward, but the Red Army and the Home Guard remained defiant.

Finally, the early winter cold froze the mud, and the Germans could move forward again. On November 15 the battle was joined. Within days the killing Russian winter reached a new fury, freezing tank engines, rifles, and submachine guns. The Germans used summer-grade lubricants; supplies did not get through as the snows fell; and soldiers, who had not been issued overcoats or heavy boots, suffered from frostbite. In early December temperatures dropped to 40 degrees below zero, and the Germans succumbed to exposure. Perhaps 100,000 of Hitler's men suffered disability, including 14,000 who had to undergo amputations. Many of the wounded froze to death. And still the Russians came back at the German invaders, dying by the thousands in never-ending counterattack waves.

End of an Illusion

"The idea that the enemy forces opposing Army Group would collapse is an illusion," a German general reported on December 1. Two nights later, retreat began, with the Germans being harried by a vigorous counterassault devised by the great Russian military hero Marshal Georgi Zhukov. For the rest of the increasingly vicious winter, the invaders could not regain the initiative. They had come within 27 miles of Moscow but failed. Leningrad remained free. While Germany did control the Ukraine's granaries and much of Russia's coal and iron resources, it had been beaten back from the vital oil supplies in the Caucasus region.

Like Napoleon, Hitler failed to conquer Russia, but his determination prevented a complete rout, for he believed that even strategic retreats were dangerous to morale. Stiffening the resolve of his panicked generals, he kept his armies fighting. The common soldier remained true to the führer's wishes, even when forced to survive by eating the flesh of dead cavalry horses. But the world had seen that the Nazis were not invincible, and the psychological effect upon the United States and Britain was bracing.

On the one hand, the Germans had slaughtered about half a million Russian soldiers, wounded twice that many, and imprisoned up to 3 million, or about the same number as their entire invading army. On the other hand, about a quarter of their strength — 830,903 men — was

During a strategic conference on May 9, 1942 (left), Hitler determined that Stalingrad and the Caucasus should be the main objective of the summer offensive. The Germans penetrated the city that autumn, although they overstretched their supply lines to do so.

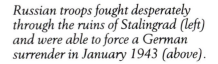

Russian troops fought desperately through the ruins of Stalingrad (left) and were able to force a German surrender in January 1943 (above).

The 900-Day Ordeal

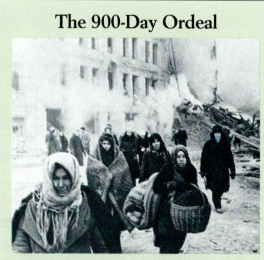

Isolated by the enemy and by geography, the inhabitants of Leningrad were forced to save themselves from the inexorably advancing Germans in the late summer of 1941. Inspired and harried by the indomitable Marshal Zhukov, about a third of the city's 3 million people labored furiously to build improvised fortifications, dig antitank ditches and defensive trenches, and set out mines and barricades.

The neighboring Finns, angry at earlier Russian incursions into their country, struck from the north, reclaiming all of their lost territories. By autumn they had joined with the Germans to encircle the Soviet Union's second most important city almost completely, beginning a harrowing siege of 900 days. Rail lines were cut, enemy troops established a foothold in the suburbs, and the Luftwaffe began bombing the city around the clock. As one officer reported, "The führer wants to avoid house-to-house fighting, which would cost our troops heavy casualties. The city is to be just shut in, shot to pieces by artillery and starved out." (Above, women leaving a bombed-out apartment building.)

Only one pathway led through the tight cordon, thanks to the occasional Russian ally, "General Winter." Lake Ladoga became frozen so hard that truck convoys could bring supplies down a narrow corridor. This lifeline eventually brought food to save the city, but not before nearly a million people died of starvation. The cold also killed many, for there was almost no fuel for heating.

In January 1942 a Soviet counteroffensive pushed the invaders back from the western shore of the lake. Tracks were laid and trains began bringing food and other essential supplies, boosting the physical health and morale of the valiant Leningrad citizenry. Enemy shelling continued, however, and the city was not liberated until January 27, 1944.

dead, disabled, imprisoned, or missing, effectively giving the lie to Hitler's claim that the Red Army was "useless in battle."

Hitler lost no time in placing the blame on his underlings. Army officers, including 35 corps and divisional commanders, were purged, and the dictator assumed even more control over military strategy. His major errors could no longer be hidden, however. He had missed the opportunity of winning the hearts and minds of the oppressed Soviet people, who were looking for salvation after seeing 20 million of their fellow countrymen killed in the aftermath of the communist revolution. He had misjudged the strength of enemy resistance and the difficulties of conducting war against Russia: long supply lines, harsh weather, and unquenchable nationalistic fervor.

The unsuccessful assault on Moscow marked a major turning point in World War II. Heartened by the disaster, growing in strength as Hitler concentrated on the Eastern Front, Britain was reinvigorated. The United States had more time to prepare to enter the conflict, and Russia — despite continuing distrust of the capitalist West — was ready to cooperate with the Allies.

The Final Assault

Weakened but undeterred, Hitler planned an ambitious offensive for the summer of 1942, including the capture of Stalingrad, the gateway to the oil fields of the Caucasus. In one air raid alone, 40,000 Russian citizens were killed. Once again, however, the Nazi dictator paused at the brink of success, diverting his forces from the exhausted city for two weeks. When the invaders returned, angry Russians were firmly entrenched in the rubble of the 30-mile-long industrial center, prepared to fight doorway by doorway for survival. The odds, augmented by superior German weaponry, were against them — until winter returned in all its savagery.

On November 19 a Russian counteroffensive began to press against the German 6th Army, surrounding it in Stalingrad. As in 1941, blizzards raged as ill-equipped soldiers faced frostbite, disease, and starvation. Hitler vowed that he would not retreat any farther, but the survivors of the 300,000-man attack force were forced to surrender on January 31, 1943. The heady weeks when Moscow's Red Square almost became another of the spoils of war were now a distant memory. On the road to the capital, as on the road to Stalingrad, Hitler's strange hesitation had changed the destiny of nations. The checkmated führer could only lament, "The God of War has gone over to the other side."

The massacre of the U.S. 7th Cavalry at the Little Bighorn became the subject of legend.

Custer's Last Stand

*Ordered to move to reservations in the winter of 1876,
thousands of Plains Indians stood their ground. The ensuing
Battle of Little Bighorn would prove to be one of the most
controversial fights in American history.*

In the first months of 1876, the Black Hills of South Dakota were alive with feverish activities. The uneasy accommodation that had existed between the Plains Indians and the white man had come to an end during the previous winter, and there was a sense that the territory was about to undergo momentous, presumably bloody, changes. Troops drilled. Indian chiefs powwowed. Everyone braced for an explosion.

The trouble had begun two years earlier when the 7th Cavalry with George Armstrong Custer in command had reconnoitered the so-called Great Sioux Tribal Roaming Spaces in the western part of South Dakota. His ostensible purpose had been to locate a new military post to protect the Indian lands from the illegal trespass of white settlers. But Custer's real mission was to find gold, and the swashbuckling young officer had not disappointed either the newspaper reporters who went with him or the hordes of Americans back east waiting for news. He sent word that there was "gold among the roots of the grass."

A stampede of prospectors had followed, and by 1876 hundreds of white men were trampling over the sacred Sioux hunting grounds with no regard for the Fort Laramie Treaty, which had expressly guaranteed the Dakota lands to the Indians "as long as the grass grows, or water runs."

The Sioux leaders had first attempted to reason with U.S. government officials, to remind them of their obligations. But when it became obvious that no protection would be forthcoming, thousands of the Indians had left the reservation to hunt and live in the still pristine hills of nearby Montana. The Indian Bureau had responded with an ultimatum that the Sioux should return immediately. After January 31, 1876, they ruled, any Plains Indian still remaining in "unceded territory" would be considered the enemy and summarily shot or taken prisoner.

Believing they had no choice but to make outright war if the Army attempted to carry out the threat, Crazy Horse of the Oglala Sioux and Sitting Bull of the Hunkpapa Sioux summoned the other Sioux chiefs and their Cheyenne allies to a meeting. Though the separate Indian tribes did not customarily live or fight together, they saw the need now to join forces. Together they agreed to encamp in a wide valley along the Little Bighorn River. With perhaps 2,500 warriors among them, they would resist to the death if necessary.

"Indians Enough for All"

The U.S. Army, for its part, was under orders to carry out the Indian Bureau's ultimatum. With General Alfred H. Terry in command, plans were made on June 22, 1876, to mount a three-pronged offensive that was supposed to surprise and engage the Indians several days later. Custer, with 10 years' experience in fighting the Plains Indians, was to lead one of the smaller contingents, the 7th Cavalry. He would have some 600 men under his command. Terry wanted him to proceed ahead of the rest of the Army toward the vicinity of the Indian encampment. Once there, he was to stay out of sight until the 26th, when the rest of Terry's forces were expected to be in position on the far side of the valley. Then all three forces could attack simultaneously. Such a strategy seemed to Terry to guarantee victory, for the Indians were traditionally guerrilla-style fighters. It was presumed that, when they were confronted with Terry's combined forces, they would flee in all directions, presenting easy marks for Army riflemen.

What Terry had not counted on was the unpredictable nature of Custer. Perhaps he should have, for Custer had a bad reputation among his fellow officers for insubordination and grandstanding. The 36-year-old officer had actually been court-martialed a decade earlier and found guilty of absenting himself from his command, disobeying orders, failing to protect his troops, and treating deserters in an unmilitary fashion. And though Custer was a West Point graduate and had gained a considerable amount of glory during the Civil War as the youngest brevet general in the Union Army, he had never shown any talent for military strategy or leadership.

As his men had learned by painful experience, Custer also showed minimal regard for safety on the battlefield. His mode of fighting was consistently one of charging the enemy; more than once he had callously endangered the lives of his men in order to execute some flamboyant maneuver. That he had managed to retain a command all these years was as much a matter of panache as it was ability, for Custer had no equal when it came to looking like a dashing cavalier, with his shoulder-length golden hair, his ruddy complexion and flashing blue eyes, his military bearing in the saddle, and his fancy uniforms. He also had a gift for making friends in high places and had been forgiven errors through the intercession of powerful allies.

The Sioux chief Red Cloud was a so-called Agency Indian, because he tried to reach an accommodation with the white men.

Perhaps it was on account of Custer's vainglorious ways that one of his fellow officers had called after him as he left base camp on June 22, "Now don't be greedy. There are Indians enough for all. Wait for us."

Dividing His Command

But as history would record, Custer did not wait. From the moment he left Terry's camp, he led his troops toward their destination at breakneck speed, marching nights as well as days until his troops and their mounts were on the edge of exhaustion. On their first night of march, his men commented among themselves that even allowing for Custer's usually snappish disposition, he was strangely tense and exhilarated. He told his

Sitting Bull (left) was no longer an active warrior at the time of the Battle of Little Bighorn, but he was still regarded as a great Sioux leader. There are no pictures of Crazy Horse, because he would not allow himself to be photographed.

officers why he had turned down Terry's offer of an extra battalion of cavalry and a battery of Gatling guns. They would not be needed, he said, because the 7th Cavalry was stronger than anything the Sioux could throw against them.

By the morning of June 25, Custer and his exhausted column were within a few miles of the Indian encampment, according to information supplied by his advance party. Despite Terry's instructions, Custer began ordering his troops into position. His first move was to detach one company to guard the slow-moving supply train. He then sent Captain Frederick W. Benteen and 125 troops on a scouting mission that took them away from the center field of action. Next he sent Major Marcus Reno and another 140 men on a separate tack that would bring them to the southern end of the Sioux camp. Finally, Custer ordered his five remaining companies of 215 men to fall in behind him as he prepared to take the enemy head-on. With him went his brothers Boston and Thomas Custer, his nephew Henry Armstrong Reed, and his brother-in-law James Calhoun.

By any measure Custer's actions are difficult to

The seemingly numberless herds of wild buffalo were the livelihood of the Plains Indians — until the senseless slaughter by white men brought the beasts to the brink of extinction. Below, railroad passengers shoot buffalo for sport.

explain, even considering his track record as an impetuous and sometimes foolhardy officer. Not only did he explicitly disobey General Terry's orders to wait for the joint assault scheduled for the next day, a major infraction of military rules, but he disregarded his own military intelligence. His scouts, having looked down from the hills upon the Sioux encampment, had counted at least seven separate Indian villages stretching across a three-mile-long section of the valley. Even Custer's favorite and most trusted scout, Bloody Knife, had warned him that there were more Sioux warriors than there were bullets in the belts of his soldiers.

What then prompted Custer to initiate his foolhardy adventure? Historians have been debating the question ever since. Some have suggested that Custer believed that Sioux scouts had seen his column coming and had tried to make the best of a bad situation by attacking before the Indians had time to defend themselves or escape. Others, less kindly disposed toward Custer, have proposed that he was merely demonstrating what his troops had often said of their commander behind his back: that he was a sorry excuse for a cavalry officer — all showmanship and vanity and no common sense.

Into a Valley of Death

All that is known for certain is that some time after noon on the 25th, as the heat of the day lay heavy over the land, Custer raised his sword in the traditional signal to advance and turned his horse toward the mouth of the valley and the assault. His 200 men, perhaps less sure of victory than he, followed him to the meeting with 2,000 or so hostile Indian warriors.

Meanwhile, carrying out Custer's orders, Reno and his detachment rode off to attack one of the villages. They were almost instantly stopped by a mass of warriors led by the Hunkpapa chief, Gall. Reno's men were driven back in disarray, with scores of them shot from their horses and left to die. To add confusion to the terrible situation, the warriors set fire to the grass between them, and there were flames and smoke everywhere.

Reno panicked. He ordered his remaining troops to make for the distant bluffs perhaps a mile away. Once there Reno saw Benteen's column approaching, and he raced forward to meet them. Benteen, having decided that he had been sent on a fool's errand, had circled back and, hearing the shooting, had presumed he would find Custer. Discovering Reno instead and learning that Custer had taken the remainder of his troops directly into the mouth of the valley, Benteen was unsure of how to proceed. Reno's detachment was in a sorry state, its numbers reduced by half, many of its horses gone, and its remaining bluecoats short on ammunition. Reno and Benteen decided that their position was extremely dangerous and that they should try to avoid further confrontations until the supply train could catch up. As night fell, they dug in as best they could, while the eerie sound of chanting warriors resounded in the distance.

A Martyred Hero?

Precisely what happened to Custer's own companies that afternoon has never been learned, but

A drawing by the Sioux Red Horse shows the Sioux and Cheyenne on horseback surrounding and shooting the outnumbered soldiers of the U.S. 7th Cavalry on June 25, 1876.

Betrayals on a Grand Scale

In 1830 Congress passed the Indian Removal Act. It gave the president legal power forcibly to remove Indians from their homelands within settled parts of the United States to regions then considered worthless, the lands across the Mississippi River.

At first the transplanted Indians were left to pursue their nomadic way of life with relative freedom. But following the end of the Civil War, the spirit of expansionism sent waves of farmers, miners, trappers, timbermen, and railroaders westward, and Indian lands once again became prime territory for exploitation. The federal government, which had solemnly promised to protect the Indians, responded with a new policy. Each Indian nation was forced into a treaty by which it agreed to become concentrated on reserved

Still proud of her American flag, this woman on the Navaho reservation typifies the continuing plight of Indians in the United States.

lands in exchange for annual payments. When these promises were not kept, the Indians made a last desperate fight for redress.

They were no match for well-armed, well-fed soldiers, and by 1880 they were effectively destroyed as independent people. All that remained of the 19-odd million acres that they had held in the 1830's was a patchwork of scattered reservations in some of the least desirable parts of the West. Circumstances have not improved. Today there are some 1.5 million Native Americans settled on 285 reservations in the United States. Unable to pursue traditional ways of life or to find employment in the white man's world, many reservation Indians endure lives of quiet desperation, with malnutrition, alcoholism, social dysfunction, and suicide widespread concerns.

---

the impetuous cavalryman apparently rode directly into the huge forces led by Crazy Horse. One of the finest battle leaders the Sioux had ever produced, Crazy Horse greeted the morning of the 25th with eager anticipation. "Ho-ka hey!" Crazy Horse called out to his men. "It is a good day for fighting! It is a good day for dying!" He then ordered his warriors to prepare themselves for battle. As the desperately outmatched Custer approached, Crazy Horse's Oglala Sioux went out in force to meet him in the northwestern end of the valley. It was now about 4 P.M. At the same time, Gall and still more Sioux, having chased Reno and Benteen from the scene an hour earlier, turned around and caught Custer's small band in a flanking attack.

According to the testimony of Brave Wolf, one of the Indians engaged in the fight, Custer's men fought valiantly to the end. But within perhaps 20 minutes of the first shot fired, there was not a single one of the 215-man contingent alive. "I have been in many hard fights," Brave Wolf recalled, "but I never saw such brave men."

The next day Benteen and Reno were attacked again, but this time in a rather desultory fashion. By now Crazy Horse and the rest were aware of General Terry's approach, and around midday they struck camp, leaving what remained of the

7th Cavalry to wonder what had befallen Custer and the rest of their forces. Finally, on the 27th, Reno and Benteen learned the awful truth. Terry and his men appeared, and soon they located the hilltop site of Custer's "last stand."

Though many officers had their private theories as to how Custer had come to such an end, they kept them largely to themselves. In the public's perception Custer was a martyred hero; and when a court of inquiry was convened to place blame for the terrible losses, Custer's supporters tried to make Major Reno the scapegoat. After 26 days of hearings, the court exonerated Major Reno but found no fault with Custer either.

In the end, only the Sioux were declared guilty of Custer's murder, and retribution against the Indians became fiercer than ever. The year 1876 was, after all, the centennial of the U.S. Declaration of Independence, and Americans were particularly full of national pride and feelings of invincibility. Within two years most of the Indians who had defeated Custer and his 7th Cavalry had been hunted down or driven into Canada. Crazy Horse, who felt that he had no choice but to lead the surviving Oglala Sioux onto a reservation in 1877, was promptly charged with instigating a revolt and shot on the spot — ostensibly while resisting imprisonment.

Power Play in Rome

**By the summer of 1943 the tide was turning against the Axis powers in
World War II. With the enemy landed in Sicily, Italy's
dictator Benito Mussolini faced a political challenge on the home
front. Would he be able to meet it?**

In the days following the Allied landing in Sicily on July 9–10, 1943, the island's inhabitants greeted the British and American soldiers more as liberators than as enemies. For them, the unwanted and disastrous partnership with Nazi Germany was happily at an end. Many if not most mainland Italians shared their feelings. Three years of warfare had drained the country of manpower and resources. The bombastic dream of empire propounded by fascist dictator Benito Mussolini had proved a sham.

When it became evident that the Italian troops in Sicily were no longer willing to die for Mussolini and that only German units there were resisting the Allied advance, Adolf Hitler was faced with a dilemma. He could ill afford to send reinforcements to the crumbling front. Yet he could not allow the military collapse of his Italian part-

*The deposition and arrest of Mussolini (left) by King Victor Emmanuel III (right)
bitterly divided war-ravaged Italy.*

ner. On Sunday, July 18, the German ambassador in Rome delivered an urgent invitation to *Il Duce*, as Mussolini was known, to meet Hitler at a villa northwest of Venice the next morning.

The daylong summit conference was little more than a harangue by the führer, who did not bother to have his monologue translated into Italian. It was clear, however, that Hitler would demand control of Italy's armed forces in return for sending reinforcements. Through it all, Mussolini sat in glum silence, occasionally sighing deeply and often pressing his left hand behind his back to relieve the excruciating pain of a stomach ulcer. He interrupted only once, to announce the alarming news brought into the room by a secretary: At that very moment, Rome was undergoing its first aerial bombardment.

Upon parting Monday evening, Mussolini asked Hitler to send all the assistance he had requested and as soon as possible. "Ours is a common cause," he reminded the führer. Hitler would never send what was needed, one of Mussolini's aides whispered to another. The duce was deluding himself that victory was still possible.

Two Conspiracies Converge

On Wednesday morning, July 21, the fascist leader Dino Grandi arrived in Rome following consultations in his hometown of Bologna. In his pocket was the draft of a letter to King Victor Emmanuel III, asking the figurehead monarch to restore Italy to the liberty, unity, and independence it had lost during the two decades of Mussolini's dictatorship. It was not a sudden impulse.

An imperious Benito Mussolini (above, center) presides over the Grand Council at Rome's Palazzo Venezia. Meeting through the night of July 24–25, 1943, the long-dormant body voted on a resolution to depose the duce introduced by Dino Grandi (right).

Indeed, two years earlier, Grandi had pressed Victor Emmanuel to demand that Mussolini reinstate the parliament and Grand Council — the duce's supercabinet — as working political bodies. If Mussolini refused, he had told the king in 1941, Victor Emmanuel should take personal command of the armed forces and assume the powers of head of state. The king had wanly remarked that he had to keep Grandi's proposal from the duce. "The time *will* come," he added. "But it has not come yet." The Allied advance in Sicily and the bombing of Rome convinced Grandi that the time had indeed come.

Before Grandi could arrange an audience with the king, he received a summons from Mussolini. The following Saturday, July 24, at 5 P.M., the duce would meet with the 28-member Grand Council for the first time in four years. "This is our chance," he said to himself. "*This* is our chance!" Grandi spent most of Wednesday enlisting other members of the Grand Council in his conspiracy, which now took the form of a resolution to strip Mussolini of his powers.

Hoping to give his plan a semblance of legality, Grandi went to see Mussolini on Thursday evening. Scheduled to last 15 minutes, the interview — an affable one, according to Grandi — lasted an hour and a half. But when he urged the duce to surrender his dictatorial powers voluntarily, Mussolini answered that he would only take such a course if the war were lost. "But in fact it is about to be won," he told Grandi, "because within a few days the Germans will launch a weapon that will transform the situation."

Unknown to Grandi, there was a second conspiracy under way, one led by Chief of Staff General Vittoria Ambrosio and Duke Pietro d'Acquarone, minister of the royal household. They planned to use Grandi's resolution to the Grand Council — by then an open secret in Rome's corridors of power — as the pretext for having Mussolini arrested by the carabinieri, Italy's national police. They had even picked the dictator's successor: Marshal Pietro Badoglio, perhaps the country's leading military figure.

A Night of Long Knives

As Mussolini left his residence, the Villa Torlonia, en route to the Grand Council meeting late

Saturday afternoon, his wife urged him to have the councillors arrested. "According to your mother," the duce joked to his son, Vittorio, "I'm surrounded by traitors, spies, saboteurs, and weaklings." So contemptuous was he of the plotters that he had released most of his personal bodyguards to assist in rescue work in the bombed areas of the capital.

The members of the Grand Council were all gathered at the Palazzo Venezia by 5 P.M. Grandi was still canvassing support for his resolution. Although 12 of the 14 members he had approached were in agreement with him, only 10 had signed his motion. Aware of the extreme peril he faced, Grandi had confessed to a priest, left a last letter to his wife and children, and strapped a hand grenade to his leg; he did not intend to be taken alive if he failed. Mechanically, he joined his fellow councillors in the fascist salute when Mussolini strode into the room. As the duce launched into a rambling two-hour defense of his conduct of the war, Grandi slid a copy of the resolution to the councillor in the next seat. After a whispered consultation, the man signed. Eleven votes. Four more needed for a majority.

Mussolini himself raised Grandi's resolution, which the councillor from Bologna supported with an impassioned attack on the duce. It was not the army that was responsible for Italy's military failure, he said; it was Mussolini's dictatorship. Across the nation, he charged, were 100,000 mothers who could cry out that the duce had assassinated their sons.

Astonished and exhilarated Italians grab for newspapers on the morning of July 26, 1943, to read that Mussolini had been deposed and replaced by Marshal Pietro Badoglio. The end of the fascist dictatorship, however, did not bring an immediate end to the miseries of war.

Toward midnight Mussolini attempted to adjourn the meeting, but the councillors refused to leave. During a break for refreshments, Grandi succeeded in gaining several more signatures, but the debate droned on until a call for the vote at 2:40 A.M. One of the duce's remaining supporters later described Mussolini's strange detachment at the crucial moment: "It seemed to me as if he had covered his head with a toga, like Caesar under the dagger thrusts of Brutus and the conspirators." Voting for Grandi's resolution were 19 councillors. Seven voted against; one abstained; one voted for his own motion. The Grand Council had deposed the fascist dictator, though Mussolini did not appear to comprehend his fate.

An Audience with Victor Emmanuel

Despite the late hour at which he had returned home, Mussolini rose early on Sunday and was at his office by 9 A.M. Toward noon he told his private secretary to ask that his regularly scheduled Monday meeting with the king be moved up to 5 P.M. that afternoon. The request was granted, with the stipulation that the duce appear in civilian attire rather than in his customary uniform. Dressed in a blue serge suit, wearing a high-crowned bowler, and carrying pearl-gray gloves in his left hand, he appeared at the royal residence five minutes before the appointed hour. Although his private automobile was admitted to the courtyard, the cars in which his bodyguards rode were detained outside the gate.

In a break with precedent, Victor Emmanuel greeted the duce at the front door, smiling and extending his hand. "You will have heard, Your Majesty," Mussolini joked, "about last night's childish prank. . . ." The king abruptly cut him off. "Today you are the most hated man in Italy. You cannot count on a single friend except me." Victor Emmanuel asked for and accepted the duce's resignation, promising that he would personally ensure the deposed dictator's safety.

During the brief interview with the king, Mussolini's driver was called into the porter's lodge and detained. An ambulance staffed with carabinieri officers was backed into the courtyard. When Mussolini emerged, he was directed to the ambulance and swept off to captivity.

Within six weeks of Mussolini's deposition, Marshal Badoglio — named by the king as the duce's successor — signed an armistice with the Allies. A few days later, on September 12, German commandos rescued Mussolini, who proclaimed a new fascist government in the north. He was little more than a puppet of Hitler.

By early 1945 the German defense of Italy was

Revealing Diaries

Voting against Mussolini in the Grand Council on the night of July 24–25, 1943, was his own son-in-law, Galeazzo Ciano, the count of Cortellazzo. The count's marriage in 1930 to the duce's daughter, Edda, was the prelude to a brilliant political career. Ciano became Italy's foreign minister in 1936 and was soon second only to Mussolini in the power structure of Italy's government. Yet he made no secret of his ambition to replace his father-in-law, whom he contemptuously called "Old Soft-in-the-Head." The count's fatal flaw turned out to be his disdain for the alliance with Nazi Germany.

On February 5, 1943, Mussolini abruptly removed Ciano as foreign minister, though giving him the face-saving position of ambassador to the Vatican. "Remember, when hard times come — because now it is certain that hard times will come," the count admonished Mussolini at their otherwise cordial leave-taking, "I can document all the treacheries perpetrated against us by the Germans." Ciano's documentation was recorded in secret diaries, which he kept as a kind of life insurance policy.

Even though he had voted against the duce, Ciano feared banishment along with Mussolini because of their long political association and their family ties. Pulling strings with her father's former allies, Edda Mussolini Ciano secured German assistance for escape to neutral Spain. On August 27, a month after the fateful Grand Council meeting, Ciano, his wife, and their three children boarded a German plane in Rome. Told that they were stopping in Munich for technical reasons, the Ciano family was taken into protective custody. Two months later Count Ciano was brought back to northern Italy, where his father-in-law had been reinstated as a German puppet. Tried and convicted of treason, Ciano and four other councillors were executed on January 11, 1944. Only two days before her husband's execution, Edda Ciano fled across the border into Switzerland — the count's explosive diaries concealed under her skirts. In 1946 she had them published.

collapsing before the irresistible Allied drive northward. Disguised as a German soldier in a truck convoy making for the border, Mussolini was seized by communist partisans and executed without a trial on April 28, 1945. The bullet-riddled body of the once omnipotent duce — along with those of his mistress, Claretta Petacci, and 13 other fascists — was hung upside down in Milan's Piazzale Loreto. Across the liberated city the joyous sound of church bells rang out.

The Unsinkable Ship

Three football fields in length, 11 stories tall, the mammoth passenger liner Titanic *was considered unsinkable, but a lone iceberg sent it to the bottom of the sea only five days after leaving England on its maiden voyage. Did hundreds of people perish because of human negligence?*

"God himself could not sink this ship," boasted a crew member aboard the White Star Line's 46,000-ton *Titanic*, an opulently appointed ocean liner larger than any ship ever built before. On April 10, 1912, to the fascination of newspaper readers around the world, the gigantic luxury craft sailed toward New York from Southampton, England, carrying 891 crew and 1,316 passengers. Some were enormously wealthy; about 700 were immigrants in steerage class; all were confident that their passage across the treacherous North Atlantic would be worry-free. With its 16 watertight compartments, the remarkable ship reflected the day's most advanced engineering techniques. Boasting such sybaritic features as Turkish baths and wide verandas flanked with potted palms, fine dining, and the best orchestra afloat, the *Titanic* was virtually a world unto itself, insensible to the buffeting of wind and wave.

In the early morning hours of Monday, April 15, 1912, the Titanic, *having been grazed by an iceberg, sank in the North Atlantic. Captain E. J. Smith (left) went down with his ship.*

On April 15, two collapsible rafts and 15 lifeboats were scattered among fields of icebergs in the choppy, frigid waters of the Atlantic. Half frozen, exhausted from shock, the survivors were fragile proof that the great *Titanic* had once existed but had sunk forever during the night. In the debris that drifted over a large area, hundreds of battered and bruised corpses floated face up, most already rendered unrecognizable. To one observer, they looked like a flock of seagulls bobbing in the waves. Many were women, rigidly clutching their babies in death. The world's first "unsinkable" ship had foundered and vanished within hours of its brush with an ancient foe of unwary sailors, a silent, implacable iceberg.

Unheeded Warnings

Contrary to standard practice today in regions where ice can be expected, the *Titanic* sped at 22 knots through the still, moonless night of April 14. Yet, since 9 A.M. on that chilly Sunday, there had been at least six ice warnings from other ships plying the same pathway to North America, known as the Newfoundland route.

First, a radio operator on the steamer *Caronia* alerted the *Titanic*'s captain, E. J. Smith, who wired back an acknowledgment. Early in the afternoon an operator on the *Titanic* delivered a specific warning from the *Baltic* to Smith: "Icebergs and large quantities of field ice today in latitude 41°51'N, longitude 49°52'W." The captain handed it to J. Bruce Ismay, the managing director of the White Star Line, who read it and put it into his pocket without comment. At least twice, the *Californian* sent messages. "Three large icebergs," was the first warning from that ship's operator. "Say, old man," he radioed in the evening, from a point 19 miles away, "we are stuck here, surrounded by ice." A testy Jack Phillips snapped back, "Keep out. Shut up. You're jamming my signal. I'm working on Cape Race."

The radio operator's response, which may sound incredible today, reveals the real mandate of radio communication on luxury liners of the period. From the Cape Race operator in Newfoundland, Phillips was receiving messages for the important passengers aboard his ship. That was his first priority. In fact, Phillips and the other radio operators were employees of a telegraph company, the British Marconi Company; they were not members of the White Star crew or subordinate to the captain of the *Titanic*.

The grand staircase in the A deck foyer gives an indication of the spacious opulence of the Titanic's *construction and furnishings.*

At 9:40 P.M. the *Mesaba* reported, "In latitude 42°N to 41°25', longitude 49°W to 50°30', saw much heavy pack ice and great number large icebergs, also field ice." If officers on the *Titanic*'s bridge received this message, a matter open to dispute, they would have realized instantly that the dangerous ice lay directly ahead of the liner. Lookouts, who were not even provided with binoculars, had been warned that ice might be encountered any time after 9:30 P.M., but no icebergs were spotted throughout the evening. The clear sky, ablaze with bright stars, revealed only a glassy smooth sea.

Meanwhile, there was an ominous sign. The water temperature fell rapidly from 43° Fahrenheit to slightly below freezing in only a few hours — always an indication in northerly waters that ice might be floating near. Yet the *Titanic* neither slowed nor turned southward to avoid the danger zone into which it was entering.

Barely a Jolt

At around 10 o'clock, for afterdinner relaxation, a few of the second-class passengers gathered to sing hymns, including a traditional mariner's chorus: "Oh, hear us when we cry to thee, for those in peril on the sea." At 11:40 P.M., lookout Frederick Fleet suddenly spied a small, dark ob-

ject, darker than the inky midnight waters upon which it floated. It grew rapidly larger. Sharply striking the crow's-nest bell three times, he telephoned the bridge: "Iceberg right ahead!" First Officer William Murdoch immediately ordered the engine room to reverse engines and told his steersman, Quartermaster Robert Hichens, to turn the wheel "hard astarboard!" In the sailing argot of the time, this meant to turn the ship's stern hard to starboard, or toward the right side of the craft, so that the bow would swing to port, or toward the left.

Racing at more than 22 knots, displacing about 66,000 tons of water, the *Titanic* could not be slowed down instantly. As the great liner finally began to turn away from the looming iceberg, the terrified Fleet breathed a sign of relief—but it was premature. Ice fell onto the deck as the iceberg sheared a 300-foot gash down the starboard side of the ship. As cold green seawater roared into the No. 6 boiler room, fireman Frederick Barrett just barely slipped into adjacent No. 5 before the watertight door slammed shut.

Yet the collision seemed little more than a slight jolt to the few passengers who noticed it. One socialite described it "as though somebody had drawn a giant finger along the side of the ship." Another woman compared the sound of impact to the ripping of a piece of calico. Some first-class travelers leaped from their comfortable leather chairs in the smoking room to glimpse the iceberg, towering above the topmost deck as it grazed their craft. But they saw little cause for

excitement, much less alarm, in the encounter.

The crew already knew better. Captain Smith conferred with the liner's chief designer, Thomas Andrews. After a quick descent into the hold, they learned that five compartments were flooded. Andrews estimated that the unsinkable *Titanic* could stay afloat for "an hour and a half. Possibly two. Not much longer."

Too Few Lifeboats

Just after midnight, about 25 minutes after the seemingly unremarkable impact, the crew was ordered to uncover the 16 lifeboats and 4 canvas collapsibles on board. At most, they could hold 1,178 people, or about 1,000 fewer than the passengers and crew who now began to crowd the decks. Ironically, regulations for stocking lifeboats had required only enough boats to carry 962 passengers, for regulators had not foreseen the construction of such a huge liner. Nor, of course, had anyone given serious consideration to the possibility that a flagship of the White Star Line would ever need to be evacuated. Not all of the lifeboats on board had been supplied with signal flares, food, or containers of fresh water, and life belts were scarce.

The situation now verged on chaos, since the passengers had never been given a boat drill and had no boat assignments. To help keep people calm, Bandmaster Wallace Henry Hartley led his musicians in ragtime music, but the horrible reality suddenly became clear as the first distress rocket shot up into the sky at 12:45 A.M.

As it went under, the Titanic *broke in two; at right, the forward two-thirds of the hull is shown collapsed on the ocean floor. Above, radio operator Jack Phillips.*

The Unresponsive Californian

Just weeks before, an international conference in Berlin had specified a new distress signal, or SOS, which operator Phillips was sending out frantically. At rest in the ice field, the *Californian* lay only 10 miles away, and some crew spotted glowing lights to the southeast. However, they did not know that it was the *Titanic* or that the liner was in trouble. Exhausted, perhaps peeved, the operator had shut off his radio after Phillips snubbed him. He was sound asleep as the *Titanic* begged for help from ships in the area.

Sometime after midnight, the radio operator of the passenger liner *Carpathia*, which was only half full, decided to call the *Titanic* about some messages from Cape Race. "CQD SOS," the startled operator heard. "Come at once. We have struck a berg." More than four hours (or 58 nautical miles) away, the *Carpathia* built up a full head of steam and raced to help. The ship's engineers illegally screwed safety valves shut in the engine room so that the craft's normal limit of 14 knots could be pumped up to 17 knots. Even so, it would not arrive until about two hours after the *Titanic* was expected to go down.

Meanwhile, distress rockets from the *Titanic* were seen aboard the *Californian*, but Captain Stanley Lord chose not to wake his sleeping radio operator, who had already worked a 15-hour day. Lord did send signals in Morse code to the unidentified ship but received no reply. According to most postmortems of the tragedy, the drifting *Californian* could have reached the *Titanic* at about the time it sank.

"Don't Waste Time!"

The enormously wealthy John Jacob Astor had sneered at first when evacuation was ordered. "We are safer here than in that little boat," he said. When one society matron agreed with him, an annoyed crewman shot back, "Don't waste time! Let her go if she won't get in." Gradually, resistance crumbled, the joking died down, and passengers set to the grim task of filling the lifeboats. Men stood stoically on the deck as women and children boarded the flimsy-looking craft. In the confusion, the first boat, which could hold 65 people, was lowered into the water with only 28 aboard. One capable of taking on 40 was allowed to pull off with only 12 persons.

Mrs. Isidor Straus, wife of the former congressman and chief executive of Macy's, refused to join the other women. "I've always stayed with my husband," she said, turning to him: "Where you go, I go." Astor helped his young bride into one of the half-filled boats and stepped back. His

The *Titanic*'s Watery Grave

Nearly three-quarters of a century after it sank, the *Titanic* was finally discovered. At about 1 A.M. on September 1, 1985, an automobile-sized submersible craft named the *Argo* began to photograph telltale debris on the ocean floor using powerful strobe lights and sophisticated video equipment. Operated by an American expedition under the direction of marine geologist Robert Ballard, the sturdy sledlike craft found one of the 29 boilers of the *Titanic* at a depth of 2.36 miles, approximately 350 miles southeast of Newfoundland. Later, the expedition would discover the two halves of the great ship lying 1,970 feet apart. Ballard, who had first proposed a search for the lost liner in 1971, felt "like an archaeologist opening a pharaoh's tomb."

A year later a second expedition was able to photograph the wreckage in much more detail, finding some of the legendary luxury items in amazingly good condition: crystal chandeliers, porcelain sinks and toilets, wine bottles, and neat rows of dinnerware (above). On the last dive of the 1986 expedition, a memorial plaque was placed on the stern. Ballard, who believes it would be disrespectful to try to raise or salvage the death ship, was able to get the U.S. Congress to declare the underwater site a memorial to the victims and make it illegal to "alter, disturb, or salvage" any part of the ship.

body was among those later recovered at sea. As the ship listed sharply to port, causing the deck to slant precipitously, millionaire Benjamin Guggenheim changed to evening dress, declaring that he was prepared to go down like a gentleman. "No woman shall be left aboard this ship because Ben Guggenheim was a coward," he added.

When no more women and children seemed to be left, Ismay, who had been helping others escape from the ship, took his place in one of the last lifeboats at about 1:40 A.M. The White Star Line's managing director would be pilloried in the press for leaving the ship while others remained behind. By 2:15, when the last two collapsibles were about to be launched, the *Titanic* tilted, making it impossible to use them. From the lower decks the forgotten steerage passengers, women and children definitely among them, streamed up to see what was happening. No one had warned them, and many would still be below as the ship went down.

Perhaps 1,600 passengers remained. Despite the popular legend that the band began to play "Nearer My God To Thee," in fact the last selection played was the Episcopal hymn "Autumn":

> God of mercy and compassion
> Look with pity on my pain;
> Hear a mournful, broken spirit
> Prostrate at thy feet complain.
> Hold me up in mighty waters. . . .

More Than 1,500 Dead

Several hundred people gathered on the stern as it raised ever higher into the air. At 2:18 A.M. the *Titanic* stood up on its bow, pausing in a vertically upright position. Then, with a horrendous noise, a funnel collapsed, the famous watertight bulkheads imploded, and everything loose on the decks — equipment as well as remaining passengers and crew — was swept into waters that were four degrees below freezing. One survivor would later recall "the agonizing cries of death from over a thousand throats, the wails and groans of the suffering, the shrieks of the terror-stricken, and the awful gaspings of those in the last throes of drowning." Incredibly, firemen swimming nearby were scalded when explosions brought the icy seas to a boil.

At 2:20, tilted now at about 70 degrees, the doomed liner slid beneath the waters, breaking in two as it fell toward the depths at about 20 knots. Moving back and forth, the sundered ship reached the great underwater river known as the Benthic Current flowing 8,000 feet below the surface. At about 2:30 the ship's two halves smacked into the ocean floor at a depth of 13,000 feet, its debris scattered over a half mile area. The shattered wreck lay under pressure of 6,365 pounds per square inch, entombed about 350 miles southeast of Newfoundland. It had proudly sailed the ocean for precisely 4 days, 17 hours, and 30 minutes.

Newspapers reported the unimaginable disaster with huge headlines. At right, a special edition of the Daily Graphic *in London.*

As news of the tragedy was published, friends and relatives of passengers and crew sought information at the White Star Line's offices in Southampton (far left). On April 19 the first of many memorial services was held at St. Paul's Cathedral in London (left).

The Lesson of History Ignored?

Surely, nothing like the sinking of the *Titanic* would ever happen again. At the Titanic Conference in 1914, the seafaring nations agreed to enforce new safety rules: for example, every ship must supply enough lifeboats to rescue all passengers and crew, and a radio operator had to be on call at all hours. New ships would have watertight bulkheads built all the way to the deck. Alexander Brehm, a German physicist, invented the echo sounder, a device that uses sound waves to locate potentially threatening icebergs. The tragedy that sent the White Star Line's "unsinkable" ship to the bottom of the North Atlantic on its maiden voyage had taught everyone vitally important lessons.

Yet, shockingly, the catastrophe was almost repeated on June 20, 1989, when the 630-foot-long Soviet cruise ship *Maxim Gorky* was ripped open shortly after midnight by an enormous piece of drift ice in the Greenland Sea north of Norway. At the time, the captain of the vessel and others were holding a party in the ship's restaurant to celebrate reaching the northernmost point of the cruise. But, as on the *Titanic*, most passengers were already in bed. As the merrymakers danced, the ice made two gashes in the side of the liner — one 20 feet long, the other 7 feet — letting in 18,000 tons of water within minutes. The 575 passengers, many of them elderly West German tourists, were told to assemble on deck and put on life jackets.

"There was some confusion about which lifeboats we were to

Shipwrecked passengers from the Maxim Gorky *use their lifeboat's oars to keep dangerous drift ice from damaging one of the craft in which they await rescue.*

go on," one passenger later reported, "but no panic." Although another passenger complained that his lifeboat was left suspended in midair over the side of the ship for two hours, most of the tourists had nothing but praise for the efficiency of the Russian crew in getting them off the ship and the promptness of the Norwegian coast guard's rescue operation.

In fog and freezing rain, with the temperature hovering at 37° Fahrenheit, many of the passengers spent up to seven hours huddled under thin blankets in the boats or on the ice floes to which some moved. But those with heart conditions and diabetes were quickly

evacuated by helicopter to the Spitsbergen Archipelago some 200 miles to the east. Deck chairs were set on the ice floes for some, but others had to lie flat on the ice, fearing it would crack to pieces otherwise. The lifeboats were well stocked with liquor but no drinking water. Amazingly, none of the passengers, who had signed up to view the midnight sun in these waters above the Arctic Circle, and none of the 377 crew were injured.

As the Norwegian rescue ship *Senje* jostled through three miles of ice to reach the stricken *Maxim Gorky*, her captain huffed, "I would hardly have sailed faster than 2 to 3 knots in such ice-clogged water." Speeding at about 18.4 knots, the cruise ship seemed to be emulating the practices of 1912, when sailors had followed a "ram-you-damn-you" philosophy regarding icebergs until the *Titanic* disaster. Even with today's advanced technology, sailors experienced in northern waters are extremely cautious, because ice gives less of an echo on radar than other objects at sea. According to experts, the *Maxim Gorky* would have needed at least 45 minutes to stop, even if an iceberg or a floe was spotted at a distance of 10 miles. Apparently, the captain of the Soviet vessel had never sailed in these waters, and it was unusual for so much ice to be drifting in the area. As Russians and Norwegians cooperated, the *Maxim Gorky* was stabilized and towed to port for repairs. Commentators could not resist asking whether the lessons of the *Titanic* had been forgotten.

About three and a half hours later, or around 6 A.M. on Monday, April 15, the *Californian* finally heard the tragic news and began to travel toward the site of the sinking. By 8:50 the *Carpathia* had taken aboard all of the survivors and set sail toward New York. When the *Californian* arrived, the captain spent about an hour searching for bodies but, almost unbelievably, would later report that he could find none. Only a week later

the cable ship *MacKay-Bennett* would retrieve 306 corpses in the area.

Less than a third of the passengers and crew, only 705 persons, survived the disaster. The number included 338 men, about 20 percent of the total, and 316 women, about 74 percent of the total. The rest were children. Among those who did not survive were Captain Smith and the radio operator Jack Phillips.

Seward's Icebox

After the Civil War, the U.S. government set out to rid North America of foreign influences and to tidy up its territorial borders. But was Secretary of State Seward's purchase of remote, desolate Russian Alaska pure folly?

By 1867 czarist Russia was in financial and diplomatic straits. Not only did the nation have huge debts stemming from a stunning defeat in the Crimean War, but Czar Alexander II's ministers were having a difficult time administering the empire's vast and scattered lands.

Alaska, which had been Russian territory ever since explorer Vitus Bering had claimed the land in 1741, was one such troublesome property. Though it had provided abundant sea otter and seal pelts, the Russian-American Company that oversaw the territory had always needed state subsidies to operate. And because of its severe climate and limited agricultural potential, Alaska had never been an attractive site for colonization. Separated from the Asian continent by the Bering Sea, the deeply indented coasts of Alaska had only a handful of fur trading bases and a few hundred Russian trappers, agents, and soldiers to maintain the czar's authority. Should either England or the United States cast a hungry eye on Alaska, the czar and his generals could not possibly mount an effective or timely defense. Rumors that Alaska possessed gold and other valuable minerals only made matters more precarious for the owners. Once Americans got wind of what lay under the surface of barren Alaska, the czar felt certain, there would be a stampede like the

Secretary of State William H. Seward (seated) negotiated the purchase of Alaska with Russian envoy Baron Eduard de Stoeckel (standing with his hand on the globe). The treaty of sale was signed on March 30, 1867.

one that had shaken California loose from Mexico in 1849. Better to sell the territory for a modest amount of cash now than let it simply slip through his fingers for nothing a few years hence.

Raising the Price Tag

Early in March the czar instructed his ambassador, Baron Eduard de Stoeckel, to offer the vast territory to U.S. Secretary of State William H. Seward for $5 million. Cordial talks began in Washington immediately.

As soon became apparent, Seward was not just interested in discussing such a deal; he was in a great hurry to conclude negotiations. A confirmed expansionist and believer in America's "manifest destiny" to extend its domain across the continent of North America, Seward was fully persuaded that Alaska, for all its remoteness, would some day turn out to be of consummate value to the United States — though it could take the people of America a generation to realize its true worth. But he had to get congressional support before President Andrew Johnson's enemies had time to gather strength and mount a counteroffensive.

Stoeckel, sensing Seward's urgency, decided to take a languid approach to the sale. He guessed that as Seward's anxiety rose, so, too, would Alaska's potential price tag. The ploy worked. Over the next two weeks Seward repeatedly upped his offer to the diffident Stoeckel. Finally, late on the evening of March 29, the Russian minister secured a promise of $7.2 million and with that the two men shook hands. Seward insisted on signing the treaty that very night. After each man had routed his staff out of bed and everyone had convened at the State Department, Stoeckel and Seward set their signatures to the 27-page treaty of sale, finishing around 4 A.M.

Outraged Opponents

Stoeckel was understandably elated with the results of his negotiations, foreseeing not only his government's praise but a substantial personal reward for services skillfully executed. Seward, however, still had to win Senate approval of the treaty and persuade the House of Representatives to pass a sizable appropriations bill. The Senate turned out to be favorably disposed, but House members were furious that the secretary of state had not consulted them before spending so much money. Critics referred derisively to "Seward's Icebox" and "Johnson's Polar Bear Garden" and accused the secretary of engineering a "dark deed done in the night."

Seward, for his part, needed more information

The Glittering Prizes

On the reasonable premise that the mountain chains that had yielded gold to the south might be equally bountiful in the north, prospectors gradually worked their way upward into Alaska. By the 1870's a scattering of veterans was panning the lower Yukon River, but with only modest returns. Then, in August 1896, while prospecting along a tributary of the Klondike River some 50 miles east of the Alaska border in Canada's Yukon Territory, an old sourdough found "raw gold laying thick between flaky slabs like cheese sandwiches."

Within weeks the population of nearby Dawson had climbed from 500 to 5,000. By the following summer, when several of the first prospectors arrived in San Francisco with $3 million in gold nuggets, some 100,000 tenderfoots took ship for the Alaska panhandle and the perilous overland trails beyond.

The Klondike bubble burst rather quickly, as newcomers found the best goldfields already staked out. But soon there was dazzling news from another quarter: Good-sized finds had been made in the black sands along the Seward Peninsula at a place called Cape Nome. By riverboat, dogsled, ice skates, and even by bicycle, the disappointed of Dawson gathered up their gear and headed 800 miles due west. Nome also faded quickly; within two years its beaches were picked bare of $2 million in gold nuggets. In the end Alaska's gold turned out to be a flash in the pan, but the brief excitement served to bring hordes of settlers — and ultimately federal law and order — to the huge territory.

about Alaska's practical value to argue his case effectively. No sooner had the treaty of intent been signed than he commissioned an expedition under the supervision of the Smithsonian Institution to make a rapid coastal survey of the place. On July 21, 1867, geologist George Davidson and a small corps of scientists sailed from San Francisco on a reconnaissance mission to gather data on Alaska's ocean currents, climate, landforms, harbors, economic potential, natural history, human habitation, and any other favorable features that they could uncover. Davidson and his party did the best they could in the short time allowed, and they were back in San Francisco with a report by the end of the year. But while those who supported the acquisition of Alaska could find much in the coastal survey to confirm their good opinion, the explorers' report was probably too vague and too incomplete to change the minds of many opponents of the purchase.

A Duel of Lobbyists

Meanwhile, Baron Stoeckel was also busy shoring up the treaty's prospects. When it became apparent to him that the deal might come unglued, he approached Robert J. Walker, a former secretary of the treasury, and proposed that Walker work secretly as a lobbyist for imperial Russia.

Walker was not only a committed expansionist like Seward, but he had powerful friends in Washington and access to the influential *Daily Morning Chronicle*. And he needed money badly, for his personal fortunes had taken a turn for the worse. Walker went at his assigned task with extraordinary vigor and a persuasive pen. Writing a column almost daily, he described Alaska as ideally situated for the coming struggle for command of the Pacific. He said the climate there was "charming" and the land filled with such an abundance of riches that the visitor could collect gold "by the handful." The clever proponent declared that while commerce was undoubtedly Alaska's first appeal, Americans could take pride in the knowledge that Christianity would follow in its wake.

Newspaperman Uriah Painter sold his talents to the anti-Alaska faction and began publishing angry denunciations of Seward's treaty. In the end, Walker's arguments proved more persuasive, and the Alaska bill was passed on July 18, 1868, by a vote of 113 to 43, with 44 abstentions.

Painter, however, decided to get even with Walker. When the U.S. Treasury drew checks totaling $7.2 million on August 1, and these were handed over to Stoeckel, Painter watched to see who among the players in and out of Congress might grow suddenly richer. He did not have long to wait. A few days later the reporter read in a New York newspaper that Walker was visiting up

The view at right of Novoarkhangelsk (today's Sitka), the capital of Russian Alaska, dates to 1830. Palisades surround the governor's fortress against feared Indian attacks.

In March 1989 an oil spill from the tanker Exxon Valdez *sent 10 million gallons of crude oil into the waters of Prince William Sound, causing an estimated $1.9 billion in damages (below, the cleanup) — dramatic proof of nature's vulnerability.*

Today, Alaska's "gold" is the oil that is brought from Prudhoe Bay on the Arctic coast in a pipeline that snakes across the state to the port of Valdez on Prince William Sound in the south. Construction of the pipeline cost $7.7 billion, more than a thousand times the purchase price of Alaska; related expenditures brought the cost to $11.3 billion.

north and that he had a nasty encounter with a pickpocket. It seemed the culprit had relieved him of $16,000 worth of gold Treasury certificates that he was carrying. When the local police managed to locate the pickpocket and recover the money, Walker mysteriously chose not to prosecute. To Painter this was proof positive that Walker had something to hide and that the money was ill-gotten. Painter publicly charged Walker with having been in the employ of the Russian government. After several Republican newspapers had taken up the cry, a congressional committee was convened to investigate corruption charges. In the end, no one succeeded in proving much of anything. No money was shown to have been exchanged for congressional votes, only for "educating" the public and members of Congress, which was hardly illegal.

A Bargain at Two Cents an Acre

Meanwhile, Russian Alaska had already become a de facto American territory. So eager had the Russians been to leave and the Americans under President Johnson's command to take over that U.S. General Lovell H. Rousseau had sailed for Novoarkhangelsk (Sitka), the capital of Russian

Alaska, in September 1867 to effect the transfer. On October 18 Rousseau oversaw the ceremonial lowering of the Russian imperial flag and the raising of the U.S. flag over Sitka.

Small cadres of American troops were posted to Sitka and a few other port settlements, just to establish a U.S. presence, but over the next decade most were brought back home where fighting between federal forces and Indians was a constant problem. Finally, concern over the lack of law and order in the neglected territory prompted Congress to pass an organizational act in 1912; it provided a governor, a body of laws, and a tiny purse for the education of Alaska's natives. The territory's true value, however, was still in doubt, and it was not until World War II that military and strategic considerations finally brought Seward's folly into the American fold. By then, the landmass that measured twice the size of Texas and cost less than two cents an acre was beginning to seem the bargain Seward had said it was.

The Emperor's Last Battle

**The greatest general of his age, Napoleon Bonaparte faced two
enemies as he sought to reestablish his imperial power. He divided his forces
so as to defeat them one by one. But his well-tested
strategy did not work this time.**

The news electrified Europe. On March 1, 1815, three days after slipping away from his place of exile on the island of Elba off Italy, Napoleon Bonaparte was back in France.

Less than a year earlier, the French emperor had abdicated after a coalition of his enemies had marched into Paris, but he had been allowed to take a 1,000-man force to Elba and had been granted a generous stipend for retiring to the island. It was not enough for the military genius who had dominated Europe for two decades. As the representatives of the restored Bourbon monarchy met in Vienna with the victorious allied powers — Austria, Britain, Prussia, and Russia — to redraw the map of Europe, Napoleon plotted his return. At first, it went as planned.

Landing on the south coast of France between Cannes and Antibes, Napoleon was joyously greeted by French citizens who yearned for a return to the glory he had brought the country but who somehow managed to forget the years of war and sacrifice. En route to Paris, he gathered regiments quick to defect from King

*After the rout of Napoleon's forces on June 18, 1815, the victors meet on the battlefield: the Duke of
Wellington (left), the British commander, and Marshal Blücher, the Prussian leader.*

Near the center of Wellington's defensive line, the farm of La Haie Sainte was stoutly defended by the duke's army and ferociously assaulted by Napoleon's. At left, the French on the brink of capturing it; below, the farm today.

Louis XVIII. Only hours before Napoleon entered the capital, the king fled to Belgium.

A Gathering of Enemies

In Vienna, Napoleon's enemies vowed to resist his return. Large Austrian and Russian armies were ordered to invade France from the east. To the north two forces were hastily gathered to stop his expected pursuit of Louis XVIII. Britain's 46-year-old Duke of Wellington, victor in the Peninsular War that had driven the French out of Spain and Portugal, commanded a polyglot European force of 106,000 — less than a third were British — at Brussels. Some distance to the east was the 120,000-man Prussian army under 72-year-old Marshal Gebhard Leberecht von Blücher, *Alte Vorwärts* (Old Forwards) or Papa Blücher to his devoted troops.

Napoleon soon had a quarter million Frenchmen under arms and from them assembled a well-balanced force of infantry, cavalry, and artillery for the campaign that was meant to oust the Bourbon monarchy and ratify his resumption of power. Many of the 128,000 officers and men he took north were veterans of his previous wars.

The emperor crossed the frontier into Belgium on June 15 and, with the goal of driving a wedge between Wellington and Blücher, formed his army into a Y-shape for the march north. In command of the left flank was Marshal Michel Ney, called "the bravest of the brave" for his heroic command of the rear guard on Napoleon's retreat

from Moscow in 1812. In command of the right flank was the Marquis de Grouchy, a hereditary aristocrat and renowned cavalryman who had never commanded infantry or artillery. The imperial guard was to be kept in reserve to be thrown into whichever flank needed additional manpower once the battle was joined.

An Interrupted Party

Attending a ball given in Brussels by the Duchess of Richmond, Wellington learned of Napoleon's rapid advance about 1 A.M. on Friday morning, June 16. Not wishing to alarm the festive assembly, he lingered for some 20 minutes before making his farewells — as if retiring for the night. But before he left the house, he asked his host for a map. "Napoleon has humbugged me, by God!" he exclaimed. "He has gained 24 hours' march on me." Asked what he intended to do, the duke said that he would concentrate his troops at Quatre Bras, some 20 miles south of the city.

Despite prodding by Napoleon, Marshal Ney failed to dislodge Wellington's force from Quatre Bras on the 16th. Riding over to see his ally at Ligny several miles to the east, the duke was horrified to see the Prussians drawn up on the forward slope of a hill and exposed to Grouchy's French artillery. "My men like to see their enemy," Blücher explained. The Prussians saw rather too much of the enemy that day, especially Blücher, who had a horse shot out from under him while leading a desperate cavalry charge. Pinned beneath the fallen beast, the valiant Prussian survived two cavalry assaults before being rescued. That evening he ordered a retreat north. Meanwhile, one of Ney's corps had been diverted to Ligny without his knowledge, but it was later recalled for the assault on Quatre Bras. Marching back and forth, it added to neither battle.

Taking Up Their Positions

Because of Blücher's defeat at Ligny, Wellington was forced to withdraw from Quatre Bras and take up a new position closer to Brussels on Saturday, June 17. Unlike his ally had done the previous day, the duke positioned the bulk of his nearly 68,000-man force back of a low ridge that rose just south of the village of Mont-St. Jean. He was determined to hold three points in front of the ridge: the chateau Hougoumont to his right; the farm of La Haie Sainte to the center; and a cluster of buildings at Papelotte to his left. The Prussians were at Wavre, 10 miles to the east and thus on the duke's extreme left. Wellington sent word to Blücher that he would make a stand at Mont-St. Jean if his ally could send two corps the next day. Blücher promised to do so.

Only 1,500 yards in front of Wellington's line Napoleon deployed his 72,000 men for a frontal assault. Because of heavy rain during the night, however, he did not open his attack until after 11 on Sunday morning, thus allowing the ground to harden and his men to dry out their weapons. In hand-to-hand combat, the 2,500 men at Hougoumont were able to resist successive waves of French assaults on the chateau, thus tying up 13,000 of the emperor's troops on that flank.

Sometime after 1 P.M. Napoleon directed a corps of 16,000 men to attack Wellington's center, believing that his artillery had weakened resistance. But the duke's men were mostly safe behind the ridge, and a cavalry charge turned the French back as they reached its crest. But even as the center attack was launched, Napoleon and his generals were anxiously looking to the east where they expected to see Grouchy arrive following his defeat of Blücher at Ligny. Instead, they

The Congress of Vienna

In September 1814 the diplomats and leading personages of Europe began gathering in Vienna to establish a new order on the continent following the turmoil of the Napoleonic age. After the French emperor's abdication and exile to Elba, France had been generously treated by the coalition that had brought about his defeat: Britain, Austria, Prussia, and Russia. The Bourbon monarchy in the person of King Louis XVIII was restored; France's borders of 1792 were again recognized; and Louis' minister of foreign affairs, Prince Talleyrand, was admitted as an equal to the discussions of a peace settlement at the Congress of Vienna.

Napoleon's return to France and brief resumption of power — the so-called Hundred Days that ended with his second abdication and surrender to the British — struck

In this caricature of the work of the Congress of Vienna, a bowed Napoleon (right) watches as crowns are restored and large portions of his empire are awarded to and carted off by his enemies.

terror into the hearts of the diplomats assembled in Vienna. Nonetheless, they were able to devise a finalizing act of the Congress of Vienna on June 8, 1815, that in effect determined the political future of

Europe for the remainder of the 19th century. Austria regained its former domains and was awarded much of northern Italy; Prussia was acknowledged to be a great power — though German unity under its leadership was postponed; Russia was awarded Poland; the Dutch republic was united with Belgium; and a number of smaller kingdoms were recognized or restored.

Although some of its provisions were short-lived, the peace settlement at Vienna spared Europe a major conflict for a century. What it ignored, however, was the rising tide of nationalism that refused to accept great-power domination of the continent indefinitely. This was the fatal flaw that caused the balance of power to be swept aside in the wake of the gunshots at Sarajevo that sparked World War I in the summer of 1914.

A portrait of defeat: the figure of Napoleon at the wax museum near Waterloo. Above, the landscape surrounding the famous battlefield is one of neatly kept farms and gently rolling hills with little to betray it as the site of the clash of arms that ended Napoleon's dream of empire.

learned from a captured Prussian courier that Blücher had managed to disengage himself from Grouchy's attack at Wavre and was en route with the promised two corps.

Fatal Delay, Confused Orders

Napoleon had already made a blunder that was to doom his chances of success. When Grouchy asked for instructions on how to follow up his success at Ligny, the emperor had delayed his reply for hours and then given him contradictory orders. The commander of the French right wing was told to pursue Blücher north and to link up with the main army — in effect asking Grouchy to move in two directions at once.

Why had the brilliant strategist who had conquered most of Europe made such a mistake? Years later, his brother Jerome — a division commander under Ney — revealed that on the day of battle Napoleon had been suffering from fever, cystitis, and hemorrhoids aggravated by long hours in the saddle. Witnesses had commented on the emperor's drowsiness and lethargy during the campaign; those who had not seen him recently were shocked to see how fat he had become and how aged he seemed, though he was only three months older than Wellington.

Committing eight battalions of his imperial guard into the frontal assault at 7 P.M., Napoleon himself led the troops to within 600 yards of the battle line before handing over command to Ney. But though his infantry captured the farm of La Haie Sainte, the emperor's time was running out.

"Look, there are the Prussians!" was the cry as the corps Blücher had promised began arriving from the east. Next came shouts that the imperial guard was retreating. "Save yourself if you can," the dispirited French began calling to one another. Atop the ridge Wellington raised his cocked hat to signal a general advance; it swept Napoleon's army from the field.

Fleeing south with but a small escort, Napoleon reached Paris three days later and signed a second abdication on June 22. Surrendering to the British at the port of Rochefort on July 15, he was sent into permanent exile on the island of St. Helena. His return to power had lasted just 100 days, and on the battlefield south of Brussels he left 25,000 wounded or dead, with another 16,000 deserting or being taken prisoner. Allied losses that day totaled 22,000.

About 9 P.M. on June 18, Wellington and Blücher met and embraced near the farm of La Belle Alliance, which had served as the emperor's headquarters during the clash of arms. Blücher suggested that their great victory be called La Belle Alliance, but Wellington insisted on naming it for the headquarters to which he then withdrew to write his report: Waterloo.

Hitler's Secret Diaries

It was, said the publishers of Germany's Stern, *"the journalistic coup of the post-World War II period." One of their reporters had discovered the führer's previously unknown private journals.*

*I*n bloodred letters splashed across the cover of its issue dated April 25, 1983, Germany's weekly magazine *Stern* announced a publishing exclusive: "Hitler's Diaries Discovered." Inside, illustrated with 10 examples of the Nazi führer's handwriting, were 42 pages of extracts from the diaries, the first of 28 installments to be published over the following 18 months. The sensational material came from 62 notebooks bound in black imitation leather that the magazine had recently acquired. Unknown to his associates at the time and historians of the era, Hitler had kept a handwritten diary from mid-1932 until two weeks before his death amid the ruins of

Berlin in April 1945. Or so said Peter Koch, the magazine's editor in chief, at a self-congratulatory press conference in Hamburg. The diaries had been obtained for the magazine by its 51-year-old investigative reporter Gerd Heidemann.

London's *Sunday Times* paid $400,000 for British and Commonwealth rights to the diaries. France's *Paris Match* and Italy's *Panorama* planned publication in their countries. *Newsweek* ran a 13-page cover story on the diaries the following week, noting that what its editors had seen "reeks of history . . . 13 years of the most hideous years in human experience are described by the man who did so much to make them vile."

Confronted with the testimony of experts, Konrad Kujau quickly admitted to having forged the alleged Hitler diaries; at left, one of his sources; at right, a sample of his work.

During a press conference at Stern*'s office in Hamburg on April 25, 1983, reporter Gerd Heidemann proudly displays several of the thin notebooks containing Hitler's secret diaries. His widely promoted discovery was shortly shown to be a fraud for which he was later sent to prison.*

Nonetheless, *Newsweek* editors had declined to buy American rights to the diaries because they disagreed with *Stern*'s plan to publish in installments over such a long period of time and because they wanted "more systematic and authoritative authentication."

Stern offered the opinions of British historian Hugh Trevor-Roper and Gerhard L. Weinberg of the University of North Carolina, both of whom had briefly examined the diaries and were on record as believing them to be genuine.

And Then the Doubts

Rising at the press conference in Hamburg, the British historian David Irving asked an embarrassing question: Had the ink in the documents been chemically tested to prove its age? It had not. *Stern*'s two experts began backing away from their endorsements. Weinberg asked *Stern* to call in handwriting experts and allow scholars to examine the diaries page by page. Trevor-Roper announced first that some of the documents in the cache might be fake and then that all were forgeries "until the opposite is proven." German historians were quick to enter the fray, one of them charging that *Stern* was only out to sell copies of the magazine. Indeed, it had increased its 1.87 million circulation by 300,000 copies with the first installment and had raised its newsstand price from $1.25 to $1.45.

Skeptics asked how Hitler had been able to conceal the diaries from his secretaries, valets, and military assistants. No one in his inner circle had ever mentioned that the führer was keeping a diary. It was pointed out that Hitler had hated to write, invariably dictating his letters to a secretary. When he did write, it was usually in pencil. From January 1943 onward Hitler was known to have been suffering from palsy, subject to severe shaking attacks that made it virtually impossible for him to write in a legible hand.

"Reason to Be Ashamed"

A handwriting expert retained by *Newsweek* studied two of the diaries *Stern* brought to New York. They were, he said, "not only forgeries, they were bad forgeries."

In Germany scientists were able to prove that the paper in the diaries as well as the ink, the glue in the notebooks' bindings, the imitation-leather covers, and the red ribbons hanging from wax seals on some of those covers all dated to the postwar period. Hans Booms, head of Germany's Federal Archives, pronounced the *Stern* diaries "a blatant, grotesque, and superficial forgery." One of Booms's associates even found a source for the material in the diaries, a 1962 book titled *Hitler: Speeches and Proclamations, 1932–1945*, by Max Domarus. Whoever compiled the *Stern* diaries slavishly followed Domarus's work, even picking up some of his errors.

In Hamburg, *Stern*'s outraged staff staged a six-day sit-in at the editorial offices, demanding to know how the magazine's top management could so easily have been duped and expressing concern about the damage done to the publica-

A Forger at Work

Lining the walls of a small, two-room gallery on a quiet street in Stuttgart, Germany, are paintings by Rembrandt, Renoir, van Gogh, Degas, Picasso, Dali, and other masters — or so it would appear. But the prices asked for them, ranging from about $50 to just under $1,000, give away the secret. They are all the work of Konrad Kujau, convicted and sentenced to prison for having forged the "Hitler diaries" that *Stern* bought for some $3.7 million in 1983.

Having developed cancer of the larynx, Kujau was released from prison in mid-1987 after serving two years of his four and a half year sentence. Since whatever money he received from *Stern* had gone to pay his legal and tax debts, Kujau was impoverished. The obvious way for him to support himself was by doing what he did best: forge. Only this time he is doing it openly. His shop is called the Gallery of Fakes, and on the back of each "Rembrandt," "Dali," or other painting in the style of a famous artist is a stamp: "Certified Fake by Konrad Kujau." The stamp is meant to avoid legal problems, Kujau explains, "but I find some customers want the stamp anyway because they say I'm as well known as the original master."

For some 10 years prior to swindling *Stern*, Kujau had been selling fake Third Reich memorabilia to Nazi buffs. His output included watercolors attributed to the führer (there are genuine Hitler paintings, dating to the time before he went into politics) and carrying a signature Kujau claims he can do as fast as his own. He began painting the works now for sale while he was still in prison and continues to turn them out, working at an easel in the upstairs study of his home in Stuttgart (above).

Kujau is quick to point out that his paintings are not copies of existing works but original creations. Before he starts each painting, he carefully studies the coloration, technique, and materials used by the artist so as to make his work closely resemble that of the master.

tion's credibility. Peter Koch was forced to resign. Henri Nannen, the publisher, sadly confessed, "We have reason to be ashamed."

Unmasking the Culprits

Stern had placed its trust in Heidemann, a 32-year veteran of the staff. An amateur student of the Nazi era, Heidemann had sold his home in Hamburg in order to buy a yacht once belonging to Hitler's second in command, Hermann Goering. On it he liked to entertain former Nazi officials and through one of them met Konrad Kujau, alias Konrad Fischer, who sold Nazi memorabilia from a shop in Stuttgart. Early in 1981 Kujau told Heidemann that his brother — an officer in the East German army — had smuggled previously unknown Hitler diaries across the border into West Germany and was offering them for sale.

The diaries, Kujau explained, had been put aboard a transport plane in Berlin in late April 1945, as Hitler's reich began crumbling around him. Along with other valuable possessions of the führer, they were to be taken to Berchtesgaden in the Bavarian Alps for safekeeping. Hitler presumably would follow in another plane to make a last stand in his mountaintop lair. However, the first plane crashed near Dresden; Hitler, of course, never left Berlin. All but one aboard the plane died in the crash. But a local farmer had been able to salvage some of the cargo — including the diaries, which he had stashed away.

Heidemann accepted Kujau's fantastic tale and in the next two years persuaded his employers to part with 9 million marks ($3.7 million) for the diaries. For his role in the transaction the reporter kept 1.5 million marks ($600,000) of *Stern*'s money. As it turned out, there had been no plane crash, and there had been no diaries hidden in East Germany and spirited across the border. Kujau himself had forged the documents over a period of years.

Kujau confessed, trying to implicate Heidemann in his scheme. The reporter, promptly dismissed by the magazine, maintained that he had been hoodwinked. Two years later, after a lengthy trial, the two men were found guilty of fraud. Heidemann was sentenced to four years and eight months in prison; Kujau's sentence was two months shorter. However, the presiding judge reserved his strongest criticism for *Stern*'s management. Blinded by wanton greed, he said, the magazine's publishers had failed to make a sufficient examination of the diaries before buying them and had actually encouraged the forger and his accomplice by so readily handing over to them such large sums of money.

Debacle in the Desert

For nearly six months the United States had been unable to gain the release of 53 American hostages held captive by fanatic Iranians in Teheran. When the superpower at last struck, its military might proved inadequate.

eheran, April 25, 1980. Trucks bearing the insignia of the Iranian army pull up to the rear entrance of the U.S. embassy. As shots break the nocturnal silence, the heavy vehicles crash through the embassy gates. Overhead six military helicopters appear out of nowhere. Three of the aircraft land in the embassy compound, covered by massive firepower from the other three helicopters hovering above. A force of 90 commandos disembark to join the ground force in storming the embassy. Together, they easily overcome the guards holding 50 Americans hostage. Another team brings three additional hostages from the nearby Iranian Foreign Ministry where they were being held separately.

While Iranian militia throughout the capital fire at one another in confusion, the commandos urge the hostages into the helicopters. The aircraft lift off and whirl away in the darkness. Soon afterward, the helicopters land at a remote desert site where transport airplanes are waiting to take the hostages and their rescuers to safety far from Iranian soil. The United States has ended its long humiliation with this bold strike; President Jimmy Carter is lauded throughout the country for the daring initiative that prompted his move.

That is how, more or less, the strategists in the White House imagined the outcome of the raid to free the hostages after 172 days of captivity. The reality, unfortunately, was far different.

Destroyed helicopters in the Iranian desert (right) bear sad witness to the failure of the mission to rescue American hostages in Teheran. The militants who seized the hostages advertised their feat in a crude caricature of President Carter (below).

A Campaign of Hatred

The crisis in United States-Iranian relations had begun 15 months earlier, on January 16, 1979, when Shah Mohammad Reza Pahlavi was forced to flee the revolutionary turmoil of his country. The Ayatollah Ruhollah Khomeini, the aged leader of the fundamentalist Shi'ite Muslims, returned in triumph from his exile in Paris to launch a virulent anti-Western and anti-United States campaign. The shah's government, bolstered for decades by U.S. financial and military support, disappeared without a trace, and the ayatollah was proclaimed the undisputed spiritual and, by extension, temporal ruler of Iran.

A disgraced and powerless outcast, the shah wandered with his family from one country to another, seeking asylum. When it became known that he was suffering from cancer, President Carter permitted the shah to enter the United States on October 22 for medical treatment in New York. In Teheran the news touched off a wave of angry demonstrations with the ayatollah's fanatic supporters marching through the streets of the capital shouting, ''Death to the shah!'' and ''Down with America!''

The ayatollah's campaign of hatred against the United States reached a climax on November 4, when a mob of inflamed young revolutionaries seized control of the American embassy and took the staff as its hostages. They would be freed only in exchange for the shah's extradition from the United States and his return to Iran for trial on charges of crimes against the people.

Standing Firm Against Lawlessness

President Carter refused to give in to the mob's demands and was initially supported by an overwhelming majority of the American people. Relying on behind-the-scenes diplomacy, the president hoped to put pressure on the ayatollah to renounce the actions of the mob. Instead, Khomeini used the situation to consolidate his power and fend off challenges from more moderate members of the government. He knew, moreover, that the euphoria of the successful challenge to a superpower was distracting the Iranian people from the economic woes of their country.

The Ayatollah Khomeini (above) gave his blessing to the taking and holding of U.S. hostages — a virtually unprecedented action among civilized nations. After the abortive rescue, Iranian militants secured the U.S. embassy with sandbags, fearing another American strike (left).

The Coup at Entebbe

What Americans failed to achieve in Iran in April 1980, Israelis had triumphantly proved possible four years earlier: the rescue of hostages in a surprise attack.

On June 27, 1976, Palestinian terrorists hijacked an Air France passenger plane en route from Tel Aviv to Paris following an intermediate stop at Athens, Greece. Demanding the release of 53 so-called freedom fighters held by Israel, Kenya, and several European countries, the hijackers took the plane with their 258 hostages to Entebbe Airport in Uganda — there to be welcomed by the East African country's dictator, Idi Amin.

Israel began negotiating with the hijackers while planning its rescue mission. When the hijackers started releasing non-Jewish hostages, the clandestine preparations were

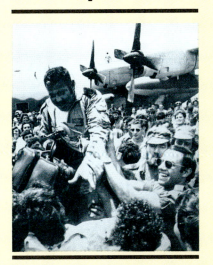

Upon their return home, the successful commandos were rapturously welcomed by Israelis justly proud of the rescue mission to East Africa.

intensified, with an Israeli army strike force conducting four days of rehearsals for the operation. On July 2 two C-130 Hercules transport planes and two Boeing 707 passenger jets, one of them equipped as a hospital, took off for the 2,000-mile flight to Uganda. While the hospital plane diverted to a friendly airport in Kenya and the other Boeing 707 remained aloft as a communications plane, the two C-130s swooped down upon Entebbe at 11 P.M.

Rushing from their aircraft, the rescuers easily overwhelmed the terrorists, killing seven of them, and herded the bewildered hostages to the transport planes for takeoff. It was all over in 53 minutes. The Israelis left behind three hostages shot by mistake and their commander, Yonatan Netanyahu, who had been killed by a sniper.

As 1979 ended with no resolution of the crisis, Carter had to think of sterner measures to take against a clearly intolerable situation. In April 1980 he broke off diplomatic relations with Iran and imposed a trade embargo on all U.S. goods bound for the country with the exception of food and medicine. A strict accounting of frozen Iranian assets in the United States would allow the funds to be used to indemnify the hostages after their release and pay off the claims of U.S. firms against Iran.

Carter's tardy moves were not enough for the American people. A new poll revealed that 65 percent of the citizenry felt his sanctions would not speed up release of the hostages; 51 percent of the respondents said that the president's actions were "not tough enough."

When reports reached Carter that the ayatollah planned to keep the hostages at least until the first anniversary of their seizure — November 4, 1980 — the president knew that he had a domestic political problem as well as one of international relations. The Democratic president would be seeking reelection to a second term on that date, and already his principal Republican challenger, Ronald Reagan, was capitalizing on Carter's apparent helplessness. "It's been wrong from the first," Reagan said of the president's cautious

policy. "The hostages shouldn't have been there six days, let alone six months."

The Military Option

The president had been considering a military solution to the hostage crisis almost from the beginning. On November 9, just five days after the mob seized the embassy personnel, Carter ordered an inner circle of his advisers to come up with various military options — among them a rescue mission. Ten days later the report was on his desk. Although he authorized the Pentagon's antiterrorist Blue Light unit to begin planning and training for such a mission, he considered it only a last resort. He wanted to be sure that he had exhausted all possibilities for a diplomatic solution of the crisis. To deceive the Iranians, Carter noted at a press conference on January 8 that any rescue attempt "would almost certainly end in failure . . . and in the death of the hostages."

By the end of March the ayatollah's intransigence was apparent; Khomeini had no intention of reining in his fanatic adherents. On April 11, as he was making his diplomatic and economic moves in public, Carter privately gave the go-ahead to the rescue mission. It would ultimately involve all four branches of the armed services, Army, Air Force, Navy, and Marine Corps.

Iran's Islamic Republic

The Iranians are an Aryan people who migrated to their desert plateau between the Caspian Sea and the Persian Gulf sometime before 1000 B.C. Although their language, Persian, or Farsi, is written in an Arabic script, it is related to European languages. The overwhelming majority of the people are Muslims, belonging to the smaller Shi'ite branch of that religion as opposed to the Sunnite Muslim sect of most Arab nations. The Shi'ites believe that Caliph Ali Ibn Abi Tabib, a cousin and son-in-law of Muhammad, is the only rightful heir of the prophet and that he is represented today by ayatollahs, spiritual leaders who interpret and enforce orthodoxy.

When he returned from exile in 1979, the Ayatollah Ruhollah Khomeini assumed leadership of the campaign to purge Iran of pro-Western influences. His first enemy was the exiled shah; his second, the U. S. government that had long supported him. To Khomeini the seizure of the hostages was a legitimate maneuver to humble and defeat those enemies.

Although the constitution adopted by Iran in 1979 provides for an elected president and legislature, final power remained with Khomeini, who was named the country's spiritual leader for life. The ayatollah's death in 1989 touched off a nationwide demonstration of hysterical grief from a people who considered him the divinely inspired leader of a revolution that had created the world's first Islamic republic.

It was an intricate and daring plan. Six C-130 Hercules transport planes were to leave an Egyptian air base, circle below the Arabian Peninsula, and land in a remote area of the Iranian desert, nicknamed Desert One, some 250 miles southwest of Teheran. There they would be joined by eight RH-53 Sea Stallion helicopters flying in from an aircraft carrier just beyond the Persian Gulf. The helicopters would take the commandos — an elite force of 90 volunteers — to the capital, where the landing and assault would be coordinated with pro-American Iranians arriving in disguised trucks. The freed hostages and commandos would be airlifted back to Desert One by the helicopters and loaded on the transport planes for the flight back to Egypt and safety. After refueling from the C-130s, the helicopters would return to the carrier.

It all called for meticulous planning, intensive training, clockwork coordination, tight security, and — perhaps — more than a little luck.

What Went Wrong

On Thursday afternoon, April 24, the C-130s took off from Egypt on schedule and skimmed across Iran at a height low enough to avoid radar detection. But almost as soon as the helicopters from the aircraft carrier crossed into Iranian airspace, two of them developed mechanical trouble. One returned to the carrier, but the other was forced to land. Its crew was taken aboard one of the remaining six helicopters for the low-level flight to the staging area at Desert One.

During refueling in the desert, a third helicopter was discovered to have a severe hydraulic malfunction that made it inoperable. The ground commander, U.S. Army Colonel Charles Beckwith — a 51-year-old Green Beret veteran of Vietnam — faced a dilemma. Six helicopters had been considered minimum for getting the hostages and their rescuers out of Teheran; he was now down to five. Across 8,000 miles went the request to Washington for a decision on whether or not to proceed. The answer: Abort and leave Iran. "At least there were no casualties," Carter told his aides, "and there was no detection."

The president was almost immediately proved wrong on both counts. A bus carrying some 40 Iranians suddenly appeared at Desert One; the Americans decided that they would have to be taken aboard the C-130s for the return flight to ensure that the mission remained secret. However, as it was refueling, one of the helicopters lifted too abruptly, its rotary blade ripped into the transport, and both aircraft burst into flame. Five Air Force crewmen in the C-130 were killed; three Marines in the RH-53 died. Four other Americans sustained severe burns. There was no time to let the wreckage cool in order to reclaim the bodies or to load the Iranians who had stumbled upon Desert One. The commandos piled into the remaining C-130s for a speedy departure.

In the aftermath of the tragic rescue mission, the Iranian militants dispersed the hostages to sites throughout the capital so that another mission would be deemed impossible. Carter went on national television to take full responsibility for the debacle. "It was my decision to attempt the rescue operation," he said. "It was my decision to cancel it when problems developed."

In the view of most commentators, the failure of all his efforts to free the hostages — and in particular the ignominious end of the rescue mission — cost Jimmy Carter reelection to the presidency. Ronald Reagan easily defeated him in the November balloting. The very day Reagan was sworn in as president, January 20, 1981, Iran released the last of the hostages.

A Victory Thrown Away?

When a high-living, cocky youth inherits the Swedish throne,
three powerful nations eagerly join the effort to steal his lands. Charles XII swiftly
smashes all three, but he fails to pursue his Russian
adversaries to Moscow.

The Great Northern War began in 1700 with the spectacular victory of Sweden's King Charles XII over Czar Peter the Great of Russia at the strategically important Baltic town of Narva. Sweden, known as the Mistress of the North for its firm stranglehold on northern Europe, seemed destined to become Empress of the East as well, for no obstacles lay between its highly disciplined, undefeated armies and poorly defended Moscow. Yet Charles XII, the enigmatic young military genius who had become a world hero overnight, paused. Did he throw away the richest opportunity of his career? For nine years he conducted draining campaigns against a lesser enemy while Peter was able to build a modern army as well as his country's first navy. The result was the landmark Battle of Poltava on June 28, 1709, in which the Swedish forces were overwhelmed and their proud king was wounded and forced to flee in humiliation to the outer reaches of the Ottoman Empire.

A statue of Samson overcoming the lion stands in the midst of a great fountain at the palace of Peterhof outside St. Petersburg (formerly Leningrad); it represents Russia subduing Sweden.

Born to Wage War

When King Charles XI died of stomach cancer at the age of 42, his 14-year-old son was not unprepared for leadership. Taken from the company of women at the age of six, the boy had learned to delight in rough sports, military games, and self-imposed tests of endurance. When he was 11, his mother died; that same year he shot his first bear. Soon he decided that it was unsportsmanlike to use firearms against bears and used only a pitchfork. Aside from one flirtation, he never pursued female companionship and never married. For Charles XII, his obsession was victory on the battlefield. Unusually intelligent, the boy tried to mold himself after Alexander the Great, whose biography he carried with him throughout his life. Thoughtful, convinced that justice and truth should be honored above all else, he avidly studied the Bible and made sure as king that his Lutheran armies prayed twice daily. Even so, his rowdy behavior as an adolescent was the scandal of Stockholm.

Although a regency council was supposed to oversee the young king until he reached 18, it soon became clear that he was determined to rule in fact. To the horror of liberty-loving Swedes, he publicly crowned himself at the age of 15. Embarking on new debaucheries, he would drink himself into a stupor or slice off the heads of living sheep until the palace hallways flowed with fresh blood. "Woe to thee when thy king is a child!" preached three pastors on the same Sun-

The movements of Charles XII during the Great Northern War are traced in broad outline on the map above. In reality, the Swedish campaigns were far more complicated, with some of Charles's forces following independent routes.

day. After that, Charles subdued his behavior for a while, but a visit from his pleasure-loving brother-in-law sparked even wilder behavior. Awakened from a drunken stupor by his grandmother after getting a pet bear so inebriated it fell out of a window to its death, the mortified ruler took a temperance oath and never again drank anything stronger than watered-down beer.

His pledge was fortuitously timed. Appetites whetted by the rumors of this feckless boy-king, the leaders of Denmark, Saxony-Poland, and Russia conspired to take advantage of the situation. All three countries decided to invade Sweden at once and share the spoils.

The Wolves Circle

When his enemies attacked in 1700, the newly sober king was startled and angered, but not confounded. "I have resolved never to begin an unjust war," he declared, "but also never to end a just war without overcoming my enemy." His first strategic decision was brilliantly simple and effective, for he decided to concentrate on one invader at a time, certain that God was on the side of Sweden.

On April 13 he left for Denmark, little knowing that he would never see Stockholm again. With a daring maneuver that frightened his advisers, he was able to join his fleet with the allied English and Dutch ships sent by William III of England. Within two weeks Copenhagen had been surrounded on land and the Danish navy rendered useless. Chastened, Denmark's King Frederick was obliged to sign a treaty restoring the status quo prior to his ill-starred invasion.

Charles immediately led his army, outfitted with the new flintlock muskets and circle bayonets, toward the Russian forces poised near the Baltic. Winter storms, the scorched-earth policy of Czar Peter's retreating forces, and scarcity of supplies caused the young king's commanders to advise against continuing this winter campaign. The same factors convinced the czar that the Swedes could not soon reach him at the town of Narva. He had not yet experienced the nearly superhuman determination of his youthful adversary. On November 13 Charles began marching his 10,500 men toward the fortified town, where almost 40,000 Russian soldiers lay in wait. When word came that the Swedish army was near, Peter took an action that has puzzled historians. Did he choose this moment to travel off to confer with his remaining ally, Augustus of Saxony-Poland? Or did he flee in terror? In any event, he left his soldiers in the hands of a commander who could not even speak their language.

On the bitterly cold morning of November 20, Charles had his forces in place. When a howling snowstorm rose at midday, the Swedes wanted to stay put, but Charles instantly saw that it was a great stroke of luck. The blinding snow was blowing toward the Russians, perfect for obscuring a Swedish onslaught. At 2 P.M. the excited young king launched an attack that is one of history's most famous. Outnumbered four to one, his army, having marched at breakneck speed through many obstacles, swiftly vanquished the defending Russians. Perhaps 10,000 of the czar's forces drowned in the river as they fled; others were killed when two bridges collapsed. So many prisoners surrendered that Charles had to work secretly through the night to rebuild a bridge for their escape; otherwise, they could have turned on their captors, many of whom were either exhausted from the struggle or incapacitated from celebrating with strong spirits.

The rout became the talk of Europe. Hailed as a hero and a genius, Charles XII had a medallion struck showing Peter fleeing in tears. The enemies of Sweden quailed, and the legend of the invincible king was born. Unfortunately, 19-year-old Charles came to believe this legend himself, and it would prove his undoing.

The Crucial Decade

Charles pondered an immediate attack upon Moscow, for Russia looked almost helpless, but he did not take the opportunity. Hunger and disease were certainly taking their toll among his men, but his decision was made on a more personal basis. The Saxon leader Augustus, still undefeated in this war, was the king's first cousin, and his role in the allied invasion of Sweden was unforgivable treachery — at least in the eyes of Charles XII. The victor of Narva felt that he could ignore the defeated Russians and more profitably turn his attention toward the West.

No one better understood the depth of the Swedish king's blunder than Peter the Great,

who would later write in his diary that the disaster at Narva forced him and his people "to be industrious, laborious, and experienced." While Charles harried the Saxons with his tactical inventiveness, such as burning manure and damp hay to create a smoke screen for an attack across a river, Peter concentrated his autocratic powers on forging a national war machine. Perhaps 90 percent of the state's resources were devoted to the military. Equally significant, the czar — despite entrenched opposition from his nobles and the Russian people — created a new city in swampland beside the Baltic. By building St. Petersburg, he demonstrated his determination to stand and fight on the coast.

For about six years, Charles chased after the elusive Augustus, the elector of Saxony who had also made himself king of Poland. At one point, the desperate Saxon sent the most beautiful and wily of his mistresses to convince his cousin to negotiate, but the confirmed bachelor politely waved the woman away. His tenacity paid off. In the autumn of 1706, Augustus was forced to resign the kingship of Poland, allowing Charles to

After he was shot in the foot at Poltava, Charles XII had to be carried through the battle on a litter.

install a puppet of his own. Self-confident to the point of arrogance, the Swedish warrior-king had now defeated the second of the three leaders who had the temerity to invade his empire in 1700. In 1707 he planned to dispose of Czar Peter.

To Punish the Czar

During his respite Peter had achieved a few minor victories, including retaking Narva and ensuring that the Swedes there were "butchered in heaps." His troops had learned discipline; and he had, like Charles, supplied himself with a mobile gun that could fire a three-pound shell, as well as the latest musketry and bayonets. Still, the 70,000 Swedes who began the thousand-mile march toward Moscow in 1707 seemed invincible, feared for their ferocious reliance on cold steel in hand-to-hand combat. Indeed, they were well fed and splendidly decked out in yellow-and-blue uniforms, but they soon came against Russia's most powerful ally: the vast and forbidding countryside with its treacherous weather.

As Peter beat a tactical retreat, laying waste the towns and crops in his wake, the Swedes were harried by sniper fire from skilled native hunters. Eventually, desperate for food, the invaders took to killing infants to force peasants to reveal their

hidden supplies. Halfway to Moscow, after a remarkable victory against a superior number of Russians, Charles rested his troops, while Peter tried to predict his opponent's next move.

There were three possible routes to the capital; Peter destroyed everything in all three directions so that the Swedes could not live off the land. The contest was drawn between 110,000 Russians and perhaps 62,000 Swedes, but the latter were succumbing to the harsh conditions of the scorched land. Charles, deciding that he now needed more supplies before attempting an assault on Moscow, veered toward the fertile south in the summer of 1708. This was another blunder. To do so, he moved 90 miles away from reinforcements heading his way with food and matériel; about half of the 12,000 Swedes marching toward him were killed or captured. Worse, the

In 1703 Peter the Great (right) began building a grand new city — his so-called window into Europe — where the Neva River flows into a gulf of the Baltic Sea. He moved Russia's capital there from Moscow in 1712; the view of St. Petersburg below dates from the following century and shows the Ships' Bridge leading to the Isaac Cathedral.

Death in Battle or Murdered?

Charles XII seemed pensive and sad on the evening of November 30, 1718, as he watched the diggers in the trenches at Fredrikssten. At about 9:30 the king raised his head above the lip of the front-line trench to view the firefight, resting his chin on one hand. Terrified friends knew better than to warn their warrior-monarch of the danger. Suddenly, his companions heard a sound like a stone being thrown vigorously into mud. The king's hand dropped; his body did not move. He had been killed instantly by a musket ball that pierced his left temple.

But had he really fallen to an enemy marksman? Rumors spread that someone in the Swedish ranks had assassinated him. The obvious beneficiaries were his younger sister, Ulrika Eleonora, and her husband, Frederick, duke of Hesse, who was with Charles at Fredrikssten. Before leaving Stockholm, the duke had ordered his wife to have herself crowned queen if anything should happen to the king. When the news of Charles's death reached the capital, she promptly assumed the throne. In 1722 an ailing King Frederick flung open the windows of his royal apartment and shrieked that he had indeed murdered Charles. Was this the raving of a delirious patient, or was it truly a deathbed confession?

Russians had foreseen his move and once again devastated an area where he expected to find forage and foodstuffs.

All across Europe, the winter of 1708–09 was considered the worst in memory. Some 3,000 of Charles's men succumbed to the weather, but the king stubbornly held his ragged, dwindling army together, sharing their meager food supplies. By April he had begun a siege of the Russians holed up in Poltava, a little cliff-top town about 200 miles southeast of Kiev. He now had only about 19,000 men to mount an assault on the 42,000 Russian defenders. The king's advisers wanted to turn around and go home. Only Charles's fortitude could convince his discouraged soldiers that victory was possible.

Death of a Legend

Suddenly, a thrill of horror raced through the Swedish forces outside Poltava. King Charles had been shot in the foot. Characteristically stoic, he had continued to lead his men for three hours and then had cut away some of the flesh himself when surgeons hesitated to probe for splinters — never showing pain throughout the ordeal. Soon he was feverish, however, and lay close to death. Although he would recover, he had to lie on a litter, unable to see the order of battle. Nevertheless, he ordered an assault on the town at 4 A.M. on June 28, 1709. It was a disaster.

Envious of each other, his commanders did not communicate their moves clearly. Without their king's guiding genius, chaos reigned as the superior Russian firepower mowed down the Swedish infantry. In the melee, 21 of the 24 men carrying Charles's litter were shot down. By the end of the day, half of Charles's army was dead, wounded, or taken captive.

Depressed, perhaps feverish again, Charles lay silent as he was conveyed off the field in his litter. Furiously pursued by the gleeful Russians, he was barely able to escape across the Dnieper River, race across the steppes to the Bug River, and then cross the frontier of the Ottoman Empire.

By this victory, Russia took Sweden's place as the colossus of northern Europe. For years Charles would be forced to live as a prisoner-guest with the Turks, whose hospitality was encouraged by his war chest. Eventually, in 1714, he escaped and rode horseback to Sweden in only two weeks, disguised as "Captain Frisk." Trying to bolster the spirits of his battered country, now attacked on all sides, he began a campaign against Norway, the first step in a projected new war against Russia, but Charles was shot to death at Fredrikssten on November 30, 1718.

Credits and Acknowledgments

2–3 Bridgeman/Art Resource, New York. 11 E.R. Degginger/Animals Animals/Focus. 12 Painting by Nicolas Monsiau, Musée des Arts Africains et Occidentaux, Paris. Archiv für Kunst und Geschichte. 14 M. Seemuller/Istituto Geografico de Agostini. 15 *bottom* Roger-Viollet; *bottom right* Seraillier/dpa. 16 Archiv für Kunst und Geschicte. 17 *top* Meh/Contact/Focus; center right Musée de la Marine, Paris. 18 *bottom* The Bettmann Archive. 19 Claus Hansmann. 21 AP/Wide World Photos. 22 *left* Ben Weaver/ The New York Times; *right* Antiquariat Heribert Tenschert. 23 Zefa UK/ Zefa. 24 *top* Painting by Ferdinand Theodor Hildebrandt, 1835, Kunstmuseum, Düsseldorf, Bildarchiv Preussischer Kulturbesitz; *bottom right* Archiv für Kunst und Geschicte. 26 Thomas Hopker/Anne Hamann. 27 Bilderdienst Süddeutscher Verlag. 28 Engraving after a painting by John Beys, Ullstein Bilderdienst. 29 *left* Damm/Zefa; *right* Bilderdienst Süddeutscher Verlag, 30 Keystone. 31 Dr. Georg Gerster. 33 Woodcut, National Library of Australia, Canberra. 34 *top* The John Oxley Library, Brisbane; *center* Mitchell Library. 35 Smith/Zefa. 37 Illustration by Rex Whistler, Tate Gallery, London. 38 *top* Historia-Photo; *center left* Painting after G. Kneller, 1714, Cambridge University, Bildarchiv Preussischer Kulturbesitz; *center right* Painting by Jacques Vaillant, 1691, Bomann Museum, Celle; *bottom left* Watercolor by Wilhelm Kretschmer, Historisches Museum am Hohen Ufer, Hannover. 40 Painting by Kristian Zahrtmann, 1873, Gisselfeld Klosters Kontor, DK-Hasley. 41 Illustration by Rex Whistler, Tate Gallery, London. 43 *left* Christina Thomson-/Woodfin Camp/Focus; *right* Peter Frey. 44 amw/Bilderdienst Süddeutscher Verlag. 46 *all* Bilderdienst Süddeutscher Verlag. 47 Raoul-Wallenberg-Föreningen, Stockholm. 49 Bilderdienst Süddeutscher Verlag. 50 Bilderdienst Süddeutscher Verlag. 51 *left* New York Public Library; *right* Dare County Tourist Bureau. 53 *both* Illustration by John White, 1585, The Granger Collection, New York. 54 Historical Pictures Service, Chicago. 55 *top* Culver Pictures. 56 *top* Imperial War Museum, London; *left* Bilderdienst Süddeutscher Verlag; *right, from top to bottom*, The New York Times, John Frost Newspaper Collection/Sunday Mirror, John Frost Newspaper Collection/The Mail on Sunday. 58 *both* Collection of George T. Simon. 59 Bilderdienst Süddeutscher Verlag. 60 *top* Ullstein Bilderdienst; *bottom* Archiv Dr. Karkosch. 61 Memory Shop, New York. 62 From "The Icy Sleep," vgs Verlagsgesellschaft Köln, Photo: Owen Beattie. 65 *top* E.R. Degginger/Animals Animals/Focus; *bottom* Bildarchiv Preussischer Kulturbesitz. 66 Dan Guravich. 67 *top* MacDonald/Aldus Archive; *bottom* Verlag Das Beste. 68 Woodcut after a painting by Thomas Sumth, Archiv für Kunst und Geschichte. 69 *top* Eugen/Zefa. *right* Publifoto. 70 *bottom left* Bilderdienst Süddeutscher Verlag; *center right* Luca Servo/AFE. 71 Farabolafoto. 73 dpa. 74 *bottom left* Thomas Pfündel; *right* Verlag Das Beste. 77 *top* Bildarchiv Huber; *bottom left* Painting by Franz Piloty, 1865, Schloss Herrenchiemsee, Bildarchiv Preussischer Kulturbesitz; *bottom right* Painting by R. Wenig, circa 1880, Marstallmuseum, Schloss Herrenchiemsee, Bayerische Verwaltung der staatlichen Schlösser, Gärten und Seen, Munich. 78 Painting by Kurt von Rsozynski, 1890, Archiv für Kunst und Geschichte. 79 *left* Bildarchiv Süddeutscher Verlag; *bottom right* Contemporary illustration by Joseph Watter, Ullstein Bilderdienst. 81 *top* United Nations; *bottom* Bilderdienst Süddeutscher Verlag. 82 *center* Keystone; *bottom* Bilderdienst Süddeutscher Verlag; 83 Keystone. 84 Bilderdienst Süddeutscher Verlag. 85 Reportagebild/action press. 86 Patrick Thurston. 87 *top* Michael S. Yamashita/Focus; *right* Alleged portrait of Marlowe of the French School, Corpus Christi College, Cambridge, Robert Harding. 88 *bottom left* Painting by John de Critz the Elder, The National Portrait Gallery, London; *right* Verlag Das Beste. 89 Contemporary painting, Scottish National Portrait Gallery, Edinburgh, National Galleries of Scotland. 91 *center left* Bildarchiv Preussischer Kulturbesitz; *bottom* Painting by W. W. Meschkow, Central Museum of the Revolution, Moscow, Novosti (APN)/Soviet Union Today. 92 Archiv für Kunst und Geschichte. 93 *left* Bildarchiv Preussischer Kulturbesitz; *right* Ullstein Bilderdienst. 94 *left* Ullstein Bilderdienst. 94–95 Bildarchiv Preussischer Kulturbesitz. 95 *right* Historia-Photo. 97 Painting by an unknown artist, 16th century, Penshurst Palace, Kent, Archiv für Kunst und Geschichte. 98 Österreichische Nationalbibliothek, Vienna. 99 *bottom left* Anonymous lithograph, 19th century, Archiv für Kunst und Geschichte; *right* Oil painting by Joseph Lange, Mozart-Museum, Salzburg, Erich Lessing/laenderpress. 100 Anonymous oil painting, Gesellschaft der Musikfreunde, Vienna, Interfoto. 101 Oil painting by Ignaz Unterberger, 1784, Historisches Museum, Vienna, Erich Lessing/laenderpress. 102 dpa. 103 UPI/dpa. 104 *bottom left* dpa; *right* Macmillan Publishing Co., from Stephen White, *Should We Now Believe the Warren Report* © 68 Columbia Broadcasting Systems, Inc. 105 Historia-Photo. 106 Sipa-Press/action press. 107 Ullstein Bilderdienst. 109 *bottom left* Open air festival Schwäbisch Hall, Wilhelm Pabst; *right* Painting by Diego Velázquez, circa 1625, Prado, Madrid, Bildarchiv Preussischer Kulturbesitz. 110 Painting by Francisco Rizzi de Guevara, 1683, Prado, Madrid, Archiv für Kunst und Geschichte. 111 Tinted copper engraving, 18th century, Bildarchiv Preussischer Kulturbesitz. 113 *both* Bilderdienst Süddeutscher Verlag. 114 dpa. 116 dpa. 117 Peter Turnley/Black Star/Transglobe Agency. 118 Aubert Prytanée National Militaire. 120 Lithograph after a painting by Dumesni, 18th century, Bildarchiv Preussischer Kulturbesitz. 122 *bottom left* Heinz Eschmat; *right* J. Oster/Musée de l'Homme, Paris. 123 Engraving by Schiavonnetti after Guttenbrunn, Archiv für Kunst und Geschichte. 125 *top* Painting by Antonine Jean Gras, 1810, Musée Versailles, Archiv für Kunst und Geschichte; *center right* Drawing by L. Kratky, 1894, Bilderdienst Süddeutscher Verlag. 126 *top* Caricature, Musée de la Ville de Paris/SPADEM 1989; *center left* Portrait by Wyvil, 1832, Historia-Photo; center *right* After a painting by J. Sant, Bilderdienst Süddeutscher Verlag. 127 Guner/Sipa-Press/Transglobe Agency. 128 Painting by Jung, Musée Carnavalet, Paris, J. Guillot/Edimedia. 129 Ullstein Bilderdienst. 131 *center left* Painting after the school of F. Clouet, 16th century, Victoria and Albert Museum, London, Archiv für Kunst und Geschichte; *bottom* Mary Evans Picture Library. 132 Tinted woodcut after a drawing by Sieben, 1889, Archiv für Kunst und Geschichte. 134 *bottom left* Bilderdienst Süddeutscher Verlag; *center and bottom right* Ullstein Bilderdienst. 135 Bildarchiv Preussischer Kulturbesitz. 137 *both* Archiv für Kunst und Geschichte. 138 Painting by Edouard Manet, Kunsthalle, Mannheim, Joachim Blauel/Artothek. 139 *top* Copper engraving by Rothgiesser, 1656, Historia-Photo; *bottom* After an engraving by Kilian, 1606, Historia-Photo. 140 *top* Bildarchiv Preussischer Kulturbesitz; *center left* Damals-Verlag. 142 Bilderdienst Süddeutscher Verlag. 143 Deutsche Oper, Berlin, Story Press-Jochen Clauss. 144 Collection of Merrill K. Lindsay. 145 *left* Portrait by Charles Willson Peale, Independence National Historical Park Collection, Philadelphia; *right* H. Steenmans/Zefa. 147 *top* Nathan Benn/Focus; *center right* From *The Assassination of Winston Churchill*, Colin Smythe (Gerrards Cross) Ltd., Buckinghamshire. 148 Tinted engraving, Bildarchiv Jürgens. 149 Bildarchiv Preussischer Kulturbesitz. 150 Story Press-Jochen 151 Sipa-Press. 153 *top* Interfoto; *bottom* Ullstein Bilderdienst. 155 Bavaria/BAVARIA. 156 Ullstein Bilderdienst. 157 Interfoto. 158 Andrej Reiser-/Bilderberg. 159 *bottom left* Archiv für Kunst und Geschichte; *right* Archiv Gerstenberg. 160 Historia-Photo. 161 Keystone. 162 *bottom left* Mary Evans Picture Library; *right* dpa. 163 Historia-Photo. 164 Archiv Dr. Karkosch. 165 Lithograph, 19th century, Keats Shelley Memorial House, Rome. 166 Painting by Eugene Delacroix, 1822, Musée des Beaux Arts, Bordeaux, Archiv für Kunst und Geschichte. 167 *bottom* Oil copy by Schnorr von Carolsfeld after a painting by Anthony Van Dyck, Bildarchiv Preussischer Kulturbesitz. 168 Painting by Jan Asselyn, circa 1650, Herzog-Anton-Ulrich Museum, Braunschweig (Brunswick), Bildarchiv Preussischer Kulturbesitz. 169 Larry Downing/Woodfin Camp & Associates/Focus. 170 Kunsthistorisches Museum, Vienna. 171 Historia-Photo. 172 Fred/IFA Bilderteam. 173 *top* Copper engraving from Merians *Theatrum Europeum*, 1635ff, Archiv für Kunst und Geschichte; *right* Kunsthistorisches Museum, Vienna. 174 *center* Copper engraving by an unknown artist, 1562, Archiv für Kunst und Geschichte; *bottom* Contemporary painting, Museum of London, London, Bridgeman/Art Resource. 175 EPU/dpa. 176 K. Reinhard/Transglobe Agency. 177 *bottom left* H.J. Kokojan/Black Star/Transglobe Agency; *right* dpa/Ullstein Bilderdienst. 178 *bottom left* Los Alamos National Laboratory; *right* Verlag Das Beste. 179 Deutsches Museum, Munich. 180 Keystone. 181 Bilderdienst Süddeutscher Verlag. 182 J. Robert Oppenheimer Memorial Committee. 183 G. Hahn/IFA-Bilderteam. 184 *left* Westermann-Archiv; *right* Bilderdienst Süddeutscher Verlag. 185 Historia-Photo. 186 *left* René Burri/Magnum/Focus; *right* Bildarchiv Preussischer Kulturbesitz. 187 *both* Bilderdienst Süddeutscher Verlag. 189 *left* Georg Fischer/Bilderberg; *right* Painting by A.M. Wasnezow, 1897, Tretiakoff Gallery, Moscow, Bildarchiv Preussischer Kulturbesitz. 190 Richard K. Dean. 191 Painting, Fort Ticonderoga Museum, Fort Ticonderoga Association. 192 Ullstein Bilderdienst. 193 Historia-Photo. 194 Volker Hinz/Black Star. 195 *center* Dr. David Millar/Science Photo Library/Focus; *bottom left* Bilderdienst Süddeutscher Verlag. 196 Popperfoto. 198 *top* Charles Neider; *center left* Bilderdienst Süddeutscher Verlag. 199 Archiv für Kunst und Geschichte. 200 Bilderdienst Süddeutscher Verlag. 201 dpa. 202 dpa. 203 Ullstein Bilderdienst. 204 *left* dpa; *center right* Bilderdienst Süddeutscher Verlag; *bottom right* Heinrich Hoffmann/Interfoto. 206 Camera Press/dpa. 207 dpa. 209 *top left* Sipa-Press; *right* AP/Wide World Photos. 210 *top* Robert Llewellyn. 211 *bottom left* Smithsonian Institution; *right* The Bettmann Archive. 213 Bildarchiv Preussischer Kulturbesitz. 214 *top* Joachim Messerschmidt/Ullstein Bilderdienst. 215 dpa. 216 *top* Michael Ventura/Transglobe Agency; *left* National Archives. 217 *bottom left* Keystone; *right* Bilderdienst Süddeutscher Verlag. 219 *center and bottom* Bildarchiv Preussischer Kulturbesitz. 220 Lewis Morley-/Camera Press, dpa. 221 *top* Bilderdienst Süddeutscher Verlag; *right* Historia-Photo. 223 *bottom* Painting by Giorgio Vasari, Palazzo Vecchio, Florence, Scala. 224 Picard/Mainbild. 225 Städtisches Museum, Braunschweig (Brunswick). 226 *center* Archiv für Kunst und Geschichte. 227 Historia-Photo. 228 *bottom left* Luis Castaneda/The Image Bank; *right* Portrait by Elisabeth Vigée-Lebrun, 1778, Chateau Versailles, Bildarchiv Preussischer Kulturbesitz. 229 Tinted copper engraving by C. Guerin, 1776, Archiv für Kunst und Geschichte. 230 Historia-Photo. 231 *bottom* Bilderdienst Süddeutscher Verlag. 232 Lithograph after a drawing by Léon Faurat, Bildarchiv Preussischer Kulturbesitz. 233 *bottom left* Gerald Davis/Contact/Focus. *right* Hoerskel/IFA-Bilderteam. 234 Ullstein Bilderdienst. 235 dpa/Ullstein Bilderdienst. 236 *bottom* Painting by Vigilius Erichsen, circa 1770, Musée des Beaux Arts, Chartres, Archiv für Kunst und Geschichte. 237 *bottom left* Painting by A.P. Antropov, Trinity Monastery, Sagorsk, Novosti (APN)/Soviet Union Today; *right (both)* Hermann-Josef Müller/Berlin Tin Figures. 238 *left* Copper engraving by Schwerdgeburth after Heideloff, Archiv für Kunst und Geschichte; *right* Timm Rautert/Visum. 239 Bildarchiv Preussischer Kulturbesitz. 240 Aquatint page by Wagner after a drawing by E. Karnejev, 1812, Kunstbibliothek, Berlin, Bildarchiv Preussicher Kulturbesitz. 241 *bottom* Klaus D. Francke/Bilderberg. 242 *bottom left* Archiv für Kunst und Geschichte; *right* Bilderdienst Süddeutscher Verlag. 243 Wolfgang Kunz/Bilderberg. 244 Ullstein Bilderdienst. 245 Ullstein Bilderdienst. 247 *top left* Illustration by Harry Clarke, Mary Evans Picture Library; *center* Ullstein Bilderdienst. 248 *top left* Copy after a painting by Paul von Somer, St. John's College, Cambridge, Bildarchiv Preussischer Kulturbesitz; *center* San Zarember/The Image Bank; *right* Painting by N. Hilliard, 1585, The National Portrait Gallery, London. 250 Copper engraving by Reynald Elstrack, 1614, Archiv für Kunst und Geschichte. 251 *top* Eckebrecht/Bavaria; *right* Engraving by W. Otto after a painting by F. Leutze, Ullstein Bilderdienst. 252 *top (both)* AP Associated Press. 253 Frieder Blickle/Bilderberg. 254 Bildarchiv Preussischer Kulturbesitz. 255 *both* Ullstein Bilderdienst. 256 *bottom* Painting by Sir George Hayter, 1820, The National Portrait Gallery London. 258 *top* Painting by Sir Thomas Lawrence, 1804, The National Portrait Gallery, London; *bottom* Bohnacker/

IFA-Bilderteam. 259 *left* Painting by Sir Thomas Lawrence, 1814, The National Portrait Gallery, London; *right* Bildarchiv Preussischer Kulturbesitz. 260 Peter Hendrie/The Image Bank. 261 *bottom (both)* Bilderdienst Süddeutscher Verlag. 262 Verlag Das Beste. 263 *top left* Ullstein Bilderdienst; *top right and center* Bilderdienst Süddeutscher Verlag. 264 Bilderdienst Süddeutscher Verlag. 265 David Irving. 266 Ullstein Bilderdienst. 267 Archiv für Kunst und Geschichte. 268 Bildarchiv Preussischer Kulturbesitz. 269 *both* Bilderdienst Süddeutscher Verlag. 271 *center right* Ullstein Bilderdienst; *bottom* Bilderdienst Süddeutscher Verlag. 272 *left* Keystone; *top right* Ullstein Bilderdienst; *bottom right* Bilderdienst Süddeutscher Verlag. 273 Bilderdienst Süddeutscher Verlag. 274 Archiv für Kunst und Geschichte. 275 Archiv Dr. Karkosch. 276 *Center* Tapestry by Herbert A. Bone, 1879, Vigo Sternberg Galleries. 277 English Heritage. 278 Siegfried Lauterwasser/Bildarchiv Bayreuther Festspiele. 279 *left* Michael Holford; *right* Bildarchiv Preussischer Kulturbesitz. 280 Book illustration in the manuscript of the Parsifal legend, Amiens, 1286, Universitätsbibliothek, Bonn, Claus Hansmann. 281 *left* Armin Maywald/Silvestris; *bottom* From "Nosferatu, Phantom of the Night" by Werner Herzog, 1979, Archiv Dr. Karkosch. 282 Oertel/IFA-Bilderteam. 283 *top right* Archiv Dr. Karkosch; *center* Painting, Ambras Castle, Kunsthistorisches Museum, Vienna. 284 Wolfgang Kunz/Bilderberg. 285 *bottom* A. Prenzel/IFA-Bilderteam. 286 Mary Evans Picture Library. 287 Interfoto. 288 *center* Studio Perathoner. 289 *top right* Archiv Dr. Karkosch; *center left* Studio Perathoner. 290 *bottom left (both)* Studio Perathoner; *right* Claus Hansmann. 291 Claus Hansmann. 292 Archiv für Kunst und Geschichte. 293 *top* Woodcut, 16th century, Bildarchiv Preussischer Kulturbesitz. 294 Detail from the fresco "Resurrection" by Pinturicchio, Vatican Museum, Bildarchiv Preussischer Kulturbesitz. 295 *top* Bildarchiv Huber; *right* Verlag Das Beste. 296 *bottom* André Gelpke/Focus. 297 Fresco by Schnorr von Carolsfeld, 19th century, Residenz, Munich, Claus Hansmann. 298 *bottom left* Kopetzky/IFA-Bilderteam; *right* Archiv Dr. Karkosch. 299 Book illustration from the Great Heidelberg Song Manuscript (Codex Manesse), 13th century, Universitätsbibliothek, Heidelberg, Archiv für Kunst und Geschichte. 300 Bildarchiv Preussischer Kulturbesitz. 301 *bottom, left and right* Buffalo Bill Historical Center, Wyoming; *center* Culver Pictures. 302 Jack B. Wymore Collection. 303 State Historical Society of Missouri. 304 Bildarchiv Süddeutscher Verlag. 305 *top left* Bildarchiv Preussischer Kulturbesitz; *center* Pinkerton's, Inc. 306 *center* E. Morell/Helga Lade. 307 *bottom left* Painting by Roqueplan, Musée Carnavalet, Paris, Bulloz; *right* Pictor International. 308 Pastel painting by Maurice Quentin de la Tour, Musée du Louvre, Paris, Archiv für Kunst und Geschichte. 309 *top left* Archiv für Kunst und Geschichte; *center* Verlag Das Beste; *right* Bildarchiv Preussischer Kulturbesitz. 310 *center* Hans-Jürgen Burkard/Bilderberg; *bottom* Copper engraving, 1590, Archiv für Kunst und Geschichte. 311 Archiv für Kunst und Geschichte. 312 *top right* Westermann Archiv. 313 Stuckey/Photofile/Zefa. 315 *bottom* Walter Mayr/Focus. 316 *bottom left* Steel engraving. Zentralbibliothek, Lucerne; *right* Ernst Wrba/Helga Lade. 317 *center* Fresco, Tell Chapel, Sisikon, Wilkin Spitta. 318 Bilderdienst Süddeutscher Verlag. 319 Wilkin Spitta. 321 Oil painting by John Collier, circa 1898, Herbert Art Gallery, Coventry, Bridgemann/Artothek. 322 *all* Etchings, circa 1850, Bildarchiv Preussischer Kulturbesitz. 324 Seebach/IFA-Bilderteam. 325 Interfoto. 326 *center* Ann Münchow. 327 Toni Schneiders. 328 F. Gohier/Nature. 329 *bottom* Tinted picture postcard, circa 1905, Archiv für Kunst und Geschichte. 330 Camera Press/Ullstein Bilderdienst. 331 *top right* Luftbild Klammet & Aberl; *center left* R. Grosskopf/Zefa. 332 Camera Press/dpa. 333 U.S. Navy Department. 334 *top left* Pen and ink drawing by Johann Georg Laminit, 1828, Stadtbibliothek, Nürnberg. 335 *top* Foto-Atelier Beer; *right* Foto-Atelier Beer/Johannes Mayer. 336 Contemporary color lithograph, 1830, Stadtbibliothek, Nürnberg, Foto Hilbinger. 337 *top center* Pastel by Johann Friedrich Karl Kreul, 1830, Martin-von-Wagner-Museum of the University of Würzberg; *left and right* Contemporary copper engravings, W. Kraft/Johannes Mayer. 338 *top left* H. Kunzendörfer/Johannes Mayer; *center* Germanisches Nationalmuseum, Nürnberg; *right* Head study by Heinrich Adam, Germanisches Nationalmuseum, Nürnberg, H. Kunzendörfer/Johannes Mayer. 339 AP Associated Press. 340 Contemporary portrait of the English school, Private collection, Newberry Smith Associates. 341 *bottom* U.S. Navy; *bottom right* Verlag Das Beste. 342 *bottom right* Bildarchiv Preussischer Kulturbesitz. 343 & 344 Bilderdienst Süddeutscher Verlag. 345 Bildarchiv Preussischer Kulturbesitz. 346 Bilderdienst Süddeutscher Verlag. 347 *bottom background* dpa; *bottom left* Copy of a contemporary painting, 1731, The National Portrait Gallery London, Bildarchiv Preussischer Kulturbesitz; *center* Anonymous portrait, The National Portrait Gallery, London, Bildarchiv Preussischer Kulturbesitz; *right* Copy after a painting by Abraham von Blyenberch, The National Portrait Gallery, London. 348 *bottom left* Photographers International/action press; *right* Bilderdienst Süddeutscher Verlag. 349 Bilderdienst Süddeutscher Verlag. 350 Walter Mayr/Focus. 351 Cover for B. Traven, *The Death Ship*, rororo 126, cover design Karl Gröning, Jr./Gisela Pferdmenges. 352 *bottom, left and right* University of Hartford,

Museum of American Political Life; *center* Culver Pictures. 353 The Granger Collection. 355 Historia-Photo. 357 J. Belcher/Zefa + Interfoto. 358 Camera Press/Ullstein Bilderdienst. 359 *bottom (both)* Keystone. 360 *bottom left* Bildarchiv Preussischer Kulturbesitz; *right* From *The Burning of the Reichstag, Legend and Reality* © 1962 by Grote'sche Verlagbuchhandlung KG, Rastatt. 361 Bilderdienst Süddeutscher Verlag. 362 Keystone. 363 *top* Bildarchiv Preussischer Kulturbesitz; *center* Ullstein Bilderdienst. 364 *bottom left* Contemporary etching, Musée Carnavalet, Paris; *right* Painting by Hyacinth Rigaud, 1701, Musée du Louvre, Paris; *(both)* Archiv für Kunst und Geschichte. 365 *top right* Daniel Faure/Scope. 366 Grimm/dpa. 367 *center* After a miniature by Jean Petitot, Historia-Photo; *bottom* From "The Man with the Iron Mask" by Mike Newall, 1976, Archiv Dr. Karkosch. 368 Painting by Vigée Le Brun, Musée d'Art et d'Histoire, Auxerre, Hubert Josse. 369 *center* Drawing by Felix Schwormstädt, Bildarchiv Preussischer Kulturbesitz. 370 Bildarchiv Preussischer Kulturbesitz. 371 *top* Ullstein Bilderdienst; *center right* Bildarchiv Süddeutscher Verlag. 372 *bottom left* Andrej Reiser/Bilderberg; *right* dpa, 375 *center left* AP Associated Press; *bottom* Bilderdienst Süddeutscher Verlag. 376 Ullstein Bilderdienst. 377 Bilderdienst Süddeutscher Verlag. 378 *bottom left* Otello Pagliai; *right* Bilderdienst Süddeutscher Verlag. 379 Bohnacker/IFA-Bilderteam. 380 Mary Evans Picture Library. 381 *top center* Otello Pagliai; *right* Giuliano Cappelli. Painting by Antonio Lonza, Archiv für Kunst und Geschichte. 383 *left* Bildarchiv Preussischer Kulturbesitz; *right* Bundesarchiv, Koblenz. 384 Bildarchiv Preussischer Kulturbesitz. 385 *top left* Ullstein Bilderdienst; *right* Bilderdienst Süddeutscher Verlag. 386 & 387 Bilderdienst Süddeutscher Verlag. 388 *bottom left* Engraving by Boul, Ullstein Bilderdienst; *right* Engraving by Rouargue, 19th century, Bibliothèque Arts Deco, Paris, G. Dagli Orti. 389 Verlag Das Beste. 390 Copper engraving by Martinet, Historia-Photo. 391 *bottom left* Painting by Elisabeth Vigée-Lebrun, Bulloz; *right* Bilderdienst Süddeutscher Verlag. 392 P. Graf/IFA-Bilderteam. 393 Bildarchiv Preussischer Kulturbesitz. 394 *bottom* Aquatint by Jacques Philippe Loutherbourg, British Museum, London, Bildarchiv Preussischer Kulturbesitz. 395 *top left* Robert Royal. 396 Painting by John Seymour Lucas, "The Armada in Sight, 1588," oil on canvas 126.4 x 182.8, Art Gallery of New South Wales, Sydney. 397 *bottom left* Illustration from a contemporary English manuscript, Bildarchiv Preussischer Kulturbesitz; *right* Mike Beazley/Transglobe Agency. 398 Eileen Tweedy/Reader's Digest/ Plymouth City Art Gallery. 399 *bottom left* Bildarchiv Preussischer Kulturbesitz; *right* Bilderdienst Süddeutscher Verlag. 400 *bottom left* Bildarchiv Preussischer Kulturbesitz; *right* Bilderdienst Süddeutscher Verlag, 401 dpa. 403 *center left* Bilderdienst Süedeutscher Verlag; *right* Archiv für Kunst und Geschichte; *bottom left* Bildarchiv Preussischer Kulturbesitz. 404 Bilderdienst Süddeutscher Verlag. 405 *top* Woodcut by Waud, end of the 19th century, Bildarchiv Preussischer Kulturbesitz. 406 Smithsonian Institution/UPI/dpa. 407 *center left* Library of Congress; *center* T. Stone/Silvestris; *bottom* Bilderdienst Süddeutscher Verlag. 408 National Anthropological Archives, Smithsonian Institution. 409 Eberhard Grames/Bilderberg. 410 Bilderdienst Süddeutscher Verlag; *flag* Lueticker/Zefa. 411 *top* Bilderdienst Süddeutscher Verlag; *right* Ullstein Bilderdienst. 412 Bilderdienst Süddeutscher Verlag. 414 *bottom left* Keystone; *bottom* Tinted drawing by Willy Stöwer, 1912, Bildarchiv Preussischer Verlag. 415 The Titanic Historical Society, P.O. Box 51053, Indian Orchard, Mass. 416 *bottom left* Archiv für Kunst und Geschichte; *right* Madison Press Book. 417 Agence France-Presse/dpa. 418 *all* Archiv für Kunst und Geschichte. 419 Scanfoto/dpa. 420 *bottom left* Silvestris; *right* After a painting by Leutze, Bildarchiv Preussischer Kulturbesitz. 421 Keystone. 422 Ullstein Bilderdienst. 423 *top left* Aberham/IFA-Bilderteam; *right* Paul Fusco/Magnum/Focus. 424 *bottom* Painting by Adolph von Menzel, 1858, Neue Pinakothek, Munich, Bildarchiv Preussischer Kulturbesitz. 425 *top left* Watercolor by Reinhard Knoetel, circa 1900, Archiv für Kunst und Geschichte; *right* Koch/dpa. 426 Bilderdienst Süddeutscher Verlag. 427 *top left* dpa; *right* Mike Beazley/Transglobe Agency. 428 *center* Klemens Beitlich/Ullstein Bilderdienst; *bottom left and right* Poly-Press/Ullstein Bilderdienst; *right* Pohlert/dpa. 430 Konrad Kujau. 431 *bottom left* Lothar Kucharz/Ullstein Bilderdienst; *right* Lehtikuva Oy/dpa. 432 *center right* Hans-Peter Kruse/Ullstein Bilderdienst; *bottom left* dpa/Ullstein Bilderdienst. 433 UPI/Ullstein Bilderdienst 435 *center* van Phillips/Zefa. 437 Drawing by C. Häberlin, Ullstein Bilderdienst. 438 *center left* Copper engraving by Legrand, 18th century, Archiv für Kunst und Geschichte; *bottom* Engraving by G. Lory, Bernisches Historisches Museum, Bern, Gottfried Keller-Stiftung. 439 Painting by D. von Krafft, Nationalmuseum, Stockholm.

Illustrations: Willi Rieb/Margot Klingler: 17, 104, 353, 365. Werner Neidhardt: 167. *Illustrations (on maps):* Milada Krautmann: 13, 32, 48, 52, 64, 84, 149, 154, 197, 312, 342, 373, 395, 402, 436. *Cartography:* Karl-F.Harig: 13, 32, 48, 52, 64, 84, 149, 154, 197, 312, 342, 373, 395, 402, 436. *Cartographic vignettes (at beginning of each story):* Rolf Salzmann."

Index

Page numbers in **bold** type refer to illustrations.